For decades balloonists have tried to break the last world-span
March 1999, Bertrand Piccard and Brian Jones broke that recor
in 20 days in Orbiter III, the balloon featured on the text cover
technology played a crucial role in the historic flight. Systems he
patterns so the pilots could guide the balloon swiftly and sa
communication with ground crews and monitored the balloon's position and altitude.

The pilots' personal success translated into business success for Breitling, Orbiter III's sponsor, and for balloonmaker Cameron Balloons. The flight was also a success for society. As President Ruth Dreifuss of Switzerland said, "It is a success for technology, but also the realization of a dream that many children—and adults—have shared with you."

Just as the Orbiter III pilots relied on information systems to achieve their dream, Gupta's

INFORMATION SYSTEMS

shows how people, business, and society rely on information systems to succeed.

B. Bloomfield

Information Systems

Information Systems

Success in the 21st Century

Uma G. Gupta
Creighton University

Prentice Hall
Upper Saddle River, NJ 07458

Acquisitions Editor: David Alexander
Developmental Editor: Charlotte R. Morrissey
Editor-in-Chief: Mickey Cox
Managing Editor: Lucinda Gatch
Assistant Editor: Lori Cerreto
Director of Strategic Marketing: Nancy Evans
Senior Marketing Manager: Kris King
Production Editor: Marc Oliver
Permissions Coordinator: Monica Stipanov
Associate Managing Editor: Sondra Greenfield
Manufacturing Buyer: Lisa DiMaulo
Senior Manufacturing Supervisor: Paul Smolenski
Senior Manufacturing/Prepress Manager: Vincent Scelta
Senior Designer: Cheryl Asherman
Design Manager: Patricia Smythe
Interior Design: Amanda Kavanagh/Ark Design
Photo Research Supervisor: Melinda Lee Reo
Image Permission Supervisor: Kay Dellosa
Photo Researcher: Teri Stratford
Cover Design: John Romer
Cover Illustration/Photo: AP/Wide World
Composition: Omegatype Typography, Inc.

Credits
Credits and acknowledgments for materials borrowed from other sources and reproduced with permission, in this textbook appear on page 427.

Library of Congress Cataloging-in-Publication Data
Gupta, Uma G.
Introduction to information systems / Uma Gupta.
p. cm.
ISBN 0-13-010857-X
1. Management information systems. 2. Information technology—Management. I. Title.
T58.6.G814 1999
658.4'038—dc21

99-43259
CIP

Prentice-Hall International (UK) Limited, London
Prentice-Hall of Australia Pty. Limited, Sydney
Prentice-Hall Canada, Inc., Toronto
Prentice-Hall Hispanoamericana, S.A., Mexico
Prentice-Hall of India Private Limited, New Delhi
Prentice-Hall of Japan, Inc., Tokyo
Pearson Education Asia Pte. Ltd., Singapore
Editora Prentice-Hall do Brasil, Ltda., Rio de Janeiro

Printed in the United States of America
10 9 8 7 6 5 5 4 3 2 1

DEDICATION

To my beautiful and talented daughter, Priyanka. Being your mother is the greatest privilege and honor God bestowed upon me. May your generation create a future, digital and otherwise, that will take human achievements to new heights.

Brief Contents

Contents

Chapter 2: How Businesses Use Information Systems 31

PART TWO TECHNICAL FOUNDATIONS OF INFORMATION SYSTEMS 62

Chapter 3: Computer Hardware 63

LIZ claiborne

PLANTERS
DRY ROASTED
PISTACHIOS
PLANTERS
PEANUTS
PLANTERS
HONEY ROASTED
PEANUTS

Chapter 10: Information Systems for Managerial Decision Making 265

PART FIVE APPROACHES TO DESIGNING, DEVELOPING, AND MANAGING IS 294

Chapter 11: System Analysis and Design: Methodologies and Tools 295

Chapter 12: **Computer Security 327**

Chapter 13: **Managing Knowledge, Change and IS Personnel: The Next Challenges 353**

Preface

We're in the midst of an information revolution that is transforming society, business, and our personal lives. Changes in the information systems field are awe-inspiring, yet so rapid-fire that we wonder how to keep pace.

The changes are also transforming the introductory IS course for which this text is designed. The patchwork of terms and concepts that an introductory IS book covers often overwhelms students. And keeping IS issues current and relevant enough to engage students is a Herculean task. Here are six ways this text helps to overcome these challenges.

#1 Demonstrates How Businesses, Individuals, and Society Use "IS for Success"

Information Systems has an IS for Success framework that opens, closes, and infuses every chapter. The IS for Success content theme is based on the idea that people and organizations must carefully plan their use of information systems to accomplish a wide range of goals. In a business setting, those goals are usually to minimize costs, maximize value, and achieve a competitive advantage in the global marketplace.

But how can professors make such a pivotal topic come alive for students? *Information Systems* places information systems in context, examining more than just business implications of IS. Readers also explore the societal and personal implications of information systems, giving the subject more immediate relevance to their lives. This examination might take readers to the aftermath of Hurricane Mitch, the midst of the Balkan War, or to a physician's office in Bangladesh to see how IS and IT are helping to improve lives. It also might take them to the boardroom of GE or to a small online business in Idaho where businesspeople grapple with the power of information systems and its effects on business processes, employees, business partners, and customers.

#2 Involves a Diverse Audience with Traditional and Nontraditional Business Examples

Information Systems is designed for the introductory IS course. Students in that course may be strictly business and IS majors. However, the course may also include a mix of majors with varying degrees of technical experience. To reach such a diverse audience successfully, the text provides a mix of traditional and nontraditional business examples that run the gamut from fields such as health care and law enforcement to entertainment, aerospace, and education. Traditional business examples cover all business areas in a balanced way to accommodate students' varied interests and give a broad view of business.

#3 Practices What It Preaches: Using IS to Keep Pace

To help you keep up to date with IS and IT topics, we've included the most current material to support the IS concepts. But we also practice what we preach. The text has its own information system that offers emerging technology issues on an ongoing basis. The Prentice Hall Companion Web site provides updates and new technology issues in real time. Case updates and expert insights on current topics are also available on the Web site. The Web site is the ultimate resource, serving as a teaching assistant that keeps your instructional material up to date and linked to the text.

#4 Provides Coverage Where It Counts

This 13-chapter text is organized to give students a foundation in IS that will serve them in their careers and in additional MIS and business coursework. First, we analyzed current business practice and then we sought market feedback. We learned, for instance, that databases are crucial to business, yet have many concepts that are difficult for students to grasp, such as data mining and data warehousing. We developed the text content with these challenges in mind, balancing clear explanation with applications and supporting exercises. In addition, we developed supplementary Web site projects to provide as much hands-on experience as possible.

Reviews and research also show that this text's telecommunications coverage is richer than that of any other text on the market. We start with a chapter on telecommunications foundations (Chapter 6). Chapter 7 covers the Internet, Intranets, and Extranets; Chapter 8 explores Electronic Commerce; and Chapter 9 covers Client/Server Computing. These chapters offer the breadth, depth, and practical coverage that they'll need to succeed in the electronic business world. In addition, the text shows through examples the potential effect of telecommunications on business. Students explore how and why Liz Claiborne uses global networks to link its far-flung designers and manufacturers, juice maker Odwalla's Internet strategy in a public relations crisis, and how electronic commerce transformed a small business in Florida into a Fortune 500 firm.

#5 Illustrates That Many Paths Lead to IS Career Success

The current shortage of IS specialists means that businesses want skilled professionals to handle a broad array of IS-related jobs. However, the traditional IS jobs are expanding well beyond the stereotypical, solitary ones of programmer and database manager. Organizations the world over need people with a blend of business and technical skills to shape business practices and implement change. Nine chapters feature a section on "Careers for Success" that showcases careers such as financial technologists, relationship managers, and Web masters. In addition, the last chapter discusses changes in IS Careers and the ways IS personnel fit in an organization. The Web site also has career information.

#6 Offers a World View of IS

Information systems are breaking down the barriers of culture, time, and space. To do business effectively, IS users and specialists should understand the cultural and technological challenges that confront a world connected electronically. *Information Systems* offers the strongest global coverage of any introductory IS text. Chapter 1 introduces global concerns as they relate to IS, and then those concerns are revisited as they relate to concepts in each chapter. For instance, Chapter 2 explores the cultural and technology challenges of setting up a global information system. Chapter 8 examines the cultural, linguistic, and technology infrastructure issues that affect electronic commerce in regions as varied as Africa and Asia.

In addition to the integrated text coverage, eleven Global IS for Success feature that showcases how companies grapple with cross-cultural IS issues.

Other Highlights: Text Features and Supplements

To help make your course a success, the text features and ancillaries make teaching and learning from Gupta, *Information Systems* a multidimensional experience that will appeal to a diverse audience.

In-Text Pedagogy

Pedagogy in every chapter includes a *table of contents, "Technology Payoff" opening vignette, learning objectives, summary points* that link to those objectives, easy-to-find *definitions* in the margin, and *review questions.* The text also includes the following distinguishing features:

1. **"For Success" Chapter Introductions:** Each chapter begins with an examination of the societal, business, and personal implications of the chapter subject matter. This opening sets the stage so students can see the forest before becoming involved in the trees.

2. **"Global IS for Success" features** serve as short, real-world cases within the chapter that address specific global IS issues, including the cultural and technological concerns that can affect a company's success. These features complement the text's thorough global coverage. The end result? This text offers the most extensive, integrated international coverage found in any IS text.

3. **"Ethics for Success" features** address critical topics for IS users and managers. The ethics scenarios, based on actual events, end with "You Decide" questions that illustrate how thorny IS ethical issues can be. The topics range from the ethics of outsourcing to maintaining privacy in an EC transaction to developing fair punishment for teenage hackers.

4. **"Careers for Success" segments** spotlight emerging IS careers and the skills needed to succeed in those fields. They are designed to inform and broaden students' view of the role of IS in the organization. Reviewers told us that students develop interest in IS careers seeing by examples. You'll find attention-grabbing examples in these features that show students the realm of IS career possibilities.

5. **Business Guidelines for Success:** The guidelines that close each chapter serve as a bookend to the introductory section and help students focus on the "big picture" from a business perspective. The guidelines give suggestions designed to aid IS business decisions about the chapter's subject matter.

6. **Discussion Questions and Exercises:** This question set is designed to build communication, application, and presentation skills. It uses thought-provoking questions and short scenarios to build on chapter concepts. The exercises range from software and Web exercises to group presentation exercises. Supplementary Web-related questions are offered on the Gupta *Information Systems* Companion Web site.

7. **Critical-Thinking Cases for Success:** These real-world end-of-chapter cases underscore the chapter themes and examine the strategic implications of IS. Because the cases ask students to apply the knowledge gleaned from the chapter to a new scenario, they build critical-thinking skills that are so important in an information-based business world.

Companion Web Site

Located at *www.prenhall.com/gupta*, the text's Companion Web site offers resources for both students and instructors. **Faculty** can sign up for an electronic mailing list to receive a monthly newsletter from the author concerning current updates. The PowerPoint Presentation Slides and the Instructor's Manual are available for instructors to download from the faculty area of the site. Please contact your local Prentice Hall representative for a password to the instructor downloads.

Student resources on the Web site include:

- *Interactive Study Guide* with Multiple Choice, True/False, and Matching style review questions to help students review material in each chapter and prepare for exams. Student responses are graded and the "Results Reporter" can be printed or e-mailed to the instructor.
- *Internet Exercises* that provide students with the opportunity to further explore text topics on the Web. Responses to these essay style exercises can again be printed or e-mailed to the instructor.

- *Technology Updates* on the site appear monthly and are designed to bring current events to students' attention in light of the appropriate chapters of the text.
- Students can also participate in nationally based *mailing lists, bulletin boards,* and *chat rooms.*

Additional Instructor Resources

To make your teaching and learning experience an effective one, we designed each supplemental resource to work hand-in-glove with the text.

Instructor's Manual with Test Item File

Instructors will find a wealth of resources in the Instructor's Manual with Test Item File. Features include sample syllabi, teaching objectives and suggestions, key terms, transition notes, and more. In addition, answers to Review Questions, Discussion Questions/Exercises, and suggested answers to the Critical Thinking Cases are provided. The Test Item File is a comprehensive collection of Multiple Choice, True/False, and Essay questions designed to reinforce key concepts and terms covered in the text.

Windows Prentice Hall Test Manager

The Windows PH Test Manager is a wonderful suite of tools for testing and assessment. With five basic databases, Test Manager allows instructors to easily manage student records, course information, question content, test portfolios, and test results. The questions are taken from the printed Test Item File found in the Instructor's Manual.

PowerPoint Presentation Slides

PowerPoint Presentation Slides have been created for each chapter to highlight key text coverage and illuminate classroom lectures. The slides can be downloaded from the Web site at prenhall.com/gupta in the password-protected instructor area.

Prentice Hall MIS Video Library

The **Prentice Hall Management Information Systems Video Library** provides a mixture of video segments chosen and designed to illustrate concepts in the IS curriculum. A **Correlation Video Guide with case study questions** appears on the Instructor's portion of the Companion Web site. Additional video segments will be added in the coming years to keep the text and cases fresh for students and instructors alike.

Acknowledgments

A project like this is a major undertaking and a labor of love. The book went through an extensive review process at all stages of development. Special thanks go to the faculty that reviewed multiple drafts of the manuscripts, and those that responded to our on-line survey. Your valuable feedback helped steer the project in the right direction.

John E. Anderson	*Northeastern State University*
H. Michael Chung	*California State University, Long Beach*
Carol Clark	*Middle Tennessee State University*
Charmayne Cullom	*University of Northern Colorado*
John Deichstetter	*DeVry Institute of Technology*
Laurie Eakins	*East Carolina University*
Orlano K. Johnson	*University of Utah*
Magdi Kamel	*Naval Postgraduate School*

Richard Lee Kerns	*East Carolina University*
Lynne Koenecke	*University of Georgia*
Paul Krause	*California State University, Chico*
Joseph R. Mason	*SUNY College at Brockport*
Emmanuel U. Opara	*Prairie View A&M University*
Rocco Paolucci	*Cabrini College*
Richard E. Potter	*University of Illinois at Chicago*
Hailin Qu	*San Francisco State University*
Sasan Rahmatian	*California State University, Fresno*
Sally K. Scott	*Illinois State University*
Kan Sugandh	*DeVry Institute of Technology*
John R. Tarjan	*California State University, Bakersfield*
Madjid Tavana	*La Salle University*

The people at Prentice Hall also deserve accolades for their hard work and vision. Thanks to Editors-in-Chief PJ Boardman and Mickey Cox for supporting this project wholeheartedly, and to Acquisitions Editor David Alexander. Without David's vision, sound judgment, and direction, this project would never have gotten off the ground. His passion, single-minded focus and commitment to develop a strong introductory textbook in information systems that would appeal to a wide range of students was an inspiration. David, when you hold this book in your hands, remember that your role in making this project a success was pivotal. Much appreciation also goes to Managing Editor Lucinda Gatch who jumped in with both feet and problem solved like a professional CEO. Her fresh ideas contributed to the book from cover to cover.

Charlotte Morrissey, my developmental editor, never let me forget that the ultimate goal is to help the student understand and appreciate the power of information systems. She brings honor to her profession and raises the bar of excellence for others in the field. Thank you, Charlotte. May all authors be so blessed as to have an editor like you on their side.

A big thank you to former Editorial Assistant Keith Kryszczun, who managed key details with amazing good humor and attention to detail, and Assistant Editor Lori Cerreto, who handled the supplements program with grace, ingenuity, and a can-do attitude. Lori's respect for details made a substantial difference to this project. Thanks also to Editorial Director Jim Boyd and Business Division President Sandy Steiner for their support.

Kudos to the efforts of our crack marketing team and the Prentice Hall sales force—truly, you are the best in the business. A sincere vote of thanks to Nancy Evans, who helped brainstorm at every stage of the process and provided energy, insight, and added motivation whenever needed. Many thanks to PH Sales Directors Iain MacDonald, Matt Denham, Sharon Turkovich, and Dana Simmons for your feedback from the market and for your continued support of the IS list and all of our many customers. Greg Christofferson continues to lead our technology efforts in Companion Web sites and Testing software. Brian Kibby, Director of Marketing, thank you for supporting this project and hiring such talented people.

The hard work of the production and design team was essential to this text. Marc Oliver attended to all the niggling details with style, patience, and flexibility. Your calm and steady hand guided the project through the production process with speed—despite the inevitable bumps in the road. Cheryl Asherman's ability to translate what we said we wanted into something better than what we asked for and her patience as we thought through oh-so-many ideas was incredible. Cheryl, the interior design of this text is more beautiful than we envisioned. Lisa DiMaulo handled all of our manufacturing and budgeting issues with professionalism and grace.

Finally, I would like to acknowledge Ashok, my dearest friend, confidant, and soul mate. As the song goes, you are the wind beneath my wings who motivates and encourages me to dream and to dare to live life to its fullest. You are my rock, my sunshine, and my greatest blessing. As I reflect on my life, you are the reason for all the good times, laughter, and cherished moments. Who could ask for more? Thank you. I would also like to acknowledge my parents, who made great sacrifices so that I received a good education. Thank you for laying the foundation.

Information Systems

Part 1 Organizational Overview of Information Systems

Inspiration is everywhere, if you're willing to recognize it and let it move you.

James Bell, IT freelance writer

CONTENTS

INFORMATION SYSTEMS FOR SUCCESS

Numerous social, political, and economic forces are changing the world at a rapid clip. One reason for the breakneck pace of change is computer-based systems and technologies. "Welcome to the Information Age, where we will all have to operate at three speeds: fast, faster and faster. Information has changed the rules of the game."[1]

Once only trained specialists used computers as sophisticated work tools. Today, people play games, manage finances and schedules, stay connected with friends and family, or do schoolwork on computers at home. In 1997 the information technology market generated revenues of $899 billion, making it the largest business sector in the United States. This number is staggering, given that the market did not exist 50 years ago.[2] "By the time [information] technology matures, we will have fundamentally changed the nature of work and what we look for from life," explains Warren McFarlan, a business professor at Harvard and an information systems specialist.

As we see in Figure 1-1, information systems decisions have the power to enhance the quality of our personal and business lives. They will change the way we learn, work, and play. If used success-

FIGURE 1-1

IS Decisions Affect Individuals, Businesses, and Society

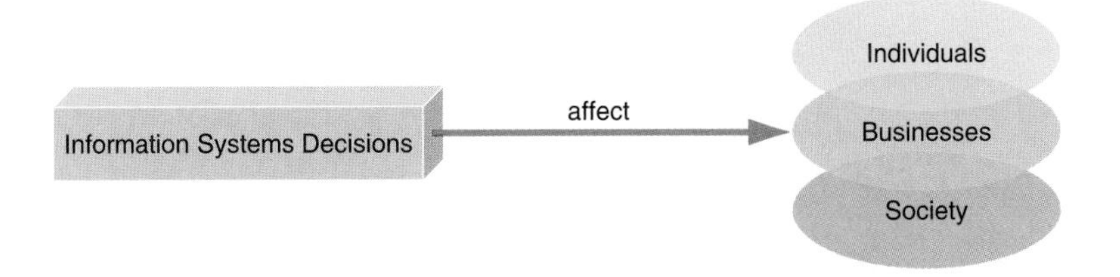

Chapter 1

Information Systems: A Framework for Success

AFTER STUDYING THIS CHAPTER, YOU WILL BE ABLE TO:

- Explain the two meanings of information systems
- Describe a system's characteristics and components
- Outline how data becomes information and the characteristics of information
- Summarize the effect of information systems on decision making
- Discuss the opportunities and challenges of information systems

fully, they can also improve society. As James P. Grant, the late executive director of UNICEF, noted: "With today's communications capacity, it is possible to put the basic benefits of scientific progress at the disposal of the vast majority of the world's people."

Dr. Michael Loots, founder and director of the Humanities Libraries Project in Antwerp, Belgium, puts Grant's words into practice. Dr. Loots took action when he learned that children in Bangladesh were dying because it was so difficult to get health-related information in that country. The project distributes CD-ROMs containing a library of about 3,000 books to hundreds of hospitals, schools, municipal administrations, and women's groups in developing countries. According to Dr. Loots, the library covers "most of the solutions, know-how and ideas that anyone involved in the development, planetary well-being and basic needs (of human beings) requires."[3]

Information systems can have other positive effects on society. They can improve the speed and quality of cancer research, improve weather prediction to save millions of lives around the world, and provide better education facilities to children in remote parts of the globe.

Information systems are also a tool for building successful organizations. They can help firms improve customer relations, provide

To aid countries that need basic health information, Dr. Michael Loots of Belgium developed a library of scientific information to distribute on a CD-ROM. Has he used information and technology successfully?

TECHNOLOGY PAYOFF

Staying Ahead of the Game

They're young and reckless. Their idea of fun is a long night of pillage. But today's on-line gamers are tomorrow's on-line customers and they have a few things to teach people working in information systems. When Origin Systems, a Division of Electronic Art Inc. in San Mateo, California, launched Ultima, an on-line role-playing game, thousands of young players swarmed to the game's virtual world. But soon the systems were bursting at their seams, threatening to slow the game down.

Keith McCurdy, vice president of technology at Origin Systems, understands that speed and fluidity of movement are critical for a game's success. He knew that if his systems slowed down, the game would lose its drama—and its customer base.

McCurdy and his staff worked to improve the performance of the network (hardware and software that links different computers), which indirectly affects the performance and speed of the game. The strategy worked: The company sold more than 80,000 CD-ROMs in the first three months and broke the record for the fastest-selling PC title in the division and in the company, all without spending a dime on advertising. "You have to be prepared for success," McCurdy says. The ability to grow as the number of system users increases "will make you either a success or a failure. We now build all our plans with this idea in mind."

Source: Alex Frankel, "Ahead of the Game," *CIO Web Business,* Section 2, May 1, 1998, 51–54.

Keith McCurdy, vice president of technology at Origin Systems.

better information for decision making, strengthen productivity, and promote global competitiveness. The Technology Payoff, for instance, shows how Origin System's sophisticated technology helped Keith McCurdy respond to customer preferences for fast, dramatic action in Ultima, Origin's top-selling on-line game.

Effective information systems can also help businesses provide outstanding customer service that can lead to more market share. For example, Dallas-based Pinnacle Brands, a marketer of sports trading cards, uses information systems to provide better customer service. The system tracks customer reactions to its cards, so the company can provide its distributors with merchandise that sells well. "[Our information system] is a good way to protect our shelf space at an outlet because as demand peaks and ebbs, we're constantly replacing one hot product with the next," says Dan Barth, Chief Information Officer.[4]

However, the expanding role of information systems offers as many challenges as it does opportunities. The key, then, is learning how to use computers and related technology to achieve and sustain success for society, the organization, and the individual.

The Field of Information Systems

The acronym "IS" stands for **information systems.** However, IS has two meanings, as Table 1-1 indicates. First, **IS** is a **field of study,** which means that IS is a specific area of expertise with a common body of knowledge. Second, IS also refers to a system that provides information. In this section we explore the IS field, the key skills that prepare IS professionals, and career opportunities. In the section that follows, we investigate the second meaning of IS.

IS, a relatively new field, focuses on the relationships between information, technology, people, the organization, and society. IS specialists draw principles from many disciplines to address IS issues, as Table 1-2 shows.

This cross-disciplinary perspective enriches the information systems field and means that IS job seekers can prepare with one of many majors combined with a study of computers and information systems. For example, an information systems specialist with a psychology background could explore the effects of information system speed on the decision-making process.

TABLE 1-1 The Two Uses of the Term *Information Systems*

As a field of study	IS is an interdisciplinary field influenced by computer science, political science, psychology, operations research, linguitics, sociology, and organizational theory.
As a type of information system	IS is a broad class of information systems that provide information to aid organizational decision making.

TABLE 1-2

Disciplines and Principles Used in the IS Field	
Discipline	**Key Principle**
Computer science	Identify and understand the scientific principles of computing. Learn to develop more powerful and interactive computers.
Political science	Examine the political impact of information, both inside and outside the organization, and the effects of information systems on society.
Psychology	Understand and study how human beings reason and apply information to solve problems. Explore how to help human beings use information to become better decision makers.
Operations research	Develop tools, techniques, and methods to gather and process information efficiently and effectively. Understand the scientific and mathematical principles to get the maximum benefits from IS investments.
Linguistics	Understand the role and power of language in communications. Focus on developing more "humanistic" ways to communicate with computers.
Sociology	Identify the principles that govern society as they relate to information. Develop meaningful ethical guidelines for individuals, businesses, and society to work in an information-intensive world.
Organization theory and behavior	Assess how the influence of organizations and their culture influence individuals and society. Develop guidelines to help individuals succeed in different organizational settings.
Ergonomics	Determine ways to improve the interaction between human beings and machines. Explore ways to make computers a natural extension of human beings.

Field of information systems
The study of information and its effect on the individual, the organization, and society at large.

Information system
A system that creates, processes, stores, and generates information to help individuals make meaningful decisions.

Information System Knowledge and Skills

Technical knowledge and skills are necessary to work in the field of IS, but they are not sufficient. The IS professional—and those who work with IS specialists—should also have business knowledge, creative problem-solving skills, communication and interpersonal skills, the ability to work in teams and manage group projects, and a sensitivity to ethical and cultural issues. Figure 1-2 shows the knowledge and skills that IS professionals use.

Technical Knowledge and Skills

Although no person can be an expert at everything, and this is certainly true in the field of IS, a good grasp of the technology—whether it is systems programming, databases,

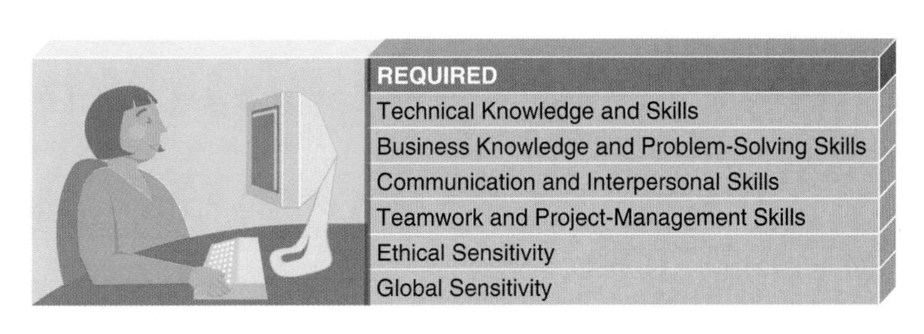

FIGURE 1-2

The Skill Set of an IS Professional

networks, the Internet, or software—is essential. Also, just as medical professionals must regularly update their knowledge through classes and special training programs, IS professionals must continually learn about technological changes or they will be left behind.

Computer literacy

Knowledge of how a computer and its elements work.

This technical knowledge starts with **computer literacy,** the knowledge of how a computer and its parts work and how the computer integrates and interacts with other technologies. Computer literacy requires a foundation in the principles of computer hardware, software, networks, peripherals such as printers, and other computer-related technologies. Specific skills include how to write and implement effective computer programs, connect two or more computers, create and maintain a database (a collection of related files containing data), and spot issues related to managing and maintaining networked computers. This knowledge is an essential foundation for IS specialists. "You've got to have the base down to work your way up the pyramid," counsels Richard Swanborg Jr., an IS consultant.[5]

Business Knowledge and Problem-Solving Skills

Almost every IS decision affects business performance. IS professionals, then, must have sufficient business knowledge to make technology decisions that solve business problems. Specifically, IS specialists must have **information literacy**—sufficient understanding of the business to be able to apply technological know-how in creative ways to help a company meet its business goals. This type of knowledge also requires a "big picture" view of how decisions made in one area of a business can influence the performance of another. As Figure 1-3 shows, computer literacy is the building block for information literacy. That is, computer literacy is a necessary and integral part of information literacy, but it is only one part. In this book we help you become information literate.

Information literacy

Knowledge about how to use computers and information systems to achieve the goals of an organization or an individual.

Lucy Cabrera is president of Food for Survival, the largest food bank in the United States. Her organization counts on a paging system to make sure that food donations are picked up and distributed to the hungry efficiently.

To illustrate how information literacy can help organizations solve problems, let's look at Food for Survival. This nonprofit organization collects and distributes more than 31 million pounds of food each year to help feed the hungry in New York City. Some time ago, a donor tried to give 1,000 cases of highly perishable, ripe tomatoes to Food for Survival but the dispatcher was unable to contact a driver to make the pickup. "At the end of the day, the donor became so angry that he pledged never to make another donation," recalls Warehouse Supervisor Robert Savino. Then RAM Mobile Data, a company that helps companies manage their data, assessed the nonprofit's information needs and stepped in to help.

Today, all Food for Survival drivers carry a palm-sized pager that receives and sends text messages to the dispatcher. Drivers now have timely information about what food is perishable so they can adjust their routes accordingly. "Food for Survival may be a not-for-profit agency, but it's still a business that needs business solutions to meet its growing challenges," explains William F. Lenahan, RAM's President.[6]

Communication and Interpersonal Skills

IS specialists must be able to communicate difficult technical concepts in a clear, concise manner to people with varying levels of technological expertise and interest. Communication riddled with technical terms confuses listeners and almost guarantees that others will not understand the issues at stake.

FIGURE 1-3

Computer Literacy and Information Literacy

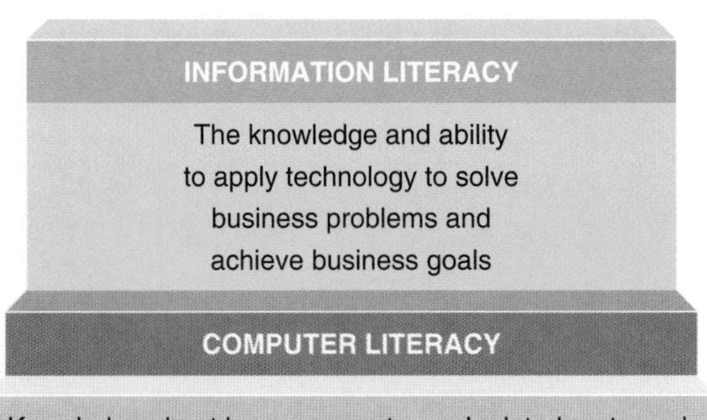

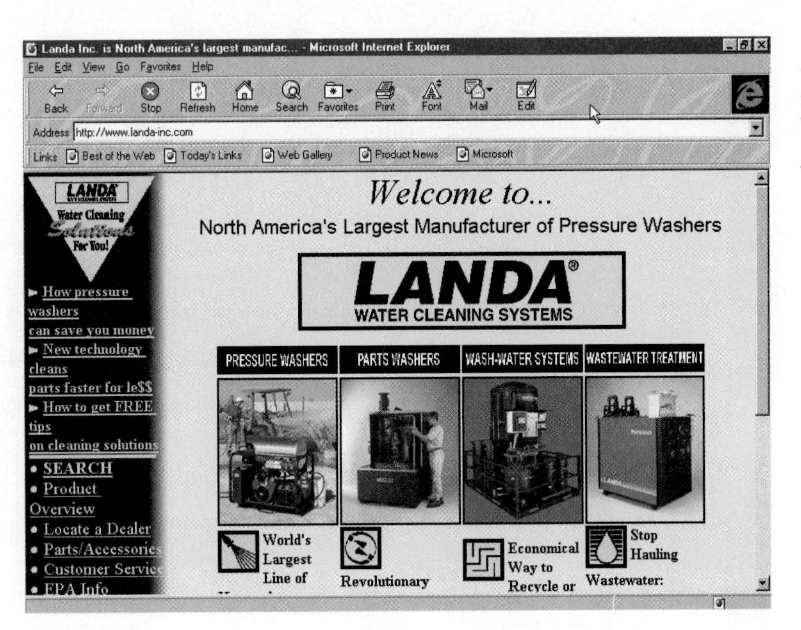

IT manager Lonnie Knotts convinced Landa's management team to develop a customer Web site with a compelling, jargon-free presentation.

Take, for instance, Ken White's experience as a managing director of oil and gas at Torch Energy Advisors in Houston. White says he needed foreign language classes to understand some of the sales presentations he sat through when his company was trying to choose business software. "Some of the [technology] salespeople literally spoke in tongues. It was difficult to get people to talk at a level that was understandable."[7]

IS professionals must learn to put themselves in the shoes of the businessperson and feel their pain, urges Nimish Mehta.[8] They should devise ways to make technical concepts simple and relevant to the listener. Information technology manager Lonnie Knotts of Landa, a water cleaning systems manufacturer based in the northwestern part of the United States, developed a compelling story to convince upper management that the Internet could improve the company's bottom line. Instead of citing facts, figures, and technical information, Knotts created "A Day in the Life of a Landa Customer," a presentation that demonstrated how customers would use the Internet. The story was persuasive because the benefits were easy to understand. Landa's president decided to invest in Knotts' initiatives.[9]

Because information systems are designed to meet the information needs of employees, business partners, or customers, learning how to listen to and interact with end users is essential. That way, IS specialists can learn about end users' needs, invite their participation in the systems development process, and work with them after the system is developed and installed to improve the system or smooth out problems.

Teamwork and Project Management

As IS professionals move up the corporate ladder, they become responsible for successfully completing IS projects that meet the company's needs, deliver information to the right people at the right time in the right format, and stay within an allocated budget. Project management requires both the technical knowledge to develop, install, and monitor a product and the ability to manage a group of intelligent, creative individuals. In fact, project management is such a difficult job that good project managers are in high demand in the IS field.

Ethical Sensitivity

Staying sensitive to IS ethical issues helps professionals plan and develop systems that treat users' privacy and other rights in a socially responsible way. Failure to do so can lead to serious repercussions, such as angry customers, a public relations fiasco, or a costly lawsuit. As technology advances, new ethical issues arise, so businesspeople must anticipate and respond to these concerns. Table 1-3, a set of ten ethical "commandments," offers recommendations to help managers avoid ethical problems such as

TABLE 1-3

Ten Commandments of Computer Ethics for Managers

1. Thou shalt not use a computer to harm other people.
2. Thou shalt not interfere with other people's computer work.
3. Thou shalt not snoop around in other people's computer files.
4. Thou shalt not use a computer to steal.
5. Thou shalt not use a computer to bear false witness.
6. Thou shalt not copy or use proprietary software for which thou hast not paid.
7. Thou shalt not use other people's computer resources without authorization or proper compensation.
8. Thou shalt not use other people's intellectual output.
9. Thou shalt think about the social consequences of the program thou art writing or the system thou art designing.
10. Thou shalt always use a computer in ways that demonstrate consideration and respect for thy fellow humans.

Source: Computer Ethics Institute, http://ei.cs.vt.edu/~cs3604/lib/WorldCodes/10.Commandments.html.

privacy, theft, and copyright violations. These guidelines work well for anyone who uses information systems in business.

We examine ethical issues in Ethics for Success features and in discussion throughout the text. The issues we explore touch on individual, business, and societal standards of right and wrong. The Ethics feature in this chapter questions how society should react to wrongdoing that violates citizens' privacy and jeopardizes safety.

Global Sensitivity

Becoming global is becoming commonplace. In fact, with the advent of the Internet, the number of companies that are purely domestic is shrinking. IS people need to master cross-cultural issues so that information systems communicate well with diverse users

Ethics for success

Does the Punishment Fit the Crime?

A teenager in Massachusetts allegedly disabled an entire local telephone loop for 6 hours, disrupting emergency response services and all but shutting down the control tower at a local airport. He also broke into a local drugstore's computers four times and copied customer records. As a punishment for this crime, the teenager's parents were charged a small fine and the youth was asked to do community service and give up his modem.

Many in the computer industry are shocked at the leniency of the punishment. "The message is disturbingly clear: If you commit vandalism with a computer, you're less accountable for your action than if you throw a rock through a window or shimmy up a telephone pole and cut the cable," says Paul Gillin, editor of *Computerworld.* Some say that one of the reasons why computer break-ins are increasing is because the punishment is not severe. Others say that teenagers are just that and need to be shown some leniency.

YOU DECIDE

1. Should all individuals, regardless of age, be expected to act responsibly with computers?
2. What kind of punishment would you have recommended?
3. Do you think the punishment in this case sent the right message?

Source: Adapted from Paul Gillin, "Slap on the Wrist," *Computerworld,* March 23, 1998, 1.

around the globe. Many experts advise new IS specialists to "Think locally, act globally," as the Global IS feature describes.

For instance, Citibank has operations all over the world, so the company must manage a global workforce. To help, the company has developed a global database that provides basic information about all employees, including their compensation, a talent inventory bank of 10,000 managers, and information on compensation and benefits packages in the 98 countries where Citibank has offices.

Even if a company is not global, chances are that the IS team is international. Due to the shortage of IS professionals, companies hire individuals from all over the world. The profile of an IS department is likely to be more diverse than any other department in the company. Learning to interact with people from different cultures can improve communication, reduce misunderstanding, and benefit the company that harnesses creative talent.

We explore how these IS knowledge and skills apply in practice in other chapters. Next we introduce career issues in the information systems field.

Information Systems Careers

To many, jobs in the information systems field conjure images of nerdy-looking people programming in small cubicles who rarely interact with others. Fortunately, this image is inaccurate. In fact, the jobs of many IS professionals require extensive interaction

Global IS for success

Think Locally, Act Globally

"The difference between a multinational company and a truly global one is like the difference between a tourist and a world traveler. The latter knows you don't tip bartenders in London, like you do in the U.S. He knows that in Paris, you need a special phone card to make a public phone call and that when dining in Iran, he might be served a sheep's eye as the guest of honor," says Mary Brandel, a freelance writer for *Computerworld.*

Building a global business is no small challenge. It is a classic struggle of balancing the desire to have a single, recognizable corporate image while meeting individual expectations of customers around the world. Global information systems can help, but such systems can run into both cultural and technological obstacles. One nation may forbid satellites because of privacy concerns and another may not have the resources to link to a standard information system. "There is no perfect answer to mixing and matching business systems, culture, and technology," explains John Parkinson, a partner in the Center for Business Transformation at Ernst & Young in Las Colinas, Texas.

But many companies are trying to think locally by staying sensitive to cultural issues in the various communities they target and act globally by presenting a strong brand image. Take London's Guinness PLC, which operates in 140 countries and sells its namesake beer throughout the world. Being a vendor of intoxicating liquor, Guinness has to be sensitive to local customs and must strike a balance between central control and letting overseas operations apply their local knowledge.

For example, the company relies on a new information system for its marketing personnel to help smooth the relationship between local marketing groups and the central marketing department. "Sometimes the central marketing department and local marketing groups clash," he notes. When local companies operate on their own, they can sometimes cause problems for the company. "Information systems help to ease these kinds of tensions by giving employees a consistent and timely flow of information."

QUESTIONS AND PROJECTS

1. What steps can you take to become more sensitive to cultures in other countries?
2. How can information systems help companies to become truly global?
3. Singapore is renowned for its use of information systems. Conduct library or on-line research to see how companies in Singapore think locally but act globally. Write a brief paper summarizing your findings.

Source: Adapted from Mary Brandel, Philip Sims, Ron Condon, and Joanne Taaffe, "Think Global, Act Local," *Computerworld,* March 10, 1997, www.computerworld.com.

with a wide range of people both inside and outside the company. A world of opportunities awaits those who have the right knowledge and skills!

Chief information officer (CIO)

The highest-ranking IS executive in a business.

Careers in information systems cover a wide spectrum. They range from executive and other managerial jobs, such as **chief information officer (CIO)** (the highest-ranking IS executive in a business), to a project manager (the person responsible for managing a specific systems project), to a Webmaster (the manager of a company's World Wide Web site). Other jobs involve developing and designing systems, such as software developers, database developers, and Web designers. Still others involve maintaining all or part of the system, including information security professionals and database administrators.

The information management workforce, the portion of the workforce that contributes to managing information, now comprises 55 percent of U.S. employment and earns a remarkable 64 percent of all wages and salaries. Further, this group has been growing twice as fast as all other occupations and wage increases have surpassed all other career fields.

Who is working in the IS field? Statistics show that by 1996 (the last year for which such numbers were available), 13.3 million women and 13.9 million men were working in this field.[10] The backgrounds of those in this field are diverse, with people from all walks of life and every level of education actively pursuing IS careers, including many who are transitioning from other careers such as nursing, art, pharmacy, teaching, and law.

The attraction to this field is motivated in part by the shortage of workers in this area and the salaries they can command. The Information Technology Association of America (ITAA) found that about 346,000 positions (approximately 10 percent) for programmers, systems analysts, and computer engineers in the United States are currently vacant.

Will the shortage stop soon? Not unless the supply of trained personnel can keep up with demand. The U.S. Department of Labor projects that during the next 10 years, 1.3 million information technology jobs will be created in the United States. One effect of the labor shortage is higher-than-average salaries for IS professionals. A salary survey conducted by the National Association of Colleges and Employers found that the average salary for a computer science or MIS graduate was about $41,000 in 1998, compared to $36,000 in 1997. And offers in the $50,000 to $60,000 range aren't uncommon, especially in the Northeast.[11] The job market and prospects for those with an IS background are better than they have ever been.

Careers for Success features in each chapter give a snapshot of some emerging careers and the skills you need to work in those professions. However, as we see in Chapter 13, the IS field is so dynamic that career choices and descriptions are constantly changing.

Information Systems: Systems That Deliver Information

Information systems also refer to systems that deliver information to individuals and organizations. Although these systems can be manual, such as a handwritten bookkeeping system, in this book we focus on computerized systems. These systems are like a big puzzle: A number of pieces must come together in a meaningful way for the system to be effective. The main pieces of the information system puzzle include hardware, soft-

FIGURE 1-4

The Information System Puzzle

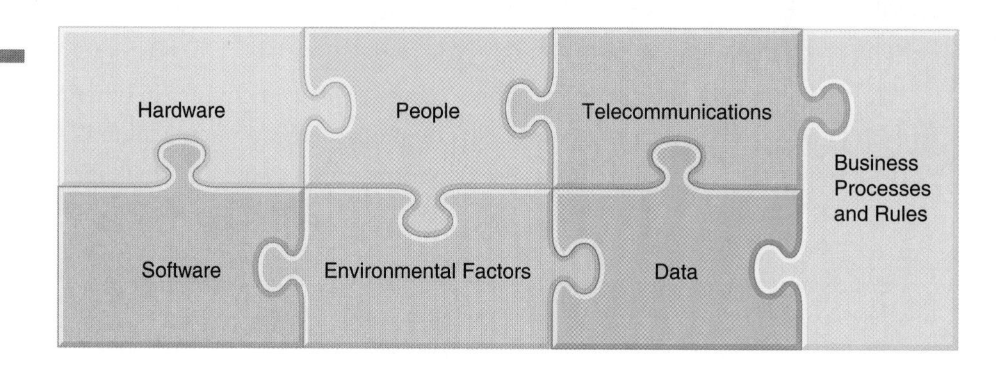

Careers for success

Michael Bell of Novartis, IS Relationship Manager

Michael Bell is an IS relationship manager at Novartis Pharmaceuticals Corp. in East Hanover, New Jersey. As a relationship manager, Bell works to improve communication and understanding between the IS department and other departments in his company, such as accounting and marketing. And he's not alone.

A study by Meta Group in Stamford, Connecticut, shows that about 30 percent of U.S. companies have IS/business relationship managers. Relationship managers may have many different titles, such as account manager, business consultant, or business information officer.

What is the job of a relationship manager like? "My job is 80 percent to 90 percent political and 10 percent technical," explains Bell. "I listen to what everyone has to say, and in the end, I'm almost like a judge." Relationship managers help non-IS people determine their information needs and articulate those needs to the IS department, but are usually not responsible for making technology decisions.

Relationship managers must have excellent writing, interpersonal, and negotiation skills. They should also understand how technology influences the overall success of the business. The question remains, however, whether they should have an information systems background or not. Although Bell does not have a technical background, technical individuals with good people skills can do well in such careers.

Source: Barb Cole-Gomolski and Thomas Hoffman, "Bridge Over Troubled Waters," *Computerworld,* March 23, 1998, retrieved on-line at www.computerworld.com/home/print.nsf/all/98032332FE; *see also* Alan S. Horowitz, "IT Ambassadors," *Computerworld,* April 20, 1998, www.computerworld.com.

ware, data, telecommunications, business processes and rules, people, and environmental factors, as we see in Figure 1-4.

As Figure 1-5 illustrates, information systems can be formal or informal. **Formal information systems** are those designed specifically to meet the information needs of the organization. In contrast, **informal information systems**—think of it as the grapevine—provide employees with information that they may not get from formal information systems. Although informal systems can often play an extremely useful role, we concentrate on formal information systems.

Formal information systems

Computer systems that the organization invests in to implement its information policies, procedures, and principles.

Informal information systems

Communication systems created informally to meet information needs; often referred to as the "grapevine."

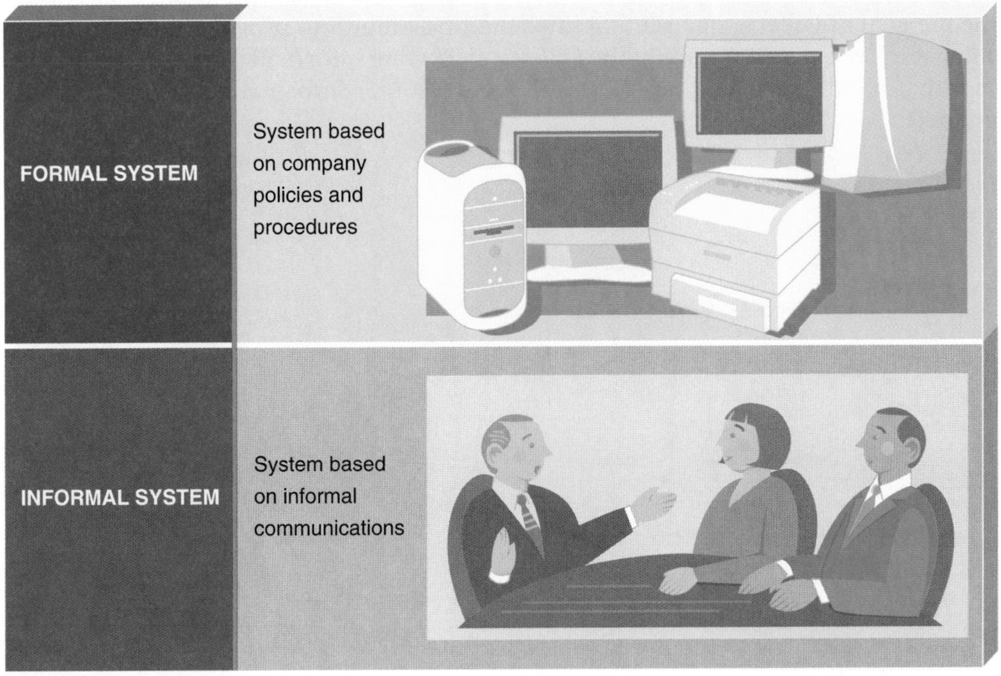

FIGURE 1-5

Formal Information Systems versus Informal Information Systems

The information system of Minnesota's Department of Public Safety, which is responsible for both drivers' licenses and car registrations, is an example of a formal system. The Department of Public Safety planned and designed the system to meet state employees' needs in processing citizens' vehicle licensing and registration. The system helps them process, store, and retrieve information related to drivers' licenses and vehicle registrations quickly and efficiently.

Although computers are often the heart of a formal information system, a number of other elements form parts of information systems. An information system consists of software, hardware, telecommunications, data, system processes, and people. The environment of an information system usually includes the organization, its specific business environment including industry regulations and competitors, and society.

Understanding each element and how they interconnect helps us plan for, develop, and use information systems successfully. To understand how these elements interconnect, we explore systems in more detail. Then we investigate how a system helps to create, process, and store information.

What Is a System?

System

A collection of parts that work together to achieve specific goals and function in an environment.

Subsystems

Units in a system that share some or all of the characteristics of the system.

We are part of many systems, ranging from our families to business organizations to galaxies. According to general systems theory, a **system** is a unit that functions in an environment and has many parts that work together to achieve a common goal. The major parts of the system are known as **subsystems.** A shopping mall is an example of a system; each store in the mall is a subsystem. A music concert is a system and the drummer, say, is a subsystem.

With an information system, the subsystems depend on the goals of the system. To demonstrate, suppose you work for Gillette, a $10 billion company that manufactures and markets a wide range of shaving gear. Gillette strives for global market share leadership. It has a portfolio of impressive brand names, including Sensor, PaperMate, Oral-B, Right Guard, Duracell, and Braun. Its products are manufactured in 27 countries and sold in over 200. Your assignment is to work with the IS team to design and develop a marketing information system.

Figure 1-6 shows that a system usually has one or more subsystems and an environment. The boundaries separating the systems, subsystems, and its environments are logical, not physical, boundaries. That is, the boundaries do not depend on physical location. For instance, all members of Gillette's Sensor marketing team, even though they are dispersed throughout several countries, would be part of the Sensor system.

First, let's identify the Gillette marketing information system parts and goals. In this case the goal of Gillette's marketing information system is to provide outstanding customer service. The subsystems in the Gillette marketing information system include the parts that handle information about pricing, customer information, warranties, and products.

FIGURE 1-6

The Subsystems and Environment of a System

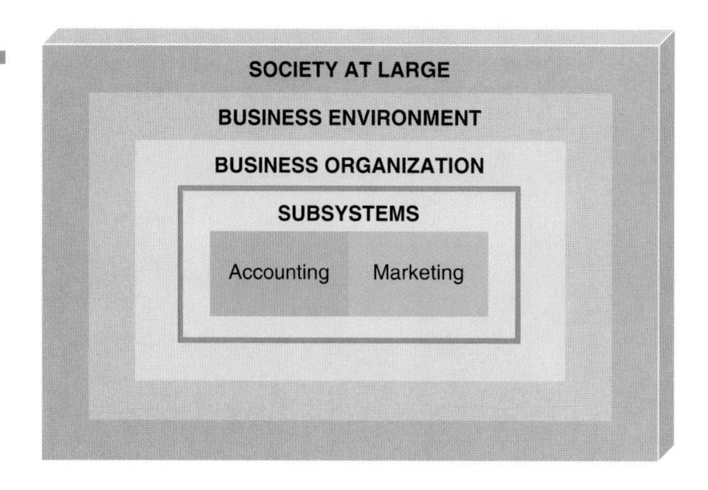

All systems operate in an **environment.** Gillette operates in a competitive global business environment governed by numerous laws and regulations. The mall operates in the business environment of the state it's in. The environment greatly influences the behavior of the system by imposing various constraints on it, such as limitations on financial resources, competitive forces, market conditions, and economic factors. Conversely, it is rare that a single system can influence the behavior of its environment.

Environment

The surroundings or the context in which the system operates.

How do we know if something is a system or a subsystem? That depends on the perspective of the user. To the CEO of Gillette, each division or brand name is a subsystem. That is, the Oral-B division is a subsystem of Gillette. To the Oral-B Division President, Oral-B is the system, the marketing department the subsystem, and Gillette becomes the environment.

System Components

Almost every system, including information systems, has five main components:

- *Input* (machines, manpower, raw materials, money, time, and so on)—Inputs for every system should be carefully defined. The input of an information system is data. In the Gillette system, the data consists of customer name, address, phone number, products purchased, price of the product, and so on.
- *Processes* (policies, procedures, and operations that convert data into information)—For example, Gillette may have a policy that it will honor a warranty up to 30 days after the warranty has expired. The system will check to see if a customer's warranty is still valid if a customer files a product malfunction claim. The process converts the warranty number and expiration date (data) into information (warranty coverage does or does not exist).
- *Output* (information in the right format, conveyed at the right time and place to the right person)—Example: Gillette's marketing managers receive daily reports on all product sales and salespeople get weekly reports on the products their division sells.
- *Feedback* (data about the performance of the system)—For instance, someone who detects an error in the system's output should report it immediately to the IS department.
- *Control* (processing the feedback and taking the necessary action, such as modifying the processes, input, or output)—An example of a control mechanism is a policy that once the IS department is notified of an error, its staff will rectify it within 24 hours.

Figure 1-7 shows the interaction among the five components of a system.

A business such as Gillette is an example of an **open system** because it is capable of interacting with its environment, receiving feedback, and acting on it. Good businesses seek many types of feedback at frequent intervals. Without feedback, businesses cannot survive. Imagine if top managers at Gillette received no information about any of its product sales! In contrast, a **closed system** does not receive or process any input from the external environment. Few, if any, fully closed systems exist in the world. Each system—whether it is IS, accounting, or marketing—is an open system that receives feedback from its environment for its survival.

Open system

A system that is able to interact with its environment and receive feedback.

Closed system

A system that is incapable of receiving feedback.

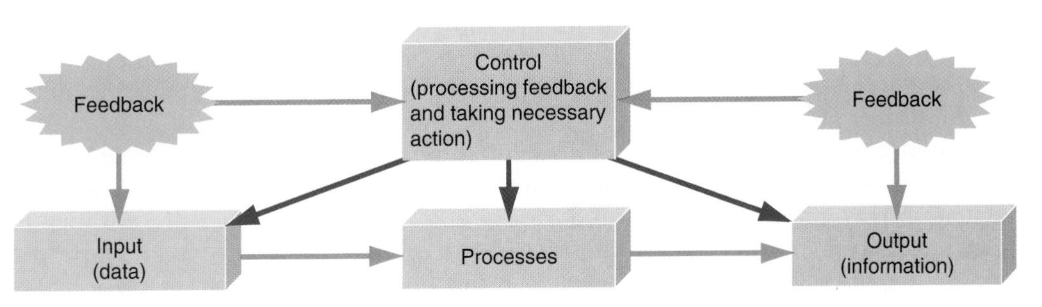

FIGURE 1-7

The Five Components of a System and Their Interaction

Characteristics of Open Systems

Systems are goal-driven. Effective open systems have several characteristics:

- Every system has a purpose.
- Open systems have the five components of input, processes, output, feedback, and control.
- Systems are made up of subsystems, whose goals are referred to as subgoals.
- The goals of a system are more important than the subgoals of its subsystems.
- Subsystems are guided both by their individual goals and by their relationship with other subsystems within the system.
- Subsystems must work together in harmony to achieve system goals.

Now that we have explored the components and characteristics of systems, let's examine what information is.

What Is Information?

Although most of us take information for granted, good information is not easy to come by. Let's investigate the difference between data and information, the characteristics of good information, and the process of transforming data into useful information.

Data

Text, numbers, graphics, audio, video, images, or any combination of these.

Information

Data that are processed and converted into a form that is useful and meaningful to the decision maker.

To make sound decisions, managers need reliable, accurate **data** that can be transformed into information. Organizations use many methods to collect data, including surveys, interviews, document reading, and even brain-wave monitoring. Sophisticated voice-activated technology is available that allows people to store data merely by speaking into a computer.

Raw data may or may not be useful to the decision maker. Human beings apply facts, principles, knowledge, experience, and intuition to convert data into **information** so that it is useful for making decisions. An example highlights the difference between data and information. Efforts are under way to create a national information system that would allow employers to determine whether a job applicant is qualified to work in the United States simply by keying the applicant's Social Security number into a computer. The information system compares the Social Security number with other relevant data, such as the candidate's immigration status and work permit. Here, data (the Social Security number) are converted into information (work eligibility) that an employer can use to make hiring decisions. Another example is class grades. To a potential employer, the grades on exams are data, whereas the overall grade in the course is information.

How Data Becomes Information

The process of converting data into information that decision makers can use is shown in Figure 1-8. Whether all seven steps in the process apply depends on the decision that problem solvers face, but all should be considered to produce the most meaningful information. We discuss these seven steps next: (1) *collection;* (2) *classification;* (3) *sorting, adding, merging,* and so on; (4) *summarizing,* (5) *storing,* (6) *retrieval,* and (7) *dissemination.*

The first step is to *collect data* through surveys, interviews, sensors, documents, newspapers, or any other appropriate means. (Data collection can sometimes be a tedious, time-consuming, and labor-intensive process. As a result, managers should carefully assess the time and cost of data collection.) Forrester Research estimates that within a year, 75 percent of all data are likely to be digital—in other words, the origins of data will be electronic, not paper, so it should be much faster to collect.

Next, data are *classified* and *sorted* in a meaningful way. For example, data about students can be sorted alphabetically based on last names for easy retrieval. Sometimes the process may include steps other than sorting, such as adding values, merging files, deleting duplicates, and so on.

When processed data becomes information, it can be *summarized* to make it more useful to the decision maker. The information is then *stored* carefully for future use. (Information may get damaged if stored improperly.) We explore the different ways to store information in Chapter 3 (Computer Hardware). Decision makers rely on proper storage to *retrieve* the information when they need it. Finally, information must be *dis-*

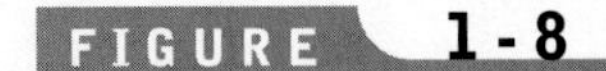
FIGURE 1-8

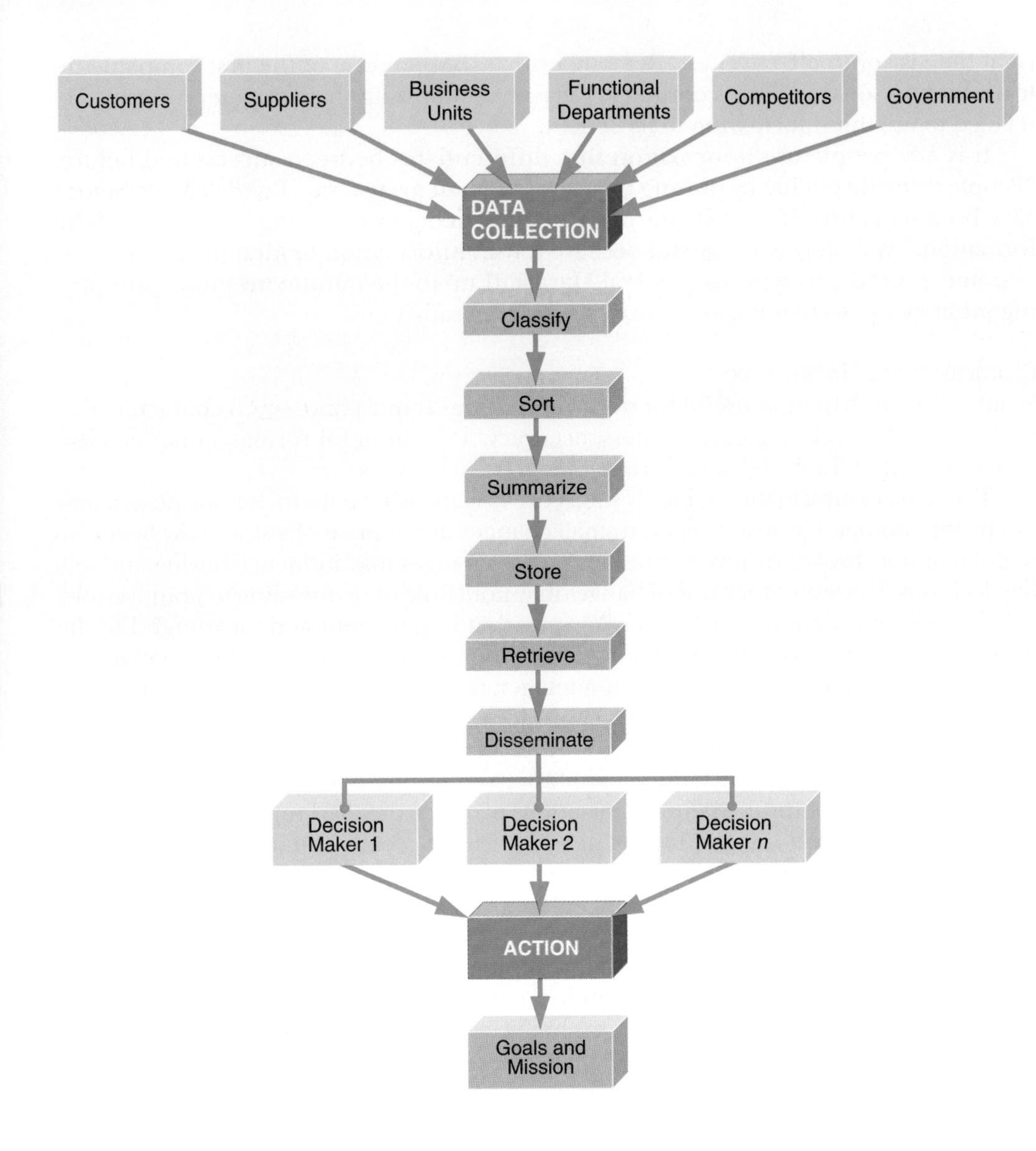

The Steps in the Data Collection and Information Gathering Process that Lead to Decision Making

seminated or distributed in the right format, at the right time, to the right place, and to the right people to be useful.

Simply executing all seven steps does not guarantee that data will become information. If the processing is inaccurate or inappropriate, its output may be useless to the decision maker. The principle GIGO—garbage in, garbage out—refers to bad data or to bad processing.

Let's look at how the Massachusetts Department of Revenue uses data from an individual's taxes and employment records and converts it into information that helps government employees identify and track parents who have defaulted on their child support payments. The state collects data on such parents and classifies and sorts the data based on factors such as the name of the employer or residential address. This information is then summarized, stored, retrieved, and disseminated to the appropriate agencies and employers throughout the state. The tax and employment records (the data) are of limited value until the state processes them into information that helps government employees identify, track, and bring these parents into court.

Once data are processed into information, that information is used for decisions. Assume for the moment that perfect information exists. Does perfect information mean individuals can make perfect decisions? Far from it! "[P]erfect information has never meant perfect decisions," explains Laurence Prusak, co-author of the book *Working Knowledge: How Organizations Manage What They Know.* Instead, using the right information at the right time is key to effectiveness. Remember that IBM was one of the first companies to learn that personal desktop computers were revolutionizing the computer industry. Yet it failed to use this information to its benefit.

It is *how* people use information that differentiates between success and failure. "People think we got big by putting big stores in small towns," says Randall Mott, Senior Vice President and CIO of Wal-Mart. "Really, we got big by replacing inventory with information." Wal-Mart is successful because it uses information to identify and meet its customers' needs. Its systems give Wal-Mart staff up-to-the-minute inventory and pricing information so that it can make decisions that satisfy customers.

Characteristics of Information

What makes information useful for decision making? It must have seven characteristics: subjective value, relevance, timeliness, accuracy, a meaningful format, completeness, and accessibility. Table 1-4 summarizes these characteristics.

The value of information is highly subjective because what is useful for one person may not be for another. For instance, even small changes in the price of a stock may be meaningful to a stockbroker or investor because these changes may influence buying and selling decisions. However, stock price changes may hold little or no meaning to noninvestors.

Information is good only if it is relevant—that is, pertinent and meaningful to the decision maker. Suppose a plant manager is trying to determine why a certain machine breaks down frequently. For that plant manager, the number of units that the machine has produced in the past 5 years is probably not relevant to the problem.

Information must also be timely. In our example if the manager gets information about the causes of machine failure a year after requesting it, the information is so untimely that it is not helpful. Many organizations produce detailed reports but do not pay attention to *when* the information is needed, which greatly diminishes the reports' value. Or employees fail to deliver customer complaints in a timely manner to the person with the authority to handle them.

Customer relations manager Shelly Halfpap knows that timely, meaningful information helps Bath & Body Works service its customers effectively.

Only 2 years ago telephone operators at nationwide retailer Bath & Body Works took notes by hand when customers called to praise or pan the latest violet balm. That process usually meant that only the loudest complaints or compliments were heard. Even then, they weren't always passed on to upper management, says Shelley Halfpap, manager of customer relations at the 1,000-store chain in Reynoldsburg, Ohio. The retailer receives more than 100,000 calls and letters from customers each year.

Today, operators type detailed notes on all calls into their personal computers. The system collects those notes in a common database so everyone throughout the company can search for and find information about customer attitudes. "We've changed so much in the last year that we've gone from crawling to running in terms of development of the customer relations department," Halfpap notes. The change has made customer attitudes more visible, requiring everyone to consider ways to incorporate the new input into buying decisions and other plans.[12]

TABLE 1-4 Characteristics of Information

Characteristic	Description
Subjective value	The value of information differs from individual to individual.
Relevance	Information should be pertinent to the decision maker.
Timeliness	Decision makers should receive the information at the right time.
Accuracy	Information should be free of errors.
Meaningful format	Information should be presented so that it can be readily used in decision making.
Completeness	The decision maker should have all necessary information to make a good decision.
Accessibility	Information should be readily available to those who need it.

Information must be accurate because erroneous information can result in poor decisions and may erode users' confidence. Just how accurate the information must be depends on the context. For example, great precision is critical for planning a space mission. Decision makers require less precision to plan a company picnic.

Information must be well formatted to be useful to decision makers. The format should allow decision makers to apply the information directly to the problem at hand without further processing. To illustrate, let's say that a manager wants to know the total sales of its leading product last year. One appropriate format for that information would be an annual summary of sales figures for the product.

Information is complete if the decision maker can solve a problem satisfactorily using that information. Although completeness is desirable, it is often unattainable. Managers often have to make decisions based on incomplete information, especially when novel problems force managers to use intuition and judgment to solve a problem.

Businesses have to strike a balance when making information accessible. On the one hand, information is useless if it is not readily accessible to decision makers when needed. On the other hand, information that is too easily available can fall into the wrong hands. Furthermore, too much accessible information can create **information overload,** a sense of being overwhelmed by the volume of available information.

Information overload

A sense of being overwhelmed by the volume of accessible information.

The Relationship between Information Systems and Technology

IS professionals must have both technical and business knowledge to guide decisions about how technology can solve business problems. In this section, let's examine the technology needed to build systems and the importance of the fit between information technology and information systems to meet business goals.

Information Systems versus Information Technology

What is the relationship between information systems and information technology? Computers and other information technologies are tools used to build information systems. **Information technology** includes hardware, software, databases, networks (technology that connects two or more computers), and other related components, as shown in Figure 1-9. With advances in information technology, the number and types of technologies available to organizations have increased dramatically.

Information technology (IT)

The tools and techniques used to build information systems.

Information systems use and integrate technologies to meet the information needs of different users. Technologies by themselves do not do anything for users. It is only when they are applied in meaningful ways that they can be used effectively.

However, technology decisions have grown more complex. Managers often have to decide whether the organization should invest time and money for new, more advanced technology that will enhance its business operations but may or may not mesh well with existing technology. "It's like running a marathon and part way through needing a heart-and-lung transplant. That's really the job we face," says Robert Walker, former vice president and CIO at Hewlett-Packard.[13]

Decisions about the technology to build information systems are difficult for several reasons. First, companies find it difficult to keep up with rapid advances in hardware and software. Today's technology stays current for a very short time. Second, technology

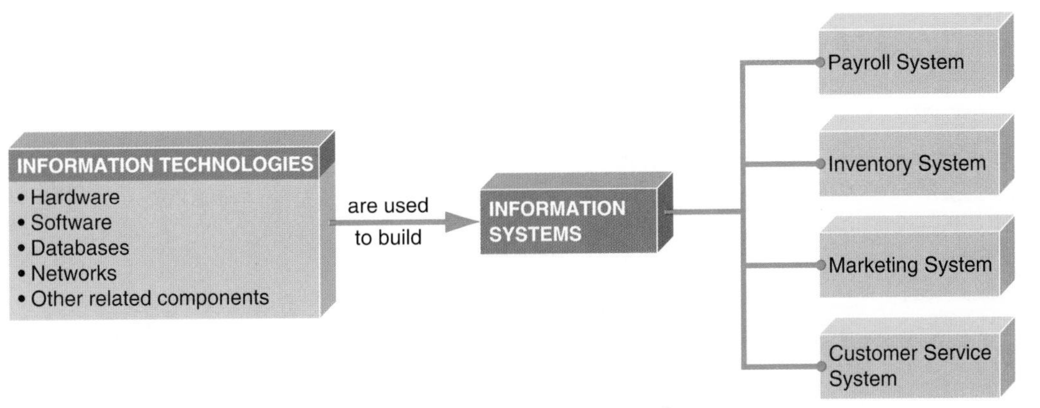

FIGURE 1-9

Information Technologies That Build Information Systems

decisions can make or break companies. Developing and implementing information technology is often expensive. Also, investments in the wrong technology can easily become a serious setback for a company. Third, the window of time for technology decisions is small because nimble competitors will outrun companies that fail to keep pace.

Finally, technology is about people and how they adapt to change. Companies that view technology simply in terms of hardware and software often fail miserably in the marketplace. Employees must use technology effectively before a company reaps benefits. It is important, then, to address people's fears, concerns, insecurities, and other emotions when considering technology investments.

The Right Fit between Information Technology and Information Systems

When a business uses IS to achieve its mission and goals, it is using information systems in a strategic way. Businesses need the right technologies to build information systems that can meet the goals of the organization. For example, American Greetings Corporation successfully uses IS to capture new markets through its unique products. This $1.7 billion Cleveland-based company launched a line of electronic cards that allows customers to create and send greeting cards from their computers. This system relies on a number of technologies, including personal computers, mainframe (a large computer), networks, sophisticated software, printers, and touch-screen monitors (monitors that are sensitive to touch), to name a few.

The company's goal is to build a $500 million electronic card business through innovative uses of computer technologies. If American Greetings relied on software that couldn't handle the graphics that illustrate the cards or its program was too tough for customers to learn, the company couldn't meet its ambitious goals.

The right systems are those that meet users' information needs. That is, they give decision makers access to relevant, complete, accurate, timely, and well-formatted information that the user values. A poorly designed system, such as one that fails to meet users' information needs, can't be saved by top-notch technology. The technologies and the systems must fit to satisfy users' needs and meet the business goals.

Computer architecture

The major components needed to build a system and an analysis of how the components fit together.

IS managers ensure a fit between information systems and technologies through **computer architecture.** The task is similar to building a house. An architect creates lists of materials and blueprints that show the sizes, types, locations, and number of rooms and how they fit together. IS specialists rely on computer architecture that identifies the *what* of a system (the technology components such as computers, databases, networks) and *how* those components fit together.

For example, the computer architecture for a firm might indicate that all the 150 computers in the company should be networked. The architecture may specify that

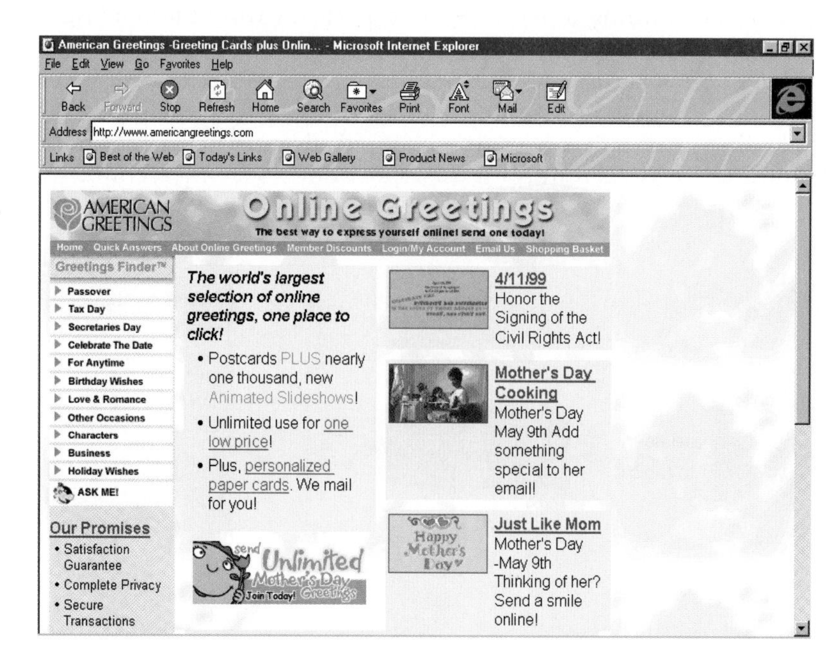

American Greetings Corporation uses its information systems to create a competitive edge. Its systems allow customers to create an electronic greeting card for every occasion with the click of a mouse.

Just as an architect draws up blueprints that show the materials needed to build a house and how they fit together, computer architecture identifies the technology components and how they fit to build a system.

each department in the company requires a separate database: one for human resources, one for manufacturing, and so on. The architecture may specify that the company needs a mainframe at its corporate headquarters and so on.

Once the design of the system is complete, information technologies help build the **information infrastructure.** The infrastructure consists of the physical components required to implement the architecture, such as wiring, cables, specific software, the type of computer, and so on. The infrastructure specifies what type of wiring and cabling is required to link the 150 computers in the company. The infrastructure addresses the issue of what kind of database to build and the functions of that database. The infrastructure also dictates how all the 150 computers and the company's mainframe (a big, general-purpose computer with strong processing capabilities) should be integrated.

Information infrastructure

The physical components necessary to implement the architecture.

Because infrastructure decisions have long-term implications (sometimes 5 to 10 years), they cannot be changed easily and can affect an organization's performance dramatically. As a result, organizations should make these decisions with great care. However, many organizations fail to give infrastructure decisions their due. "For many companies . . . infrastructure is the Rodney Dangerfield of the computing world: It gets no respect. Nobody wants to think about infrastructure because, let's face it, glamorous it isn't. Building a solid infrastructure forces a company to pay attention to the basics before it tries to get fancy, and it's not easy." [14]

Let's review some of the concepts we just discussed. Companies need information technologies to build information systems that effectively meet the information needs of different users. How do companies build systems using information technologies? The road map requires an architecture that identifies what technologies the company needs to build one or more information systems. Infrastructure helps companies to see the big picture and address how different technologies will work together to achieve business goals.

The cement that binds information systems, information technologies, and infrastructure together is the application of business knowledge and technology skills. Patrick Zilvitis, vice president of corporate information technology at Gillette in Boston, explains how understanding the relationship between business and technology helps him lead Gillette's IS initiatives more effectively. "I can't apply technology to improve business environments unless I understand both."[15]

Information Systems and Decision Making

Remember that the reason for developing information systems is to help employees make better decisions. Decisions may be related to company finances, inventory, customer service, market analysis, product promotion, employee benefits, and a wide range of other issues. Because different decisions require different types of information in different formats, it is quite a challenge to build systems that effectively meet the needs of all employees. One way to address this problem is to study who makes what types of decisions in the organization and the impact of these decisions on the organization. Obviously, some decisions, such as Where should we build our next manufacturing plant? are far more serious than Where should we hold the company Christmas party?

Different individuals in an organization make different types of decisions, depending on the nature of their jobs. Though many different options exist, the management structure in most organizations looks like a pyramid with the chief executive officer (CEO) and top managers at the apex. Nonmanagerial employees (staff) form the base. If the organization is large enough, it may have middle managers between top management and staff.

However, the pyramid structure is changing in some organizations and is giving way to what is called either the task-based or team-based organization. In this type of organization, projects and other related tasks are accomplished by bringing together groups of people based on their skills to accomplish the task, rather than their position or level in the organization. Figure 1-10 depicts the pyramid and team-based structures.

A surgical team in a hospital is an example of a team-based organizational structure. A group of medical specialists and physicians come together to accomplish a task, regardless of their levels within the structure of the hospital. Task-based teams work well for companies that operate in a dynamic business environment. Intel, a leading manufacturer of computer chips, and W. L. Gore, manufacturer of Gore-Tex material, frequently use the task-based approach to its projects. A manager at Intel describes the work of a task-based organization as similar to "planning and executing a play in football before regrouping, with substitutions or perhaps an entirely new line-up, and running another play."[16] Because the pyramid is a simple and common type of organizational structure, it is the focus of this section.

Individuals at different levels make different types of decisions. If information systems are to be truly useful, they must support decisions at all levels. This section looks at the different types of decisions people in organizations make and the role of IS for each decision type.

Structured and Unstructured Decisions and Information Systems

Structured decisions

Decisions that are routine, easily understood, and do not require the decision maker's intuition or judgment.

Typically, lower-level managers and staff are responsible for the day-to-day operations, activities, and transactions of an organization. Some of these activities may include inventory control, payroll, processing sales transactions, and keeping track of employee work hours. These employees are responsible for the short-term performance of the company and make many **structured decisions.**

FIGURE 1-10

Pyramid and Team-Based Business Structures

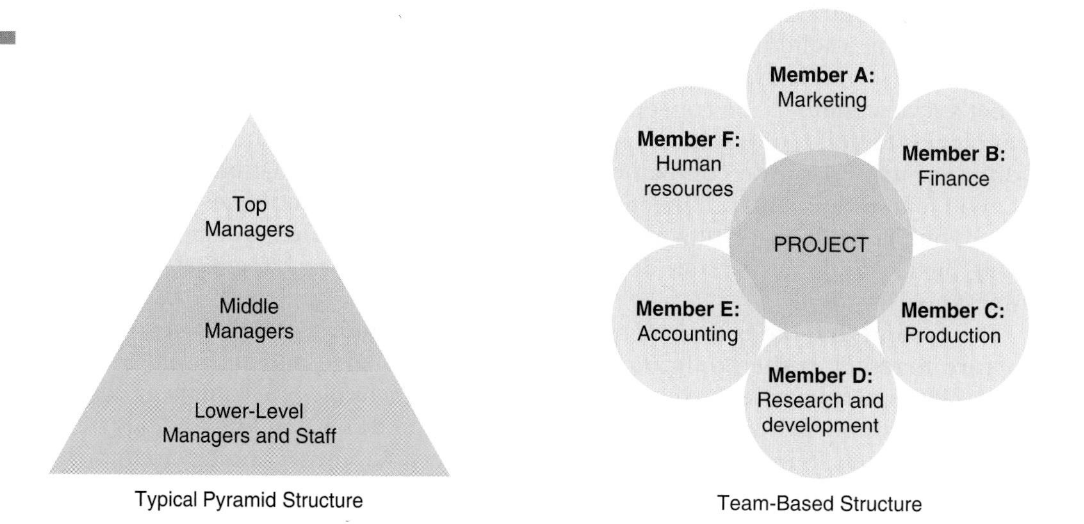

TABLE 1-5 The Difference between Structured, Semistructured, and Unstructured Decisions

Structured decisions	Routine, easily understood decisions that do not require intuition or judgment.
Semistructured decisions	Decisions that are part routine and part intuitive.
Unstructured decisions	Decisions that rely heavily on judgment, intuition, and experience.

Usually, employees who make structured decisions have access to information that is easily applicable to the given problem. Calculating the simple interest on a loan is an example of a structured task because it is routine and requires no intuition. Keep in mind that lower-level managers and staff use judgment and intuition in some decisions, but many decisions don't require it because they are based on set rules and procedures.

Generally, middle managers in an organization coordinate, control, and monitor various activities—or tactics—in an organization and act as liaison between those in charge of day-to-day operations and top managers. Middle managers make many semistructured decisions that are partly structured and partly ambiguous or unstructured. Examples of **semistructured tasks** include assessing the effect of different marketing strategies on product sales, determining the effect of an increase in operational costs on company profits, and appraising the effect of a new tax law on return on investments.

Semistructured tasks

Tasks that are part routine and part intuitive.

Finally, the top of the pyramid consists of high-level managers whose major responsibility is to establish the vision, long-term goals, and course for the company—the business strategy. The decisions of top managers are mostly **unstructured.**

Unstructured decisions

Decisions that rely heavily on intuition, judgment, and experience.

Unstructured decisions may include analyzing how competitors will respond to the company's new marketing strategy, predicting the effect of changes in the economy, and developing new products and services. Sometimes it is difficult to identify the kind of information needed to solve unstructured problems. The relevant information may be incomplete, inconsistent, or unavailable. Table 1-5 outlines the difference between structured, semistructured, and unstructured decision making.

To make good decisions, individuals at different levels in the organization use different types of information. Top and middle managers are more likely than lower-level managers to use external information—information that people or entities outside the organization generate. Managers may gather external information from the government, lawyers, regulators, competitors, stockholders, or customers. Lower-level managers, in contrast, typically need information to address short-term problems such as the number of units to produce, how to eliminate defective parts, how to schedule part-time employees, and so on. Figure 1-11 shows the three management levels and identifies the kinds of decisions made at each level.

Individual, Group, and Organizational Decisions

In this section we look at decisions that individuals, groups, and organizations make and the role of IS in each type of decision. Systems can be grouped into three types depending on whether they support individuals **(personal information systems),** groups

Personal information systems (PIS)

Systems that support the information needs of individual decision makers who must make structured, semistructured, and unstructured decisions.

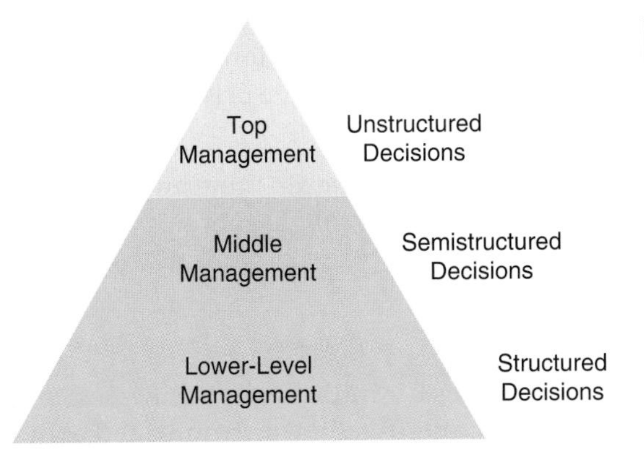

FIGURE 1-11

Types of Decisions Made in Organizations

FIGURE 1-12

Personal, Work-Group, and Organization-Wide Information Systems

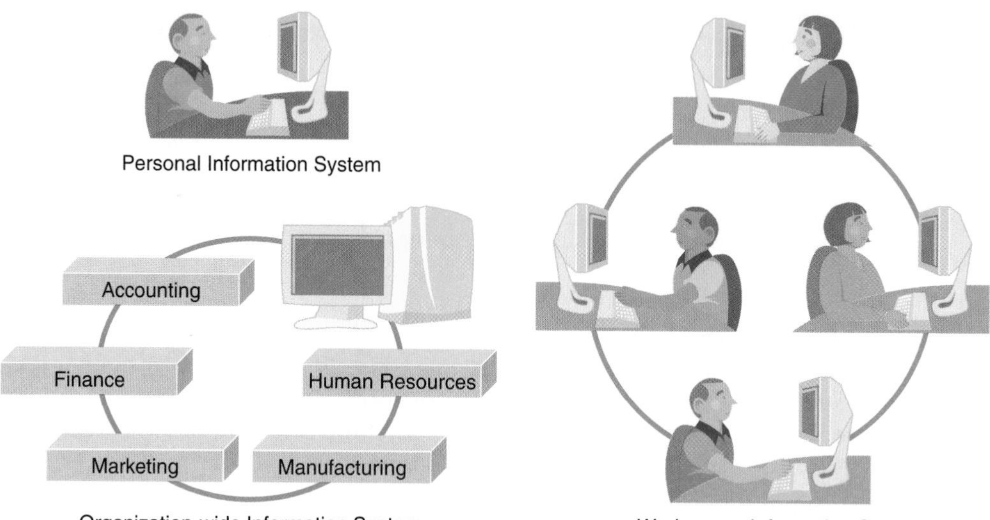

Work-group information systems (WIS)

Systems that support group decision making.

Enterprise-wide systems (EWS)

Systems that support decisions about the entire organization and provide comprehensive, long-term company information.

(work-group information systems), or the entire organization **(enterprise-wide systems).** A primary reason for the sustained growth of information systems is their ability to support and enhance the quality of decision making at all three levels. Figure 1-12 shows the differences among these three types of systems.

For example, a manager may use a personal information system (PIS), to calculate the total amount due on a set of invoices (structured decision), or to analyze market trends over the next 5 years (semistructured), or to evaluate the impact of a competitor's marketing strategy (unstructured). Note that individuals can use a PIS to make any type of decision.

Groups and teams, rather than single individuals, make many important decisions in organizations. Launching a new automobile, for instance, requires team effort and free sharing of information among group members. The work-group information system (WIS) is designed to support such decision-making activities.

For example, the Getty Education Institute for the Arts uses an e-mail–based group software program to provide information and idea exchange on special art-related topics. These topics show art educators how to teach students to understand art from multiple perspectives. Teachers involved in the arts are easily able to connect, communicate, and collaborate with one another with the help of this program. Art educators, who are often underpaid, greatly appreciate the opportunity to exchange ideas with experts around the world at no cost. Teachers have ready access to thoroughly developed lesson materials that they can use immediately in their classroom.[17] Although groupware (software for group communication) is a special kind of WIS, it shows the power of systems that support group decision making.

The third type of system is an enterprise-wide system (EWS) that supports organizational decisions. An example of an EWS is one that allows members of the organization to respond to general customer queries. If a customer wants to know the status of an order, for instance, an employee will need information on product availability (manufacturing), product discounts (marketing), payment policies (finance), damaged items (quality issues), and so on. The employee must integrate information from different departments. The EWS provides tools that offer integrated information. Table 1-6 summarizes the key differences between personal, work-group, and enterprise-wide systems.

Information Systems: Opportunities and Challenges

Information systems offer many benefits to organizations. However, they can have some negative effects on people and organizations. This section highlights key opportunities and challenges that information systems pose to individuals and organizations, as outlined in Table 1-7.

Opportunities

Information systems open up a world of opportunities for individuals, businesses, and society. For example, the Internet allows individual patients to be more informed about

TABLE 1-6

Comparing Personal, Work-Group, and Enterprise-Wide Information Systems

	Number of Users	Tasks	Size of Computer (usually)
Personal information systems	Single	Individual-based	Small
Work-group systems	Group	Group-based	Medium
Enterprise-wide systems	Larger groups	Organization-wide	Medium/large

their illnesses, possible treatments, and the pros and cons of those treatments. Businesses use information systems to create better products, serve their customers better, and empower employees. Society uses information systems to locate criminals, serve rural citizens effectively, and encourage global trade, to name a few advantages. Let's examine some key business opportunities next.

Enhance Global Competitiveness

Information systems play a critical role in helping multinational organizations meet their diverse information needs. Global companies and governments must receive and act on timely, accurate information about products, people, and procedures around the world. Information systems serve to connect people separated by time and space. Even more important, it helps people to share a common vision of the company's goals, objectives, and mission.

Consider how the Swedish government relies on IT to help cut costs. In 1994, a new Social Democratic government with Goran Persson as Prime Minister understood the importance of IT and relied on it as a means to enhance the quality of government services. Now 70 to 90 percent of all government contracting is done over the Internet. Administrative processing costs were cut by more than 50 percent thanks to the efficient use of technology. Staffan Sundstrom, the project manager, described his vision: "We had high security ambitions as well as high savings goals for the (government) organizations. And it was all to be done in just a few years. We had to set these goals so high in order to start the change wheels rolling."[18]

Capture Opportunities in the Marketplace

Successful companies quickly identify market opportunities and translate them into meaningful products and services. For example, when Wal-Mart discovered that retail customers were interested in good-quality, inexpensive merchandise in a clean, friendly environment, it acted on the information quickly. As a result of sophisticated information systems that captured even small details about customers' preferences, such as preferred color of shirts, preferred size for water hoses, and so on, Wal-Mart became a retail

TABLE 1-7

Information Systems: Opportunities and Challenges

Opportunities	Challenges
Enhance global competitiveness	Workforce downsizing
Capture market opportunities	Information overload
Support corporate strategy	Employee mistrust
Enhance worker productivity	Difficult to build
Improve quality of goods and services	Security breaches

giant. Further, because it has shared this information with its suppliers and made them partners in its quest for success, Wal-Mart has one of the most efficient inventory systems in the world.

Support Corporate Strategy to Gain a Competitive Advantage

According to strategic management researcher and author Michael Porter, several competitive forces put pressure on businesses—such as threats from old and new competitors, substitute products and services, and the bargaining power of buyers and suppliers.[19] In response to these forces, companies try to gain a competitive advantage in the marketplace by using one or more of these four basic strategies:

- They stay ahead of their competition by providing goods and services at lower cost.
- They produce highly specialized or unique goods and services that allow them to stand apart from their competitors.
- They find a market niche and focus on meeting the needs of this special group better than their competitors do.
- They develop ways to create meaningful, binding ties to customers, suppliers, and other business partners.[20]

As we see throughout this text, information systems can help companies implement their chosen business strategy successfully to develop a competitive advantage.

Enhance Worker Productivity

Information systems can help employees be more productive in the workplace by improving their decision processes. By providing them with accurate, timely information that helps them see the "big picture," employees can contribute more to the organization's success. At Dallas-based electronics vendor Texas Instruments, information systems inspire employees to learn and innovate. The company offers employees virtual classrooms, content, tools, and brainstorming space. Employees can even use information systems to post classified ads seeking help with a project.[21]

Improve Quality of Goods and Services

Quality concerns almost all companies, regardless of the products or services they produce. Total quality management (TQM) is one of the most popular approaches for enhancing quality in an organization. TQM refers to a company's comprehensive program designed to address all aspects of quality, both technical and managerial, from an organizational perspective, rather than from a departmental perspective. Quality-oriented efforts and decisions often rely heavily on information systems that deliver product quality information to the right people at the right time.

State Street Bank and Trust Company in Boston relies on its information systems to acquire and process data from around the globe. In fact, State Street Bank views technology as its core business. Under the leadership of its Chief Information Officer, Marshall N. Carter, State Street transformed itself from a bank that uses technology to serve customers to an information technology company that provides state-of-the-art tools and services to its customers. The results are impressive. The bank's total revenue, profits, and earnings per share more that doubled during Carter's first 5 years, and last year revenue was up 17 percent and business grew by 23 percent.[22]

Challenges

In spite of the many benefits, information systems also pose some challenges. Because information systems greatly influence the people in the organization and business performance, managers need to recognize and anticipate both the upsides and the downsides of IS. We explore six IS challenges next.

Workforce Downsizing

When new technologies are introduced or when technology companies merge, people may lose jobs. Many industries, such as the automobile, defense, and insurance industries, have gone through periods of massive layoffs because of intense automation efforts. Even Silicon Valley is not free from job layoffs. California-based Sybase laid off

Even companies in Silicon Valley, such as Sybase, have felt the effects of layoffs.

workers after its Japanese division misstated results. Disk drive maker Seagate Technology, in Scotts Valley, California, cut 800 jobs in the United States and thousands overseas to restructure its operations. IS can help improve business profits and productivity, but the technologies may displace workers, which is a high cost.

Information Overload

As information systems become more sophisticated and user-friendly, reports can be generated easily and quickly. However, excessive amounts of information can overwhelm managers, causing information overload. Unlike in the past, today it is easy to get information from different sources, such as a company's information systems, external or paid-for systems such as the Dow Jones, the Internet, and an overabundance of trade journals and magazines. But the ability of the human mind to digest this vast volume of information is limited. As a result, managers often feel that they have not done their "homework," simply because they have not read all the information accessible to them.

Employee Mistrust

Employee mistrust of IS develops for several reasons. First, employees may fear that computers will eventually replace them. Some companies anticipate this problem and take measures to assure employees that they will not be replaced by technology or that they will be retrained and placed in a new position. Second, some companies use information systems and technologies to monitor the activities of employees, such as reading private e-mail. Though legal, such acts generate a sense of violation of privacy. In addition, some companies use IS to gather customer information that the general public would rather keep private. America Online was nailed a few years ago for trying to sell data about its subscribers to direct marketing outlets.

Difficulty of Building Information Systems

Information systems are not easy to design and develop. In spite of the large number and variety of development tools available today, few companies develop systems on time and within budget. As a matter of fact, estimates indicate that fewer than 30 percent of information systems are delivered on time and under budget.

Security Breaches

Protecting computers and information from theft, pilferage, and security breaches is a challenging task. Take a look at some of the statistics about security violations. Hackers attack the average corporate network 12 to 15 times each year, according to a survey by the Computer Security Institute and the FBI. Of the 563 users polled, 73 percent said hackers had penetrated their networks. But 18 percent said they had no idea if, or how often, their systems had been invaded.[23]

The more sophisticated the technology, the more difficult and expensive it is to protect it. Computer break-ins and loss of information can be very damaging to an organization. "The time has come for IS executives to turn fearful. CIOs must become as aggressive about information security as the professional spies and thieves who threaten them," says Paul Strassman, an IS consultant and ex-CIO of Xerox. The simple fact is that risks from IT malfunction now rank with earthquakes (a $30 billion to $60 billion exposure) and hurricanes ($5 billion to $15 billion per incident) in potential economic losses. And if one takes into account various failure scenarios, such as a global software virus or deliberate acts of information terrorism, the estimate of financial damage approaches that from an accident at a nuclear power plant.[24]

In summary, like other tools, information systems have advantages and disadvantages. An awareness of the pros and cons is the first step toward using and managing IS effectively.

Business Guidelines for Information System Success: A Framework

Information system success depends on numerous circumstances, rather than a black-and-white formula. These systems are open systems so they are dynamic, affected by the environment, and influenced by the people who use them. However, these systems are also goal driven, so we can measure IS success by focusing on whether the system achieved the goals of the organization.

Each chapter integrates examples that show how businesses use IS successfully, often to gain a competitive advantage, and closes with guidelines for success. We focus on goal-driven, effective uses of information systems to help you become a more educated information systems user no matter what profession you choose.

SUMMARY

1. **Describe the field of information systems.** The information systems field is cross disciplinary. Those who work in the field must have technical and business knowledge, also referred to as computer and information literacy. IS specialists must have technical, communication, problem-solving, teamwork, and project management skills, and a sensitivity to ethical and cultural issues. Contrary to stereotypes, IS career options are wide-ranging, exciting, and creative.
2. **Discuss the characteristics and components of a computerized information system that provides information to users.** An information system consists of hardware, software, networks, processes, data, and people, and functions in an environment. The system receives data—the raw material from which information is generated. It converts the data into information by processing, storing, and disseminating it to help people make decisions. Note that information systems consist of more than technology. They also include data and people and function in an organizational, business, and societal environment.

   An information system, as with any type of system, is a collection of interrelated parts that work together to achieve one or more common goals. A formal system is one that follows set rules, processes, and procedures to deliver information. Effective systems typically have five basic components: inputs, processes, outputs, feedback, and control.
3. **Summarize the relationship between information systems and information technology.** Information technologies are tools used to build information systems. Information technologies include hardware, software, databases, networks, and other related components. Information systems use and integrate technologies to meet the information needs of different users. The information technology, then, must support the goal of the information system, which is to provide accurate, timely, relevant, complete, well-formatted information that users value. Computer architecture ensures a fit between information systems and technologies.
4. **Summarize how IS supports decision making.** Information systems should support structured, semistructured, and unstructured decision making in an organization. They should also support individual, group, and organization-wide decision processes. Personal information systems support individual decision making, work-group information systems support group decisions, and enterprise-wide systems support organization-wide systems.
5. **Outline the opportunities and challenges of IS.** Information systems offer opportunities, such as more global competitiveness, faster responsiveness, strong support for corporate strategy, improved worker productivity, and better-quality goods and services. IS challenges include layoffs, information overload, difficulty in systems development, employee mistrust, and security breaches.

KEY TERMS

chief information officer (p. 10)
closed system (p. 13)
computer architecture (p. 18)
computer literacy (p. 6)
data (p. 14)
enterprise-wide systems (p. 22)
environment (p. 13)
field of information systems (p. 5)
formal information system (p. 11)
informal information systems (p. 11)
information (p. 14)
information infrastructure (p. 19)
information literacy (p. 6)
information overload (p. 17)
information system (p. 4)
information technology (p. 17)
open system (p. 13)
personal information systems (p. 22)
semistructured tasks (p. 21)
structured decisions (p. 21)
system (p. 12)
subsystem (p. 12)
unstructured decisions (p. 21)
work-group information systems (p. 22)

REVIEW QUESTIONS

1. Describe the field of information systems. What are some of the disciplines that have influenced the study of information systems?
2. What is an information system? What are some benefits that organizations can derive from information systems?
3. What is the difference between computer literacy and information literacy? Suppose a student designs and implements an information system for a video store. Is this an example of computer literacy, information literacy, or both?
4. *Computer architecture* and *information infrastructure* help us to create good information systems. Explain what these two terms mean.
5. How does understanding the five components of systems help us to build better information systems?
6. What is the difference between data and information? Identify some activities in the process of converting data to information.
7. Identify any three characteristics of information that were important to you in selecting your school and your major.
8. Can a business be a closed system? Why or why not?
9. What is the difference between an information system and an information technology? Can one exist without the other?
10. Is your bank ATM an example of an information system, information technology, or both? Discuss.
11. What are the differences between structured, semi-structured, and unstructured decisions? Give an example of each.
12. What are the main differences between personal, work-group, and enterprise-wide systems? Give an example of each.
13. What are some opportunities and challenges that information systems pose for society?

DISCUSSION QUESTIONS AND EXERCISES

1. Look at your university or college as a system. Identify any subsystem in this system. Also, identify and describe the environment in which the educational institution operates. What are some of the inputs, processes, and outputs of your system? What kind of feedback and control mechanism would be appropriate for this system?
2. Give an example of a personal information system and a work-group information system in a large organization.
3. Identify a company that has felt the negative effects of computers and information systems and list the negative effects. Identify a company that has become a market leader because of its innovative use of information systems.
4. Describe the control-and-feedback mechanism that your teacher uses in this course to assess and evaluate your class performance and his or her performance as a teacher.
5. **(Software exercise)** Create a spreadsheet using the data in Table A below. Find the average quiz score and average exam score for each student.

TABLE A

Name	Student ID	Q1	Q2	Q3	Q4	Q5	Q6	E1	E2	E3
Kriegler	600091	80	85	90	80	100	95	87	89	94
George	600054	67	90	84	94	98	89	65	76	77
Stella	600079	98	88	87	79	99	97	88	80	98
Nathan	600049	92	68	87	91	89	80	92	89	88
Jeffrey	600092	82	88	89	90	91	92	79	65	91

Case 1: Technology to Monitor Stress

Some industry experts think computers cause stress in the workplace; others are using computer technology to track stress levels of employees and be proactive in tackling this issue. A new e-mail service allows employees to anonymously rate their overall satisfaction about their companies and the quality of their work life.

Al Braut, Director of the Human Resources Department at the University of Rochester, decided to give the service a try. His 65-member staff gives him feedback on a regular basis about the department and issues that are important to them. "A vehicle like this provides employees an opportunity to communicate some things they usually would not say in other venues," says Braut.

Moshe Mor, CEO of SPL World Group in San Francisco, also believes in this service. "I want to use technology to create an informal communication mechanism for employees. This is an early warning system," says Mor.

Typically, e-mail service is better than paper-based surveys because they are less tedious to administer, less costly, and less time-consuming. For instance, an analysis of survey results may take several months before management finds out about employee issues, and by that time it is too late to do anything about them. Even with timely information, success is not guaranteed. "Management has . . . to be prepared to hear both good news and bad news and take action on it," says Bob Felton, CEO of Indus International, Inc., another subscriber to the e-mail service.[25]

1. **(Web exercise)** Visit the Web site www.stressrelease.com and identify some factors that lead to work-related stress.
2. Is this an innovative use of existing technology? Is this example particularly useful for global companies? Discuss.
3. Are there any ethical dilemmas that can arise in this situation?
4. **(Software exercise)** See if you can use your current e-mail system to send mail anonymously. If so, what could be some potential drawbacks to and benefits of this capability? What would be the drawbacks to and benefits of not having this capability?

Case 2: Computer Crime Costs on the Rise

The cost of computer crime is rising. The average losses from theft of proprietary company information has leaped 68 percent in the past 2 years, according to a recent survey of 250 businesses conducted by the Computer Security Institute in San Francisco. Some companies are taking an aggressive approach to this problem.

Charles Schwab, for example, has about 15 security staffers and is constantly trying to hire more. Ed Ehrgott, Director of Internal Audit at the discount brokerage firm, says, "We constantly assess and monitor network traffic operations both internally and externally. In the event the worst happens and we get hit, we're ready with a trail of evidence to turn over to the proper authorities."

Christine Snyder, a vice president at Price Waterhouse LLP in Baltimore, said she considers the biggest security threat to be from company insiders. As a result, she believes that educating employees of the consequences of security breaches is a top priority. A comprehensive survey reported the six most common computer-related abuses reported by security directors of 150 major U.S. corporations. Those top six problems and the percentage of companies that reported the problems follow:

- Credit-card fraud, 96.6
- Telecommunications fraud, 96.6
- Employees' personal use of company computers, 96.0
- Unauthorized access to confidential files, 95.1
- Cellular phone fraud, 94.5
- Unlawful copying of software, 91.2

"It's extraordinarily widespread," said survey researcher David Carter, a criminal justice professor at Michigan State University.[26]

1. **(Web exercise)** Visit www.computerworld.com. Use this site's search link to identify any recent developments in the area of computer crime.
2. **(Software exercise)** Use a spreadsheet to show how computer crimes have increased in the past 5 years in the United States.
3. How can organizations ensure that trust in their employees is not misplaced?
4. What are some possible reasons for the increase in computer crimes?

Case 3: A Million-Dollar Question!

BC Telecom in Vancouver, British Columbia, was preparing to develop a new database system and decided to get some input from users. "If you knew something you don't know today, or had easy access to information you don't have now, what opportunity could you create, and how much revenue would it generate?" They received 49 ideas for new business opportunities for the new system; so far about one-third have resulted in actual applications. Suggestions include ideas for using marketing information to retain customers and to identify the kinds of products and services that might be of interest to individual customers. Early estimates are that those ideas could bring in $42 million in revenue over 3 years.[27]

1. Pick a company for which you would like to work. How would you answer the question that was posed to the employees of BC Telecom?
2. What are the benefits of asking employees for their input about the development of a new system? Are there any drawbacks?

Case 4: NATO Buys into Technology

At NATO's headquarters in Brussels, the offices are cramped as diplomats from the member nations negotiate mutual defense plans. The ability to negotiate and be flexible are also hallmarks of the IS department at NATO, where the staff consists of military officers borrowed from the armed forces of 16 countries.

NATO is like any other large organization: tight budgets, strict schedules, and a whole host of technologies to manage, all operating within an environment of rapid and unpredictable change. Even so, the IS department at NATO is a model of efficiency and responsiveness. Why?

NATO does not buy technology for the sake of technology. Instead, it takes existing information systems and adapts them to meet its unique needs. For example, instead of building a financial system from scratch, NATO bought its system from military services of member nations and tweaked the system to meet its needs. The result? A sophisticated system that cost less, was delivered faster, and remains highly responsive to a user's needs.

Flexibility is key to the success of NATO's IS department. Unlike many other business organizations, at NATO an IS project can be suspended if technology is changing, users won't be ready, or a more important project comes along. When the time is right, the department will restart the project. The payoff from such flexibility is information technology delivered better, faster, and more cheaply.[28]

1. What leadership traits are necessary to run a successful IS department?
2. NATO does not buy technology for the sake of technology. Why is this a meaningful approach for any organization?

The era of evaluating IT value based on the skin-deep pizzazz of technology is over. These days, the technology still needs to shine, but the CIO must also demonstrate how the new system will open new markets, add revenue and increase customer loyalty.[1]

Christopher Koch, information systems writer

CONTENTS

INFORMATION SYSTEMS FOR SUCCESS

In this and other chapters we explore how information systems affect the way we think, learn, perform, and share knowledge. We also investigate how information systems (IS) affect individuals, businesses, and society. These effects are dramatic, as evidenced by the worldwide growth of the information technology (IT) industry.

According to a study sponsored by the American Electronics Association and NASDAQ, IT (a combination of the computing and telecommunications industries) is the largest industry in the United States. The IT sector produces 6.2 percent of the country's goods and services and employs 4.3 million workers, who earn 70 percent more in average wages than other private sector workers.[2] European companies employ roughly 400,000 IT professionals and invest more than 2 percent of their annual revenue in IT staff, infrastructure, and projects. Germany, the United Kingdom, and France top the list of high spenders in Europe. Top honors, in terms of highest-spending European companies, go to Germany's Siemens AG and the joint U.K.–Dutch operation Royal Dutch/Shell.

Information systems and technologies offer individuals opportunities to enhance their personal productivity and communication. People complete tax returns or do investment research quickly and accurately using personal financial software. To learn a new language, art, or skill, people turn to computer CD-ROMs. Students make pen pals around the world, and avid travelers use the Internet to find cheap fares to their chosen destination.

Businesses also rely on IS and IT to achieve their goals. Companies invest huge amounts of money in computers and IS because they have become "the electronic nervous system" of business. They use IS and IT to improve their efficiency, speed, and customer service

Chapter 2

How Businesses Use Information Systems

AFTER STUDYING THIS CHAPTER, YOU WILL BE ABLE TO:

- Describe basic business structures and functional areas
- Identify four types of information systems
- Explain the role and function of marketing information systems
- Summarize the purpose of manufacturing and service information systems
- Outline the purpose of financial and accounting information systems and how they support a business
- Explain the role and function of human resource information systems
- Discuss the purpose and effects of cross-functional systems
- Define and describe global information systems

to gain a competitive edge by serving customers anytime, anyplace, and at the best price.

This may sound like a challenge; it is. First, technology is both a curse and a blessing. It can help a business improve its operations. However, constant technological developments force companies to respond or risk losing to competitors who harness the technology to work better, faster, and harder. Second, companies face an ever-changing business environment due to a global economy, shifting and exacting customer expectations, and agile competitors. To succeed in the face of such change, businesses must have clear goals, innovative yet flexible strategies, and a strong sense of mission.

The IS effects are not limited to business. Information systems play an important societal role—from aiding people affected by natural disasters to enriching education in rural communities to exploring Mars. On hearing of the devastation wrought by Hurricane Mitch in his father's homeland of Nicaragua, Ronin Corp.'s help-desk administrator Pete Sequeira immediately requested family leave so he could fly down to help. What he didn't expect was that his boss, CIO Bob McCracken, and several colleagues would want to go, too. "We felt we had to do something instead of sitting around," McCracken explains. An estimated 4,000 people were killed in Nicaragua and 800,000 became homeless after a week of torrential rains that peaked at four inches of rainfall per hour. The team flew to Nicaragua to quickly put together networks and databases to help track missing people, medicine inventories, and disease outbreaks.[3]

In this chapter we examine how companies can harness the power of cross-functional information systems to create a competitive advantage. What do we mean by cross-functional systems? Every

TECHNOLOGY PAYOFF

The Ritz-Carlton's Savvy Salesforce

The Ritz-Carlton, a privately held international chain of 33 hotels based in Atlanta, depends on exemplary sales, service, and customer relations to succeed. Its highly trained, 700-person sales and service staff relies on marketing information systems to help meet the company's customer service and sales goals. Those systems include a central database and a common sales and marketing information system.

Before the system was installed, the salesforce would compete against one another and against other local hotels for bookings. In many cases, more than one sales representative called a corporation to drum up sales, explains Lisa Fearon, Ritz-Carlton's manager of sales system development. This redundancy of effort often caused awkward moments for both the sales reps and the hotel chain.

The new system has eliminated the duplication of effort, resulting in time and money savings. Today, sales reps share account information on reservations and catering. Armed with occupancy data and a customer's reservation history, salespeople can target top-tier corporations, gauge missed sales opportunities, and access historical information to anticipate what a customer will want before making the first sales call. The marketing system has helped the Ritz compete effectively in a tight marketplace and become more responsive to its customers' needs.

Source: Adapted from Kim Girard, "Streamlining Sales at the Ritz," *Computerworld,* December 15, 1997, 23–24.

IS specialists provide vital assistance to people in Nicaragua in the aftermath of Hurricane Mitch.

business has certain key functions such as production, finance, accounting, marketing, and so on. Each function often has its own information systems. For example, the accounting department may have an information system to process accounts receivable. Cross-functional systems integrate information between different functional systems (such as accounting) with that of other functional systems (such as marketing) so employees can share information easily and readily.

As the Technology Payoff shows, the Ritz-Carlton relies on cross-functional information systems to outdo its stiff competition. Its systems combine information from different areas, such as marketing and finance, to help employees understand the big picture and avoid duplicating efforts. Customers, in turn, receive better service. Next, we explore the structure of business and the role of information systems in marketing, finance and accounting, manufacturing and services, and human resources. We also examine global information systems, which are networks that link different business units around the world.

Structuring the Business to Work Effectively

A business is a complex entity that must be organized well to operate effectively. One type of business structure is to organize departments according to business functions. Several common functions are marketing, manufacturing (or production), finance and accounting, human resources, and information systems, as we see in Figure 2-1. Because the focus of this text is information systems, we will not explore IS as a separate function here. Instead, we look briefly at the other functions and how they use information systems.

Marketing

The cornerstone of marketing theory is how to mix product, price, distribution (also called place), and promotion strategies—known as the "marketing mix" or the "4 Ps." Marketing activities include selling, pricing, distributing goods and services to a place where customers can buy them, advertising or other promotional activities, and customer service. The marketing department supports the company goals relating to profits, growth, public relations, and market share. How a firm mixes and matches the 4Ps of the marketing mix can determine whether the firm is or is not successful.

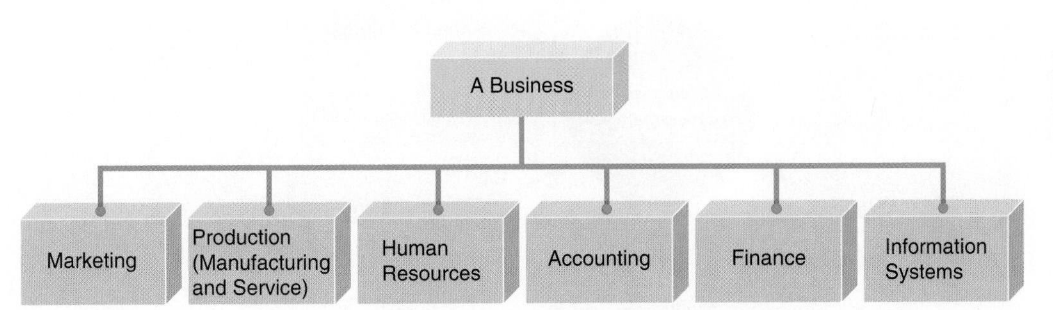

FIGURE 2-1

Key Business Functions

Manufacturing and Services

The manufacturing department is responsible for all activities related to producing and delivering a product or service. Activities include the design, manufacture, and delivery of a product or service. Manufacturing is also responsible for identifying and purchasing raw material (although in most large organizations purchasing is a separate unit in the manufacturing department) and for logistics, which ensures that the right product reaches the right customer at the right time.

Managers in this department are responsible for ensuring that the right products in the right quantities are made on the right machines using the right amount of raw materials. This set of responsibilities is sometimes referred to as "production scheduling." Personnel scheduling requires that people be scheduled to do jobs that match their skills.

Finance and Accounting

Accounting and finance cover a wide range of activities and business functions such as short- and long-term budgeting, cash and asset management, portfolio analysis, general ledger, accounts receivable, inventory control, and payroll systems. Types of information systems that support this department include record keeping, account analysis, cash management, financial analysis, leasing options, insurance underwriting, insurance claims processing, and investment management.

Financial institutions such as banks use specialized financial and accounting information systems, including commercial loan analyzers, credit approval and credit application systems, commercial account rating systems, automated teller control, and securities trading. Finance and accounting departments also develop the company's financial statements, which are written records that provide accounting information to people inside and outside the company.

Human Resources

The human resources (HR) department helps manage, train, and staff the employees in an organization. Managers in human resources develop policies and procedures concerning recruiting, hiring, layoffs, employee evaluation, promotion, transfers, salaries, job descriptions and responsibilities, training, and affirmative action and equal employment opportunities.

This department ensures that the company follows tax and labor laws and payroll policies, handles health and child care benefits and grievance procedures fairly, and collects but safeguards other personal information that affects employees. It must also communicate company policies and procedures to all employees and help to maintain a safe workplace. HR information systems must be highly responsive to employees' needs and support the activities of HR managers.

Although we study a business by looking at the functional areas, this approach may not always be the most effective way to structure a business, particularly in a highly

FIGURE 2-2

A Business Structured by Cross-Functional Teams

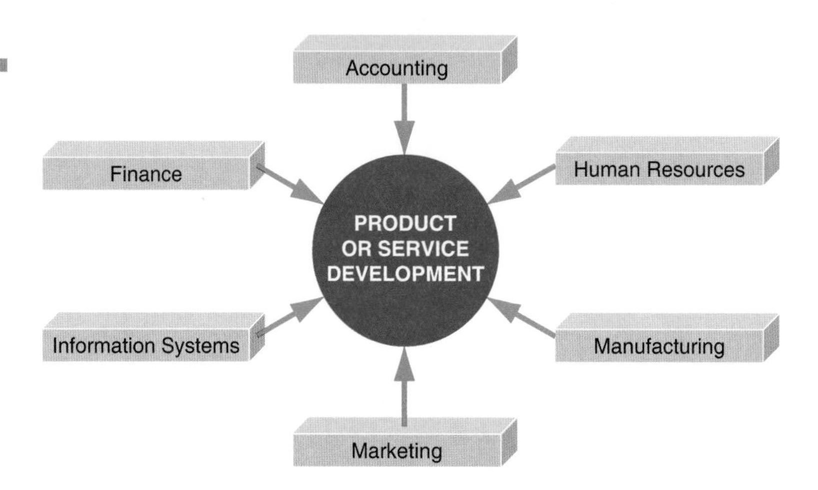

competitive, uncertain environment. In fact, organizing the business according to function is on the wane. According to a survey by the Information Management Forum (IMF), half the surveyed companies are moving or planning to move from a functional to a cross-functional orientation—that is, organizing staff not by traditional departments, but according to the nature of the task that needs to be accomplished. Figure 2-2 illustrates this type of structure.

Suppose, for example, an automobile manufacturer wants to introduce a new model every two years. This requires that a team of people with different areas of expertise, also referred to as a "cross-functional team," work together to design, produce, market, and sell the model. Together, the team tackles various issues, such as:

- Can we produce this model? (a manufacturing issue)
- What are the needs of our customers? (a marketing issue)
- How much money can the company afford to invest in a new model? (a finance issue)
- Do all activities comply with accounting rules? (an accounting issue), and
- How many people do we need to produce this model and what kind of skills should they have? (a human resource issue)
- What information do employees need to make good decisions? (an IS issue)

Compare the cross-functional and functional approaches. With the functional structure, designers would model the car and pass on the designs to manufacturing specialists, who would look into the model's feasibility and then pass on the model to marketing and so on, as we see in Figure 2-3. This assembly-line approach is not always the most efficient way to conduct business. For instance, the design might be impossible to manufacture, finance, or market because the designers did not have input from other functions.[4]

Because cross-functional systems are helping companies compete, it is likely that you will work on a cross-functional team, so understanding how these teams work is crucial. Further, many exciting IS career opportunities exist for individuals who are creative, technologically savvy, and team oriented. Those who have some IS and other business expertise can become "business technologists," as shown in the Careers feature. Business technologists take a cross-functional approach to solving problems that affect the entire organization.

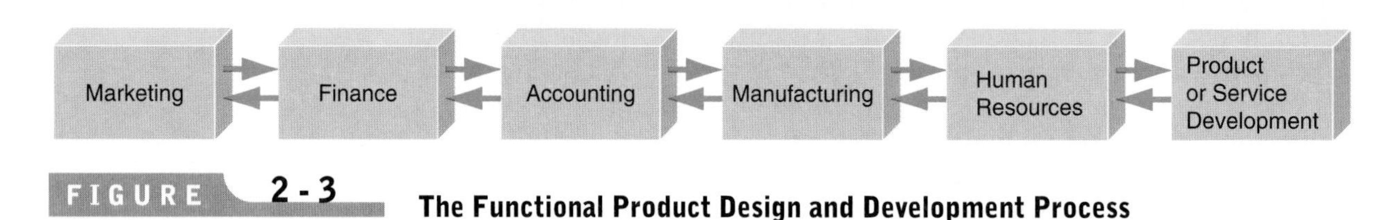

FIGURE 2-3 **The Functional Product Design and Development Process**

Careers for success

Business Technologists

David Kramer's ability to use technology to recognize and capture business opportunities attracted the attention of top managers at Fidelity Investments. They created a new position to put his talent to full use. Today, Kramer is director of operations for a custom-publishing subsidiary. He is responsible for making sure the technology supports the company's operations.

He reports to the president and the organization reports to him about technology issues. "If you have both business and technology skills, good things will happen," Kramer says. Kramer is a member of a growing class of information technology staffers dubbed "business technologists." Able to communicate with nontechnologists, and thoroughly versed in business operations, these people quickly rise to the top.

One company that grooms and promotes business technologists is Sears, Roebuck and Co. in Hoffman Estates, Illinois. Joseph Smialowski, vice president and CIO, says that when he recruits senior executives he looks for people with both business and IT backgrounds. Business and IT, he notes, "are the skills you need to foster a business partnership and meet business needs. If you aren't able to evolve into those roles and responsibilities, you are in jeopardy. You will not be going where the IT profession is going," he says.

David Foote, managing partner at Cromwell Foote Partners LLC, a management consulting and research firm, says this is a trend that extends well beyond Sears. He predicts that "seven to 10 years from now, there will be no information technology organization as we know it. . . ." Instead of a technology division, there will be teams led by MBA-types who understand the interplay of business and IT. "The demand for that layer between the pure technologist and the business [specialist] has increased tenfold," says Matthew Corbett, who recruits computer consultants for Winter, Wyman Contract Services, the computer-consulting wing of a placement firm in Waltham, Massachusetts.

Source: Adapted from Natalie Engler, "The New Business Technologists," *Computerworld,* November 16, 1998, www.computerworld.com.

Next we look at ways to classify information systems. Then we consider how information systems support each business function by providing functional managers with accurate, timely information that promotes better decision making.

Types of Information Systems

There are several ways to classify information systems. In this section, we look at four classifications.

1. Personal, Work-Group, Enterprise-wide Systems:

As we saw in Chapter 1, sometimes information systems are grouped into categories based on the number of individuals who use them. For example, information systems can be grouped into personal systems (one user), work-group systems (a group of users), or enterprise-wide systems (the entire organization).

2. Systems Based on Type of Decision:

Information systems can also be grouped based on the type of business decision they support. Decisions can be classified as operational, tactical, and strategic. For instance, systems that process transactions in a company are called "transaction-processing systems" and these support lower-level, operational decision making. Other types of decision-oriented systems include management information systems, decision support systems, and so on. We cover these briefly in this section and in greater detail in Chapter 10.

3. Strategic Information Systems:

Strategic information systems, a broad classification of information systems, are information systems that give a company a significant strategic advantage over its market competitors. So a strategic information system may be a transaction processing system, a management information system, a decision support system, and so on, or any combination of these systems. A system becomes strategic, not because of the underlying

Strategic information systems

Any information systems that use information technology to give firms a strategic, competitive advantage in the marketplace.

technology or who uses it, but because of how that technology is applied to give the company a competitive edge.

A commonly cited example of a strategic information system is the ATM. Citibank was the first bank to use a transaction processing system (TPS) to allow customers to bank anywhere, anytime. The use of the TPS gave Citibank a tremendous market advantage until competitors responded with similar systems. Another example is the SABRE airline reservation system developed by United Airlines. By giving travel agents information about all flight times, availability, and fares through a database system, United achieved a significant competitive edge in the travel industry.

4. Function-Oriented Information Systems:
We can also classify information systems according to types of business function: marketing information systems, manufacturing information systems, financial information systems, and so on. These systems are the focus of this chapter.

The categories of size of user, type of decision, strategic use of information technology, or type of business function are not mutually exclusive. For example, a transaction processing system may also be an enterprise-wide system or a strategic information system. A marketing information system may also be a personal information system. The reason for categorizing information systems is to find an easy way to discuss the nature and scope of information systems. In a real-world setting, however, most systems can be classified in numerous ways. In the following sections, we examine two information systems classifications: those based on type of decisions and functional information systems.

Information Systems Based on Type of Decisions

People in organizations make different types of decisions to achieve operational, tactical, and strategic goals. Operational goals are those that relate to the everyday operations of a company. Operational goals are supported by operational decisions. This may include decisions such as "How many units of Product A should we manufacture on Machine C?" "How many temporary workers should we hire for next week's night shift?" "How many units of Product B should we ship to our New York store?" and so on.

Operational decisions focus on the day-to-day operations of a company and are usually made by lower-level managers operating under the guidelines and procedures established by top management. These low-level decisions, or "structured decisions," are fairly routine, are easily understood, and require only limited intuition and judgment.

Middle managers set tactical goals and relate to the short-term (one to two years) success of the company. Middle managers must coordinate, control, and monitor various activities in an organization and serve as an effective liaison between lower- and top-level management so that the efforts of all employees combine to support the overall goals and mission of the organization.

Tactical decisions support tactical goals. Examples of tactical decisions include "What advertising strategy should we use to respond to our competitor's promotion campaign?" "What kind of a benefit package should we offer our employees so that we can attract and retain the best people?" "Should we build another production facility to meet our growing demand?" "What is the impact of the new tax law on our foreign investments?" and so on. Tactical decisions, by nature, are part structured and part ambiguous so they are sometimes called semistructured decisions.

Finally, strategic goals focus on the long-term (more than 3 years) growth and success of a company. Companies achieve strategic goals by planning for and making decisions about the company's general course. Strategic decisions include predicting industry trends and growths, developing new products that meet untapped customer needs, identifying how technology can contribute to greater profits, and locating new markets for growth and expansion.

Strategic decisions are sometimes called unstructured decisions because they rely heavily on intuition, judgment, and experience. Sometimes it is hard to identify the information a manager needs to make a strategic decision. For example, what kind of information would a manager need to predict critical technologies in the year 2005? Table 2-1 compares the three types of decisions.

TABLE 2-1

Comparison of Types of Decisions

Types of Decisions	Description
Operational	Structured decisions. Routine, require minimal judgment, focus on day-to-day operations.
Tactical	Semistructured decisions that support tactical goals. Often made by middle managers.
Strategic	Unstructured. Rely heavily on intuition, judgment, and experience. Usually made by top-level managers and executives.

Systems that support operational, tactical, and strategic decisions are broadly classified into the following categories:

1. Transaction processing systems (TPS)
2. Management information systems (MIS)
3. Intelligent support systems (ISS), which include decision support systems (DSS), executive information systems (EIS), and expert systems (ES)

Figure 2-4 shows what level of decision each of these systems support. We discuss these systems in detail in Chapter 10. Here, we briefly examine how these systems relate to marketing, manufacturing, human resources, quality control, and finance and accounting.

Transaction processing systems record, validate, process, and store transactions that take place in the different functional areas of a business for future retrieval and use. Management information systems (MIS) refer to a group of general-purpose, well-integrated systems that monitor and control the internal operations of an organization. They provide middle managers with the information necessary to make tactical decisions, which assess the impact of daily operations on the long-range goals of the company. The transaction processing system and other internal sources in the company serve as the main input to management information systems.

The typical outputs of an MIS are summary reports and exception reports. A summary report simply summarizes a set of events or occurrences in a company. For example, it may show the total number of defective products produced last week in each of the three shifts. An exception report is designed to bring immediate attention to some event or occurrence. For example, a company is likely to document an accident on the shop floor as an exception report.

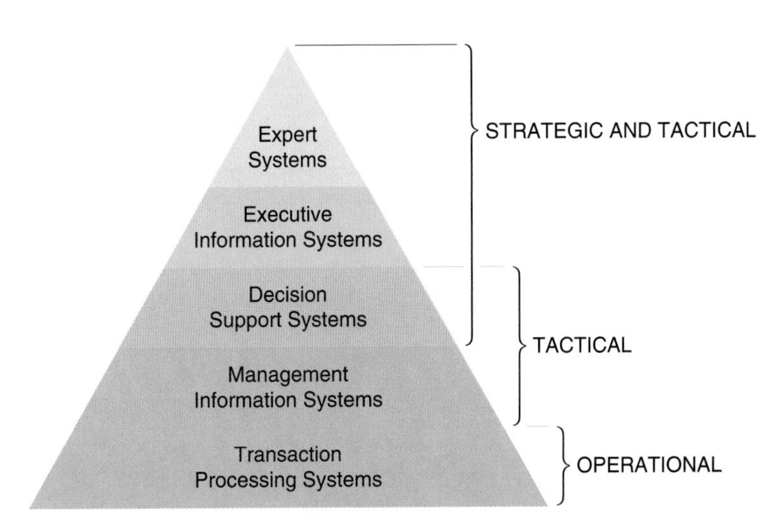

FIGURE 2-4

Systems That Support Stratetic, Tactical, and Operational Business Decisions

Intelligent support systems (ISS) refer to a group of systems that support decisions requiring the use of knowledge, intuition, experience, and expertise. The following systems fit in this category:

- Decision support systems (DSS)
- Executive information systems (EIS)
- Artificial intelligence (AI) and expert systems (ES)

DSS, EIS, and ES and AI are intelligent support systems because they support decisions that require intuition and judgment. In Chapter 10 we examine ISS in detail.

How do these three types of information systems help businesses meet the information needs of people working in various functions? They support operational, tactical, and strategic decisions in different functional areas in the organization, aiding managers throughout the entire business.

Functional Information Systems

Information systems can also be classified according to function in these four areas:

1. Marketing
2. Manufacturing and service
3. Accounting and finance
4. Human resources

Neither management nor information systems are listed because each of the four functional areas integrates managerial and IT tasks.

Although we classify information systems by separate functional areas, most departments do not function in isolation, nor should their information systems. Companies that take an integrated approach to IS typically develop a strategic plan that supports the company's mission and objectives. The IS team then develops a strategic information plan for all business functions that supports the strategic plan, as we see in Figure 2-5.

However, many companies lack completely cross-functional information systems because truly cross-functional systems are extremely difficult to build in a dynamic business environment. As a result, understanding the role of each functional system is still critical. We explore marketing, manufacturing and service, accounting and financial, and human resources information systems next.

Marketing Information Systems

Most businesses consider **marketing information systems** crucial for success. Originally, marketing systems focused on periodically gathering information about key local or regional market indicators, such as sales volume, profit margins, and discounts. Today, marketing systems provide continuous and instantaneous access to key market indicators on a global basis.

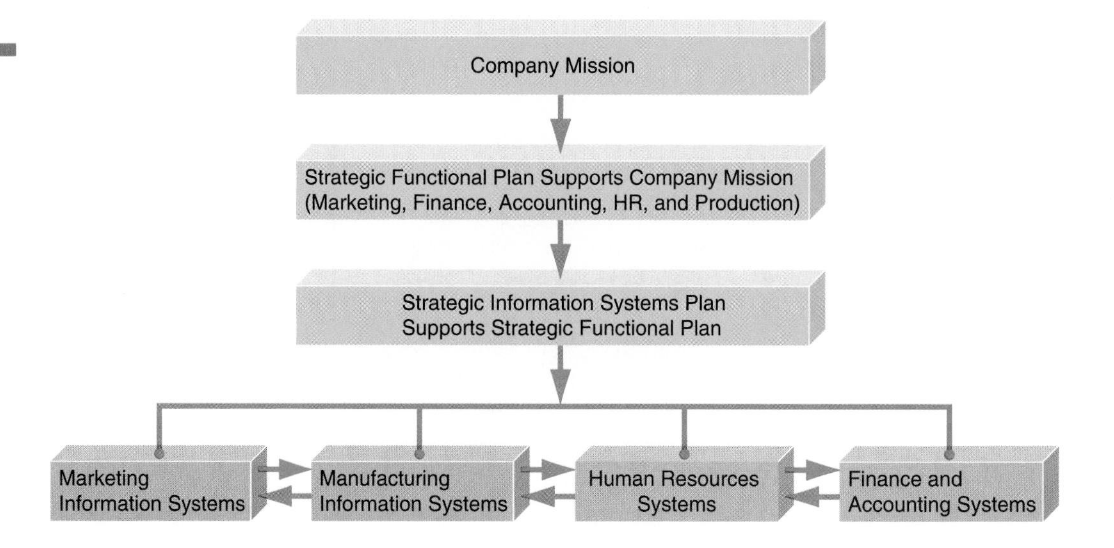

FIGURE 2-5

Developing a Strategic Information Plan in a Company with Integrated Information Systems

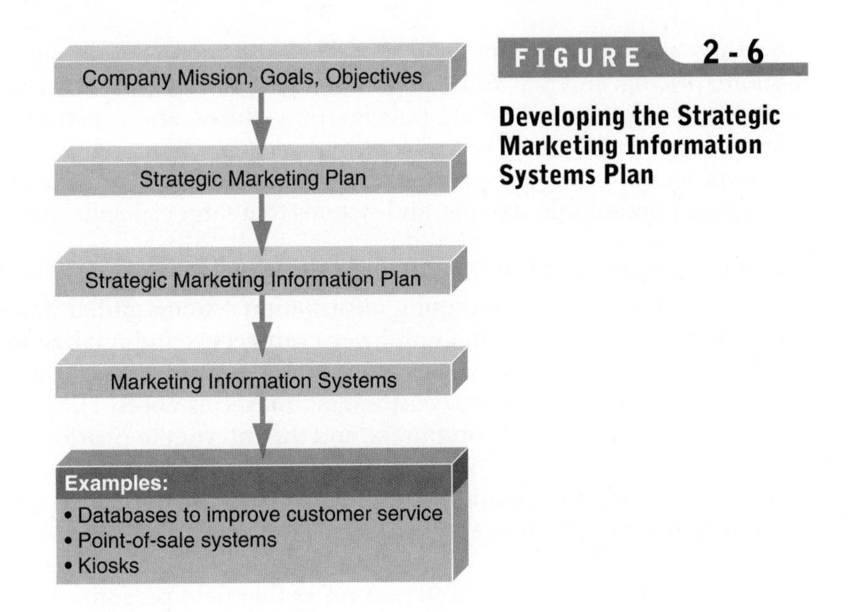

FIGURE 2-6

Developing the Strategic Marketing Information Systems Plan

The focus of a marketing system is to help a company provide exceptional service to the customer by ensuring that customer needs such as quality, price, reliability, availability, and product features are fully and effectively met. Companies make sure the marketing information systems meet these goals through careful planning. A business organized according to function typically has a business plan that sets the overall course of the company. It also requires each department (marketing in this case) to develop a strategic plan that outlines the goals and objectives of the department that support the company's general goals.

Marketing information systems

Information systems that meet the information needs of an organization in the areas of sales, distribution, advertising and promotion, market analysis, market intelligence, product research, service management, and other marketing functions.

Those in charge of the marketing information systems decisions examine the goals of the strategic marketing plan and develop a strategic marketing information systems plan that supports those marketing goals. Figure 2-6 summarizes the process of developing the strategic marketing information systems plan.

A key decision that planners must grapple with when developing the marketing information systems plan is how much to invest in technology. Experts suggest that organizations evaluate technology investments from the perspective of how they affect the customers' feelings toward the company.

Improved customer service, traditionally a marketing activity, is one of the top benefits of good business processes. Service is the basis for trust between a business and its customers. Historically, companies such as L. L. Bean, Federal Express, and 3M that have a strong customer focus have become market leaders. Poor customer service can result in significant losses for a company. Take a look at these facts:[5]

- A whopping 90 percent of a customer's contact with a company is through its marketing department
- A dissatisfied customer generally tells three or four people about a bad experience that he or she had with a company
- A satisfied customer tells at most one other person about a good experience
- Recruiting new customers is five times more costly than retaining customers

Marketing information systems should help companies provide exceptional, timely service to their current and future customers. What kind of information helps achieve the goal of top-notch customer service? A good marketing information system should give marketing managers "actionable data," which are current information that helps managers meet customer demands, develop better products, reduce costs, and compete in the global marketplace. Systems that provide actionable data are so powerful that they can help companies realize a significant increase in sales each year.[6]

Marketing systems, unlike other functional systems, cannot be standardized for all companies. Just as every individual has a unique fingerprint, every company has a unique way of researching, targeting, and servicing customers; developing products and promotions; pricing; and delivering its goods and services. Marketing systems should be tailor-made to meet the marketing policies, procedures, and practices of the business. To give you a sense of the variety, let's look at three types of marketing information systems that improve customer service: systems in which databases provide critical customer information, point-of-sale systems, and systems that target specific market segments.

Databases That Improve Customer Service

Many customer-oriented marketing information systems gather and store key product information in a database that employees can access and analyze to serve customers' needs. Hewlett-Packard Co. uses a marketing system called K-Mine that helps service technicians provide answers to customers' questions about HP products. The system uses a database, networked computers, and the Internet to provide thousands of HP engineers in 34 call centers in 31 countries answers to customers' questions.

The marketing information system contains detailed records on more than 20,000 parts and products, with precise diagrams for about one-third of those parts. It also stores thousands of "solution" documents entered by call center personnel from around the world listing specific fixes and user notes that field personnel submit to the system. The system also stores voice and video recordings. According to Paul Primmer, support technology lab manager for HP's worldwide customer support operations in Roseville, California, "The vision is to make knowledge available anytime, anywhere, anyway." Anytime means that it is available 24 hours, seven days a week anywhere in the world.[7] To ensure complete accessibility no matter what happens, HP has three customer service backup systems in Singapore, Brussels, and Atlanta.

At British Airways flight attendants carefully observe the preference of their valuable customers. They enter this information into their onboard laptops, which are connected to the airline's marketing information system. Flight attendants access the system before each flight "so that the next time the passenger in seat 3B flies with the airline, she automatically receives an extra pillow."[8]

Point-of-Sale Systems

A point-of-sale (POS) system is a computerized, transaction-oriented information system that captures information generated at the point the sale was made. A POS system captures information such as the store where the item was bought, quantity, customer address, and so on. When customers buy a candy bar or beer, a large database at Catalina Marketing makes note of what is bought and how frequently it is bought by gathering information from the POS system at the checkout. The POS information helps supermarket retailers customize their promotions so that they can meet the unique buying habits of their customers.

The Florida-based Catalina Marketing has almost 16 billion rows of data about customers and their buying habits. This storehouse of data allows managers to collect extensive marketing data, typically providing 12 weeks of data in about 1,800 stores for anywhere between 100 and 15,000 random products. The system also provides detailed information on items such as which cracker brands are purchased more often with which brand of sardines or peanut butter. These systems help marketing managers around the world cater to the unique needs of their customers through better product offerings, distribution, and promotions.

Segmentation Systems

Today companies are using their marketing information systems to treat each customer as a unique individual. Instead of mass marketing to all customers, companies are using informations systems to segment—or divide—its market into smaller groups so that marketing can meet the specific needs of each group more effectively. BMG Direct, the direct marketing division of BMG Entertainment, creates about 50 variations of each of its marketing promotions to appeal to its 8 million club members. Its marketing information system classifies customers by musical category. Within each of the 14 musical categories, members are divided into groups based on their length of membership. Customer loyalty is rewarded through deeper discounts. According to Elizabeth Rose, vice president of strategic planning and electronic commerce, BMG's business depends on its ability to segment its customers "so that members receive catalogs and offers with the right kind of music, a feature selection we think they would like and at a discount level in line with their membership in the club."[9] IS helps BMG target and market to customers successfully.

An effective marketing information system answers these questions:

- What is the best way to capture customer data at the point where the sale is made?
- What types of goods and services do our customers want and at what price?
- What does "customer service" mean to our customers?
- Are customers interested and willing to use information technology as part of the service?
- How much more are customers willing to pay for better service?
- What key product or service features will attract and keep customers?

Marketing information systems that can help companies answer these questions play a vital role in helping a company earn profits and achieve its desired market share, two components of business success. These systems can also raise ethical issues, as the Ethics for Success features shows.

Ethics for success

Two Giants Collide

Wal-Mart Stores, the discount retailer, sued Washington-based Amazon.com, a pioneer of high-tech retailing, accusing the Internet bookseller of stealing its computer secrets. In a suit filed in Washington state court in October 1998, Wal-Mart argues that Amazon.com and several of its affiliates tried to recruit Wal-Mart IS employees and business partners to copy Wal-Mart's massive information system.

The system, which analysts say is second in size only to the U.S. government's, collects extensive consumer data, determines how Wal-Mart stocks its shelves, and controls how it runs its distribution network. The nation's largest retailer is seeking an injunction, damages, and revenue that Amazon.com gained from using Wal-Mart secrets. Wal-Mart accuses Amazon.com of seeking Wal-Mart IS employees "in an attempt to obtain access to trade secrets and other confidential information that is unique to Wal-Mart," according to the suit.

The suit also names as defendant Richard Dalzell, who worked in Wal-Mart's information systems division until becoming Amazon.com's chief information officer in September 1997. A Wal-Mart spokeswoman said the recruiting of at least 15 current and former Wal-Mart employees and employees of vendors who all have intimate knowledge of Wal-Mart's computer system began after Mr. Dalzell left the Bentonville, Arkansas, firm. Bill Curry, a spokesperson for Amazon.com, explains, "We're not interested in other people's trade secrets. We're interested in hiring the brightest, hardest-working and most talented people wherever they might be." He adds that Wal-Mart is "about 300 times our size and probably sold more yesterday than we sold in the last 12 months."

Betsy Reithemeyer, a spokeswoman for Wal-Mart, counters that high-tech concerns typically don't seek talent in Wal-Mart's rural patch of northwest Arkansas. "There's a lot of computer talent out there in the Valley. If you're coming to Bentonville, you're looking for something specific."

YOU DECIDE

1. Is there anything a company can do to prevent its technology and IS trade secrets from leaking to competitors through employees who leave the company?
2. Do you think Wal-Mart's case could restrict the market for skilled IS professionals?
3. Imagine that you work for Wal-Mart and are a star employee in the IS department. Dalzell, your ex-boss, learns that you're unhappy at Wal-Mart and makes you a job offer to work at Amazon.com. Would you hesitate? Explain.

Sources: Emily Nelson, "Wal-Mart Accuses Amazon.com of Stealing Its Secrets in Lawsuit," *Wall Street Journal,* October 19, 1998, B10; *See also,* David W. Johnson and Kenneth K. Dort, "Wal-Mart's Case Against Amazon.com," *Computerworld,* March 8, 1999, www.computerworld.com.

Information Systems for Manufacturing and Service

The manner in which businesses offer services and manufactured goods to customers has undergone and continues to undergo significant, rapid changes. Until 15 to 20 years ago, for instance, manufacturing was dominated by mechanical equipment, most of which was not fully automated. Most information was hand computed. Today, computers, robots, and information systems dominate the shop floor. In fact, many manufacturing plants around the world are run without employees. Computers make many tactical decisions about how many products to make and how to make them.

Like marketing information systems, manufacturing information systems are guided by the company's strategic manufacturing plan, which in turn, is derived from the company's overall strategic plan, as we see in Figure 2-7. The strategic manufacturing plan outlines the role of the manufacturing department in achieving the company's overall goals.

Note, however, that the phrase "manufacturing information systems" is a misnomer because it applies to both manufacturing and service environments. An automobile factory and a travel agency both use manufacturing systems, even though one provides a product and the other a service. In this chapter we use the terms *manufacturing* and **manufacturing information systems** in the context of goods and services environments.

Manufacturing information systems

A set of systems that support the manufacturing and service functions of purchasing, receiving, quality control, inventory management, material requirements planning, capacity planning, production scheduling, and plant design.

Manufacturing information systems help companies automate the development process to improve efficiency, deliver goods and services more efficiently, and speed up the product development process. They also improve product development by allowing more customization.

Automation Systems

Numerous manufacturing information systems use automation to cut production costs and speed manufacturing time. Digital and other computer technology often combine to automate the manufacturing process. After lagging behind rivals for years in new-car development, General Motors Corp. now competes effectively in global markets. The automobile maker uses an automated manufacturing process that relies on sophisticated computer and digital-imaging tools to cut product development costs by as much as $200 million for a single global car or truck program.

The GM manufacturing system takes a designer's computer drawings of a new car or truck and develops the model digitally, with all its features, until it is ready to go into production. This digital model saves the company time and money by eliminating the need for building physical models, allowing changes to be made easily, and making it possible to solve manufacturing problems in "virtual" factories instead of real ones. It

FIGURE 2-7

Developing a Manufacturing Information System Plan for Manufacturing and Service Businesses

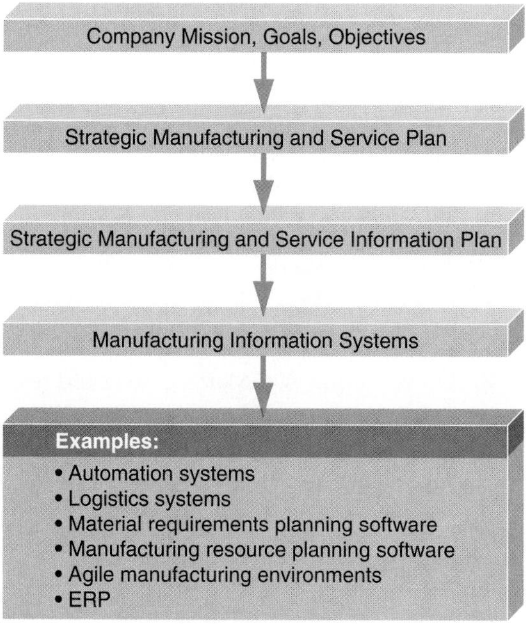

Company Mission, Goals, Objectives
↓
Strategic Manufacturing and Service Plan
↓
Strategic Manufacturing and Service Information Plan
↓
Manufacturing Information Systems
↓
Examples:
- Automation systems
- Logistics systems
- Material requirements planning software
- Manufacturing resource planning software
- Agile manufacturing environments
- ERP

GM's manufacturing information system uses digital-imaging tools to cut costs and time spent developing new cars and trucks, such as we see in this Brazilian GM plant. GM's speed and efficiency makes it a formidable global competitor.

now takes GM an average of 24 months from the time a vehicle's design is approved until the start of production, down from 42 months. Even though 24 months is now the world standard, GM plans to reduce that time frame to 18 months.

GM spends about $1 billion on its manufacturing information system. Is it worth it? The answer is a resounding yes. It costs most auto makers $2 to $4 billion to engineer and build one new vehicle. GM's manufacturing information system means that its new-vehicle development costs are 5 percent to 10 percent less than that—a saving of $1 million to $4 million for each new car or truck. In addition, the speed to market of the new models gives GM an edge in responding to changes in customer demands and tastes, thereby increasing its market share.[10]

In contrast to two decades ago, most manufacturing companies fully automate their manufacturing processes. This South Korean manufacturer uses robots and other automation tools to manufacture circuit boards.

Logistics Systems

Manufacturing managers are responsible not only for producing goods and services, but also for delivering them to the right customer at the right time. These delivery systems are sometimes called logistics systems. Retailer Office Depot has nearly perfected its manufacturing information logistics systems, leading the company into double-digit growth and high customer satisfaction. Every year for the past decade the company has sold more office supplies to more businesses than any of its competitors because it offers telephone, fax, and Web ordering capabilities, an information system that tracks inventories and product prices in all stores, and next-day delivery.

Office Depot's logistics systems provide value to its customers such as Kaiser Permanente, an HMO. Before Office Depot contracted to meet Kaiser's office supply needs, the HMO allowed 10 different service areas to purchase supplies from local stationery suppliers and outlets of their choosing and also allowed individuals to buy supplies from nearby office supply stores as needed. Diversity abounded. "We identified over 500 types of pens that were being bought," recalls Sarah French, director of contracting at Kaiser. "That's just outrageous."

Now Kaiser Permanente personnel across the country place orders as they choose—by telephone, fax, or the Office Depot Web site—and receive their supplies the following day. The combination of reliable next-day delivery and customized mini-catalogs has shrunk ad hoc purchases from local outlets dramatically, notes French. Tom Cross, Office Depot's senior vice president of marketing and advertising, explains: "We're in a just-in-time business. . . . When customers want office supplies, they want them now—and at competitive prices."[11]

Sophisticated manufacturing information systems keep Office Depot's costs down and customer satisfaction levels high by knowing which store in the region has the right product at the lowest price. The system also helps deliver products to the customer in the shortest time possible.[12] The company has 700 stores across the United States and Canada and a company-operated fleet of 2,000 trucks outside North America. International growth is strong, with 58 outlets open in eight countries.

Office Depot's use of a logistics system has translated into business success in eight countries, including Israel.

Material Requirements and Manufacturing Resource Planning Software

Today, many manufacturing environments operate with the help of a powerful software called MRP—material requirements planning. This software automates the process of production planning by collecting information that helps managers make decisions about these and related production issues:

- "How much of a specific product should I make?"
- "On what machine should I make this product?"
- "How many units should we make in Shift A and how many in Shift B?"
- "What part of the product can I make on Machine A and what part on Machine B?"

These decisions become extremely complex when managers have to build hundreds of products on hundreds of machines that have diverse specifications and requirements.

An extension of MRP software is MRP II—manufacturing resource planning. MRP II software helps managers determine the resources required to manufacture a product. The resources include personnel and items such as machines, raw materials, and money.

Although MRP and MRP II software are powerful and can yield excellent benefits, they work only if companies can see how manufacturing supports the overall business goals. George Stalk, Jr., a time-management expert at the Boston Consulting Group, notes that many companies use MRP and MRP II software on a piecemeal basis with the goal of reducing costs or achieving incremental improvements in efficiency. But the most effective use of MRP and MRP II is to integrate these systems with other non-manufacturing ones in the organization, such as finance, accounting, and marketing. The integration allows decision makers to see how manufacturing efficiency can enhance production, marketing efforts, and financial investments.

Agile manufacturing: Manufacturing environments that are dynamic and flexible enough to produce customized goods and services in different quantities quickly.

Agile Manufacturing and Enterprise Resource Planning

A term given to highly automated manufacturing environments is "agile manufacturing." In agile manufacturing, managers use existing machines to switch from making one product to another, enabling them to produce customized goods and services in varying quantities. Unlike traditional manufacturing environments, where one machine can make only a given set of products at a given time, agile manufacturing focuses on agility of the entire manufacturing process. Agile environments rely heavily on information systems so that the product can be made on the best possible machine in a time-efficient manner and delivered to the customers as needed.

The key feature of agile manufacturing is mass customization, a concept quite different from mass production. Mass customization is a novel concept in which goods are produced in mass quantities, yet they are customized to the unique needs of each individual. McDonald's and Burger King are good examples of mass customization because although the goods are produced in mass quantities, they are customized to meet the unique needs of each individual. With mass customization:

> [p]arents can buy dolls that look like their own children. Dozens of vitamins can be customized into just a few pills. Even Barbie dolls sport the cheerleading uniform of the nearest university. Instead of simply stamping out the same thing every day, many companies are revamping their production lines to make them flexible enough to spin hundreds of variations on a single product from the same assembly line.[13]

Agile manufacturing allows companies such as Mattel to create products that meet their customers' needs on a more personal basis.

Steven L. Goldman, technical director of the Agile Manufacturing Enterprise Forum at the Iacocca Institute at Leigh University in Pennsylvania, draws an analogy between the emergency room at a hospital and agile manufacturing. Hospital emergency rooms have special equipment and staff that provide highly skilled services to patients on short notice. When the same idea is transferred to a manufacturing environment, we have an agile organization—one that can respond quickly and effectively to a wide variety of customer needs.

HealthGate Data Corporation is using an agile manufacturing system in the health care field with great success. Located in Massachusetts, the company delivers medical information on-line, customizing it in different ways for different audiences. In 1994 William Reece, founder of the company, teamed up with Rick Lawson, a medical librarian, and Dr. Barry Manuel, an associate dean of the department of continuing education at Boston University's School of Medicine. This exceptional team understood that doctors were under great pressure to reduce the time they spent with each patient, so delivering customized, accurate information to physicians via the Internet provided a benefit.

The company has 160,000 registered users and estimates that it gets 35,000 visitors a day. Articles cost anywhere from $2 for a short overview of a particular drug to $50 for the complete text of an article from a medical journal. Annual subscription fees for customized packages can cost from $25,000 to $200,000.[14]

What are some differences between traditional manufacturing and agile manufacturing? Two key differences exist.

- ***Agile manufacturing products can meet the needs of each customer:*** Unlike traditional manufacturing, which measures success by rising product sales, agile manufacturing measures a product's success based on how well it meets the unique needs of each customer. Acumin Corp. president Bradford Oberwager founded his business after watching his sister swallow dozens of pills each day following her cancer radiation treatments. Acumin offers customized multivitamins to customers. It has the technology to put all the vitamins a customer wants in dosages tailored to the individual's needs, age, and lifestyle—and the company can usually fit them into two or three pills instead of the customary seven or eight.[15]
- ***Agile manufacturing integrates customer service as a competitive weapon:*** Most agile manufacturers understand the true meaning of customer service. Japanese eyewear manufacturer Paris Miki, whose U.S. headquarters is in Seattle, has interactive software that helps people create custom-shaped lenses. The interactive software program allows customers to customize their glasses to their precise needs and preferences. Sales associates take a digital picture of the customer's face and measure the distance between her eyes as well as the length of her nose. The customer then chooses from a list of "desired images"—such as intelligent, sexy, distinctive, dramatic, playful—to describe the look they are after. The software recommends the most complementary lens shapes and displays the results onscreen over a digital three-dimensional image of the customer's face. Customers who have used this service to select their lenses are often reluctant to go elsewhere.[16]

Enterprise resource planning

Software designed to help businesses quickly identify and integrate the resources and raw materials required to turn incoming orders into outgoing shipments.

Now that we have looked at the nature of an agile manufacturing environment, let's explore the information systems and information technology that support agile environments. One type of software used in agile manufacturing and other manufacturing environments is **enterprise resource planning** (ERP) systems. This software helps decision makers consider all the resources, such as labor, raw materials, money, equipment, and time required to produce a product and deliver it to the customer. Because decision

TABLE 2-2

How to Prepare for ERP Implementations

- Expect to spend 10 percent or more of your total project budget on end-user training
- Training may have to begin 4 months or more before you go live
- Start with general classes on the way ERP works, not job-specific training
- Trainers must be versed in business processes as well as the technology
- End users may need 3 to 6 months of actual usage to become proficient
- Be willing to change employee productivity measurements to fit the software

Source: Craig Stedman, "ERP User Interfaces Drive Workers Nuts," *Computerworld,* November 2, 1998, 1, 24.

makers rely on this information, the business is better able to coordinate and control the resources needed to deliver a product to the customer successfully.

ERP software integrates a number of core business systems, such as general ledger, accounts payable, and manufacturing. Warner-Lambert uses an ERP system for its Listerine product. Listerine is a complex concoction. Its ingredients are extracted from several continents and its production process requires the coordination of countless individuals and business partners. Warner-Lambert's ERP system coordinates sales, marketing, manufacturing, finance, and quality control decisions around the world. Decisions may originate anywhere from Australia, famous for its eucalyptus tree oil, a key Listerine ingredient, to New Jersey, where Warner-Lambert's sales team forecasts demand for the product.

The ERP software helps the company share strategic plans, performance data, and market insight with leading retailers such as Wal-Mart Stores. The software has been so successful that Warner-Lambert increased sales by $8 million because it was better able to keep store shelves fully stocked, says Jay Nearnberg, director of global demand management.[17]

In spite of its many benefits, ERP is not simple to implement. It takes a long time for companies to adapt to the technical and business requirements of ERP. Take for example Hydro Agri's Canadian fertilizer stores in Tampa, Florida. It used to take workers 20 seconds to process a farmer's order. But installing enterprise planning software a year ago changed things—for the worse. The average order-processing time ballooned to 90 seconds because workers had to navigate through six screens to enter all the required data. At Hydro Agri, the increased order-entry times "basically threatened to be a showstopper for us," explains Andy Hafer, director of information management.

This slowdown occurred because ERP software is so complex and tries to integrate information from a wide variety of sources. It is a problem faced by many companies: Enterprise resource planning applications promise many corporate benefits, but they have unwieldy user interfaces that can frustrate employees, sap their productivity, and hurt customer service. "We take 45,000 orders during a six-week period, and clicking from screen to screen was a killer," says Hafer.

The order-entry delays forced Hydro Agri to throw more personnel into its Canadian stores to handle the spring-planting business rush. For end users on the ERP firing line, it can take as many as 6 months to get comfortable with the software, notes Hafer and other executives involved in ERP projects. The company is scaling back on its ERP implementations.[18]

What are some things that companies can do to be better prepared for ERP implementations? Table 2-2 offers some general tips.

Financial and accounting information systems

Computerized systems that provide accounting and financial information to improve decision making.

Financial and Accounting Information Systems

Financial and accounting information systems (FAIS) are a set of systems that provide information related to the accounting and financial activities in an organization. These systems should be tightly integrated with other functional information systems because finance and accounting are interwoven into all business operations.

FIGURE 2-8

Developing the Strategic Financial and Accounting Information Systems Plan

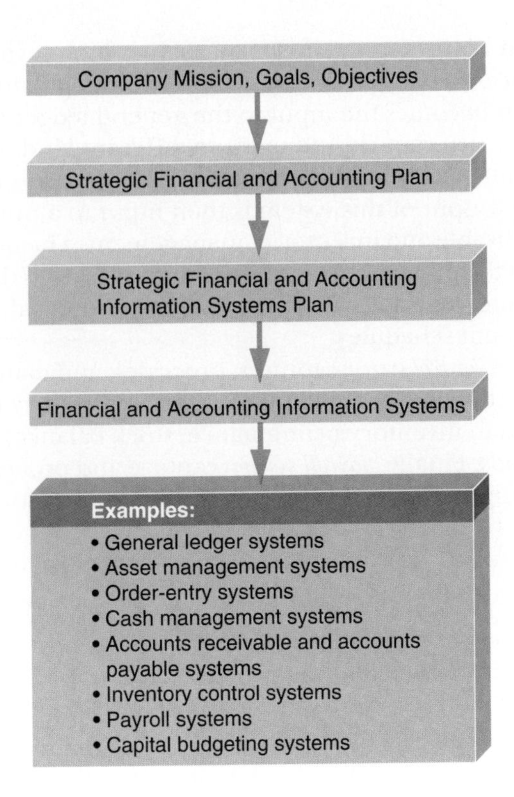

Figure 2-8 shows how financial and accounting systems support the strategic financial and accounting plans. These strategic plans outline how the finance and accounting function can help a business achieve its goals. Although most financial and accounting managers respond to urgent issues on a daily basis, they must have a strategic plan to ensure that their activities support the organization's goals.

Next we examine six financial and accounting information systems and the functions they perform: (1) general ledger, (2) asset management, (3) order-entry, (4) accounts receivable and accounts payable, (5) inventory control, and (6) payroll systems. *General ledger systems* generate the company's income statement and balance sheets and are responsible for managing the new and old accounts in the company. *Asset management*

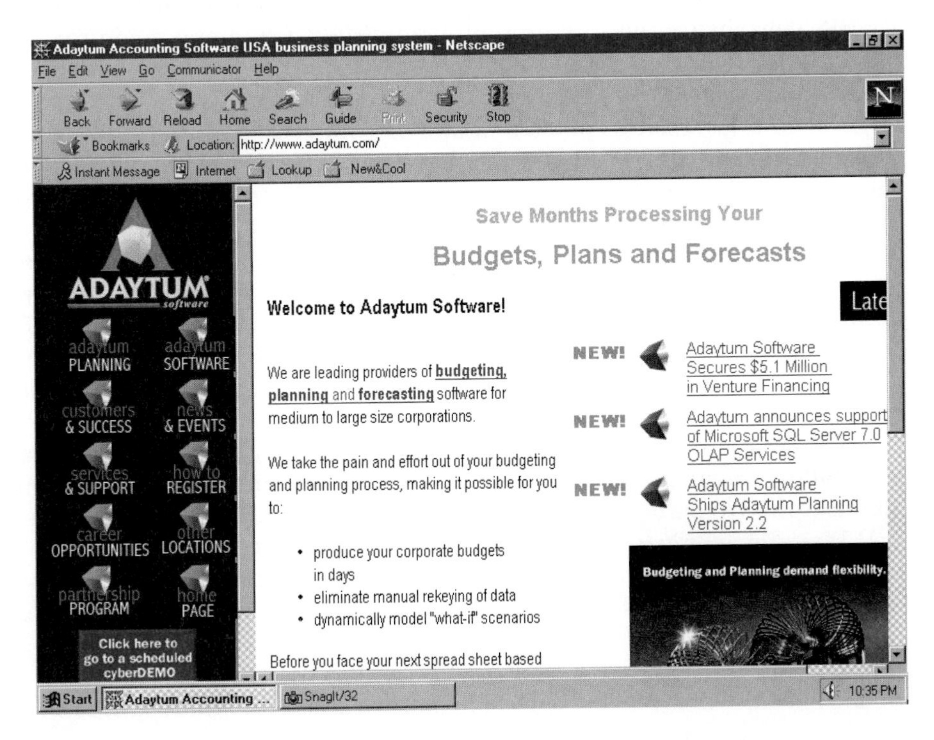

Adaytum accounting software is an example of a budgeting and financial forecasting system.

systems maintain an inventory of the company's long-term assets and ensure that accounting practices for company assets comply with regulatory standards. The output of this system often becomes the input to the general ledger system.

Order-entry systems capture and manage different kinds of data relating to a transaction such as number of units sold, customer billing, credit history, sales tax, and inventory levels. The output of this system is then input to a number of other systems, such as accounts receivable and inventories management. The *accounts receivable and accounts payable system,* as the name implies, captures and processes data such as creditor and customer billing information, payments received and owed, credit terms, account balances, and payment schedules.

The *inventory control system* captures, processes, and manages all issues related to the company's inventory such as items in inventory, inventory levels and costs, accounting practices related to inventory maintenance, stock balance, and data on lost, damaged, or returned goods. Finally, *payroll systems* capture and process data related to wages and salaries, including federal and state taxes, other deductions, employee benefits, overtime, and other related data.

Besides these six systems, many businesses use other types of financial and accounting systems such as the following:

- *Cash management systems* (that is, systems that ensure the organization has enough cash to conduct normal business, receive the best possible return on its short-term cash deposits, and sufficient cash flow to achieve good ratings in financial markets).
- *Capital budgeting systems* (for example, systems that ensure the acquisition and disposal of capital assets such as land, buildings, and so on).
- *Investment management systems* (such as systems that ensure that the organization gets the best possible returns on its long-term investments).

Although financial and accounting systems are critical for all businesses, they become more so for financial institutions. David Pottruck is president and CEO of Charles Schwab & Co., the brokerage subsidiary of San Francisco–based Charles Schwab Corporation. He says, "To our view, technology is the solution. . . . Whenever I give speeches, I say, 'We are a technology company that happens to be in the brokerage business.' I like to believe the people who come here to work within [the IS organization] aren't just hired help; they are the heroes of the company. They create opportunities for the business people to be successful."[19]

Pottruck claims that information technology has helped Charles Schwab maintain a competitive edge. For example, his team developed a new information system called VoiceBroker, a voice-recognition tool that satisfies customers' call-in request for stock quotes. The system recognizes 16,000 variations of the names of 5,000 registered stocks, so customers can request a quote for "International Business Machines," "IBM," or "Big Blue." It costs less than 20 percent of what it would cost a Schwab employee to provide the quotes personally. The latter project is particularly noteworthy, Pottruck says, because it originated in IS. "More and more, ideas come from the technology people saying, 'can you imagine this?' "[20]

One function that many financial and accounting systems perform is to send customers bills showing how much they owe the company. However, the traditional bill is becoming outdated. Companies such as Working Assets Long Distance (WALD), a long-distance telephone carrier, are finding new ways to transform invoices from monthly nuisances into featured attractions that market new products and maintain customer loyalty, explains Carol Hilderbrand, a freelance writer for *CIO* magazine.

WALD's phone bill beautifully illustrates how smart companies are transforming their billing function from cost centers to tools that can build long-term customer relationships. "We barely view it as a phone bill," says Laura Scher, chair and CEO of WALD's parent company, Working Assets Funding Service in San Francisco. "It's a piece of mail you get every month that tells you, the concerned citizen, what you can do about certain issues. And all this information happens to be in a phone bill. It's a very important tool for us."[21]

A satisfied WALD customer notes: "I can't say I'm thrilled when the long-distance phone bill lands in my mailbox, but I do have to admit to a mild spark of interest. That's

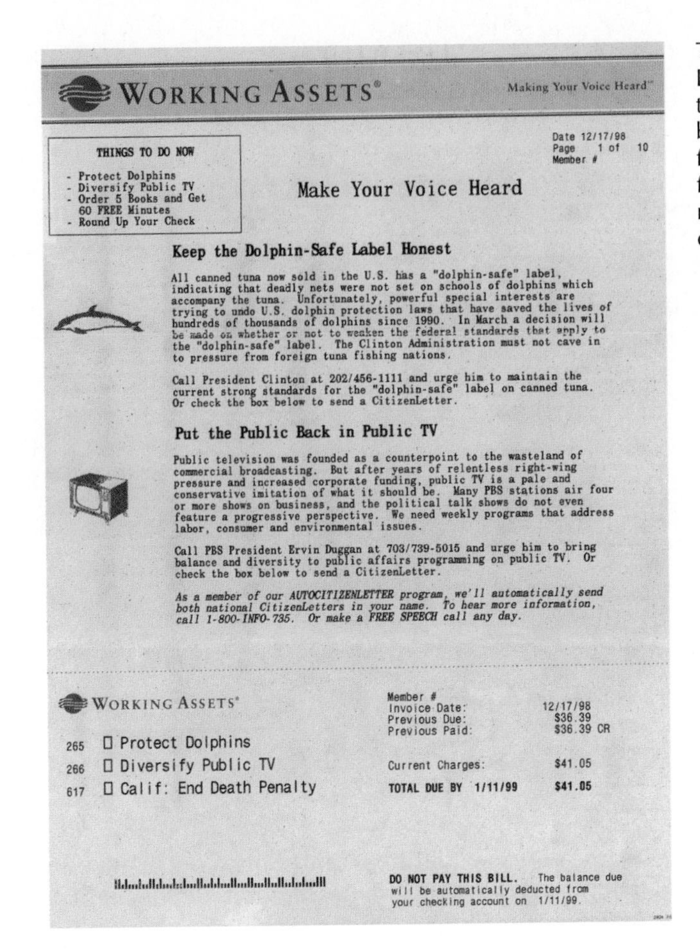

WORKING ASSETS®
Making Your Voice Heard™

THINGS TO DO NOW

- Protect Dolphins
- Diversify Public TV
- Order 5 Books and Get 60 FREE Minutes
- Round Up Your Check

Date 12/17/98
Page 1 of 10
Member #

Make Your Voice Heard

Keep the Dolphin-Safe Label Honest

All canned tuna now sold in the U.S. has a "dolphin-safe" label, indicating that deadly nets were not set on schools of dolphins which accompany the tuna. Unfortunately, powerful special interests are trying to undo U.S. dolphin protection laws that have saved the lives of hundreds of thousands of dolphins since 1990. In March a decision will be made on whether or not to weaken the federal standards that apply to the "dolphin-safe" label. The Clinton Administration must not cave in to pressure from foreign tuna fishing nations.

Call President Clinton at 202/456-1111 and urge him to maintain the current strong standards for the "dolphin-safe" label on canned tuna. Or check the box below to send a CitizenLetter.

Put the Public Back in Public TV

Public television was founded as a counterpoint to the wasteland of commercial broadcasting. But after years of relentless right-wing pressure and increased corporate funding, public TV is a pale and conservative imitation of what it should be. Many PBS stations air four or more shows on business, and the political talk shows do not even feature a progressive perspective. We need weekly programs that address labor, consumer and environmental issues.

Call PBS President Ervin Duggan at 703/739-5015 and urge him to bring balance and diversity to public affairs programming on public TV. Or check the box below to send a CitizenLetter.

As a member of our AUTOCITIZENLETTER program, we'll automatically send both national CitizenLetters in your name. To hear more information, call 1-800-INFO-735. Or make a FREE SPEECH call any day.

WORKING ASSETS®

265 ☐ Protect Dolphins
266 ☐ Diversify Public TV
617 ☐ Calif: End Death Penalty

Member #	
Invoice Date:	12/17/98
Previous Due:	$36.39
Previous Paid:	$36.39 CR
Current Charges:	$41.05
TOTAL DUE BY 1/11/99	**$41.05**

DO NOT PAY THIS BILL. The balance due will be automatically deducted from your checking account on 1/11/99.

This bill from Working Assets Long Distance (WALD) illustrates how one company combined billing—a traditional financial information system function—with customer information to give its company a competitive advantage.

because my long-distance carrier, Working Assets Long Distance (WALD), uses its bill as far more than an invoice."[22] Information accompanies the bill that explains how congressional representatives are voting on environmental and social issues. Working Assets' customers can request that Working Assets send personalized advocacy letters to representatives on a variety of topics. "I can also help fund 50 non-profit groups, such as Ecotrust and the NAACP, by checking off a box that rounds up my bill to the nearest dollar. Best of all, Working Assets donates 1 percent (about $3 million last year) of its revenue to those same advocacy organizations," explains a WALD customer.[23] WALD uses its financial system creatively to gain a competitive edge and satisfy its customers.

Human Resource Information Systems

Human resource information systems (HRIS) provide managers with information relating to all human resource functions, such as policies and procedures concerning recruiting, layoffs, employee evaluation, promotion, termination, transfers, salaries, job descriptions and responsibilities, training, Affirmative Action, and equal employment opportunities. These systems also provide vital information about items such as payroll, federal and state income and Social Security taxes, benefits, grievance procedures, and other personal information that affects employees.

Human resource information systems (HRIS)

Computerized systems that support the planning, control, coordination, administration, and management of the human resource assets in an organization.

Human resource information systems will become key resources for managers who must keep up with voluminous governmental employment regulations and need to find talent in an economy facing severe labor shortages. Like other functional systems, HRIS is derived from the strategic human resources plan, as we see in Figure 2-9. That plan describes human resources' role in helping the company achieve its overall goals. Systems that deal with the following areas are considered human resource information systems: personnel data, payroll, benefits administration, equity monitoring, processing applications, monitoring positions, training and development, safety and workers' compensation, union negotiations, and collective bargaining.

The core of a human resource information system is the database that contains detailed personal and professional information about each employee in the organization.

FIGURE 2-9

Developing the Strategic Human Resource Information Systems Plan

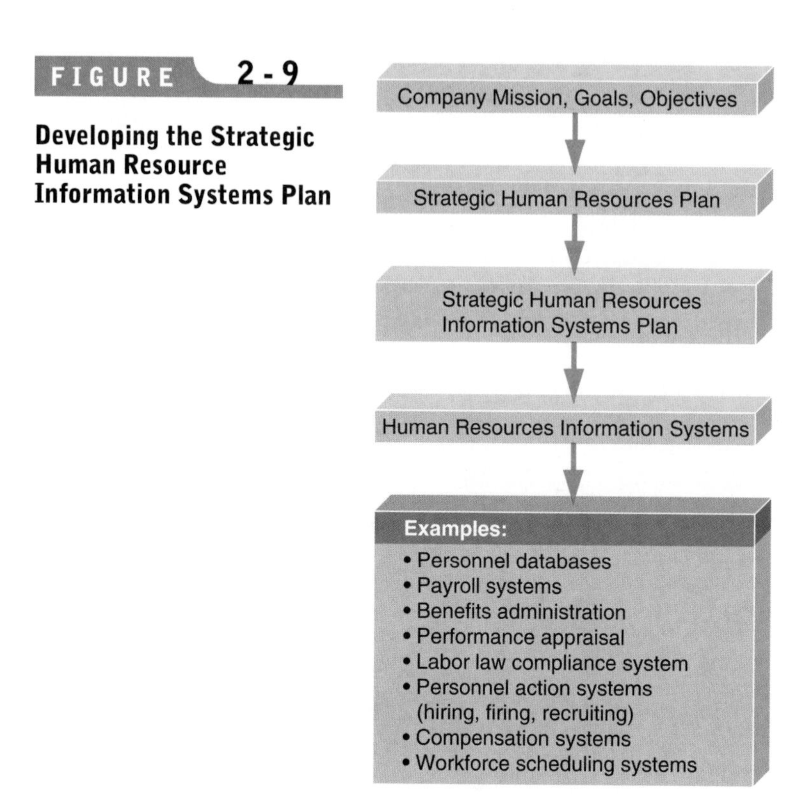

Personal information includes name, age, sex, address, and Social Security number. Professional data includes education level, job title, job description, department code, years of employment, number of promotions, performance evaluations, and the like. All other human resource subsystems take their information from this core database.

An important subsystem of the HRIS is the compliance system that closely tracks and monitors the organization's compliance with government laws and regulations, such as Affirmative Action, equal employment opportunities, health and safety codes of the Occupational Safety and Health Administration (OSHA), and others. In the past two decades, the amount of regulatory paperwork has increased many times and organizations are searching for ways to cut the hours and money devoted to these activities.

Another vital HRIS subsystem provides information regarding the recruitment, transfer, promotion, layoff, and termination of employees. Often when any of these situations occur, the HR department generates a large amount of information that should be carefully stored to comply with the legal requirements of state and federal governments. As the number of lawsuits on improper hiring, promotion, and firing policies increases, accurate and timely record keeping becomes even more important.

Other subsystems of the HRIS include developing and maintaining job titles and job descriptions for all jobs in a company, compensation and benefits information systems, and personnel planning systems. Performance appraisal systems that provide employees with real-time information on corporate performance measurements, thus making continuous performance improvement a way of corporate life rather than an annual chore, is another important subsystem in a HRIS. Pretesting compensation policies, ensuring that employees meet requirements, identifying problem areas in employee turnover, administering drug and alcohol policies, and providing training and employee empowerment programs are some other modules in an HRIS.

One reason for the growing importance of human resource information systems is their ability to provide valuable information to managers in all functional areas of the organization. Such information can help companies cut costs, increase efficiency, improve employee morale, and achieve a competitive advantage in the marketplace.

In some companies, HRIS is tightly integrated with financial and accounting systems to help financial analysts and accountants better measure employee-related cost factors. For instance, accountants may be able to assess the financial implications of hiring full-time versus part-time employees.

Another example of the use of HRIS is to recruit good employees. Human resource information systems are responsible for publicizing job openings and hiring personnel. Many companies today submit job openings over the network and encourage employees to submit computerized resumes. Resumes are then matched with existing, on-line skill inventories or "competency libraries" of employees that identify relevant skills, work experience, qualifications, and educational background. This matching process greatly increases the efficiency and effectiveness of recruitment.

Recruiting IT talent is a game at Inacom Corp.—literally. This Omaha-based technology management services company finds the smartest technical employees by enticing them to play "Techno Challenge," a high-tech skills assessment tool disguised as a Web game. The company's Web site (www.inacom.com) houses the game, which has three levels of difficulty. Technically savvy people who get to the third level are entered into a quarterly drawing for a $1,500 gift certificate and are identified as potential employees. "We get a list of people who get to the third level—and those are the ones we want to call right away," says Eva Fujan, vice president of technical recruiting.

More than 3,000 people have played the game since it went on-line a year ago. Of those, a couple of hundred have hit the third level, Fujan notes. The game is also used to prequalify information technology candidates who use traditional channels. "If we're interviewing for 20 systems engineers, we can say, 'Play the game first, and see how you did,' " Fujan says. The game is part of the company's new approach to recruiting, called Inacom World Tour, designed to appeal to young techies.[24]

Another important function of human resource systems is workforce scheduling. Airlines, for example, go through a juggling act of scheduling 18,000 flights per year using 2,500 pilots while monitoring compliance with excruciating regulatory details. Toss in the fact that each pilot has his or her own schedule preferences and you end up with a scheduling nightmare. "We used to build the schedules almost by hand," recalls Mary Pedrosa, manager of crew allocation at TWA in St. Louis. "It took five people between four and five business days to put together the schedule each month—it was hideous."[25]

The company now uses a software package that automatically schedules pilots, after taking into account their seniority and other regulatory guidelines (such as how many hours a pilot can fly per week and how much downtime they must take after transcontinental or overseas flights). Pilots can even use computer kiosks set up just for crew scheduling at TWA hub airports. The airline hopes to save 2 percent of its annual $210 million payroll with the system.[26]

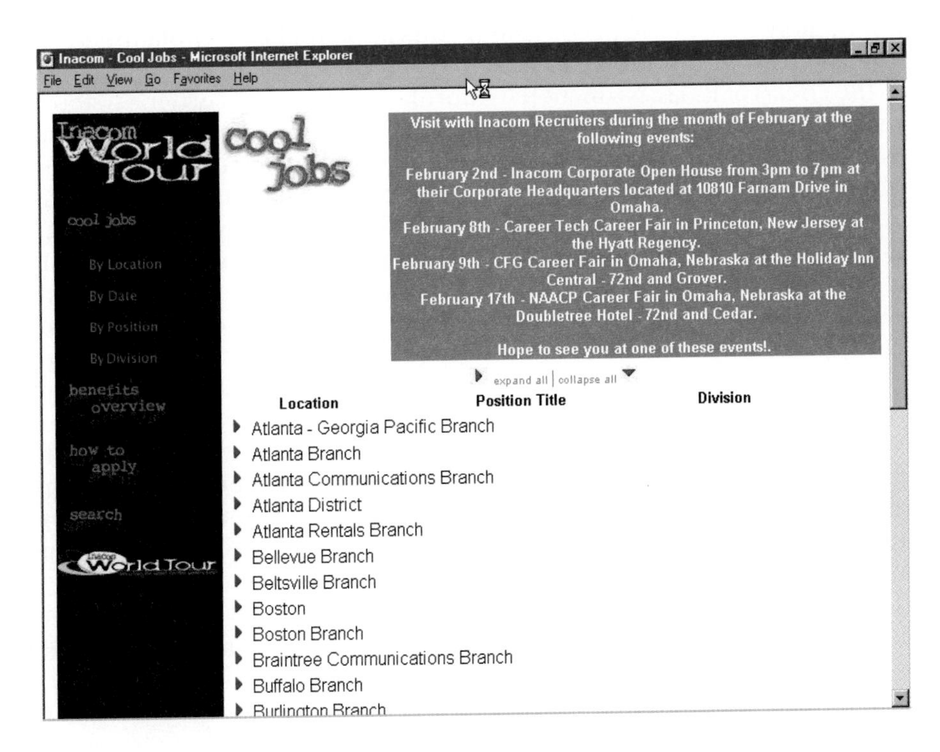

In an innovative use of human resource information systems, Inacom recruits and prequalifies candidates with its "Techno Challenge" game.

TWA relies on a human resource information system to schedule its pilots and flight crew.

Workforce diversity is another critical issue facing employers. HRIS can play a key role to help a company achieve its diversity goals by tracking and monitoring diversity measures. Why is diversity monitoring so important? In a recent survey of 440 CEOs, Coopers & Lybrand LLP in New York City found that 54 percent of the respondents felt that having good representation of women and minorities on their management team was important to maintaining business growth. "CEOs who acknowledge the importance of women and minorities on their management teams appear to be leading the more progressive and productive growth firms," says James P. Hayes, partner and director of diversity at Coopers & Lybrand. "Compared with other firms over the past five years, these companies have grown 22 percent faster and expect to increase their revenues 2 percent faster over the next 12 months."[27]

Now that we have investigated how functional information systems play an important role in helping an organization achieve its goals, we examine a company that uses cross-functional information systems to achieve and retain its quality image.

Putting the Functions Together: Cross-Functional Systems

Many companies striving to produce high-quality goods and services recognize that they must give employees access to timely, reliable information. Systems that integrate separate functional systems give end users more complete information for decision making when they need it. The result of these cross-functional systems is faster, more accurate decisions that can give businesses a competitive advantage.

Louisiana-based Turner Industries Ltd., a $600 million organization that specializes in large-scale construction and repairs at petrochemical plants, is a case in point. The company offers "efficiency, accuracy, profitability and customer satisfaction," due to the effects of its cross-functional information system.[28] Turner's system integrates finance, accounting, scheduling, production, and human resources information systems. System users can generate reliable time and cost estimates, project task schedules (some projects have more than 40,000 tasks), and personnel requirements.

Because Turner's decision makers provide customers with realistic, dependable estimates, the company has a sterling service reputation. Because the scheduling program is so efficient, Turner's project managers can spot problems and opportunities early, which allows the company to finish projects on time or ahead of schedule—an important aspect of client satisfaction. For instance, when Turner finished a project for Exxon ahead of time, it saved Exxon $8 million. This speed and reliability translate into repeat customers, additional revenue, and growing market dominance.[29]

The case for cross-functional information systems is even stronger in global companies. Multinational companies rely heavily on information systems to receive, process, and disseminate information to their global units. A strong and consistent flow of information is essential to project a uniform "face" to all people who have a stake in the business, as the Global IS for Success feature shows.

In this chapter and throughout the book we highlight global companies. Why is it important for today's student to have a good understanding of global issues? The answer is simple. Global companies are becoming the norm in many industries. With the growth of the Internet, even a small mom-and-pop shop in a remote corner of the world

Global IS for success

An All-Star Team at Tambrands

The trick to achieving growth in business is extending your reach without losing your grip. Tambrands, based in White Plains, New York, has mastered this principle. The company, a dominant player in the feminine hygiene products market, faced a big challenge: to develop standard business procedures that would allow a plant in Auburn, Maine, to perform the same processes in the same way as a plant in Kiev, Ukraine.

Managers believed that developing uniform manufacturing, marketing, and financial processes dictated by the best practices in the company would allow the company to freely exchange information among all its divisions and units. Dianne Forrest, vice president of information technology, explains that the aim of developing the business information systems in an integrated way was to create the feel of everyone working in the same building, despite the disparate office locations.

The company has manufacturing plants in seven countries, including France, China, Ukraine, Ireland, and the United Kingdom. The independent operations of these locations was hurting the company. The goal was to move from independent, country-centered groups to an integrated global organization—a huge task. Although the units in different locations used the same hardware, the software and operating procedures were quite different.

Beginning in the early 1990s, Tambrands implemented a cross-functional system that integrated information from all functions and departments in the organization. This system allowed employees to study key performance measures worldwide—profits, costs, employee turnover, cost of advertising, and so on—and use this information to allocate resources. The new system enhanced the role of employees, shifting the emphasis from number crunching to analysis. The company also improved its manufacturing operations by establishing uniform production standards.

The company also stays flexible about the system's implementation. Sites in China and the former Soviet Union were not large enough to warrant the use of large computers, so the company compromised with personal computers. In Kiev, where most people are trained in local accounting practices that bear little resemblance to U.S. and European models, the company installed a software package that allows employees to use local methods and then translates their results into the language of Western accounting.

QUESTIONS AND PROJECTS

1. What was the goal of Tambrands in restructuring its business information systems? Explain the sequence of steps that the company took to achieve this goal.
2. Outline some benefits that the company achieved by restructuring its business information systems.
3. What do you think are some challenges in developing integrated information systems for a global organization?

Source: Leigh Buchanan, "A Process-Change All-Star Team," *CIO,* March 15, 1994, 46–52. Reprinted through the courtesy of *CIO.*

can participate in the digital revolution. So, regardless of whether you work for a small or a large company, chances are that you will confront global issues. The next section discusses the role and importance of global information systems and identifies some critical IS-related issues for global companies.

Global Information Systems

A few years ago, the digital revolution and the power of automation were the exclusive privilege of the Western world. Only Western countries could afford to invest significant sums in technology innovation. However, in the past few years that has changed. Many countries recognize the power of the digital economy and are eager to participate in it.

Global spending on information technology has skyrocketed to approximately $2 trillion. In fact, IT has become so critical to global growth and progress that even financial crises cannot curtail IT growth, according to an International Data Corp. study. The study also found that more than 118 million PCs are now in use in homes and schools globally, representing a more than threefold jump, compared with 5 years ago.[30]

Even with the Asian crisis in full bloom, market researcher Killen & Associates estimates that Asian spending on IT, including hardware, software, and services, will grow at a compound annual rate of 9 percent from $353 billion in 1997 to $542 billion in 2002. "It's the biggest of the growth markets and probably the most attractive because of the sheer size of the potential market," says Bob Goodwin, senior vice president of Killen, Palo Alto, California.[31]

Although we often use the words "global" and "multinational" synonymously, some argue that there is a big difference between the two. "Today, multinational companies merely have a presence in different international markets, while global companies fuse their worldwide manufacturing, marketing and distribution operations into a single, seamless whole."[32] A global company understands that the world is just one large marketplace. For these companies, time, distance, language and cultural differences, infrastructure limitations, and political obstacles must be managed to compete.

The difficulties of being a global company abound. Every country has its cultural, political, and societal norms, values, and customs that business people must appreciate to conduct business globally. For example, in Thailand, the word "yes" can have several meanings, such as one that suggests the listener is paying attention to the speaker's words and another implying agreement. In Italy, balancing work and home is sacred so employees are reluctant to work overtime, even under the most pressing business conditions.

"In every country we deal with, there are different cultures and conditions," says Adrian Seccombe, manager of Eli Lilly and Co.'s IT infrastructure in Europe, Africa, and the Middle East. Global managers should encourage employees to learn about different cultures. Seccombe cites the tremendous difference between German and Japanese professionals and how they deal with ambiguity in negotiations. "In Germany, ambiguity is anathema," he explains. "In Japan, there are degrees of 'yes' and 'no,' and it's a journey to get from a middle 'yes' to an unequivocal one."[33]

Labor rights and employee attitudes toward work are also quite different as we travel between continents. For example, in Europe labor rights are so strong that managers cannot ask technicians to put in overtime—even when there is risk of potential losses. One network manager, who declined to be identified, relates an example of potential problems in such a highly charged political environment: "The company was throwing a Christmas party on two different floors when a manager decided everyone should get a chocolate Santa Claus. He sent one person from each floor to get them. They apparently went to two different stores and came back with two different-sized chocolates. The ones who got the smaller Santas actually brought it up as an issue before the work council."[34]

Global information system

A system that links people, systems, and business units located around the world through the use of telecommunications (hardware and software that links two or more electronic devices that are geographically separated).

Global information systems are systems that help companies share information freely across national boundaries through the use of telecommunications. They help address the problems of time, currency, social, and cultural differences; offices in separate locations; the business effects of local policies, procedures, and government regulations; and differences in the way in which people receive and process information. We see that global information systems issues consist of more than technology. They encompass a wide range of cultural concerns—all of which must be addressed with care and sensitivity.

So what should information system managers and technical employees operating in a global environment do to be successful? Discussions with several global consultants suggest the following 10 points are critical to global success:[35]

1. **Incorporate diversity into your organization.** Recruit team members from across geographic lines, business functions, and corporate experience. Diversity is a powerful tool when you're trying to gain acceptance. It also brings insight about local conditions that may affect a project's success.
2. **Build trust.** Take time to cement relationships among members. Plan regular get-togethers, such as meals off the corporate premises. Such activities help transform "us" and "them" into "we."
3. **Create team identity.** Any special program that will help the group to gain corporate recognition will heighten participants' sense of importance in the company.
4. **Build consensus.** Make sure that members at all levels share the corporate vision; otherwise, you'll keep coming back to that issue every time there's a disagreement.

IS employees often work in a multicultural environment, such as these IS managers who work for an international technology firm and have different cultural backgrounds.

Don't underestimate the value of confrontation. If used correctly, it keeps issues from festering and sabotaging success.

5. **Teach sensitivity.** Formal instruction goes a long way in eliminating ignorance that could set a project back. When everyone is in sync about the proper protocols for processes that differ from one location to another, the project runs more smoothly.
6. **Establish ground rules.** To avoid misunderstandings and frustration, global teams need to follow common ground rules for communication, conflict resolution, running meetings, and other project activities. If necessary, use a facilitator to identify significant differences among members and suggest the most effective rules for the group. Although ethical values and principles may vary from one region to another, it is important to clearly establish ethical practices.
7. **Be fair.** Be consistent in compensating team members. They will talk. Boost morale by offering incentives when they meet project milestones.
8. **Communicate progress.** Make sure you share critical data among team members in a timely fashion. Keep management or other interested parties aware of successes and setbacks. Toot your own horn when things go well. Solicit new ideas when you're stymied. Flag problems that need resolution.
9. **Designate responsibilities.** Especially when time and distance separates participants, it is easy for tasks to fall through the cracks. Avoid finger pointing by documenting exactly who is responsible for what.
10. **Go face to face.** No matter how well you keep in touch, time and distance often cause minor problems to escalate. It is important to get global team members together in one location on a regular basis. That promotes more productive brainstorming and helps participants iron out difficulties, realign priorities and, most important, reinforce a sense of community.

The next section identifies some guidelines for companies that want to use information systems to achieve organizational goals successfully.

Business Guidelines for Information Systems Success

What does it take to build effective business information systems? How can companies ensure that their functional systems give managers the "big view" of the company rather than a narrow, department-oriented focus? What should companies do to ensure that its investments in information systems yield high returns? How can companies be successful in the global marketplace? The answers to these and similar questions depend on the company's ability to follow these success guidelines.

Give Employees Information Access for Improved Decision Making

Many companies that use information systems successfully do so because they trust employees enough to give them access to information so they can make decisions that affect their jobs. Take for example, 3M Corporation, the $14 billion manufacturer based in St. Paul, Minnesota. The company has a policy of letting employees devote 15 percent of their time to conceiving new products and systems. 3M employees are not required to tell management what they do with this time. In fact, employees often keep management in the dark until an idea emerges as a product, as happened with an innovative mouse pad product that improves mouse precision and tracking.

"As vice president, I can walk into a room, ask a guy what he's doing, and he can say, 'I'm not going to tell you; it's my 15 percent,' " says Geoffrey C. Nicholson, staff vice president, corporate technical planning and international technical operations. "This requires trust on our part and trust on their part that they're not going to get fired. Even I don't tell my boss [the CEO] everything I do." This policy has helped the company meet its goal of earning no less than 30 percent of its annual sales from products introduced in the past 4 years, notes Nicholson.[36] Believing in employees' creativity has helped 3M use technology to achieve a competitive edge.

Problems Won't Go Away. Opportunities Will. Be Prepared to Act on Both.

Companies that build successful information systems are those that catch the "technology bull by the horns." A recent survey by Chicago-based management consulting firm Diamond Technology Partners surveyed 430 CEOs and found that many suffer from a severe case of high-tech inertia. According to the survey, technology falls into the same category as annoying-but-important tasks (like changing a car's oil) that are often postponed. "What the survey says is that CEOs are aware of technology and its potential impact," says Mel E. Bergstein, the chair and CEO of Diamond. "However, they don't know how to approach the problem. There's a bit of paralysis." For example, 54 percent say technology is a key part of achieving revenue growth and 69 percent strongly agree that "information technology is redefining the market place in ways that can either upset a company's plans or create new opportunities."[37]

However, when it comes to implementing technology those same executives who talk the talk don't necessarily walk the walk. Thirty percent of the participants do not have a company Web site. Bergstein thinks those executives' foot-dragging stems from a fear of making decisions riddled with uncertainty. The problem is that opportunities to apply technology to achieve competitive advantage slip away quickly. Further, when companies miss such opportunities it is often difficult, if not impossible, to make up for time lost.[38]

Use Information Systems to Improve Customer Satisfaction

The most successful information systems are those that are focused on customers. The key question when approving an information system project should be "How will this help our company better serve our customers?" Customer satisfaction is not just about how pleased the customer is; instead, it is about finding new ways to please the customer. An old joke sums up the problem with measuring customer satisfaction: A Boy Scout, hoping to earn a badge, submitted to the scoutmaster his list of good deeds for the week—2 hours spent shepherding pedestrians safely across the street. Commendable work indeed, said the scoutmaster as he handed the scout his new badge, but why did it take so long? Replied the scout: "They didn't want to go." Like the badge-hungry Boy Scout, most satisfaction surveys focus on how well, or how badly, a company performs. But surveys should focus on customer sacrifice: the difference between what the customer wanted and what that customer settled for. That is the only way to become outstanding at customer service.[39] Once the business understands the measure of customer sacrifice, then it can assess how its information system can help offer customers the type of service they want.

Integration Leads to Success

Companies that invest in systems that are isolated from other internal systems often create complex problems. For example, the retail industry is paying a high price to integrate its different systems. Older systems do not communicate well with more modern ones, with the result that decision makers cannot get the information they need as and when they need it. "Right now, a huge amount of money and effort is spent on integration in the retail industry. Everyone would rather be putting that energy into creating new products," says Michael Campbell, president and founder of Campbell Software, which develops retail applications.[40] To stay fast and nimble, businesses should plan for an integrated system rather than piecing one together as problems arise.

Take Calculated Risks

Many new and innovative information systems are also risky investments. Because there is no easy way to avoid risk, IS managers must learn how to assess and manage risk. "Managers face risk every day, in every decision they make. Put away the Maalox. Although you can't eliminate risks, there are ways to ensure you're taking intelligent ones. The problem is that smart risks are best determined with 20/20 hindsight. After all, if this stuff were easy, everyone would have an income to match Madonna's.[41] "James Lam, chief risk officer for Fidelity Investments, has a handy method for helping company executives remember the four questions they should ask to assess the risk of a proposed initiative. Naturally, he uses the acronym "RISK."[42]

- "R" is for return: Are we achieving an appropriate return for the risks we take?
- "I" is for immunization: Do we have the controls and limits in place to manage risk?
- "S" is for systems: Do we have the systems to measure and report risk?
- "K" is for knowledge: Do we have the right people, skills, culture, and incentives for effective risk management?

The saying "no risk, no return," applies to information systems, so managers should learn how to manage the risk inherent in their information systems.

SUMMARY

1. **Describe basic business structures and functional areas.** The different functional areas of a business include management, marketing, manufacturing or service production, finance and accounting, and human resources. Some businesses organize its employees and resources according to a functional structures in which the business would have departments for each functional area. Still other businesses organize themselves according to project, using cross-functional teams of people with various types of expertise.
2. **Identify four types of information systems.** Information systems are grouped into categories. One category is based on the number of individuals who use them: personal systems (one user), work-group systems (a group of users), or enterprise-wide systems (the entire organization uses the system). The second category is based on the types of business decision the information system supports. Transaction processing systems process basic transactions and support lower-level decision making. Other types of decision-oriented systems include management information systems and decision support systems. Strategic information systems provide companies with a competitive advantage because of how the technology is applied to solve business problems. The fourth category is based on the type of business function the information system supports: marketing information systems, manufacturing information systems, financial and accounting information systems, and human resources information systems. In most companies the goal is to develop cross-functional systems that improve customer service.
3. **Explain the role and function of marketing information systems.** Marketing information systems are a set of information systems that meet the information needs of an organization in the area of sales, distribution, advertising, market analysis, market intelligence, product research, service management, and other marketing functions. These systems provide decision makers with marketing information that is key to providing excellent customer service. Marketing information systems, if used effectively, can help companies be responsive to customer complaints, requests, and needs.
4. **Summarize the purpose of manufacturing and service information systems.** Manufacturing and service information systems are designed to help companies get optimal results from its manufacturing plants and service facilities. Manufacturing information systems provide decision makers with all the information necessary to make good decisions on the shop floor. This includes deciphering the amount of various resources required to make a product and determining how best to make that product and deliver it quickly and effectively to the customer. Today, traditional manufacturing is being replaced with agile manufacturing, which allows companies to mass customize products to meet the unique needs of its global customers.
5. **Outline the purpose of financial and accounting information systems and identify how they support the business.** Accounting and financial information are key to the survival and growth of any business because they provide data about assets, liabilities, cash flow, debt, inventories, and so on. Often, this information is then integrated in a meaningful way with other systems in the company.
6. **Explain the role and function of human resource information systems.** Human resource information

systems provide a broad and comprehensive view of information related to company employees and other external entities that the company may deal with. Also, human resource information systems are responsible for ensuring compliance with laws and regulations so they must be robust and reliable.

7. **Describe the purpose and role of cross-functional information systems.** Cross-functional systems integrate the information being generated by different functions. The primary purpose of cross-functional information systems is to give decision makers a unified, comprehensive view of information. Finance, accounting, marketing, manufacturing, and human resources may be separate functions, but like wheels on a cog, must work together to achieve the company's goals.
8. **Define and describe global information systems.** Global information systems are systems that integrate people, systems, and business units from around the world. They rely on telecommunications to achieve this goal. The development and implementation of such systems require technology and sensitivity to cultural, legal, and business issues from other parts of the world.

KEY TERMS

agile manufacturing (p. 44)
enterprise resource planning (p. 45)
financial and accounting information systems (p. 46)
global information system (p. 54)
human resource information systems (HRIS) (p. 49)
manufacturing information systems (p. 42)
marketing information systems (p. 38)
strategic information system (p. 35)

REVIEW QUESTIONS

1. What are some of the benefits of information systems to an organization? Identify at least three business benefits of IS.
2. How did the Ritz-Carlton's sales and marketing information system (see Technology Payoff, p. 32) benefit its salesforce? Its customers?
3. Briefly describe the types of functional information systems. Is any one system more important than the other is? Discuss.
4. A functional system can be a personal, work-group, or enterprise-wide system. Discuss.
5. How can IS be classified by decision type?
6. What is a marketing information system and what are some of its functions?
7. What are some key questions that a marketing information system should address?
8. Why should manufacturing information systems be integrated with other systems in the organization? Describe MRP and MRP II.
9. Describe agile manufacturing. What distinguishes agile manufacturing from traditional manufacturing?
10. Manufacturing information systems also refer to service information systems. Discuss.
11. What is an ERP system? How can it help a company make better decisions?
12. What are some types of financial and accounting information systems?
13. What are some issues that IS managers should consider when developing global information systems?
14. What are some benefits of global information systems?
15. What are some guidelines that can help companies be successful in developing business information systems?

DISCUSSION QUESTIONS AND EXERCISES

1. Salespeople often don't want to learn complicated software programs that they must use on a sales call, according to Kurt Johnson, an analyst at Meta Group, Inc., a consulting group based in Stamford, Connecticut. As if user resistance isn't enough, consider the following: More than three-fourths of the businesses that install a salesforce automation system are dissatisfied and about 61 percent of those implementations fail to produce any measurable benefits, according to Gartner Group. What's more, if the vice

president of sales isn't included in the project, expect a 90 percent failure rate. At a cost of about $3,500 per user at the high end and 6 months to 1 year to implement, a failed project is hard to swallow.

a. What are some steps that you would take as a marketing manager to enlist the participation of your salesforce?

b. Top management often views systems development as an IS function. How would you encourage your manager to ensure the success of your project?

2. Here are some tips for companies about to embark on a salesforce automation project:

- Enlist the vice president of marketing to help develop the project.
- Get your top salespeople to use the software first. That way the rest of the sales team can hear the success stories.
- Get IS and sales working together. Have an IS manager assigned to the project follow a sales executive around for a day.
- Hire an integrator or consultant to push the project forward.[43]

a. Interview sales executives in a local firm about their daily activities and write a one-page report on how you would automate some of the functions the sales executives perform.

3. Can the ideas of agile manufacturing be applied to a service industry? How would the travel industry benefit from the ideas of agile manufacturing?

4. Many companies are not reaping the full benefits of an ERP system because they do not plan how they will use the information generated by ERP to better serve their customers. Tom Davenport, a "guru" in IT management says, "When I ask, for example, "What are you doing about management reporting with ERP, I get one of two answers. . . .'We're using our ERP to generate the same old reports we used to.' At least the ERP implementers have the good taste to say this with some sheepishness. The second, 'We haven't decided yet.' "[44]

a. Interview a local company that uses ERP to see how they are reaping the benefits of ERP. Write a one- to two-page paper analyzing the company's approach.

b. What recommendations would you make to ensure the best use of ERP?

5. Although experts emphasize the importance of developing integrated, customer-oriented systems, many organizations have difficulty developing such systems. Identify three reasons why organizations may have such difficulties.

6. Some questions confronting top management are, "Does the salesforce spend time on the activities that bring the highest return? Does the operations staff waste time on tasks that are not worthwhile? One way to find the answers to those questions is to use activity-based management (ABM) tactics. ABM is the accountant's version of a basic law of physics: For every business action or activity, there is a cost. ABM identifies what activities, policies, and technological applications consume resources, generate costs, and cause work to be performed. By identifying which actions and processes create costs, managers can decide whether discrete activities are worthwhile and cut accordingly. For example, Boise Cascade Office Products applied ABM to analyze which customers added the most to Boise's bottom line. One result: Salespeople are no longer paid commission on orders that do not achieve a gross margin big enough to cover the costs of recording, processing, and delivering the order. If Boise loses money on the customer, why should the salesperson be paid?[45] What would be your reactions to working for a company that used ABM to decide how much you get paid? What are the strengths and weaknesses of such an approach?

7. A fundamental requirement for building integrated, customer-oriented information systems is the willingness of managers and employees to share and disseminate information. However, in many organizations, information is viewed as a currency that can be used to achieve job security, promotions, and power. Some employees feel that giving away information may reduce their value and power in the organization and may resist change and even provide inaccurate information to stall the process of building integrated systems. Would you, as a manager, be sympathetic toward an employee who hoards information to protect his or her job?

8. **(Software exercise)** Your teacher keeps an accurate record of your scores using a spreadsheet. Create a spreadsheet that computes the class grade for you and five friends. Suppose the following formula is used to calculate your course grade.

4 quizzes	20%
First exam	10%
Second exam	15%
Third exam	15%
Final exam	25%
Assignments	20%

Calculate the final score for each student and select the top three students. Can you calculate the grade that the student is making at any given point in the semester?

Case 1: The Japanese Are Reluctant to Automate

Kiyoshi Maenaka had a feeling Daiwa Bank was not up to the rigors of modern, high-tech finance. Then in July 1995, a bond trader at Daiwa's New York office sent a letter to headquarters disclosing that for 10 years he had been hiding trading losses by forging documents that most U.S. banks had computerized a long time ago. The ensuing scandal cost the bank $1.1 billion in the United States. Even worse, Daiwa's managers were doling out $7.3 billion in loans they now cannot recover, part of a mountain of bad debt that has shaken Japan's financial system.

For Mr. Maenaka, deputy general manager at Daiwa's systems-planning division, the revelations proved that the bank's computer systems were not up to date. He took action to remedy this problem. Today, Daiwa is the first Japanese bank to farm out its computer operations to a foreign company—IBM. In Japan the banks traditionally build their own systems. Mr. Maenaka had to get the nod not only from the Ministry of Finance, but from holdouts within the bank that worried that outsourcing would breach Daiwa's "social responsibility." He eventually struck a compromise. IBM would hire 260 Daiwa technicians to work with 40 IBM employees in the same building where Daiwa ran its own networks.

No amount of technology can make up for bad financial judgment. But running a modern bank requires complicated computer systems, systems most Asian banks, from Tokyo to Bombay, India, do not have. Despite huge investments in computer hardware during the boom years, Asian banks are behind the West in using computers to do everything from preventing and detecting fraud to making smart loans. "They're trailing U.S. and European banks by three to five years," says James Fiorillo, a banking stock analyst at ING Barings Securities (Japan).

Asian banks are so far behind that many bankers say the easiest solution is to turn over their entire computer operations to foreign experts. For example, many Japanese banks have remained quaintly labor-intensive. In a typical branch, an usher still helps customers find their way to seats, the bank doors shut at 3 P.M., and only this year did the ATMs stop shutting down at night. Loan approvals must still bear the personal red-ink stamps that have served for centuries in lieu of pen-and-ink signatures. Electronic mail is rare. A desk employee at a bank in Asia is only half as likely to be on a networked personal computer as an employee at a U.S. bank, says market-research firm International Data Corp. of Massachusetts.

Asian bank employees use fewer computer systems to make decisions. They lag in using systems that slice and dice data about customers to help craft new financial products. Computerization also conflicts with Asia's notion of lifetime employment. "They love the concept of automation," says Mitsuo Matsunaga, a manager at U.S. consulting firm A. T. Kearney. "But when we get down to details and it's going to affect certain people, it's a different story."[46]

1. In spite of lagging behind in computerization, Japan is still a global economic force. What do you think are some reasons for this?
2. Some argue that if the Japanese hesitate any further to automate their banks, the banks will eventually shut down. How would you convince a Japanese manager that automation is good for the bank?
3. What, if any, is the link between automation and "social responsibility," as the Japanese see it. Do you agree?

Case 2: Viacom International

Recent surveys by Gartner Group and Forrester Research show that CIOs overwhelmingly favor finance as their top priority for achieving a competitive edge in the marketplace. Many CEOs view financial information systems as a key tool for making effective decisions. There are many reasons for the growing interest in developing financial information systems and using them to achieve business goals. First, many financial systems are becoming antiquated since they were built long ago. As companies rethink how to design and develop new systems, it gives them an opportunity to make these systems more powerful and effective. Second, more and more managers need financial information to make decisions concerning every aspect of the business, from marketing to quality control to human resources. Many financial systems do not provide the information at the level of detail that managers would like to see. Hence, managers are looking at how to get more from their financial systems.

At Viacom International Inc., the New York-based parent of MTV, Nickelodeon, and other entertainment

continued

Case 2: Viacom International, *continued*

interests, the Chief Financial Officer (CFO) teamed with executives from sales, marketing, and contracting to lead the company in new directions. Because financial processes are so intertwined with the processes in other departments, top managers felt that redesigning finance should ideally be part of a company-wide project. Although some turf wars were inevitable, executives involved in this large-scale effort to reorganize the company were persuaded to support cross-departmental process change. In the case of Viacom, the company targeted its financial systems to find better and smarter ways to handle the financial reporting of its wholly owned subsidiaries. The new system has reduced the company's dependence on paper, particularly financial transactions, which often involve rekeying, rechecking, and doing accruals. Further, it gives managers time to analyze the data and to use it to make better decisions, rather than spending their time collecting the data.[47]

1. Identify two reasons why financial information systems are excellent tools for improving decision making.
2. Explain why financial information systems were at the center of initiating change at Viacom.

Case 3: Bean Counters

Building and maintaining information systems is a costly proposition. This often puts the IS department at loggerheads with the finance department, which approves all IS projects. Finance executives are used to being called "bean counters," "corporate cops," "number crunchers," and so on. They simply view it as part of the territory, fully realizing that their number-one responsibility is the financial well-being of the company.

When faced with corporate technology concerns, however, CFOs find that they must reconcile their role as supervisor of the IS department with that of financial watchdog (not to mention to their position as major IS user). The need to balance all three perspectives makes for a complex and challenging task for many finance executives. Is IT a function to be managed, a cost to be contained, or a strategic asset to be exploited?

CFOs insist that they must view and study technology from a business point of view rather than from a budgetary point of view. "It's not about cutting costs; it's more about making sure that technology gives us the information to run the business better," says Dorothy D. Hayes, director of internal audit at Hewlett-Packard Co. in Palo Alto, California. She adds, "But if we spend lots of money on IT and we're still not getting the [return on investment], we get kind of irritable." Other CFOs also complain that IS project requests often fail to show a high probability of returns. "We have no idea whether [the IS department is] making those numbers up," says Christian D. Weiss, controller at The Franklin Life Insurance Co. in Springfield, Illinois. "They could be sandbagging for all we know." Hayes agrees. "It's really a leap of faith."[48]

1. Assume that you are responsible for obtaining some funds for your favorite IS project. What are some issues that you would present to the CFO to convince him or her that this is a worthwhile project?
2. Top management is often skeptical of the numbers that IS departments present for funding requests. What are some steps that IS employees should take to win the trust and confidence of top management?

Part 2 Technical Foundations of Information Systems

I regard information technology as a precocious teenager: full of energy, irreverent, unpredictable, a source of both joy and heartache—and frequently in need of close supervision.

Kent "Oz" Nelson, Chair and CEO of United Parcel Service

CONTENTS

HARDWARE FOR SUCCESS

Every day, in one form or another, computers and other related hardware, such as printers, modems, wireless communication devices, scanners, voice-recognition systems, and so on, touch our personal and professional lives. In fact, computers are invading our kitchens. Feeling bored while waiting for your microwave dinner to heat up? Here's help. NCR Corp. has a prototype microwave oven that doubles as a TV and a voice-activated computer. "As soon as you shut the door, and the pizza is happily spinning around, you can talk to the microwave and check your bank balance, send an e-mail or even watch the last 5 minutes of the TV sitcom *Friends,* says Stephen Emmott, director of NCR's Knowledge Lab, the computer maker's London center.[1]

The prototype version—which looks like a regular countertop microwave—comes with a 10-inch monitor built into the door. The computer is voice activated, letting users order a particular TV channel, visit a favorite Web site, or conduct home banking. For those who prefer typing, the touch-activated screen can display a virtual keyboard. There is also a built-in bar-code scanner that can read your favorite brand of microwave popcorn and add it to a shopping list if you are buying groceries on-line.[2]

Computers are also changing our commute to school or work. Intel Corp. has teamed up with Microsoft Corp., Ford Motor Co.'s subsidiary Visteon, and other key players in the automotive industry to develop PCs for automobiles. Initially, the computers will offer drivers voice-activated access to e-mail, a cellular phone, and navigation devices. Eventually, passengers will be able to surf the Web from the back seat. Prices for auto PCs should run about the same as those for desktop PCs, according to Intel.[3]

Chapter 3

Computer Hardware

AFTER STUDYING THIS CHAPTER, YOU WILL BE ABLE TO:

- Discuss the fundamentals of data representation
- Describe the five hardware components in a computer system and their main functions
- Compare and contrast different types of computers according to size and speed: supercomputers, mainframes, minicomputers, workstations, and microcomputers
- Explain the process of buying a personal computer

Computers can serve as productivity tools for individuals and businesses. Memory, recall, search, and processing—often difficult or tedious tasks for the human mind—are simple ones for computers. In addition, a study on the effectiveness of technology in schools found that students who use computers tend to feel better about themselves, learn faster, communicate better with teachers and peers, and achieve more than nonusers.[4] The study suggests that these effects occur because computers free students from boring tasks, help them to learn difficult material at their own pace, enhance communication with their peers and others around the world, and sharpen their problem-solving skills.

One of the great ironies of our times is that not everyone has access to new technologies. "We will have a two-tiered system . . . a great divide created by technology," warns Rich McGinn, CEO of equipment maker Lucent Technologies. The trouble has already started, says William Kennard, chairman of the Federal Communications Commission. Only 27 percent of U.S. classrooms have the infrastructure to support computers. Only 14 percent of minority schools and 4 percent of rural schools are prepared. "It goes to our competitiveness as an economy," he says. "If we don't educate [students] how to use these products . . . our customers, shareholders, and employees will be someplace else," says Michael Dell, founder of Dell Computer.[5]

Despite the benefits, even the most sophisticated computers cannot THINK. Intelligence and creativity are still exclusive, endearing hallmarks of the human mind. Creativity, vision, leadership, and common sense are skills that human beings have but computers do not. As a result, human beings and computers complement each other in powerful ways.

TECHNOLOGY PAYOFF

Everest Is the Limit

Armed with equipment specially designed by the Media Lab at MIT in Cambridge, Massachusetts, a U.S. expedition climbed the 29,000-foot-high Mount Everest to gain a better understanding of its climate and geology. However, the effort to outfit the climbers showed the importance of tailoring technology to its environment.

The scientists behind the expedition had to wrestle with the design and operation of the climbers' computer equipment, tackling issues from power conservation to real-time monitoring of systems in remote locations. Temperatures can go from subzero to uncomfortably hot; the oxygen level is only one-third the normal level. Robert Poor, a Media Lab graduate student, explains: "Logging a week's worth of data and beaming it wirelessly down the mountainside is a substantial challenge."

Obtaining sufficient power without using bulky equipment was probably the biggest obstacle. The batteries carried in the climbers' backpacks had to be long-lasting without being too heavy or numerous, Poor notes. To solve the problem, Media Lab created computer batteries that sleep for five minutes and awaken every sixth minute to provide power to sensors that take readings and radio the data back to base camp. Even at base camp, more than 10,000 feet below the summit, the technology must be rugged. Mt. Everest is a far cry from the climate-controlled offices that most computers call home.

Source: Rebecca Sykes, "Everest Tests Technology," *Computerworld,* May 18, 1998, 37–38.

Despite the growing importance of IS in society, less than a third of U.S. schools have the technology resources to support computer instruction.

Developments in computers and other hardware are often tantalizing. However, as Richard R. Roscitt, president and CEO of ATT Solutions says, "It's not about hot technology or showcasing the latest neat application of technology; it's really about improving the value of the company using technology."[6] As we see from the Mt. Everest example, people can use computer hardware in innovative ways. The mountaineers on this expedition used a variety of computer hardware such as laptops, wireless equipment, computer power conservation devices, and powerful batteries. We also see that computer hardware is more than just the computer and its parts. Computer hardware refers to all tangible parts of an information system that help a computer to function effectively and to meet users' needs.

Users of information systems should understand computer hardware for several reasons. First, many employees will work with computers that are part of information systems on the job, so a working knowledge of hardware is helpful. Second, as people move up the corporate ladder, they often become involved to varying degrees in decisions about computer hardware purchases. Third, many of the terms used in this chapter have become part of the professional's dictionary. For example, someone may ask you, "How much RAM does your machine have?" Familiarity with these terms is useful. Fourth, the home-PC market is booming. To make effective decisions about a home computer, we need to understand computer hardware well.

This chapter provides a broad overview of computer hardware, which consists of the physical components of information systems. First we examine how data are represented in all computers, regardless of the size and type of computer. Data representation and its requirements are the foundation of our computer hardware discussion. Then we examine the five key components of a computer, types of computers, and how to buy or lease a personal computer. We also explore ways to use hardware technology to enhance business success and to avoid the pitfall of using new technology for its own sake.

Fundamentals of Data Representation

How are data represented in a computer? How does computer hardware understand a program written in a specific language? All data, be they numbers, symbols, graphs, images, or alphabets, are represented in a computer using a string of binary digits (represented

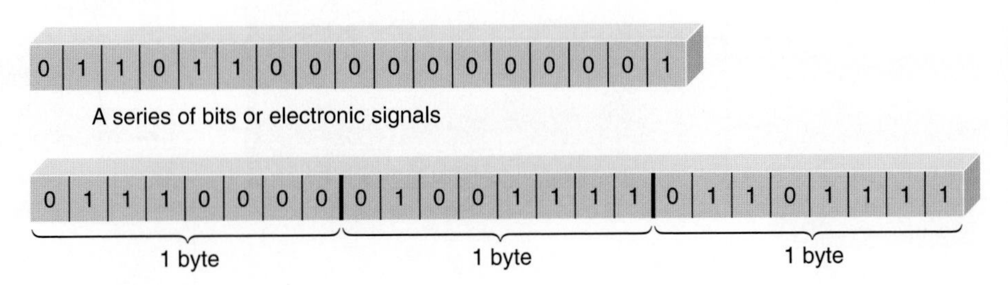

FIGURE 3-1

The Relationship between Bytes and Bits

A byte is made up of eight bits, and a bit, which is an electronic signal, is represented as 0 or 1.

using zeroes and ones) or **bits.** A one indicates the presence and a zero the absence of an electronic signal. Note that electric signals when used in computers and telecommunications are referred to as electronic signals.

It takes a unique combination of eight bits, or one **byte,** to represent a character in a computer, as shown in Figure 3-1. For example, to represent the letter *P*, the number 7, and the symbol *!* in a computer requires eight bits per character. A thousand bytes (1,024 to be exact) is called a kilobyte (kB). Approximately one million bytes equal a megabyte, a billion bytes is a gigabyte, and a terabyte is 1,000 gigabytes. Table 3-1 summarizes the memory size units used in a computer.

Two important considerations influence the performance of a computer: *speed* (the time it takes to process data) and *memory size* (the amount of memory required to store data and instructions). Speed is measured in fractions of a second whereas memory size is measured in bytes. **Million instructions per second** (MIPS) is the speed at which a computer executes instructions. For example, 2 MIPS is 2 million instructions per second. Faster computers have higher MIPS than slower ones. Because some computers need more instructions than others to do the same task, MIPS alone cannot be a deciding factor.

Bit

The smallest unit of data in a computer, which is represented using zeros and ones.

Byte

A combination of eight bits.

MIPS

The number of millions of instructions a computer processes per second.

TABLE 3-1

Memory Size Units for Computers

Unit	Amount of Memory
Byte	8 bits
Kilobyte (kB)	1,000 (10^3) bytes*
Megabyte (MB)	1,000,000 (10^6) bytes
Gigabyte (GB)	1,000,000,000 (10^9) bytes
Terrabyte	1,000,000,000,000 (10^{12}) bytes

*This number is an approximation. The exact value is 1,024 bytes.

The Five Computer Components

A computer system consists of five basic components:

1. The central processor (central processing unit and primary storage)
2. Secondary storage
3. Input devices
4. Output devices
5. Communications devices

Figure 3-2 shows these five components and how they relate to one another. We examine each of these components next to give you an overview and then describe each part in more detail in the following sections.

FIGURE 3-2

The Five Basic Components of a Computer

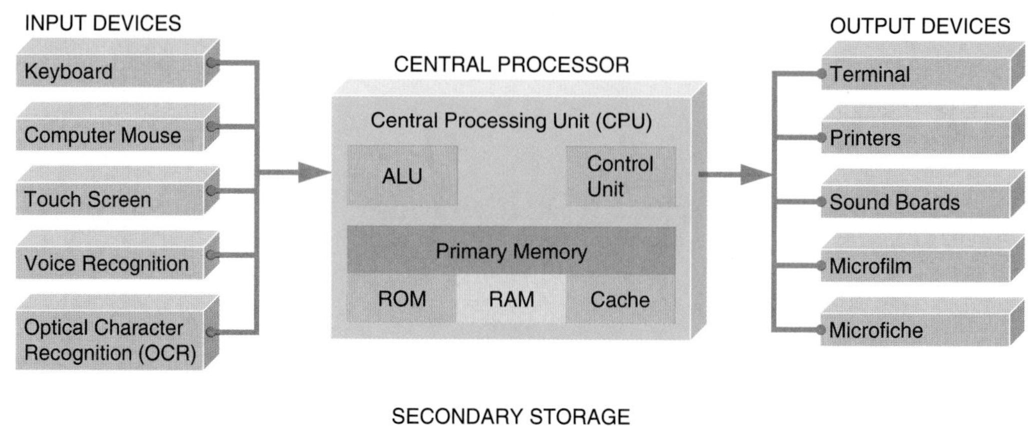

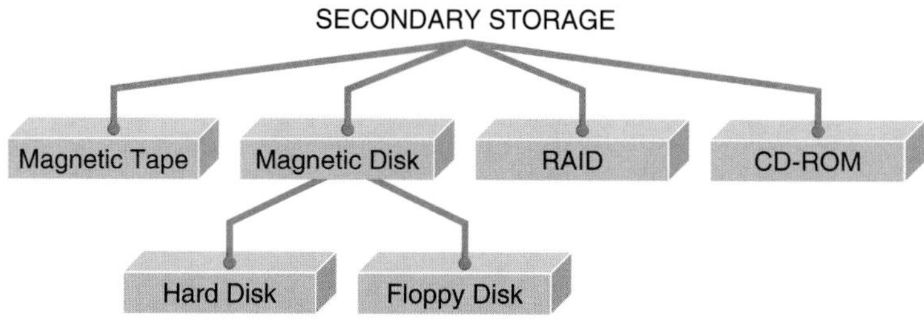

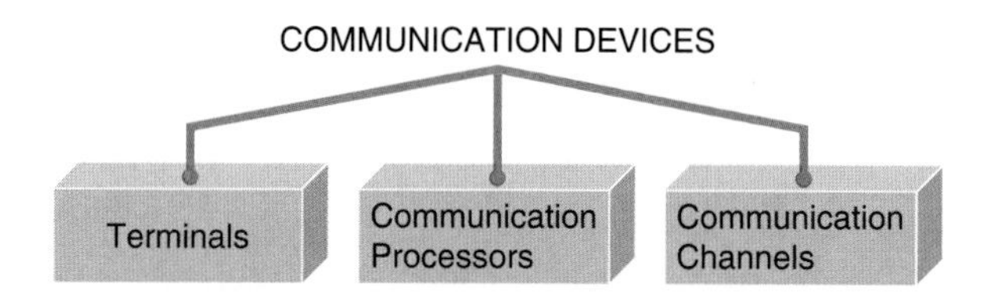

Central processing unit (CPU)

The unit that does all the processing work in a computer, also called the chip.

Arithmetic-logic unit (ALU)

The part of the computer processing unit (CPU) that performs basic arithmetic operations (such as adding and subtracting) and logical operations (such as assessing which number is greater than, equal to, or lesser than another number).

Control unit

The part of the CPU that accesses the data and instructions stored in the computer and transfers it to the arithmetic-logic unit.

Instruction

A command that tells a computer how to accomplish a given task.

Primary memory

A group of memory cells that temporarily store data and instructions.

The Central Processor

The central processor and its components provide "intelligence" to the computer. The components of the central processor handle all processing operations and store and retrieve the software residing in a computer. Without the central processor, the computer will not be able to do any tasks that we now expect our computers to perform. The central processor consists of two parts:

1. The central processing unit (the CPU)
2. Primary storage

The **central processing unit (CPU),** also referred to as microprocessor in smaller computers, is a critical computer component. Without the CPU, the computer cannot function. The CPU has two main parts:

a. **Arithmetic-logic unit** (ALU)

b. **The control unit**

When the computer is given a problem that involves any kind of mathematical operation, such as adding two numbers, the CPU directs the arithmetic-logic unit to perform the calculations. How does the arithmetic-logic unit know how to perform these calculations? The control unit obtains the data and **instructions** necessary to do the processing and gives it to the ALU. An instruction tells the computer in a structured, step-by-step fashion how to accomplish a given task. The control unit and the ALU work closely to process information efficiently.

The second main component in the central processor is **primary memory.** Recall that the control unit in the CPU fetches the data and instructions. Where does the control unit get the data and instructions? Primary memory is a place to store data and in-

The CPU (also known as the "chip") houses the arithmetic-logic unit and the control unit and is the "brain" behind the computer.

structions. Each cell in primary memory consists of one byte. Storing a character in a computer—regardless of whether it is a number, an alphabet letter, a blank space, or a symbol—requires one byte. Like an apartment complex where the tenant may change but the address remains the same, the contents of the memory cell in primary memory may change but the cell's address remains the same. The computer finds a piece of information by going to the right cell address.

The memory cells consist of several electronic components called semiconductors or "chips." A semiconductor consists of several thousands of transistors, devices that can open or close a circuit. Think of it as an electronic switch, or bridge, that can turn the electronic signal on or off. We classify chips according to the number of transistors or circuits etched on them. A chip with a small number of circuits is called an integrated circuit (IC), and as the number of circuits increases, the chips are referred to as large-scale integration (LSI), very-large-scale integration (VLSI), or ultra-large-scale integration (ULSI).

Table 3-2 summarizes the different types of primary memory classified according to type and volatility. These are the three types of primary memory:

1. **random access memory** (RAM) (volatile memory)
2. **read-only memory** (ROM) (nonvolatile memory)
3. cache memory (volatile memory)

The computer can both read and write instructions to random access memory (RAM). Note that primary memory holds data and instructions only temporarily. When the computer is turned off or when there is a power failure, RAM loses its contents. This temporary storage feature is why primary memory is considered volatile. The word

Random access memory (RAM)

A part of primary memory that acts as temporary storage for data and instructions.

Read-only memory (ROM)

A permanent part of primary memory that contains instructions the computer can read, but to which it cannot write.

TABLE 3-2 **Different Types of Primary Memory**

Types of Primary Memory	Volatility	Description
RAM (random access memory)	Volatile	Memory in which data and instructions are stored temporarily
ROM (read-only memory)	Nonvolatile	Memory in which some basic instructions are permanently stored
Cache memory	Volatile	Memory used to complement RAM. Speeds up retrieval of data and instructions

FIGURE 3-3

Contents of a RAM Cell before and after a Power Failure

Because RAM is volatile, it loses its contents after a power failure.

An empty address in RAM.

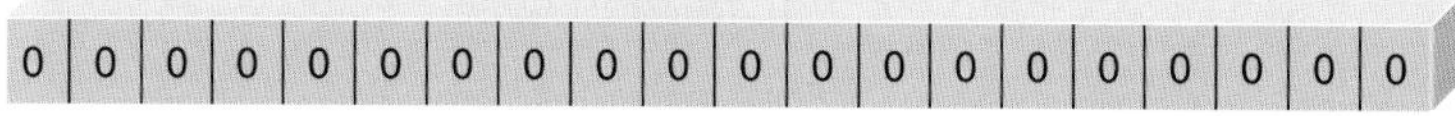

Before power failure: An address that has something stored in it.

0 0 0 0 0 0 0 0 0 0 0 0 0 0 0 0 0 0 0 0

Oops! RAM after a power failure.

random in RAM implies that the computer can directly—that is, it can "randomly"—access any cell (say cell address 99) in memory without reading all the cells before it (cells 1 through 98). Figure 3-3 shows the volatile nature of RAM.

Programs and instructions that are frequently used, but not frequently changed, are etched or "burned into" ROM by hardware vendors. ROM is nonvolatile memory and does not lose its contents when power to the computer is switched off or lost. ROM has two variations, PROM and EPROM. PROM (programmable read-only memory) allows users to permanently etch certain software programs into primary memory using special equipment. However, instructions etched on PROM cannot be erased. Another kind of ROM memory is EPROM (erasable programmable read-only memory), which allows users to erase and reprogram customized instructions etched on the chip through the use of ultraviolet rays.

Cache memory (pronounced "cash") is the third type of primary memory. Note that in addition to cache memory, other types of cache exist, such as disk cache, browser cache, and so on. The fundamental purpose of all types of cache is the same: to improve the performance of the computer.

The CPU searches cache memory for data and instructions before it searches RAM. Cache, then, acts as a temporary storage for frequently used information. The bigger the cache, the faster the computer will perform, assuming all other factors are constant. Not only is cache memory faster than RAM, if it's large enough, more instructions can be stored there and the computer will be able to find instructions quickly and efficiently. In addition, cache memory is physically located closer to the CPU than RAM, so the computer can retrieve information from cache memory more quickly.

The computer uses a formula or guiding principle to identify instructions that should be loaded in cache. This formula helps the computer predict the next set of instructions that will be required and transfer those instructions into cache in blocks.

In this section, we have seen that the central processor manages and processes data. Its two key parts are the CPU and primary storage. The CPU, in turn, consists of the arithmetic-logic unit and the control unit. Next, we examine secondary storage.

Secondary storage

Long-term memory that resides on storage devices outside the CPU.

Sequential storage

A type of secondary storage in which users can only access and retrieve data in the order in which it was stored in the system.

Direct access storage

A type of secondary storage in which users can directly access and retrieve data in any sequence.

Secondary Storage

Primary memory alone is inadequate to meet the information needs of an organization. Also, computer users need memory that is nonvolatile so that when there is some power disruption, the data are not lost. This type of memory is called **secondary storage,** or secondary memory. Recall that the control unit fetches data from primary memory. Hence, the data and instructions from secondary memory must be transferred to primary memory before they can be processed. Storage is already the most costly hardware component in IT. Three years ago, storage represented 30 percent of hardware purchases. Today that figure is 35 percent, reports Dataquest, a California research firm.[7]

The two main types of secondary storage are **sequential** and **direct access**. For example, if a file containing 100 names is stored in a sequential storage device, then the 98th name can be accessed only after reading the 97 names that precede it. Payroll is a good example of an application well suited for sequential storage because companies rarely issue checks in a random manner to their employees.

Systems in which information must be immediately processed when received require direct access storage. For example, an airline reservation system will simply not work in a sequential storage device because the computer will have to read all the records preceding the record that is being searched. Suppose your last name was Zephyr. The computer would have to access all passengers preceding the letter *Z* in the alphabet. Clearly, sequential storage is an inefficient way to process airline records.

Although hardware developers have made considerable progress in the area of secondary storage, many experts believe the revolution in data storage has just begun. For the past few years, storage device developers have embraced the "smaller and faster" principle: Storage devices should be as small as possible and work as fast as possible. In the following sections we look at some popular secondary storage devices such as magnetic disks, magnetic tape, and CD-ROM.

Magnetic Disks

A popular storage medium, both for large and small computers, is the **magnetic disk.** You can read from and write to magnetic disks. Because magnetic disks are a direct access storage device, they are essential for on-line systems in which data have to be stored and retrieved almost instantaneously. Magnetic disks come in two forms: floppy disks and hard disks.

Magnetic disks

Direct access storage devices that use magnetic technology to store data and information. Also known as hard disks and floppy disks. Disk drives are used to read from and write to disks.

Floppy disks are an integral part of the PC world. Floppy disks are the 3.5-in. diskettes that are used mostly on PCs. These disks are reliable, portable, and have fairly large memory capacities. Today some floppy disks can hold about 120 MB of data. This is 80 times more data than the 1.44-MB storage capacity of a few years ago. The new floppies are fairly inexpensive and are excellent for backups and archiving.

A revolution is taking place in the computer storage industry. IBM's giant magnet resistive (GMR) technology is a 3.5-in. floppy disk drive that holds up to 16.8 gigabytes of data. Current storage problems are similar to having too few closets in your home. IBM's director of storage performance argues that home PC buyers shouldn't experience storage problems with GMR technology because it will improve storage capacity by about 60 percent per year over a 3-year period.

A magnetic disk such as this one gives users direct access to stored data and information.

Large computer systems may use multiple hard disks to store data. Hard disks access data more quickly and efficiently than floppy disks and are highly reliable. Hard disks are made up of several "hard" disks or rigid, thin glass or aluminum platters that are coated with iron oxide. In large systems, several hard disks may be vertically mounted to form a single unit. On each platter, information is stored in what is referred to as tracks that are concentric circles etched on the platters. The information is then retrieved using read/write heads, which are small and sensitive mechanical devices that retrieve information based on the track's address. All hard disks used to be fixed disks that were not portable. However, removable cartridge disks are now gaining in popularity.

Older hard disks held as little as five megabytes and used platters up to 12 in. in diameter. Today's hard disks can hold several gigabytes and generally use 3.5-in. platters for desktop computers and 2.5-in. platters for notebooks. In 1956, IBM's RAMAC, which was a part computer, part tabulator, was the first machine with a hard disk. It was an extraordinary technology for its time. The disks were 24 in. in diameter and held a whopping 100,000 characters (they were not called bytes then), for a total of five million characters. Today, a 3.5-in. drive can hold five gigabytes of data. In 1995 IBM researchers created a model of a disk with a bit density of 3 gigabytes per square inch, 1.5 million times more dense than the first hard disk.[8]

Magnetic disks have advantages and disadvantages. Magnetic disks provide quick and direct access to data with fairly large storage capacities (anywhere from 20 megabytes to 7.5 gigabytes). Also, on-line systems cannot function without magnetic disks. Magnetic disks have some disadvantages, however. They are relatively expensive and are not always reliable. Further, their speed is much slower than the CPU (this is true for other secondary storage devices, too), so magnetic disks can slow down the processing speed of the computer.

This 3.5-inch hard disk platter has tracks that store information.

Managers must consider the advantages and disadvantages of magnetic disks and make decisions about storage devices carefully. If storage devices do not have enough capacity or if the storage mechanism does not meet the processing needs of the

SABRE, a huge airline reservation system, crashed when a circuit breaker tripped at its underground data center. The crash halted business at travel agencies, airlines, and reservation Web sites such as Travelocity.

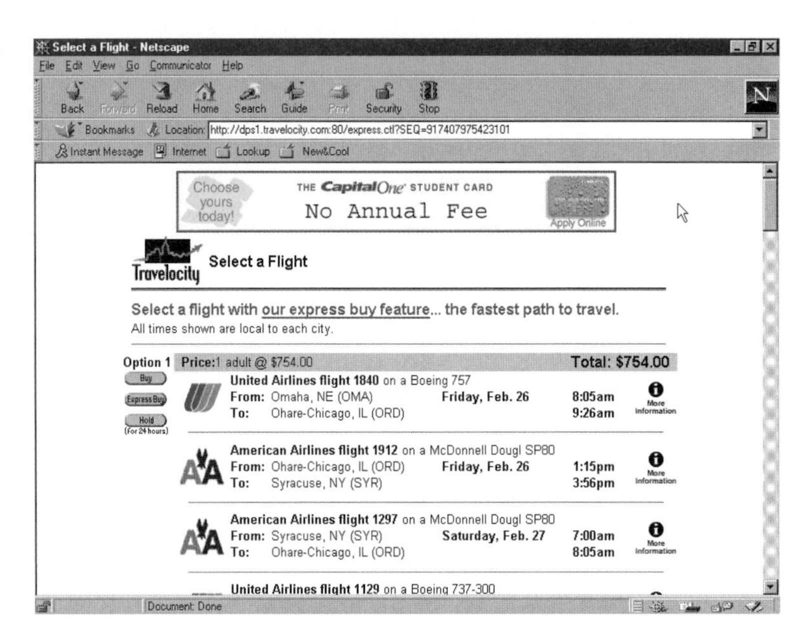

organization, it can affect the organization's productivity through delays in information flow. Further, because companies must back up all their important files, slow or unreliable storage devices can also cause significant productivity problems.

Take the example of the travel systems giant, Sabre Group. When the company's data storage system crashed in June 1998, it caused a 3-hour outage, which delayed flights and froze reservations nationwide. The system crash left travel agents and airlines without access to the SABRE airline reservation system. "This is the lifeblood—our system," recalls Jennifer Hudson, a spokeswoman for the Sabre Group in Fort Worth, Texas. Hudson explains that for reasons not yet known a circuit breaker tripped at Sabre's underground data center. That cut the power to the disk system and left agents and travelers in the lurch.[9]

RAID

RAID, or redundant array of independent disks, refers to two or more drives that work together to provide storage, increased performance, and error recovery. RAID developers wanted to bring together a number of inexpensive and small hard drives so that they could yield the same capacity and power of a single, reliable large drive.

RAID has become a mainstay for many companies. Businesses that need large amounts of data storage or guarantees that their storage system will not fail rely on RAID systems because they are fast, reliable, and have the ability to recover quickly from errors and failures. A North Carolina manufacturer needs to double the amount of data it stores every 6 months as a newly installed financial, human resources, and manufacturing system kicks in. A New York daily newspaper, which can't afford a system failure on deadline, needs a reliable backup for its publishing process. In each case, the users deployed storage systems that rely on RAID technology.

Further, RAID drives allow users to boost system performance because they can access several hard drives simultaneously via a faster channel than the drives support directly.[10] As a result, they increase the efficiency of data retrieval and storage. RAID also has other features, such as the ability to share the same disk space among multiple systems or the ability to add to existing disk volume without having to bring the computer server down, a procedure a single drive requires.[11]

Magnetic tape stores digital data and information sequentially.

Magnetic tapes

Tapes used to store digital data and information in a sequential manner.

Magnetic Tape

Magnetic tape is used most often in large computers for storing historical data or keeping a backup of important files. PC users and network administrators also use magnetic tape as a secondary storage device. **Magnetic tape** is a sequential storage medium well suited for batch applications—tasks that are accumulated and processed periodically. It has several key advantages. It is a low-cost, portable, fairly reliable storage device that holds a large amount of data and information. When carefully handled, magnetic tape can be reused many times. Magnetic tape's main disadvantages are its sequential rather than random access (although for some applications this isn't a problem) and the need for careful handling and for keeping it in a controlled environment.

CD-ROM

Compact disk–read-only memory (CD-ROM), used both in small and large computers, is based on optical disk technology that uses a laser device to "burn" data into optical disks. They are particularly well suited for storing large volumes of static data, such as historical facts and figures, telephone directories, and dictionaries. The amount of data that can be stored physically on other media, such as floppy disks, is very limited compared to CD-ROM, which enjoys high storage capacity (around 600 megabytes) given its relatively low cost. One CD-ROM can store the equivalent of 300 or more floppy disks.

Compact disk–read-only memory (CD-ROM)

A special kind of optical disk on which data are recorded using laser devices and read using CD-ROM drives.

CD-ROMs are optical disks that have huge storage capacity compared to other storage devices, such as floppy disks.

Once, CD-ROMs were mostly read-only devices, meaning that you could only read the data on a CD-ROM but could not write data to it. That is no longer the case. Two different types of CD-ROMs are CD-R (read only), and CD-RW (read and write). Each performs different functions.

Users can use their CD-R drives to compile family photos and videos or even record their favorite music using a special device. Once the information is etched on a CD-R, users can only read the information but cannot change or write new information to the CD. Special programs allow CD-R users to customize their CD-ROM recordings. For example, you can modify pitch levels to make Celine Dion's voice sound like a baritone—or a chipmunk—without changing the music's duration. You can also "age" a musical piece, making it sound like it's coming from an old 78—or add a futuristic techno-edge.[12] Unlike a CD-R, a CD-RW is rewritable so users can write to the same CD many times.

Many industries, such as travel, entertainment, finance, and motion picture, have enthusiastically embraced the CD-ROM technology because of its ability to integrate different types of data. Companies spend between $200,000 and $300,000 to produce training CD-ROMs that contain video, animation, catchy scripts, and stereo music. CD-ROMs help learners interact with a system that is fun. "Multimedia has a real power to it that nothing else does," explains Bruce Clark, project manager of a CD-ROM that trains technicians at Mitel Corp., a telecommunications company in Ottawa, Canada.[13]

For example, in the Mitel CD-ROM, technicians are given quizzes in a game format. The company estimates that CD-ROM training cut a week off a proposed 3-week training class and saved the company travel and lodging expenses, Clark notes. Consultants Marita Decker and John Faier of OmniTech Consulting Group in Chicago created an interactive CD-ROM to help thousands of AT&T Corp. managers learn about technology. Jonathan Jones, multimedia production manager at AT&T, claims that the CD-ROM works because of games that made the CD more interactive. "Users have more control, and it's more motivational."[14]

"Don't bug me!" "Cool!" "What's the idea?" This is everyday talk for most 14-year-olds, but foreign expressions to deaf kids. And the signs expressing the sarcasm and superlatives of teen language are foreign to hearing kids. But a CD-ROM called "Street-Signs: A City Kid's Guide to American Sign Language" helps both deaf and hearing students grasp these and other complex concepts. The CD-ROM was produced at JHS 47, a school for the deaf in inner city New York. With its ability to show action, facial expression, and emotion, the CD-ROM is a superior way to teach American Sign Language, which is based on concepts, not words. For example, the sign for "Cool, man," expresses approval, rather than indicating the ambient temperature.

The CD-ROM contains more than 650 sign movies divided into 24 language categories. Using their computers, students roam the streets of New York. They learn number and money concepts on a virtual Wall Street and travel to Central Park to learn signs for nature concepts. They travel to the United Nations to learn signs about different countries and to St. Mark's Place in Greenwich Village, New York, to learn street language. When they click on a word, the signer-actors who appear on-screen are students. That lends credibility and immediacy that line drawings cannot imitate. Best of all, the movies can be exported into student reports, databases, and slide shows.[15]

CD-ROM technology helps deaf teenagers communicate with their peers.

Source: http://www.evolvingtech.com/susan/ssmain.html

CD-ROM is also playing an integral role in interactive advertising, which helps manufacturers, retailers, and advertising agencies reach consumers, advertise products, and sell goods. Consumers rely on CD-ROM drives to access product information and obtain detailed information on a variety of products.

Interactive CD-ROMs are becoming the norm for many users. For example, many Web sites offer interactive CDs for a wide variety of products and services, from music to computer training. Take, for example, d-Rom, an interactive dance music store on the Web. This site allows visitors to sample various dance tracks, including upcoming releases. Users can listen to interviews with various DJs and visit a series of dance rooms.[16] Another interactive CD-ROM that captured the attention of many in the retail industry is the Harry Rosen CD-ROM on fashion. Filled with video, sounds, and tips designed to help users with fashion-related questions, the CD provides information on everything from "tying a loose fit tie to picking the perfect band collared shirt."[17]

The CD-ROM industry is still advancing. California-based Zen Research has found a way to increase the performance of CD-ROM drives and other optical storage devices. Currently, the technology reads one track at a time and focuses on spinning the disks faster to achieve higher performance. But Zen Research's TrueX technology reads more than one track at a time. CEO Emil Jachmann predicts that TrueX will shatter optical performance barriers, making the CD-ROM so fast that it will no longer slow down the personal computer (most secondary storage devices are the slowest component of the PC). "We want to push the bottleneck back to the CPU."[18]

Write-once, read-many (WORM)

A special kind of optical disk on which data once written can be read many times but cannot be rewritten without special equipment.

Besides CD-ROMs, another type of optical disk is **write-once, read-many (WORM),** an excellent storage document for archives and backups. Once information is written to the disk, it cannot be erased but it can be read many times.

Digital Versatile Disk (DVD)

Many experts consider the digital versatile disk to be the successor to the CD. It is a silvery platter that stores from 2 to 17 gigabytes of information. Like the CD, it can store different kinds of media such as audio, video, and other data. Unlike the CD, which records information only on one side, the DVD stores information on both sides of the disk. There are different types of DVDs, such as DVD-R (read-only) and DVD-RW (read and write). Companies use DVDs to distribute software, movies, and video games; transport files; and create backups of existing files and information. Will the DVD overtake the CD immediately? "My take is that it will be more like 2005 before rewritable DVD takes over rewritable CD," predicts Wolfgang Schlichting, an analyst at International Data Corporation in Framingham, Massachusetts.[19]

In summary, storage is crucial for many organizations because data loss can cause serious time and financial drains. An understanding of data storage and its organizational implications, then, is essential for IS managers and users. Now that we have investigated the central processor and secondary storage, we turn to the third hardware computer component: input devices.

Input Devices

The third component in a computer system is the input device, through which a computer accepts data. Input devices help human beings to interact with a computer and convey to the computer what they want the computer to do. To interact meaningfully with the computer, then, users must have a thorough understanding of input devices.

From the mundane devices of the 1950s, 1960s, and 1970s, to the ultra-sophisticated devices of the 1990s, input devices have come a long way. Today, most of you are familiar with a keyboard and a mouse, "the point-and-click" device that revolutionized the way we create and generate data and information. The mouse, invented by Douglas Englebart in the 1960s, is essential for terminals that use graphical user interface (GUI)—computer interfaces that rely heavily on menus and graphs.[20] Let us look briefly at other popular input devices such as the touch screen, voice recognition, and optical character readers.

Touch Screens

One popular, easy-to-use, intuitive, and inexpensive input device is the **touch screen.** Even users with little or no computer background can easily use a touch screen. The only disadvantage of touch screens is that the input data are limited to the choices on the screen. The many applications of touch screens in organizations range from fast food restaurants to video stores to entertainment parks. At Disney theme parks, visitors can obtain information on entertainment program offerings by touching a computer screen menu. At Grace Hospital in Morgantown, North Carolina, doctors enter patient data using touch screens.

Touch screen

An input device that allows users to execute commands by touching a specific location on the screen.

Hallmark Cards, one of the largest greeting-card producers in the world, creates more than 11 million cards *per day* that generate sales of $2.3 billion a year. Touch screens in Hallmark's 1,200 in-store kiosks allow card buyers to design and print their own customized cards all over the world. Hallmark's Touch-Screen kiosk has a computer, a CD-ROM, and a printer. The customer uses the touch screen to answer questions the computer asks, such as "Who is the card for?," "What is the occasion?," "Is the recipient male or female?," and so on. Once customers input the information, they print a customized card.

Voice-Recognition Systems

An input device that converts the human voice into a digital pattern, compares that pattern to a set of prerecorded patterns, and executes a command if a match is found is a **voice-recognition system.** If no match is found, the system may ask the user for more

Voice-recognition system

An input device that analyzes and interprets the human voice to follow instructions.

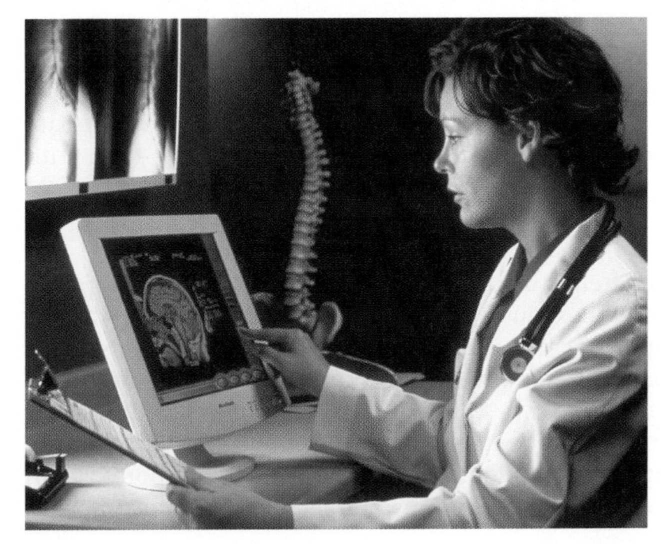

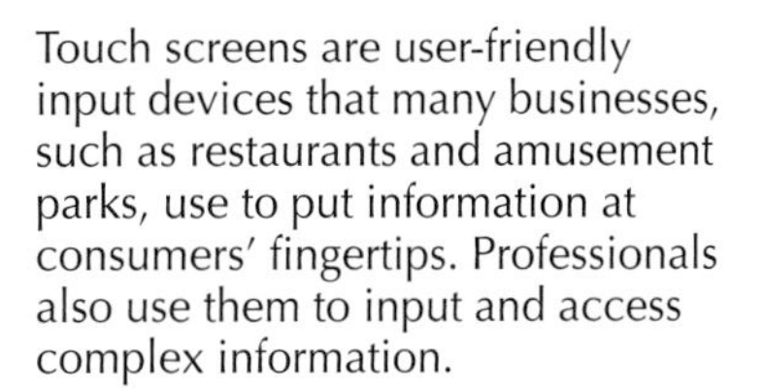

Touch screens are user-friendly input devices that many businesses, such as restaurants and amusement parks, use to put information at consumers' fingertips. Professionals also use them to input and access complex information.

Voice-recognition systems allow users to input information hands-free.

input. Although voice-recognition systems have been around for many years, until recently they were not commercially viable because they were too expensive and too ineffective at recognizing speech variations. Today, thanks to artificial intelligence and pattern-recognition software, voice-recognition devices have become powerful, viable, affordable, and more common.

David Barton, president of AcuVoice, sums up a key advantage of this input device: "The most normal way for us to communicate is by voice. Reading and writing are acquired skills, but hearing and speaking are animal instincts."[21] In addition, voice-recognition systems allow hands-free browsing of on-line catalogs, airline schedules, and other types of documents. "A keyboard is a pretty clumsy way to enter information, especially for people who aren't good typists," explains Charles Hemphill, a senior scientist at Texas Instruments.[22] Analysts estimate that in the near future voice recognition will be a standard feature in many computers.

"Speech recognition is now ready for prime time because the accuracy level is finally above 90 percent," explains Donna Fluss, a Gartner Group technology analyst. Experts estimate that 30 percent of new customer service systems will be voice-based by 2003. UPS, the Atlanta-based package delivery company, uses voice recognition for its customer package tracking system. The system handles 120,000 calls per day, and the company's six-figure investment paid for itself within four months. The cost is roughly one-third what the company would have had to pay operators to handle the same number of calls, according to a UPS spokeswoman. "One of the things we've proved is that customers prefer this method of communication because it's timely, predictable and accurate," says Carl Skonberg, project manager at UPS.[23]

In spite of its many advantages, voice-recognition systems have some disadvantages. Experts say that as users begin to "talk or even yell" at their computers, users may become burdened with sore throats and hoarseness. As one expert observes, new users, in particular, tend to "speak louder to make sure the system understands!" The problem with voice injuries is even more acute for those who smoke, have stress, or suffer from allergies. In fact, some users seek the help of speech therapists to learn correct posture, breathing, and relaxation techniques. Speech therapists recommend the following measures to avoid voice injuries:

- Sip water frequently
- Sit up straight (or stand)
- Relax the neck, shoulders, and jaw
- Speak softly and in a conversational tone
- Take frequent rests. [24]

Optical Character Reader (OCR)

Documents such as utility bills, insurance premiums, legal documents, and credit cards, are ideal applications for **optical character readers.** The most widely used OCR is the bar code reader that scans a pattern of bars marked on products. The pattern on the bars represents information about the product. Bar code scanners are used extensively in many companies around the world. For example, Toyota Vehicle Processors, a Toyota subsidiary, uses bar code scanners to make sure that shipments of thousands of automobile parts arrive at the parent company as needed rather than storing parts until they are used.

Optical character reader (OCR)

An input device that scans data from paper documents into a computer and then converts the data into digital form.

Output Devices

An output device is any device that helps the user to view the output of the computer. The most popular output devices are computer screens (also known as a video display terminal) and printers. The computer screen uses a cathode-ray tube (CRT) to shoot a stream of electrons on the computer screen, which allows us to see text and images.

Printers are based on three different types of technology: dot matrix, inkjet, and laser. The cheapest in terms of price and operational costs is the dot matrix printer, which uses a column of printing wires, also called pins, that strike an ink ribbon to form characters on a paper. The greater the number of pins, the better the quality of print.

TABLE 3-3

Features of the Three Types of Printers	
Type of Printer	**Features**
Dot matrix	Cheapest type of printer. Uses pins to press on a ribbon to make characters. Noisiest type of printer.
Inkjet	Higher-quality output than the dot matrix. Uses a nozzle to spray ink onto a page. Produces about 2 to 8 ppm. Can print documents in color. Quieter than a dot matrix printer, but more expensive to operate.
Laser	Highest-quality output, comparable to magazine output. Quietest printer. Typically the most expensive printer. Produces 4 to 16 ppm or more.

Printing speed is measured in characters per second, or cps, although many consumers look to the ppm—the estimated number of pages per minute.

Inkjet printers lie somewhere between dot matrix printers and laser printers in terms of price and print quality and are quieter than the dot matrix printer. Inkjet printers can also print color documents. They use a print-head nozzle to spray drops of ink that form characters on the page. Laser printers are quick, efficient, and sophisticated printers that can produce print of the same quality as a magazine or newspaper. Laser printer speed measures from about 4 to 16 pages per minute or more for network printers. Table 3-3 describes the three types of printers.

Ports connect a printer, or any other peripheral device such as a CD-ROM, to a computer. The two types of ports are parallel and serial. A parallel port or a serial port can be either a socket on a computer or a circuit on an expansion card that is then plugged into the expansion slot found on the inside of most computers. An **expansion slot** is a small storehouse inside a computer that is designed to accept certain kinds of circuit boards, also called **expansion cards.**

Expansion slot

A space in the computer that allows users to expand existing features and capabilities on their computer, such as memory, video cards, fax modems, and other input and output devices.

Expansion card

A circuit board designed to fit in the expansion slot of a computer.

The difference between a parallel and a serial port is that a serial port transfers data in sequence whereas a parallel port transfers data in parallel bits. A serial port is designed primarily to connect a modem to a computer. In a modem, data are transferred serially. A parallel port is designed to connect peripheral devices, such as printers. The parallel port can transmit information to a printer in parallel over eight lines (one bit per line).

Microfiche and microfilm are two relatively inexpensive output devices. Many libraries use microfiche and microfilm to store large volumes of information in a small amount of space. An entire issue of a newspaper, such as the *New York Times,* can be stored on a piece of microfilm that is only a few inches long. Unlike the microfilm, which is stored on a file, a microfiche is stored on a 3-by-5-inch index card and can hold several hundred pages of output.[25] They are ideally suited for outputting information related to transaction processing applications such as invoices, checks, and accounts receivable.

Communication Devices

Devices that help users separated by distance and time to communicate with each other electronically are **communication devices.** These devices help us to transmit text, images, graphics, voice, and video. Some basic communication devices are *terminals* (used to input and output data); *communication channels,* such as telephone lines, cables, and so forth (used to transmit information between the sending and the receiving parties); and *communication processors,* such as modems (which support the transmission of data and information). These devices, along with communication software, help companies to send and receive information electronically around the world. Communication devices are covered in detail in Chapter 6 on telecommunications.

Communication devices

Devices that allow users separated by distance and time to exchange documents, files, graphics, and other digital information.

We have explored the five hardware components of a computer: the central processor, secondary storage, input devices, output devices, and communication devices.

Global IS for success

An International Appeal

The World Congress on Information Technology held in June 1998 in Fairfax, Virginia, attracted more than 1,600 people from around the world. Naftali Moser, Director of the Peres Center in Tel Aviv, Israel, also attended the event. The Peres Center, established by former Israeli Prime Minister Peres, was designed to foster joint economic development projects among Israelis and Arabs, with an emphasis on information technology (IT). The center will train Palestinian University graduates in information systems' specialties to help meet the region's technology needs and boost the Palestinian economy. The center also has more ambitious goals. "By making sure that there are contacts between the Palestinians and Israel, you are promoting world peace," Moser says. That desire, Moser observes, has helped motivate Israel and its Arab neighbors to cooperate on economic development projects. "IT is the fast route to economic development."

But what about the rest of the world's ability to grow its IT industry? Statistics for most of the world's population are grim. Only 15 percent of the 5.8 billion people in the world live in so-called developed nations with per capita incomes of $25,000 or more. The remaining 85 percent earn up to $1,000 annually, according to Jeffrey Sachs, the director of Harvard University's Institute for International Development. Sachs notes that IT and telecommunications represent the most effective way to spur globalization and improve the economies of developing nations. He adds that the large attendance at the conference "is a testimony—if anybody needed it—that there is a desperate hunger all over the world to be part of (the IT) industry. . . . Nobody wants to be left behind."

Mikhail Gorbachev, former president of the former Soviet Union, who spoke at the event, said multinational companies must pay attention to conditions in the underdeveloped world. He warned of "unpredictable consequences" if human concerns are subordinated to profit. Gorbachev said lagging information technology in the Third World could aggravate those countries' enormous economic gap with industrialized nations. "Many Third World intellectuals believe that this gap is an expression of expansionism in a new form, and they call it electronic colonialism." He continued, "I would not recommend that you dismiss such concerns. . . . Those of you who work in transnational companies certainly know that this gap carries a tremendous potential for conflict."

QUESTIONS AND PROJECTS

1. Identify some specific ways by which technology can promote economic development.
2. Developing nations have bigger problems to worry about than staying on the leading edge with technology. Discuss.
3. Electronic colonialism or the "digital divide" is a problem in the United States also. How would you address this problem?

Source: Patrick Thibodeau, "Global IT Meeting Holds Promise for Many," *Computerworld,* June 22, 1998, 45, www.computerworld.com.

Recent developments in computer hardware have led to lower cost and increased accessibility. These developments have occurred because various nations recognize the market for affordable computing technology and work to provide ever-cheaper, ever-faster computers. However, even with these developments, people in some countries may not be able to keep up with the developments, as highlighted in the Global IS for Success feature. Now that we understand the computer's basic components, let's explore different types of computers classified according to size and processing speed.

Types of Computers

We classify computers into different types based on memory and processing speed. Typically, the larger the user group, the greater the demand for memory and processing speed. Supercomputers and mainframes are enterprise-wide systems, midrange computers and workstations are work-group systems, while all other types of computers are personal information systems. Recall from Chapter 1 that enterprise-wide systems support the needs of the entire enterprise; work-group systems allow groups of decision makers to process and exchange information; and personal infor-

FIGURE 3-4

Computers That Support Different Work-group Sizes

COMPUTERS THAT SUPPORT DIFFERENT WORK-GROUP SIZES

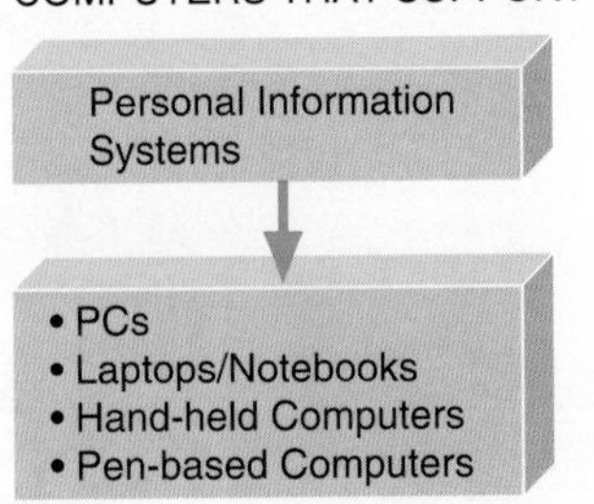

Work-group Systems

• Midrange or Minicomputers
• Workstations

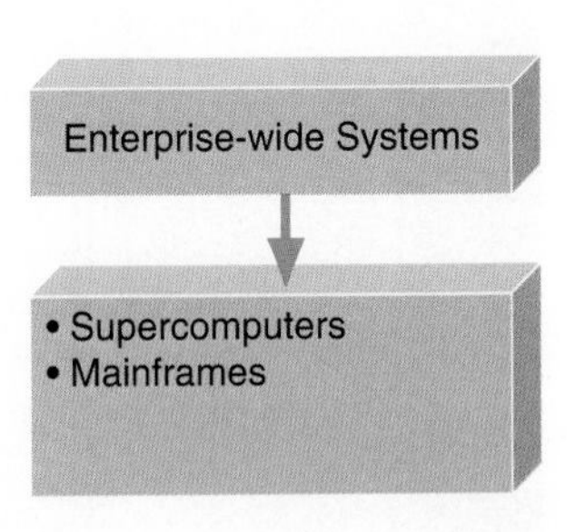

mation systems meet the information needs of individual decision makers. Figure 3-4 shows this relationship.

Supercomputers

Some of the fastest and largest computers available today are supercomputers. They are used in a wide variety of applications, such as processing large files and performing large-scale mathematical calculations. For example, the University of Oklahoma uses a supercomputer at the Pittsburgh Supercomputing Center to forecast weather storms. Supercomputers help weather experts to extend the forecasting period from 30 minutes to 4 or 5 hours.

Supercomputers
Computers with very large memories and high processing speeds that are capable of processing more than a billion instructions per second.

Supercomputers have two common characteristics: the ability to process instructions in parallel (parallel processing) and the ability to automatically recover from failures (fault tolerance). Personal computers usually have a single processor that processes one instruction at time. (Some PCs do have multiprocessors, especially those used for intense computations.) In contrast, supercomputers have multiple processors (or CPUs) that process multiple instructions at a time. This type of processing is known as **parallel processing.** Some business applications that are ideally suited for parallel processing include programs that help determine the best way to distribute the limited resources that an organization has, financial portfolio analysis, image processing such as processing photographs, and creating complex graphics.

Parallel processing
The computer's ability to process more than one instruction at a time using more than one processor or CPU.

Other computers may or may not have fault-tolerant features, but supercomputers have always been fault-tolerant. That is, supercomputers use a backup mechanism to automatically isolate and reconfigure hardware failures during system operation. The Securities and Exchange Commission uses fault-tolerant computers to analyze massive amounts of financial data that U.S. corporations submit to the Commission. The White House has installed four high-security, fault-tolerant computers to process a wide variety of applications. Goodyear Tire & Rubber Company in Akron, Ohio, uses a supercomputer for modeling tire designs. "(The designs) have been a significant breakthrough for us," says Loren Miller, director of tire performance modeling at Goodyear. "We are talking about reducing computing time from years to days."[26]

This Cray supercomputer is one of the fastest, largest computers available today.

Computer scientists at Sandia National Laboratories and Los Alamos National Laboratory are determined to push the frontiers of computing to what, quite simply, may sound unimaginable to the less adventurous. The goal is to develop by 2004 supercomputers that can perform 100 trillion (1,000,000,000,000) instructions *per second,* a speed that is 100 times faster than today's speediest machines.[27] To accomplish their goal, the scientists must triple the real performance of their computers every 18 months.

The main disadvantage of supercomputers is their high cost. A supercomputer costs anywhere from $250,000 to $3 million and the software to run supercomputers is also very expensive. The cost is one reason why fewer than 200 supercomputers exist in the United States.

Mainframes

Mainframe
A large, general-purpose computer with a large memory and excellent processing capabilities that is smaller than a supercomputer.

Mainframes, which are frequently enterprise-wide systems, are so called because of the "main frame" that once housed the CPU. They are ideal for transaction processing, financial applications, payroll, investment analysis, weather forecasting, airline reservations, and other applications that require extensive computations. Unlike a personal

The mainframe computer is a large computer with excellent memory and storage capabilities that allows multiple users to work on the system simultaneously. A midrange computer is smaller, slower, and cheaper than the mainframe. Although midranges sometimes look like PCs, they are more powerful than PCs.

computer where only one person can use the computer at a time, many users can simultaneously use the mainframe.

One of the main disadvantages of the mainframe is that it is expensive to purchase, operate, and maintain. Mainframes often require customized software and highly trained computer personnel to run and operate them. In spite of this disadvantage, mainframes have been around since the late 1950s and continue to be used for a wide variety of applications.

Minicomputers (also known as midrange computers)

Small yet powerful multiuser systems with excellent memory capabilities and processing speeds.

Midrange, or Minicomputers

In the 1970s, Digital Equipment Corporation (DEC) first introduced the concept of a **midrange computer,** or **minicomputer,** called the VAX series. Although midrange computers are slower and often have less memory than mainframes, they are workhorses that can deliver excellent "bang for the buck." The introduction of midrange computers allowed corporations that were unable to afford mainframes to enter the computing age.

Workstations are a productive alternative to PCs for many architects, engineers, and designers because of their power and speed.

Workstations

Workstations lie somewhere between midrange and personal computers. They can be used by individuals or groups, are faster and more sophisticated than PCs, and include numerous productivity tools that increase efficiency. Some workstations now handle tasks that supercomputers and mainframes handled 2 years ago. Engineers, designers, architects, and film industry animators are big users of workstations. For example, Pitney Bowes, a company that manages the movement of business messages and packages, uses workstations to develop renderings of advanced office products before they are manufactured. As we see in the Ethics for Success feature, companies must grapple with ethical problems that involve all types of computers.

Network computers

Computers that do not have storage capacity because they access whatever data and programs they need from a network when needed.

Network Computers

The network computer, also known as "thin clients," is a simplified version of a personal computer. Network computers were designed as an alternative to the personal computer, which can be expensive to operate and maintain.

Network computers have become the technology to watch in the next few years. **Network computers** are used mainly to access programs that reside on a company's network or on the Internet. In many companies they are replacing terminals connected to the mainframe and PCs. Larry Ellison, CEO of Oracle Corp., a high-tech company, observes: "The mainframe is not dead; it is just not at the center of the universe. The PC

Ethics for success

Hardware's Role

It's true: Computers do get more than their fair share of the blame when things go wrong. A survey of ethical behavior in the workplace found that 14 percent of workers admitted to wrongly blaming an error they made on a technological glitch. Another 13 percent admitted to using office equipment to shop on the Internet. About 1,000 workers, covering a broad range of industries, responded to the survey.

It is hard to separate ethical violations into hardware violations and software violations, because one cannot be done without the other. Here, we showcase how IS ethical violations often involve the use of one or both. The survey, conducted by the American Society of Chartered Life Underwriters and Chartered Financial Consultants and the Ethics Officer Association also found the following:

- 4 percent of those surveyed admitted to sabotaging systems of former or present employers. This could be things such as disabling a cable (hardware violation) or changing the software (software violation).
- 5 percent admitted to using the office computer to visit pornographic Web sites (both a hardware and software violation).

"Every manager needs to sit up and take notice that these things may be going on their workplace," cautions Edward Petry, executive director of the Ethics Officer Association.

In all, 45 percent of those who responded admitted to some unethical behavior involving technology. But workers were evenly divided about whether it's okay to play computer games at work—51 percent said games are a go. However, workers were opposed to Big Brother–like oversight, such as random e-mail monitoring, but they were willing to accept less invasive solutions, such as Internet-blocking software and clear policy guidelines from employers.

YOU DECIDE

1. Blaming one's error on technology is harmless, so it shouldn't be considered an ethical violation. Discuss.
2. Computer games are relaxing and may help some employees be more productive. As a result, companies should not prevent employees from playing computer games. Discuss.
3. Divide the class into groups of four to six. Assume your business has a midrange computer system and several people have reported ethical violations similar to those mentioned in this case. The violations are not only taking up employee time—they're slowing down an overtaxed system during your busy season. Spend 10 minutes devising a set of ethical guidelines for employees. Now join another group. One group should play the role of employees and the other the employer. Employers offer their policies and employees give feedback. Then the groups switch roles. Together, the groups should develop and report to the class a final policy with their rationale.

Source: Patrick Thibodeau, "Technology Takes Rap for User Mistakes," *IT Career News,* April 28, 1998, www.computerworld.com.

is not dead; it is just not at the center of the universe. At the center of the universe is the network (computer)."[28]

Network computers are well suited for task-oriented jobs, such as data entry, order entry, and assembly line work that constitute about 50 percent of the jobs in large and medium-sized companies. People in task-oriented jobs can use network computers effectively because the programs they typically access are stored on a central computer rather than on the individual's machine. For example, U.S.–based retailer Sears Roebuck and Co. plans to deploy more than 2,000 network computers nationwide as point-of-sale computers in its automotive centers.[29]

Network computers function by downloading all applications from a central computer and obtaining and storing all data back on the central computer. They are similar to a diskless computer that has no floppy or hard disk storage. Network computers usually have less processing power than a personal computer. They also require less individual care than the PCs because software updates are done from a central location so users can't meddle with them, resulting in fewer problems and breakdowns.

Some companies buy network computers and then upgrade them to contain more memory and local storage. This often defeats the purpose of a network computer because then the company will inherit all the problems of using PCs, which is why they chose to invest in network computers in the first place.

Opinions in the information systems community are divided on the benefits of network computers. On one hand, many adopters of network computers find them efficient and effective. They help cut maintenance costs, centralize support, and in some cases, find new uses for old equipment that might otherwise have been discarded. Because all programs and data are maintained on one computer, maintenance is simple on network computers.

"We were able to keep our investment in PCs from years past," explains Karl Gouverneur, director of technology architecture at Uarco in Barrington, Illinois. "We salvaged 400 older computers by turning them into [network computers]. We are realizing a savings of between 70 percent and 90 percent of the cost of maintaining a shop of strictly PCs." Uarco's experience is not unique. Zona Research, a research firm based in Redwood City, California, estimates that the network computer costs about $1,200 per user per year compared with $3,000 per PC user per year. Think for a moment about these figures. A company with 1,000 desktops could reap huge savings.[30]

On the other hand, some users believe that network computers simply exchange one set of problems for another. Because network computers rely heavily on the network, they can cause bottlenecks in network traffic. Some networks are not designed to handle traffic associated with having all the programs and data on a central computer. "NCs are a bad idea. Sure, they promise the dream of . . . less risk and lower maintenance costs. Just let me know how that balances with the increase in network demands," says Mark Peugeot, General Partner, Lancaster Internet Services. Regardless of how we weigh the advantages and disadvantages, network computers are on the radar screen for many CIOs as a technology to watch.

Microcomputers or Personal Computers (PCs)

Microcomputers, also known as PCs, are regarded by many as one of the greatest inventions of the 20th century, revolutionizing the way corporations around the world do business. Although the memory size and processing capabilities of microcomputers are less than mainframes and midrange computers, hardware technology advances have made the PC a compact, powerful, and versatile machine. In fact, advances in hardware technology have equipped many microcomputers with the same, or even better, memory and speed capabilities as the mainframe of a few years ago, with the result that some companies are replacing their mainframes with client/server systems (the topic of Chapter 9) to run sophisticated applications.

A PC can be customized to meet the specific needs of users. This customization is referred to as configuration. For example, one user may opt to have fax capabilities built into the system, while another user may prefer to have an external communication device, such as a modem, to fax documents.

Plug-and-play

A personal computer hardware capability that allows users to plug different hardware components into their PC without having to perform technical configuration procedures.

PCs also have **"plug-and-play"** capability. This capability gives PCs the limited intelligence to automatically install, remove, and configure different input, output, or communication devices without having to perform any technical procedures, making the customization process simple. Some people humorously refer to plug-and-play as plug-and-PRAY to indicate that with the proliferation of new hardware, plug-and-play is not always simple!

Plug-and-play also allows users to run different kinds of software on various types of desktop machines manufactured by different vendors. Today, several vendors are working hard to create plug-and-play standards that will make computers even easier to use. So those without a technical background can customize their PCs with a few simple keystrokes.

Mobile Computers: Laptops, Notebooks, Handheld, and Pen-based

Laptop, pen-based, notebook, handheld, and wrist computers are examples of mobile computing technology. These computers are battery operated so they can be used anytime, anywhere. Table 3-4 offers a brief summary of mobile computers. Laptop com-

TABLE 3-4

A Comparison of Types of Mobile Computers

Type	Description
Laptop	Fits on a user's lap and is slightly larger than a notebook. Has full PC functionality with a reduced keypad and screen. Has floppy drive.
Notebook	Has full PC functionality with a reduced keypad and screen and no floppy drive.
Handheld	Smaller than a laptop or notebook computer. Has a built-in monitor that can be operated from the palm of one's hand so the keyboard and screen are smaller than a laptop. Often, the keyboard requires an electronic pen to input data.
Pen-based	Uses an electronic writing pad and a light-sensitive electronic pen to input data.
Wrist	Can download text, photos, and other applications from PCs and transmit data via infrared rays; users input information on the LCD watch face that turns into a small keyboard.

puters are small enough to fit on a user's lap; notebook computers are the size of a notebook. The primary difference between these computers is their size and weight.

Notebooks are smaller than laptops; handheld and pen-based computers are even smaller. Wrist computers are still smaller. However, regardless of the size, mobile computers are equipped with powerful microprocessors, excellent communication devices, graphic capabilities, good memory size, mouse-driven input, and CD-ROM drives. Prudential, the insurance company in Newark, New Jersey, uses mobile computers to ensure the productivity of its agents and field associates. The company's 12,000 agents and field associates are equipped with laptops that are expected to improve productivity and customer service. The laptops have a database and a networking software that help agents complete policy applications via e-mail. Sales reps are also able to access the company's systems for customer needs analysis, sales illustrations, marketing brochures, and other relevant materials.[31]

Pen-based computers use an electronic writing pad and a light-sensitive electronic pen to input data. When the user writes on the pad, the writing is converted into digital input and stored as files in the computer. Pen-based computing is becoming increasingly popular because many people feel comfortable using a pen, especially sales and service representatives, insurance agents, retail suppliers, delivery people, and health care providers who are constantly on the move.

Workers—from farmers to executives—that need easy access to information outside a traditional office use mobile computers to increase productivity and save time.

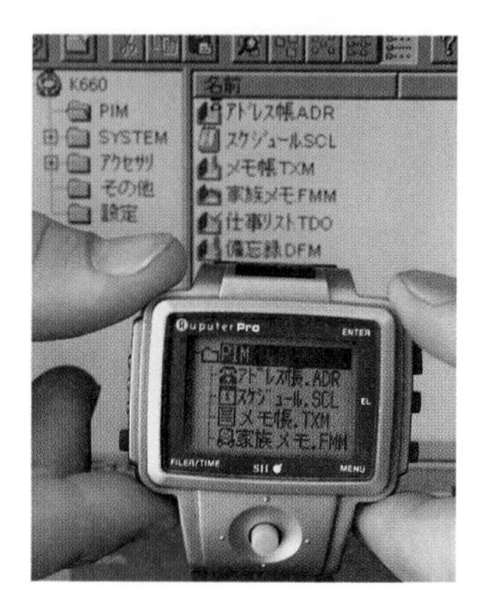

Seiko's Ruputer, the world's first wrist-watch computer, is a wearable PC that can download data from other PCs.

The portability of notebook and handheld computers has increased the productivity of many employees, particularly workers who travel extensively or do not spend much time in an office. Help desk employees at the city of Palo Alto, California, rely on handheld computers to do their job as they service 1,300 of the city's computer users. The workers use handhelds to download customer help requests from a central PC each morning. Throughout the day, technicians use electronic pens on their handhelds to jot down how they solved a problem. The computer has handwriting recognition software so users can input, store, and access notes. As a result, technicians don't need to create formal report documents from their daily notes. "It saves us an hour a day," explains Napone Phommachakr, the city's IT support manager. "It's a godsend."[32]

Japanese developers have devised a new mobile computer that weighs barely 67 grams (about 2.5 ounces) and can be worn on your wrist. Called Ruputer, this wrist computer can download text, photos, and other applications from PCs and transmit data via infrared rays. Users input information on the LCD watch face that readily transforms into a miniature keyboard. Users, besides telling the time, can also play games, store names and addresses, and keep track of appointments. Developed by Seiko Instruments, Ruputer has a 16-bit CPU, 128 KB of RAM, and 512 KB of ROM.[33]

In this section we examined the different types of computers. In the next section, we explore how to buy a personal computer.

How to Buy a PC

For those of us who do not already own a PC, the task of buying one can sometimes be daunting because the microcomputer world changes so rapidly. However, it is important to understand the basics of buying a PC. In this section we investigate six technical factors that affect the PC-buying decision: processor, clock speed, RAM, secondary storage, removable storage, expansion slots, and monitors. Figure 3-5 highlights these six factors.

Processor

The CPU determines the overall processing capabilities of a computer. The higher the number, the faster the processor. Past generations of processors or chips based on the 8086 chip that Intel Corp. developed in the early 1970s are represented as 80286, 80386, 80486. Pentium Pro, Pentium II, and Pentium III chips perform almost 90 percent better than the 486 chip.

Careers for success

Financial Technologists

Hardware touches all career fields, including business, science, health care, engineering, and the arts. For example, for the many individuals who are experts in financial products, their jobs now have a new and growing component, namely hardware and software technology. Finance professionals must know what hardware to use for different financial problems. Further, many finance professionals have to work closely with teams of IT professionals, so a good understanding of hardware and software issues is critical. Conversely, IT professionals working in the financial industry find that their jobs often require in-depth knowledge about financial products and services, which they often lack. As a result of the merger between finance and technology, companies now hire a financial technologist who has knowledge of both fields.

Financial technologists act as a liaison between experts in finance and technology experts who understand and build computer hardware and software that supports financial activity. Financial technologists know how to translate requirements about financial models into specifications that programmers understand and give advice on what hardware should support the modeling program.

Those who want to enter this field should take classes in both finance and computer science. Courses include computer hardware, telecommunications, programming languages, project management skills, risk management, modern portfolio theory, and capital markets. If you have an interest in finance and technology, consider becoming a financial technologist to achieve a happy medium.

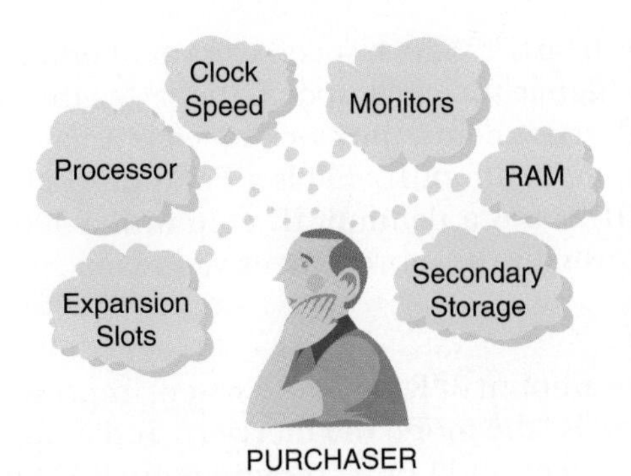

FIGURE 3-5

Six Technical Considerations in Buying a PC

Processing power is increasing at a dramatic rate. According to Moore's law, a technology axiom, processing power doubles every 18 months. Consider the advances of the PowerPC, which IBM, Motorola, and Apple Computer jointly developed to rival the Intel 8086 series. The PowerPC uses a technology called RISC (reduced instruction-set computing) that processes instructions more quickly than older chips. How? RISC chips contain only those instructions that are fundamental to operating the computer. In contrast, older chips contained a vast number of instructions in addition to the fundamentals. It reduces the complexity of chips by using simpler instructions.

What does the future hold for processors? Pluck a hair from your head. Imagine slicing it lengthwise into 555 strands. Each would be 0.18 micron thick, the same thickness as a wire destined for Intel Corp.'s new Merced chip. In fact, they are not even called wires—*traces* is the term—and you need an electron beam to arrange them in the specific layout that will become a Merced microprocessor. Merced is the code name for the first chip to be built from a new 64-bit microprocessor design, dubbed IA-64, created by Intel and Hewlett-Packard Co. (64-bit refers to the amount of data a CPU can process at once. A 32-bit system can handle 4 bytes; a 64-bit system can handle 8.) The IA-64 chips will incorporate a joint Intel/HP design called EPIC, or explicitly parallel instruction computing. EPIC chips perform tasks in parallel instead of sequentially, which will make them at least twice as fast as today's chips, analysts say.[34]

A CPU should be chosen based on the volume and complexity of work to be done, rather than on the price of the CPU. So, let's say you want to buy a PC to meet your college educational needs. Most students perform word processing, spreadsheet analysis, graphics, and e-mail functions. The CPU power required for such applications does not have to be the highest on the market.

When you graduate, however, let's say you get a job working with a team of marketing professionals. Now, in addition to your basic computing activities, you are responsible for extensive market data analysis of large files that require large accounting and marketing software programs. You are also involved in putting together a marketing newsletter that requires extensive graphics. Further, the response time for all programs should be quick. The CPU power that your work machine needs is much greater than what you needed in college.

Price should never be the only consideration when buying a computer. Instead, a good understanding of your application needs and their relationship to CPU processing power is needed.

Another consideration when buying a CPU is its compatibility with the software and hardware that you plan to buy. Today, chips are being customized to meet entry-level tasks. Instead of forcing users to buy a bulldozer to pull out a weed, chip makers are building chips exclusively for basic tasks such as word processing, simple spreadsheet analysis, and basic e-mail so that the systems have power that matches their intended use.

Clock Speed

The second factor in buying a computer is clock speed, or the speed of the processor, measured in megahertz (Mhz). "When referencing CPU speed, the megahertz rating is really the heartbeat of the computer, providing the raw, steady pulses that energize the circuits. If you know any German, it's easy to remember this. The word "Herz," pronounced "hayrtz," means heart."[35] Clock speed can vary between 25 MHz and 450 MHz, or more for PCs. The higher the clock speed, the faster the computer executes instructions. In computer advertisements, the clock speed is usually indicated after the type of processor. For example, Pentium II/450 is a Pentium II chip with a 450 MHz clock speed. The Pentium III/500 is a Pentium III chip with a 500 MHz clock speed. The higher the clock speed, usually the more expensive the machine.

RAM

The third consideration is the amount of RAM in the system, represented in megabytes. The simple principle to follow is "the more, the merrier." Today application programs (such as Word, WordPerfect, Excel, and Lotus) require more RAM than ever before so RAM is critical. Note that additional RAM can be added to the motherboard. A motherboard is the main circuit board in a computer. It houses the CPU, any coprocessors, data transfer mechanisms (also called the bus), memory sockets, keyboard controller, and other circuits for miscellaneous things. On some motherboards, we may find chips for video display, serial and parallel ports, and input devices. If they are not on the motherboard, they can be plugged into an expansion slot (a small storehouse designed to accept expansion elements) on the motherboard.

Usually there are one or two expansion slots on a motherboard. RAM is a function of the amount of memory that the operating system needs to function given the memory requirements of your applications, such as word processing, spreadsheets, and so on. Because every person uses different applications, no set guidelines exist for deciding how much memory your computer needs.

For example, you need 12 megabytes (MB) of RAM to run the operating system Windows 95 or Windows 98. The Windows NT operating system requires a minimum of 64 MB, although experts recommend 128 MB of RAM. This is simply to start and run your computer. Each application that you run on your computer has additional requirements. For most users, 32 MB of RAM is sufficient. Programs such as photo editing or sophisticated graphics packages usually require 64 MB of RAM.

The prices of RAM have dropped significantly in the last few years so that today you can get 1 MB of RAM for under a dollar. If you are planning to buy a laptop, RAM becomes even more critical because laptops have very limited expansion slots, so it is not easy to expand RAM in a laptop.

Secondary Storage

Secondary storage on PCs is relatively inexpensive, but this was not always the case. In 1983 a 10 MB disk drive for an IBM PC added $1,100 to the system cost. Translation? Each megabyte of storage space cost roughly $110. It now costs between 6 and 8 cents per megabyte of secondary storage and access times are now about 6 to 8 milliseconds, compared to older versions with access times in excess of 100 milliseconds. Given that secondary storage is relatively cheap, it is advisable to invest in it.

Expansion Slots

The fourth consideration is the number and type of expansion slots in the computer. Recall that an expansion slot is a small storehouse inside the computer that is designed to accept expansion devices, known as expansion cards. Low-end PCs may have only one expansion slot, but other PCs may have more. A user can increase the amount of RAM by adding a memory expansion card to an expansion slot or the user can add an input/output (I/O) device such as a sound card that records and plays back sound. The sound is then output through speakers or an external amplifier that is connected to your computer. The de facto standard for sound card compatibility in PCs is Creative Labs' Sound Blaster.

The most widely used type of expansion slot is the PCI, which stands for peripheral component interface. The USB, or universal serial bus, is another type of expansion slot that is found in the rear of the computer. It allows users to connect multiple devices to the computer without opening the computer case. Users can hook digital cameras, digital speakers, keyboards, a mouse, and other devices to the USB and can remove a USB device without rebooting the computer, unlike devices linked to other types of slots.

Monitors

The fifth consideration in buying a PC is the monitor. Quite frequently, buyers pay a great deal of attention to other factors but overlook the importance of monitors. The right monitor can do wonders for the eyes, however. Monitors can be flat or curved. A flat screen reduces the distortion especially at screen edges, but is more expensive. Most monitors currently in use are curved.

Like TV screens, monitors are measured diagonally. A 15-inch monitor is adequate for most tasks although a 17-inch monitor is much easier on the eyes. Nineteen and 21-inch monitors are excellent. The size of a monitor can be confusing, however. Even though vendors may indicate the size to be 15 or 17 inches, the "viewable area" may differ from one vendor to the next, so be sure to find out the monitor's viewable area before buying one. Typically, the bigger the monitor, the more expensive it is.

Resolution of a monitor refers to the capacity of the monitor for displaying pixels (short for picture elements), which affect the sharpness of screen images. Two numbers such as 640 by 480 usually express a resolution. The first number is the horizontal capacity and the second is the vertical capacity of the monitor to display information. The higher the resolution, the crisper the letters and graphics will appear on the screen. Common resolutions are 640 by 480, referred to as VGA (video graphics array) and 1,024 by 768, known as super VGA. Currently, the highest resolution available is 1680 by 1280. Monitors work in tandem with a video card that fits in an expansion slot on the motherboard, so the type of video board (also called video card or graphics adapter) used with the monitor is also important. The greater the memory on the video card, the more colors and resolution it can capture.

If you like good sound and want it incorporated into your PC, some monitors have three-way sound systems. These monitors have subwoofer, midrange speakers, tweeters, and three-dimensional sound. This type of monitor is called an integrated monitor.

Timing Your PC Purchase

With the technological changes that are taking place, when is a good time to buy a PC? As Table 3-5 shows, hardware prices have plummeted over time.

To wait as long as possible without hampering current information needs, some users are making system upgrades in which some parts of an existing PC are updated or replaced. Upgrades allow users to improve the performance of existing systems, although they do not work beyond a certain point. The easiest way to address that problem is to upgrade your motherboard, CPU, and RAM. However, the problem with upgrading the motherboard is that since most off-the-shelf machines are proprietary, this automatically requires replacing the computer case also.

What components should you buy to upgrade? That depends on your applications and performance expectations. Adding more memory, installing a faster CD-ROM, replacing an older, slower, smaller hard drive with a larger, newer, and faster model, or some combination thereof can enhance performance. A good rule of thumb is, if you have to spend more than $600 on an upgrade, a new computer is a better choice. Now that we have examined six technical considerations for buying a PC, let's turn to considerations for leasing a PC.

TABLE 3-5

Plummeting PC Costs

Year	Processor	RAM	Monitor	Cost
1981	Less powerful than a 80286 chip	256 kilobytes (Kb) of RAM	1-color monitor	$5,000
1992	80386 chip	2 MB of RAM	Color monitor	$1,000 to $2,000
1999	Pentium II with 233 MHz	64 MB of RAM	Color monitor	under $1,000

Leasing a Computer

According to the Equipment Leasing Association of America, in 1997 just under one third of businesses leased computers. Leasing computers is complicated, and if you make a mistake, you could be stuck with a technology albatross for 2 or 3 years. "The only people who should lease instead of buy are those without the cash," says Stephen Canale, a consultant in Ann Arbor, Michigan. "Leasing is a no-holds-barred, buyer-beware market. If you don't know who you are dealing with or have a good idea of how the lessor operates, not only won't you get your best deal, but chances are you'll be taken for a financial ride," says Richard M. Contino, author of *Negotiating Business Equipment Leases*.[36]

If you decide to lease a computer, here are some questions to ask: Will the lessor assume responsibility for upgrades or service? Can you renew the lease at the end on a month-to-month basis? Do you want protection if you decide to terminate the lease early? And do you have the option of owning the computer at the end of the lease? Leasing companies are virtually unregulated across the country. What sounds like a great deal might have some surprises in store, or turn out to be a lot more expensive if anything goes wrong.[37]

Caring for the Environment

On a final note, many of us have become environmentally responsible citizens. Or as consultant Jacquelyn Ottman puts it, "An environmentalist is just an efficiency expert in a green cloak." There are many simple things that you can do to protect the environment while buying and using your PC. In the words of Tim Mann, program manager for IBM's office for environmentally conscious products, "the most important ways to save the environment are probably the easiest."

1. **Hit the switch:** Save energy by turning off computers, monitors, printers, and other office equipment at night and on weekends. Because computer equipment generates heat, you will also save money and energy on air conditioning.
2. **Shop for Energy Star seals:** Buy only energy-efficient computers, monitors, and printers that bear the EPA's Energy Star logo.
3. **Let your PC sleep:** If you let an idle computer sleep, or move into a low-power mode, you will consume less energy. A technician can adjust the computer's sleep modes.
4. **Share printers:** In a typical office, the average printer is on 24 hours a day, yet it operates for a total of only 1 hour, according to EPA and industry studies. Sharing printers saves energy, space, and money.
5. **Print in duplex:** Duplex copying means printing on both sides of the page. This saves paper and money. However, duplex copying also drastically cuts down on pollution because it takes many times more energy to actually manufacture a piece of paper than it does to make a copy.

Business Guidelines for Hardware Success

Hardware is the foundation that makes information systems happen. However, paying undue attention to hardware while neglecting other key elements involving people, processes, and the business goals can lead companies down the wrong path in a hurry. This section identifies some critical success factors that can help a company with its hardware decisions.

1. **Cost is only part of the story.** Often, when companies think about building a new system or replacing an existing one, the focus turns to hardware costs. Top management often wants to see hard facts and figures that show the return on investments. However, many benefits resulting from information systems are intangible and tough to measure, such as increased productivity, improved decision making, and faster customer service. Many industry experts argue that companies overemphasize the cost of hardware technology. In the last decade or so, hardware costs have plummeted from being significant to negligible. To succeed, then, businesspeople need to view hardware costs as just one thread in a complex, intricate fabric.

2. **Don't compromise on capacity and reliability.** In many business environments, the motto is "if it ain't broke, don't fix it." However, this does not apply to hardware capacity and reliability, which can make or break companies. Many people in the IS community remember when America Online offered its customers an all-you-can-download Internet pricing scheme. Although at first glance it appeared to be a great service, AOL soon found itself in hot water. The press had a field day: AOL had underestimated the capacity requirement of its computers and its networks, resulting in busy-signal nightmares. Customers were so upset with the poor service that they took AOL to court in 38 states to get better service. What went wrong? AOL decided to implement a business strategy without checking to see if its machines had the capacity and reliability to meet new customer demands. Gerry O'Connell, senior vice president of systems and CIO at the Chicago Board Options Exchange "pinch themselves regularly to make sure they aren't dozing off into AOL land."[38]
3. **Infrastructure, infrastructure, infrastructure.** Machines no longer work in isolation. Instead, they are interwoven and interconnected through the infrastructure. Unfortunately, as we explored in Chapter 1, infrastructure is not glamorous and CEOs are often reluctant to invest in technology infrastructure, such as networks. "There's a general aura of bad karma around infrastructure: The stuff is invisible unless there's something wrong with it, in which case all hell breaks loose. Put simply, if infrastructure were a product, no self-respecting salesperson would want to be stuck selling it."[39] But for a CIO, infrastructure keeps the business running, so all business decisions—including hardware changes—should consider the technology infrastructure and IS professionals should be prepared to sell its importance to top management.
4. **Support is crucial.** "Ghostbusters" isn't the answer when someone asks "Who ya gonna call?" for information systems support.[40] The dazzling array of technologies that now resides in offices around the country is quite overwhelming. Each system comes with its own nuances and complexities. Furthermore, users have neither the time nor the patience to wait for help. When there is a problem, users expect the problem to be fixed almost immediately. As a result, hardware decisions should always consider the technical support issue. Hardware support should address questions such as "Who will provide support?" "What is the nature of support?" "When will the support be provided (24 hours a day, 7 days a week versus weekday support)?" and "Who will pay for the support—the user or the IS department?"

SUMMARY

1. **Describe the five main hardware components in a computer system and their main functions:** The five main components in a computer are the central processor, secondary storage, input devices, output devices, and communication devices. The central processor converts data into information. Primary storage, which is a part of the central processor, temporarily stores data and instructions. Secondary storage is nonvolatile memory that resides outside the CPU. Input devices include keyboards, the mouse, touch screens, voice-recognition systems, and optical character readers. The functions of input devices are to help human beings interact with the computer and input data into the computer. Output devices include computer screens, printers, microfiche, and microfilm. Their function is to help viewers see the output of the processing done by the computer. Finally, the fifth component in a computer is communication devices that allow communication between two or more computers separated by time or place.
2. **Compare and contrast different types of computers according to size and speed:** Computers can be classified into different types based on their memory size and processing speed. Supercomputers have large memories and high processing speeds and are capable of processing up to a billion instructions per second. A mainframe is a large, general-purpose computer that has a large memory and excellent processing capabilities. Minicomputers are small, powerful, multiuser systems and are excellent workhorses. Workstations lie between midrange computers and personal computers and are faster and more

sophisticated than PCs. Engineers, scientists, and others whose work entails extensive data analysis or graphics usually use workstations. Network computers are diskless computers that access all programs and data from a central computer. Personal computers are versatile machines that are less powerful than microcomputers. Finally, laptops, notebooks, handheld, wrist, and pen-based computers are battery operated so they can be used anywhere, any time.

3. **Explain the process of buying and leasing a personal computer:** Buying a personal computer is an important decision that requires careful thought. A user must consider a number of factors before making this decision. Some considerations include the CPU, the clock speed, RAM, expansion slots, and monitors. Decisions about the CPU and clock speed are tied to the kind of applications that will run on the computer. Some programs require a more intensive CPU than others. When it comes to RAM, more is generally better, given that many programs today use a lot of memory and RAM costs have decreased. Finally, monitors should be carefully chosen to promote better user interaction with the computer and to avoid eyestrain. Businesspeople who decide to lease computers should know who is responsible for upgrades and service, the lease renewal and termination terms, and whether a lease-to-own option is available.

KEY TERMS

arithmetic-logic unit (ALU) (p. 66)
bit (p. 65)
byte (p. 65)
communication devices (p. 75)
compact disk–read-only memory (CD-ROM) (p. 71)
control unit (p. 66)
CPU (p. 66)
direct access storage (p. 68)
expansion card (p. 75)
expansion slot (p. 75)
instruction (p. 66)
magnetic disks (p. 69)
magnetic tapes (p. 70)
mainframe (p. 77)
minicomputers (midrange) (p. 78)
MIPS (p. 65)
network computers (p. 78)
optical character reader (OCR) (p. 74)
parallel processing (p. 77)
plug-and-play (p. 80)
primary memory (p. 66)
random access memory (RAM) (p. 67)
read-only memory (ROM) (p. 67)
secondary storage (p. 68)
sequential storage (p. 68)
supercomputers (p. 77)
touch screen (p. 73)
voice-recognition system (p. 73)
write-once, read-many (WORM) (p. 72)

REVIEW QUESTIONS

1. Describe how data are represented in a computer. What are the two important hardware considerations in representing data in a computer system?
2. Identify the time and space units of a computer. What does MIPS stand for?
3. Identify the five basic components of a computer system and briefly describe their functions.
4. Describe the central processor and its two main elements.
5. Name any two differences between primary storage and secondary storage. Describe at least two reasons why we need secondary storage.
6. Identify three types of primary storage and briefly describe each type.
7. What is the difference between RAM and ROM? What are the two types of ROM?
8. What is the difference between volatile and nonvolatile memory?
9. There are two types of secondary storage: sequential storage and direct access storage. Briefly describe each type.
10. Describe a CD-ROM and its characteristics. What are some applications of CD-ROMs?
11. Name and describe two input and output devices.
12. Computers are classified into different categories based on memory size and processing speed. Identify the different types of computers discussed in this chapter from the most powerful to the least powerful.
13. Describe parallel processing. What is the difference between a parallel processing machine and a PC?
14. What is the difference between a network computer and a PC?

15. Why is the information systems community divided in its opinion about network computers?
16. What are some technical considerations that a PC buyer should take into account before buying a PC?
17. What are some guidelines that will ensure business success in using hardware?

DISCUSSION QUESTIONS AND EXERCISES

1. For many IS managers, the proliferation of PCs in their organization is a mixed blessing. With advances in user-friendly software, users are now capable of developing their own systems to meet their unique information needs. But as PCs proliferate, managers are concerned that they may be losing control over the growth and application of PCs in their organizations.

   Managers are taking two different approaches to manage the growth of PCs in their organizations. Some are taking a conservative approach by authorizing only limited software packages to users, such as spreadsheets and word processing, only from certain vendors. In fact, some organizations are so strict about this policy that employees who are found using unauthorized software can be fired. Other managers believe that the full power and potential of PCs can be achieved only by giving users full freedom to develop their own applications on whatever software packages they choose. In such organizations, users determine the applications and the software packages to use.
   a. What are the two approaches for managing the growth of PCs in an organization? Which approach would you advocate and why?
   b. What are some of the pros and cons of each approach?
   c. Develop a middle-of-the road approach. Do you think this approach is better? Why?
2. **(Web Exercise)** Fiber Channel technology represents a significant, fundamental change in the way storage is purchased, implemented, managed, and perceived within IT organizations. It is a new and evolving technology that allows users to connect multiple storage devices to multiple servers, without having to rely on a network. Fiber Channel is a communication and interconnection technology that provides high-speed, point-to-point transfer of large volumes of data among numerous devices. These devices can include PCs, workstations, servers, mainframes, supercomputers, and storage devices.

   Search the Web to find more information about Fiber Channel. Write a two-page report on this technology and identify any companies that are working with fiber technology.
3. **(Software and Web Exercise)** You want to buy a computer with the following requirements:

   Pentium II Processor at 266 MHz

   21-in. monitor

   64 MB SDRAM

   4 GB hard drive

   24× CD-ROM

   56 K modem

   Microsoft Windows 98

   a. Visit the Web site or store of a computer seller and find a computer that meets your requirements for the cheapest price.
   b. Gather information about the PC's processor, clock speed, monitor, RAM, and price. Then find the price for a PC with a 17-in. monitor, and 32 MB of RAM. Develop a spreadsheet that compares the model that you selected with the Pentium II model just outlined. Calculate the difference in price between the two models as a percentage.

Case 1: Insurance Agents Spiral toward the Future . . . Slowly

Compared with other regulated financial industries, the insurance market is light years behind in technology. While use of PCs and networks is prevalent among small insurance companies, the equipment and software tends to be several generations old. Few have discovered the Internet, or even e-mail, so paper and fax machines remain the cornerstones of how individuals work and communicate. "To this day, I have [agent] friends that can't do anything on a PC but turn it on," describes Gordon Harden, Jr., a 27-year insurance agent veteran currently operating a three-employee Nationwide Insurance brokerage. Harden is also the founder of Insurance Quote.Net, a Web-based insurance quote service, and has been leading the wave to educate other agents/brokers about the benefits of technology.

Perhaps the biggest hurdle is the insurance provider. Small insurance agencies acquire their mission-critical software from the provider, rather than developing their own. With no control over their most important software, which generates quotes, policies, and claims information, insurance agents have little or no incentive to seek out software alternatives or to spend on technology as a whole. Agents typically resist being brought into the present, until the insurance provider forces them to, says George Wieland, president of Biometrics Services Corp., a company that specializes in insurance agents, brokers, and providers. "Agents don't like to spend money on PCs, although a few are PC enthusiasts with PCs as hobbies. Most of them, though, are only interested in running a business. There's a tendency in agencies to be penny-wise and pound-foolish," he notes. "Over the past year or two, many insurance companies now provide software to their agents and brokers. The software has certain minimum requirements and forces agents to upgrade—perhaps kicking and screaming—but upgrade nonetheless." Once convinced, the insurance market has been known to embrace technology wholeheartedly, particularly technology that sells insurance with other financial planning services.[41]

1. You have been asked to make a presentation to an insurance agent about the benefits of computer technology and its effects on the bottom line. Identify three key factors that you would highlight to make your point.
2. An insurance agent is trying to decide if she should buy a new computer or upgrade her existing ones. How would you advise this agent?
3. What are some reasons why insurance agents are reluctant to embrace technology?

Case 2: Southwest Airlines Flies High

Southwest Airlines is taking computing to a higher plane by using new onboard technology that it says will increase safety, lengthen the life of an aircraft, and save airlines money. The system, known as an aircraft onboard performance system (OPS), will assist captains and first officers in calculating maximum takeoff and landing weights in real-time under all combinations of environmental, airport, and aircraft systems conditions. Southwest, the fifth-largest domestic carrier in the United States, plans to equip its entire fleet of 250 Boeing 737-series jets with the system.

The system works this way: The first officer enters data such as atmospheric pressure, temperature, and wind direction and speed into the PC. Based on the input, OPS spits out the most efficient equipment settings and speeds for takeoff and landing. Experts say the precision of those calculations will minimize engine strain over time, resulting in longer engine life and fewer costly overhauls. In addition to enhancing aircraft safety and reducing engine repair cost, Southwest expects to increase revenues by calculating how much cargo can be added safely to each flight.[42]

1. What type of a computer would be well suited for this application?
2. What is fault-tolerance and is it an essential feature in this system? Discuss.
3. Should the intuition and judgment of the pilot override the recommendation of the system? Why or why not?

Case 3: Culture Change

The Japanese have a great appreciation for knowledge and information but not for using IT to create and share it. They are reluctant to use computers, networks, or the Internet because of the complexity of their language. One reason for this problem stems from the difficulty of keyboard typing in Japanese because its Kanji characters are much more complex and numerous than the 26-letter English alphabet. The reluctance to use a keyboard bars many Japanese from using computer technology. This is not to say that the Japanese do not invest in IS and IT. Many Japanese companies do invest significant dollars in IS and IT. However, their rationale for doing so is to catch up with global competitors, rather than to increase productivity. [43]

1. What are some input technologies that can help the Japanese overcome the barriers associated with keyboards?
2. What are some of the disadvantages that a company or a nation may face if it is always playing catch-up?

Case 4: Unbelievable, But True

What if you discovered that your expensive new television set was rigged at the factory so that every time you turned it on, the TV automatically tuned itself to the same predetermined channel? What if it was a channel whose owners had paid the TV maker to stick it in front of your face? And what if the only way to disable this "feature" was not explained in the manual? Most of us would be pretty steamed. Yet that is exactly what is happening with a far more expensive item, the home personal computer. Pieces of the PC are being prewired to link to certain sites on the World Wide Web whose owners have paid the computer manufacturer for this privilege.

For example, in its new Presario PC line for consumers, Compaq Computer has placed special quick-access Internet buttons on the keyboard, supposedly to make it easier for novices to get on-line. But three of these four buttons are prewired to take you to Web sites whose proprietors are paying Compaq to drive traffic to them. Originally, the company planned to make it impossible for users to reconfigure these three so-called Easy Access Internet buttons. But after receiving criticism from reviewers and test users prior to the machines' release date, it devised a method that technically allows users to program the buttons with their own favorite sites. But the method is so obscure and so poorly explained in the manual that only a few individuals will be able to figure it out.

In other words, the computer that is sitting on your desk continues to bring in revenue for the manufacturer, although you are not getting any special benefits. "If they want to sell services instead of products, they should slash prices deeply, or even give the PCs away, on the model used by the cellular-phone systems, which make phones cheap in order to woo more service users," says one outraged computer user.[44]

1. What would your reaction be if you bought a computer that was pre-wired to certain Internet sites? How would you handle such a situation with the vendor?
2. If the vendor gave you a deep discount for such a PC, would you buy it? What are some problems with this approach?

As a great social leveler, information technology ranks second only to death. It can erase cultural barriers, overwhelm economic inequalities, even compensate for intellectual disparities. In short, high technology can put unequal human beings on an equal footing, and that makes it the most potent democratizing tool ever devised.

Sam Pitroda, Telecommunications Consultant

CONTENTS

SOFTWARE FOR SUCCESS

Hardware and software are like a successful marriage: One cannot exist without the other. **Software** (also called a program), a set of step-by-step instructions that enables a computer to perform a specific task, must be combined with hardware in a relevant, useful way to build effective information systems. Software's power to help people solve problems, make decisions, and accomplish tasks affects every IS success story, as the Technology Payoff shows. However, software costs have escalated, making it one of the most expensive parts of an information system.

As the tasks for which we use software increase in scope and complexity, writing error-free software becomes more difficult and expensive. Consider some tasks that software handles—from assisting doctors with surgery to conducting scientific research and doing space exploration. In cases such as these, software is "mission critical" because lives can depend on the proper functioning of the software.

Testing software is also difficult and costly. The more complex the software, the harder it is to test. For instance, the software that operates a space mission has millions of lines of code embedded in thousands of programs guiding the space shuttle. All these programs must work in unison for the mission to succeed. A simple error in any of the programs can lead to a disaster.

Software development and maintenance is intense, creative work that requires patience, artistry, and discipline. Expert programmers who can tackle software development issues are expensive and often in short supply, as evidenced by the shortage of IS professionals in Canada, the United States, and many European countries. To further aggravate the labor problem, consider this: A software pro-

Software

A set of step-by-step instructions that enables a computer to perform a specific task and is used to control, coordinate, and manage different hardware components in an information system.

Chapter 4

Computer Software

AFTER STUDYING THIS CHAPTER, YOU WILL BE ABLE TO:

- Describe different types of system software, including operating systems
- Discuss important types of application software
- Explain the concept of programming and identify different programming languages

gram is never complete. It must be changed and maintained to keep up with the dynamic needs of its users.

To alleviate some software cost issues, some programmers are joining forces to develop and share software with the rest of the world—for free. These teams of experts collaborate to develop reliable software programs, such as the Linux operating system (a Microsoft Windows competitor), that are not owned by a single company, but are instead maintained by a loose confederation of programmers who work together over the Internet. Linux is popular among technically advanced computer users, because the programs are free, compact, reliable, and easy to modify. Much to the concern of major commercial software developers, this movement is gaining momentum.[3]

In this chapter we investigate different kinds of software, their functions, and their role in helping an organization achieve its goals. We also explore operating systems, a special type of software that operates and manages the computer system. Finally, we examine issues that affect the use and management of software in organizations.

System Software

In this chapter we examine the two broad categories of software: system software and application software, as shown in Figure 4-1.

System software controls and monitors the different activities and resources in a computer and makes it easier and more efficient for users to operate computers. Without this software, we would not be able to run our computers. The three types of system software are system control software, system support software, and system development software.

System software
Software that performs the basic functions necessary to start and operate a computer and controls, coordinates, and manages the operations of all computer-related resources such as the CPU, monitors, printers, and other peripherals.

TECHNOLOGY PAYOFF
A Delicate Balancing Act on the Internet

When Johannes Guttenberg invented the printing press in 1448, politicians denounced the press as a machine that could corrupt young minds. "Since then, the invention of every new communications medium has been followed by public debate over its impact."[1] The Internet, classified as "the most democratic medium yet devised by man," creates its own unique set of problems.

One gnawing problem—the unfettered access to sexually explicit material—has parents, politicians, and Internet advocates worried. How can society balance the interests of freedom and free speech against the interest of protecting children? Should the government step in to regulate the Web? Or should it allow Internet providers to self-regulate the medium? Though the debate is far from over, the answer may be, let technology solve the problem by offering Internet users a choice.

Several companies have developed software to help parents and educators control and monitor what children view on the Net. Microsystems Software has developed a series of software programs that allow parents to choose what children can access, how much time they spend, and what information they give out on the Internet. Its "Cyber Patrol" software allows parents to filter Internet material they do not want their children to view. In simplest terms, the Cyber Patrol screening software works like a guard standing at the door of a house to keep out unwanted guests and protect those inside. Instead of blocking guests, however, the software blocks sites deemed inappropriate by referring to the CyberNOT list, a list of inappropriate sites that the parent or educator creates.

Many such software programs begin by identifying categories of sites that parents and educators can block—such as sexually explicit material, violent content, nudity, alcohol and tobacco, hate speech, and so on. Once blocked, the child cannot access material that fits in the category. For instance, if a parent has blocked sexually explicit material, her child will discover that an on-line search for *Playboy* results in the message "Restricted by Cyber

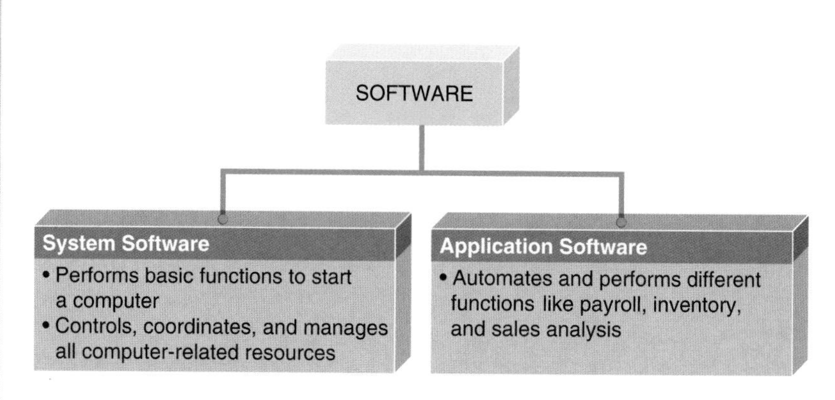

FIGURE 4-1 The Two Main Types of Software

System software helps to start and run a computer. Application software helps run the business by performing numerous functions.

As highlighted in Table 4-1, the three types of system software are similar to a hospital team of administrators, doctors and nurses, and researchers who help improve health care procedures. The hospital administrators who coordinate resources, including surgeons, nurses, other hospital staff, operating rooms and other facilities, supplies, and money are akin to the *system control software* that manages and coordinates all computer resources (such as printers, terminals, CPUs, networks, and so on).

TABLE 4-1 The Three Major Categories of System Software

Software Type	Description
System control software	Programs that manage the resources in a computer, such as memory and printers
System support software	Programs that implement different programs, such as payroll and credit card processing
System development software	Programs that help developers create information systems

Hospital personnel manage the smooth execution of different health care programs (emergency care, operating room facilities, nutrition and fitness, pediatrics, and so on). Like the doctors, nurses, and other staff in a hospital, *system support software* runs, manages, and supports large programs such as payroll, student registration, motor vehicle registration, and so on.

Finally, a hospital often seeks the help of researchers and consultants to improve health care procedures and implement the latest medical discoveries. Similar to these researchers and consultants, *system development software* helps software developers create and build new programs and information systems. In the sections that follow, we explore the three types of system software illustrated in Figure 4-2.

Patrol." In addition, parents can tailor access for each individual child, so that a teenager could have access to sites–for example, sex education—that might be blocked for a younger sibling.[2]

Such software also helps parents and educators manage *when* children access the Net. Cyber Patrol software helps with time management in two ways. First, it can limit the total hours that each family member can spend on-line on a daily and weekly basis. Second, parents and educators can set the specific hours a child can go on-line, such as the hours that a working parent is home.

Several companies have also developed software that restricts information that a minor can give out on the Net using sophisticated filtering technology. If a child participating in a chat room inadvertently gives a stranger his surname, age, phone number, address, or school name, the software converts the information to a series of XXXs, thereby protecting his privacy while still letting him participate on-line.

Washington Post reporter John Schwartz recently observed: "This category of software is more important than ever. The very existence of such tools was part of the reason that a panel of three federal judges struck down the Communications Decency Act (CDA) in 1997." The law, which proposed criminal penalties for those who made indecent materials available to minors via computer networks, was turned down because the judges felt it was overly restrictive, given the available option to use screening software to limit a minor's access to such materials. Software such as Cyber Patrol, then, offers protection without relying on government regulation (for the time being) that could restrict everyone's Internet access. This innovative, creative software is helping society address a complex problem.

Source: "Cyber Patrol, Innovation Collection," *Computerworld Smithsonian Technology Awards,* Innovation Network, 1997, www.thunderstone.com/texis/si/sc/innovate/+ToeX2an+wBme6rvyXenqwww/full.html

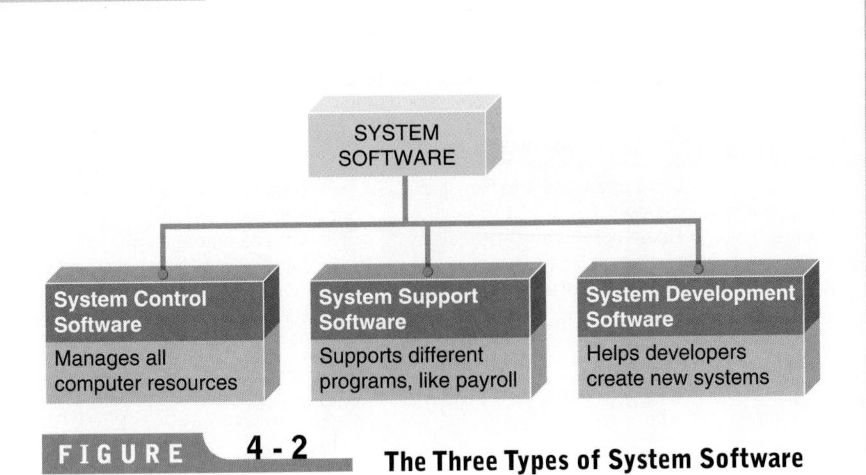

FIGURE 4-2 The Three Types of System Software

System Control Software

System control software helps the computer to function and it increases the efficiency and effectiveness of a computer system. The most critical type of system control software is the **operating system,** which is a set of programs that works together to make the computer appear "intelligent." Without an operating system, we could not do simple things such as start the computer, locate a file, or resolve conflicts when, say, two users want to use a resource such as a printer at the same time. Without an operating system, the computer will not be able to recognize input from a keyboard or run different programs such as word processing, graphics, or spreadsheets.

An operating system is a versatile type of software that performs many functions, the number of which depends on the type of computer (mainframe, personal computer, and so on) for which the software is used. Generally, operating software acts as a manager, a housekeeper, and a traffic cop for a computer system. As Figure 4-3 shows, the basic functions of an operating system can be divided into the three broad categories that we examine next: resource management, file management, and user management.

Resource Management

The overall purpose of resource management functions is to manage all resources in a computer system efficiently and effectively. These functions include:

- Managing computer resources such as CPU, primary memory, secondary storage, input and output devices, and other computer resources so they are put to the best use
- Ensuring the efficient use of primary and secondary memory to prevent waste
- Ensuring that input and output devices, which are significantly slower than the CPU, do not slow down the CPU's performance
- Tracking different resources that a program consumes and reallocate different resources based on need. Say computer memory is overused whereas the CPU is underused. The operating system may recommend expanding computer memory to improve operational efficiency

System control software

Software designed to monitor, control, coordinate, and manage computer resources.

FIGURE 4-3

The Three Main Functions of an Operating System

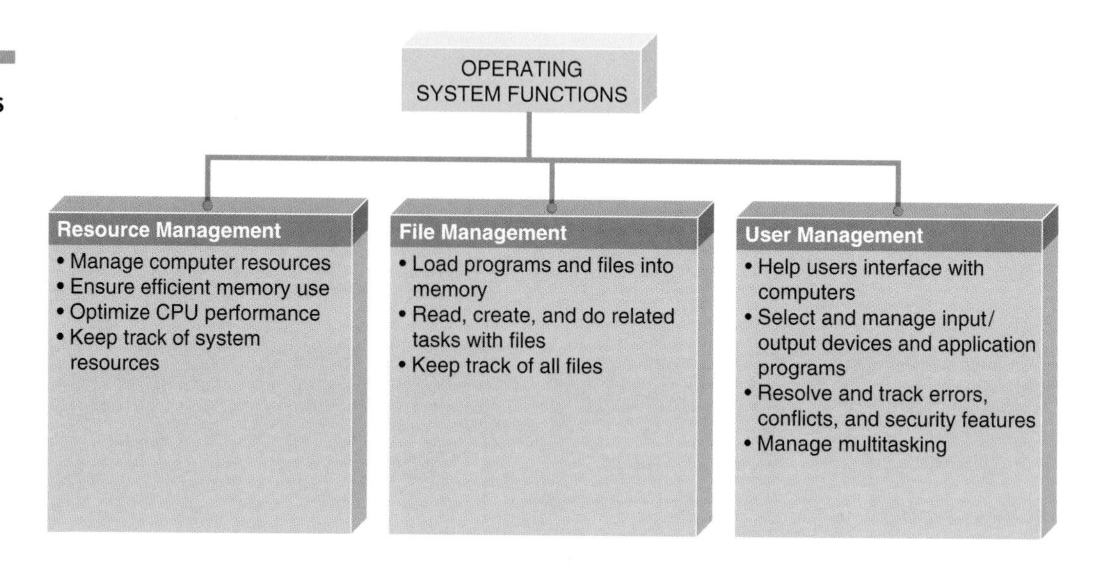

Operating system

A software program that manages the computer's operations and resources.

File Management

File management functions work to create, organize, and manage computer files. Some functions include:

- Loading programs and files into the main memory and sending a user a message when the program is complete
- Reading, creating, deleting, merging, renaming, and performing other tasks related to computer files
- Keeping track of files located in primary and secondary memory

User Management

Basic user management functions improve and simplify computer use. They perform the following functions:

- Serve as an interface between the user and the computer
- Select the appropriate input/output devices and the application programs that the user wants to execute
- Perform and manage input and output operations and "release" or free up the I/O device when no longer needed
- Resolve errors and conflicts if two or more programs vie for the same resource
- Manage computer system multitasking—the ability of the computer to do multiple tasks at the same time such as editing one document while printing another or running two different application programs at the same time; the multitasking speed depends on the CPU's power and the amount of memory in the system
- Keep track of system errors and failures
- Manage and monitor any system security features

Now that we have reviewed the functions of system control software, we consider the system control software environments of multiprogramming and multiprocessing.

Multiprogramming environment

A feature of an operating system in which users can simultaneously run multiple programs on a single-CPU computer.

Operating System Environments

Some operating systems can support running multiple programs at the same time, which increases the efficiency of computer operations. This system capability, known as a **multiprogramming environment,** ensures that the slow processing speed of input and output devices does not affect the performance of the CPU, as we see in Figure 4-4.

To understand how a multiprogramming system increases time efficiency, let us assess how such a system works. Many of us are in a "multiprogramming" mode while

NONMULTIPROGRAMMING

Operating System
Program A
Program B

MULTIPROGRAMMING

Operating System
Program A
Program B
Program C
Program D

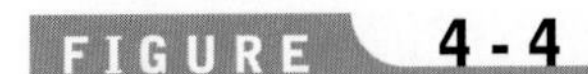

Operating Systems with and without Multiprogramming

In a system without multiprogramming capabilities, the operating system is dedicated to executing one program at a time. With multiprogramming, the operating system executes several programs concurrently, increasing the efficiency of the CPU, the memory, and the input/output devices.

we work. A chef at a restaurant switches between multiple tasks, giving each task a slice of his or her time. While the food is simmering, the chef chops, garnishes, and supervises the efforts of those who work for the chef, and so on. In a multiprogramming environment, the CPU switches between multiple programs although at any given time the CPU is executing only one program.[4]

This is how multiprogramming works: First, the operating system keeps programs that are waiting to be executed in primary storage. The operating system selects the first program and begins to execute the first program instruction. When it encounters an input or output operation, such as when a user inputs characters from a keyboard or when a user sends a file to the printer, the operating system passes the instruction to the appropriate input or output device. While the input or output device is processing the instruction, the CPU selects the second program from the queue and starts to execute it. In the meantime, when the input or output processing of the first program is complete, the operating system notifies the CPU, which then switches back and continues executing the first program until it encounters another input or output instruction, at which time the process is repeated.

Some computers have multiple processors, or more than one CPU, to handle jobs that are computationally intensive, as Figure 4-5 demonstrates. In such cases, the operating system should make full use of multiple processors. The operating system Windows NT, for instance, can handle up to 32 processors. Note that multiprogramming

Multiprocessing system

An operating system that can support multiple CPUs in a computer.

Just as a chef switches between several tasks to prepare a meal, a multiprogramming system allows the CPU to switch between multiple programs, although at any given time the CPU is executing only one program.

FIGURE 4-5

Difference between a Single versus a Multiprocessing Environment

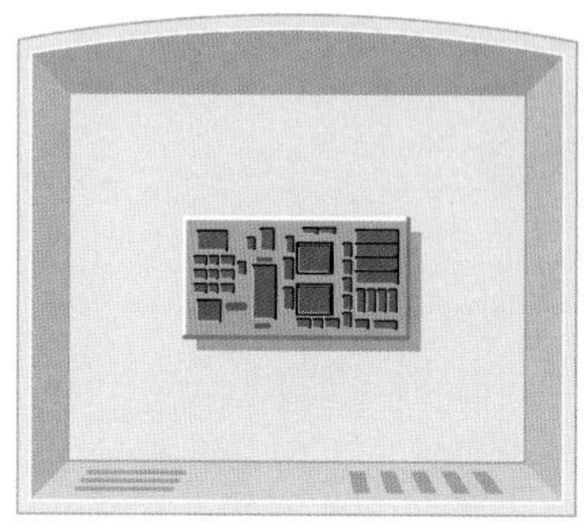

One CPU is a single-processing environment

Multiple CPUs is a multiprocessing environment

and multiprocessing are not mutually exclusive. In fact, many operating systems have both characteristics. Table 4-2 summarizes these two operating system characteristics.

Today, different types of operating systems exist. Some operating systems are designed for microcomputers and workstations whereas others are designed for mainframes and minicomputers. We investigate different types of operating systems next.

TABLE 4-2 Operating System Environments

Environment	Description
Multiprogramming	Multiple programs can be run on a computer at the same time. The CPU switches between programs. However, at any given time it is executing one program.
Multiprocessing	A multiprocessing system has a number of CPUs that process data and instructions, unlike systems that have only one CPU. Ideally suited for complex and computationally intensive operations that require extensive processing.

Types of Operating Systems

Apart from performing basic functions, operating systems help determine the user-friendliness of the computing environment. A good operating system can help employees become comfortable with the company's information systems and save money due to security features, back-up mechanisms, efficient resource allocation, and other features. Conversely, a poor system can frustrate users and make the system difficult to use. The choice of an operating system, then, is crucial.

Many operating systems work exclusively on PCs. Some accommodate single users, such as one of the earliest PC operating systems, MS-DOS. Still others, such as UNIX, can accommodate multiple users. Windows, Windows NT, UNIX, and OS/2 are popular operating systems for PCs. Linux is also growing in popularity.

MS-DOS

MS-DOS (disk operating system), a single-user system, was once a popular operating system for PCs. DOS is cryptic and not user-friendly. For example, to copy a file "MyName" from your floppy disk (a:) to a folder called "YourName" in the c: drive, the command is "copy a:\MyName c:\YourName." Some DOS commands are shown in Table 4-3.

In 1994 the PC software industry began to put the final nails in the DOS coffin because by then many end users had become familiar and comfortable with user-friendly point-and-click commands and preferred them to cryptic commands. "I love DOS . . . but the reality is that all our new application development work is being done [on newer operating systems] Windows and OS/2," mourns Rock Blanco, director of in-

TABLE 4-3

Five Popular DOS Commands

Command	Description	Examples
CD	Allows you to switch between subdirectories. CD changes the current directory and allows access to any subdirectory.	cd\reports cd\reports\annual cd\
COPY	Allows you to copy files. You can copy files from one diskette or hard disk to another, from one directory to another, and so on.	copy a:\friday c:\ copy c:\mon c:\reports copy a:*.* c:\reports
DEL	Allows you to remove one or more files from a hard disk or diskette.	del Friday del C:*.* del c:\reports*.*
DIR	Allows you to see what files are on a disk. The DIR command lists all files and subdirectories in a directory. For each file, the system displays the name, the size (in bytes), and the date and time you last changed the file. DIR also displays the total number of files and the amount of free space (in bytes) on the disk.	dir dir c: dir\reports dir *.wyz
RENAME	Allows you to change one or more filenames and/or extensions. Renaming a file does not change the contents of the file.	rename c:memos letters rename*.old *.new

formation systems at Garber Travel Services in Boston. Many technical people such as Blanco like DOS because they are comfortable with the cryptic commands, they prefer the flexibility DOS gives users to perform certain operating system functions—as compared to recent operating systems—or both. Still other users prefer DOS because it doesn't require sophisticated hardware to run on, as our Global IS for Success feature spotlights.

Windows Operating System

Windows, the most widely used operating systems for personal computers, is driven by **graphical user interfaces** (GUI). These highly graphical and user-friendly symbols replaced the need for typed commands. The Macintosh operating system pioneered the use of GUIs for the PC, although Microsoft marketed the idea heavily and made huge profits.

Graphical user interface

A software program that allows users to interact with a computer using graphical icons, symbols, and pictures. Users can perform different functions on their computers by clicking these icons with the mouse.

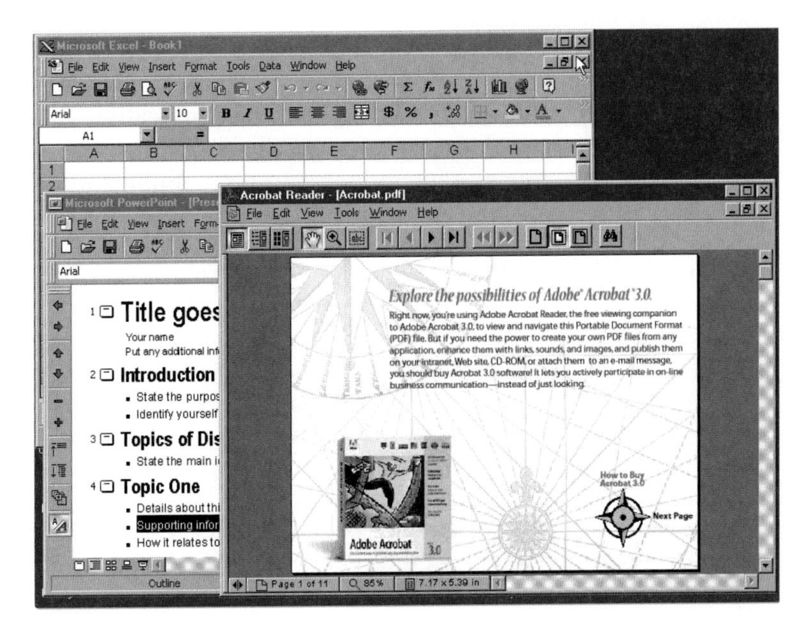

Graphical user interfaces make it easy for users to interact with their computer system, especially applications that use many similar icons.

Global IS for success

P&G Strikes Gold!

Would you be comfortable using an information system that depended on old 386 PCs and outdated software to break into markets of more than 4 billion people? Procter & Gamble did—and won big in emerging world markets. As an added bonus, P&G learned some lessons about speed, simplicity, and dealing with cultural resistance. The Cincinnati-based consumer products giant developed a software system called Distributor Business Systems (DBS), which consisted of ordering, shipping, billing, inventory management, and financial software. Most of this software was purchased off the shelf. DBS has transformed P&G's shaky and inefficient overseas distribution channels (wholesalers, retailers, and others that a company uses to distribute its products in the marketplace) into a competitive advantage in the emerging markets of Asia and Central and Eastern Europe.

In 1992 Procter & Gamble executives knew they couldn't meet their corporate growth goals with the product distribution system in growing markets abroad. In Asia, more than half of P&G's business was handled by 1,500 non-P&G distributors (also called third-party distributors), many of them tiny family-run shops that processed orders, bills, and inventory statements manually. Without data about how and where products were distributed, P&G lacked sales information about its shampoos and detergents. "We lost touch with our products as they went to the distributors," says Stephen Goodroe, vice-president of global customer marketing for P&G worldwide.

The situation in former Iron Curtain countries of Europe posed a similar problem with its 78,000 wholesalers. "The reliability of supply dropped exponentially through each step of the distribution system. By the time products got to the shelf, we had virtually no control over the supply or pricing accuracy," says Robert L. Fregolle, Jr., vice-president of customer business development and customer marketing in Europe. "That was not going to be a winning strategy versus our competitors."

P&G had to find a solution quickly. "Simplicity" became the watchword for DBS development. "We wanted ready-made software that wasn't too sophisticated, didn't cost a lot, that was bullet-hardened," says Wayne Matthai, vice-president of management systems worldwide. Accordingly, P&G in Asia and Central and Eastern Europe chose a DOS-based ordering, shipping, and billing software system that would run on 386-based PCs. "This is not bleeding-edge technology, it's tried-and-true mainstream technology used to gain tremendous reach into new markets," says Christopher Hoenig, director of the Information Management and Technology Division of the U.S. General Accounting Office.

Graphical user interfaces revolutionized the PC industry because users could conduct basic computer operations (such as opening a file or printing a document) using a mouse to point and click on an *icon*—a pictorial representation of an action or application. GUIs made computers accessible to novices. Once vendors began to use the same set of icons from one application to the next—for example, many icons in Microsoft's word processing package are identical to those in its spreadsheet package—users could easily transfer knowledge of one application to another. GUIs are the standard for desktop and laptop computers worldwide.

Microsoft, the largest independent software company in the world, and the "Windows industry" that it spawned, created Windows and its related products. In this section we explore four Windows operating systems: Windows 3.0, Windows 95, Windows 98, and Windows NT. Windows 3.0, introduced in 1990, had DOS as its foundation. It is a 16-bit architecture that runs on 286 Intel processors and above. A 16-bit operating system moves data in chunks of 16 bits versus a 32-bit operating system, which moves data in 32 bits. Figure 4-6 shows the differences between these two architectures.

Windows 3.0 allowed users to activate DOS commands from the Windows operating system using its graphical user interface. Windows 3.0 also had multitasking capabilities, which DOS did not have. It also had applications that shared many GUIs and applications such as word processing and spreadsheets. Applications appeared as windows, making it easy to navigate between windows and applications. By the early 1990s Windows became the major desktop operating system worldwide.

To make certain all parties had a stake in the new software, P&G brokered a deal with the distributors. They would pony up for the PCs and provide employees to operate the system; P&G would take care of the software, including local customization to accommodate language differences and government-mandated financial reporting. It also agreed to cover the costs of installation, training, and support. The company also needed to face resistance and foot-dragging from some third-party distributors and its own country managers. L. D. (Mike) Milligan, senior vice-president and a 37-year P&G veteran, had heard the "uniqueness" mantra a million times—that each country has distinct needs and that a one-size-fits-all approach is a mistake. But he dismissed those arguments for DBS. "When you come down to it," he says, "things like cash flow and inventory are spelled the same everywhere."

The company diffused resistance by explaining the tremendous profits that distributors would reap from the new software system. In fact, distributors using DBS have doubled their growth rates and as a group have slashed tens of millions of dollars in costs. When managers dragged their heels, top management led by example. "The track I took was to encourage first and then insist. I'd push and push in a country, and if they still didn't get going, I'd push somewhere else and achieve a success there that I could show to the others," says Goodroe.

P&G's investment in this software has helped it to increase sales in Eastern and Central European sales from virtually nothing to $1 billion in 4 years, and Asian sales from $3 to $4 billion in 3 years. Even more important, P&G is the unquestioned leader in these emerging world markets.

QUESTIONS AND PROJECTS

1. Identify some reasons why doing business on a global basis can pose a challenge for an information systems manager.
2. Resistance to new software systems is quite common. What are some measures that managers at P&G took to alleviate this situation? What would you have done if you were the global manager?
3. Is it easier to implement new software in the Western world than it is in Asia? Research the issue and write a one-page report to this comment.

Source: Richard Pastore, "Continental Shifts—Standardized Low-End Distribution Technologies Help Procter & Gamble Penetrate Global Frontiers," *CIO*, February 1, 1998, 44–47.

Windows 95 upgraded Windows 3.0 and its related versions. It has plug-and-play capabilities (the ability to automatically install and configure different computer components without having to perform any technical procedures) and additional features such as the ability to use filenames that are longer than eight characters. Its 32-bit operating system requires at least a 386 machine to operate. Windows 98, in turn, upgraded Windows 95. The new operating system, introduced in 1998, offered an embedded Internet Explorer browser designed to give consumers direct access to the Internet.

Windows 98 loads applications faster than Windows 95 and includes tighter Internet integration. The Active Desktop interface on Windows 98 is a feature that helps integrate data on users' PCs with Internet data—in effect merging the Internet with Windows

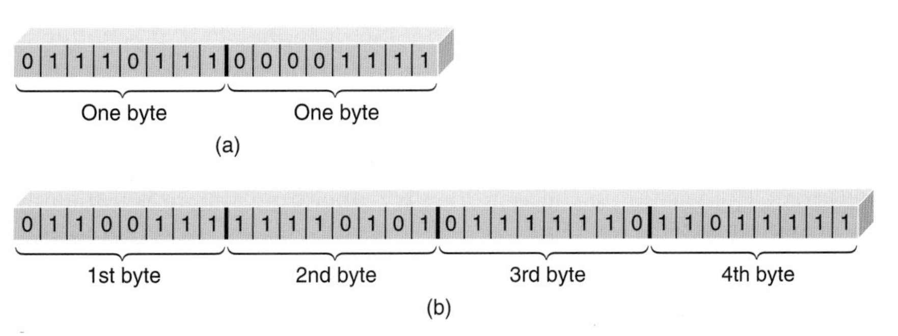

FIGURE 4-6

A Comparison of 16-Bit and 32-Bit Architecture

(a) In a 16-bit architecture, data moves inside the computer in 16 bits, or 2 bytes. (b) In a 32-bit architecture, data moves in 32 bits, or 4 bytes, so it has more speed and power than a 16-bit.

The Windows 98 operating system offers tighter integration with the Internet, has better systems recovery features, and loads applications faster than its predecessors.

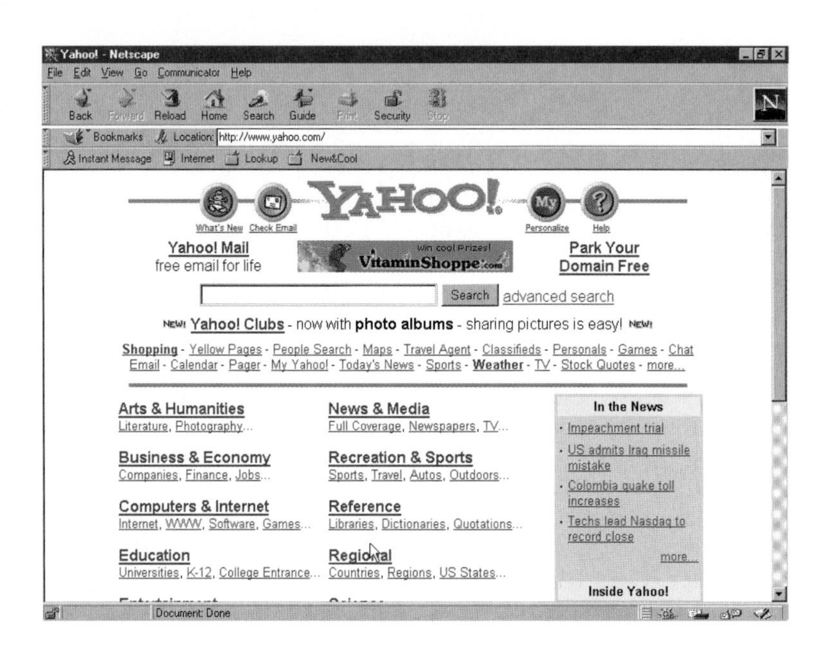

applications. Windows 98 also supports newer hardware and is better equipped than Windows 95 to recover from errors and system failures. Users can add many of the Windows 98 features to Windows 95 systems at minimal cost by downloading different software from the Microsoft Web site. The system also provides automatic upgrades.

Should users upgrade to the newest Windows system? That depends on the needs of the company. Proponents claim the new operating system is worth the upgrade. Rob Enderle, area director at business research firm Giga Information Group's Santa Clara, California, office, believes that Windows 98 is a "must have" product for many organizations because it eliminates many problems he found in Windows 95. "Let's be honest, Windows 98 is really the first maintenance release for Windows 95," he says, noting that during the past 3 years, CIOs have been forced to endure versions of the operating system that still had many software glitches in it.[5] Opponents argue that many Windows 98 features are unnecessary and eat up so much memory that the system upgrade would force companies to upgrade their hardware. The benefits of such an upgrade, they claim, do not outweigh the costs.

Windows NT

Microsoft's Windows NT (Windows New Technology), introduced in 1993, is an advanced 32-bit operating system that is totally independent of the DOS operating system. It runs both 16-bit and 32-bit Windows applications and DOS applications.

Windows NT has a number of sophisticated features such as outstanding networking capabilities and fault-tolerance. This operating system works well for transaction processing because it has excellent security features. Further, it makes it easy for companies to manage different users. System administrators can create a variety of group and individual user accounts with different rights and privileges. Windows NT 4.0, and 5.0 upgrades of Windows NT, have the same user interface as Windows 95 but do not support plug and play as Windows 95 does.

Although Windows NT can run on 486 or higher PCs, it is better suited for workstations and minicomputers. Ideally, it is suited for large business applications that run in a networked environment. It provides mainframe-like capabilities in a microcomputer environment and can support up to 32 multiple processors.

Computer industry professionals are divided on the value of Windows NT to organizations. Converting to the Windows NT operating system is not always an easy task. Information systems managers at Anheuser Busch Cos., who had to administer 15,000 users on 700 Windows NT–based machines, discovered that they needed 15 rather than 5 experts to keep the machines running on the new system. Even then, they still could not provide timely support. Other companies have experienced similar problems. The

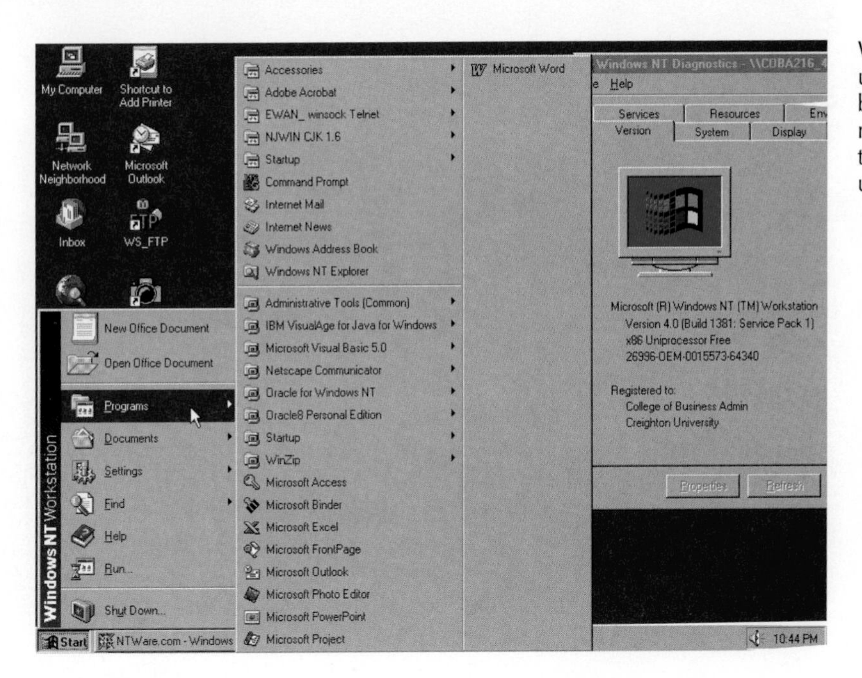

Windows NT has the same user interface as Windows 95 but has several features that make it easier for organizations to manage multiple users.

"eccentricities, peculiarities, and failures" of Windows NT made it an enormous struggle to keep the systems running, observes Valerie O'Connell, a systems and network management analyst at Aberdeen Group Boston.[6]

Several reasons explain why managing Windows NT is not easy. Managing users and what they do in the system is a challenge. In addition, Windows NT still does not have all the tools necessary to successfully maintain and manage the system, so companies often spend more money than initially anticipated. O'Connell notes that Aberdeen had to buy another piece of software to simplify the task of running the NT operating system and do routine tasks such as changing passwords.[7] Further, because Windows NT is a complex operating system, companies must spend huge amounts of money in training employees to use it.

If an organization wants to use a Microsoft operating system, what criteria should it use to decide which system to select? Decision makers should consider several points. For instance, if a company is running Windows 3.1, it should consider transitioning from a 16-bit to a 32-bit architecture because 32-bit applications are more reliable, generally deliver more robust performance, and offer a greater range of security features. "If you're still in a Windows 3.1 environment, the smoothest transition to the 32-bit Windows world is going to be via Windows 98," recommends Michael Gartenberg, research director for Gartner Group in Stamford, Connecticut.[8] But find out if the company's computers have sufficient memory or fast enough CPUs to handle a 32-bit architecture. If not, Windows 3.1 may be a better choice.

UNIX Operating System

UNIX is an operating system that allows multiple users doing multiple tasks to work on the computer at the same time. It comes in both 32-bit and 64-bit versions. While Windows dominates the PC world, UNIX dominates other areas. UNIX is written in a language called "C." AT&T developed both UNIX and C and distributed UNIX freely to government and academic institutions, which led to its prominence. However, it is a fairly cryptic operating system. For example, to copy a file, users type the command "cp," which stands for copy.

Despite the attempts to standardize the UNIX operating system over the years, standardization has not been successful because UNIX runs on so many different hardware platforms. The lack of standardization is one disadvantage of UNIX. In spite of this disadvantage, UNIX is widely used in mission-critical applications for transaction processing systems and has become a mainstream operating system for many businesses.

Western Publishing Company, publisher of the Little Golden Books series of children's stories, chose UNIX as its operating system because of networking capabilities,

UNIX is the operating system for many businesses in part because it allows multiple users to work on many different tasks at the same time.

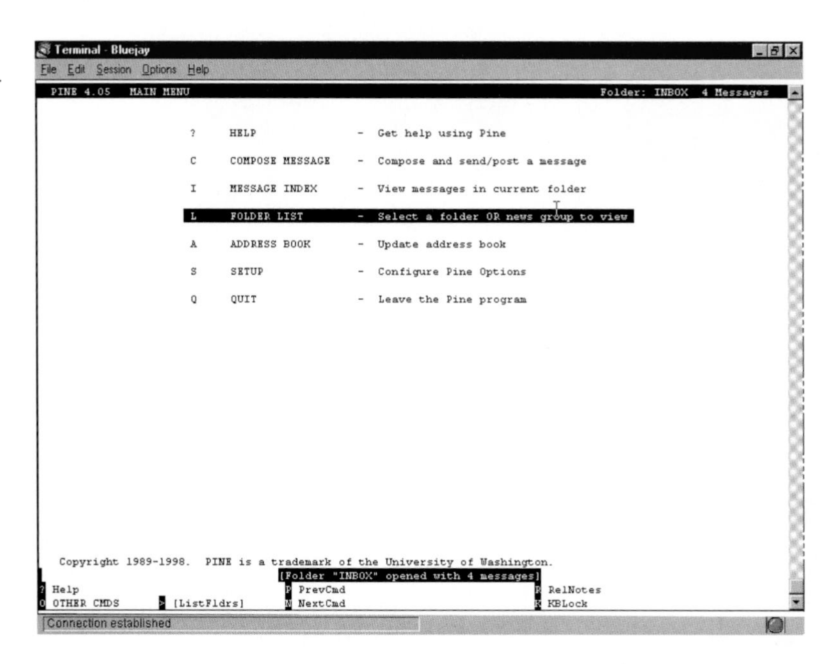

numerous applications, flexibility, and reliability. "We always look for the best application first, and then (and only then) we bring in the technology that supports it. Very often, that supporting technology is UNIX, which directly contributes to our bottom line."[9]

Western Publishing uses UNIX in various departments, but its application in the 16-person telemarketing group illustrates UNIX's power. The group markets various product lines, including children's books, games, toys, videos, and books on tape. It formerly relied on a word-processing system and traditional card files to track sales contacts and prepare orders. The system was isolated from other company applications and its information was often outdated. Western used UNIX as the operating environment to run software that automated sales tracking and order preparation.

UNIX improved the flow of telemarketing data in the department and throughout the company. When the workload on telemarketing increased, the scalability (the ability to move to a more powerful version) of UNIX enabled the company to upgrade in a fast, easy, and cost-effective manner. After its installation, telemarketing boosted sales contracts by a full 30 percent and increased personal productivity by roughly 35 percent.[10]

Today several products integrate UNIX and Windows NT, allowing users to reap the best of both worlds. The most compelling reason for UNIX/NT integration is that it lets users retain their investments in UNIX while tapping into NT's benefits. However, the operating systems are highly dissimilar, so melding the two environments is technically daunting. "It's in Microsoft's best interest to create as many barriers to integration as possible so users will get fed up trying to connect Unix and NT and just say, 'Let's go all native NT,' " says Glenn Gabriel Ben-Yosef, president of Clear Thinking Research, a Boston-based consulting firm.[11] Despite the barriers, several third-party vendors are creating software products that make it easier to integrate these two operating systems.

The OS/2 Operating System

The OS/2 (Operating System/2) is a 32-bit, single-user operating system from IBM that supports multitasking. It can run programs written for OS/2 and other operating systems such as DOS and Microsoft Windows. In fact, many OS/2 and DOS commands are identical. Its 32-bit capability makes it faster than DOS and ideal for applications that require networking and multimedia features, such as playing sound files or movies. OS/2 comes with a number of small programs, called applets, that range from time scheduling to appointment calendars to card game programs. It provides both a graphical user interface and a means for users to enter verbal commands.

IBM and Microsoft jointly developed the first version of OS/2, which was written for 286 machines. OS/2 provides a dual boot feature—a feature that allows users to select either OS/2 or DOS when they first "boot" (start) their computers. In late 1994, IBM

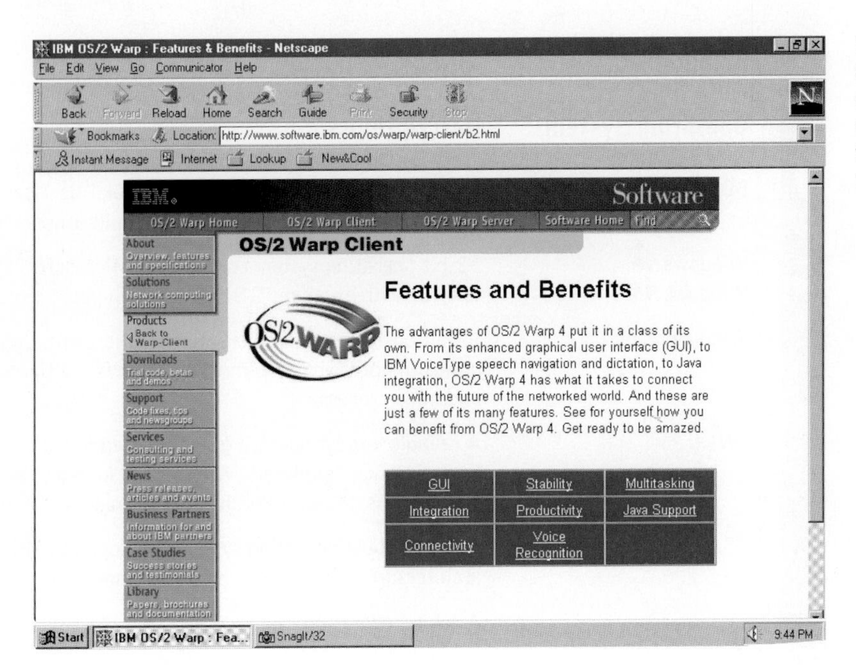

IBM's OS/2 Warp is a later version 3 of its sophisticated OS/2 operating system. It supports multitasking and applications that require networking and multimedia features.

introduced Version 3 of OS/2, known as OS/2 Warp. Since OS/2's Achilles' heel has been a lack of applications, IBM addressed this problem by creating more than 2,500 applications that run on OS/2 Warp. Warp can also run all applications written for DOS and Windows, thus increasing the number of applications available to users who choose the OS/2 operating system. OS/2 Warp comes bundled with 12 OS/2 applications, collectively known as BonusPak, which include a word processor, spreadsheet, personal information manager, Internet access, and other on-line services.

First Union National Bank has used OS/2 for over 10 years. During that time, the bank has deployed nine commercial and imaging applications under OS/2. The bank now has approximately 6,000 OS/2 desktop systems, although that figure could soon swell to 10,000. Two projects, the Commercial Banking Solution (CBS) and the Corporate Call Center (CCC), also use OS/2. CBS allows loan officers to use notebook computers to start the loan process in the customer's home. Managers then send documents back to the home office, where they are routed to workers through a software program that transfers documents from one worker to the next worker once a task is finished, resulting in a fast turnaround time.[12]

First Union Bank relies on the OS/2 operating system to keep the bank functioning smoothly.

The Corporate Call Center (CCC) allows customers to call a single telephone number to get answers to questions about basic bank services and products. The application, which resides on an OS/2-based workstation, intelligently routes hundreds of thousands of calls over the course of a year to support people who can best answer the questions. In the long run, OS/2 has proven to be an outstanding operating system for First Union.[13]

Linux

Until a few years ago, few people had heard of Linux. Today, it is a fast-growing, popular operating system that has attracted the attention of technical gurus and business leaders from around the world.[14] Linux is the brain child of Linus Torvalds, who created his system in the early 1990s after working with other operating systems such as UNIX while a student at the University of Helsinki. Defying traditional thinking that encourages software programmers to hoard their work for commercial gain, Linus shared his creation on the Internet so that software developers from around the world could study it and build on his work. Soon an army of programmers was donating time and talent to make this free operating system one of the best in the world. Linux is becoming a stable operating system with many of the same features and functions as Windows NT. In fact, because some of its features are more advanced than the current version of NT, Microsoft is keeping a close watch on this system.

TABLE 4-4

Summary of Different Types of Operating Systems

Operating System	Description
DOS	One of the earlier operating systems for PCs. Uses cryptic, text-based commands. Windows 3.1 was built around DOS.
Windows 98 Windows 95	32-bit operating systems created by Microsoft. Popular software for PCs with excellent GUI features. Support multiprogramming.
Windows NT	32-bit operating system created by Microsoft. Considered a powerful operating system that supports multiprogramming and multiprocessing.
UNIX	A reliable, robust operating system used in PCs, workstations, and midrange computers. Widely used in many large-scale applications. Supports multiprogramming and multiprocessing.
OS/2	A solid, robust operating system developed by IBM. Uses 32-bit architecture and supports multiprogramming.
Linux	A robust operating system (can run on 64–bit systems). Developed by Linus Torvalds. Ongoing development by other programmers must be shared free of charge. Supports multiprogramming and multiprocessing.
Mac OS	A powerful, multitasking operating system with excellent graphical capabilities and user-friendly features. Uses a PowerPC chip developed by Apple, Motorola, and IBM. Can run many applications.

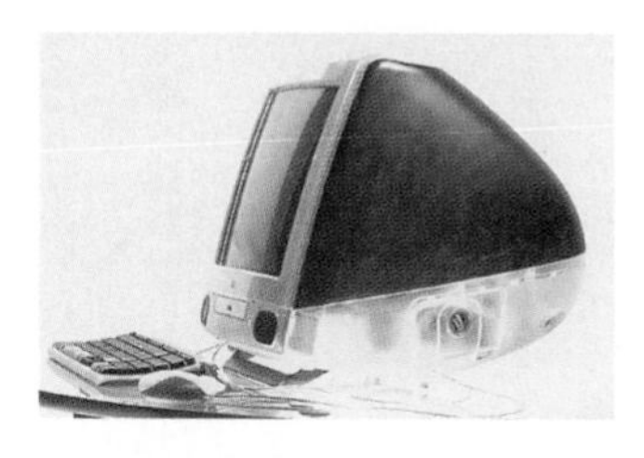

Macintosh computers, such as this iMac, use versions of Mac OS, an operating system that supports numerous application software programs.

Mac OS

Macintosh is the name of a family of personal computers from Apple. Unlike PCs that rely on Intel chips, Apple's PowerMacs and iMac rely on the PowerPC CPU chip, a family of CPU chips designed by Apple, IBM, and Motorola. PowerMacs and the iMac run Mac, DOS, and Windows applications using special software.

Mac OS, the operating system for Macintoshes, is a multitasking operating system with numerous features and graphical capabilities that make Macintoshes popular in publishing, marketing, and educational organizations. QuickTime is a piece of software that further enhances the operating system, providing excellent multimedia extensions with its sound and video capabilities.

Table 4-4 summarizes the different types of operating systems. As we have seen, no operating system is superior to another. Rather, users should select the operating system that works best for their situation, considering the number of applications they use, the number of end users, and their hardware and network requirements. Note, also, that users can load more than one operating system in a computer, such as Windows operating system and UNIX.

To Upgrade or Not to Upgrade to a New Operating System?

The system software upgrade question challenges many decision makers. As software companies release new versions of existing operating systems or develop new operating systems, business managers are forced to consider several factors, such as the following:

- **The budget.** Almost all software upgrades include more than the cost of the software. They also require hardware changes, such as increased memory and more powerful processors. In large companies, updating the hardware on hundreds of machines can quickly become an expensive proposition.
- **Training and learning costs.** Software upgrades also cost time and money to train employees to use the new system. Cost of training is a significant part of the IS manager's budget, given the rapid technological changes. Upgrades also cost in terms

of employee productivity. When the employee is away at training or spending time after training to become proficient, productivity suffers.

- **Technical support.** The help desk staff in an organization also needs extensive training to deal with the problems and challenges of a new operating system. This is no small task. Help desk personnel must be prepared to deal with a wide variety of problems quickly and efficiently.
- **Standardization.** Standardization in this context means that all employees in the company use the same software or the same operating system. Standardization helps companies achieve uniformity, thereby making it easier to share applications and transfer files from one user to another. It also means that all employees receive consistent training. In cases in which companies opt to upgrade only some computers, standardization problems may result.
- **The size of the business.** A small business with fewer computers has different upgrade needs than a large business with many computers. The impact of company size varies from one situation to the next. On the one hand, if the company is small, it may not need to upgrade as often as a company with more complex information needs. On the other hand, in small companies, it is easier to upgrade because it influences a smaller number of users.
- **Security issues.** New operating systems typically offer different levels of security that may or may not benefit the business. Make sure the OS offers the type of security you need. Some new systems may provide better security than existing systems, while others may not. Further, the security features offered by that of one operating system might be different from that offered by an earlier system. Be sure to identify security features that are important to your company before you upgrade.
- **The nature of applications the operating system supports.** Be certain the operating software supports the applications software the business requires. Not all operating systems support all applications. This lack of support could cause frustration for users and productivity losses for the business.
- **Amount of downtime that the organization can afford.** Each time the computer is down, some work comes to a halt in an organization. Depending on the nature of the application, such computer downtime is tolerated or not tolerated. For instance, in a hospital surgery room, computer downtime is simply out of the question. In contrast, in a health club, the consequences of computer downtime are far less serious.

Table 4-5 provides the questions decision makers should ask when faced with an upgrade decision. We have explored the importance of, types of, and decision criteria for system control software upgrades. In the next section, we investigate the second type of system software, system support software.

TABLE 4-5

Questions to Consider for an OS Upgrade Decision

Factor	Question
Budget	What is the total cost of the upgrade?
Training	How much training is required to learn a new system?
Technical support	How much technical support does the vendor provide?
Standardization	Does the system fit with the company's standardization policies?
Business size	What is the effect of company size on the upgrade decision?
Security issues	What kind of security does the upgrade provide?
Applications	Do our current application needs match the new system?
Computer downtime	What is our tolerance for computer downtime due to system crashes?

System Support Software

System support software

Software that supports or helps with the smooth and efficient operations of a computer.

Recall that there are three kinds of system software. The second kind, known as **system support software,** is software that helps the computer to perform efficiently. The four main types of system support software are utility programs, language translators, database management systems, and performance statistics software.

Utility programs perform tasks such as formatting disks, locating free space on a disk, retrieving lost or damaged files, sorting and merging data, managing files, converting files from one format to another, backing up important data and files, and providing simple on-line help.

Language translators are support programs that convert the programs written by software developers into bits and bytes that the computer understands. Database management systems help create, manage, and maintain data. Another example of system support software for organization-wide systems are performance-monitoring programs. These programs monitor system performance by collecting data about various computer activities such as idle CPU time, use of different input and output devices, memory use, amount of time users are logged on to the system, and so on. By collecting data on system performance, managers can ensure that their systems are put to good use. They can also correct problems that have a negative effect on system performance.

System Development Software

System development software

Software designed to help system developers design and build better systems.

The third type of system software is **system development software,** which is software that helps programmers and system developers to build better systems. Compilers, programs that translate higher-level programming languages into basic machine language, are an example of system development software. Another example of system development software is computer-aided software engineering (CASE), which helps developers design and develop solid, sophisticated information systems.

Recall that two main types of software exist: system and application. So far, we have studied types of system software: system control, system support, and system development. In the next section, we examine application software.

Application Software

Application software

Software designed to perform people-related tasks such as payroll, inventory, and sales analysis.

Figure 4-7 showcases the two types of **application software:** general-purpose (designed for general applications, such as payroll and sales) and dedicated software (designed for specific applications, such as the space shuttle). Organizations use general-purpose software for common business functions such as word processing, spreadsheets, and

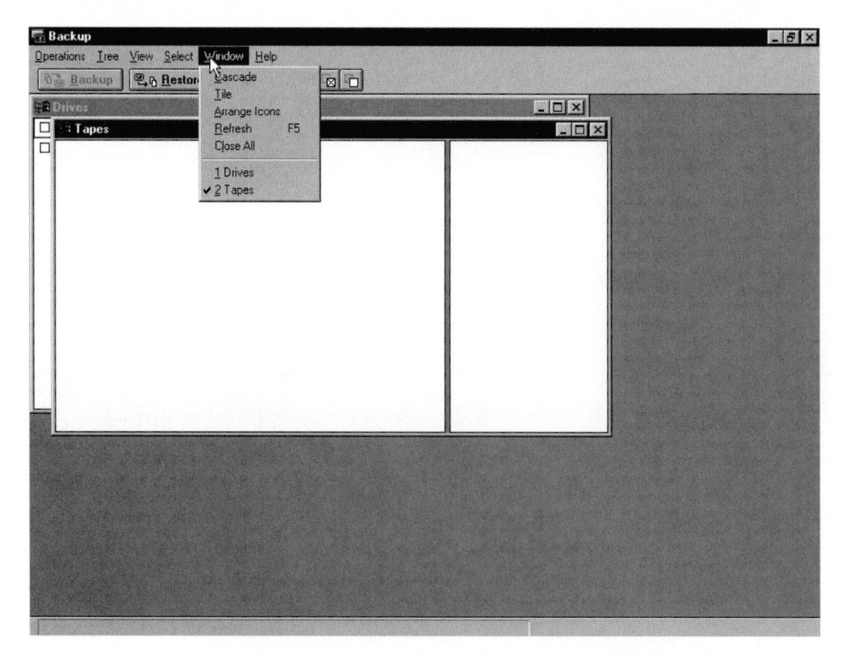

Utility programs help users with some activities, such as checking to see if there are any viruses in the system.

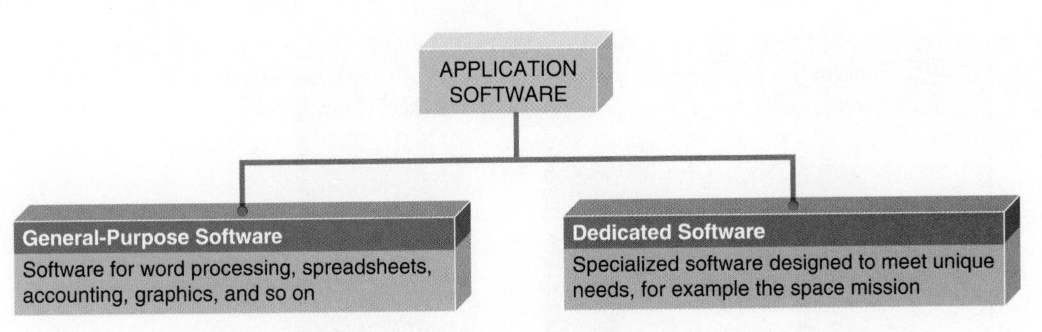

FIGURE 4-7

Different Types of Application Software

electronic mail. Dedicated software helps organizations meet their unique information needs, such as inventory software for a global jazz music company.

General-Purpose Software

You may be familiar with some type of **general-purpose software,** such as e-mail (software for sending electronic mail) or software for general office functions like an electronic address book and so on. We look at five types of general-purpose software, outlined in Table 4-6: word processing, desktop publishing, computer graphics, spreadsheet, and imaging.

General-purpose software
Software mass produced for a broad range of common business applications such as word processing, graphics, payroll, and accounting.

To communicate in a print format, people use word-processing software, which creates, manages, corrects, and manipulates text efficiently. Desktop publishing software builds on word-processing features and adds text and image placement features. Some additional features include color layouts and easy integration of photos and images. This type of software is suited for newsletters and pamphlets that require the integration of text and complex graphics. Although many word-processing packages can produce simple graphics, desktop publishing offers tools to draw sophisticated figures and graphs.

Computer graphics software allows users to communicate information in the form of graphical images and pictures. Many sophisticated graphic packages offer extensive features that include drawing features, powerful paint applications (programs that allow you to create and paint pictures with an electronic paint brush), and animation programs (software that allows you to create electronic animations such as a hand waving goodbye). Some graphical packages such as Corel Draw have a powerful tool for creating realistic natural textures such as wood, marble, clouds, stone, and metal.

TABLE 4-6

Five Types of General-Purpose Application Software

Type of Application Software	Description
Word processing	Allows easy creation, management, correction, and manipulation of text documents.
Desktop publishing	Produces documents such as memos and pamphlets. Has many word-processing features but has more sophisticated text and graphics capabilities.
Spreadsheets	Uses electronic calculators for extensive number crunching, such as financial analysis, budget preparation, other numerical analysis, and "what-if" analysis.
Computer graphics	Provides for the creation and management of sophisticated graphics, charts, and figures. Often comes with extensive color capabilities and clip art.
Imaging	Scans text and graphics from paper documents and converts then into digital images.

FIGURE 4-8

Graph of Salary Differences

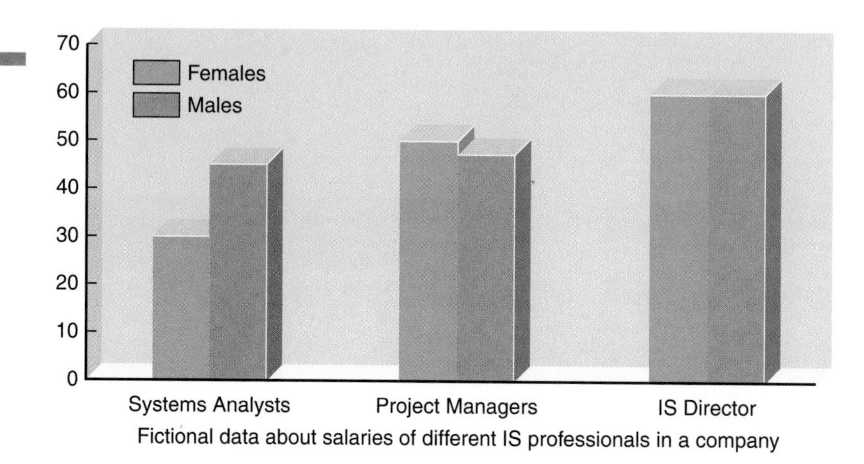

Some packages allow users to create a three-dimensional effect or capture screens of different applications. Suppose you were writing a software training manual for Windows 98. The graphics software allows you to capture a screen from the program, including menu lists, toolbars and so on, to make it easy for readers to follow the training manual.

Businesspeople often use graphic programs to provide visuals that summarize text or numerical decision-making information. For example, human resource departments closely monitor salary differences to avoid a discrimination lawsuit if salaries differ because of race, gender, or other non-work-related factors. Figure 4-8 graphically depicts a fictional company's salary differences based on gender. The graph is easier to understand than the underlying numerical data showing the relationship between salaries and gender in each job type.

Spreadsheets are a third type of general-purpose software. They simplify computationally intensive tasks, such as financial analysis, budget preparation, and grade calculation. Spreadsheets can sort and analyze data; create charts, graphs, and figures; and perform what-if analysis to assess the effect of input changes. For example, a spreadsheet is ideal for tracking and calculating a year's worth of financial activities for tax purposes. Users can create a spreadsheet of all income and expenses that are input as they occur and can calculate the taxes owed at year's end with a few simple keystrokes.

A fourth kind of application software is imaging software that scans text and graphics from paper documents and converts them into digital images. Imaging is becoming

	A	B	C
1	**Name**	**Type**	**Description**
2	student ID	number	the unique student ID, generally equals social security number
3	student name	text	the name of the student, no more than 255 characters
4	student birth date	date	the date of the student's birth
5	student major	text	the major of student, 1-2 from 109 choices of the university
6	student score	number	the final score of the student
7	faculty name	text	the name of the faculty, no more than 255 characters
8	course	text	the name of the course student selected this year
9	tuition payment	number	the residual tuition the student needed to pay this year
10	HI status	y/n	the status of whether the student has bough the health insurance plan
11	company name	text	the name of the company who plans to recruit this year
12	applicant	text	the name of the student who is applying for the position
13	B team member	number	the ID of the student on the baketball team
14	scholarship	text	the name of the scholarship
15	value of scholarsh	number	the value of the scholarship
16	receiver of schola	number	the student ID of the receiver of the scholarship
17			

Spreadsheet software simplifies the task of keeping track of annual income and expenses.

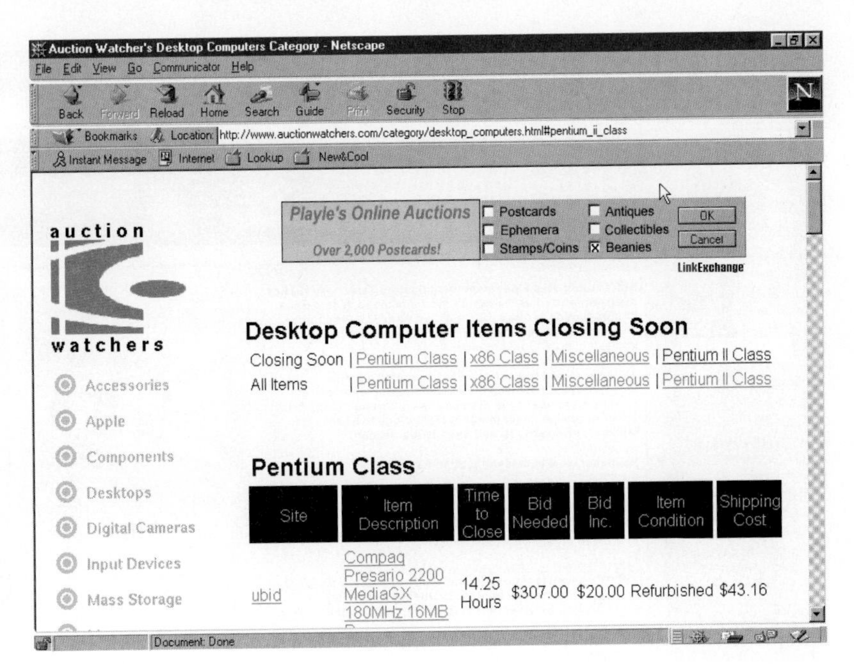

Auction Watchers offers its customers a convenient, quick way to find and bid on the items of their choice.

more popular for four reasons. First, it decreases the need to store paper documents because all images are digitized and stored in the computer. Second, it decreases copying costs. For example, Norfolk Southern, a 168-year-old railroad whose tracks cover 14,500 miles in 20 states and Canada, uses an advanced imaging system to digitize paper records such as maps and deeds. The copying cost saving is substantial: About 250 users access these images over the company's network to make decisions.[15]

Third, it reduces problems with lost or misplaced data. Unlike paper documents that can be ravaged with time and mishandling, digital images can be preserved for a long time. Finally, imaging software has become more affordable.

Companies use imaging for a variety of tasks. Auction house Auction Watchers uses imaging software to display and auction its items electronically. Compared to the print catalogs that traditional auction houses offer, buyers do not have to sort through hundreds of pages to get details on a specific item. Instead, viewers can click on their category of choice, such as laptops or software, and scan a list of all items in that category. When the viewer clicks on a specific item, an image and detailed description pops up. The software lets the viewer examine and bid on the item if wanted.

The software has helped Auction Watchers minimize the costs of doing business: The company does not need to hold a live auction, print an expensive paper-based catalog, or spend money mailing these catalogs to parties around the world. More important, customers everywhere can access items they want to view quickly, at any time, and for as long as they wish from their home or office computer.

Another example of an imaging application occurs in law enforcement. Officials use imaging software to catch criminals by capturing fingerprint images. The digitized images of criminals' fingerprints are stored in a database, making comparison easy to do when the need arises and prevents the print from fading with time or suffering the ravages of human touch. Further, the human eye can only see about 60 shades of gray, whereas imaging software detects 256 or more shades of color on a fingerprint, thus increasing the chances of finding a match with a suspect's fingerprints.

We examined five types of general-purpose software that help companies meet basic information needs. In the next section we discuss application-dedicated software, which is software that addresses an organization's specific needs.

Application-Dedicated Software

Application-dedicated software cannot be easily modified or adapted for other applications because it is highly customized to meet specific, and often unique, information needs. The types of dedicated software are as varied as each organization's needs,

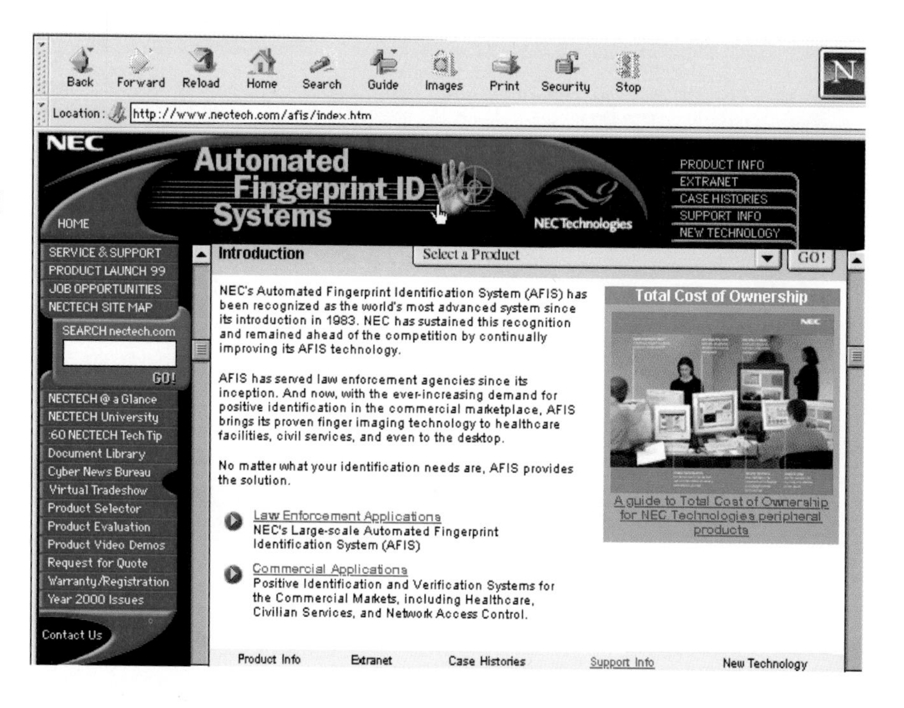

NEC's Automated Fingerprint Identification System (AFIS) imaging software has helped law enforcement officers match fingerprints more efficiently because the digitized prints do not fade with age and the software can match more shades of gray than the naked eye can.

Application-dedicated software

Specialized or customized software designed to meet specific information needs of users.

as we see in examples from government, business, sports and entertainment, police departments, and health care. The National Aeronautics and Space Administration (NASA) uses many application-dedicated software packages in its space shuttles that are crucial to the mission. Some space missions have used software that consist of more than 14 *million* lines of code written in 15 different languages that run on 170 different computers. Overall, it takes about 6,000 hours of labor to develop application-dedicated software for a single space flight.[16]

NASA also uses application-dedicated software to train astronauts and monitor their vital signs, replicate actual flight conditions, and process data gathered in space. Some other examples of application-dedicated software that NASA uses include computerized alarms and global maps that indicate the nearest landing sites. In fact, the NASA software team is on standby during a space launch so that programmers can immediately correct a problem that occurs during flight.[17]

Cigna Investment Services in Hartford, Connecticut, uses application-dedicated software to automate some parts of its sales function. The sales software helps the com-

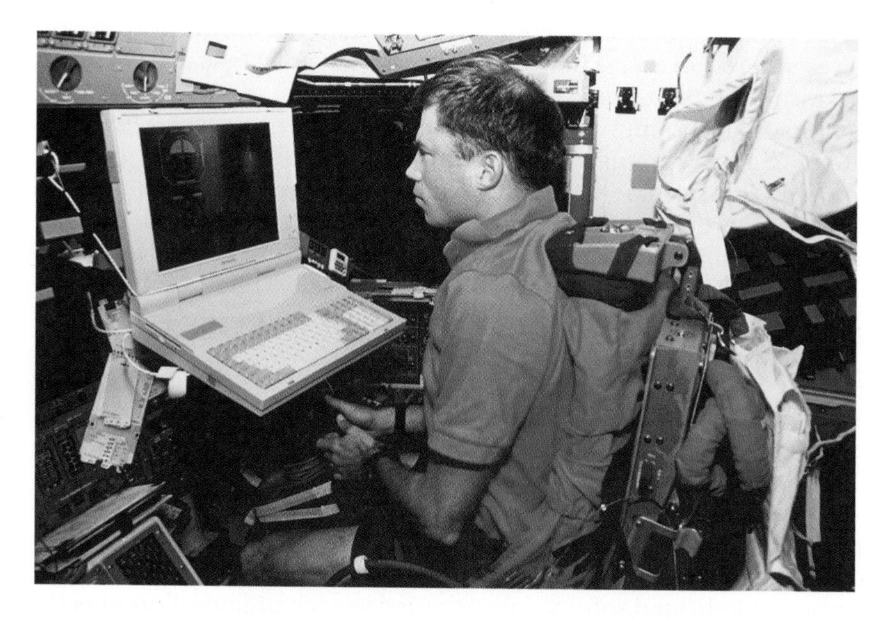

NASA astronauts use application-dedicated software to train and simulate flight conditions. Here, an astronaut is measuring the effect of space on pilot proficiency with the help of Portable Inflight Landing Operations Trainer (PILOT) software.

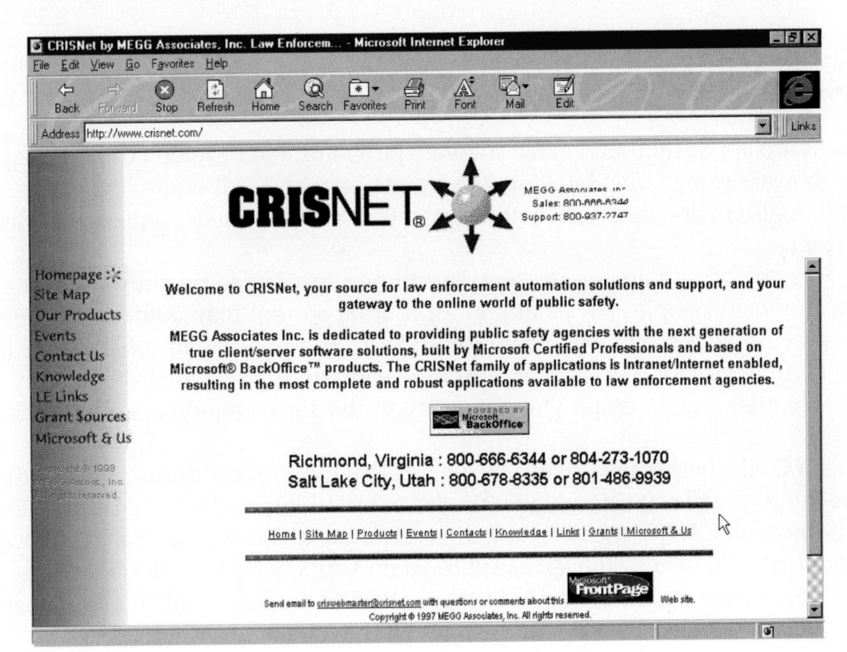

Law enforcement agencies often rely on application-dedicated software such as RECAP and CRISnet to serve the specific needs of the community. This type of software has helped police departments target prevention efforts.

pany respond quickly to requests for proposals. For example, when a potential client asks Cigna for a bid, employees at the company use the software to access more than 600 documents and other related materials from previous bids. The software also helps the company customize its proposals, rather than send out boilerplate proposals based on earlier documents. "If it takes longer just to pull up standardized information and not even customize it, you are not meeting the specific needs of your customers," says Ann Swanson, Cigna's assistant director of sales and marketing.[18]

Businesses often rely on dedicated software to save money. To reduce mailing costs, companies develop or purchase dedicated software that checks the accuracy of mailing addresses, adds bar codes to letters for easy post office sorting, and presorts mail to get postal discounts. The savings from such efforts can be significant: ITT Hartford's use of such software saves about $135,000 a year on its 23 million mass mailings.[19]

The Minneapolis police department uses RECAP, application-dedicated software, to help police analyze 400,000 emergency 911 calls and gain a better understanding of community problems. The *Re*peat *C*all *A*ddressing *P*olicing ("RECAP") system captures caller identification and delivers it to the police officer, who then initiates the appropriate action. Reports showed that 10 percent of the addresses accounted for nearly 60 percent of calls for police intervention. By working with people in these communities, police resolved many local problems. In one instance, 75 of the 105 calls were made during a short period of time from one building and involved one apartment. RECAP counseled the main caller and averted future calls.

A popular type of dedicated software for IT specialists trying to reduce help desk calls is called self-healing software. This type of software automatically restores desktop applications to their original state by reinstalling application components damaged, removed, or modified by other programs. The end user may not even realize that the self-healing program is running. Why is this type of software growing in popularity? Almost two-thirds of help desk calls involve users who need their applications restored, according to research firm Hurwitz Group. Self-healing systems bypass help desk administrators because they work automatically with the end user's operating system.[20]

Despite the benefits of application-dedicated software, it does have downsides. First, it can be expensive to develop, maintain, and upgrade. Second, planning application-dedicated software requires a thorough understanding of the business goals and activities and tremendous time. Third, as the Ethics for Success feature shows, some dedicated systems can open the door to ethical violations.

We have examined general-purpose and application-dedicated software. Next we examine programming languages.

Ethics for success

Profiling Systems

Profiling systems are application-dedicated software programs that develop customer profiles. They are used in many industries, including banking, travel, retailing, and real estate. Passenger-screening software is a profiling system designed to help travel agents and airlines better understand travelers' profiles to serve them better.

However, like any other software program, profiling systems can be abused. They can also affect the privacy of innocent people. For example, a profiling system may automatically profile a cash-paying customer who buys a one-way plane trip to Syria as a possible terrorist whose luggage needs to be thoroughly searched for a bomb. Or a profiling system in a credit-card company may interpret a visit to a psychiatrist and an employment agency in the same month as an indication of pending bankruptcy.

The American Civil Liberties Union (ACLU) worries that the airline industry's new Computer-Assisted Passenger Screening (CAPS) software unfairly singles out passengers of Middle Eastern descent for extra scrutiny. The purpose of CAPS software is to help spot potential terrorists and is mandatory at all major U.S. airline terminals. But since January 1, 1998, when CAPS went from the pilot stage to live use at Northwest Airlines and other airlines, the ACLU has gotten "scores of complaints" from passengers, most of whom complained of racial discrimination. Says Greg Nojeim, an ACLU lawyer in Washington, "A profile that targets as potential terrorists people who travel frequently to a country on the State Department's terrorist list would have a disparate impact on people who trace their national origin to that country. Who, after all, visits Syria? It's not a big tourist destination. Not a lot of business travelers go there. But people do visit their families."

Hassan Abbass, a U.S. citizen born in Syria, and his wife filed a $4 million lawsuit last July against U.S. Airways, alleging discrimination and a subsequent "humiliating" luggage search. The Cleveland couple was stopped apparently because of multiple trips to Syria, the suit claimed. The case was later dropped and each side agreed to pay its own legal fees. But the ACLU, among others, expects many more cases like it.

Take another example. Some banks and other lenders use credit-risk evaluation software that picks out credit-card charges for, say, marriage counseling and an employment agency in the same month. The thinking is that a troubled marriage combined with a lost job can signal coming bankruptcy or, at least, serious money problems, explains a spokeswoman at HNC Software, a profiling software vendor in San Diego. Such profiling systems can help save money, reduce credit risks, and boost profits for corporate America. For instance, First Union Corp. raises rates and late fees for bank customers whose profiles show increasingly "bad" behavior, such as months of missed payments, notes Chris Hamilton, a portfolio management coordinator at First Union.

Experts in computer ethics say there are several ways to encourage responsible use of profiling systems. One is to make sure a red flag in a computer doesn't trigger an automatic action against people. Actions should only be taken after further review. Another technique is to make sure end users are trained to understand the sensitive legal issues and to recognize that a computer's conclusions aren't gospel. "There's a tendency to put more credence in [computers] instead of personal judgment," says Don Gotterbarn, a computer ethics expert at East Tennessee State University in Johnson City, Tennessee.

YOU DECIDE

1. If you were the president of a company that profiles customers, how would you convince your employees of the system's benefits? What objections do you think employees will raise, and how will you respond?

2. Profiling systems success depends on the intuition, judgment, and good sense of the decision maker. Discuss.

3. If you were unfairly treated because of a profiling system, how would you respond?

Source: Kim S. Nash, "Electronic Profiling," *Computerworld* (February 9, 1998), www.computerworld.com.

Programming Languages

Regardless of the software type, all software—systems or application—is written in specific programming languages. A programming language is necessary to communicate with a computer, so to pick the right language for the right application we must understand the differences between programming languages.

A **programming language** is a computer language with its own syntax and grammar. There are two types of programming languages: procedural and nonprocedural. A **procedural language** tells the computer in a step-by-step fashion how to accomplish a given task. Think for a moment about how you would instruct a 4-year-old child to stick a stamp on an envelope. You have to give the child step-by-step instructions. In contrast, **nonprocedural languages** simply indicate what needs to be done, and the 'how' part is implicit. This is comparable to telling your roommate to stick a stamp on a letter. You omit the step-by-step instructions for accomplishing that task.

Now let us look at a business example. Suppose the CEO of a worldwide clothing company would like to know the stores with the top five highest sales. In a nonprocedural language, the CEO would simply tell the computer, "Determine the stores with the top five highest sales." The computer automatically figures out how to retrieve this information. In a procedural language the CEO must give specific instructions to the computer for accomplishing this task, including where to find the data, how to process the data, and how to format and output the data. Although early programming languages were completely procedural, today several powerful and user-friendly, nonprocedural languages exist.

There are four generations of computer languages. As we review the generations, we can see how much progress the software industry has made in a short time.

- **First generation:** In the early years of the computer revolution, programs were written in **machine language,** which was the first generation of computer language. It was tedious, time-consuming, error-prone, and machine-dependent. Machine-dependent implies that programs written on one machine cannot be executed on other machines. However, the only language that a computer understands is machine language, so there are special programs that convert a program written in any programming language into machine language.
- **Second generation:** In the early 1950s this generation of computer language, known as **assembly language,** emerged. Although assembly language is machine-dependent, it is easier to use than machine language because it uses words such as *add* and *sub* (for subtract), instead of the 0s and 1s used in machine language. An assembler is a special program that converts assembly language into machine language.

Programming language

A computer language with its own syntax and grammar that is used to write computer software.

Procedural language

A computer language that explains step-by-step how to accomplish a given task.

Nonprocedural language

A computer language that focuses on what needs to be done, without specifying exactly how it is to be done.

Machine language

A first-generation computer language that is written in binary code (zeros and ones) and is the only language that the computer understands.

Assembly language

A second-generation computer language that uses meaningful abbreviations of words or mnemonics to represent basic computer instructions.

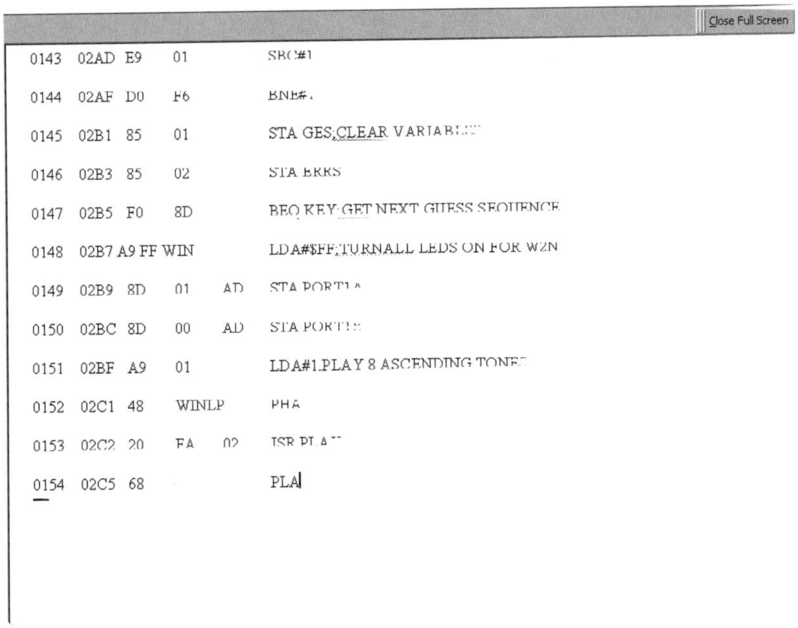

Close Full Screen

```
0143  02AD  E9   01          SBC#1
0144  02AF  D0   F6          BNE#.
0145  02B1  85   01          STA GES;CLEAR VARIABL
0146  02B3  85   02          STA ERRS
0147  02B5  F0   8D          BEQ KEY GET NEXT GUESS SEQUENCE
0148  02B7 A9 FF WIN         LDA#$FF;TURNALL LEDS ON FOR W2N
0149  02B9  8D   01    AD    STA PORT1A
0150  02BC  8D   00    AD    STA PORT1
0151  02BF  A9   01          LDA#1.PLAY 8 ASCENDING TONE
0152  02C1  48   WINLP       PHA
0153  02C2  20   FA    02    JSR PLA
0154  02C5  68               PLA
```

Assembly software is tedious to code with, although it was an improvement over first-generation language.

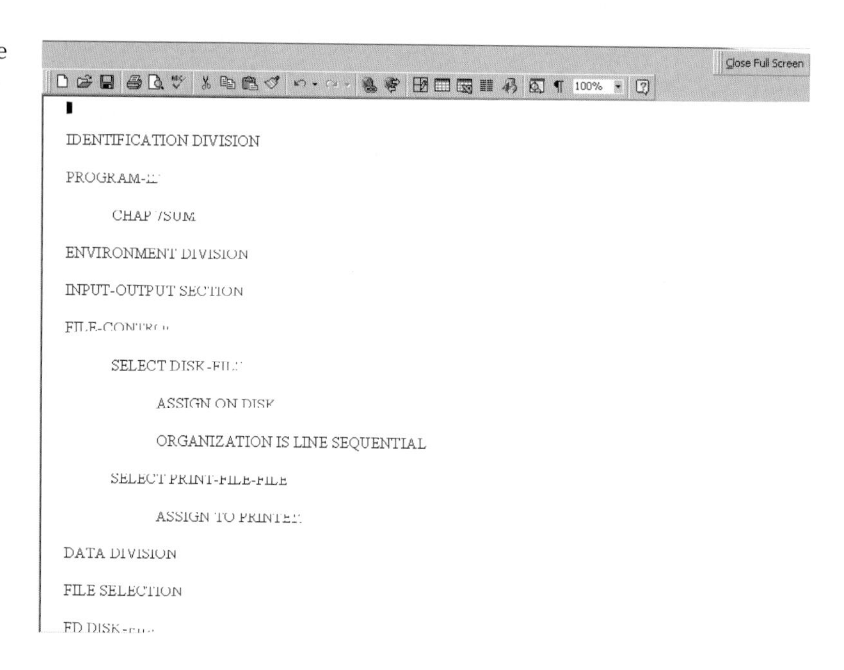

COBOL, a high-level language that is not as powerful as C, is still widely used.

- **Third generation:** From the mid-1950s to the 1970s, developers devised a new set of languages called **high-level languages (HLL),** or 3GLs (third-generation languages). These languages were easier to use than assembly and machine language because they relied on natural language (such as words in English) and used fewer lines of code to execute an instruction. Some popular high-level languages are BASIC, COBOL, FORTRAN, and C. Although high-level languages are a considerable improvement over earlier languages, becoming an expert programmer in any high-level language still takes years of training and experience.

High-level languages, or 3GLs

Third-generation computer languages that use English-like instructions that require fewer lines of code than earlier-generation languages to perform an instruction.

One of the most widely used high-level languages is COBOL. Many people predicted almost a decade ago that newer and more powerful languages, such as C, would replace COBOL. However, COBOL is still widely used. In fact, its popularity is probably at an all-time high. Today, COBOL comes with several nice features, including the ability to access COBOL applications over the Web.

3GLs are machine-*independent* languages—that is, they are portable from one machine to another. A special program, called the **compiler,** converts all programs written in 3GL to machine language.

Compiler

A type of system software that reads a program written in any 3GL and converts it into machine language.

- **Fourth-generation languages: Very-high-level languages** or 4GLs (fourth-generation languages) as they are popularly called, emerged in the late 1970s. 4GLs overcome some of the limitations of high-level languages. Many languages called fourth-generation languages are actually a combination of third- and fourth-generation languages.

Very-high-level languages, or 4GLs

Nonprocedural languages that require users to simply specify what needs to be done, rather than how it is to be done.

A word of caution about the generations of languages. The terms *first-, second-, third-,* or *fourth-generation language,* or *machine* or *assembly language* do not refer to a specific programming language. Rather, they are general descriptions of a generation of computer languages. Table 4-7 describes some popular types of third- and fourth-generation programming languages.

Some examples of fourth-generation languages are SQL, FOCUS, and SAS. Query languages (languages that help users ask specific questions of and receive answers from a database) are also examples of 4GLs. Fourth-generation languages are efficient, user-friendly, easy to learn, and very much like English. For example, in a 4GL language called dBASE, a user who gives the command "List," will see a list—an automatic display of all the items in a database. In second- and third-generation languages, the user must issue several commands to accomplish this same task.

One of the main advantages of 4GL is that it is easy to use, allowing even non-programmers to develop fairly complex applications. This ease of use not only reduces the cost of development but also means businesses can trim programming staff and re-

TABLE 4-7 Different Generations of Software Programming Languages

Generation of Language	Description
First Machine language	The only language that the computer understands. It is represented in 0s and 1s.
Second Assembler language	A symbolic language that uses abbreviations and symbols. An improvement over machine language.
Third BASIC COBOL FORTRAN PASCAL	An improvement over assembly language. It is closer to the human language than earlier languages. They are machine-independent.
Fourth INTELLECT FOCUS	Programming languages that require users to specify only *what* needs to be done, not *how* it has to be done.

duce the time it takes to develop systems. As a result, many organizations have switched to 4GLs. People with 4GL skills are always in demand.

The Santa Fe Railroad company's Corwith yard in Chicago was in desperate need of a computer system to track its complex and growing railroad operations. Although the company had a detailed plan to computerize the operations, its programmers on the West Coast were busy with many other projects, so Corwith opted to switch to 4GL languages. It asked four mid-level managers with no programming experience to become its 4GL programmers. In less than 3 months, the first part of the system was operational and before long it was adapted for use in other Santa Fe yards. The finished system has helped the company save more than $100 million a year.

The Santa Fe Railroad switched to 4GL languages to keep its trains in Chicago running smoothly.

If 4GLs are so efficient and user-friendly, why aren't all programs written in 4GL? The reason is, companies have already invested millions, if not billions, of dollars in their software systems. Many programs were written in BASIC, COBOL, FORTRAN, and other third-generation languages. It is difficult, if not impossible, and financially impractical to rewrite all these programs in fourth-generation languages. Companies, then, continue to update and maintain systems written in older languages. Remember, though, that staying with an older-generation programming language poses several

Microsoft Access - [Query2 : Select Query]

File Edit View Insert Format Records Tools Window Help

id	name	exam1	exam2	exam3	final exam	Score
600007	Dave	90	78	89	90	87.4
600009	Nathan	89	88	86	78	83.8
600039	Felix	69	92	93	90	86.8
600045	Eric	92	93	92	89	91
600048	Todd	91	95	89	96	93.4
600050	John	79	81	92	89	86
600072	Peter	67	90	90	89	85
600076	William	89	97	92	91	92
600079	Jennings	90	78	93	91	88.6
600088	brenna	98	78	89	99	92.6
600089	Cindy	99	98	67	96	91.2
600089	Ginger	88	99	99	98	96.4
600091	Wang	91	96	91	99	95.2
600096	Henry	89	91	88	78	84.8
600099	Darcy	98	78	96	99	94
600100	Alex	97	90	89	69	82.8
600100	Linda	56	60	61	80	67.4
600101	Peng	81	88	78	90	85.4
600560	George	82	64	92	83	80.8
0		0	0	0	0	

Record: 1 of 19

Datasheet View

A query provides answers to a user's specific questions. This screen shows the answer to a query for student exam scores and final averages.

disadvantages. Compared to a 4GL, programmers may have to write more lines of code, cope with more-limited development features, and experience restriction in the language's ability to interface with other programs.

In the next three sections, we investigate a new breed of programming languages: object-oriented languages, visual programming languages, and Java. These languages are distinct from other programming languages in their fundamental approach to problem solving.

Object-Oriented Programming

Object-oriented programming

A programming language that treats different real-world entities (places, persons, things, or ideas) as objects. Each object comes with its own data and code that specifies how the object should behave.

Object-oriented programming, also known as OOPS (object-oriented programming systems), is a programming language that looks at the world as a set of objects. Each object interacts with another object based on the messages it receives. An example can help illustrate how object-oriented programming works. Scotiabank, which operates branches in Canada and 45 other countries, used object-oriented design and programming to develop a software application that helps new customers choose services and gathers detailed customer information for the bank. This, in turn, helps salespeople better market the bank's products.

In this application a residential customer is an object class and a commercial customer is another object class. Each class has its own set of properties, such as a commercial customer must have a business address, or a commercial customer should list the Chief Financial Officer as a cosigner, and so on. Each object can send a message to another object. For example, the "commercial customer object" could request the "residential customer object" to print the names of all customers who also have a commercial account with the bank.

The principal benefit of OOPS is code reusability, which means that the same piece of programming code (lines of instructions that a programmer writes) can be reused for different applications. For instance, a print function in a word-processing file can be reused in a spreadsheet. Today, code reusability is not only desirable, but essential. Companies can develop applications much faster and can simplify maintenance because reusable code is standardized and widely understood. It is estimated that half the required code already exists and about 40 to 60 percent of all new code can potentially come from software libraries of reusable components.

Raytheon Co. of Massachusetts has such a strong software reuse program that 80 to 90 percent of new business applications comes from reusable components. Raytheon has also built a library of nearly 2,000 reusable software modules—chunks of reusable code that can be used over and over again for a number of basic business functions.

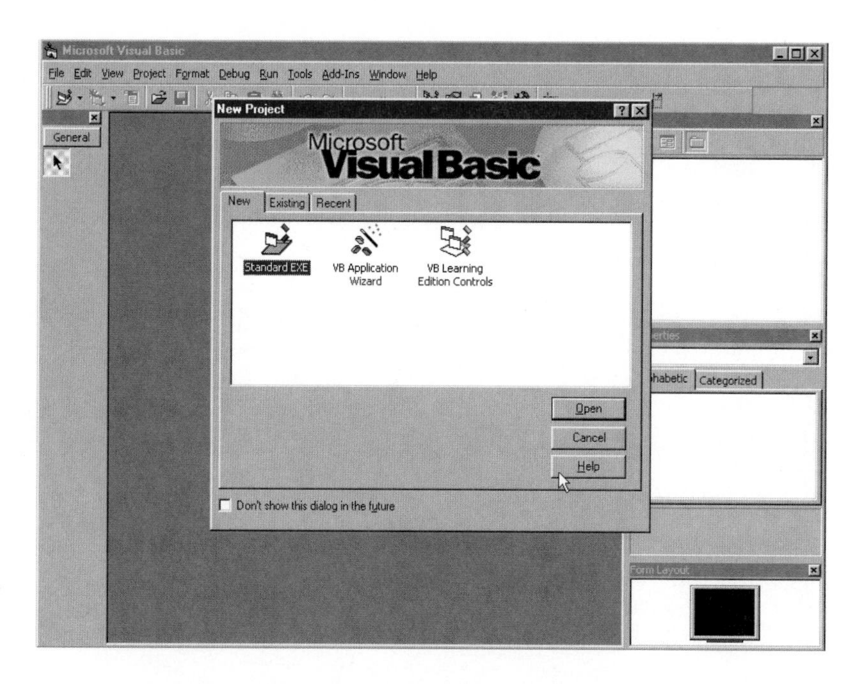

Microsoft Visual Basic, a popular visual programming language, serves as a common programming language for Microsoft's software applications, such as Access and Excel.

Microsoft's Visual C++ is one of the most popular object-oriented languages. Users can develop applications for both DOS and Windows applications using Visual C++, which combines traditional C programming with OOPS capability.

Although OOPS have many benefits, such as shorter development time, reusability, and ease of maintenance, they have some limitations. First, many experts feel that OOPS has been oversold as a panacea for all software development problems. Such high expectations lead to customer disappointments. Second, businesses cannot reap short-run benefits with OOPS; the benefits come only over the long run as they generate and reuse more OOPS code. Further, companies can reap the full potential of OOPS only if they are willing to start from scratch—a process many companies are reluctant to endure.

Visual Programming

Visual programming helps users create powerful and less error-prone applications in a shorter time span. It allows users to write special programs that in turn help users to select menus, buttons, and other graphics elements from a palette. This selection can then be embedded into any application.

Visual programming

Programming languages that allow users to visualize their code and its impact on the system.

One of the most popular visual programming languages is Visual Basic, a version of the BASIC programming language that Microsoft developed for Windows applications. It allows users to easily integrate Microsoft Windows applications and develop Windows applications quickly. A Visual Basic programming environment first converts the Visual Basic program into an intermediate language called byte code and then translates the byte code into machine language. Visual Basic serves as a common language for Microsoft's Access, PowerPoint, Word, and Excel applications. Because the same language can be used for a wide variety of applications, it reduces development time.

In recent surveys of application development managers by International Data Corp. (IDC) and *Computerworld,* Visual Basic and Java (see next section) were identified as the languages of the future. Experts estimated that there will be more than 6.8 million Visual Basic users in the next year or so. Forty-five percent of managers in the survey identified one of the two languages as the most important for their future development efforts.[21]

Nabisco relies on Visual Basic to track employee work flow and collaboration among different employees working on different projects. About one-third of the company's 300 developers use Visual Basic.[22]

Java

Java is a programming language for Internet (World Wide Web) application that is modeled after C++. Java programs can be either called from within Web documents that are written in a language called HTML (Hyper Text Markup Language) or launched as stand-alone programs. Java is an interpreted language, like Visual Basic, that uses an intermediate language, called byte code, which is then converted into machine language. Java programs do not depend on any specific hardware and can work with any operating system, which are big advantages. Because Java is a highly portable language, applications written in Java, unlike other languages, can be executed on any computer and any operating system. It also allows code reusability. Java is a fairly difficult, complex programming language that requires significant programming expertise. The JavaScript language from Netscape is a little easier to use than Java.

"Nothing like [Java] has existed before," says Mark Benerofe, vice-president of programming and platform development for Sony Online Ventures. "It's not only rapid deployment, but the promise and delivery of write once, reuse everywhere. For Sony, a worldwide company, there are now lots of opportunities to eliminate overlap with common components," he says.[23] So, for example, once Sony writes a program to print a document in color, the same program can be used across all its applications. This eliminates the need to write the same code over and over again for different applications.

Visa International has just embarked on its first large-scale Java project, updating its Visa Access Point system. These systems are like telephone company switches, handling thousands of credit-card transactions per second from around the globe, each of which must be processed instantly and error-free, says Art Machado, the project's chief technologist. "We're handling 2,000 transactions *per second* worldwide. We're

Careers for success

What's in a Title?

The Bank of Montreal is changing the job titles and reporting relationships of its information systems employees. Previously, every IS employee had a standard title, such as programmer or system analyst. Now the bank's IS leaders are "resource managers" if they handle IS people issues, "application portfolio managers" if they focus on users, "project managers" if they lead projects, and "business technology specialists" if their job is to stay on top of new hardware and software technologies. The standard title of programmer is gone, conveying that the job is now more than just programming!

The advantage is that each manager can focus on one key area—people inside the business, customers, or technology. Under the new career paths in the bank, an IS employee may now have multiple reporting relationships, taking direction for project work from the project manager and for career development from a human resource manager. This change gives programmers the chance to interact with many individuals, so they can get a better sense of the business and their role in helping the business achieve its goals.

Source: Gary H. Anthes, "Moniker Mania," *Computerworld,* May 18, 1998, www.computerworld.com.

looking at 10,000 per second in the next few years." A year ago, developers had no choice but to use C or C++ for such applications. Today Java is the unanimous choice for many companies. "It gives us the power we need, does away with the pain of C++. If we tried to do this application in C++ it would take three to four times as long," says Machado.[24]

Business Guidelines for Software Success

Software decisions can make or break a company. Investing in software that helps the business reach its goals effectively can help companies acquire a leadership position in the marketplace, enhance customer loyalty, and even lead to innovative product development. However, installing the latest software and walking away is not the road to organizational success. To ensure that software investments flourish, businesses must focus on business needs, vision, creativity, and ethics and individuals must research the costs and benefits of software investments, as we see next.

Assess the Values of Software

In the past few years, the computer has become an integral productivity tool, both at home and in our offices. Adults use computers to do a wide range of activities from tax returns to paying bills, while children use computers to play games, do math, and surf the Web. Regardless of the use, buying computer software has become a critical decision for many home users.

One key to success in the home office is to understand that software investments require careful thought. Like a business that seeks returns from its investments, individuals should carefully assess the expected returns from software. Research the software, its quality, and reputation before investing in it and understand the nature and scope of the warranty and technical support that the company provides.

Plan for Quality

Computer programming has been a "type-out-code-as-fast-as-you-can, shoot-from-the-hip endeavor. Accepted practice is to quickly bang out code of unknown quality and count on compiling and testing to find and fix the defects," observes Watts Humphrey of the Software Engineering Institute at Carnegie Mellon. Programmers are not encouraged to plan their program or produce quality products because they are evaluated on the number of lines of code produced rather than the quality of the code.

Quality usually requires teamwork. Teams of software experts develop almost all software of any significance, so software professionals need to be outstanding team players. "When you train professional musicians to play their instruments flawlessly, you still have to train them to play with others in a symphony," explains Humphrey.[25]

Make or Buy?

One of the decisions that IS managers frequently face is whether to make or buy software. In the past decade or so, off-the-shelf software has increased in both sophistication and versatility. Software is available for a wide variety of business functions, making it more meaningful to buy software, rather than develop software within the company. Developing software is a complex, labor-intensive, error-prone, and expensive process. In many cases, companies can customize off-the-shelf software to meet unique information needs. Unless the reasons are compelling, companies should strongly consider buying rather than developing software.

The military is relying more and more on prepackaged software. Buying, rather than making some types of software, will help the military to cut costs, increasing purchasing efficiency and simplifying training. "It's all about war-fighting efficiency," says Lt. Cmdr. Dan Shanower, an intelligence officer with the Navy's Third Fleet.[26]

However, these critical decisions have the potential to make or break a company, so the advantages and disadvantages of the make-or-buy decision must be thoughtful. "We always need to weigh the cost advantages of packaged software against the desire to differentiate your products. In some areas, particularly when it comes to product delivery, when you want to distinguish yourselves and your products from those of the competition, packaged programs may not always give you the flexibility that you need to be competitive," says Frank Wobst, Chairman and CEO, Huntington Bancshares.[27]

If a global company buys software, it should determine what kind of support the seller will provide. For example, in Eastern Europe and Latin American countries support from the seller may be rather weak. Neil Hawthorne, product manager for the Australian operations of J. D. Edwards & Co., a U.S.–based supplier of business applications, suggests that vendors should prove that they can support their software around the world. "Get them to show you their statistics for resolving problems within [so many hours]. Find out what percentage is resolved locally and what percentage is sent overseas," he suggests.

However, these statistics and promises may not sufficiently guarantee good service. Erik Keller, vice-president and director of research at Connecticut-based Gartner Group Service, cautions that "A great office now might be gone in six to 12 months." So, buyer beware![28]

Develop Criteria for Software Investments That Support Business Goals

Businesses use many different criteria to make software investment decisions. The kind of criteria that an organization uses (or does not use) has important implications. However, using finances as the dominant criterion has several limitations. First, it encourages managers to manipulate the numbers to fit the need, resulting in a "numbers game." Second, because many benefits of software are intangible, it is difficult to isolate and accurately measure the monetary value of such systems.

Third, hidden software costs are hard to estimate. For example, few organizations measure the cost of training help desk personnel to deal with the new software, the time and productivity lost in moving files from the old software to the new software, or the added stress of becoming proficient with a new application. Fourth, different departments in an organization may use different methods to measure the costs and benefits of software, leading to difficulties in assessing its true value. In sum, financial analysis is useful but should be tempered with qualitative factors and judgment.

Remember That Software Is More Than Just Automation

Software does more than help your company automate its business functions. In many cases, software plays a key role in helping a company maintain its corporate image or gain a competitive advantage. Potomac Electric Power Co. relied on its software to avert a public relations fiasco. Customers accused the Washington, D.C., utility of fixing the power lines of customers in well-to-do areas outside the city before those of inner-city customers. Concerned citizens took their case to a Washington commission.

Ken Cohn, the utility's highest-ranking IT executive, demonstrated the company's dispatch software to the commission to show how the company prioritizes repairs. Its software system maps reported outages, tracks the problem to the local generator, assesses all the homes and businesses likely to be affected, considers mitigating factors (simultaneous problems, the number of people affected, and whether there is a live wire on the ground), and then dispatches repair crews. The software demonstration convinced the commission officials and the public that the utility was dispensing service fairly. Cohn's demonstration averted further erosion of consumer confidence.[29]

Keep It Simple

Even though software is capable of performing complex tasks and functions, it does not have to be complex. Simple software is typically more affordable and easier for people of all levels to learn and use. To achieve simplicity, Du Pont's David Pensak recommends that programmers spend more time thinking and less time coding.

"Elegance. Simplicity. Beauty. How often do we have such poetic words applied to software? What often escapes notice these days in the bustle of user demands is the underlying craft of creating elegant, well-organized code. . . . Users actually expect the software they buy or download from the Web to be half-baked with annoying bugs," says the editor in chief of *Computerworld*.[30]

Thomas Sorgie at American Management Systems uses C++ to create a complex transaction processing module in only 450 KBs. The same application developed in another language or another system can take up to 30 MB. "One is a graceful ballet dancer, the other a hulking sumo wrestler," says Maryfran Johnson, senior editor of *Computerworld* magazine.[31]

Because software is so complex, the number of calls to help desks has increased exponentially. Commercial software vendors fielded more than 200 million calls for technical support in 1996—a $4.6 billion expense. About 38 percent of those calls occurred because of software program problems, according to software quality expert Cern Kaner.[32]

Follow Software Development Guidelines

Almost every organization has guidelines for developing and maintaining software. The problem is that very few developers follow the guidelines, which are "usually in a fat binder on the bottom shelf of a remote cubicle." The consequence of deviating from the guidelines is high development and maintenance costs.

In addition, there are guidelines for inspecting and testing system design and code. Complying with the guidelines can reduce software defects by 50 percent, according to Software Productivity Research (SPR), an information technology consulting firm. But getting developers to do this is next to impossible. "[It] is about as easy as collaring a cat. A large number of developers view process as the extraneous activities that have to go on to get to the cool part of writing Java or C++," notes Roger Pressman, a software engineering consultant in Orange, Connecticut.[33]

The goal of establishing guidelines is not to create more paperwork or burden programmers with unproductive activities, but instead should be viewed as a necessary step in developing high-quality systems. However, even the best guidelines will be used and implemented only if people are rewarded for using them. Most developers are not paid to stick to procedures, explains an IT project manager at a large Midwestern retail company. "People are rewarded for getting projects done, not following a process." As a result, programmers finish a project any way they can get it done fast.[34]

Pay Attention to Ethics If You Want Long-Term Profits

Organizations should consider several ethical factors while buying or installing software. The most important consideration is respecting the software copyright. Companies that prevent employees from copying software unless they have a proper license protect themselves in the long run. Copying software (also referred to as "shoplifting") is illegal, violates U.S. copyright laws, can result in dire consequences for the firm and the employee, and can cause prolonged and expensive legal battles. In fact, a single copyright infringement may result in civil damages of up to $100,000.

When is the copying illegal? Copyright violations occur if a copy of a single-user piece of software (software licensed for use on only one computer) is installed on several computers or if the company installs an illegal copy of a licensed software (for instance, software that is licensed to another company). Both situations can result in an injunction or a court order to search the company's premises and seize illegal copies.

Software piracy is no small matter and can have serious negative consequences for companies and even countries. "We have been telling the U.S. Congress that software piracy is dragging down the U.S. economy in a really significant way," notes Marcia Sterling, vice president of business development at Autodesk Inc. "We asked PricewaterhouseCoopers to assimilate the data to help us understand what the cost of software piracy really is."[35]

According to the Business Software Alliance (BSA), a watchdog group, software piracy can negatively influence future growth and innovation. When software piracy becomes an issue, companies shy away from developing new products and further feeding of the black market. About 40 percent of the PC business software used or sold worldwide in 1997 was pirated, a $11.4 billion loss for the economy. In 1997 alone, piracy rates for PC business software alone ranged from a low of 27 percent in the United States to as high as 98 percent in Vietnam. The study found that about 620,000 people in the United States were employed directly in the software industry last year, accounting for about $7.2 billion in taxes. But there would have been about 140,000 more jobs and about $1 billion more in tax revenue if piracy could be curtailed, according to the report.[36]

Such violations can prove both costly and embarrassing for a company. Budget Rent-a-Car Corp. agreed to pay $400,000 to the Business Software Alliance (BSA) for unlicensed software installed on its corporate computers. BSA, a Washington vendor alliance, works to reduce the illegal use of unlicensed software. In 1997 alone, the BSA settled copyright claims with about 50 U.S. companies and 500 companies worldwide, according to a BSA spokesperson.[37]

An organization can take several measures to prevent software copyright violations. In particular, a business must ask three questions to ensure that it is obeying the law:

1. Does the company have a published and well-understood policy statement educating employees about software copyright infringement and prohibiting them from making or accepting unlicensed copies of software?
2. Is there a set of original user manuals at each computer where a software product is installed?
3. Is the purchase, installation, and license registration of all software controlled at a central point in the company?

If the answer to any one of the above three questions is "no," then the company risks software copyright laws violation.

Here are five steps an organization can take to ensure that employees do not violate copyright laws:

- Educate all employees and managers about copyright infringement.
- Make one individual, or a group of individuals, responsible for acquiring software for the entire organization.
- Conduct regular audits of company software. The Software Publishers Association has a free software packet called SPAudit that searches all computer systems for about 700 products of SPA members.
- Keep a careful record of all documentation related to the purchase, legal ownership, and registration of purchased software.
- Destroy illicit copies of software and delete invalid installations from computers.

SUMMARY

1. **Describe different types of system software, including operating systems software.** System software performs the basic functions necessary to start and operate a computer and controls and monitors different activities and resources. System software can be classified into three categories: system control software (programs that manage system resources and functions), system support software (programs that support the execution of different applications), and system development software (programs that assist system developers in designing and developing information systems). The most important type of system control software is the operating system. An operating system is a complex set of software modules

that manage the overall operation of a computer. It acts as a manager, a housekeeper, and a traffic cop for a computer system. Some of the functions that it performs are loading programs, performing and managing input/output operations, managing files, managing computer memory, detecting errors, allocating resources, monitoring resource usage, and resolving conflicts. Some popular operating systems for PCs are Windows, Windows NT, OS/2, and Mac OS.

2. **Discuss important types of application software.** Application software refers to software designed to perform people-related tasks such as payroll, inventory, and sales analysis. The two types of application software are general-purpose (designed for general applications, such as payroll and sales) and dedicated software (designed for specific applications, such as the space shuttle). General-purpose software helps organizations perform common business functions, such as word processing and spreadsheets, quickly and conveniently. Dedicated software helps organizations meet their specialized and unique information needs.

3. **Explain the concept of programming and identify the different programming languages.** A software program is a set of step-by-step instructions that enables a computer to perform a specific task. There are two types of programming languages: procedural and nonprocedural. Procedural languages specify how a certain task must be accomplished while nonprocedural languages simply specify what needs to be done. There are four generations of programming languages: machine language, assembly language, high-level language (3GL), and very-high-level language (4GL). Each generation of language is an improvement over the earlier version in terms of coding, user-friendliness, and efficiency. Object-oriented programming languages are called such because they treat each entity as an object. Each object comes with its own code, or message, that specifies and directs the behavior of the object. Object-oriented languages promote code reusability for different applications. Visual programming is a programming language that allows users to visualize their code and its impact on the system. It helps users create powerful and less error-prone applications in a shorter time span. Java is a programming language for Internet (World Wide Web) application that is modeled after C++. Java programs can be either called from within Web documents that are written in a language called HTML (Hyper Text Markup Language) or launched as stand-alone programs.

KEY TERMS

application-dedicated software (p. 112)
application software (p. 108)
assembly language (p. 115)
compiler (p. 116)
general-purpose software (p. 109)
graphical user interface (p. 99)
high-level languages (p. 116)
machine language (p. 115)
multiprocessing environment (p. 97)
multiprogramming environment (p. 96)
nonprocedural language (p. 115)
object-oriented programming (p. 118)
operating system (p. 96)
procedural language (p. 115)
programming language (p. 115)
software (p. 92)
system control software (p. 95)
system development software (p. 108)
system software (p. 93)
system support software (p. 108)
very-high-level languages (p. 116)
visual programming (p. 119)

REVIEW QUESTIONS

1. What is a software program? Why do we need both hardware and software to build an information system?
2. What are the two major types of software? What is the primary purpose of each type of software?
3. Identify one of the most important types of system control software. Can a computer function without system control software? Discuss.
4. What is an operating system and what are its primary functions?
5. What is the difference between multiprogramming and multiprocessing? Can you do multiprocessing with your PC? Discuss.
6. Multiprogramming and multiprocessing are mutually exclusive. Discuss.
7. Name any three operating systems for PC-based environments and briefly describe each system. Are these systems mutually exclusive?

8. What is application software? What is the primary difference between general-purpose software and dedicated software?
9. Give examples of general-purpose software.
10. What are the four generations of programming languages?
11. Identify any two differences between 3GLs and 4GLs.
12. What is object-oriented programming and what is the biggest benefit of OOPS? How does code reusability affect software development?
13. What is visual programming? How does it differ from other programming languages?
14. Describe Java, the programming language. Why is it called an interpreted language?
15. What are some measures that organizations can take to prevent software copyright infringements?

DISCUSSION QUESTIONS AND EXERCISES

1. The buying habits of most purchasers of PC software are undergoing a radical change. Microsoft and other big companies are promoting an electronic software distribution system that allows customers to purchase software directly from the vendor rather than through resellers, such as retail outlets.

   The advent of electronic delivery systems, along with the growing interest in the CD-ROM as a medium for storing software, promises to change the buying habits of most PC users. Instead of purchasing floppy disks loaded with an individual software package, users will purchase multiple software packages on a single CD-ROM disk.

   Customers can browse through a CD-ROM that contains all products that a given software vendor offers. When a customer decides to purchase a specific package he or she can call the software vendor, who provides the customer with a password that gives the customer direct software access from the CD-ROM. The sale is then recorded using an electronic delivery system.

   a. **(Web exercise)** Visit Microsoft's Web site at http://www.microsoft.com. Study the company's electronic distribution system and give your comments.
   b. What are some reasons why customers may be reluctant to use software distribution systems, and what can companies do to overcome this resistance?
   c. What type of software is an electronic distribution system? What are some main characteristics that such software should have? For example, security is critical in such systems. Name three more desirable characteristics of such systems.

2. According to a study of 16,000 information technology professionals in 28 nations, U.S. programmers are more complacent and less productive than their international counterparts. The study, released in April 1999, was led by researcher Howard Rubin for Meta Group Inc., a research firm in Stamford, Connecticut. One way to measure programmer productivity is to count the number of lines of code by a programmer per year. Based on this measure, U.S. programmers wrote an average of 7,700 lines of code, compared with 16,700 lines for non–U.S. programmers. In other words, the average U.S. IT organization delivers software at "half the rate of the rest of the world," Rubin says.

   There are several reasons for this complacency, according to experts. First, there is a tremendous labor shortage so companies are reluctant to fire individuals. Second, the economy is good and this makes many U.S. IT professionals "fat and happy," according to Rubin. "My programming staff are 9-to-5ers, and complacency is a big problem," comments Paul Garrin, CIO at Holy Name Hospital in Teaneck, New Jersey. In contrast, programming expert Ed Yourdon suggests that the reason for the decline is stress and burnout resulting from putting in 70-hour workweeks. "What I'm seeing are programmers saying, 'To hell with it. I'm tired, I'm frazzled, and I'm not going to push as hard as I used to,' " says Yourdon, chairman of Massachusetts-based research firm Cutter Consortium.[37]

   a. Do you agree with the productivity measure used in this case? How would you improve this measure?
   b. What are some ways of improving programmer productivity?

3. **(Software and Web exercise)** Use the search engine Lycos and click on the link for "Entertainment" and then "Music." Pick any link under Music. Create a spreadsheet showing the choices available to users.

4. **(Software exercise)** You are a sales manager of a computer company. Customers get a 15 percent discount based on the total value of their purchases. Discounts are given to the customer at the end of every six months. If a customer is related to a store employee, he or she will receive an additional 3 percent discount. Using a spreadsheet, create five fictional customers, and show the dollar value of their purchases for each month over the past 6 months. Two of the five customers that you create must be related to a store employee. Show the total discount that the store gave to the customers over the past 6 months.

Case 1: "The Tao of Goo"

For the typical child, it's a plaything. For the disabled child, it opens a new, critical line of communication. The Baby Babble Blanket, brainchild of two Northeastern University professors, builds on the technology of musical greeting cards to allow infants to play digital recordings. It integrates simple hardware with innovative software. By twitching a muscle atop a specially wired blanket, babies activate supportive messages recorded by their parents.

Designed for babies who cannot wave an arm or kick a leg to elicit parental coos, the Baby Babble Blanket can also help any child develop understanding of cause-and-effect and motor movement skills. The blanket is wired with microswitches fed into a small switchbox in which a parent can record encouraging words, music, or any other pleasant sounds. By moving even slightly on one of the switches—say, by flexing a neck or buttock muscle—the infant triggers the recorded response. Harriet Fell, the computer scientist who developed the Baby Babble Blanket with speech pathologist Linda Ferrier, says it tested successfully with several disabled children. One 5-month-old boy with poor muscle tone, clubfeet, and hydrocephalus became more active when he learned he could roll over and hear his mother's encouraging voice. Another infant, who communicated mainly by screaming, became more at ease when he discovered how to trigger the sound of his dad's voice.[38]

1. What is the type of software (system versus application) used in this blanket?
2. Innovative software has the capability to make the world a better place. Comment.

Case 2: Gerber Takes Giant Steps

Gerber Products Co. is working with grocery stores to make sure their shelves do not ever lack for strained peas. But writing the required software left the baby food maker feeling a bit strained itself. Although this application-dedicated software was complex and difficult to develop because of its many functions and features, Gerber now has a successful software package that allows it to manage the inventory for 40 big grocery chains.

This is how the software works. Using networks, the grocery chains simply feed information on sales of Gerber products to the company. Gerber then uses its software package to schedule new deliveries of products to grocery chains, relieving grocery chains of the burden of managing inventory for Gerber products. Because different grocery chains have different information systems, Gerber's software program had to be equipped to read input from a variety of systems.

The software program is so successful that Gerber plans to triple the amount of inventory it manages for grocery stores. Of the $700 million worth of baby food Gerber sells in the United States each year, Gerber today manages around 27 percent. The company plans to manage 80 percent within two years.

Tightening inventory management is a top priority for cost-conscious retailers and their suppliers, said Ann Grackin, an analyst at Benchmarking Partners, a retailing consultancy in Cambridge, Massachusetts. "A store is one big sinkhole of inventory," she said. "You obviously want stuff to be available for customers to buy, but you don't want too much." Gerber does not charge for the inventory management service, treating it instead as a way to build customer loyalty and get sales data that can be used to fine-tune baby food production plans. "Forecasting and planning is where we think we can get a competitive advantage," Dennis Kline, an IS project manager at the company.[39]

1. Why is this an example of application-dedicated software? Why would an off-the-shelf software package not work in this case?
2. What are some reasons why building such software is a difficult and complex task?
3. What are some reasons why this software may give Gerber an edge in the marketplace?

Case 3: United Nations Faces a Formidable Task

When the United Nations General Assembly gathers its 184 member nations under one roof, the diversity of this world body is evident. But that united front crumbles in the computer room, where tracking down specific information on even one UN employee once proved formidable. "We once had more than 20 different systems between 20 and 30 years old that did not talk to each other, so we were not able to get updated information on employees and finances," explains Gian Piero Roz, an IS specialist for the UN Secretariat in New York.

Today the United Nations has an integrated management information system (IMIS), a sophisticated application software system that addresses financial and human resource information needs. Eventually, IMIS will be extended to Secretariat branches in seven other nations and to the United Nation's 20 or so peace-keeping missions worldwide, bringing the number of users to 2,100.

Mainframes in New York are used to store information on more than 20,000 U.N. employees, including payroll, cost-of-living allowances, and school costs. Employees had to manually search through multiple databases to find even basic employee-related information. The international scope of the United Nations made this work even more challenging. Consider that the accounting department of the United Nations administers an annual budget of $3 billion, encompassing 90 different currencies. Building a system to meet such diverse information needs was no small task.

One of the biggest advantages of the software is that it provides decision makers around the world easy access to consistent information that can be customized to meet local needs. U.N. organizations from one country can view and analyze data from other countries and assess the United Nations' overall operations. To accommodate users' varying technical skills, the system is highly user-friendly and flexible. In addition, users can customize the system to meet local requirements and regulations. So, for example, if hazardous duty pay in dangerous peace-keeping regions needs to be added to the payroll system, the entire program does not have to be updated or rewritten, only the local software module. This dedicated software is a boon for the United Nations.[40]

1. What are some challenges in building a truly global and complex financial information system?
2. Why is it important to provide consistent information to decision makers in different parts of the world? Why should software be customized to meet local needs?
3. What operating system features would you recommend for this application and why?

If data cannot be correctly understood, it cannot be combined with other information. Instead, it is just data pollution.

Ken Sloan, freelance writer, *Computerworld*

CONTENTS

USING DATABASES FOR SUCCESS

The Battle of Waterloo in 1815 between Napoleon's army and the Allied forces led by Great Britain launched one of the most ingenious stock market schemes in history. As legend has it, Englishman Nathan Rothschild planted contacts equipped with carrier pigeons across Europe, hoping to hear the outcome of the battle before any of his merchant banking competitors in London. When he received the first word on Wellington's victory over Napoleon, Rothschild dumped his British-backed government securities on the market, making it seem as though Britain had lost. Competitors followed his lead, dumping their securities too. When the market bottomed out, Rothschild bought back every security at fire-sale prices and made a killing. What made Rothschild tick? He understood the value of information.[1]

Information is a powerful decision-making tool. Remember that information is processed data. Databases, the focus of this chapter, are data reservoirs. For instance, almost all companies have a database of employee data, such as last names, first names, Social Security numbers, emergency phone numbers, and so on. Most companies also have a database management system (DBMS), which is software that helps users manipulate data in the database to retrieve specific information needed to make good decisions.

Databases contain organized information, a critical resource for individuals, businesses, and society in a world of information overload. Databases can help individuals with personal decisions. Say you wanted to research information systems jobs that offer a decent salary, a good location, and do not require a master's degree. A query to a database of employers would provide you that information quickly, resulting in a list of jobs that match those criteria.

When government organizations such as the U.S. Environmental Protection Agency (EPA) develop high-quality databases, society

Chapter 5

Database Design and Management

AFTER STUDYING THIS CHAPTER, YOU SHOULD BE ABLE TO:

- Explain how data are stored and managed in a database
- Describe a database management system (DBMS) and its components
- Outline how structured query languages affect decision making
- Describe data models
- Discuss data warehousing and data mining
- Explain how distributed databases help organizations

can reap the benefits. The EPA's pollution database has cut operating costs, increased employee productivity, and helped the agency achieve its mission of reducing pollution on a regional level.

The EPA's Environfacts Warehouse database system stores pollution data on more than 700,000 U.S. sites that handle potentially dangerous chemicals. The system, accessible through the World Wide Web (earth1.epa.gov), allows EPA staffers and the public easy access to the data—a vast change from the days when the data were housed in seven unconnected databases residing on a mainframe. Now

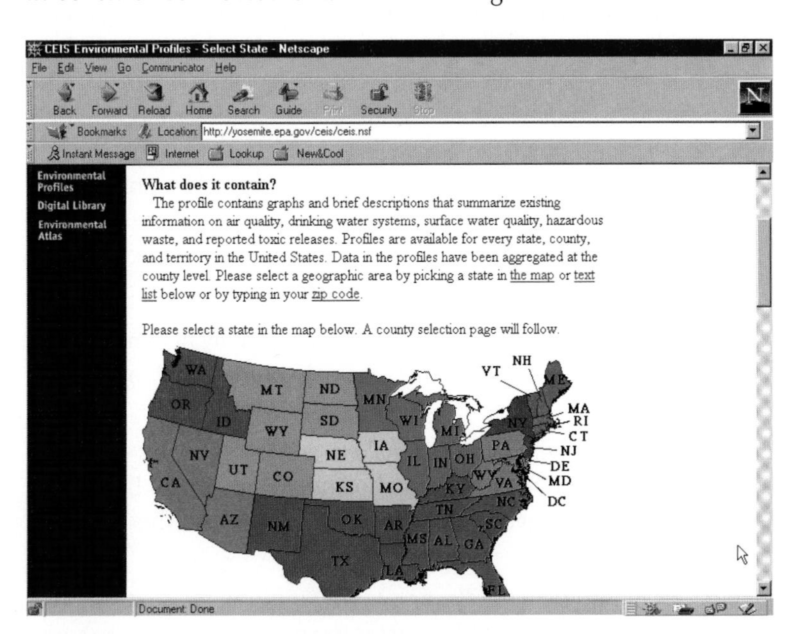

The Environfacts Web site offers interested citizens and EPA staff access to a database of 700,000 potential pollution sources.

TECHNOLOGY PAYOFF
Disney Won't Go Up in Smoke

Let's set the scene: The 911 line rings in the emergency dispatch center near Walt Disney World's Epcot Center in Orlando, Florida. Smoke has been spotted coming from the tea cups attraction. The dispatcher enters the caller's information onto a computerized screen and determines that firefighters should check it out. That's when a database application—a software program that manages data—kicks in to help the dispatcher figure out where the emergency is and whom to send.

Based on the caller's location and report, the database recommends how many trucks and which trucks from the area's three firehouses should respond. The database takes the incoming data, combines it with stored information (such as the materials used in the tea cups ride), and gives dispatchers recommendations about the necessary fire equipment and skill sets for firefighters dispatched to the scene.

Tracking 21,000 alarms and 10,000 fire inspections per year requires plenty of detailed data, notes Craig Loftin, manager of information services at the Reedy Creek Improvement District, the government authority that oversees Disney World. The rich database is vital for Disney to maintain its exemplary safety record and to respond immediately to any concerns that visitors may have about their safety.

Source: Stewart Deck, "Database Helps Put Out Fires at Disney," *Computerworld,* November 2, 1998, 57, 61.

Health care professionals such as these doctors rely on databases to help treat their patients.

concerned citizens can research potential pollution sources in their communities by company name, address, or ZIP Code in a matter of seconds.[2]

Businesses and professionals also use databases to make decisions, often to consumers' benefit. A database that connects physicians with pharmaceutical data is helping doctors treat cancer patients. Linking patients with new cancer drugs may seem simple, but without the database, doctors rely on their memory to match the right patient with the appropriate test for new and upcoming drugs. "It sounds bizarre when you tell people how things are done in health care, because it's so archaic," notes Dr. John Benear, President of Cancer Care Associates in Tulsa, Oklahoma.

Now physicians enter data about each cancer patient, including age, sex, overall health, and location and stage of the cancer into the database. The database then matches the patient and the appropriate drug test. "It's allowed us to participate in trials we wouldn't have otherwise found," says Benear, citing one patient who "would not be alive if she couldn't get into a research trial."[3]

Accurate, timely data are the backbone of good decisions, regardless of the kind of business. As we saw earlier, Disney World relies on databases to ensure the safety of its visitors. Managers decide on the price of a firm's product based on cost factors and market conditions, stockbrokers decide how and where to invest based on investment data, and bankers decide whether to approve a loan based on credit report data. In all these cases, data make the decision-making process more effective. Businesses, then, should create databases to ensure sound decisions.

Three key principles guide database creation and use:

- The main purpose of databases is to help a company become so fast, responsive, and useful to customers that it becomes the "company of choice."
- Databases should help decision makers assess how their decisions influence the overall health of the business. The typical byproduct is more committed involvement to the business and the decision-making process.
- Databases should deliver relevant, timely information in a way that meets users' needs. Information that is too much, too little, too soon, or too late will doom the communication process.

In this chapter we examine what databases are, how data are stored, the characteristics of effective data, and the relationship of data and decision making. We also explore how organizations use data warehousing, data mining, and distributed databases to improve decision making.

Storing Quality Data

To meet users' information needs, companies gather and store data in a database in an organized way that allows easy access to information. Gathering and inputting good-quality data are crucial to any database system. First, bad data lead to poor information, which in turn leads to poor decisions. Second, it is best to gather accurate data at the outset because time spent correcting data errors is unproductive and costly. "You must go back to the source system, examine not only the original data, but see how it is being pushed through the system," explains Richard Kachur, a consultant at NewThink, a database and Internet consulting firm in Calgary, Alberta. He adds, "From day one, people should be looking at data integrity and data movement. But they typically don't." The result can be huge and unnecessary losses for the company.[4]

To illustrate, let us say you were building a database on cars for sale. Alphanumeric characters, known as VIN numbers, would be critical data. One VIN number might read 0100HONDA09171000HIO4200118955. Once processed to produce the following output, the data become meaningful information for the car buyer.

MAKE	TYPE	YEAR	PRICE
HONDA	4 Doors	2001	$18,955

If one character in the VIN number is wrong, the processed information becomes unreliable. Having to search through thousands of VIN numbers to find the incorrect ones would be a tedious, time-consuming task.

The Data Hierarchy

Once gathered, the data are stored and organized in the database system. In a computer, data are organized in a hierarchy that looks similar to an organizational chart. The hierarchy in ascending order is bits, bytes, fields, records, files, and databases. Figure 5-1 shows the relationship between these elements.

To demonstrate how a data hierarchy works, imagine you work at a company that has just converted to new hardware and software. Employees are taking training courses from six outside companies to get up to speed. Your manager supervises 26 employees and is finding it difficult to track who has taken certain training courses, when, and at what cost. She has asked you to build a database to help her make better training decisions.

You begin by figuring out how to represent data in the computer. Recall that eight bits represent a byte and a byte represents a character (a number, a letter of the alphabet, and the like). Four bytes represent the name *Mary,* so the word *Mary* requires 32 bits (4 bytes × 8 = 32 bits). A **field,** which is a meaningful grouping of characters or bytes, is the smallest unit of data.

Field

A meaningful grouping of characters or bytes.

An employee's last name, first name, phone number, and the name of a training program are examples of a field. Fields (also known as attributes) are an important part of storing data because users can only retrieve data using a field name, such as "Last_Name." Suppose your manager wants to know the last names of all employees who were sent to a specific training program (Program A). She would retrieve the data using two field names: last name and name of training program. The value of the field called "Last name" could be Carter for Mary Carter.

Mary's last name, first name, Social Security number, phone number, and home address viewed together as one piece of data are an example of a **record** because it groups

Record

A group of interrelated fields that are viewed as one piece of data.

FIGURE 5-1

The Data Hierarchy

A partial credit card database consisting of files, records, fields, bytes, and bits.

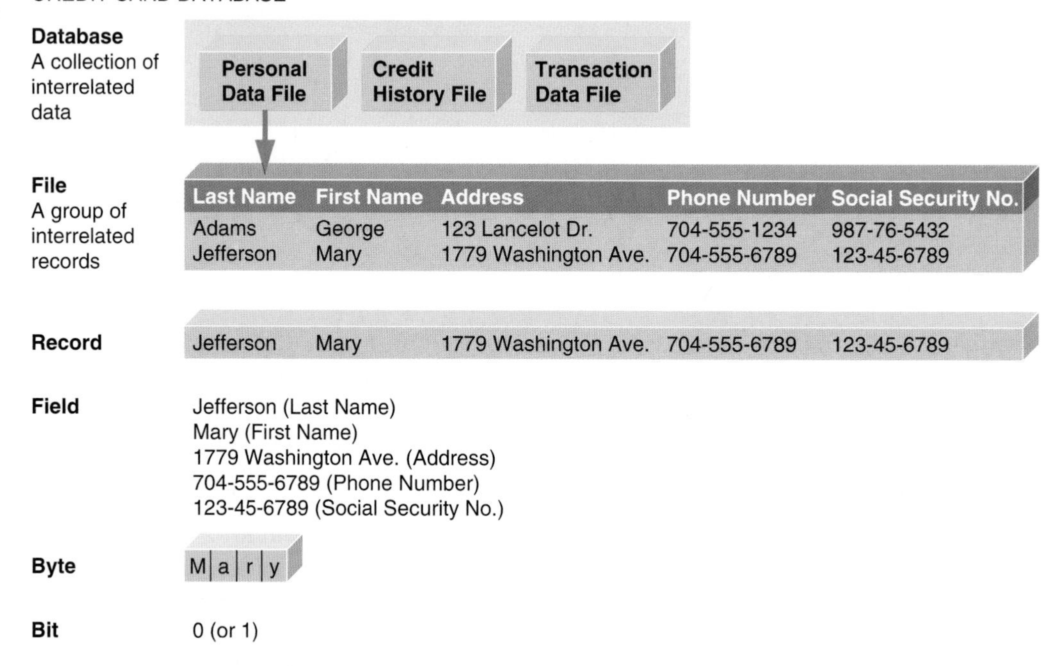

relevant data about Mary. In this example, you would have to build 26 records, one for each employee. You would input *values* into each field. For example, Mary's last name, Carter, is the value that is input in the last name field on Mary's database record. Once the values are input, a user simply has to look at a specific record to know its values. An example is shown in Figure 5-2.

Entity

A person, place, thing, or idea.

Attributes

Characteristics that describe an entity.

Primary key or key field

The field that uniquely identifies any given record in a database.

Another way to look at a record is to view it as a description of an object or **entity.** In our example, the 26 employees become the "EMPLOYEE ENTITY" and each employee becomes a record in that entity. To build a database you must identify all the entities about which you need to collect data. For your training database, employees are one entity and training companies are another. Once you identify the entities, the next step is to identify the records that make up the entity. There are 26 records of employees and six records of training companies.

Primary Keys

When storing data, we make sure users can retrieve data effectively by creating a unique identifier for each record in the database, known as **primary keys.** Social Security num-

FIGURE 5-2

An Example of Two Records in the Employee Entity

An entity consists of a set of records, such as Mary. Each record is described using a set of attributes or fields.

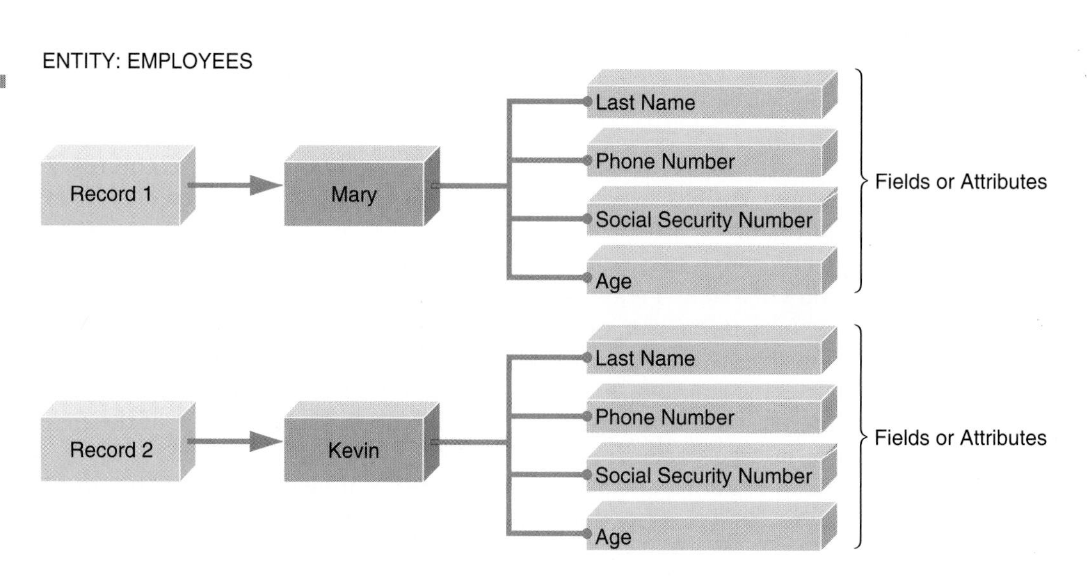

ber is a common primary key. These identifiers prevent confusion if, for instance, two employees in your department have the last name of Lambert. Users simply search by primary key to find the right Lambert.

A **file** is a collection of related records. Records of the 26 employees in your company are a file. Note that the records in a file relate to each other. For example, it would be meaningless to store employee records and the number of parking decals the company issues in the same file.

File

A collection of related records grouped together.

A collection of interrelated files is a **database.** Personnel data, employee benefits, and employees' salary files are a group of interrelated files that provide information about employees, so they are a database. In contrast, a combination of a business inventory file, employee benefits file, and suppliers' address files are not interrelated, so they would not be a database.

Database

A collection of interrelated files.

In summary, to design and develop a database we represent data and organize it in a hierarchy of bits, bytes, fields, records, files, and databases, where a database is data about a related set of entities (employees, training companies, and so on). Each entity has a set of records, each record is a group of fields, and each field has characters consisting of bytes. Next, we look at database management software that helps us to create, process, store, and retrieve data.

Database Management System

Before we examine the functions of database software, we need to explore what a database management system is. As we see in Figure 5-3, think of a **database management system** (DBMS) as a messenger between a user and the data in the database or between an application program and the data. The application program (such as a payroll program) communicates to the DBMS its data needs. The DBMS then gets the data (such as employee records) from the database and passes it back to the application program or to the user who requested the information.

Database management system (DBMS)

A group of programs that helps to create, process, store, retrieve, control, maintain, and manage data.

A DBMS also helps users query the database so that they can receive customized information to meet their unique needs. The ability to query and receive customized information is one of the biggest advantages of a database. Table 5-1 describes some DBMS functions.

As databases become large, even the most sophisticated database management system can become crippled. For example, Delivery Information Automated Lookup System (DIALS) is a large tracking database for United Parcel Service. The huge database is more than 1.5 terabytes (1,500,000,000,000) in size. One way to avoid unwieldy databases is to break the data into slices of 10,000 to 20,000 bytes, with each slice containing related data. However, the tasks of breaking data into slices and defining what a slice should be are difficult.

Database management systems are available for computers of all types and sizes—from supercomputers to handhelds. The National Football League uses databases designed for palmtop computers to help players manage their finances during their career, which on average lasts just 3 to 4 years, to provide future income. Former New York Giants player George Martin, now a marketing executive at New York–based

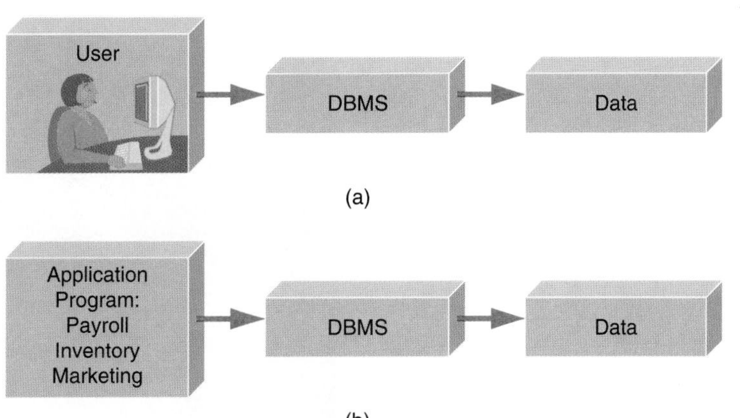

FIGURE 5-3

The DBMS Acts as a Messenger

(a) A DBMS helps the user interact with the data in the database. (b) A DBMS also links application programs to data in the database.

TABLE 5-1

Five Main Functions of a DBMS

Function	Description
Define, create, and organize a database	Establish the logical relationships among different data elements in a database and define schemas and subschemas using the data definition language (DDL).
Input data	Enter data into the database through an input device, such as a data screen, a touch screen, or a voice-activated system.
Process data	Process and manipulate data using the data manipulation language (DML).
Maintain data integrity and security	Limit database access to authorized users.
Query database	Provide decision makers with information they need to make dependable decisions. Query the database using structured query language (SQL).

investment company Mutual of New York (MONY), helped create an investment software for New York Jets players. Banks communicate the team's fund strategy to Martin, other MONY executives, and Jets players and management using a wireless network. The database of financial information ensures that Jets players can access the information they need to make effective money decisions.

Professional sporting scouts use databases extensively, too. The Seattle Mariners baseball team stores scouting reports about players on personal digital assistants (small handheld computers that individuals use to manage their everyday lives) and refer to that information during Mariners games, explains Benny Looper, the national scouting supervisor for the Mariners.[5]

Advantages and Disadvantages

Database management systems have two main advantages. First, they eliminate redundancy because businesses do not have to store the same data in different files or locations. Second, a DBMS provides data independence, which means that users can access the data they need without knowing where the data are physically located. Your boss could retrieve the records of all employees who had attended e-mail training without knowing on which machine or in which file that data are located. If data were moved from one machine to another, the programs that use that data do not have to be modified, nor is it necessary to notify users of the move. This independence makes it considerably easier to maintain databases.

The key disadvantage of a DBMS is the resources it requires. The hardware is often expensive. Plus, the cost of managing these databases and training users how to work

UPS employees collect data continuously to keep the company's database current.

Ethics for success

The Database Trail

Company databases are often used in lawsuits as evidence. As the government argued its antitrust case against Microsoft Corp., state and federal lawyers relied on sales and pricing evidence fresh from Microsoft's own databases. Lawyers for the U.S. Department of Justice and 20 states visited the vendor's Redmond, Washington, headquarters with a court order allowing them to examine sales data stored in the company's databases. Microsoft had earlier indicated that the databases were too complicated and proprietary to reproduce.

"By examining original data firsthand, the government gains more control," says Harvey Saferstein, an antitrust lawyer at Fried, Frank, Harris, Shriver & Jacobson in Los Angeles. For example, Microsoft claims it didn't charge some PC vendors more and others less for Windows licenses based on whether they also accepted Microsoft's Web browser. But if the government uncovered a query that tracks that very information, it could incriminate Microsoft.

YOU DECIDE

1. Do you think it is ethical for the government to study Microsoft's internal databases? Why or why not?
2. Simply because a company collects certain types of data doesn't mean it is unethical in its business practices. Do you agree? Discuss.

Source: Kim S. Nash and Patrick Thibodeau, "What's in a Database? Microsoft Sales Evidence," *Computerworld,* October 19, 1998, 4.

with them requires a substantial outlay of time and money. The Ethics for Success feature also spotlights another potential disadvantage: Records in databases may contain information damaging to a business.

Components

A DBMS has four main components that work together to make a powerful database: data definition language (DDL), data manipulation language (DML), the data dictionary, and reports and utilities. The DDL defines and creates the data, the DML helps to manipulate them, and the data dictionary keeps records of all data in the database. The reports and utilities component helps users generate and customize database reports. Figure 5-4 shows these components and functions.

Data Definition Language

The **data definition language** (DDL) helps users define the data in a database. It also helps users create the names of database files, identify different fields and what those fields should contain (such as text, numbers, and so on), and identify the default values of different fields (such as area code is always 402 for local phone numbers and so

Data definition language (DDL)
A DBMS language used to define data and relationships between data.

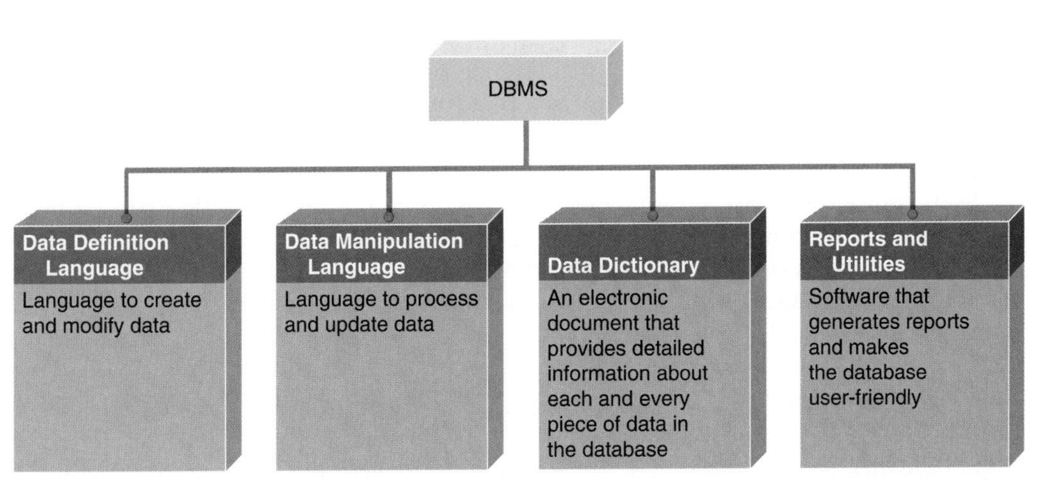

FIGURE 5-4
The Four Main DBMS Components

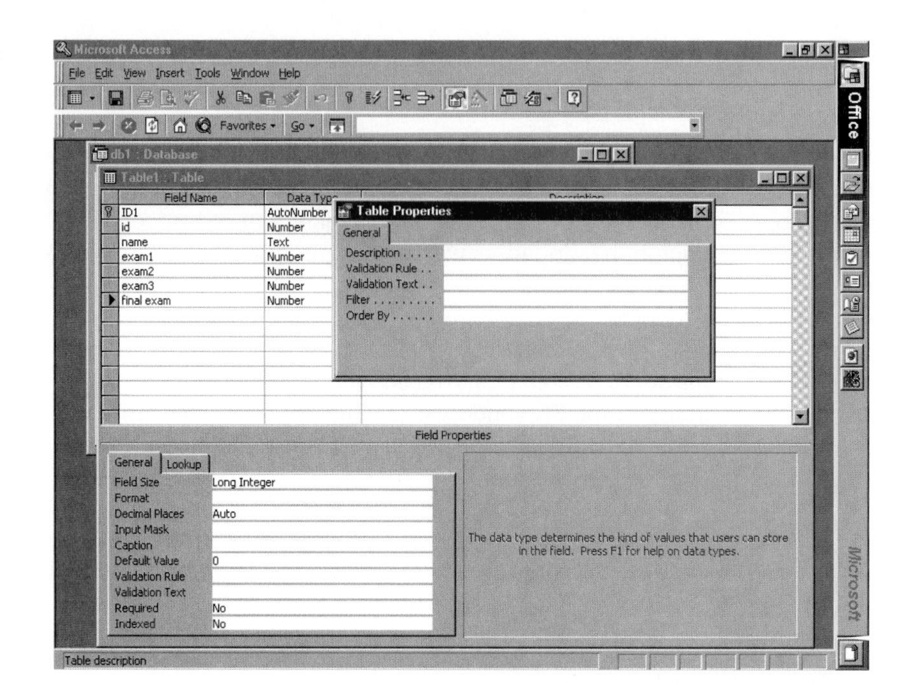

In Access, the data definition language relies on graphical user interfaces.

on). A default value is a value that automatically appears in a cell, such as "NY" for code for the New York City residents' cell.

A user also defines the relationship between different data elements using the DDL. For example, if a payroll program needs the Social Security number of an employee, the DDL defines the logical relationship between Social Security number and other data in the database—that is, it establishes that each employee has only one Social Security number. The DDL thus serves as the interface between the payroll program and the files that contain the Social Security numbers.

There are different ways to define data in a database. Data can be defined using graphical user interfaces or text commands. In Microsoft Access, the database management system shown in the screen shot, the DDL is a graphical user interface (GUI). In Oracle, a database package developed by Oracle Corporation, data are defined using text commands. In general, in PCs and single-user database environments, the DDL is usually based on a graphical interface whereas in mainframe environments, DDL is often text-based.

Data Manipulation Language

Data manipulation language (DML)

A software language that processes and updates data.

The **data manipulation language** (DML) is a software language that consists of specific commands to process, update, and retrieve data. The DML is usually integrated with other programming languages, such as 3GLs and 4GLs, which were discussed in the software chapter. This integration adds more features and functions to the database. Finally, because the information needs of users vary, it is important to be able to query a database and get specific answers using query languages.

Structured query language (SQL)

A language that deals exclusively with data, namely, data integrity, data manipulation, data access, data retrieval, data query, and data security.

Pronounced "SQL" or "see qwill," **structured query language** is a nonprocedural language used to query a database and get specific answers to user questions. It is a nonprocedural language in that you only have to tell it what needs to be done, not how it needs to be done. Originally developed by IBM for its mainframes, SQL is now an integral part of most databases.

SQL commands work interactively with a database. Sometimes they are embedded within a programming language, such as C or COBOL. Although the American National Standards Institute standardized SQL to bring some uniformity and consistency to the language, each database vendor often has its own version of SQL with some variations.

Users can ask two kinds of questions in SQL: static and dynamic. Almost all DBMS allow both types of queries. Users use static questions to do routine and standard tasks, so a static question can be used over and over again. Such queries are appropriate for generating weekly, monthly, and quarterly reports. Software packages that generate static questions are sometimes referred to as report writers. Dynamic questions are those unique to the decision maker.

Here are the four basic SQL operations:

1. SELECT
2. UPDATE
3. INSERT
4. DELETE

The SELECT statement allows users to query the database for specific information, while UPDATE, INSERT, and DELETE allow the user to update the data, insert new data, or delete existing data, respectively. Table 5-2 shows some SQL commands and their uses.

The following SQL query selects students whose GPA is greater than 3.5 (where 4.0 is the highest GPA possible) and sorts the information in descending order. The SQL commands are underlined.

```
SELECT LAST_NAME, FIRST_NAME<SSN, MAJOR
FROM STUDENTS
WHERE GPA > 3.5
ORDER BY LAST_NAME DESC
```

Mastering SQL can take years of experience and expertise and is difficult for users unfamiliar with database technologies. For example, Deere & Co. stored human resources information for more than 1,000 salaried U.S. employees on its mainframe, but users did not know how to use SQL to pose questions. To overcome this problem, Deere installed a language query tool that allows users to ask questions in plain English.[6]

"Corporate America's databases are rich in information that most mortals can't mine because they don't speak the language, typically SQL," says Aaron Zones, an analyst at Meta Group Inc. Aside from the language barrier, SQL can be imprecise, says Zones. "It's an imperfect language. You can say the same thing twice, and it will get different results."[7]

English language querying, also known as natural language querying, is one way to solve the problem. Consider the following two ways you might pose a relatively simply question to your database. "What were the sales of high-margin products last month?" versus this query:

```
SELECT[QUANTITY],[PRODUCT NAME] FROM ([LINE ITEMS] INNER
JOIN [PRODUCTS] ON [PRODUCTS]. [PRODUCT ID] = [LINE ITEMS].
[PRODUCT_ID]) INNER JOIN [ORDERS] ON [ORDERS]. [ORDER_ID] =
[LINE ITEMS]. [ORDER_ID] WHERE [PRODUCT MARGIN] = 'HIGH' AND
(MONTH [ORDER DATE]) = 4 AND YEAR ([ORDER DATE]) = 1998)
```

It is easy to see which method users would prefer. The relative simplicity of natural language query tools explains why they are becoming more popular.

TABLE 5-2

Common SQL Commands and Their Uses

Command	Use	Example
SELECT	Query the database for specific information	SELECT LAST_NAME FROM STUDENT (Select the last name of all students from the STUDENT table)
INSERT	Insert rows of data into a table	INSERT INTO STUDENT (Student_Last_Name, SSN) VALUES (Porter, 593_65_0000)
UPDATE	Used to change values in a column in a table	INSERT STUDENT SET LAST_NAME = 'NITSH' WHERE SSN = 593_65_0000)
DELETE	Used to delete records in a table	DELETE STUDENT WHERE SSN = 593_65_0000

A data dictionary, shown here, describes and manages every piece of data in a database. Why do you think it is so important?

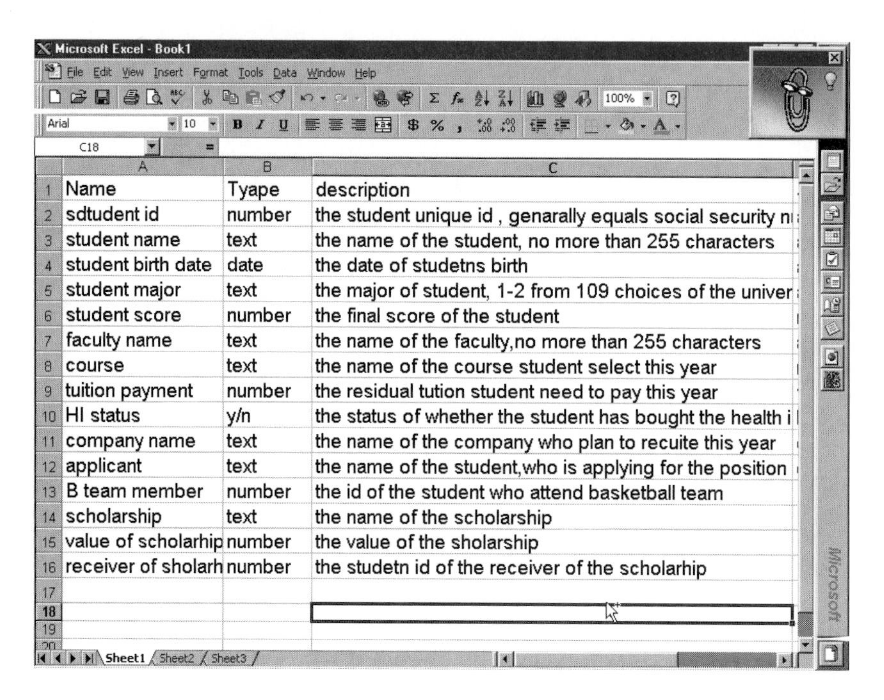

	A	B	C
1	Name	Tyape	description
2	sdtudent id	number	the student unique id , genarally equals social security n
3	student name	text	the name of the student, no more than 255 characters
4	student birth date	date	the date of studetns birth
5	student major	text	the major of student, 1-2 from 109 choices of the univer
6	student score	number	the final score of the student
7	faculty name	text	the name of the faculty,no more than 255 characters
8	course	text	the name of the course student select this year
9	tuition payment	number	the residual tution student need to pay this year
10	HI status	y/n	the status of whether the student has bought the health i
11	company name	text	the name of the company who plan to recuite this year
12	applicant	text	the name of the student,who is applying for the position
13	B team member	number	the id of the student who attend basketball team
14	scholarship	text	the name of the scholarship
15	value of scholarhip	number	the value of the sholarship
16	receiver of sholarh	number	the studetn id of the receiver of the scholarhip
17			
18			
19			

Data dictionary

An electronic document of every piece of data in an organization that acts like a database about an organization's data.

Data Dictionary

The third component in a DBMS, the **data dictionary,** describes, identifies, locates, controls, and manages each and every piece of data in the organization. The data dictionary ensures that data are defined and used uniformly and consistently, an essential ingredient of database success.

A data dictionary describes each piece of data in a business. It also describes in detail the characteristics of the data, which include the following:

- location of the data (in what file and machine the data are located)
- size of the data (how many bytes)
- range of acceptable values for each field
- type of data (number, character, audio, and so on)
- source of the data (where the data originated)
- usage (who uses the data)
- ownership (who has the right to view or modify the data), and
- methods for accessing and securing data.

Figure 5-5 depicts this information.

The data dictionary also identifies all the application programs that use a specific unit of data. If the characteristics of the data are modified, then the data dictionary will

FIGURE 5-5

Contents of a Data Dictionary

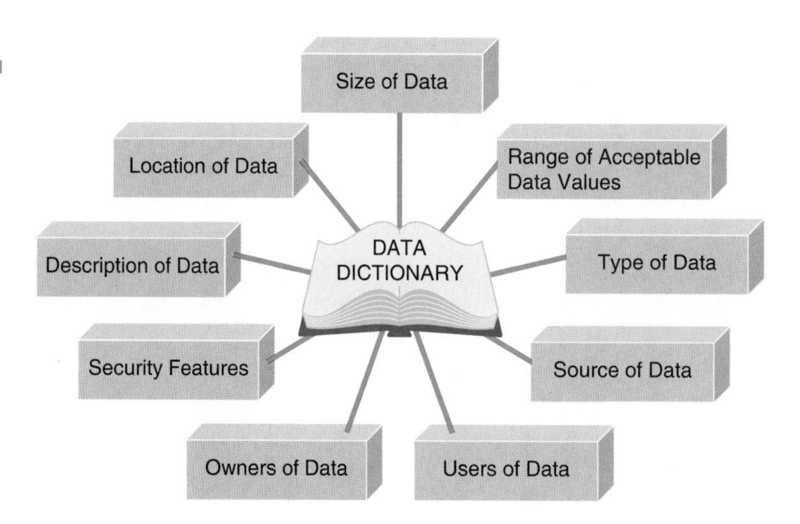

automatically identify the programs affected by the change. The data dictionary may be a stand-alone file or an integral part of the DBMS. An integrated data dictionary avoids update problems. When a change or update is made to the database, the data dictionary is automatically updated. Data are created, stored, and updated in the data dictionary using the DDL.

A good data dictionary ensures consistent definition of data across different databases and application programs. A poor data dictionary, or lack of one, can cause serious problems. For example, inconsistencies in a government data dictionary caused an accounting blunder during the 1991 Gulf War with Iraq. The term *submarine* was defined differently in various databases so decision makers were not able to get an accurate count of the number of submarines during wartime. A good data dictionary would have prevented this glitch.

Database experts stress that businesses should standardize both data terms and process terms in the data dictionary to prevent input inconsistencies. For instance, some years ago Aetna Life & Casualty Co. of Hartford, Connecticut, found that agents in different business divisions interpreted and processed the term *participant* differently, causing headaches for decision makers.[8] To one user, *participant* meant an individual whereas to another user *participant* meant a business customer. When top management needed some simple information about the company's customers and their profiles, confusion broke loose. By modifying the process data dictionary, the company took care of this problem.

Reports and Utilities

The fourth component in a database is reports and utilities. This module in the system helps users to generate database reports and customize them to meet their unique needs. The kind of utilities available in a database program may vary from vendor to vendor. Utilities refer to software programs that help with routine and repetitive functions of a database, such as creating backups, deleting old files, upgrades, system documentation, and so on. These programs can be shared by multiple users.

This section described the different components in a DBMS. The next section explores different views of data that help IS managers build effective databases.

Logical View versus Physical View of Data

Every database has two views: a logical and a physical view. A good analogy to distinguish these views is an automobile. Although many of us drive cars, few of us are well versed in the vehicle's intricate internal workings. The logical view of an automobile is what you see when you sit in your car and get ready to drive. You can see the gas gauges, the speedometer, the gears, ignition, and so on. How these things work or where they are located in the automobile is the physical view, which is probably not of much interest to an average driver.

Similarly, in the case of a database the **logical view** is data viewed from a user's perspective and the **physical view** shows the internal workings of a database. Figures 5-6 and 5-7 depict the logical and physical views of a database of classroom assignments.

Logical view of data

A view that shows the logical relationship(s) between different pieces of data in a database.

Physical view of data

A view that shows how and where data are physically stored in a storage medium.

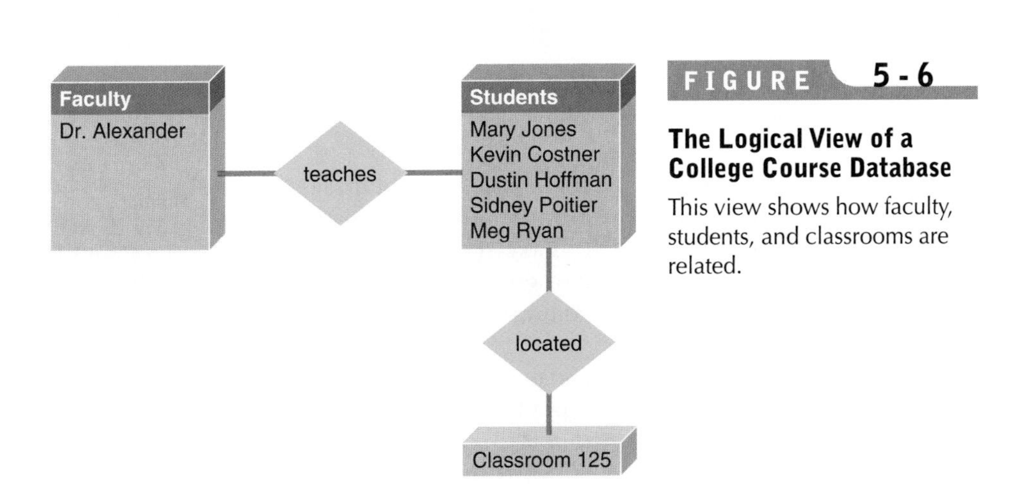

FIGURE 5-6

The Logical View of a College Course Database

This view shows how faculty, students, and classrooms are related.

FIGURE 5-7

The Physical View of a Database

This view shows where the data are stored in memory.

Physical Location	Filename
C:\Database\Student	Fall_Grades
Magnetic Disk D471	Payroll_Records98
Hard Disk A34	Customer Data
CD-ROM B36	Employee Digital Photos

Schema

A logical description of each piece of data and its relationship with other data in the database.

How does a database present the logical view to the user? It uses a **schema,** a textual or graphical representation that identifies each piece of data and its relationship with other data elements. A schema consists of the following:

- Name and description of the data (*Example:* customer name, credit card number)
- Type of data (*Example:* customer name is alphabetic)
- Length of the data (*Example:* name cannot be more than 20 characters long)

It does *not* identify the actual values of the data. A schema may show that Social Security number is related to an employee's name. However, it will not show the actual value of the Social Security number or the name of the employee. Figure 5-8 provides a graphical view of a schema. Schemas are usually generated using visual modeling tools and these tools, in turn, generate the code to represent the data and its relationships.

Subschema

A database subset that represents a user's partial view of a database.

A schema presents a logical view of the database—a picture of the entire "pie." A **subschema** is a subset of a database—a slice of the pie—that represents an individual user's partial view of the database, unlike the schema, which shows the entire database. A marketing manager, for example, may want to view only the marketing aspects of the database, so she views the marketing subschema.

Once the schemas and subschemas are defined, the DBMS automatically generates the placeholders in memory for this data. A placeholder is a place or a slot for holding the value of given data, such as a placeholder that stores the value of the last name of a customer.

We have just explored the physical and logical view of data. As a database gets larger, however, one of the challenges users face is to understand and visualize the relationships between all the different entities in a database, the subject of the next section.

FIGURE 5-8

Example of a Personnel Schema

SCHEMA NAME: PERSONNEL	
RECORD NAME: **JOBS**	RECORD NAME: **DEPARTMENTS**
JOB CODE	DEPARTMENT CODE
WAGE CLASS	DEPARTMENT NAME
JOB TITLE	MANAGER ID
MINIMUM SALARY	PROJECTS
MAXIMUM SALARY	BUDGET

Relationships: The Crux of Databases

Relationships link different entities in a database, so a database user must understand how those entities are interrelated. Suppose a veterinary hospital with five veterinarians hires you to build a new database to make sure the hospital has what its patients need. This database will have a number of entities, including pet owner, pets, office staff, suppliers, inventory, and so on. What are the relationships between these entities, if any?

Think about the nature of the relationship between pet and pet owner first. One pet owner may have many pets, but each pet typically has only one owner. What is the relationship between a pet owner and the veterinarian? Some hospitals may have a policy in which each customer is assigned to one veterinarian. In other cases, a patient may

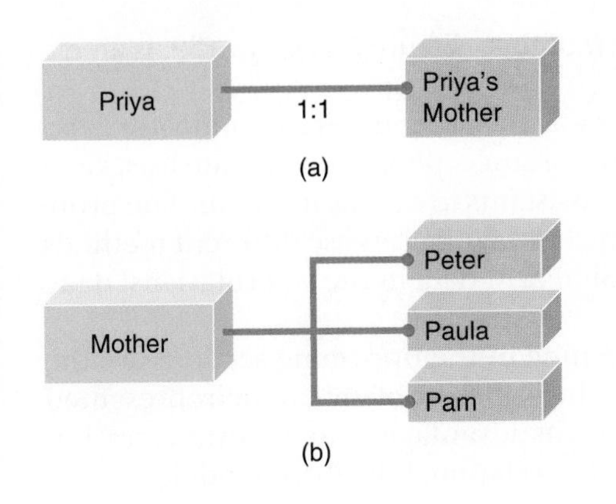

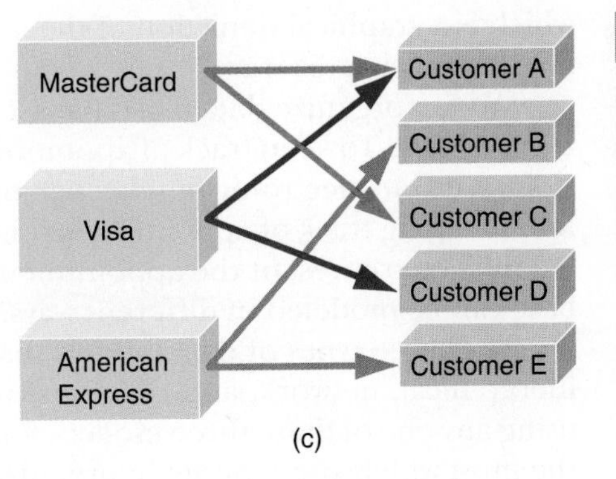

FIGURE 5-9

The Three Types of Relationships among Entities

(a) One-to-one. (b) One-to-many. (c) Many-to-many.

see whichever one is available. An understanding of these relationships provides the foundation for accurate data representation.

Let's look at three types of relationships between entities: One-to-one, one-to-many, and many-to-many, as shown in Figure 5-9.

If two entities have a **one-to-one relationship,** it implies that there is a one-to-one association between the two entities. The relationship between name and Social Security number is a one-to-one relationship because every individual has only one Social Security number. Table 5-3 shows additional one-to-one (1-1) relationships.

One-to-one (1-1) relationship

A relationship in which a unique relationship exists between any two given entities.

One-to-many relationships are common in organizations. Here are some examples:

- A mother can have many children but each child has only one biological mother
- A teacher has many students but each student has only one teacher for any given course
- A flight has many passengers but each passenger has only one flight number
- A customer can place many orders, but each order has only one customer

One-to-many (1-M) relationship

A relationship in which a given entity can have multiple relationships with other entities in the database.

In a **many-to-many relationship,** each entity has multiple relationships with other entities in the database and vice versa. Several examples of this type of relationship follow:

- Each airport caters to many airlines and each airline has access to many airports
- Each credit-card company has many customers and each customer may have many credit cards
- Each vendor may supply many products and each product may have many vendors

Many-to-many (M-M) relationship

A relationship in which each entity can be related to multiple entities and vice versa.

Many-to-many relationships cannot be represented in a database.

We have analyzed the different views and components of a database, schemas, and relationships among entities to help us better understand databases. In the next section we investigate data models, tools that represent data relationships so that the computer understands and implements them.

Data Models Help Represent Problems

A **data model** is a way to organize and represent data and the relationships between data. Let's revisit our veterinarian example for a moment. What is the best way to visually represent the relationship between the different entities so that the developer can accurately model the veterinarians' office? One way to do this is using an **entity relationship diagram,**

Data model

A model that describes how the data are organized in the database.

Entity-relationship diagram

A graphical tool that identifies and represents the logical relationships between entities in an enterprise or system.

TABLE 5-3

Examples of One-to-One Relationships	
A child and a biological mother	A President and a country
A VCR and a movie running in that VCR	An automobile and a driver
A course and the final course grade	A husband and a wife

which is a graphical depiction of the logical view of data. Figure 5-6, on p. 139, is an example of such a diagram.

We can organize data in a database in many ways by using different models to keep track of data. To keep track of appointments, for instance, people may create lists, keep a diary, use an electronic timekeeper, or rely on assistants to do this for them. The problem (keeping track of appointments) is the same but people can use different methods (models) to represent the appointment data. Similarly, data in the veterinarians' database can be modeled in different ways.

The three types of data models that we examine in the upcoming sections are the hierarchical, network, and relational models. The same problem can be represented using any one of these three models. Each one has its advantages and disadvantages, but the most widely used model in organizations is the relational database model.

Hierarchical Data Model

Hierarchical data model

A model in which the logical relationship between different data elements is represented as a hierarchy.

A **hierarchical data model,** illustrated in Figure 5-10, looks similar to an organizational chart. Each box in the hierarchical model is a record and the relationship between different records is referred to as a parent-child relationship. Each record in a hierarchical model can have only one parent (with the exception of the topmost record from which all other records originate). This makes it ideally suited to represent one-to-many (1-M) relationships, although other types of relationships can also be represented with some restrictions.

An example of a hierarchical DBMS is IBM's Information Management System (IMS) database package. The hierarchical model, used mostly in older mainframe-oriented databases, is ideally suited for problems in which the data elements have a natural hierarchical structure, such as a hierarchical organization.

It has several disadvantages. First, it is somewhat rigid because relationships between different data must be clearly identified *before* development begins to avoid adding a child or a new level in the hierarchy. This process is difficult because databases are highly dynamic. Second, to access data at lower levels, such as a student in Figure 5-10, users must access data at the top first and work their way down, a time-consuming process. Third, it cannot support users' ad hoc needs for specific information.

Network Model

Network model

A logical model that is well suited to represent many-to-many (M-M) relationships.

The **network model,** a variation of the hierarchical model, represents many-to-many relationships. Databases can be translated from hierarchical to network and vice versa. However, the network and hierarchical models differ in this way: A child can have mul-

FIGURE 5-10

A Hierarchical Data Model for a University

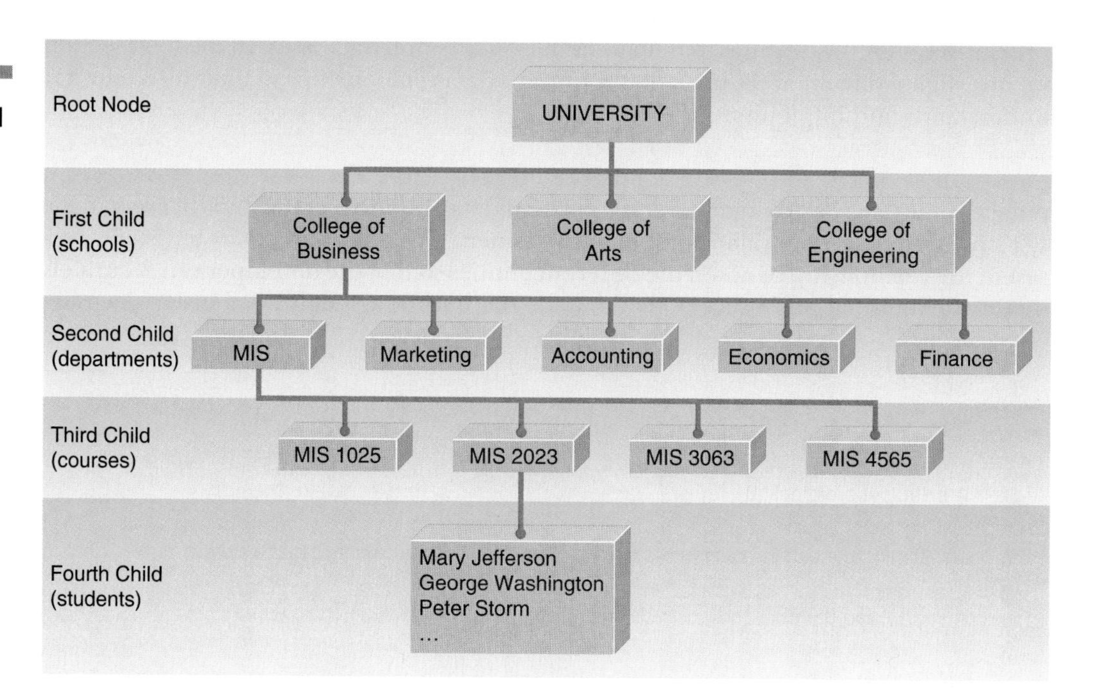

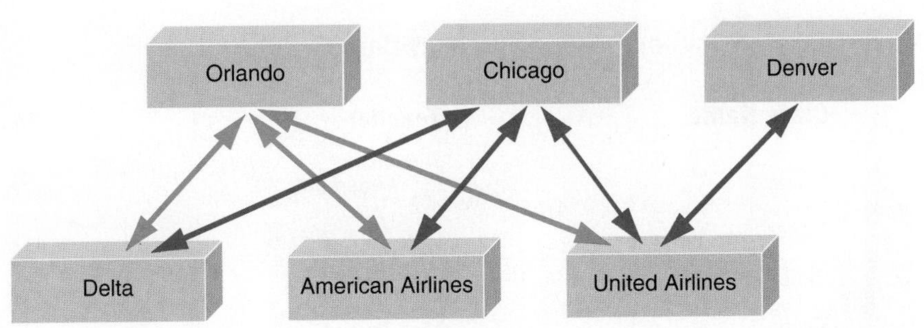

FIGURE 5-11

Network Data Model of Airports and Airlines

tiple parents in a network model, instead of only one parent, as in a hierarchical model. As we see in Figure 5-11, one parent (Orlando) can have many children (different airlines flying into Orlando). For example, Delta (child) arrives and departs from Orlando (parent), but it also arrives and departs from Chicago (parent). Thus one child can have multiple parents.

The network model is more flexible than the hierarchical model. However, it is complex to design and develop and must be fine-tuned often, which can make it tedious and time-consuming to use. As a result, the network model does not work well in dynamic environments where changes need to be made frequently. To make significant changes to the network model, the entire model has to be stripped and rebuilt, which requires significant programming. In addition, the network model cannot support on-the-fly information needs of users. An example of a network-based DBMS is Integrated Database Management Systems (IDMS), which is marketed by Computer Associates International.

Relational Model

The third and most popular type of data model is the **relational model.** Almost three decades ago, Dr. Edgar E. Codd, then a researcher at IBM Research Labs, published a paper that outlined the power of representing data in the form of tables. This seminal paper, in which Dr. Codd discussed the theoretical and scientific principles behind the relational model, eventually led to the model's development and widespread use.

Relational model
A logical database model that represents data using two-dimensional tables.

A relational model is based on relations. A *relation* is a table that satisfies three criteria:

1. Each cell in the table has one and only one value
2. Each row in a table is unique
3. All entries in a column must be of the same kind

Microsoft Access — Table1 : Table

ID1	id	name	exam1	exam2	exam3	final exam
1	600050	John	79	81	92	89
2	600560	George	82	64	92	83
3	600072	Peter	67	90	90	89
4	600091	Wang	91	96	91	99
5	600100	Linda	56	60	61	80
6	600101	Peng	81	88	78	90
7	600045	Eric	92	93	92	89
8	600076	William	89	97	92	91
9	600048	Todd	91	95	89	96
10	600039	Felix	69	92	93	90
11	600079	Jennings	90	78	93	91
12	600096	Henry	89	91	88	78
13	600089	Cindy	99	98	67	96
14	600100	Alex	97	90	89	69
15	600088	brenna	98	78	89	99
16	600099	Darcy	98	78	96	99
17	600007	Dave	90	78	89	90
18	600009	Nathan	89	88	86	78
19	600089	Ginger	88	99	99	98
(AutoNumber)	0		0	0	0	0

Record: 19 of 19

This relational table is from Access, Microsoft's database software program.

TABLE 5-4

A Relational Model Table for a Day Care Facility

Class Name	Teacher	Teacher's Aide
Pooh	Ms. Anderson	Mrs. Scoobee
Tigger	Mrs. Rodriguez	Ms. Costner
Rabbit	Mr. Dodge	Mrs. Rampart
Kanga	Mrs. Huang	Mr. Nahavandi

A table is made up of columns and rows. Each column represents a field or an attribute, and each row represents a record, also called a tuple. Each column has a unique name.

The relational model offers more flexibility than the other two models. Users can easily add, delete, or modify a table's contents. Also, users can query a table easily to obtain specific information. More important, unlike the network and hierarchical models, the relational model allows users to build relationships between entities and data elements "on the fly" instead of being forced to do this during database design.

To demonstrate how the relational model works, consider a day care facility where each of its four classes has a teacher, a teacher's aide, and a group of children. Tables can present this information easily and efficiently, as we see in Table 5-4.

The beauty of the relational model is that no matter how large or complex the information, it can be presented in a simple table format that is easy to comprehend. Relational databases have helped detectives track down people responsible for crimes committed decades earlier. A single bloody fingerprint left 23 years ago was stored as evidence in a murder case. The victim, Gerrit Weynands, was a 46-year-old Seattle timber salesperson who was shot during a 1973 robbery. Anthony Lowe was arrested on a drug-related charge long after the murder and fingerprinted. Those prints were added to a large law enforcement fingerprint database. When detectives reopened the Weynands case 23 years after the original crime, they ran the old fingerprint through the database. The detectives found a perfect match between Lowe's prints and the bloody print from the murder scene. The relationship between the two prints was decisive evidence that led to Lowe's murder conviction.[9]

Note that there is a difference between relation and relationship. A relation is a table that satisfies certain criteria and conditions. A relationship shows how two or more entities (entities are represented as table or relations) are related. Relationships between tables can be easily established as long as the two tables (or files) have at least one attribute or field in common. (For example, "last name" is an attribute.) This simple yet powerful idea has made the relational model almost a database standard.

This model has great flexibility and accessibility. Users can retrieve data from multiple tables easily and can generate *ad hoc* queries to find answers to specific questions. Further, programs that rely on the relational databases can be easily integrated with other programs such as word processing, spreadsheets, and even the World Wide Web. Some popular programs include Microsoft Access, dBase IV and Paradox by Borland, and IBM's DB2. Finally, many relational databases come with excellent user interfaces and powerful features.

However, the relational model has drawbacks. It is slow compared to other data models, as it has to access data from different tables. This slow speed can become tedious, particularly for large databases. Hardware and software advances are helping to overcome this limitation. Another disadvantage of large relational databases is its data redundancy (data duplication) because the same data are likely to be stored in several tables.

In the day care example, the teacher's names also have to be stored in a student table that shows the teacher for each student. While some redundancy is necessary and unavoidable, large redundancies can slow down the database and hog memory. Despite these drawbacks, relational models continue to grow in popularity, as the Global IS for Success feature shows.

Global IS for success

B&V Goes High Tech

Twenty years ago, Black and Veatch (B&V) was a modest-sized engineering firm struggling for a piece of the U.S. domestic marketplace. Today, the $1.4 billion, 83-year-old firm based in Kansas City, Missouri, is a global force, competing with world-renowned engineering firms. It controls 30 percent of the domestic and 24 percent of the international construction and engineering market. The key difference between yesterday and today? Powrtrak, a custom-built relational database that helped the company gain a competitive advantage.

P. James Adam, the company's current chairman of the board, started developing Powrtrak in 1979. Adam was stymied by the amount of paperwork that the company generated for internal use and to comply with laws and regulations. He visualized a single information system that stored all this information and provided easy access to everyone who needed it, both internally and externally. "I described the concept to the technical staff, who came back and said that what I wanted was a relational database," he recalls. His staff told him that the model was easy for users with nontechnical backgrounds to understand and could be changed as business conditions change. Also, because it is one of the most widely used industry models, it would have strong support from vendors.

At any given time, Black & Veatch oversees hundreds of projects worldwide, each consisting of up to 250 people, 40,000 documents, 8,000 activities, and $1 billion in installed cost. Before the database was built, all this information was stored in separate, segregated files, and was unavailable to multiple users. Today, this information is kept in a central database that can be viewed in whatever form the user needs: document, drawing, or three-dimensional model. Further, through Powrtrak, project teams have access to the most current version of a design or schedule. The database is also updated continually and is accessible via the Internet and satellite to remote users anywhere in the world.

Since its initial rollout in 1983, B&V has used Powrtrak for nearly 500 projects, each worth over $100 million in value. The company has benefited from the database, which coordinates all key elements in a construction project and keeps everyone up to date with the latest data, thereby reducing cost overruns by $100,000 to $500,000 per project. Further, data access means project managers can estimate the length and cost of a potential project accurately, so B&V has been able to bid for jobs more aggressively.

QUESTIONS AND PROJECTS

1. User acceptance is one of the most critical issues that affect database system success. What are some measures that you would take to gain user buy-in when introducing a new database?
2. How can a system, such as Powrtrak, provide competitive advantage? Do you think B&V could have achieved market success without Powrtrak? Why or why not?
3. What are some intangible benefits that the database provides?

Source: Adapted from Tom Field, "Reengineering the Engineering Business," *CIO,* February 1, 1998, 40–42. Reprinted through the courtesy of CIO. © 1998 CIO Communications, Inc.

One problem that plagues all data models is the size of the database. As databases increase in size, they become more difficult to manage. One way to handle this growth is to use data warehouses, the focus of the next section.

Data Warehouse

Data warehouse

A large database that is a collection of smaller databases containing useful data designed to support decision making.

Imagine a warehouse that contains a large number of items from which you can pick and choose to make good decisions. That description is the essence of the **data warehouse,** a database that is often a collection of other databases, as shown in Figure 5-12.

What are the similarities and differences between a database and a data warehouse?

1. In many, though not all cases, data warehouses are significantly larger than databases because the warehouses are often a collection of meaningfully interrelated

FIGURE 5-12

The Data Warehouse

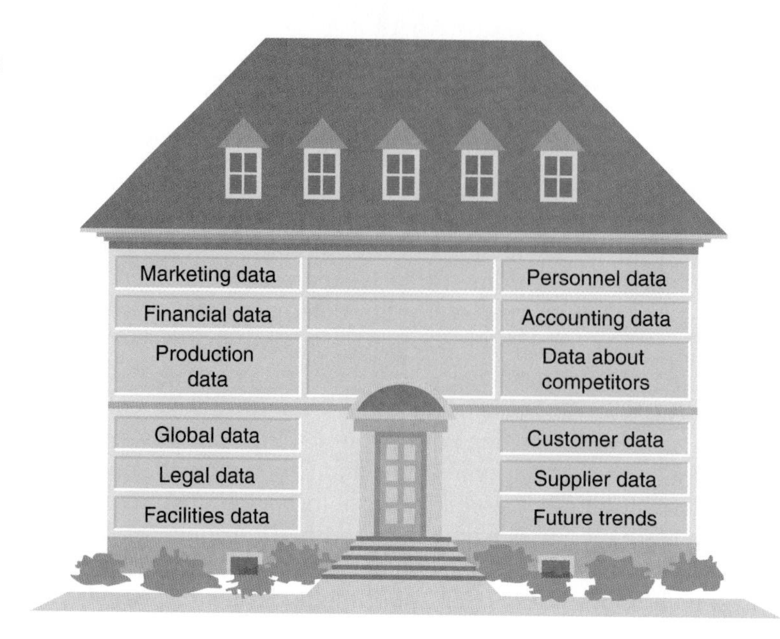

databases. By bringing together all relevant databases in one central warehouse, the user can pick and choose among a variety of data.

2. Databases are often updated frequently, some even instantaneously. Data warehouses are not. Data warehouses are often an archive of databases, so data are collected over a certain period of time and then the warehouse is updated. Data warehouses, then, are unsuitable for applications that require up-to-the-minute data such as an airline reservation system that must be updated within a few seconds after a customer books a seat.
3. Like databases, data warehouses support fast on-line queries and quick summaries for managers.
4. Data warehouses are ideal for large volumes of data because the software that supports them is designed to hold sizable amounts of data.
5. Databases are usually organized around a department, say public safety, or around a function, say marketing. Data warehouses, in contrast, are often designed to gain a view of the entire organization.

Data mart

A subset of a data warehouse that provides data about a specific function or department.

When a data warehouse is organized for one department or function, it is called a **data mart** rather than a data warehouse. Executives at Houston-based Pride International, a $1 billion on- and offshore drilling contractor, uses a data mart system to track the financial performance of its entities and the productivity of its drilling equipment. Pride needed the system because it had no easy way to gather and analyze information from the 15 companies that it has acquired during the past 4 years, explains Pride CIO Yvonne Donohoe.[10]

A data warehouse offers several benefits. First, decision makers can gain access to company-wide information quickly in summary form. Second, users see a broader view of data and how those data affect the organization, so it is ideal for applications that forecast sales, growth, or the financial health of an organization. Third, it allows users to "drill down" into several layers of data to locate a problem or an opportunity.

To illustrate the drill-down process, suppose you work for a health care organization as a regional manager responsible for 11 health care centers. You are interested in the number of patients the region's health care centers treated. After you review the data, you are puzzled by the performance of new Health Care Unit 8. You also decide that you want to review how a new hire, Dr. Chong in Health Care Unit 11, did last month. A data warehouse can drill down through the layers of the database for more detailed information about Unit 8 and Dr. Chong.

Tools that help users to drill down and get specific information are also known as on-line analytical processing (OLAP) tools. Because a data warehouse contains summaries of different data, such databases can respond to queries quickly. A relational OLAP, or ROLAP, tool extracts data from a traditional relational database.

Many health care organizations are investing in data warehouses. Kaiser Permanente, based in Oakland, California, is building a national prescription data warehouse that will hold data from 113 regional pharmacy systems and three claims-processing systems to track and manage drug use. New York Care Plus Insurance Co. is also developing a data warehouse that combines financial and administrative data. The warehouse will help the insurance company develop and price new health plan products more efficiently. St. John's Medical Center, a 570-bed hospital in Tulsa, Oklahoma, is building a data warehouse that will automatically detect drug interactions and notify doctors of procedures that an insurance policy does not cover.

Many physicians are skeptical of some data warehousing applications that may interfere with their medicine, notes Keith Fraidenburg, director of education and communications at the College of Healthcare Information Management Executives, an industry group in Ann Arbor, Michigan. "But I've also seen some highly successful data-warehousing applications," Fraidenburg says. For instance, some systems let doctors benchmark their patient ratio with other doctors in their area. "That's really valuable to them because in addition to being physicians, they are also running a business."[11]

Although the idea behind a data warehouse may seem simple, building and maintaining one are anything but. A number of hardware and software elements must mesh to build a data warehouse, including computers, networks, operating systems, database management software, and software to interface with other application programs. In a world where technology often changes in unpredictable ways, data warehousing decisions can be daunting. "Unless you can guess all the technology pieces you're going to need—and you will not be able to—you've got to be flexible," says Sam Alkhalaf, senior vice president of technology and strategic architecture at MasterCard, a company that has built several cutting-edge data warehouses.

The task of maintaining a data warehouse is also difficult because data usually lead to a demand for more data, causing the warehouse to grow. Such growth can increase

Careers for success

Architects for Data Warehouses

You will find a number of high-paying, challenging careers in databases, such as database administration, database programming, and database security. An emerging database career area is data warehouse architecture. A data warehouse architect, like a building architect, designs the structure of a data warehouse.

Data architects look at the hardware, software, networks, and user interfaces that must be brought together in a meaningful way to build a successful warehouse. They have intimate knowledge about databases, database design, relational models, programming, how people use data to make decisions, and how the different pieces in a data warehouse work together. The best architects also understand how to use data warehouses to solve business problems.

Many information systems professionals are jumping into data modeling and data warehousing as a natural next step to hone their technical skills. "Any kind of company that can use some kind of math tool for data manipulation can benefit from data warehousing," says Ken Taylor, a business analyst at The Berkshire Group, a financial services company in Boston. Taylor says he was attracted to the challenge and newness of data modeling work. "You're always in project meetings, and you're doing something new and challenging. You're starting from scratch, where you get to do a lot of re-engineering, process flow design and that sort of thing."

Cliff Calderwood, a business information services specialist, observes that data modeling professionals tend to be near the top of the IS pay scale and are in high demand. Calderwood says that he's "heard $2,000 a day quoted" on the contracting side.

How do architects get their training? Although they can take a course, "you get the bulk of your training on the job. . . . You either learn from your peers or you learn by actually getting involved in it."

Source: Kerry Lee, "The Darlings of Data," *Computerworld,* December 22, 1997, http://www.computerworld.com.

maintenance costs rapidly. To avoid needless cost, the company should train employees to assess what data they truly need to make effective decisions.[12]

Sometimes a data warehouse can become so complex that metadata—data about data—are necessary to maintain the warehouse. Metadata are a set of facts about data and other elements in the warehouse, such as where the data came from, what happened to that data on the way to the warehouse, and what business definitions or formulas apply to it. "Our warehouse architecture is so complex that we consider metadata to be the glue to hold it together," notes a manager of the data management group at the Royal Bank of Canada.[13]

Data Mining

Of what use is a warehouse if you cannot find what you need when you need it? Just as gold miners looked for gold by digging through layers of soil, data mining experts search through data warehouses to find the data they seek. This search can sometimes be as hard as digging for gold. Meaningful data are often hidden in relationships between different data, relationships that the naked eye cannot detect. Data mining software automatically searches through a data warehouse to locate specific data. Data mining experts also develop tools so users can more easily find data in a warehouse.

Data mining

The automated analysis of large data sets to find patterns and trends that might otherwise go undiscovered.

Data in a data warehouse that cannot be found when needed by a decision maker are useless. **Data mining** helps decision makers automatically detect patterns and trends that may otherwise go undetected, a process that can be as valuable as gold. From predicting responses to a new musical CD to identifying the most effective advertising campaign, data mining helps decision makers leverage data for organizational success.

Chase Manhattan Bank used data mining to assess its minimum balance requirements. The mining results? Increased profits and stronger customer service.

Chase Manhattan Bank in New York used data mining to understand the needs, preferences, and behaviors of its customers. Data mining revealed that customers who have difficulty maintaining a minimum balance may take their business to competitors with lower minimum balance requirements. Once customers take their accounts elsewhere, they stop buying other products from the bank as well. In response, Chase reduced required minimum balances in customers' checking accounts for two consecutive years.

Specifically, Chase used data mining to find answers to questions like, How many checks do customers draw per month? Do they use ATMs or conduct most of their business with tellers? And what other accounts and products do they hold? Chase determined who their profitable customers were, estimated how to set the minimum balance to retain them, and saw its profits rise.[14]

Although these questions may sound like traditional database queries, they are not. Unlike queries that retrieve relevant data to select questions, data mining tools search for patterns that may not be obvious to the naked eye. In simple terms, the primary job of query tools is to retrieve relevant data, whereas the primary job of data mining tools is to search for patterns. Searching and identifying patterns are challenging intellectual tasks because you should first identify the key variables that may produce unique insights into the business. If the wrong set of variables is chosen, the data mining tool may not be able to find a meaningful pattern. Dick's Supermarkets has carefully chosen its variables to gain better insights about its customers' shopping patterns. "It has made us smarter about our customers, smarter marketers—and made us more efficient in our marketing and merchandising investments," says Kenneth L. Robb, senior vice president of marketing.[15]

At Bank of America, customer service representatives—equipped with customer profiles gleaned from data mining—pitch the most relevant new products and services to their callers. A customer in a certain age group who has children and a home equity loan with the bank is a good candidate for taking out a student loan. Data mining helps the bank identify such customers.

"Data mining is a powerful technology, but it's not magic," says Herb Edelstein, cofounder and president of Two Crows Corp., a data mining consulting firm based in Maryland. "It doesn't sit in your computer, find things in your databases and tell you what to do with them." Instead, managers and users should know how to use data mining tools, when to use them, and how to interpret the results. Ultimately, no tool can replace human intuition and judgment. It can only enhance and strengthen these skills.

Although data mining offers significant business benefits, decision makers should be careful not to violate any privacy laws when they obtain detailed private information about their customers. The Sabre Group, the leading software vendor for travel agents, received strong and stinging criticism for its plans to build a vast data warehouse of its travel reservation information. The company was planning to use data mining tools to obtain specific information about travelers and then sell some of the data to outside organizations, such as resorts, hotels, and restaurants. The value of the data is large: Fifty million travel reservations pass through Sabre's system each day.

"This has to be one of the most remarkably insensitive and naive proposals I have ever heard," thundered one writer in a post on the rec.travel.air Usenet newsgroup. "A commercial firm with no contractual tie to fliers [only to airlines and travel agencies] plans to routinely market private information about the travel plans and personal preferences of individual citizens who fly."[16]

Sabre's plans to sell private information about travelers without the customer's knowledge raised several concerns. First, customers could receive a barrage of unsolicited sales contacts. Second, unscrupulous companies could resell the private information to others. More important, Sabre would profit at the expense of innocent customers.

Jennifer Hudson, spokeswoman for Sabre in Houston, disputed the charges of privacy violations. "[W]e do not sell passenger names or other private information to third parties without the consent of the passenger, and have no intention of doing so in the future." Hudson added that Sabre complies with all privacy regulations in the United States, the European Union, and the rest of the world and will continue to do so.[17]

Many groups argue that privacy laws are deficient because the rights of consumers to protect their data are limited and ambiguous. Dave Banisar, staff counsel at the Electronic Privacy Information Center in Washington, notes: "There's a clear need for the consumer to have some kind of enforceable rights rather than being left at the whim of [a] company over what will be done with their personal information." Companies that use data mining should be sensitive to privacy issues or risk customer dissatisfaction.[18]

Distributed Databases

Distributed database

A database distributed over computer hardware located in different geographical areas.

A **distributed database** system manages the entire system as if it were a single database. Assume the same company data are stored in different locations. With a distributed database system an update to one database results in automatic updates to the other databases. Ideally, a distributed database user in a given location can access any database on any hardware located anywhere on the network.

Although the phrase *distributed database system* conjures images of thousands of pieces of data being transmitted over a network, the goal of a distributed database is quite the opposite. Its purpose is to *localize* the data and the processes that operate on those data in the location where it is most meaningful.

There are several ways to distribute data, as shown in Figure 5-13. For example, a central database can be divided into smaller databases. Each of the smaller databases can be stored in the most relevant location. Alternatively, the central database can be replicated and stored in various remote locations, giving multiple, yet duplicate, copies of the same database. One method is not necessarily better than the other; the choice depends on the nature and type of application, number of users, frequency of data use, and other situational factors.

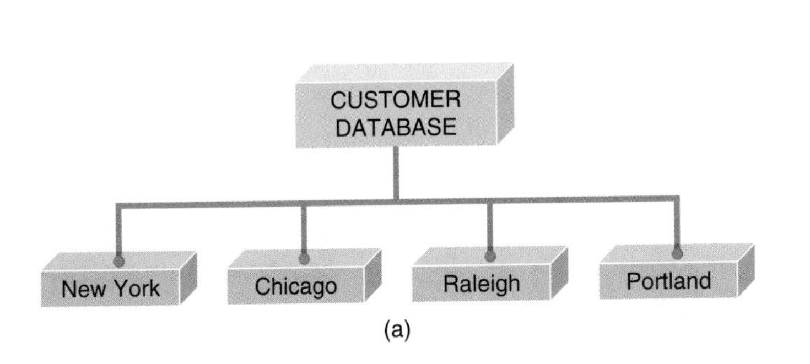

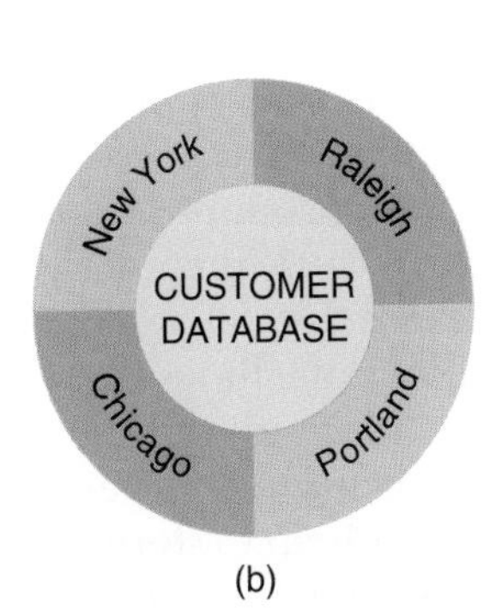

FIGURE 5-13

Different Ways to Distribute Databases

(a) Duplicate copies of the customer database in different locations (b) Dividing a customer database and locating portions in relevant locations

Tupperware relies on distributed databases to connect its far-flung employees and keep track of its global operations.

Let's look at a company that relies on distributed databases for its global success. Tupperware Corporation, maker of plastic containers, works solely through direct sales, having pioneered the idea of the party demo where an agent persuades someone to host a small gathering at home. This simple process has allowed Tupperware to grow to a multinational corporation operating in more than 100 countries and with annual revenue of $1.4 billion.

But not so long ago, according to Richard Henchoz, marketing services director at Tupperware in Europe, the Middle East, and Africa, the company's information systems were failing to keep up with the business. The core problem: The database systems could not produce useful information from the mass of data Tupperware gathered. Managers did not know who was selling what, where, or when. "Everyone had their own little database, which they'd built up in their own way. Half the time, you could never discuss on a rational basis what the real facts were because everybody had different views," says Henchoz.[19] Also, product managers were not informed about products.

Tupperware is close to solving its data problems and may save millions of dollars a year due to a distributed database that keeps accurate records of sales and other related data. This database is distributed to each country where Tupperware has regional offices. Independent regional distributors collate sales data from weekly demos or parties and upload that data via modem to keep everyone abreast of company activities.

The database also gives accurate data about top products, which is "a real hit with product managers, who have statistics for the first time," reports Henchoz. The new distributed database has improved inventory management by about 20 percent. Henchoz estimates Tupperware will save between $40 million to $60 million a year as a result. The system is likely to be adopted soon by Mexico, Canada, and five countries in the Far East.[20]

Distributed databases have become popular for two reasons. First, in the early years of computing many organizations created individual databases for different applications such as payroll, personnel data, and employee benefits. Many of these databases cannot communicate with one another because they were created on different systems or because their design is so different. Distributed databases overcome this problem because they allow a database developed on any machine to be duplicated and stored on other machines.

Second, different units of a business may be geographically dispersed, so the information needs and demands of each location are likely to differ. Distributed databases help to store the data where they are most needed or used and help to customize the data to meet the needs of individual business units.

Advantages

Distributed databases promote a sense of ownership, foster accountability, and provide a meaningful way to allocate operating costs of computing to different business units in the organization. In a distributed environment, although the CIO may retain control over the enterprise data, end users are responsible for updating and maintaining their local databases.

Distributed databases also help to minimize the impact of system failures because at least part of the network is always operational. For example, suppose a database is duplicated and stored in four different cities: Toronto, London, Tokyo, Omaha, and Portland. If the machine in Portland were to fail for some reason, the other four sites are still up and running.

Disadvantages

Distributed databases have four main disadvantages. First, they disseminate company information in a way that makes it hard to manage, coordinate, and control. Many organizations have a large number of PCs with valuable corporate data stored on them. Once data are distributed, they are difficult to centralize it again. Second, distributed databases typically give a large group of users access to proprietary data, so security risks increase.

Third, the tools required to efficiently manage distributed databases are still in their infancy, which means that managing distributed databases is terribly hard. Vendors are just beginning to develop sophisticated distributed management tools that can meet the needs of corporations. Fourth, backing up data can become an arduous task. In nondistributed environments, data are backed up in one location. In distributed environments, they have to be backed up in multiple locations and synchronized with the central database, if necessary.

Business Guidelines for Database Management Success

Databases are a powerful technology that can be the "wings to success" for an organization or its rapid demise and downfall. Why? All decisions require data. The ability to see value in data and to use them in innovative ways plays a key role in business success. This section offers guidelines for designing and maintaining databases that create a competitive advantage.

Use the Database to Improve Decision Making

Timely, relevant data are the cornerstone of all good decisions. Although many companies collect mammoth amounts of data, few put them to good use. British Airways, once dubbed "Bloody Awful" because of its dreadful customer service, used its database to make more timely, effective customer service decisions.[21] Service representatives used to take 12 weeks to respond to customer complaints. This poor customer service resulted in more than $600 million in lost revenue. The company realized that it had to improve its customer relations to survive in the competitive airline industry.

Along with establishing new performance standards, better rewards for employees, and extensive employee training, the company invested in a database that helped highlight customer complaints so that a manager could act on them promptly. A former 13-step investigation process was reduced to five meaningful steps: listen, apologize, express concern, make amends, and record the event. The database kept a detailed record of all complaints, which were then passed on immediately to the person accountable for taking appropriate steps to address the grievance. The database also helped managers locate problem areas and fix them. The airline was better able to pay attention to specific flights or locations that had more problems than others.

Professor James Cash of Harvard University points out that invaluable data lie hidden in any company's "complaint iceberg."[22] By carefully analyzing data and taking appropriate action a company can win and keep customers, thereby creating a competitive edge.

Recognize That Databases Are Competitive Weapons for All Businesses

Databases can help a company compare its strategies to those of its competitors. In many cases, companies are delving into public databases with a fine-toothed comb to find valuable competitive information. Competitive intelligence, the ability to closely monitor your competitor's strategies and next moves, is a growing field that relies on internal and external sources of data. More than 50 percent of Fortune 500 companies have competitive intelligence programs, estimates Leonard Fuld, president of competitive intelligence consultancy Fuld & Co.[23]

Databases help companies dig up vital information on archenemies. The means are legal, the data are accessible, and the returns can be stunning. The competitive intelligence group at SmithKline Beecham Corp. solved a mystery that could have proved disastrous if left unsolved. First, data about rival Bristol-Myers Squibb Co. indicated that it was planning to increase 200-fold its harvest of the pacific yew tree, whose bark is used to produce the experimental anticancer drug Taxol. Second, SmithKline Beecham tracked advertising databases that showed a sharp rise in the number of Bristol-Myers recruitment ads for oncologists in cities where the company had experimental cancer clinics. Third, financial analyst reports revealed that Bristol-Myers planned to step up oncology group funding.

When the competitive intelligence team at SmithKline pieced together the clues, it became apparent that Bristol-Myers was planning to substantially accelerate its development of Taxol. Sure enough, the company filed its application with the Food and Drug Administration 18 months earlier than outsiders had predicted. By then, however, SmithKline had accelerated the development of its own anticancer drug. "Because of the competitive intelligence, our project team was able to respond much more quickly than ordinarily," says Wayne Rosenkrans, who headed competitive intelligence at SmithKline's research and development group at the time. "It meant we didn't lose 18 months."[24]

Design the Database to Meet Users' Communication Needs

Database developers must remember that the purpose of a database is to communicate useful, valuable information so that people can make better decisions. That means the information has to be simple and accessible to everyone involved in the decision. David Clarke, Chief Information Officer at W. L. Gore and Associates, in Newark, Delaware, says that the emphasis has to be on communication rather than data transmission. For example, Clark's team doesn't think of a database management system in the traditional way. Instead, he explains, "We think of it, literally, as a communications system"[25] All database decisions at W. L. Gore are tied to one key question, "Does it help the company to communicate better with customers, employees, and other stockholders?"

Just like W. L. Gore, businesses should make sure their focus is on communicating information to decision makers in a way that supports their customers, employees, and stockholders.

Show Decision Makers How Their Choices Affect the Business

Databases enable decision makers at all levels of the business to see how their decisions affect the entire business. Motorola, one of the largest manufacturers of computer processors, integrates the company's marketing, finance, accounting, human resources, quality control, and production databases so that all managers can see how their decisions affect the company's well-being. Further, in each division all data are tightly coordinated and updated so that each employee knows what colleagues are doing.

Use the Database to Become Consumers' Company of Choice

For the past decade, CIOs have considered aligning IS and corporate goals as their top challenge. This challenge affects the design, development, and maintenance of databases. A company that quickly learned the value of aligning business strategy with its database is Daimler-Chrysler. In the early 1990s the company found that its sales volume had dropped by more than 40 percent over a 5-year period. A piecemeal approach to understanding and meeting customer needs was at the heart of the problem.

The company quickly developed and integrated its databases to support its business strategy of providing outstanding customer service. When Steve Liebhoff, the owner of a Mercedes-Benz 560 SEL, got a flat tire in midtown Manhattan, he used his car phone to call Mercedes' nationwide 800 number. By accessing the customer database, the customer service representative could address Mr. Liebhoff by his name and note that he had owned several Benzes. Within 20 minutes the representative had a service truck arrive to help Mr. Liebhoff. The database helps build customer loyalty.

Plan for Appropriate Security

The days of seeing IT systems as vaults and dungeons of information hidden from customers and employees has ended. These days, database systems are more like ticket takers at the football stadium: They make sure no one is coming in armed or with malicious intent. Many private databases are now open to anyone with a Web browser who can pass the security check at the turnstiles. A database with valuable data must be guarded.[26] Businesspeople must plan and budget for appropriate security and expect to upgrade security as technology improves.

Plan for Database Maintenance

Designing and developing a database is only half the job. The other half is to maintain the database so that it continues to meet the needs of end users. Database management and maintenance can become a tricky and time-consuming issue as business conditions, the needs and expectations of users, and technology change. But Wayne Rosenkrans, now competitive intelligence coordinator at Zeneca Pharmaceuticals in Wilmington, Delaware, cautions, "Some companies build the mother of all databases, and two things happen. First, no one is there to feed it, so maintenance becomes a nightmare. Second, it's so poorly focused, there are a jillion things in there, most of which are worthless, and there's no one to figure out what's good."[27] Managers, then, must allocate resources for database management and maintenance even as they think about building databases.

SUMMARY

1. **Explain how data are stored and managed in a database.** When data are processed, they become information. However, the accuracy and reliability of data depend on the data quality. Poor-quality data, no matter how well processed, result in unreliable information. A database is managed by ensuring that the quality of data in the database is accurate and timely and that all processes for analyzing the data are sound and error-proof. The database hierarchy in descending order is files, records, fields, bytes, and bits. A field is the smallest unit of data and a collection of related fields is a record. A set of records is a file and a set of meaningful and interrelated files is a database.
2. **Describe a database management system (DBMS) and its components.** The DBMS is the heart of a database and is responsible for the accessing, processing, managing, and maintaining data. A DBMS is used to define, create, organize, process, maintain, and secure data. The four main components in a DBMS are the DDL, the DML, the data dictionary, and reports and utilities. The DDL helps users to define the data and their structure and the DML is used to process and update the data. The data dictionary is a database about data in the organization and plays a critical role in ensuring the consistent use of data terms in an organization. Reports and utilities help users generate and customize database reports.
3. **Outline how structured query languages affect decision making.** Structured query language is nonprocedural language that is used to query a database and get specific answers to user questions. SQL commands can be used to work interactively with a database or they can be embedded within a programming language. Users can ask static or dynamic questions. Static questions are routine, standard questions that, once defined, can be used over and over again. Dynamic questions are *ad hoc* questions.
4. **Describe data models.** A data model is a logical organization of different entities in a database and its relationships with other entities in the database. The three data models are the hierarchical, network, and relational models. The most popular data model is the relational model, in which data are represented using two-dimensional tables. The entity-relationship diagram is a graphical tool that helps to capture the logical design of a database.
5. **Discuss data warehousing and data mining.** A data warehouse is a large database of relevant data that are closely tied to decision making. A data warehouse allows decision makers to analyze information that is summarized and presented in multidimensional views quickly. It is ideal for applications such as trend analysis on sales and financial information and for "drilling down" into several layers of data to locate a problem or an opportunity. Although the data may not be up-to-the-minute, the data warehouse supports

fast on-line queries and quick summaries for managers. Users can find data using data mining tools.

6. **Explain how distributed databases help organizations.** A distributed database is a number of databases distributed over different computers in different geographic locations. This allows a user access to any database on any hardware platform that is located anywhere on the network. There are several ways to distribute data, such as dividing a central database into smaller databases that are then stored in the most relevant location. A central database can also be replicated and stored in various remote locations.

KEY TERMS

REVIEW QUESTIONS

1. Why are data considered so important to a business? What are some consequences for organizations that may not realize the value of data?
2. Databases are all about effective communications. Comment.
3. GIGO stands for "garbage in, garbage out." How does GIGO apply to databases? Refer to the example on Envirofacts. How critical is good data in that system?
4. A fitness club has a membership database. Give an example of a field, a record, and a file in that database.
5. What is a primary key? Why do databases need a primary key?
6. What is a DBMS? What are its four main components? What is the difference between DDL and DML?
7. What does SQL stand for and what are its uses? Would you buy a database package that does not have SQL? Discuss.
8. What is a data dictionary and why is it an important and valuable tool for organizations?
9. What is the difference between the logical view and the physical view of data? What is one way to represent the logical view?
10. Define a schema and a subschema and give an example of each.
11. What is a data model? What are the three popular data models and what is the nature of the relationship (1-1, 1-M, M-M) of the data elements in these models?
12. The owner of a video store would like to develop a data model of her store. The model should reflect the relationships between movies (name of movie and videotape number of the movie) and customers (customer name, address, phone number, and account number). Develop a data model for this problem.
13. What is data warehousing? What is a data mart? What are some of the benefits of data warehousing?
14. What is data mining? How did data mining help Chase to retain existing customers? What is the difference between data mining and querying?
15. What are some principles of data mining?
16. What is a distributed database and when is it useful?
17. What are some guidelines for successful databases?

DISCUSSION QUESTIONS AND EXERCISES

1. A significant problem in databases is poor data quality. The time spent checking and fixing data errors can take its toll on productivity. Some organizations spend between 30 percent and 40 percent of their IS time on data correction and revision. The CIO must take the lead in ensuring that data quality is never compromised. He or she must convince and educate all employees that corrupt data have far-reaching implications. Make a presentation asking top management to invest in a $100,000 training program to educate employees about the value of clean data.
2. Congress is considering providing protection for databases created from publicly available information, such as data generated by various departments in the government, public records, such as birth and death certificates, and other public data. Data that are available to the public cannot be copyrighted, so unscrupulous individuals and organizations can use them to their advantage.

   The Collections of Information Antipiracy Act, sponsored by U.S. Rep. Howard Coble (R-N.C.), would allow companies and database providers to bring suit against a party that used a database to adversely affect the party that first created the data. Without this legislation, companies may lose their interest to compile valuable public information, says Dan Duncan, a vice president at the Software and Industry Association in Washington.

   For example, Doane Agricultural Service Company in St. Louis, Montana, assembles an Agricultural Forecast database from raw government data and could lose its edge if other companies manipulate Doane's database without compensating the company. However, Charles Phelps, the provost of the University of Rochester in New York, opposes the law as being "overly broad" and contends that it will "impede the core academic activities of research and teaching."[28]

   a. Would you support this law or oppose it? Why?

   b. What are some measures by which a company can protect its investment in its databases?
3. The IS staff at Federal Express creates, manages, and maintains several hundred databases that keep track of seven million packages per month, or 21 percent of FedEx's total deliveries. To complicate matters, managers from various departments require answers to customized queries on a regular basis. For example, the marketing department often wants specific information about a recent promotion or advertising campaign, while production wants information on the efficiency of new automated equipment. "This can feel like rush hour on the interstate," writes Patrick Thibodeau, freelance writer on technology issues at *Computerworld*. One way by which companies are addressing this problem is to encourage end users to create their own reports. There are a number of Web-based tools in the market that allow end users to tap into a database and create customized reports. One such tool is Web Focus, by Information Builders.[29]

   a. Do a one-page memo on tools that allow users to create their own reports.

   b. What are the advantages and disadvantages of this approach?
4. (**Software exercise**) Suppose you are the IT manager of a record company. Information about your employees is given next:

Name	Age	ID	Title	Join date	Department
George	46	0076	Supervisor	94/5	Sales
Frank	42	0057	Representative	97/3	Sales
Cindy	29	0089	Secretary	98/6	Advertising
Johnny	34	0090	Representative	97/2	Sales
Jackson	56	0079	Supervisor	94/3	Advertising

   a. Use the previous information and create a table called EMPLOYEES.

   b. Create a report that shows the ID and employees' ages.

   c. Present the information just shown, but in ascending order of date of employment.

   d. Create a query to search by which you can search for employees by their first name.
5. (**Software Exercise**) Refer to Discussion Question 4. The salaries of each employee are given next. Create a new table called SALARY.

ID	Salary
0076	$67,000
0090	$45,800
0079	$65,000
0057	$44,000
0089	$42,000

   a. Present the salaries in ascending order.

   b. Give each employee a 10 percent bonus. Create a separate column to show the bonus and a column that reflects their total salary.

   c. Create a query to find all employees who make more than $60,000

Case 1: Fraud Busters

Physician, police thyself. You may have helped heal thousands, but if you've gotten greedy in the process, your indiscretions may catch the eye of a no-nonsense former New Jersey State trooper named Louis Parisi. Vice president of fraud investigation and detection for Empire Blue Cross and Blue Shield (an independent member of the Blue Cross and Blue Shield association) in New York City, Parisi used to patrol his beat in a cruiser with a gun. Now he uses a PC and a data mining program. And, thanks to the technology, Parisi's aim is true.

Take the case of Dr. Leon Cantor, a Long Island ear, nose, and throat specialist. Over a 9-year period, he cheated a number of health insurers, including Empire, of more than $1.4 million. He did this by billing for bronchoscopies—an invasive respiratory procedure that is normally done only once or twice in a lifetime for those who need it—at the rate of as many as one per patient per week. Parisi caught up with him early in 1996, and Dr. Cantor served time in a federal prison in Lexington, Kentucky. Cantor has paid $58,000 in fines to Empire and turned in his medical license.

"Could we catch these people without computers? Sure, but it would take a lot longer, and we'd catch a lot fewer people," says Parisi. Manning the tackle at Empire is Parisi's 70-person fraud squad of auditors, analysts, and investigators. This team scours Empire's claims databases, mining for peculiar patterns in bills submitted not only by physicians but also by skilled nurses, pharmacists, physical therapists, and other licensed caregivers.

They uncover leads by running queries through IBM Corp.'s Fraud and Abuse Management System (FAMS). The software separates routine billing patterns from unusual ones by profiling the bills against one another and checking for aberrant patterns that have pointed to fraud in the past. It automatically flags potential indicators of fraud, such as how often providers perform various diagnoses and therapies vis-à-vis their peers in the same city. And it gets more street-smart by the day: Every successful investigation means more patterns are incorporated into the system, and are automatically flagged the next time they appear.

"My people are very enthusiastic about using technology because they like the results," Parisi says. "They have everything they need to make a difference, and it's only getting more sophisticated." Last year, the crew recovered—or held onto before paying—$38.5 million. This year the savings will easily top $40 million.[30]

1. What are some measures that you would take to prevent false charges?
2. If the database becomes too large, what are the steps that can be taken to make it more manageable?
3. (**Software exercise**) Create a table in any database showing how medical claim frauds have increased between 1995 and 1999. Identify an entity and its attributes in this database. (The following data are fictional.)

	New York (in billions)	Number of cases	Chicago (in billions)	Number of cases
1995	$1.2	212	$1.4	154
1996	$1.5	145	$1.3	121
1997	$1.6	120	$1.8	111
1998	$1.7	68	$1.6	129
1999	$1.9	123	$1.8	212

Using a spreadsheet, display the data graphically.

Case 2: Staying in Touch

Bad weather spurs a flurry of in-flight telephone calls from one-time or occasional callers, but the people who make up the bread and butter of GTE Airfone's business are travelers in business and first class heading cross-country or between continents. That is just some of the information GTE Airfone in Oak Brook, Illinois, is uncovering with its new data mart. GTE is using the system to better target its customers and improve service. The analysis is based on the credit-card information gathered when customers' place calls.

"In the past, we implemented new marketing promotions and weren't very well targeted, and [so] we didn't get much payback," explains Shekar Vengarai, senior advisory systems engineer at GTE Airfone. "The air traveler requires specialized marketing programs, and to achieve success, we need access to accurate, timely data." About 100 gigabytes of data about customers now rests in the data mart.

The data, which are customer's credit-card numbers, are pulled from GTE's billing system. From that informa-

continued

Case 2: Staying in Touch, *continued*

tion the company can pinpoint which travelers are using the system, their average income, age levels and other useful marketing information. Once GTE Airfone has the user's name, it can find out if the person is a member of frequent-flier programs and attach special telephone-use offers to the mileage packages.

GTE Airfone is not stopping at using its new data mart simply to find new marketing opportunities. The company also uses the information to monitor the quality of its service. That is being done by letting "dirty data" (data is from partial records with incomplete or missing data) show the phone calls that did not go through properly. The so-called dirty data are flagged in the billing system and sent on to the data mart. GTE's business analysts use the data to improve the quality of service. For example, the data can be used to see if a particular plane has a high number of incomplete calls, which could signal a problem with the system.[31]

1. What is the role of "dirty data" in enhancing customer service?
2. How can databases help companies get a bigger bang from their advertising dollars?

Case 3: No Place Like New York

New York City has cleaned up the way its financial information travels. New York City's Department of Finance and its Department of Information Technology and Telecommunications (colloquially known as DoIT) have collaborated on a digital infrastructure for the city's complicated system of revenue collection. Developed by the Department of Finance's System Architect Alfred Curtis, the database (called the City Agencies' Management Information System [CAMIS]) has become the city's best advocate, diplomat, and public relations machine. It helps business owners pay licensing fees and fines on time, lets city workers quickly record fine payments, and even simplifies law enforcement agents' hunt for criminals. CAMIS has allowed New York City to maximize revenues and untangle its massive bureaucracy at the same time.

At the Department of Consumer Affairs (DCA), which collects fines and fees from practically every business in the city, employees depend on CAMIS to keep track of payments for the hundreds of New Yorkers who visit the office every day. The department once held boxes of uncashed checks—all lost revenue for the city—because the workers could not post payments fast enough to keep up. Now it takes less than a minute to post a check and record its receipt, and it is easy for employees to do—so easy that the database captured the attention of other departments within the city.

Employees from all parts of the city's infrastructure have access to the database. Health inspectors use it to plan their restaurant visits, and municipal workers post every payment of fines and licensing fees in the system. But CAMIS also keeps all the city departments in communication with one another. When a change in the record is typed in at the licensing office in lower Manhattan, every city employee from Queens to the Bronx can see it. "You can search for information using any scrap of data," Curtis says. Just punch in any distinguishing characteristic of a business—its name or the owner's name, a number relating to a violation, complaint or business license, or even something as vague as its neighborhood—you'll get the history of its dealing with the city. Says one system user: "If you, as a business owner, tell us your address, we can tell you how much you owe in about a second." A business's status is not available only to city government officials, either. The moment anyone applies for a license or permit, or receives a citation or a complaint, that information becomes available to any interested party. The city's integrated voice response system, accessible through a touch-tone telephone, reveals how much debt a business has, the status of its license, and when all of its payments were received and posted.

There are 30,000 terminals in the Big Apple, and they can all be connected to CAMIS. About 500 people use the application routinely. CAMIS can hold 32 million records per file—about eight times its current volume—so it's capable of dishing up data as fast as city agencies can generate them. When someone submits a query to the database, response time is almost immediate. If you were to divide information technology into degrees of difficulty, organizing the city of New York would rank high on the scale, just on the basis of the city's size. As CAMIS expands and becomes more citywide and less agency-specific, city employees will be able to manage the city's affairs the way good businesses manage theirs: accurately, fairly, and securely.[32]

1. Is CAMIS a distributed database? If so, why do you think it is distributed?
2. Is the database aligned with the city's business strategy? Explain.
3. Is there a potential for any ethical violation in CAMIS and if so, what measures would you take to close any loopholes?

Part 3 The Telecommunications Revolution

Bandwidth is going to be the silicon of the 21st century.

Gigi Wang, senior vice president, International Data Corp.

CONTENTS

TELECOMMUNICATIONS FOR SUCCESS

Today it is easy to "reach out and touch someone," no matter where that person lives. Information, created at a rate that is 200,000 times faster than the growth of the human population, can easily be accessed and delivered usually in a few seconds between any two points on the planet. Human ingenuity and the development of computer technology have made telecommunications, the technology that allows us to electronically transmit data and signals from one computer to another, one of the most powerful technologies of our times.

We see the power of telecommunications in our personal and professional lives and in society. Automated teller machines (ATMs), airline reservations, live broadcasts, remote health care, and distance learning are made possible through telecommunications. Coffeehouses in San Francisco have set up a telecommunications network called SF Net to link patrons of more than a dozen cafes. Using computer screens and keyboards in coffeehouse tabletops, patrons pay 50 cents for 20 minutes of electronic conversation with others in similarly equipped coffeehouses. Conversations are arranged by topic, including politics, books, and philosophy.

Many business organizations around the world could not survive without telecommunications. Take Kmart, a company that relies on telecommunications to manage its inventory and respond to customer needs effectively. Employees in the retail stores use small devices that have a keyboard, a display monitor, a bar-code scanner, and a radio unit to collect detailed data about customer reactions to store items. They then transmit the data to a central computer at Kmart's headquarters in Troy, Michigan.

The backbone of tomorrow's "knowledge power," telecommunications is an agent of change so powerful that it dictates corporate

Chapter 6

Telecommunications and Networks

AFTER STUDYING THIS CHAPTER, YOU WILL BE ABLE TO:

- Describe the basic components in telecommunications
- Explain telecommunication protocols
- Discuss channel providers and their function
- Describe different types of telecommunication media
- Identify different types of telecommunication networks
- Explain key telecommunication applications
- Summarize what a global network is and its effects on business

management styles and shapes business trends. Telecommunications is helping General Electric Co. (GE) build an effective learning organization—an organization in which employees learn continuously because the company shares information openly. GE is passionate about sharing and learning. "Sharing [our] best practices [with everyone] in this company is a religion, " says Mark Mastrianni, manager of technology at GE's corporate offices in Fairfield, Connecticut. "If you are a CEO in GE and you mention, 'We've developed a great new business procedure,' the chairman will first ask, 'Who have you shared this with?' People who hoard an idea for personal glory simply do not do well at GE."

Learning organizations are often built on telecommunications. Such an organization demands that any employee located anywhere in the world can communicate or access information that helps others learn. The organization typically has a culture of "boundarylessness," which means that whatever one person knows, everyone knows. GE Chair and CEO John Welch says, "At GE, you are as well regarded for borrowing a best practice as inventing it."[1]

General Electric's CEO John Welch advocates a corporate culture in which people use telecommunications to share knowledge with colleagues.

TECHNOLOGY PAYOFF

Liz Claiborne Goes Fashionable with Global Networks

What do you do if your Manhattan fashion model can't fit into a factory sample garment that just came from Hong Kong? If you're the apparel and accessories giant Liz Claiborne, information systems can provide an answer. Liz Claiborne faced a problem similar to that of other U.S. garment makers. Designs originate in the United States but production is often farmed out overseas, making product timing and quality a challenge. Plus, trimming cycle times cuts down on excess inventory and allows more time to concentrate on new fashions.

In addition, Liz Claiborne needed to curb declining profits. According to company officials, the company had stagnated, both in design work and business practices. The time was ripe for change. But how? Liz Claiborne's management team developed a potential answer called LizFirst.

The LizFirst project aims to transform the company into one that's first in responsiveness, service, and total value. The project relies on an information system that links designers and manufacturers so they can share digital versions of design and manufacturing ideas. The key technology of this system is telecommunications, which refers to a mixture of hardware and software that helps to electronically transmit different types of data (such as text and graphics) to computers and other related electronic devices anywhere in the world.

The project has helped the company slash $70 million in operating costs and reduce the time for most business processes. The savings are mainly the result of better coordination and faster communication with worldwide business partners. Further, by being able to develop new designs more quickly, the company gains the advantage of speed in the competitive fashion industry.

A global telecommunications network knits together U.S. designers with manufacturing representatives in the Far East. In addition, apparel divisions, manufacturing representatives, design liaisons, and the mills in Asia can access design files stored in the company's headquarters in New Jersey via their desktop PCs any time the need arises.

Liz Claiborne relies on networks for applications such as electronic mail and faxing. The office in Hong Kong is connected through networks to offices in Taiwan; Djakarta, Indonesia;

Society is changing because of telecommunications, which can link individuals, schools, research institutions, industry, and governments. It fosters the free exchange of ideas and information in real-time. Value Health, a health care provider, uses telecommunications to link doctors to patient pharmaceutical information stored in a central data bank. Seven to 10 percent of all hospitalizations for people under the age of 65 and 14 percent for people over age 65 occur when a patient takes a drug that aggravates an underlying medical condition.

Telecommunications helps doctors tap into the central data bank and check the patient's prescription against his or her records to determine if there is a potential problem, thus improving the quality of health care for all patients.[2]

But advances due to telecommunications mean that some may get left behind. "Our global society has created this technological revolution, and unless we meet the needs of all our student populations, we will soon have electronic ghettos," warns William Mulvey, a technology and communications teacher at Geneva High School in Geneva, New York. He emphasizes the importance of delivering technology to all segments of the population. If we fail to do so as a society, we will create digitally illiterate second-class citizens who will face closed doors when it comes to good jobs and growth opportunities, eventually leading to economic deprivation for these individuals.

In this chapter we explore ways in which telecommunications affects business. In particular, we investigate the definition and characteristics of telecommunication channels and types of telecommunication media. Then we consider different types of networks and electronic data interchange. Finally, we examine global networks and effective corporate network management.

The Technical Foundations of Telecommunications

The *tele* in telecommunications means "at a distance" and is derived from the Greek word for *far away*. As Figure 6-1 shows, **telecommunications** is similar to face-to-face communications: there is a sender, a receiver, a message, and a medium through which the message is trans-

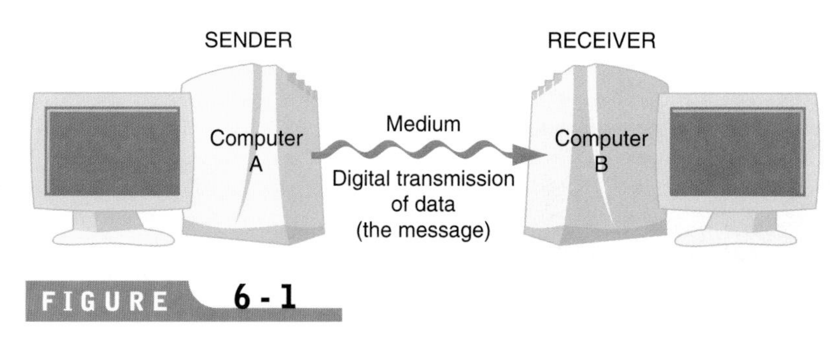

FIGURE 6-1

Telecommunications Transmit Data from One Set of Electronic Devices to Another

mitted. The sender and the receiver in this case are computers, such as a mainframe or a midrange computer. Telephones, radio, cellular phones, the Internet, cable television, home shopping and banking, ATMs, and e-mail, to name just a few, are all made possible because of telecommunications. Networks refer to a system of interconnected computers, terminals, and communications channels and devices. Information technology personnel often use the word *networks* interchangeably with the word *telecommunications,* and we, too, will treat the terms as synonyms even though the meanings are not identical.

The message is sent through a **channel.** Think of the channel as a mailperson and the transmission rate as the number of messages that the mailperson can carry. Channels have five characteristics: transmission rate, bandwidth, transmission mode, transmission direction, and transmission signals.

1. **Transmission rate:** This characteristic is the rate at which a channel carries data from one computer to another and is measured in bits per second. The higher the transmission rate, the more efficient the network. However, faster transmissions come at a price as we see later in this chapter.
2. **Bandwidth: Bandwidth** refers to the volume or capacity of data that a channel can carry. The higher the bandwidth, the more data the network can carry. Full-motion videos usually require much higher bandwidth than text or simple graphics.
3. **Transmission mode:** Data are transmitted as bits and bytes across the network. There are several ways to transmit data. Data can be transmitted one byte at a time, which is referred to as asynchronous transmission. Each byte has a "starting" bit and an "ending" bit, so that the receiving computer knows when a byte begins and when it ends. Asynchronous transmission is like a mailperson carrying one letter at a time. Data can also be transmitted in blocks of bytes, which is referred to as synchronous transmission. Synchronous transmission is faster than asynchronous because the computer reads blocks of bytes at a time. Users rely on this method when they need to transmit large volumes of data.
4. **Transmission direction:** Users can transmit data in three directions: simplex, half duplex, and full duplex (Fig. 6-2). In **simplex transmission,** a data communication device can either send or receive data, but cannot do both, so transmission occurs in only one direction. News wires, for instance, can only send information to newspapers, but cannot receive information from them. Also, television broadcasting information moves from the TV station to the TV set, not vice versa. In **half-duplex transmission,** the sender and receiver can alternate sending and receiving data. Think of a walkie-talkie. Both parties can send and receive data, but only one of them can send data at any given time. In half-duplex mode, when one party completes a transmission, control of the channel switches to the other party. In **full-duplex transmission,** both parties can send and receive information at the same time. An example of a full-duplex device is the telephone, where both parties can speak and be heard at the same time.

and New Jersey. In countries such as Sri Lanka, where the telecommunications infrastructure may not be very sophisticated, the company installs simpler networks. Shortly, Liz Claiborne hopes to use the telecommunications service to give its 250 workers in the Asia-Pacific region access to core business systems.

Liz Claiborne's efforts seem to be paying off. "They've cut cycle time, they've lowered costs, they've gotten more efficient," observes Laurence Leeds, managing director at the Buckingham Research Group in New York.

Source: Adapted from Sari Kalin, "Global Net Knits East to West at Liz Claiborne," *Computerworld,* June 9, 1997, www.computerworld.com.

Telecommunications

The transmission of different forms of data (such as text, audio, video, images, graphics) from one set of electronic devices over media to another set of geographically separated electronic devices.

Channel

The link that transmits data between the sender and the receiver.

Bandwidth

The transmission capacity of a channel, which is measured as the difference between the highest and lowest frequencies of the channel, and is measured in bits per second or in Hertz (cycles per second).

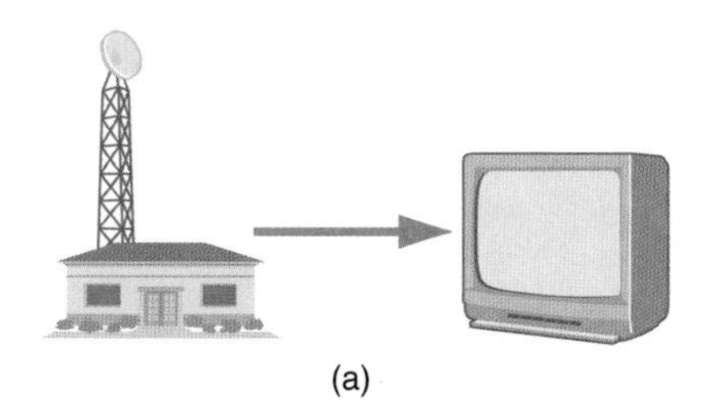
(a)

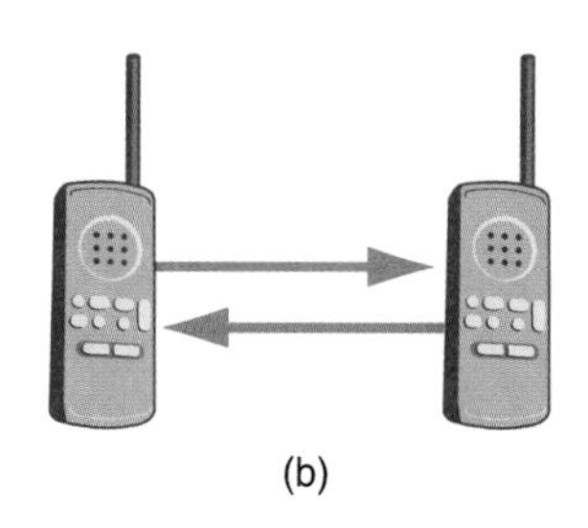
(b)

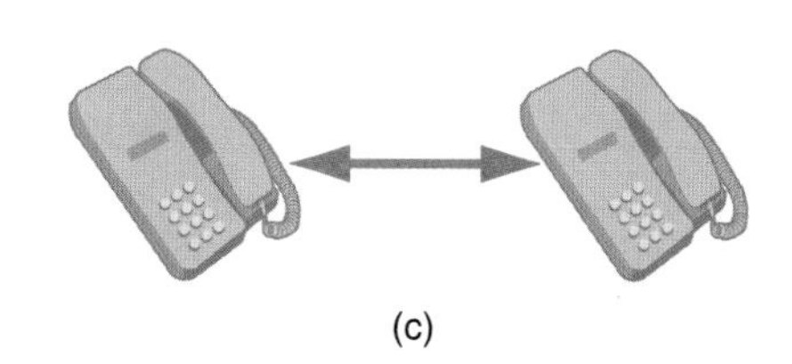
(c)

FIGURE 6-2

The Three Directions in Which Data Can Be Transmitted

(a) Simplex (one direction only) (b) Half-duplex (two-way flow of data but data can flow in only one direction at a given time) (c) Full-duplex (data flows in both directions at the same time)

Simplex transmission

A process in which data flows in only one direction over the communication channel. The computer can send or receive data, but cannot do both.

Half-duplex transmission

A process in which two parties alternate sending and receiving data. When one party has completed a transmission, control of the channel switches to the other party.

Full-duplex transmission

A process in which both parties can send and receive information at the same time.

Analog signal

A continuous signal that is represented in the form of waves.

Digital signal

A discrete signal represented in the form of zero bits or one bit.

Modem (shorthand for modulator-demodulator)

A device that converts digital signals into analog signals and vice versa.

5. **Transmission signals:** How does information travel through a channel? It travels in the form of electromagnetic signals. As Figure 6-3 illustrates, the two types of signals are analog and digital. **Analog signals** are continuous signals, represented as waves. For example, the human voice is represented using analog signals to reflect the ups and downs in the human voice. **Digital signals** are represented as either zero bits or one bit, which is represented as an on-off condition like that in an electrical switch. Unlike analog, digital signals are discrete signals. "Living" or "dead" can be best represented as discrete signals, whereas weather temperature is analog because it is better represented as a series of values than a single value. As you already know, computers communicate in digital form. Table 6-1 summarizes the five characteristics of channels.

TABLE 6-1

The Five Characteristics of Channels

Characteristics	Description
Transmission rate	Rate at which channel carries data from one computer to another.
Bandwidth	Volume or capacity of data that a channel can carry.
Transmission mode	Ways by which data are transmitted. Two ways include asynchronous (one byte at a time) and synchronous (blocks of bytes).
Transmission direction	Three directions for transmitting data include simplex, half duplex, and full duplex.
Transmission signals	Information travels as analog or digital signals.

So, what happens if we have to convert analog signals to digital or vice versa? For example, how does a computer recognize a human voice, which is an analog signal? A modem helps with the conversion process. A **modem** is a popular communication device in which telephone lines transmit data as analog signals. If two computers try to communicate with each other over telephone lines, the computer's digital signals must first be converted into analog, and at the other end reconverted into digital so that the receiving computer can recognize and accept the signals. Figure 6-4 depicts this conversion process.

Faster modems, although more expensive, result in lower long-distance charges because they take less time to transmit data. The speed with which a modem sends and receives data is measured in bits-per-second (bps). Older modems transfer data at the rate of 300 to 2400 bps, while newer models transfer data at rates ranging from 9,600 bps to 56,600 bps or higher. A 14,400 bps modem with data compression capabilities can effectively transmit 57,600 bps.

FIGURE 6-3

Analog and Digital Signals

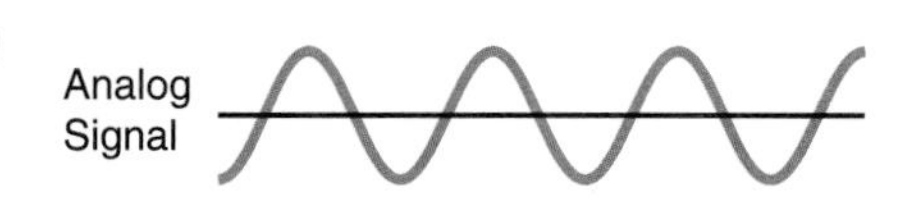

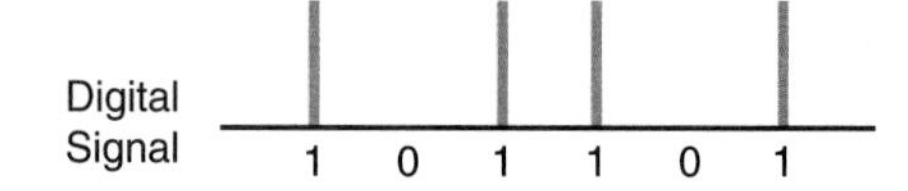

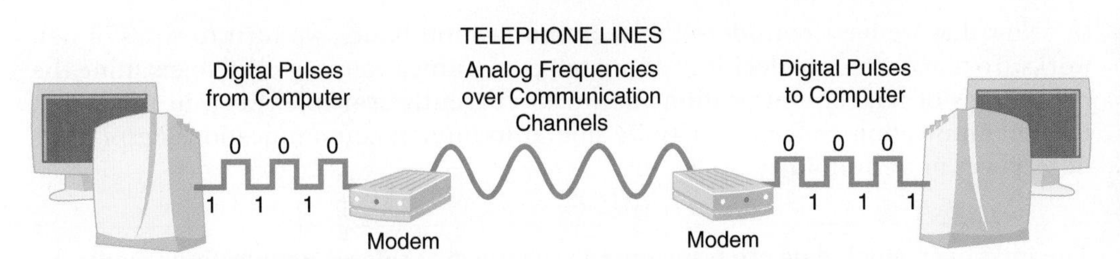

FIGURE 6-4

Modems Convert Digital Signals into Analog Signals and Vice Versa So Computers Can Transmit Data over Telephone Lines

Modems that come with fax capabilities are called fax modems. Such modems can send and receive a computer-generated document to or from any standard fax machine and offer several advantages over standard fax machines. First, sending a document to a number of recipients over a fax modem is a simpler process than doing so through a fax machine because the pages do not need to be fed manually into the machine. Second, special software makes it possible to convert a fax received over the modem into a computer file. Documents received via the fax machine must be rekeyed or scanned to convert the data into a digital file.

Telecommunication Standards: Protocols

In international relations, protocols are guidelines for behavior and communications between nations. Similarly, in telecommunications protocols are standards that ensure efficient and error-free electronic communication. Protocols range from simple rules that show how two networks must be connected to complex rules that establish international guidelines for the exchange of ideas, programs, and messages. Protocols help individuals and companies around the world communicate using a common, uniform, and consistent communications standard. Without protocols, digital communications may simply break down.

Here's an example of a simple protocol: A character should be viewed in the same way by both the sender and the receiver. For example, if I send the name "CHARLES' across the network, the alphabet characters *C, H,* and so on should mean the same for the receiver. Another example of a protocol deals with error handling. If a transmission does not go through, then both the sender and the receiver should receive a consistent error message.

Telecommunications protocols have three major components:

Telecommunication protocols
Rules and formats that ensure efficient and error-free electronic communications between two or more computers.

1. A set of characters that mean the same thing to both the sender and the receiver
2. A set of rules for timing and sequencing messages
3. A set of methods for detecting and correcting errors

The main purposes of protocols are to accurately identify each device, to ensure that each message is transmitted accurately to the correct destination, and to detect and correct errors as they occur. Some popular protocols are TCP/IP (Transmission Control Protocol/Internet Protocol), Integrated Services Digital Network (ISDN), Systems Network Architecture (SNA), System Application Architecture (SAA), XMODEM, YMODEM, and Kermit.

Channel Service Providers

Telephone and telecommunication companies that move data and information from one location to another are called data communication carriers. The two types of carriers are **common carriers** and **special-purpose carriers.** Companies such as AT&T, MCI, Sprint, GTE, and ITT are common carriers that offer long-distance voice and data communication services.

Common carriers
Companies that furnish telecommunication services to businesses and to the general public and are regulated by state and federal agencies.

Special-purpose carriers offer the basic services that common carriers provide and add features such as e-mail, videoconferencing, transmission-error correction, the ability to solve compatibility problems between different computer systems and terminals, backup services, and network management. America Online is a special-purpose carrier because it provides some of the features just listed, such as e-mail and videoconferencing capabilities.

Special-purpose carriers

Carriers that add special features to the basic communication services a common carrier provides.

Now that we have considered telecommunication basics, we turn to types of networks. To make effective decisions about telecommunications, we need to examine the many types of telecommunications networks currently available. Keep in mind that telecommunication concepts are quite similar to human communications despite the differences in terminology.

Telecommunications Media

Telecommunications media

The medium through which data are transmitted; may be either bounded or unbounded.

The links over which data are transmitted are known as **telecommunications media**. So if your company is thinking about installing a telecommunications network, the type of media that will transmit the data becomes an important consideration. Every medium has pros and cons that should be weighed carefully before making a decision. Cost, transmission speed, reliability, and transmission volume are a few factors that should be assessed before installing a network. Next, we explore the two types of telecommunications media: bounded and unbounded. Table 6-2 lists different types of bounded and unbounded media.

Bounded Media

Twisted pair

A type of bounded medium in which two insulated strands of copper wire are twisted together. A number of twisted pairs are grouped together and enclosed in a protective sheath.

Coaxial cable

A cable that consists of a central conducting copper core, surrounded first by a layer of insulating material and then by a second conducting layer of braided wire mesh.

Fiber-optic cable

A cable that consists of thousands of hair-thin strands of glass or plastic, bound together inside a glass cylinder covered by a protective sheath.

Microwave radio

An unbounded medium that uses radio signals to transmit large volumes of voice and data traffic.

In bounded media, the signals are confined to the medium so that data travel through it. Figure 6-5 shows the three most popular types of bounded media—**twisted-pair, coaxial cable,** and **fiber-optic cable.**

Fiber-optic cable carries signals in the form of modulated light beams. It is popular because it is smaller, lighter, and faster than twisted-pair or coaxial cable. Further, because it does not radiate energy or conduct electricity, it is virtually free of all forms of electrical interference. Finally, fiber-optic cable can handle much higher transmission rates than twisted-pair and coaxial cable.

For example, the American Association of Retired Persons (AARP), a nonpartisan nonprofit organization with 1,200 employees, 34 million members, and 400,000 volunteers, uses fiber optics to link its two data-processing centers, one at its Washington headquarters and the other in California. It processes voice and video in real-time and provides videoconferencing capabilities. AARP uses networks to run its membership information-processing system and its financial systems, which include about 20 LANs, 1,355 PCs, and 400 laptops at 15 sites all over the country. The network allows AARP volunteers to obtain research and publications on-line from area offices within 48 hours, instead of the usual 6 weeks. Communication networks help keep AARP's volunteer lobbyists up to date and vocal regarding legislation that affects health insurance, Social Security, or other related matters.

Unbounded Media (Wireless Communication)

In an unbounded, or wireless, medium, the signals are not confined to the medium. Wireless media transmit signals through the atmosphere, the ocean, and outer space. The four types of wireless communication are microwave radio, communication satellites, cellular phones, and high-frequency radios.

Microwave radios are useful for connecting networks that are short distances apart. The tall towers depicted in Figure 6-6 with large horns, disk antennas, or both that are seen across the country are devices for ground transmission and transmission between ground stations and satellites. The antenna on a microwave radio converts high-frequency radio signals into a beam—a line-of-sight transmission—that provides much

TABLE 6-2 Different Types of Bounded and Unbounded Media

Bounded Media	Unbounded Media
Twisted pair	Microwave radio
Coaxial cable	Communication satellites
Fiber-optic cable	Cellular phones
	High-frequency radios

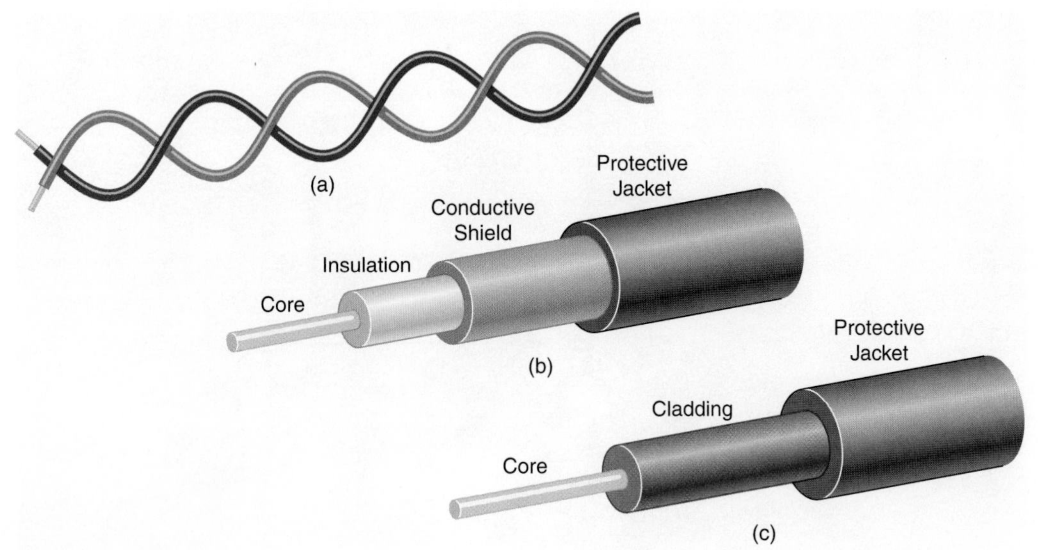

Three Types of Popular Bounded Media

(a) Twisted pair. (b) Coaxial cable. (c) Fiber-optic cable.

greater signal strength at the receiving end. Microwave radios are ideal for high-volume data transmissions. Schools, in particular, are embracing microwave technology because it transmits data, voice, and full-motion video for a fraction of the cost of fiber-optic cable.

Communication satellites move at the same rate at which the earth rotates so they remain stationary in relationship to the earth's surface, as we see in Figure 6-7 on p. 166. Solar panels power satellites and carry a variety of signals, such as standard television broadcasting, telephone transmissions, and even high-speed data. Surface stations all over the world use dish antennas to transmit data to communication satellites, which amplify the signals and transmit them to other surface stations. Because there is some delay between the transmission and the arrival of data, satellites cannot be used for real-time data processing. However, they are ideal for one-way transmission of large volumes of data.

Communication satellites

Satellites that orbit the earth and act as relay stations for microwave signals.

Consider the case of Carnival Cruise Line. It offered customers every amenity—except for access to cash. Customers could not access their ATMs on board, so almost two thirds ran out of money by the fifth day of a seven-day cruise. Vacationers use their credit cards for most expenditures, but some activities—such as gambling at the casino, day trips, and tips to crewmembers—require cash. When vacationers run out, the activity at casinos and other profitable centers drops considerably, resulting in losses for the cruise line.

Carnival needed a data link between ATMs on their ships and a host bank on land. It decided to expand its satellite technology—used to carry digitized voice signals so passengers could call friends and families—to become the first cruise line to provide shipboard ATMs. Customers appreciate the convenience of the ATMs and Carnival's revenues have increased as a result.[3]

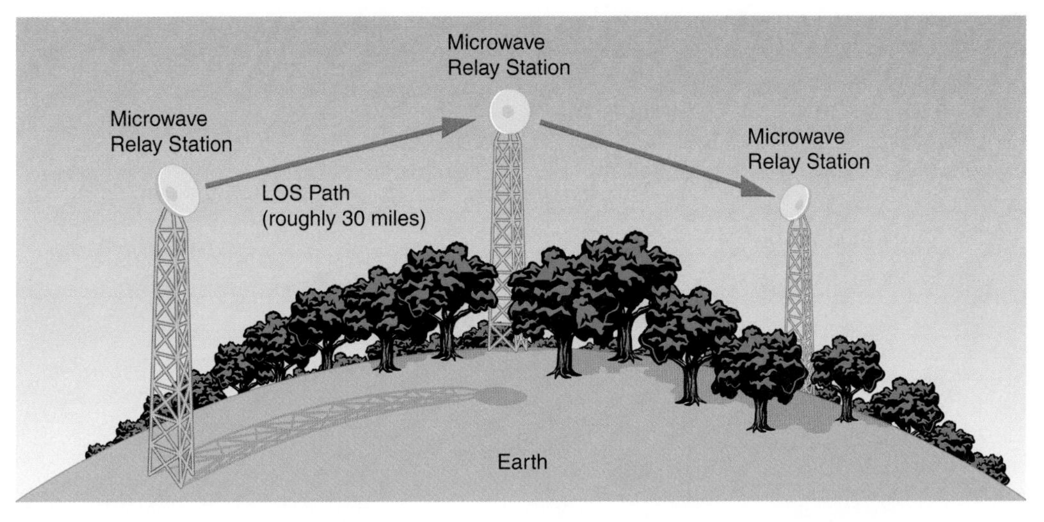

FIGURE 6-6

Microwave Radio Towers Sending Line-of-Sight (LOS) Transmissions

FIGURE 6-7

Communication Satellites Act as Data Links All Over the World

Cellular phones

Telecommunication devices that use radio waves to transmit voice and data to radio antennas in different geographical locations.

High-frequency radiophones

Phones that use radio waves to transmit information over great distances. High-frequency signals radiate from an antenna using ground waves and sky waves.

Cellular phones are wireless personal telephones that use radio waves to communicate with radio antennas. A cellular system, shown in Figure 6-8, partitions geographical areas into cells. Each of those cells has a base station with a radio transmitter, a receiver, an antenna, and a computer. Instead of having one high-powered base station for a given geographical area, cellular phone technology uses a low-power transmitter attached to each cell. As the number of power transmitters increases, the number of frequencies available to mobile phone customers increases. Incoming calls are transmitted to a caller's telephone with radio waves, using a unique set of radio frequencies for each cell. A central computer and other communication devices send, receive, track, and manage calls and handoffs from one cell to another.

High-frequency radiophones use radios to transmit information over great distances. High-frequency signals radiate from an antenna using two paths: a ground wave that follows the earth's surface and a sky wave that bounces between the earth and the ionosphere. The ground wave can communicate over distances of up to 400 miles; the sky wave can reach points up to 4,000 miles away and the reliability of data transmission is over 90 percent.

FIGURE 6-8

How Cellular Technology Operates

Cellular technology partitions geographical areas into cells in which low-power transmitters are used to send incoming telephone signals.

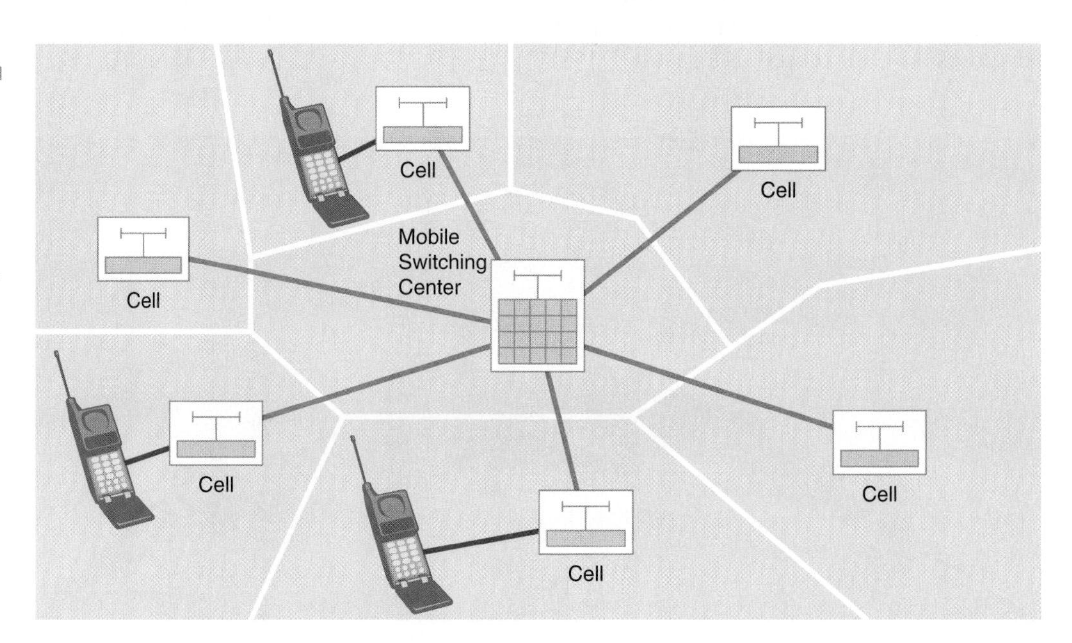

For example, the Swedish police rely on high-frequency radio telephones to improve communication between officers. All officers have a mobile workstation in the glove compartment of their police cars. The workstation allows officers in the field to send information to or receive it from the main investigating unit via high-frequency radiotelephone communication.

Types of Telecommunication Networks

Numerous devices work together in a telecommunications network. Networks can be classified into different types based on the geographical distances that the networks can service or based on how the devices are arranged on the network, also referred to as their topology or structure. In this section we examine types of networks based on the geographical distance they serve.

PBX, ISDN, LAN, WAN, MAN, and VAN

We can classify networks into types based on the geographical distances they service. In this section we look at private branch exchanges (PBX), integrated services digital network (ISDN), local area networks (LAN), wide area networks (WAN), metropolitan area networks (MAN), and value-added networks (VAN).

Private Branch Exchanges (PBX)

An electronic switching device (or a special computer) that is often located on the premises of a company is a **private branch exchange (PBX).** This small telephone exchange, typically owned and operated by the company, automatically switches calls between the company's telephone lines and that of the local telephone company.

Private branch exchange (PBX)

An electronic switching device that connects the company's telephone lines to those of the local telephone company.

A PBX performs a number of functions, such as call routing, call forwarding, redialing, storing data, tracing the origins of calls for statistical purposes, and automatically determining the least expensive route for a long distance call. Networks that carry only voice and data from PBX are referred to as PBX-based networks. Those that integrate voice, data, and images are known as integrated services digital network (ISDN).

PBXs are becoming an integral part of the "smart office." This type of network has the ability to coordinate, control, and communicate data among various devices on the network, which results in several advantages. Suppose a user wants to fax a word-processing document from her computer. A PBX can retrieve this document, automatically dial the fax number, and fax the document. Also, a PBX does not need extensive wiring—it only requires a simple telephone jack. The two main disadvantages of a PBX are its restricted geographical reach and its inability to handle large volumes of data.

Integrated Services Digital Networks (ISDN)

Carriers can also provide communication services using a digital network called the **integrated services digital network (ISDN).** ISDN uses a commercial telephone system to provide users with a wide array of telecommunication services, such as transmitting data and voice in digital form. Unlike telephone lines that are analog, ISDN is digital, eliminating the need to convert analog signals to digital so that the computer can process it. ISDN is a critical technology that is growing at an exponential rate. Experts predict that it will become the international standard for data and voice communications.

Integrated services digital network (ISDN)

A digital network that uses commercial telephone systems to transmit voice and data.

The benefits of digital networks are numerous. First, they eliminate the need for converting analog signals into digital signals and vice versa. Second, they use the coaxial or fiber-optic cables that are already used in telephone networks, which eliminates the need for rewiring. (Of course, new digital telephone equipment must replace the existing analog telephone.) Finally, they use standard interfaces that promote uniformity, standardization, connectivity, flexibility, and manageability. The major disadvantage of ISDN is cost. It is more expensive than other forms of transmission.

A major airline has realized huge savings by using ISDN to link its seven reservation centers. ISDN routes customer calls to the appropriate reservation center based on the time of day, the day of the week, and the volume of calls. If a call is not answered promptly, ISDN can reroute it to another agent or another center. The airline also plans to use ISDN to deliver client account information to the reservation agent to avoid redundant questions and improve customer service.

Northwest Airlines uses ISDN to link seven of its reservations centers. The linkage means Northwest can route customer calls to the best place for prompt, efficient service.

Local area network (LAN)

A network that links a number of independent electronic devices located within a relatively small area (usually within a radius of 1 to 10 miles).

Local Area Networks (LANs)

Local area networks (LANs) link a number of independent electronic devices located within a moderate-sized geographic area, usually within a radius of 1 to 10 miles. LANs are used primarily to share data, information, messages, software, and even peripherals, such as printers. Generally, they connect devices within office buildings. Many companies use LANs, so you are likely to work with a LAN. This section describes a LAN and answers the following two questions: How are devices on a LAN connected? What does a LAN use to transmit data?

LANs are commonplace in organizations of all sizes throughout the world. A whopping 88.1 percent of Scandinavian companies use LANs. Almost 60 percent of U.S. companies use them.[4] Why are they so common? LANs allow users to share resources so they increase efficiency and help keep costs down. They link PCs to mainframes or other large computers so users can access, process, and share large volumes of data quickly. For example, a LAN means that several users can share a laser printer. Also, organizations can store commonly used applications such as word-processing or spreadsheet packages on a LAN so that any user on the network can access the software when needed.

LANs improve communications through the rapid dissemination of files, programs, and messages. The National League for Nursing, a major Washington lobbying organization for health care reform, credits part of its success to LANs. Hundreds of PCs installed on three LANs in the league's New York headquarters download data from a central mainframe to local PCs, giving members access to information on nursing schools, patient management techniques, and political news related to health care. Applications including membership services, nursing school accreditation, accounting, and research are also available on the LAN.

Peer-to-peer relationship

A relationship in which all devices on a network have equal status and privileges.

Besides providing members with valuable and timely data, networks save the league 30 percent of its annual IS expenditures. The LAN eliminates the need to mail documents to members around the country. Further, multiple copies of documents can be distributed to all decision makers with a few keystrokes, saving photocopying and mailing costs.

Baseband

A technology that transmits digital signals directly over the network, one signal at a time.

Broadband

A technology that transmits multiple streams of analog signals over the network and is useful for transmitting large amounts of data over long distances.

Electronic devices on a LAN are linked using twisted-pair, coaxial cable, and, in recent years, fiber optics and wireless communications. The most popular ways to connect devices are Ethernet and token-ring. Ethernet uses coaxial cables whereas token-ring uses twisted-pair cable. Devices on a LAN, such as PCs, printers, and modems have a **peer-to-peer relationship.** This relationship means each and every device on the network has equal status and privileges. Compare this with a master-slave relationship in which a central computer dictates the behavior of other computers and devices on the network.

Unlike PBXs that use existing telephone lines, a LAN relies on private communication channels to transmit data. The two ways to transmit signals over private communication systems are **baseband** and **broadband.** Baseband technology is more commonly used in LANs. This technology transmits digital signals directly over the network, one signal at a time. Broadband transmits multiple streams of analog signals over the network at the same time, so it is more suitable for transmitting large amounts of data over long distances. Broadband is usually used to connect one or more LANs.

Wide area networks (WAN)

Networks that transmit data and voice communications to large geographical areas.

Wide Area Networks (WANs)

A **wide area network (WAN)** is a network that transmits data and voice communications over wide geographical areas, sometimes even countries. The key difference between a LAN and a WAN is that a WAN covers greater geographical distances than a LAN. Also, a single company usually owns a LAN, whereas both a company and a common or special-purpose carrier own a WAN. WANs often require special-purpose carriers because the technical requirements of establishing a WAN are more complicated than those for LANs. Requirements include dealing with different types of infrastructures in different locations or even countries, meeting domestic and global regulations for data transmission, and ensuring data integrity and security and so on.

How are WANs set up? There are several ways to establish a WAN link, including direct-distance dialing (DDD), wide-area telephone service (WATS) lines, leased lines, satellites, and *frame relay*. Frame relay is a technology device used to connect one LAN with another, where the two LANs are geographically separated. It organizes data into bundles for transmission from one network to another. All major carriers provide frame relay services. These services are suitable for data and image transfer. For example, we saw in our opening case how Liz Claiborne uses telecommunications to link designers and manufacturers from around the world. In this case, the company used frame relay to achieve its goal.

Many organizations and institutions, such as the Centers for Disease Control and Prevention (CDC), rely on networks to meet their communication needs. The CDC, an organization that monitors the health status of citizens around the world, gathers massive amounts of data, such as the health effects of the famine in South Africa, cholera in South America, or AIDS in the United States. The CDC's 7,000 staff members depend on a WAN to access and analyze large volumes of scientific data residing on different computers around the globe and to send and receive more than 10 million electronic messages a year.

Before the WAN was established, researchers had to rely on the postal service and fax machines to receive and transmit information. Documents often got lost or did not reach the individual at the right time. Further, there was very limited sharing of information. Today, any authorized employee can click on the right document, view it, edit it, and share his or her views and knowledge with other employees working on a similar problem or case.[5]

WANs have many of the same advantages as LANs, such as allowing users to share resources efficiently and speed of information transmission. In addition, WANs can transmit data to a wider geographical region.

However, WANs have two disadvantages. First, a WAN is difficult to manage. Because no two WANs are alike, there are few guarantees that a network environment will function smoothly. Further, when things go wrong, it is difficult to identify the source of the problem because so many elements come together in so many different ways to make the network operational. Adding to the challenge is the onslaught of a wide and growing variety of network products from vendors and changing services from carriers. One IS manager wryly commented, "When you thought your job couldn't get any harder, you suddenly inherit a wide area network. Your first inclination is to run. Your second is to sign up for primal scream therapy. After the panic subsides, you realize what you already knew: You can't escape."

Metropolitan Area Networks (MANs)

Metropolitan area networks (MANs) are high-bandwidth WANs that link electronic devices distributed over a metropolitan area. They are used for LAN-to-LAN connections, high-speed data transmission, backup network facilities, full-motion video, and image transmission.

Metropolitan area networks (MAN)

High-bandwidth WANs that link electronic devices distributed over a metropolitan area.

Client/server systems are network-based information systems that rely on telecommunications for their implementation. A client is a computer that requests a service, such as a request for the total sales figures of all new products within the last 3 weeks. A server is a machine that provides the service, such as the list of those sales figures. Several popular applications, such as the Internet, rely on the client/server model. Client/server applications may use LANs, WANs, or MANs.

Value-Added Networks (VANs)

Value-added networks (VANs) are public data networks that add value to the basic communication services that common carriers provide. VANs offer specialized services such

Value-added networks (VANs)

Public data networks that add extra services to basic communication services.

as access to commercial databases and software, correction of transmission errors, establishing compatibility between previously incompatible computers and terminals, e-mail, and videoconferencing. They allow companies to derive the full benefits of telecommunications because they facilitate the smooth flow of information, which in turn, can lead to good decisions.

Suppose you are responsible for the financial portfolio of your company. Your duty is to ensure that your company earns the best returns from its financial investments. This duty requires monitoring a number of internal and external databases, such as the Dow Jones and the New York Stock Exchange databases. It also means that your decisions must be communicated in an effective, timely manner to all employees who work for you. By electronically transmitting the right information to the right people, you can not only save your company time and money, but also help your company efficiently respond to market needs.

Companies and governments understand the importance of VANs. For example, South Africa is a country of contrasts, "a world in one country," as local tour operators love to call it. Here, telecommunications is having a profound impact as mainstream corporations invest heavily in VANs. They view this as key to successful business partnership with the rest of the world.[6]

In summary, we can classify networks into different types based on the configuration of network components or the geographical distances they serve. However, these classifications are not mutually exclusive, although they follow a certain sequence. For example, you cannot decide the topology of your network before deciding on the type of network (LAN, WAN, MAN, or VAN). Think back for a moment to the opening case about Liz Claiborne. The company could not have chosen LAN because it had to connect individuals from around the world. It first had to decide on the type of network, namely WANs and ISDN. Once this decision was made, the company focused on how to link the devices on the network.

Topology

The physical configuration of devices on a network.

Bus topology

A network configuration in which all computers on the network are connected through a single circuit, such as twisted-pair cable. Messages are transmitted to all computers on the network, although only the targeted device responds to the message.

Ring topology

A network configuration in which computers are arranged in the form of a ring using twisted-wire, coaxial cable, or fiber optics. Messages are transmitted in one direction to all devices between the sending node and the receiving node.

Star topology

A topology in which central host computer receives all messages and then forwards the message to the appropriate computer on the network.

Network Topology

Topology is the geometric configuration of devices on a network. Three popular network topologies are bus topology, ring topology, and star topology. **Bus topology** connects all computers on the network through a single circuit (such as fiber optics or twisted-pair cable and so on) to a central channel. Signals transmitted over the channel are called messages. This topology transmits each message to all computers on the network, although only the targeted device will respond to the message. Each device has an address and each device forwards messages to the address of a given device.

Bus topology has several advantages and some disadvantages. The main advantage of bus topology is that the topology makes it easy to add or remove devices from the network without affecting network performance. Also, if one of the devices on the network fails, the network is not affected. The disadvantage, however, is that network performance decreases as the number of messages increases, because each device checks to see if the message is for it or for some other device. This topology is ideal for LANs (discussed in the previous section) and for applications such as e-mail and file transfers.

In **ring topology** network devices are arranged in the form of a ring and are connected to one another through twisted-pair or coaxial cables or fiber optics. This topology transmits a message to all devices between the sending node and the receiving node. Each computer communicates directly with any other computer on the network by specifying the address of the device; the topology distributes processing and control functions among all devices on the network. If a computer on the network fails, the message is rerouted around it.

One of the oldest network topologies is **star topology.** Here, a central host computer receives all messages and then forwards the messages to the appropriate computers or devices, such as printers, on the network. In a star topology, then, all communications must go through the main computer.

An advantage of star topology is that it is easy to expand the network by adding more computers to the network. This set-up is ideal when some information has to be centralized on the host computer and other computers on the network can download that information from the host computer.

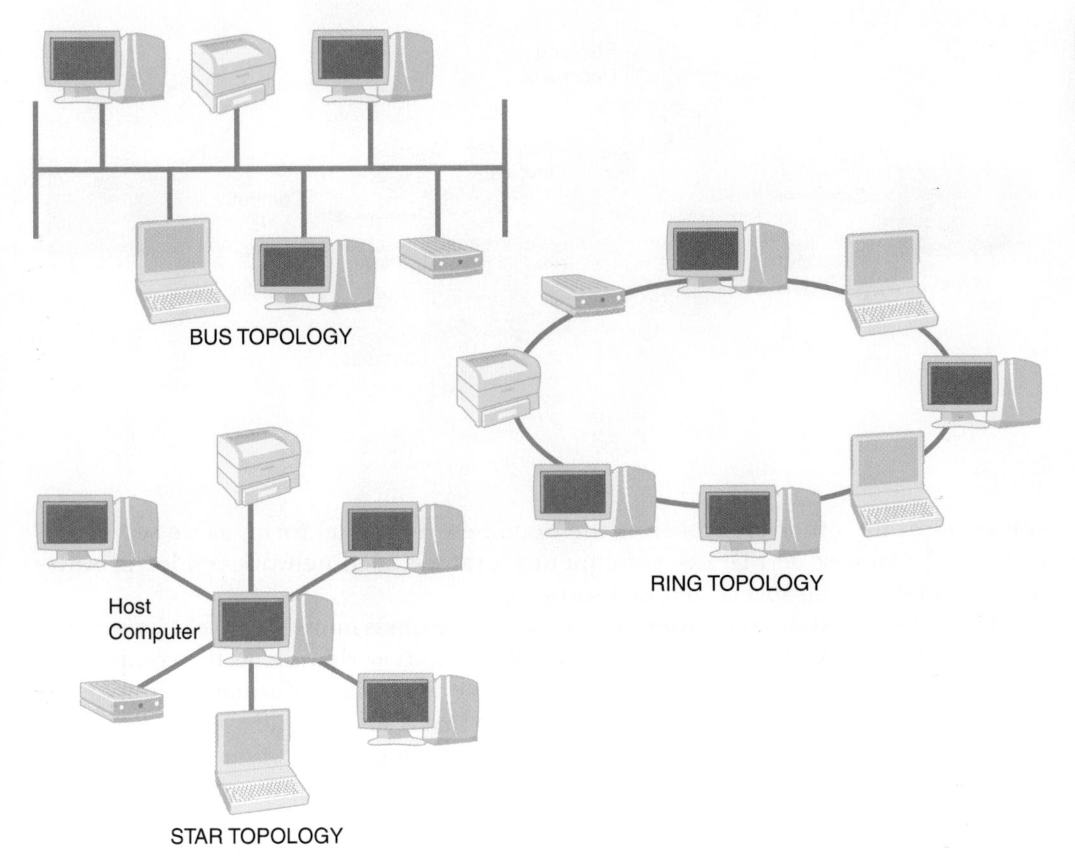

FIGURE 6-9

The Three Popular Network Topologies: Bus, Ring, and Star

This approach has two main disadvantages. If the host computer fails or malfunctions, the entire network will come to a standstill. Also, if the distance between the computers on the network and the central computer is very large, the cost of sending a message over the network increases significantly. Figure 6-9 illustrates the bus, ring, and star network topologies.

In this section we examined different types of networks. Networks can be classified based on the geographical distances that the networks can service (PBX, ISDN, LAN, WAN, MAN, and VAN) or based on how the components on the network are arranged, also referred to as their topology or structure (bus, ring, and star). Next we investigate telecommunications applications.

Applications of Telecommunications

There are many applications of telecommunications in our personal and professional lives. In this section, we look at the following applications: electronic data interchange, teleconferencing, videoconferencing, fax, and voice mail.

Electronic Data Interchange

One key benefit of telecommunications is its ability to convey the right information to the right individual at the right time. Businesses spend a large amount of time and money in creating and transmitting documents electronically as a way to share information. Note that there are internal and external business documents. Internal documents include memos, health benefits information, training class offerings, new job postings, and so on. External documents relate to the concerns of different stakeholders such as customers (proof of purchase documents or warranties), suppliers (invoices to be paid), regulatory forms (tax and environmental compliance forms), and so on.

Electronic data interchange (EDI) is a telecommunication network that allows direct computer-to-computer exchange of business documents, such as purchase invoices. Think of EDI as two computers exchanging documents without any human intervention. To implement EDI on a personal computer, all we need is a modem, a printer, and EDI software. In a simple EDI, transactions are typed into a PC on one end and the

Electronic data interchange (EDI)
A direct computer-to-computer exchange of data over a telecommunications network.

FIGURE 6-10

Electronic Data Interchange (EDI)—The Process of Digitally Transmitting Different Documents from One Computer to Another

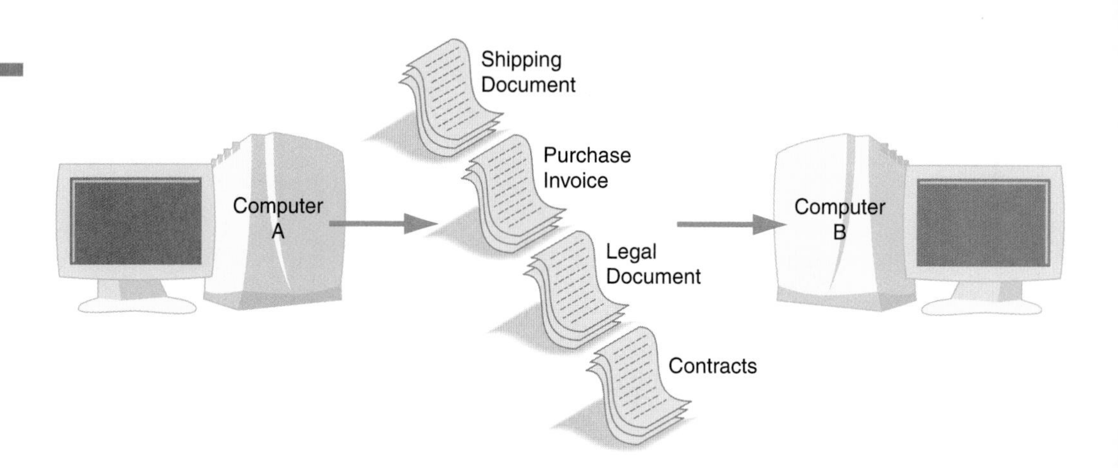

computer at the other end receives the document in digital form, as we see in Figure 6-10. In large-scale EDI cases, frequently a value-added network vendor provides the EDI service using specialized EDI software.

Tricon Global Restaurants uses EDI to conduct business more effectively. It owns and manages 30,000 KFC, Pizza Hut, and Taco Bell locations worldwide. As the company increases its global operations, it must communicate and share information in a timely, consistent manner. The company relies on EDI so that restaurants all over the world can follow uniform purchasing guidelines and order supplies through one global clearinghouse. "This is the first time we tried to unify all the brands with one system and one approach," notes John Kleban, Tricon's chief restaurant process officer. The information exchange through Tricon's EDI has helped reduce company inventory and save money.

EDI supports business and government activity in various parts of the world. The government of Singapore established TradeNet, a mainframe-based EDI system, in 1989 to help local firms process customs declarations. Now the system serves 3,500 companies, handles more than 95 percent of Singapore's trade declarations, and processes about 90,000 messages daily. Switching to EDI has saved Singapore's government and businesses about $600 million per year. The change has also reduced the time for getting key documents approved by government officials. "It is now possible for a single electronic document to be sent to all relevant government agencies and returned with the necessary approvals within 15 to 30 minutes," says a TradeNet spokesperson.[8]

EDI provides trade and market information to companies worldwide. Information such as company profiles, foreign exchange rates, government regulations, trade protocols, and other related information is now digitally available. "The future of EDI in Singapore is exciting. Like most success stories here, the accomplishments will be driven by minds open to change and a passion for excellence," claims one government official.[9]

The three types of EDI benefits are direct, indirect, and strategic. Direct benefits include reducing operating costs and increasing productivity. RCA, one of the early adopters of EDI, decreased the number of purchase orders by a factor of five when it switched to EDI. Because almost 25 percent of transaction costs are associated with data entry and reentry, savings from EDI can be tremendous.

The indirect benefits of EDI include helping companies identify and implement the most efficient way to conduct business. GE Transportation Systems, for example, used EDI to develop a better inventory policy. Before EDI was implemented, the company was forced to maintain a large inventory to meet customer demand. With the help of EDI, GE stays in close touch with its leading customers, identifies their upcoming needs, and modifies its production schedule accordingly. This improved communication has helped the company eliminate an acre of warehouse space and realize significant savings in the process.

Finally, EDI can yield strategic business benefits. By allowing suppliers to access sales data, Wal-Mart Stores headquarters in Bentonville, Arkansas, ensures that its stores do not run out of stock. This service gives the firm a competitive edge.

R. J. Reynolds Tobacco Company, owner of Salem and Winston cigarettes, with estimated sales of $9 billion, uses EDI for almost 90 percent of its purchasing transactions. The company, which purchases more than $1 billion in materials from suppliers around the world, reduced the processing cost of a purchase order from $75 to a mere 93 cents and reduced lead time for purchases from 3 weeks to less than 1 hour with the help of EDI.

In spite of its many benefits, EDI also poses some challenges. First, EDI requires the careful integration of applications that may reside on incompatible platforms. It requires integration because a company may use IBMs and its supplier may use computers from another vendor, such as Hewlett Packard. This discrepancy leads to hardware incompatibility. Also, the company's applications must be compatible with its partner's applications; otherwise, application-incompatibility problems arise. For instance, if your company has an inventory application from Vendor A and your supplier has an inventory program developed by Vendor B and the two are incompatible, this can easily become an EDI challenge. Application integration, by its very nature, is an expensive proposition.

Second, EDI forces employees to adapt to new ways of doing business and the learning curve that comes with it can be frustrating. Auditors must learn to process electronic documents; the legal department must finalize contracts without signatures. Third, training people to use EDI successfully can be both costly and difficult. Fourth, internal and external resistance to EDI can jeopardize its implementation.

Finally, EDI sometimes creates power struggles as the traditional relationship between suppliers and customers changes. For example, in some cases companies have refused to do business with suppliers that fail to use the company's EDI system. In the early years of EDI adoption, General Motors, Wal-Mart, and General Electric requested their suppliers to climb aboard the EDI ship to continue with the partnership.

Teleconferencing

Teleconferencing allows two or more people who are geographically separated to communicate over the phone. Telephone conversations usually are one-to-one; this can be a limitation when more than one person has to participate in the conversation. Teleconferencing is ideal for managing small to medium-sized projects with groups of 5 to 15 people.

Videoconferencing

Videoconferencing uses telephones, TV monitors, computers, and networks to link geographically separated decision makers. Participants can both hear and see each other, unlike telephone conferencing where they cannot see each other and only one individual can communicate at a given time. Sophisticated large-scale videoconferencing may require specially equipped videoconference rooms with facilities for computers, video cameras, microphones, and monitors. In meetings that involve sensitive information, the information can be encrypted before it is sent over the public telephone network.

This is how videoconferencing works: A computer digitizes sound and video images, converts them into analog signals, and transmits them over telephone lines to the receiver's computer. The receiver's computer then reconverts the analog signals to digital signals. The digital signals are then translated into audio and video messages and presented on the television monitor and sound system. As the price of videoconferencing equipment declines, videoconferencing has become an attractive option for many companies.

Videoconferencing is becoming a popular telecommunication business application that links people in different locations so that they can hear and see each other.

Fax

Fax, or facsimile transmission, uses telephones, modems, and scanners to transmit text and graphics to individuals and organizations with telephone access. You don't need a computer to send a fax. The idea is simple and elegant. A scanner in the fax machine scans the document at one end and a built-in modem sends it over telephone lines to the receiver; then a built-in modem in the receiver's fax machine receives the message, scans it, and prints it.

In a short time, the fax, sometimes viewed as a "long-distance copier," has become part of the home office, the work office, and even war zones. Journalists reporting on the war in Bosnia used fax machines to transmit war stories because editors wanted to see stories in hard-copy form. It is estimated that there are close to 30 million fax machines in the world today. The Japanese, in particular, rely heavily on fax communication because their language, with its thousands of ideographs, is easier to write in longhand than to type on cumbersome Japanese word processors.[10]

Voice Mail

Voice mail helps oral communication. The way it works is illustrated in Figure 6-11. The sender dictates a message over the telephone. A special device, called a codec, converts the analog signal of the sender's voice into a digitized message and transmits it over digital lines. The message is transmitted over a network and stored on a computer at the receiver's end. When the receiver retrieves the digitized message from his or her computer, the message is reconverted into analog form using the codec at the receiver's end and played back to the receiver.

FIGURE 6-11 **How Voice Mail Operates**

Global Networks

Global companies need global networks for survival. This need explains why the market for global networks is growing astronomically. By the year 2001, experts expect that the market for global networks will be $32 billion, growing at an average annual rate of about 17 percent. Although the United States remains the largest market opportunity for network services, international markets, such as Asia and the Pacific region, are growing at a fast pace.[11]

Rosabeth Moss Kanter, global-business guru and professor at the Harvard Business School, says, "Innovations come in organizations that are open to ideas coming from any place. Tapping into people's creativity requires a spirit of play." Being able to tap into anything, anywhere, anytime requires excellent telecommunications. Here are some phenomena Kanter sees driving global business and telecommunications.[12]

- **Resource mobility:** The ability to pull together global resources to accomplish a specific task is critical. For example, today the IT workforce is more global than ever before. "In the new global economy, the migrant workers are business managers that use telecommunications."
- **Simultaneity:** The best and the latest can be known anywhere in the world. Everything—every product launch, every new marketing campaign—needs to be done everywhere at once. This requires the use of telecommunications.
- **Bypass:** The threat for most companies is not from head-to-head competitors but from small niche companies offering customers exactly what they want. The tendency to bypass companies that are smaller than yours is dangerous. With telecommunications, even a small company located in a small village in another part of the world can become a threat to your business.[13]

Careers for success

Telecom Financial Analyst

The rigors of international telecommunications are causing many IT managers to reach for their foreign phrase book and their aspirin. They're also grabbing "telecom financial analysts" to help sort through the snarl of cables and currencies. "We have to have somebody that's analyzing our bills to make sure we're getting the right contracts for the right amounts," explains Jon Day, telecommunications manager at Novell, Inc, in Provo, Utah. "Five years ago, we wouldn't need this. But now we're dealing with so many types of circuits: ATM, frame relay, ISDN and home circuits. Normally, this job would be in the accounting group, but we've moved it into IT."

Salaries for telecom financial analysts start in the upper $30s but can soar into the $70s. "They can make a lot of money because they save us a lot of money," Day says. The candidate must know accounting and spreadsheets. "You don't have to tear the computer apart. Generally, we can teach the technical side, but if you have the ability already, we can really use you."

Telecom financial analysts are individuals who understand finance and financial transactions and who have the knowledge to convert this knowledge into useful digital form.

Source: Melanie Menagh, "A Breed Apart," *Computerworld,* June 8, 1998, 76.

Many companies operating in global markets fully realize the importance of establishing global networks. The networks can provide a local presence in the countries where they operate, a key to their success. Further, the networks help the business control and coordinate accurate and timely flow of information among business units in different countries. It also requires a good understanding of technical skills, business knowledge, and cultural issues. For example, an emerging career in telecommunications financial analysis employs individuals who have a good financial knowledge of currencies and a solid foundation in technology skills.

Without global networks, companies cannot get a "big picture" of what is happening in different units around the world. Think back to our opening example. Liz Claiborne's LizFirst system relies on global networks to communicate, coordinate, and collaborate with its far-flung operations and keep pace with changes in the fashion industry. Toyota also relies on information systems to achieve its ambitious quality and service goals. "Toyota, operationally, is the most amazing thing on the planet," says James Womack, former research director of MIT's International Motor Vehicle Program.[14] Toyota manufactures cars in Japan, the United States, and Europe. The company relies on global networks for gathering worldwide sales data, forecasting production requirements, and transmitting purchase orders and production schedules to suppliers all over the world.

Global networks can also help companies respond quickly to its customers' needs. Shipping firm DHL International uses global networks to notify customers of the status of their shipments. Its Electronic Shipment Advisory service, part of the DHL network, allows customers to attach an e-mail or fax message to each parcel that informs the recipient exactly what is on its way. As soon as DHL picks up the package, it transmits the message to the receiver and keeps the receiver and the sender notified, through e-mail, about the status of the package. The service handles between 30,000 and 40,000 package messages per day. DHL designed the service to eliminate the hassle of phone calls, faxes, and other mundane paperwork associated with sending and receiving packages for customers. The Advisory service also translates the e-mail or fax message into 1 of 10 foreign languages to meet the needs of global customers.[15]

Managing domestic networks is difficult; managing global networks is next to impossible. Such management requires extensive technical expertise, an in-depth knowledge of the business, knowledge about other countries, sensitivity to other cultures, and a large dose of patience. Besides size and technical complexity, other uncontrollable factors—such as poor infrastructure, monopolistic rules and regulations, and different standards of business ethics—all make global networks an extraordinary challenge for IS managers.

Many U.S. managers understand that investing in technology is only half the battle. The greater challenge is to get buy-in from individuals who may not have the same passion for technology as Westerners do. Tom Lesica, formerly the head of Pepsi-Cola International's worldwide IT operations in Somers, New York, describes a basic lesson for any corporate global network manager: "Before your company makes decisions about a new market, go ashore and take a good look around."[16]

First, telecommunication agencies in other countries, particularly developing countries, are governed by monopolistic and bureaucratic systems. Some countries have strict guidelines as to what can and cannot be transmitted over communication channels. In the Middle East, for instance, Pepsi faces tight control over the information communicated by its land-based satellites. In some cases the information is even monitored by government agencies. Says one global network administrator, "Our business is handicapped by telecommunications policy, not by technical problems. At times, you just shake your head and disbelieve what you've heard."[17]

Second, things may move more slowly in other countries as compared with the fast-paced life in the Western world. A phone connection that takes a day or so in Canada may take months, even years, in another country, and even then it may not work properly. For U.S. managers who are used to an excellent infrastructure, including reliable roads, telephones, and power, working in some countries can be daunting. Consider that machines with 486 processors are still somewhat new in China. In addition, as Tom Lesica of Pepsi-Cola North America, notes: "In China, the road infrastructure doesn't always allow for delivery trucks; you might have a cart or a bike. So you could be six years away from deploying handheld technology. Unless you take the time to understand that, you'll make mistakes."[18]

In Ho Chi Minh City, Vietnam, Lesica noticed that employees were using PCs running on 386 chips, computers so obsolete they would be hard to find in a U.S. company. Pepsi is rolling out telecommunication applications and other enterprise-wide software across the globe, and the hardware in the Vietnam headquarters could hardly be integrated into such projects. But the point, Lesica explains, "is that there's a franchise there that for its current needs has an adequate system." Weighing and choosing the right level of technological sophistication for each emerging market site, as Lesica has done, constitute one of the most fundamental decisions a global manager makes.[19]

Global networks pose more than technological problems, as McDonald's CIO Carl Drill can attest. Russian laws restricted the type and amount of data that could be transmitted over a network and the amount of electricity each restaurant could use.

Third, local laws and regulations may restrict business activities. For example, when Illinois-based McDonald's Corp. went to Moscow, it encountered laws limiting the type and volume of information transmitted over a network. It also faced laws prohibiting land ownership that dated back to Stalin's collective farming days. "We ran into problems growing potatoes—conditions were good, but we couldn't get contracts to own farms," recalls Senior Vice President and CIO Carl Dill. The Soviet legacy imposed itself again when a Russian electric utility official decided he knew best how much electricity McDonald's needed. "For our first one in Red Square, they said, 'Restaurants don't need that much power,' " Dill recalls. After a long and detailed application process, the store eventually got the necessary electricity.[20]

Cultural clashes over technology, of course, are far from limited to relations with governments. All over the world, employees from different cultural backgrounds often have attitudes toward IT that present challenges to the host company. To ensure the smoothest implementation of a global network, make sure to address the values of the corporate and national culture. In much of Asia, for example, it is best to explain new technology implementations and their value to a wide range of middle and senior managers to get them on board. The traditional Western approach, in which there is sometimes less concern with building consensus, can backfire, warns Booz, Allen's Bob Discher, a senior-level manager.[21]

Business Guidelines for Telecommunications Success

Telecommunications is the electronic nervous system of a business. This technology has profoundly influenced our personal and professional lives. However, telecommunications technology by itself is of limited value. Telecommunication decisions have to support organizational goals to create success. Let's investigate key factors that lead to successful telecommunication decisions.

Plan for the Challenge and Demands of Network Management

Telecommunications is not for the faint-hearted. Establishing the requirements of, developing, and maintaining networks are enormously challenging and time-consuming goals. In fact, network management is often identified as one of the most critical issues facing IS managers.

Network management includes a whole host of issues from making sure that the network does not fail, to ensuring proper backups and security measures, to meeting the bandwidth needs of end users. Other aspects of good network management include the following:

- Establish lines of communication among users and network managers
- Develop networking standards to establish consistency and uniformity
- Establish corporate security policies that protect critical data and other information-related resources
- Ensure that all information related to networks is carefully documented and updated regularly
- Strictly enforce backup policies and other security measures
- Invest in maintaining the network

Unfortunately, some organizations learn this lesson the hard way. They think simply investing in network hardware and software is sufficient. However, investing in experienced network managers and management tools is the key to successful telecommunications networks.

If managing domestic networks is difficult, think how much more challenging it is to manage global networks. Different political climates in different continents can affect how networks are managed, says Carol Bell, worldwide systems manager at Nalco/Exxon Energy Chemicals LP. Bell takes a unique approach to providing many of her smaller sales offices with quality technical support when it comes to telecommunications. "Whenever possible, we co-locate our offices with our customers, who, for the most part, are large oil companies," she explains. "That way, they can make use of the considerable resources those folks have." The quality of support provided in various parts of the world also varies greatly.[22]

Finally, network management is not just about managing technologies; it is also about managing people and understanding their needs. Even trinkets like T-shirts and mouse pads can help isolated technicians identify with the corporate IT mission. "Ultimately, we have to see ourselves as a single management team that just happens to have some water between us," says Andrew Kiolbasa, infrastructure chief of technology at ITT Fluid Technology Corp.

Plan for the Long Term

Network planning and investing should be long term. First, it is not easy to undo poor planning or short-term thinking once the business has invested in network hardware and software. This is because telecommunications requires a huge investment in money, time, and personnel. Second, most businesses set long-term goals, so long-range telecommunications planning means that the systems are more likely to mesh with the organization's goals.

Consider the External and Internal Effects of Telecommunications Decisions

Networks often handle the internal and external information needs of the organization. As more companies build collaborative relationships with their suppliers, customers, and others with a stake in the business, an external focus becomes critical. "Ten years ago, almost every IT job was internally focused," observes Bruce Hatz, corporate staffing manager at Hewlett Packard. "They served internal customers and supported existing applications within their companies, like payroll and inventory systems. Now, many IT opportunities are externally focused. We need people who can focus on a customer-oriented organization, understand the big picture, provide the customer with

Global IS for success

Being a CIO in a Connected World

As the management guru Tom Peters puts it, being a CIO in a world where being global is the norm is no small challenge. He offers these tips to CIOs in a connected world:

1. **Remember that your role is to lead.** Many businesses don't know how to be innovative enough to revolutionize the operations of the business. CIOs must lead and be brave enough to take the necessary risks.
2. **Develop talent wherever you find it.** Be open-minded about who can strengthen your IS team. Sometimes, the most talented people are the youngest or the ones who challenge the norm.
3. **The promise of different technologies is underhyped.** Technologies such as ERP and the Internet will radically change current business practices and will redefine every industry.
4. **The systems that must change are those that involve the corporate culture.** CIOs must confront the cultural issues directly. They are not technologists but are anthropologists. CIOs can "learn more from studying Gandhi, (Martin Luther) King, and other community and social activists" than they can from going to another business meeting or technology conference.
5. **Take time to think.** Reflect about the tools you are developing. Have they made people smarter and more thoughtful? Technology for its own sake may actually do more harm than good, so the next time you consider attending an industry conference, "go trout fishing instead or spend four days in the garden."
6. **Remember what your goal is.** Aspire to aesthetic systems, but keep in mind that a generation on the Internet or other networks may last only a few months. Elegant, coherent architecture "is at the same time a hopeless snare and a dangerous delusion. Beauty is my mantra, but 'Ready, Fire, Aim' is my calling."
7. **Stop comparing your business to your traditional rivals.** The CIO's goal is no longer to be the best of the best, but to be the only business that does what it does.

The point that Tom Peters is making is that the only rule that will guide a CIO in today's turbulent global world is the rule that says change is here to stay and only those who change will stay!

QUESTIONS AND PROJECTS

1. Do you agree with the statement that the Internet and other network technologies are underhyped? Explain.
2. Select a network technology and research any changes or advances in the technology that occurred in the last six months. Do you agree with Tom Peters that a generation in these technologies might last only a few months?

Source: Tom Peters, "Reinventing the World," *CIO,* September 1, 1998, Section 1, 26.

a total information technology solution and then support it.[23] External focus almost always requires knowledge about telecommunications, so a good foundation in telecommunications is vital for employees.

Investigate What the Telecommunications Investment Will Do for the Business

The biggest misconception about telecommunications is that it is an investment in technology. Such a view may be shortsighted. Telecommunications investments can change business processes, such as decision making and building customer and supplier relationships. There are several reasons why telecommunications can have a profound effect on a company. First, telecommunications can affect who makes decisions and how quickly. It allows employees at all levels to access the information necessary to make decisions, so many organizations shift decision-making authority from high-level managers to those most affected by the decision. Second, telecommunications helps businesses create partnerships with customers and suppliers. Telecommunications allows companies to communicate quickly and efficiently with their customers using e-mail and other telecommunication tools. As we saw earlier, applications of telecommunications such as EDI can help companies establish new and innovative partnerships with their customers.

The failure to make effective network decisions can damage a company's customer relationships. For instance, American Airlines' network decisions were supposed to translate into better customer relations, but the plan backfired because the planners hadn't anticipated customer response to new features on its Web site. The features allowed the airline's 31 million frequent flyers to look up their account, secure targeted discounts for cities they frequent, make reservations, and obtain special fares. The new features attracted much more traffic than American Airlines had anticipated, so it was forced to take the site off-line for most of the first day to reconfigure the hardware. The downtime greatly irked first-time visitors and the company's image as a technologically savvy company took a beating.[24]

Secure the Network to Protect Valuable Information

Because networks generally house extensive corporate information, inadequate security measures are equivalent to leaving the doors of the corporation wide open for anyone to come in and take what they please. Think for a moment what could happen. A network might contain the design for a new product, sensitive market research about the product, and a list of proposed customers. A competitor could take that information and invest relatively little money to develop and market the copycat product. Businesses must plan for adequate network security or risk jeopardizing the company's bottom line.

SUMMARY

1. **Describe the basic components in telecommunications.** Telecommunications is similar to face-to-face interaction in that there is a sender, a receiver, a message, and a medium through which the message is sent.

   A channel is the link between the sender and the receiver. It is the pipeline along which data are transmitted. Channels have five characteristics: transmission rate, bandwidth, transmission mode, transmission direction, and transmission signals. Transmission rate refers to the rate at which a channel carries data. Bandwidth is the volume of data that a channel can carry. Transmission signals are electromagnetic signals that travel through a channel. Two types of transmission signals are analog and digital. Transmission mode refers to whether the data is sent one byte at a time (asynchronous) or blocks of bytes at a time (synchronous). Transmission direction refers to whether both parties can send and receive messages at the same time (simplex, half duplex, and full duplex).

2. **Explain telecommunications protocols.** Telecommunication protocols help standardize digital communications. A protocol is a set of rules and guidelines used to help companies around the world communicate using a common communication standard.

3. **Discuss channel providers and their function.** Telephone and telecommunication companies that move data and information from one location to another are called data communication carriers. The two types of carriers are common carriers and special-purpose carriers. A special-purpose carrier is one that provides services over and above what a common carrier provides. E-mail is an example of one such special service.

4. **Describe different types of telecommunication media.** Telecommunications media are the links over which data are transmitted. The two types of telecommunications media are bounded and unbounded. In a bounded medium, the signals are confined to the medium and never leave it. Examples of a bounded medium are twisted-pair wires, coaxial cables, and fiber optics. In an unbounded medium, signals are propelled through the atmosphere, the ocean, and outer space. Examples of unbounded media are microwave radios, communication satellites, cellular phones, and high-frequency radios.

5. **Identify different types of telecommunication networks.** Networks can be classified according to their topology—their geometric configuration or shape—or by the geographical area they serve. There are six key types of networks based on the geographical area they serve: private branch exchanges (PBXs), integrated services digital networks (ISDNs), local area networks (LANs), wide area networks (WANs), metropolitan area networks (MANs), and value-added networks (VANs).

   A PBX is an electronic switching device located on the premises of a company that automatically switches between the company's telephone lines and that of the local telephone company, so it acts like a small telephone exchange. The ISDN is a digital network that uses the public telephone network to allow users to transmit data and voice, in digital form, over telephone lines.

A LAN, a network that links a number of independent electronic devices located within a moderate-sized geographic area, is often used to connect devices in a building or office. A WAN spans wider geographical areas than a LAN. Metropolitan area networks (MANs) are high-bandwidth WANs that link electronic devices distributed over a metropolitan area. VANs are public data networks that add value to the basic communication services the common carriers provide by offering specialized services.

The three most common types of network topologies are bus, ring, and star topology. In bus topology, computers on the network are connected through a single circuit to a central channel. The targeted device alone will respond to the message, although each message is transmitted to all the computers on the network. In a ring topology, the network devices are configured as a circular array. Each computer can communicate directly with any other computer on the network. Finally, in a star topology a host computer receives messages and forwards them to various computers on the network.

6. **Identify key telecommunication applications.** Electronic data interchange (EDI) is a powerful telecommunications application. It is a network that allows direct computer-to-computer exchange of business document data and is used by businesses to digitally transmit documents. PC implementation of EDI requires EDI software and a modem, whereas large-scale implementation of EDI requires a value-added network. Other telecommunications applications include teleconferencing, videoconferencing, fax, and voice mail.
7. **Summarize what a global network is and its effects on business.** Global companies need global networks for survival. The need for global networks is increasing at a rapid rate around the world. Global networks provide companies with a local presence in the countries where they operate. Further, the networks help the business control and coordinate accurate and timely flow of information from business units in different countries. Companies also use global networks to stay in touch with their customers and capture local market niches. Although global networks have many advantages, they are not easy to build and maintain. Cross-cultural differences, weak infrastructures, different rules and regulations, and the sheer force of time and distance make global networks a challenge.

KEY TERMS

analog signal (p. 162)
bandwidth (p. 161)
baseband (p. 168)
broadband (p. 168)
bus topology (p. 170)
cellular phones (p. 166)
channel (p. 161)
coaxial cable (p. 164)
common carriers (p. 163)
communication satellites (p. 165)
digital signal (p. 162)
electronic data interchange (EDI) (p. 171)
fiber-optic cable (p. 164)
full-duplex transmission (p. 162)
half-duplex transmission (p. 162)
high-frequency radiophones (p. 166)
integrated services digital network (ISDN) (p. 167)
local area network (LAN) (p. 168)
metropolitan area networks (MAN) (p. 169)
microwave radio (p. 164)
modem (p. 162)
peer-to-peer relationship (p. 168)
private branch exchange (PBX) (p. 167)
ring topology (p. 170)
simplex transmission (p. 162)
special-purpose carriers (p. 164)
star topology (p. 170)
telecommunications (p. 161)
telecommunications media (p. 164)
telecommunication protocols (p. 163)
topology (p. 170)
twisted pair (p. 164)
value-added networks (VAN) (p. 169)
wide area networks (WAN) (p. 168)

REVIEW QUESTIONS

1. Why is telecommunications so vital to the health of a business? Can you give one example of a company that has benefited from telecommunications?
2. What is meant by telecommunications? What are some basic components in a telecommunications model?
3. What is a channel, and what are its five characteristics? Briefly describe each characteristic.
4. What are the three types of transmission direction? Can you give an example of each?

5. What is the difference between common carriers and special-purpose carriers? When would an organization choose a special-purpose carrier over a common carrier?
6. What is the difference between bounded and unbounded media? Identify three types of bounded media and four types of unbounded media.
7. Why is fiber-optic cable becoming one of the most popular bounded media?
8. How does a cellular phone system work?
9. Identify the six different types of networks. Explain how a PBX works and identify one or two advantages and disadvantages of this type of network.
10. What does ISDN stand for? Is ISDN a digital or an analog network? What are some advantages of ISDN?
11. What do LAN, WAN, MAN, and VAN stand for? Describe a LAN and explain what is meant by a peer-to-peer relationship.
12. Does a LAN use a common carrier or a private communications channel for transmitting data?
13. What is the difference between baseband and broadband?
14. What are some differences between a LAN and a PBX? Identify any two advantages of LANs.
15. What is a WAN? What are some different ways of setting up a WAN?
16. What is the difference between WAN and MAN?
17. What is EDI? What is its primary use?
18. What are some pros and cons associated with EDI?
19. What is the difference between teleconferencing and videoconferencing?
20. What do we mean by a global network? What are some unique challenges that companies face when establishing a global network?

DISCUSSION QUESTIONS AND EXERCISES

1. ISDN revolves around five key principles: openness, modularity, intelligence, network management and control, and integrated products and services. Openness means that all ISDN products will be standardized, which will allow users to mix and match products from different vendors. Without openness, an organization can be tied to one vendor because only products from that vendor will work on its network. Modularity allows an organization to upgrade or replace any part, or module, in a network without replacing the entire network. Because the entire network is built as a set of standard modules, organizations can "mix and match" modules as the needs of the company change. Intelligence means that the network has intelligence built into it, providing users with a way to configure their network connections to meet their requirements.
   a. Can these principles be applied to other technologies too? Discuss.
   b. Can network management be simplified if companies follow these five principles?
2. As a network manager, you are responsible for the selection of a suitable network for your company. The first step is to determine the information and network requirements of your organization. Next, determine the location of the network, the amount of network traffic, and performance requirements. You must ask the following questions:

- Where will the network be installed?
- What is the geographic area that the network must cover?
- Do we need a special-purpose carrier?
- What kind of data will be transmitted over the network (data, voice, graphics)?
- What is the volume of data that will travel over the network?
- What are the peak and low periods for the traffic?
- What is the average required response time?
- What level of accuracy and reliability is required?
- How critical are the data transmitted over the network?
- What kind of security and backup measures should the organization have?

Once these questions have been asked and addressed, the next step is to determine hardware and software requirements. Set up a meeting with a network administrator in your area and identify if there are other questions that should be addressed before selecting a network.

3. You have been assigned the task of linking three business units located in New York, Los Angeles, and Orlando. What type of network and what medium would you recommend for this application and why?
4. **(Web exercise)** Use any search engine on the Web to find an international application of information systems that uses telecommunications. Summarize your findings in writing.

Case 1: Fruits Are No Small Matter

It's hard enough to get home from the grocery store with unbruised apples, oranges, and other produce. How would you like to be responsible for safely delivering 83 million cartons of oranges, plums, apples, mangos, and avocados from South Africa to a host of European countries? And make sure that the goods are on time and in good shape! Information services manager Gwynne Foster of Capespan International PLC faces this challenge.

Two South African fruit exporting companies jointly own this company, which has its headquarters in England: citrus exporter Outspan International in Pretoria and deciduous-fruit exporter Unifruco in Cape Town. The company reached $825 million in revenue in 1995 and plans to increase revenue to $1.5 billion by 2000. For Foster, managing information systems means finding solutions for marketing, distributing, and selling South African fruit to Europe. Her main challenge has been to implement a transcontinental system that ensures Unifruco's Granny Smith apples and Outspan's navel oranges make the trip to Europe safely and on time.

"The situation is becoming more complex and difficult, and we are radically rethinking some of our earlier strategies," she says. South Africa's recently renewed ability to trade with Europe, along with changing market forces in the produce industry, made it clear to Capespan in the early 1990s that it needed to change the way it moved its product. "What has happened over the last 10 years is the rise of the supermarket," Foster explains. "When you walk into a supermarket in the UK, every apple has a label on it." Partly because of such branding changes in the fruit industry, "we [rather than the retailer] have to be sure the apple is of good quality."

Several years ago, Capespan's tracking system indicated how many cartons of each kind of fruit were being shipped, but that was the extent of the information provided, and most was gathered manually. When the produce arrived in Europe, last-minute business-savvy decisions, such as customer-specific labeling requests or changes in delivery times, were out of the question. "We had to get a lot closer to the end customer," Foster explains. Through IBM Global Network, Capespan linked more than half of its 200 trading partners with a variety of PC-based tracking systems within 18 months and launched its new tracking system. To collect more information about the exported fruit, a Unix-based tracking system with bar-code readers for radio-frequency scanning was implemented in the originating South African ports.

The handheld scanners act as terminals that link directly into the computer. "From that information, we create a [record] of what is on a vessel and transmit that to Europe," Foster explains. Capespan sends the information, including details about the product's inspection, growers, packaging and chemical treatment, to sales offices and receiving ports so sales offices know what will be available for sale, and ports know what they need to off-load.

"Capespan can then do its planning of where to off-load the fruit, feeding that information further down the chain to the marketing offices so they can start allocating product to sales agents," Foster says. Once the information gets to Europe, Capespan's partners use two different PC systems to track the produce: one for European ports and cold-storage facilities and another for sales agents. All the systems link back to Capespan through the IBM Global Network, which is linked directly to Capespan's U.K. office. Electronically tracking its products gives Capespan the responsiveness and flexibility it needs in an ever-changing global market. "We have systems in place from the intake points through the ports and through to the sales agent," Foster notes. "If you get that data in right, everyone else in the chain should benefit." When a boat docks, the port already knows where to send the fruit—whether on to another port or directly into cold storage. Fruit is inspected so that any surprises, such as fruit that ripened too quickly, can be off-loaded and sold immediately.

In turn, information about any change in plans—100 cartons of peaches that won't arrive in Hamburg, Germany—is fed immediately into the information chain. "You can pre-advise and ease the work on the port," Foster says. "The whole thrust of the system is to get information about the product in the chain before the product comes through the chain." Foster hesitates to quantify financial savings accrued by the system. "A lot of what we have done is fundamental to survival, and we have not yet seen all of the potential benefit of what we've put in place," she explains. "But had we not taken dramatic steps, we would not have supported our customers."

With the unification of Europe, Capespan will have new and extensive changes to make to its tracking system. The unification of the common European trading market has meant the emergence of pan-European fruit buyers, requiring renegotiated and new trading agreements for Capespan. As these technology systems accommodate the way business is done, the technology will have to change as business relationships do. But for Capespan, adapting to a common European market would have been impossible without first installing the current system, Foster observes. "The previous view of the world—that we bring in the product en masse to local sales offices—doesn't fit the trading environment

continued

Case 1: Fruits Are No Small Matter, *continued*

moving in to the future," she notes. "Ours is not a single system. It's a process—it's a hellishly complex process—but the system is necessary to prosper."[25]

1. Explain how Capespan leveraged its telecommunications systems to achieve market leadership.
2. What types of networks would be suitable for this type of application? Explain.
3. "If you get the data in right, everyone else in the information chain should benefit." Comment.

Case 2: Shell Malaysia Goes High Tech

Shell Malaysia, a 105-year-old oil company, embarked on a reengineering journey, starting four years ago. The project involved completely reengineering Shell Malaysia Trading's (SMT) business with the objective of delivering big results, fast, leaving "no stone unturned." SMT's management team agreed that customer intimacy should be the basis on which to compete in the marketplace, with operational efficiency and product leadership also being top priorities. The reengineering journey involved continual repetition of three activities:

1. Changing business practice (invention)
2. Introducing the change (implementation)
3. Managing the change (transition)

Telecommunications and local and wide area networks provided the infrastructure to link the company's 35 offices and achieve the above goals. A state-of-the-art Customer Service Center was implemented to allow employees to take orders over the telephone, answer customer inquiries, and schedule deliveries, all on-line. Each employee has access to systems that provide information about customer contacts, advice on technical matters, and details about orders, deliveries, stocks, and other related matters. At the heart of all information systems is a hub of LANs, WANs, and global networks that allows the company to communicate effectively with all its units. For example, the Lubrication Oils Central Supply Unit (LCSU) system located in the Head Office in Kuala Lumpur helps all units in Malaysia to optimize their inventory levels by providing timely and meaningful information about customer needs. The daily stock positions are downloaded from mainframe-based order-processing and stock-accounting systems, and delivered on-line to different units, thanks to telecommunications. Shell companies in Japan and Australia access shared information about prices, suppliers, and potential deals, thus providing consistent service to customers around the world.

However, the company had to overcome several obstacles to achieve such significant results:

- Resistance to change or organizational inertia (Why change when we're doing well?).
- Unfamiliarity with new and better ways of doing things.
- Learning how to better use mainframes and other systems to support decision making.
- Lack of local technical support from suppliers for the newest technologies, such as voice response systems.
- Identifying and defining measures of performance that produce the desired behavior in all employees.
- Staff skepticism about reengineering and low morale. Was *reengineering* another word for *downsizing?*
- The belief that the IT department would not be able to deliver new technologies.
- Resistance to change from suppliers and other corporate partners.

However, by focusing effectively on both human and technical issues, Shell Malaysia achieved all its goals and showed the world how technology can be used as a strategic weapon in the pursuit of market excellence.[26]

1. Could Shell Malaysia have achieved its reengineering goals without an outstanding telecommunications infrastructure? Explain the role of telecommunications in helping the company achieve its goals.
2. Resistance to change is quite natural, especially during reengineering efforts. Identify three key steps that you would take as an IS manager to involve users and gain their participation and support for your reengineering efforts.

[T]he Internet is one of the rare, if not unique, instances where 'hype' is accompanied by understatement, not overstatement. . . . I don't think we know what has hit us.

Nicholas Negroponte, Director, MIT Media Lab

INTERNET FOR SUCCESS

CONTENTS

Many experts, like Nicholas Negroponte, consider the Internet to be the most underestimated revolution of our times.[1] If the Internet were a stock it would be considered a market phenomenon, with sustained double- or even triple-digit growth each year and no apparent end in sight to the upward spiral. Recent Internet statistics are stunning. As of March 1999 approximately 320 million Web pages existed. The estimated number of Internet users in 1998 was 122 million worldwide and 79.4 million in North America (38 percent of the U.S. population). The number of users is expected to grow to 1 billion by 2001.[2]

The Internet is a powerful information medium. It offers every kind of information imaginable: free electronic-mail services, research databases, on-line Yellow Pages, used-car price guides, maps with driving directions, kids' games, TV guides, college information, investment guidelines, and up-to-date weather information as shown in the Weather Channel screen capture on the next page.[3]

The Internet is changing our personal lives, professional lives, and society. And, like uncorking the genie in the bottle, we cannot go back. From watching the space shuttle take off to sharing one's opinions with the rest of the world to sending announcements and greeting cards, the Net has become a digital extension of our lives.

Individuals use Internet information for many reasons: to save time and money, learn, voice an opinion, join a community, read the news, and find job opportunities. We briefly focus on three personal applications, though there are thousands more: salary negotiations, on-line education, and shopping.

The Internet levels the playing field for job seekers by exposing businesses that "are way below everyone else as far as pay is concerned," notes Brian Krueger, a staffing and employee-development

Chapter 7

The Internet, Intranets, and Extranets

AFTER STUDYING THIS CHAPTER, YOU WILL BE ABLE TO:

- Describe the Internet, including the term "information superhighway"
- Identify the four types of Internet tools, including the World Wide Web
- Describe an intranet
- Describe an extranet
- Discuss Internet-related ethical issues

director for Keane, an information-technology consulting firm. Holly Peckham, a public relations account executive, negotiated a 21 percent salary increase by locating a database on the Web that contained salary information supplied by more than 16,000 communications professionals. Ms. Peckham's conclusion: Based on her qualifications, she should be making about $37,000 a year as an account executive at a PR agency serving high-tech clients. Her current employer was paying her $9,000 less than the average. Her job search began.

The weather.com site provides up-to-the minute weather information. It is the Internet's most popular single-content Web site, averaging over 135 million pageviews per month as of July 1999.

TECHNOLOGY PAYOFF

Keeping a Web Page on Ice

Consider the situation facing Odwalla, maker of natural juice and vegetable drinks, whose corporate mission is to respect the earth as it nourishes the body. When several children became ill—and one died—after drinking Odwalla juice containing apples from a supplier whose fruit was contaminated with the *E. coli* bacteria, the company knew that it had a serious health and public relations crisis on its hands.

The company turned to its public relations firm, Edelman, to seek advice on how to handle the situation quickly, compassionately, and effectively. According to Matthew J. Harrington, crisis sector and general manager in Edelman's San Francisco office, the firm had created a "dark," or inactivated, Web site for Odwalla before the crisis occurred. Once the crisis hit, Odwalla and Edelman customized the dark site to communicate with anxious consumers and Odwalla juice distributors. In fact, Odwalla's site was up and running the same day the news broke. Such timely information was clearly in demand: the site received more than 20,000 hits in its first 48 hours.

The Web site—combined with a customer hotline, press conferences, visits to the families of the ill people, and a voluntary recall of juices that might possibly have been contaminated with the bacteria—helped the company show its commitment to its customers' well-being. In fact, the company kept customers apprised of steps it took to investigate and prevent future health risks, including adopting new pasteurizing methods.

In the future, dark sites such as Odwalla's could help businesses communicate critical information with members of the general public, reporters, public officials, and business partners. The practice of keeping a Web site "on ice," ready to be filled in with crisis-related content at a moment's notice, could be one of IT's best weapons in an arsenal of crisis-management tools.

Individuals use Internet sites like monster.com to look for jobs, obtain career advice, and develop resumes.

When a company offered her a salary lower than the average during her search, she refused, citing her on-line research. "I told them the national average was between $36,000 and $38,000 . . . ," she recollects. "My hands were shaking." They upped the ante. She accepted.[4] "I wouldn't be surprised if we see a lot more [applicants] coming in, having done on-line searches" for competitive salary information, says Barbara Ewen, a principal at Chen, the firm that hired Ms. Peckham.[5]

Individuals turn to on-line education sites to learn more. One of those sites, CyberState University (www.cyberstateu.com), is an authorized technical training center for the Information Technology College Accreditation Program (ITCAP). This site allows students and other professionals to get college credit for Microsoft and other vendors' technical training courses without ever leaving their offices or homes.

The Internet is also altering the shopping behavior of individuals. Instead of trekking to the mall, people can visit merchants and businesses at home via the Internet, browsing or purchasing at their own pace. They avoid traffic, the hassle of tramping from store to store, and the aggravation of aggressive salespeople. Consider these numbers: 21 percent of those who bought new cars last year shopped for them on-line. Auto research firm J. D. Power and Associates projects that figure will double by next year. The research suggests that consumers believe they can get accurate auto data off the World Wide Web quickly, without the threat of being cheated or hassled by a dealer.[6]

Businesses, both large and small, have embraced the Internet to reach customers, obtain resources, and communicate with business partners and suppliers. Though we examine the Internet's general business effects throughout this chapter, keep in mind that Internet use may vary by size of business or gender of business owner. Studies, for instance, show that small companies and entrepreneurs use the Internet for certain applications more than large corporations. The chart in Figure 7-1 on p. 188 details the top four reasons why small businesses use the Internet.

In addition, businesswomen are more likely than men to use the Internet to accelerate the growth of their companies, according to a survey by the National Foundation for Women Business Owners (NFWBO), a nonprofit research foundation based in Silver Spring, Maryland. The survey examined the practices of nearly 800 U.S. companies during a 2-month period. The findings suggest that women who run their own companies are more likely than their male counterparts to subscribe to an on-line service, have a homepage, and use the Internet to communicate or to conduct research.[7]

The societal impact of the Internet constantly changes and grows. As the Technology Payoff shows, Odwalla relied on the Internet to provide valuable information to concerned individuals in a timely, efficient manner. What could have taken weeks or even months to convey was communicated in under a day.

A sample of the Internet's positive societal effects includes better tracking of those who fail to pay taxes. Connecticut's Internet list of the state's top 100 tax dodgers helped generate $40 million in back taxes.[8]

The Internet also connects people around the globe. The National Wildlife Federation (NWF) uses its Web site to allow people throughout the world to share their passion and concern for conserving our planet's valuable resources. The site also helps NWF members interact with one another and exchange ideas and project information. For example, one of the links on the site, called Animal Tracks, offers 55 ready-to-use classroom and outdoor education activities for teachers and environment educators. The link entitled Backyard Wildlife Habitat provides information on how people can use their backyards to enhance the quality of the environment.[9]

Now that we have examined some personal, business, and societal effects of the Internet, we explore how the Internet works, Internet tools that help a business achieve its goals, and Internet ethical issues. We also examine intranets and extranets, including strategies for their use and applications.

Just as newspapers prepare celebrities' obituaries before they die, this practice lets companies respond to events in the fastest possible way, explains Kevin Rowe, president of Eagle River Interactive. Why plan ahead? "Creating a Web site on demand overnight is nearly impossible," he says. The site has to look professional, not "like it was just thrown together," and has to be sturdy enough to handle thousands of visitors.

Sources: Adapted from L. Gibbons Paul, "From Harrowing to Heroism," *CIO,* Section 1, September 1, 1998, 40–41; *See also:* Christina Walters, "Pulp Non-Fiction," *Metro News,* January 11–17, 1996, www.metroactive.com/papers/metro/01.11.96/Odwalla-9602.

What Is the Internet?

The Net, as the Internet is popularly called, evolved from ARPANET, a now-defunct research network created and subsidized in the 1960s by the U.S. Defense Department and the National Science Foundation (NSF). The goal of ARPANET was to link research institutions and government agencies around the world so that they could freely exchange ideas, information, and knowledge. In spite of the enormous power of the Net, no one owns it. The National Science Foundation (NSF) and the Internet Engineering Task Force (IETF) formed a committee of scientists and experts and provided technical supervision, standards, and guidelines for the Net and did the main work on the Internet.

The Net
One of the oldest long-distance communication networks; a network of networks.

FIGURE 7-1

Why Small Businesses Are On-Line

Source: Small Business Computing & Communications (www.smalloffice.com), November 28, 1998, 20.

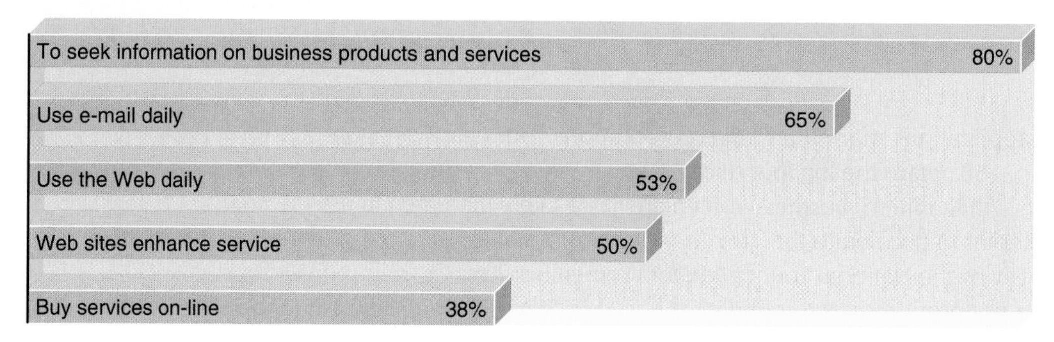

Think of the Internet as a huge repository of information on every imaginable topic (Fig. 7-2). People anywhere can access this information reservoir anytime with a few keystrokes and sufficient equipment. They can add, edit, send, retrieve, and store information residing on any computer as long as the computers involved are connected to the Internet via telecommunication lines. The Internet's expansive reach is why people often view the Internet as an electronic "Web" that links people and businesses in new ways.

The Internet is more than a database of information, however. It is a widespread communication medium. People and entities can communicate one-on-one via electronic mail or they can communicate to a large audience by posting information on a site. Posting has the same effect as placing a message on a bulletin board. Users with access to the board can read what is posted. Table 7-1 shows that the Internet has reached 50 million households in less than 5 years. That is rapid growth compared to other mediums, such as radio and television.

The growth of the Internet has profoundly affected businesses. Experts estimate revenues from Internet-related sales and other transactions to increase anywhere from 10- to 100-fold over the next 5 years. Aside from the revenues, the Internet is changing

FIGURE 7-2

The Internet Allows Access to Information of All Kinds

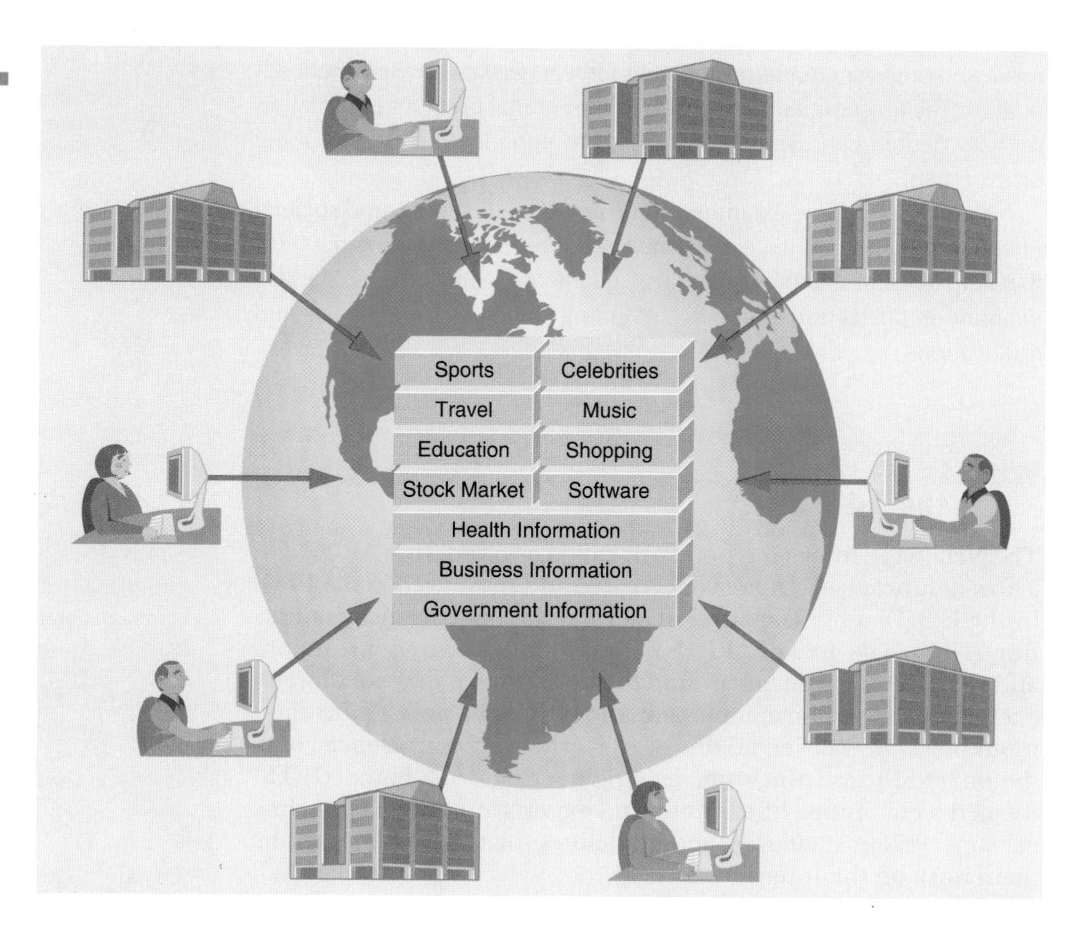

TABLE 7-1

Years Communication Mediums Have Taken to Reach 50 Million Households

Type of Medium	Number of Years
Radio	38
Television	13
Cable television	10
Internet	Less than 5

Source: Morgan Stanley Technology Research, 1997.

how companies communicate with their consumers, employees, and others who have an interest in the business. Workers can now communicate quickly, cheaply, at any time, almost anywhere, enabling them to work away from an office setting. The Internet also offers speedy access to business information, enhancing efficiency and improving relationships with those people or organizations that need such information—from customers to suppliers to coworkers in Thailand or New Zealand.

The Internet Is an Information Superhighway

In recent years, the term **information superhighway** has been used to describe the Internet. Although there is no universally accepted definition of the information superhighway, it has three key characteristics:

Information superhighway
A network of networks that is fully scalable with no central controlling entity, and its users remain anonymous.

1. It has no central controlling entity. In other words, no one individual or organization controls the superhighway.
2. It is fully **scalable,** meaning that system performance will not degrade as the number of users increase.
3. Users' profiles are kept anonymous. A user can be an individual, a machine, an organization, or some other entity. For example, an e-mail address does not always reveal whether the individual is male or female. In some cases, we may not know if the user is an individual or an organization, or if the mail is customized to one individual or mass mailed to thousands.

Scalable
Performance of the system does not diminish as the number of users increases.

The Internet has all three characteristics, so information superhighway is an apt description.

The Internet Is a Network of Networks

Although no individual or organization owns the Internet, it is one of the most powerful networks in the world. The network consists of personal users' PCs, which act as *clients,* and Internet-connected computers that store information of interest to others, which are configured as *servers.* Note that both clients and servers are computers. The only difference is that the client requests a specific type of service and the server provides the service. That means that a PC can be both a client and a server. (Client/server systems are covered in more detail in Chapter 9.)

The clients and servers are connected through a complex interconnection of networks. Sending an electronic message is quite similar to air travel. If you want to go from Los Angeles to Orlando, your travel agent determines the shortest route between the two cities. However, you may have to change planes to get to your destination, depending on the distance between your starting and ending locations. Similarly, when a user sitting at her PC sends an electronic message, it is routed first to her Internet Service Provider (ISP). The ISP forwards the message to the next most meaningful *node,* which is a computer on the network (akin to changing planes), and this process continues until the message reaches its destination.

Different companies, universities, and research institutions run, manage, and own parts of the network that link different computers. Figure 7-3 shows the structure of the Internet and who helps run and maintain it.

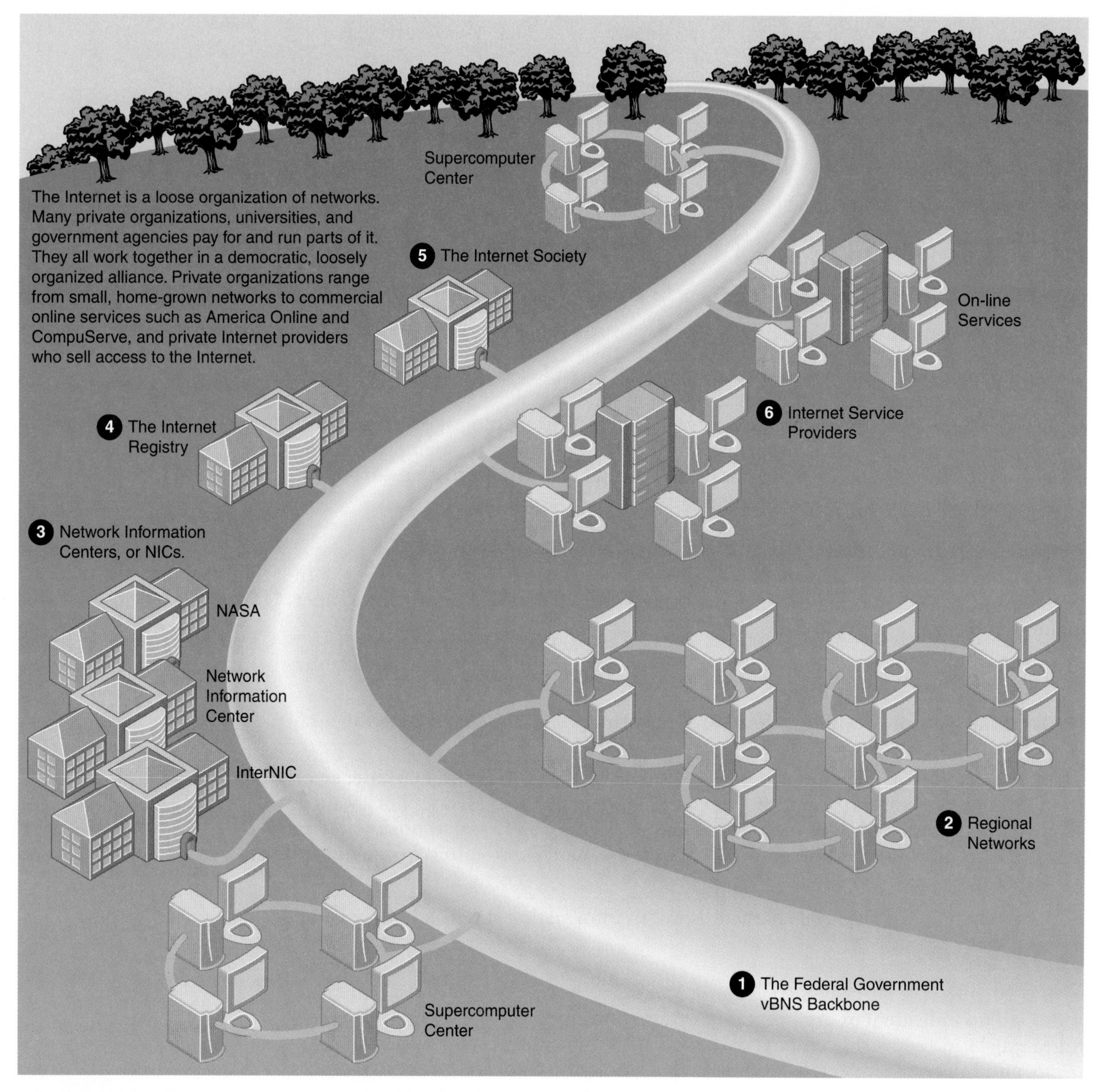

FIGURE 7-3 **Who Helps Run the Internet**

Source: Preston Gralla, *How the Internet Works* (illustrated by Sarah Ishida) (San Francisco, CA: Ziff-Davis Press, 1997), p. 6.

Figure 7-3 depicts six entities that help operate the Internet. A loose confederation of networks pays for and runs portions of the Internet. First, the U.S. government pays for some high-speed network services (known as vBNS, or very-high-speed Backbone Network Services) that link supercomputer centers. In addition, several Internet providers and telecommunication companies supply long-distance connections—known as backbones—that connect servers from around the world. A backbone refers to the part of a network that handles the major traffic on the network. Smaller networks are usually attached to the backbone. A backbone can span a large or very small geographic area.[10]

Second, regional networks offer Internet access in a limited geographic area. Often these networks include groups of smaller networks that work together to provide and maintain better Internet service. Third, to help organizations use the Internet, private and government-sponsored Network Information Centers (NICs) provide support and information. The InterNIC is an organization that assists all NICs. The National Science Foundation, in turn, supports the work of the InterNIC.[11] InterNIC, Internet Network Information Center (www.internic.net), is the most widely known of the organizations that handle Internet domain name registration. Domain names are names given to networks on the Internet.

ARIN, American Registry for Internet Numbers (www.arin.net), is an organization that was founded in 1997 to dispense Internet Protocol (IP) addresses in North and South America, the Carribean, and sub-Saharan Africa. This entity manages domain names in these areas. The European and Asian counterparts of ARIN are Researux IP Europeens (RIPE) and Asia Pacific Network Information Center (APNIC).

Who keeps track of the addresses of every person or organization on the Internet? The Internet Registry, shown in number four in Figure 7-3, records these addresses and monitors the relationship between addresses and domain names. The Internet Society, highlighted in number five, is a nonprofit entity that recommends the direction the Internet should take for maintenance and growth. The final player in Internet operation is the Internet service provider (ISP). These providers sell users Internet connections and run their own computers on the Internet.[12]

Now that we have examined what the Internet is, we explore different Internet tools.

Internet Tools

The Internet is used to retrieve and send information, search for information, and send e-mail. Each activity requires different Internet tools, which we list next:

- *Information retrieval tools:* FTP and Gopher
- *Information search tools:* Archie, Veronica, WAIS, and search engines
- *Communication tools:* e-mail, telnet, Usenet, mailing lists, and chat rooms
- *Integrating different forms of information retrieval and dissemination:* the World Wide Web (also known as Multimedia tools)

In the sections that follow, we examine each type of tool and its applications.

Information Retrieval Tools

The Internet houses such vast amounts of information that one of the biggest tasks is retrieving useful information. In this section, let's investigate how two tools help users retrieve and send information from the Internet: FTP, or file transfer protocol, and Gopher.

One of the early Internet information retrieval tools, known as **file transfer protocol (FTP),** continues to be widely used. FTP allows users to upload or download files, copy files, and list directories. A directory is an electronic folder that stores related files. For example, all class grades can be stored in a directory called GRADES.

File transfer protocol (FTP)

A protocol that allows users to transfer files, such as text, graphics, sound, and other data, from one computer to another.

FTP is a protocol that establishes a link between the computer requesting the service and the computer providing the service. Recall that a telecommunications protocol is a set of internationally recognized standards that facilitate the digital transmission of data and information. One such special protocol is FTP, a set of standards that guides how files are to be transferred from one computer to another. Special software, which the Internet service provider (ISP) sometimes furnishes, helps the user requesting the service to access the remote machine to send or receive data or files.

FTP users can transfer files by entering a command at the command prompt or using an FTP program. Some FTP programs have graphical user interfaces, making it easy for users to transfer files. Users can also use some Web browsers, such as Netscape, to transfer FTP files. In such cases, the Internet address begins with ftp:// instead of the usual http:// (where http stands for Hyper Text Transfer Protocol).

Another popular way to retrieve files is through an anonymous FTP server. The user logs onto an FTP site on the Internet and enters his or her ID as "anonymous" rather

This is a screen shot showing FTP.

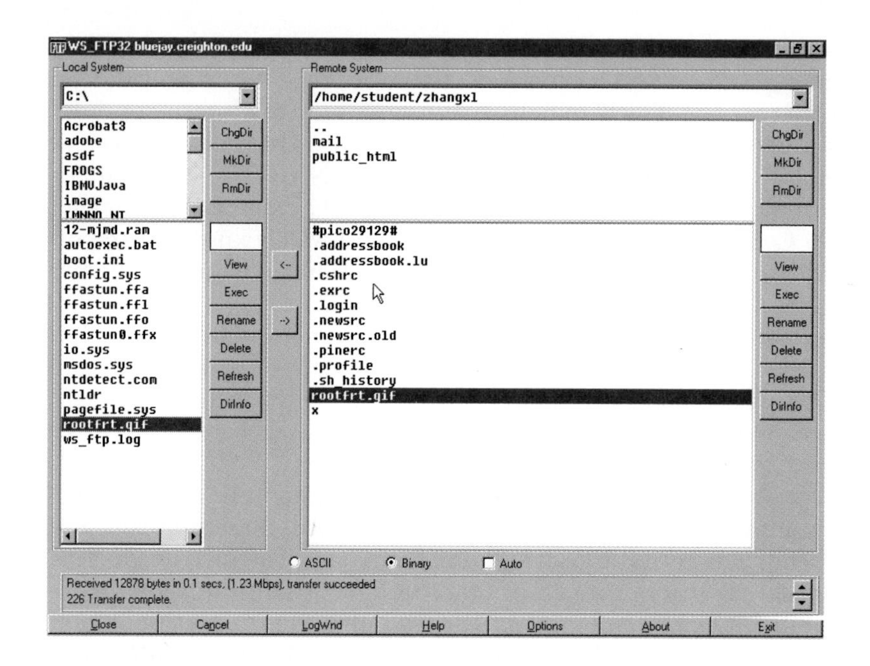

than a user ID that is often given by companies to log on to a system. In other words, an anonymous FTP allows any user to download a file. In some cases, the server may require a password. Users often obtain freeware and shareware—programs that are available at no cost on the Net—through anonymous FTP servers. Usually, anonymous FTP sites are isolated from other computer systems in the organization because anyone can access these systems.

Users can only receive files from anonymous FTP sites; they cannot send any files to them. For security reasons, this restriction makes sense because the identity of users using an anonymous FTP server is unknown. There is no way to trace who accessed an anonymous FTP server. Note that there is a difference between the "anonymity" of users on the Net versus someone signing on as "anonymous" to access a system. The former is the nature of the Net; the latter is a decision made by a company or organization to allow individuals to access a given system without checking their identity.

Gopher

A menu-based interface that provides access to information residing on Gopher sites.

The second type of Internet information retrieval tool is **Gopher.** This tool is often a menu-based interface that provides easy access to information residing on special servers, called Gopher sites—sites open to and organized for Gopher access. Although Gopher performs the same function as the FTP, its interface is more user-friendly than FTP programs, although that is changing because FTP sites are improving their user interfaces.

Further, it provides additional functions, such as links to other Internet services. By selecting an item on the Gopher menu, users can move, retrieve, or display files from remote sites. The menu also allows users to move from one Gopher site to another

FIGURE 7-4

Gopher Space: Interconnected Gopher Computers

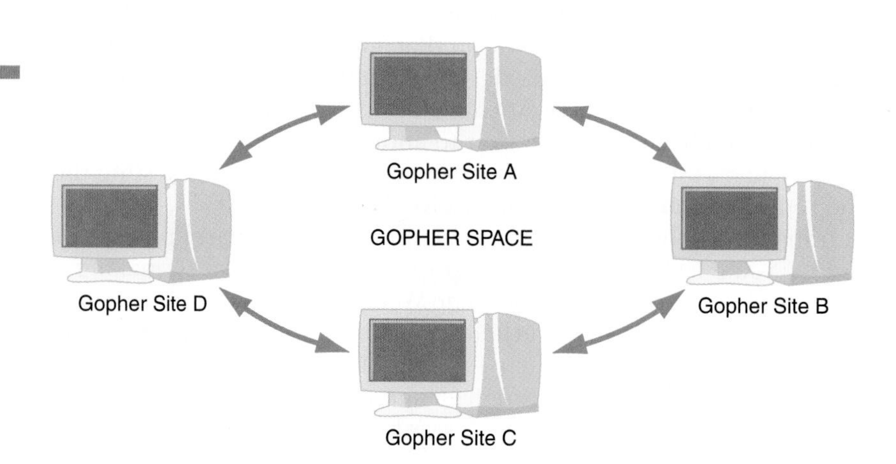

through the use of hyperlinks. A hyperlink (discussed in more detail later) is an electronic link that is built into a Web page or any other electronic document. By clicking on the link, the user can easily move back and forth from one document to another. Finally, the entire Gopher space (which refers to interconnected Gopher computers) can be easily expanded by adding more computers.

Information Search Tools

Numerous Internet search tools allow users to search for specific information. Archie, Veronica, and Wide Area Information Server are three early Internet search tools. **Archie** searches, periodically, anonymous FTP servers on the Archie database and identifies all files on these servers, which users can then access using Archie software if they know the file name. **Veronica** is similar to Archie except that it locates all files on Gopher sites, even if a user does not know the full file name. Users who have access to Gopher and Veronica can access the database. **WAIS (Wide Area Information Server),** pronounced "ways," accesses computers linked to the Internet to locate specific files using an index of keywords on various topics.

Current Internet search tools are faster, easier, and more efficient than the early tools. Users hunt for information using "search terms" that may be words, partial words, numbers, phrases, names, or concepts. World Wide Web search tools, often called **search engines,** review a database of URL addresses for specific keywords. The sophisticated software of these engines searches Web sites on the Internet that the search engine has previously identified and indexed according to keywords. If the software finds sites that contain a match with one or more of the user's search terms, it displays those sites' URL addresses and often shows site descriptions.

The engines help users locate specific Web sites or files for information on almost any topic. Depending on the sophistication of the seach engine, users can search for and download articles, demos, graphics, audio, video, and images. Many downloads can be saved directly to the user's computer and edited if desired. Search tools have become common in large part because they are so useful that users expect Web sites to have them.

Archie

An early Internet search tool that searches different networked computers, retrieves relevant files, and stores them in a database that users can access.

Veronica

An Internet search tool that locates files in databases on Gopher sites.

WAIS (Wide Area Information Server)

An Internet search tool that accesses computers linked to the Internet to locate specific files.

Search engine

An Internet search tool that searches specific sites or files, primarily on the World Wide Web, to find those that match the user's search terms.

Communication Tools

Internet communication tools are designed to improve written communication over the Internet. Users select a particular type of Internet communication tool depending on their needs. The three main types of communication tools are e-mail, telnet, and Usenet. Users who want to communicate as they would via a regular mail service use e-mail. Those who want to run a program or access a remote file rely on telnet, and those who want to post or discuss general information turn to Usenet.

E-mail

One of the earliest and most popular Internet functions is **e-mail,** which refers to sending messages or files electronically over a network. Users can send mail to a single recipient or to many recipients. The receiver can retrieve the mail at his or her convenience, or in some systems the user is automatically notified when there is mail in the electronic mail box.

E-mail

The transmission of electronic messages over a network.

An e-mail system requires a messaging system that stores and forwards the messages to the right individual and a mail program that allows the user to send and receive messages. Suppose you have a word-processing document (say, your resumé) that you would like a friend to review. You can simply cut and paste the document into your e-mail program and send it to your friend or you can send it as an e-mail attachment. In this case, there will be an icon or link on the receiver's e-mail message. When the user clicks on the icon, it will activate or open up the receiver's word-processing package and your friend can view the document as if it were a word-processing file residing on his or her system.

Sending or receiving information over the Internet is similar to sending or receiving mail. The key is to know the address of the individual or organization. All individual Internet addresses are made up of two elements: the user ID, followed by an @, and then the name of the host computer sending or receiving the mail. Internet addresses generally have the following format: userid@name-of-the-computer.type-of-organization. An Internet service provider assigns the address. For example, if Chris Green is accessing the Net from home using her American on-line (AOL) account, her Internet address

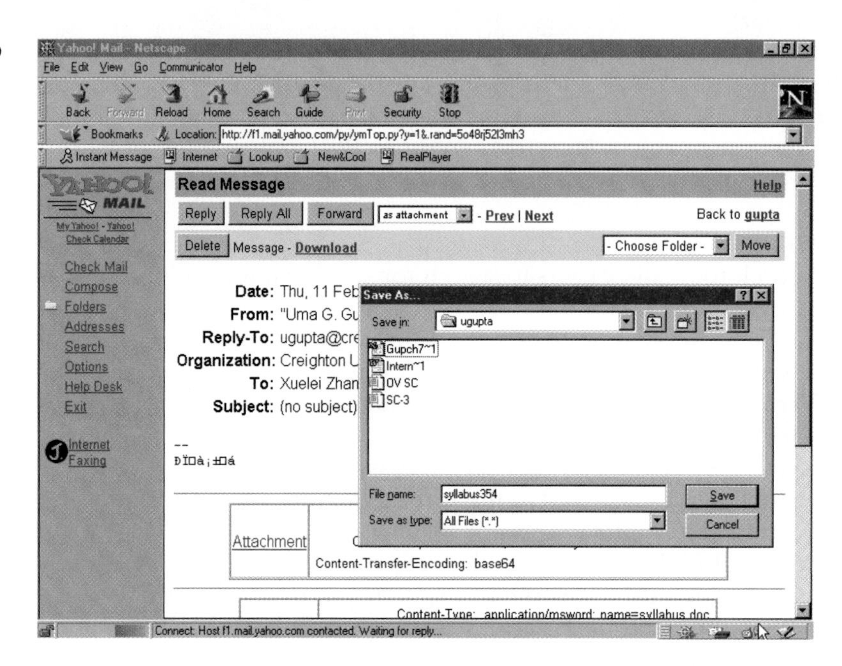

E-mail programs allow users to communicate electronically with one or several people. Users may also attach files, such as a word-processing document, which are represented by an icon.

might be green@aol.com. "aol" identifies the host computer or network; ".com" indicates that this is a commercial domain. Table 7-2 lists other domain abbreviations.

Say that Chris Green is connecting to the Internet from a machine in the computer science department at New Mexico State University, her address might be cgreen@cs.nmsu.edu. In this case, cgreen is the user's ID. The "cs" may stand for the computer science department. (Of course, this could also be represented in other ways such as "compsci," "cscience," and so on.) "nmsu" stands for the host computer receiving or sending mail, and ".edu" indicates that this is an educational institution.

Now suppose you received mail from the following Internet address: hford@hollywood.columbia.com. (This is a fictional address.) The user id is hford (Harrison Ford); the name of the computer sending the mail is Hollywood at Columbia Pictures (an organization), which is a commercial entity (represented as com). It is through this simple yet powerful idea of addresses that users all over the world are able to send and receive e-mail over the Internet (Fig. 7-5).

E-mail is almost addictive for some individuals. Once users become familiar with their e-mail software, the idea of sending mail through the post office (also called "snail mail") seems too slow. In Canada, the United States, Germany, and other parts of the world, e-mail has become as commonplace as the telephone. Companies that do not have an e-mail address are considered archaic. An IS manager recalls how the Russian accountants at the Moscow office of Young & Rubicam, the New York City ad agency,

TABLE 7-2 Domain Abbreviations

Domain Abbreviation	Stands for . . .
.org	Any organization such as the Red Cross or American Heart Association
.edu	Any educational institution such as a university, community college, or high school
.gov	Any government agency
.com	Any commercial entity
.net	Any network service provider

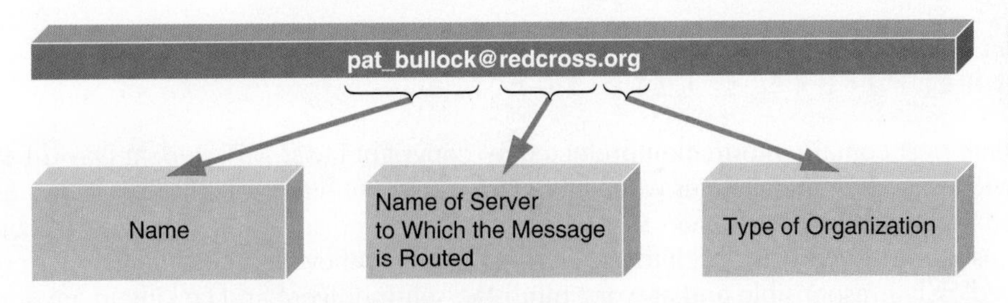

FIGURE 7-5

The Structure of an E-mail Address

fought against external e-mail access. "The whole culture of Soviet management had been one of information protection." The accountants could not believe that information from the Moscow office would stay safe. "Once we demonstrated it could be protected, they gave a hesitant nod. Six months later, they were saying e-mail is the greatest thing since bread and butter."[13]

Telnet

A command that allows users to log onto a remote computer and run a program or locate a file from their computer is called **telnet.** Telnet is part of the TCP/IP communications protocol. While file transfer protocol only allows users to move or transfer files, telnet provides broader services, depending on the host machine, such as executing programs, checking e-mail, or even developing an application.

Telnet

A protocol that allows users to connect to a remote machine and type a command, such as running a program, from their local computer.

Usenet

Internet service providers offer the **Usenet** service, which is like a public bulletin board system. Usenet consists of thousands of newsgroups. Any user can post ideas, opinions, or questions in a newsgroup and other users can read and respond directly to the author of the message by e-mail or post a reply in the newsgroup for everyone to read.

Usenet

A service that provides users with electronic discussion groups or forums for gathering information on a wide variety of topic; an electronic bulletin board.

A user can select from different newsgroups (over 30,000 groups worldwide) with the help of an Internet browser, such as Netscape Navigator or Microsoft Internet Explorer, or with the help of newsreading programs such as Pine or Agent. There are different types of newsgroups, catering to different interest groups, such as golf fanatics or nuclear physicists. And for new users to Usenet there is a newsgroup called news.newusers.questions.

All newsgroups follow certain etiquette. Readers are expected to show courtesy to their fellow members and users should understand the group, its needs, and expertise before posting a question. In fact, many members have a strong sense of community and often bond emotionally with other group members.

Many find Usenet a helpful information-gathering tool on a variety of topics. For example, computer vendors monitor technical forums to gain an understanding of issues that their customers are facing. In some cases, companies can halt misinformation or rumors about their company or its products. For instance, a calculation error in the Pentium I chip was first discussed on a newsgroup. Intel eventually addressed the problem.

Some employers monitor newsgroups to find the technically talented and then offer them jobs. One IS manager posts particularly thorny technical problems on Usenet in the relevant discussion groups and then makes an offer to individuals who give some of the best replies.

Visit the Web site www.deja.com to view some of the thousands of newsgroups that are available. Despite their great benefits, Usenet groups pose ethical dilemmas, as we see in the Ethics for Success feature.

Mailing Lists

A **mailing list** is similar to a newsgroup, except that instead of an electronic bulletin board, users rely on e-mail to communicate with each other. The first step is to subscribe to and become a member of the mailing list. Members then receive e-mail from other members in the group. Usually an individual or an organization "owns" the list and it

Mailing list

An electronic discussion forum that encourages group communication using e-mail among users with information needs on specific topics.

Ethics for success

Yo, Ho, the Pirate's Life for Me

Should a Usenet post contain information protected by copyright laws? MIT student David LaMacchia escaped conviction on criminal charges when he ran an electronic bulletin board that others used to illegally upload and download more than $1 million in copyrighted software. U.S. District Court Judge Richard Stearns wrote in his decision, "If the indictment is to be believed, one might at best describe his actions as heedlessly irresponsible and at worst nihilistic, self-indulgent and lacking in any fundamental sense of values."[14]

Current copyright law could not be used against the MIT student because the law requires proof that the copyright infringement was made "for purposes of commercial advantage or private financial gain," something LaMacchia was not alleged to have done.

"The LaMacchia case points out that we need a legislative fix to enable us to prosecute unethical bulletin board operators," notes Ken Wasch, executive director of the Software Publishers Association in Washington. He estimates that software piracy costs vendors $7.5 billion a year worldwide, and $1.5 billion in the United States. Some estimate piracy costs to be as high as $12 billion.[15] Piracy is not just a vendor's problem; it also becomes a problem for consumers, who end up paying more for the software, as vendors try to recover their losses. Wasch claims that the financial benefit requirement in the current copyright law is flawed. "The issue is not what the bulletin board operator gains, it's what the copyright holder loses."

YOU DECIDE

1. Do you think the copyright laws should be redrafted to stop bulletin board operators such as LaMacchia?
2. Let's say that you stumbled onto LaMacchia's site and could download some commercial software that you've wanted to purchase. Would you do it? What would be the ethical quandary?
3. Do you think the users who uploaded and downloaded the software should be punished for contributing to software piracy?

Sources: Jeremy Hylton, "David LaMacchia Cleared; Case Raises Civil Liberty Issues," *The Tech,* February 7, 1995, 4; See also "The Diane Rehm Show," *National Public Radio,* October 21, 1998.

is up to the list owner to establish rules and guidelines for communications. For example, some list owners may first review the message before it is posted on the list, whereas others may give members the privilege to post the message directly to the list. Members can unsubscribe from the list at any time.

Chat Rooms

Chat room

An electronic conference where participants chat with one another using their keyboards.

A **chat room** is an electronic room where people chat with each other by posting messages on a specific topic to electronic bulletin boards. Chat rooms are similar to attending a conference on the Net so they are often referred to as Internet Relay Chat (IRC). The "chat" takes place by keying in the message, not through voice communications. The messages are conveyed in real time to all visitors in the chat room. Of course, two people can participate in an electronic conversation only if both are logged on to the computer at the same time. However, there is no facility to automatically record all conversations that take place in the chat room. This requires special software, so if someone is not in the chat room they may miss some important conversations.

World Wide Web

World Wide Web (WWW)

An Internet tool that allows users to retrieve and display documents and images stored on any computer linked to the Internet.

The **World Wide Web** (WWW) is such a popular Internet tool that it has almost become synonymous with the Internet. The Web, as it is frequently called, allows users to access and display documents and images stored on any computer that is linked to the Internet. In 1989 Tim Berners-Lee, a computer scientist at the particle physics lab in CERN (the European Center for Nuclear Research in Geneva), designed WWW as a tool to help an international group of physicists exchange findings and information related to

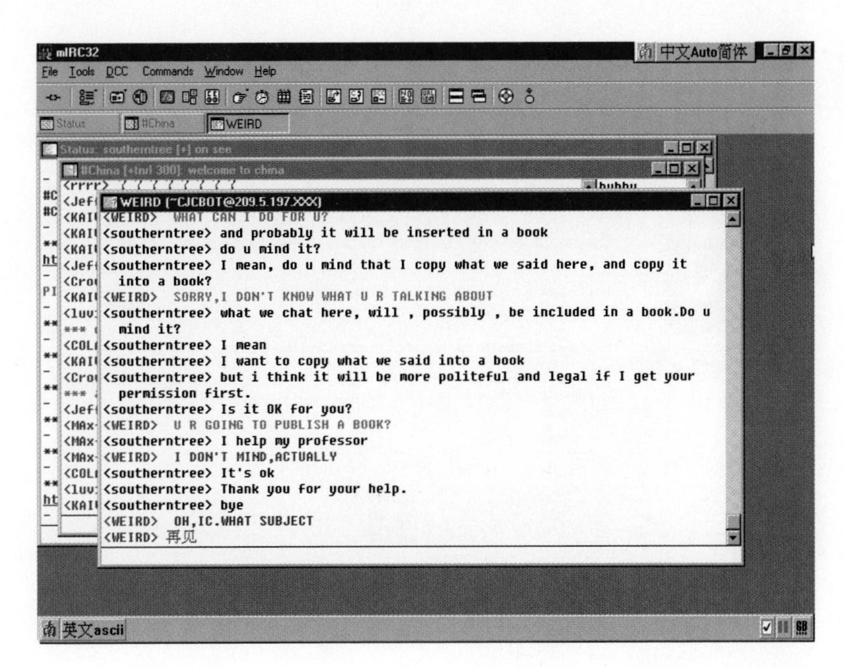

Chat rooms are venues for electronic conversations on a wide variety of topics.

their research. But it was in late 1993 when friendly PC software was developed to access the Web that its popularity soared. Table 7-3 lists some key World Wide Web terms.

Internet (or Web) Browsers

A **browser** is a program that acts as a gateway to the Internet by allowing users to "browse" through data on the Internet. Users retrieve Web pages that are electronic documents and images that provide information about an individual or an organization, with the help of their browsers.

Browser

A software program that allows users to interface with and browse the Internet in an easy, user-friendly manner.

TABLE 7-3 **Key World Wide Web Terms**

Term	Description
Encryption	A method to ensure that network exchanges are secure and reliable. In the case of data, both the sender and the receiver use a special electronic key to lock and unlock the data.
Gateway	A computer that converts data transmission protocols between networks or applications that use different protocols.
Host	A mainframe, mini, workstation, or PC that is connected to the Internet using the TCP/IP protocol.
IP Address (Internet Protocol Address)	The unique address for every computer on TCP/IP network. An IP address consists of four sets of numbers separated by periods, such as 126.201.41.8.
TCP/IP	Stands for Transmission Control Protocol/Internet Protocol. All Internet computers use the TCP/IP protocol.
T1 Line	A dedicated, digital line that transmits data over the network at a speed of 1.544 Mbps. Telecommunication companies provide T1 lines. Because the lines are much faster than cable or twisted pair, they are widely used by Internet service providers.
URL (Universal Resource Locator)	An electronic address for a Web page.
Web Server	A computer that provides Internet services and includes hardware, operating system, Web server software, and TCP/IP protocols.

Netscape is a popular Web browser that has user-friendly interfaces.

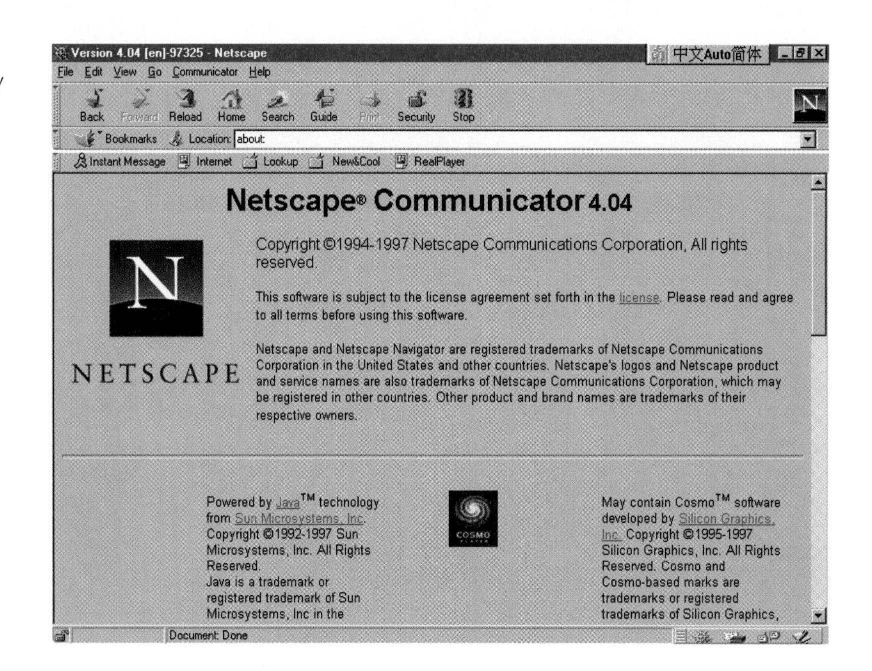

Browsers such as Netscape Communicator and Microsoft's Internet Explorer come with a number of useful features that allow users to easily navigate the Internet and access its many services. Besides retrieving or displaying Web pages, browsers have features that allow you to save any Internet document on your computer. So, for example, if a visitor finds an interesting article on jazz, she can save, edit, and print the file as a word document. In addition, visitors can search in a given document for a specific word or phrase using the browser's "find" feature.

Browsers also have a "bookmark" feature that allows users to add and edit a list of their favorite Web sites. When users want to retrieve one of their favorites, they open the list, click on a site with the mouse, and the site pops up. This feature saves users the time of remembering and keying in the address of their favorite sites each time they want to visit them. Bookmarks can also be classified and grouped into folders, similar to word-processing files or other files. That is, a user can group his favorite Web sites into such folders as games, job hunting, and shopping.

A Web bookmark such as this one saves users time by allowing them to point and click on a favorite Web site address instead of having to type it.

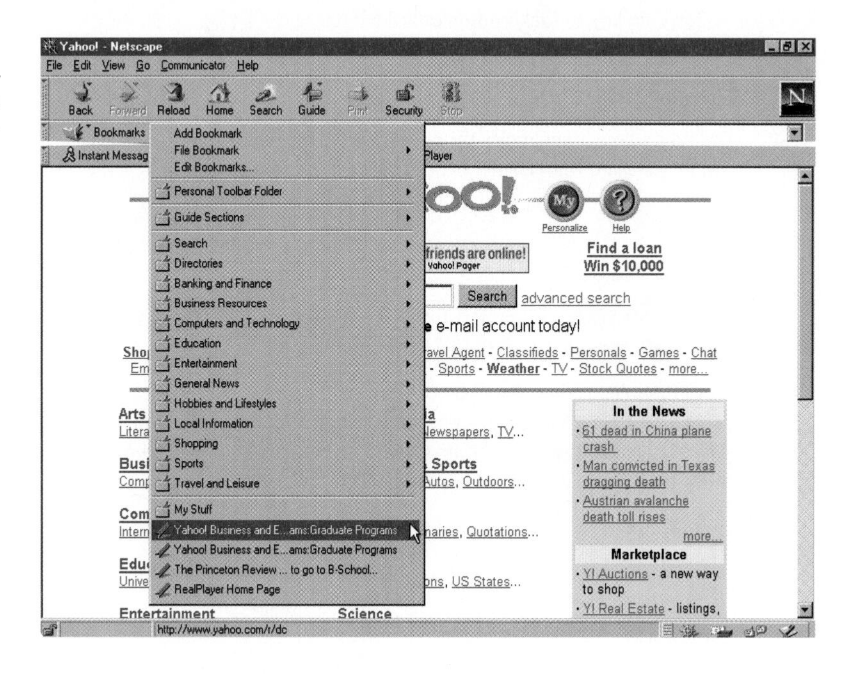

Finally, Web browsers help users to connect to powerful search engines that allow them to search the entire Internet for documents and sites that match their information needs. A number of search engines and index sites are popular with Web users, including Alta Vista, Excite, Go.com, HotBot, Lycos, and Yahoo. Although the basic functions of all the search engines are the same, each has its own unique features and strengths.

Web Sites

Web sites have become so popular that many people think only of them when they consider the Internet. A Web site is an electronic résumé of an individual or organization. It can also be a catalog of products and services that an organization offers. A Web site often consists of several Web pages, although a user may or may not see the breakdown of each page. Each link on a Web site is a Web page. The Technology Payoff featured an example of a Web page for Odwalla.

Web site

An electronic description of an individual, institution, or organization that resides on the Internet.

The address of a Web site is often referred to as the domain name. IBM's domain name is www.ibm.com, Microsoft's domain name is www.microsoft.com, and so on. Domain names are valuable because they give the company a unique Internet identity. In fact, many costly legal battles are fought over domain names.

For example, Prema Toy Co.'s efforts to retrieve rights to the pokey.org domain name from Christopher Van Allen of Pennsylvania ended up in court. Prema, which holds the trademark to the Pokey and Gumby toys, wants the pokey.org name. Van Allen, whose nickname is Pokey, received the domain registration as a gift from his father and uses it as his personal Web site. When Prema's attorneys sent a letter seeking

Global IS for success

Staying in Touch

As war raged in Bosnia and "ethnic cleansing" claimed the lives of tens of thousands, Dutch systems administrator Frank Tiggelaar says, he "knew as much about [former] Yugoslavia as your average newspaper reader." Then Bosnian refugees moved into his apartment building and told him their stories.

Today, Tiggelaar and a small team of volunteers runs an ambitious Balkan news site on the World Wide Web called Domovina Net ("domovina" means homeland). It has about 10 Gbytes of data spread over computers in four countries and includes video and audio streams from around the world. Domovina Net (www.domovina.net) also features news reports from Kosovo, the Yugoslav province where Serb forces have warred with the majority ethnic Albanian population, triggering NATO to react.

"At Domovina Net, you have everything. You have real-time broadcasts, you have multilingual renditions of the local papers, of the international press. . . . Basically, everything you want to know is there or linked to the site." Using FTP, users can exchange files and news items from anywhere in the world.

Tiggelaar met some Bosnians who had fled the onslaught of Serb nationalist forces and learned that they were desperate to contact relatives still caught in the war. He let them use his home computer and Internet connection to send e-mail to Bosnia, where there were rudimentary connections set up via satellites between besieged Sarajevo and the outside world. His Bosnian friends then asked about starting a Web site with news from their country. With Tiggelaar's help, that site was launched in May 1995.

Domovina Net now attracts 25,000 to 50,000 visitors per week. That number surged during the conflict in Kosovo. Predrag Jovanovic, an engineering technician now living in the United States, is one of many expatriates who regularly use the site. Although he is frustrated sometimes by the nationalist tone of some broadcasts from the region, Jovanovic says, "It's nice to hear news in my native language."

QUESTIONS AND PROJECTS

1. Visit this Web site (www.domovina.net) and evaluate its information content. What suggestions would you make to improve the site?
2. Search the World Wide Web for one another similar site that helps people to stay in touch with relatives in other parts of the world.

Source: Sharon Machlis, "Balkans Turn to Web for News," *Computerworld*, June 29, 1998, 51–54; see also www.domovina.net.

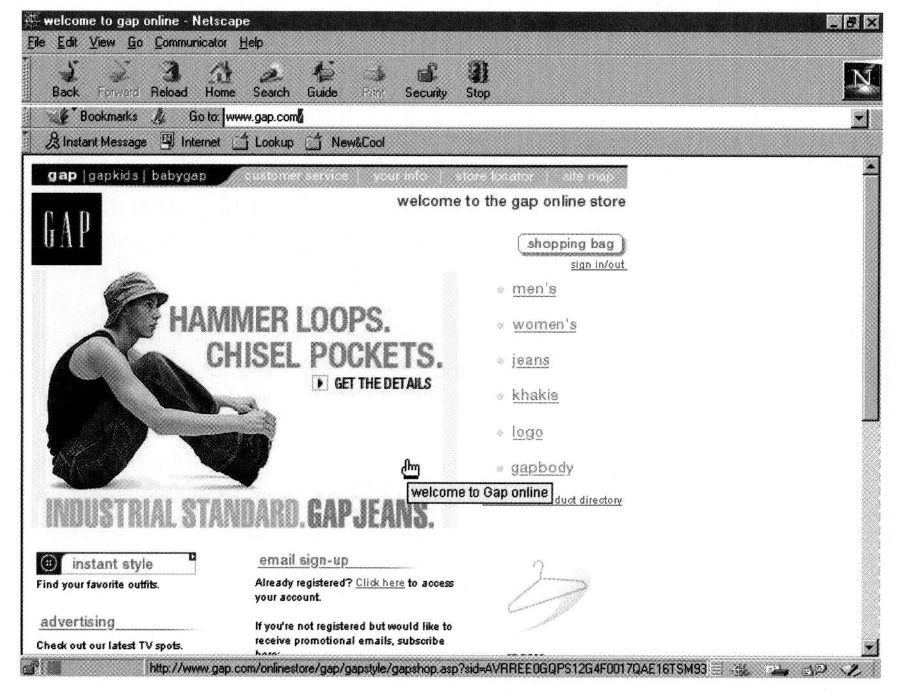

Here we see the HTML for the Gap's home page and the home page itself. If you look at the code closely, you can see specific instructions for font size (font), images (img), and the text on the page.

rights to the domain name, Van Allen retorted, "Pokey.org is mine, and THEY CAN'T HAVE IT." Prema offered Van Allen a free license to use the pokey.org domain if rights were returned to the toy company, an offer Van Allen rejected.[16]

Web pages have transformed in the past 5 years. According to the publisher of *CIO* magazine, beginning and ending in 1995 it was "cool just to have a Web site." Then from 1996 to 1997, businesses "tried to cram as many dancing applets on our home pages as possible. Thankfully, reason won out." Now we are in "a stage characterized by simplicity, ease of use and customer-centric design."[17]

All that a user needs to set up a home page is a computer, connection to the Internet, and software to generate Hyper Text Markup Language (HTML), which is the graphical interface to the Internet. Setting up an effective Web page can be expensive.

For example, the cost to build a "conservative" Web site for an organization can vary from $10,000 to $100,000. More sophisticated Web sites cost anywhere from $1 million to $10 million, according to Forrester Research. However, simple individual Web sites are inexpensive to establish and a knowledgeable individual can establish one in a matter of a few hours.

Hypertext and hypermedia are integral parts of a home page. Hypertext allows users to get additional information about a topic or a term with just a few mouse clicks. When a user clicks on a highlighted word or phrase, the system brings up more information about the word. This feature is referred to as a **hyperlink,** which is an electronic link to another related Web document. Sometimes the links may bring up information from the same file that the user is viewing or from different files that are in the same computer. They can also retrieve files that are located on other computers linked to the Internet. Hyperlinks, then, add significant value and time savings to those seeking information on the Internet.

Hyperlink

An electronic link in a Web page that connects the user with another related document or information on the same or other Web pages.

What are some do's and don'ts when it comes to Web sites? First impressions count. "Your Web site has a lot in common with a first date. It's often where your customers first learn about you and your products, so you need to make sure their impression is positive," says Dave Johnson, who writes about computing and small business.[18] If a Web page is too slow to download or if it is garish and disorganized, visitors will quickly move to other sites. Graphics for the sake of graphics or meaningless animation will only irritate visitors.

A Web site is an opportunity to present yourself or your organization to the world, so it should be developed carefully with the audience in mind. It should present the information visitors seek candidly and succinctly. Table 7-4 gives further tips on effective Web sites.

Although Web sites have many benefits, they also have some risks. By making information available, there is more opportunity for information misuse. In addition, the global nature of the Web presents cultural, legal, and ethical problems. Consider how countries try to restrict offensive material on the Web. Former British Prime Minister Margaret Thatcher cautions that governments that try to pass laws to restrain such material may go too far, thereby restricting freedom of speech. "They cut out a whole class of things and indeed make far too much illegal—which is wrong."[19]

Erik Bedo, general manager of MatavCom, a Hungarian-based networking company, agrees. He believes every country must participate to find a workable solution. "If we only have one country in the world where you do not control any information . . . that site can be looked at from anywhere in the world."[20]

Determining how and what material should be controlled on the Web becomes a daunting challenge because of differing cultural values. As Bedo observes, "What you call an obscenity in the United States is not what we call an obscenity in Europe."[21]

TABLE 7-4

Web Page Do's and Don'ts

1. Keep your pages small
2. Keep pages graphically light so downloading times are short
3. A word is worth a thousand pictures
4. Pay close attention to the graphics; reuse the same graphic as much as possible and avoid cute animations
5. Achieve a sense of balance between images and text
6. Test your site repeatedly
7. Know your customer

Source: Dave Johnson, "Put Your Site on a Diet," *Small Business Computing and Communications,* November 1998, 56.

Other countries restrict or monitor Internet access, such as countries in the Middle East and China.[22] To prevent clashes and harness the advantages of the Internet and the Web, members of the global community will need to continue developing workable protocols and remain sensitive to the cultural, political, and legal concerns of users.

In the following sections, we investigate two important variations of the Internet, called intranets and extranets. Businesses use intranets and extranets in many innovative ways that enhance productivity.

Intranets

Intranet

A private network designed exclusively to meet the internal information needs of an organization that the general public cannot access.

Firewall

A piece of hardware and software installed between two or more networks to ensure that only authorized users access the network.

An **intranet** is a private corporate network that uses Internet technology and is designed to meet the internal information needs of employees. It includes information such as telephone numbers and e-mail addresses of employees, travel expense forms, health care benefits, product catalogs and product pricing, in-house training programs, and so on. The general public cannot access intranet sites because organizations design them for the exclusive use of their members or employees. However, employers may give permission to a special group of nonemployees, such as suppliers and outside contractors, to access the intranet.

Firewalls help ensure that only authorized users access a network, such as an intranet. "When hosting a private party, you might place someone at the door to check names against the invitation list. Any person not on the list is denied access. That's essentially how a firewall works on a network."[23] For a simple firewall, a company creates an access control list that contains the IP addresses authorized to access the network. When a router, a device that connects two or more LANs and aids data exchange, receives an electronic message, it checks the IP address of the recipient against the access control list. If the address is valid and authorized, the message is transmitted. If not, the message is returned to the sender.

Firewalls provide several kinds of network security. They are often installed between networks of two different organizations to curtail unauthorized access and can also prevent employees from transmitting confidential messages from the company network to unauthorized sites, such as the competition's network.

Additionally, firewalls are used to separate a company's public Web server from its internal systems, as in the case of an intranet. To demonstrate, let's look at a hospital's information system. The hospital's public information—its location, main emergency numbers, and names of key health care specialists—does not require a firewall to prevent consumers' network access. However, private information about patients should be protected and requires a firewall. Finally, firewalls can prevent unauthorized internal users from viewing confidential information. In most companies, for instance, confidential salary data is protected through the use of a firewall.

Intranets are becoming quite common. "We want to make maximum use of the intranet in all of our business operations. Ideally we want it to be so commonplace that it's viewed like a public utility—you only notice it when it's down," explains Robert R. Walker, Vice President and CIO Hewlett-Packard Co.[24] Figure 7-6 shows the rapid rate of intranet growth.

FIGURE 7-6

Number of U.S. Users Linked to Intranets

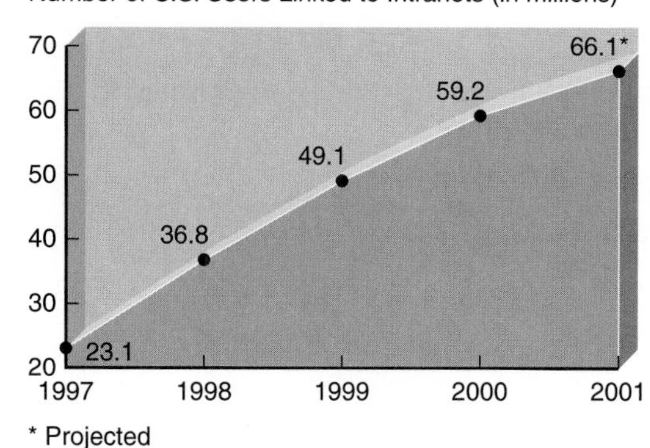

One of the biggest advantages of intranets is that they use the same communication technologies and protocols as the Web. For instance, employees may be able to visit other Web sites from their intranet through hyperlinks. The shared technologies and standards allow companies to leverage their Internet connection to meet internal information needs. How? A company with an Internet connection does not need any additional networking hardware to establish an intranet. It uses the same connection for its intranet, thereby putting its existing network infrastructure to better use.

Intranet Strategies

Many businesses jump on the intranet bandwagon before assessing the complexity and cost of the project. Many companies have lost millions of dollars in intranets because of poor planning and implementation. Even worse, the company's image in the eyes of its employees suffers and employees become reluctant to use the intranet.

Some successful intranet strategies include the following:

- **Include widely used applications and make them simple to use.** Use the intranet to simplify employee's lives. For instance, by putting travel expense reports on-line, employees do not have to waste time filling out hard-copy reports, making copies for numerous people, and sending them through regular or interoffice mail, which can take days. Instead, they can complete reports and send them to as many people as needed. The recipients receive them in moments.
- **Secure the system.** Security of intranets is vital. If the information on an intranet is corrupted (such as an inaccurate posting of company job openings) or if a competitor accesses the information (such as pricing policies for different products), it can lead to distrust.
- **Integrate databases into intranet applications.** Databases are at the heart of intranet applications. The data and information that employees access from the intranet come from one or more databases. Companies must invest the time and money to build databases that are accurate, complete, and reliable.
- **Invest in excellent network capacities.** Clearly, networks are essential for the success of intranets. Without a robust network infrastructure, an intranet simply will not be able to function. If the network is frequently down or if the network is too slow, employees will get frustrated and may not use the intranet.
- **Motivate employees to use the intranet.** Change is not easy. Many people prefer to do things the way they always have. To convince people of the benefit of change, intranets must be easy to use with user-friendly, intuitive interfaces. Further, companies should give incentives encouraging employees to use the intranet.

Table 7-5 lists these intranet strategies.

Intranet Applications

Intranets can help businesses in several ways. They can save money by eliminating paper and mailing costs, improve communications, deliver information when and where needed, train and reeducate employees, enhance the efficiency of a business, and enrich global interactions.

TABLE 7-5

Successful Strategies for Intranets
Include widely used applications and keep them simple
Secure the system
Integrate databases into intranet applications
Invest in excellent network capacities
Motivate employees to use the intranet

An intranet at Rich Products Corp., the nation's largest privately held frozen food company, serves as an illustrative example. Rich Products expects its intranet to save $100,000 or more annually on paper, mailing, and communication costs. The three key applications of Rich Product's intranet are sales reporting, order status, and a nutritional information directory.

Instead of distributing printed sales analysis reports, all sales reports are available on the intranet. Printed reports often arrived too late or when the representative was traveling, so many sales reps could not use them. Now sales representatives access up-to-date sales reports from the intranet off their laptops, regardless of where they are. The order-status application allows brokers or independent salespeople to see the status of their order with a few keystrokes. The nutritional directory about each and every product helps the company conform to regulatory requirements. Restaurant operators, brokers, and food distributors can look up the information on the intranet, saving the company unproductive time spent faxing or mailing documents.

Some other Rich Product intranet applications include the distribution of a company-wide newspaper called *Rich Week*. The paper offers hints on personal investments; sample sales presentations that employees can use to avoid creating presentations from scratch; and access to Family Scorecard, a goal-setting document for the company that tells employees how Rich Products is performing.[25]

An intranet, especially one that posts organization charts and human resource policies, is useful for new employees because they can access a wide range of company-related information at their convenience. When Andrew Jewell, a new manager in the industrial and utilities consulting group at American Management Systems, needed to answer a question about a department project, he wasn't quite sure where to turn. So Jewell logged on to the company's intranet. That intranet provides detailed information, including a list of AMS's experts. Jewell found a vice-president down the hall with the required expertise who was happy to share his ideas. The intranet "gave me a single point of contact to check all the resources of the firm," Jewell says. "Without it, I'd probably have wound up reinventing the wheel."[26]

The intranet can help train employees on an ongoing basis. Siemens Business Communications Systems is transforming itself into a company whose products combine voice, data, fax, and video. Doing so requires the Santa Clara, California–based unit of Siemens AG to train its employees in new communications technologies. It is doing so with the help of a Virtual University. Students and teachers "electronically meet" over the company's intranet to exchange documents and data via the intranet and voice systems. The Virtual University means that students can sit at their desks and learn as much or as little as they need when convenient. Says one employee, "I now have the ability to tap all of our experts in the field around the world to help deliver the learning that is necessary."[27]

Given the wide range of intranet applications, companies are investing in intranets to be more responsive to their employees' needs and to help employees better serve customers. In the next section, we look at extranets, which are systems that allow companies to interact and communicate electronically with external entities such as suppliers and customers.

Extranets

Extranet

A corporate password-protected network that provides information to people or entities in the environment of the business.

In contrast to intranets that provide employees and other selective external parties with internal company information, extranets are almost exclusively designed to meet the information needs of external parties, such as suppliers, customers, and stockholders. An **extranet** is a private network that is designed to meet the information needs of people and organizations in a business's environment, such as employees, suppliers, and customers. Access to an extranet requires the use of passwords because it is not for the general public. Our discussion about firewalls in the intranet section applies equally to extranets.

The company that owns the extranet determines who may access it and the type of access allowed. For instance, a company may give its key customers exclusive access to certain parts of its extranet, such as prices and delivery information about products, and it may give its suppliers access to other parts, such as information on current inventories.

Information on the extranet is transmitted through the public Internet system, which is why it is called an extranet. Extranets are somewhat similar to electronic data interchange (EDI) in the sense that both establish communication bridges with the external community. However, unlike EDI, which can handle only information in a predesignated format, extranets can deal with different formats, such as text, graphics, images, and so on. Also, extranet technologies are more open and flexible than EDI technologies. In the sections that follow we explore different strategies to build successful extranets and extranet applications.

Extranet Applications

Extranets can help businesses gain a competitive edge if handled properly because they can put the right information into the hands of the right people at the right time. However, access to business information and the ability to disseminate information can also have its downside, as we see shortly. Here, we explore how extranets can improve communication with those outside the organization to increase business efficiency, and improve information access, influence the behavior of those outside the organization and, conversely, how powerful external groups can use extranets to change internal business practices.

Increase Business Efficiency

Extranets can improve communications with key players who support the business to improve its business processes. How? Extranets offer speed and round-the-clock access to valuable information that can be a great advantage.

Ford Motor Co. subsidiary Visteon, an auto parts supplier, is developing an extranet to improve the efficiency of its internal and external communications. Remember that although extranets are designed primarily for external entities, employees also have access to extranets. The extranet gives Visteon, which has 82,000 employees at 81 facilities worldwide, a unified communication system rather than the patchwork of EDI systems it had previously. The extranet allows suppliers and customers to search catalogs and place orders for items. Suppliers can also check inventory levels and identify future product needs of the company. "We'll have a centralized global solution," says one manager.[28]

Change Business Partners' Practices

In addition to streamlining internal business processes and increasing efficiency, extranets can also force business partners to change their practices. General Electric Co. is constructing a massive extranet to handle billions of dollars in purchasing. In the process, it is forcing tens of thousands of its suppliers to conduct business on the Internet to improve GE's efficiency.

GE, the largest diversified industrial company in the United States, plans to launch extranets for each of its 12 operating units. The systems will serve as many as 40,000 trading partners by 2002, all of which would have to use the network to do business with the $91 billion company. The extranet strategy could dramatically boost GE's bottom line by reducing costs, according to Randy Rowe, manager of GE's corporate initiatives group. "Today, we have too many purchasing systems to count," Rowe explains. "We're looking to enable each division to manage their purchasing on extranets, with financial data funneling to a centralized platform.[29]

At full deployment, GE could save between $500 million and $750 million through reduced errors and other efficiencies, executives predict. What is different about GE is the number of industries it affects because of its extranet. According to analyst Scott Lundstrom at AMR Research, "GE's plan may ratchet up the rate of Internet development across broad sectors." Lundstrom observes: "There's a line of reasoning that would say if GE is going to put the gun to the head of 40,000 substantial industrial companies and call on them to make their enterprises Internet-ready, then those businesses are going to leverage an Internet infrastructure more rapidly."[30]

Empower Customers

Even though some businesses use extranets to force outsiders to change, extranets can also spur change in the organization. Customers and other groups have used extranets as a weapon to enact such change. In mid-September 1998, United Airlines dropped a bombshell by slicing travel agents' ticket sales commissions from 10 to 8 percent. The move was soon echoed by other major airlines. Facing the threat of a 20 percent drop in revenue, the American Society of Travel Agents (ASTA) did not turn to an attorney, but instead used its extranet, ASTAnet, to convey the displeasure of its 25,000 worldwide travel agents. The extranet helped members get the word out about the effect of the commission cuts.

Press releases, statistics of the impact of the reduction in commission, copies of national ads against the cut, and measures that the professional society were taking were all available on the extranet. The extranet page headlined "Commission Crisis" and illustrated with a photo of lightning striking an airplane also prepared members for potential consumer calls following an upcoming press conference. All this caught the attention of travel agents across the country. "We immediately saw a 149 percent increase in usage among members," says Stephanie Kenyon, VP of industry affairs and travel technology for ASTA in Alexandria, Virginia. "Members are using the information to fight the commission cut."[31]

Extranet Strategies

Extranet developers make the following recommendations for building successful extranets:

1. **Understand the return on investment.** The business should develop its extranet with specific goals in mind, such as improving customer satisfaction, reducing operating costs, increasing sales, or any other goal. Companies must establish clear goals and work toward them because extranets are expensive, costing anywhere from $50,000 to $50 million.
2. **Select your audience and meet its needs.** Extranets are designed to cater to the external entities of a business, such as customers, suppliers, government regulators, and stockholders. The company should carefully select the entity or entities that it wants the extranet to serve. The information needs of a stockholder are quite different from the information needs of a supplier. Once a decision is made about the audience for the extranet, the next step is to carefully identify specific information problems the extranet will address.
3. **Be willing to change**. An extranet is a work in progress. Companies must continue to invest in the extranet if it is to meet the changing needs of its audience. Otherwise, the extranet will become quickly outdated, defeating its purpose.
4. **Keep things simple.** People want clean, crisp, easy-to-click-on applications. Because many visitors may not be proficient with the Internet, it is important to make extranets intuitive and easy to use. Users do not want to spend an enormous amount of time on clerical functions, so such functions, in particular, should be easy to use.
5. **24 hours a day.** Extranets should be up and running 24 hours a day, 7 days a week. Visitors should be able to access the extranet anytime from anywhere. In the case of global companies, this becomes imperative, given the time difference between different countries.
6. **Work with end users.** When IT staff try to build an extranet without help, the project's chances of success sharply diminish. Successful extranets are a joint venture between IT and the business end users. Table 7-6 outlines these six strategies.

Ethics and the Internet

The Internet has raised, and will continue to raise, a whole host of ethical issues that companies and individuals may not be fully prepared to address because many are new. The anonymity of the Internet—both its strength and its weakness—has led to a number of ethical problems. First, readers can be misled about the source of an e-mail message or a document. For example, suppose you get a document that says Stock A is going

TABLE 7-6

Successful Strategies for Extranets
Understand the return on investment
Select your audience and meet its needs
Be willing to change
Keep things simple
Operate twenty-four hours a day
Work with end users

to drop by 15 points by the end of the day. It is not always easy to determine who sent the message: a competitor, a stock analyst, or a concerned stockholder. You would have to do some investigation to find the source of the message or document.

Second, like junk mail, junk e-mail also exists. Because the source is not easily identifiable, this can become a nuisance. Although there are laws in some states against unsolicited commercial e-mailing, some unscrupulous companies ignore this. Third, anonymity emboldens people to commit illegal or unethical acts, such as the development of child pornographic sites, the unauthorized distribution of private information, and market scams.

Conversely, when Intel disclosed that its new Pentium III would track the digital identities of its users by hard coding a unique serial number into the processors, the computer industry protested loudly. Many urged Intel to reject the tracking device, claiming that Internet users should be allowed to remain anonymous to prevent unscrupulous companies from collecting and selling data about their personal Internet transactions. Intel's tracking is similar to someone stealthily watching each and every computer move of every user with a Pentium III.

A company that fails to implement ethical guidelines risks legal exposure and a public relations fiasco. Why? Businesses can be held legally liable for what its employees do and say on the Internet, such as divulging trade secrets or engaging in copyright infringement. Second, as Mary J. Cronin, author of *Doing Business on the Internet,* explains, the controversial statements or the politically unpopular views of an employee can tarnish a company's image.[33]

To prepare as effectively as possible, companies should establish written Internet policies before going on-line. These policies must be communicated in a clear, candid manner to all employees, and the company should enforce the penalties. Written policies that aren't enforced are ineffective—employees quickly understand that management lacks the commitment to penalize offenders.

To avoid legal and public relations problems, businesses can require that all messages posted on the Internet must clearly specify whether the views expressed are the employee's or the organization's. A word of caution, though. Simply putting a disclaimer at the bottom of the message stating that the views are those of the individual and not the company may be insufficient in a court of law. Table 7-7 lists employee activities that Internet policies should anticipate and prevent.

TABLE 7-7

Employee Activities That Company Internet Policies Should Prevent
Solicitations for money for religious or political causes
Offensive or harassing statements, including "disparagement of others based on their race, national origin, sex, sexual orientation, age, disability, religious or political beliefs"
The distribution or solicitation of sexually oriented messages or images
The dissemination or printing of materials (including articles and software) in violation of copyright laws

Joseph Rosenbaum, a technology lawyer in New York, suggests that firms safeguard their image by making sure that they can answer "yes" to three simple questions:

- Is there a guideline?
- Do employees know about it?
- Is it enforced?

Business Guidelines for Internet Success

The Internet and related technologies, such as extranets and intranets, are some of the most exciting, dynamic technologies ever developed. Although these tools have the power to revolutionize our professional and personal lives and society, they also pose challenges. Successful companies should consider the following factors when making Internet, intranet, and extranet decisions.

View the Internet as a Survival Tool

Joining the Internet community is no longer an option for companies. In fact, many experts see the Internet as a business tool that is becoming as commonplace as the telephone. Certainly we would not do business with a company that did not have a telephone. Many customers, especially business customers, feel the same way about companies that do not have Internet access. So the Internet is no longer a competitive weapon; it is a tool for survival.

Companies that take a "wait and see" attitude may jeopardize the company's health for two key reasons. First, the Internet has become a source of revenue, a means to increase market share, and a way to cut costs through increased efficiency. Second, the Internet gives companies of any size access to the world market. Without investing huge resources in global offices, the Internet allows a company to operate as if it were global.

Plan for Security

Safeguarding a Web site is a daunting task given the ingenuity of hackers and other security violators. Some companies are reluctant to establish Web sites without guarantees about the security of the site. Security concerns become even more paramount if the business sells, purchases, or conducts other electronic transactions over its Web site. Internet, intranet, and extranet visitors will only use sites that are safe, so security should be integral to site design and development. Businesses that do not plan site security carefully risk wasting their investment in that site.

Devote Sufficient Resources to Handle Maintenance and Management

Many companies are eager to establish a Web site, but launching a site is a relatively small task compared to running a site. Like raising a child, a Web site takes continuous work and attention to be effective. Visitors expect the site to change frequently with new, unique, and innovative offerings. Many sites die a slow and deliberate death on the Internet as users reject these sites for their poor maintenance.

Do Not Forget the Basics

The best Web sites are those that follow five guidelines. First, the information on the site should be current and free of errors. Second, the information should be easy to find. Users are willing to click only a few times before they will abandon the site and move on to others. Third, to heighten viewer interest, keep graphics and animation fresh and to a bare minimum. Fourth, colors should be pleasing to the eye. Visitors do not want to get sore eyes from viewing a Web site. Finally, the computer on which the Web site resides should be functional 365 days a year.

Remember That Data Are Sacred

The information superhighway makes it easy for marketers to compile detailed information on every aspect of a consumer's life, from shopping, education, family travel, sports, hobbies, and so on. Such detailed data are invaluable to marketers, who can use the information to better target their customers. But companies must remember that such information is sacred to their customers, too. If the business sells such data without the express permission of customers, it may end up in court facing privacy violations. At the very least, treating customer data carelessly can create consumer backlash.

Today, customers demand a voice in the decision as to how personal data are used. Some marketers say, "If you give [customers] a big enough discount to divulge their life story and a say in how that information will be used, they will go along." No matter what the incentives are, companies should guard customer data gleaned from the Internet.

SUMMARY

1. **Describe the Internet, including the term "information superhighway."** The Internet, a network of networks that links computers from around the world, has revolutionized communication through its speed, efficiency, and global reach. Although the term *information superhighway* can be defined in a number of ways, it has three main characteristics: (1) it has no central controlling entity, (2) it is fully scalable, and (3) it has user profile anonymity. Because the Internet has all three characteristics, it is considered an excellent model of an information superhighway.

   The Internet is not owned or operated by any one entity. It is a loose confederation of networks of the government, universities, regional networks, Internet service providers, and some businesses such as telecommunications companies. Network Information Centers help organizations use the Internet and the Internet Registry keeps track of the connections between addresses and domain names. The Internet Society develops guidelines that direct Internet operations and growth.

2. **Identify the four types of Internet tools, including the World Wide Web.** Internet tools can be broadly divided into four categories: (1) information retrieval tools (FTP and Gopher); (2) information search tools (Archie, Veronica, WAIS, and search engines); (3) communication tools (e-mail, telnet, Usenet, mailing lists, and chat rooms); and (4) the World Wide Web. FTP allows users to upload or download files, copy files, and list directories. It is a protocol that establishes a link between the computer requesting the service and the computer providing the service over a TCP/IP protocol. Gopher is a menu-based and user-friendly interface that provides easy access to information residing on special servers called Gopher sites. Internet search tools (such as Archie, Veronica, WAIS, and search engines) allow users to search for specific information.

   Written communication tools include e-mail, telnet, Usenet, mailing lists, and chat rooms. E-mail refers to sending electronic messages or files over the network from one user to one or more users. Telnet is a protocol that allows users to log onto a remote computer and run a program or locate a file. It is part of the TCP/IP communications protocol. Usenet is a public bulletin board system that serves as a huge library of discussion topics and newsgroups. Users can join any group and post messages for others to see. A chat room is an electronic conference where participants chat with one another using their keyboards. In mailing lists members communicate with one another through e-mail.

   The World Wide Web is an interface that allows users to retrieve and display documents and images stored on any computer anywhere in the world as long as that computer is linked to the Internet. A Web browser acts as a gateway to the Internet by allowing users to browse and retrieve data using fairly intuitive interfaces. Browsers have a number of sophisticated and user-friendly features that make it easy to copy and edit Web documents. A Web site is an HTML (Hyper Text Markup Language) document on the Web that combines text, graphics, audio, and video. It is similar to an electronic résumé about an individual or organization.

3. **Describe an intranet.** An intranet is a private, corporate network designed to meet the internal information needs of employees. One of the biggest advantages of intranets is that it uses the same communication technologies and protocols as the Web. Firewalls, which are made up of hardware and software, provide security and prevent unauthorized access to an intranet. However, employees may be able to visit other Web sites from the intranet.

4. **Describe an extranet.** An extranet is a private, corporate network designed for use by a business's suppliers, partners, and customers and requires the use of passwords. It is not targeted at the general public, but at selected users in the environment of the company. The business that owns the extranet determines who has access to it and the type of access they have. Information on the extranet is transmitted through the public Internet system, which is why it is called an extranet.

5. **Discuss Internet-related ethical issues.** The Internet and the World Wide Web have generated numerous ethical issues. Anonymity may cause individuals or businesses to engage in unethical practices on the Internet. Unsolicited commercial e-mail, pornographic Web sites, and disclosure of private information are some ethical problems related to the Internet. Finally, companies can be held liable for what their employees do on the Internet during a workday, so businesses should establish clear policies and guidelines to avoid liability.

REVIEW QUESTIONS

1. How did a Web site help the beverage maker Odwalla deal with a crisis? Explain.
2. What are some implications of the Internet for businesses?
3. The Internet is more than a database of information. Why?
4. What is ARPANET? How is it related to the Net?
5. What is the information superhighway and what are its three characteristics? Does the Internet qualify as an information superhighway? Why?
6. Clients and servers make up the Internet. What is the role of each of these in the Internet?
7. What are the four categories of Internet tools? Briefly describe each type of tool.
8. What does FTP stand for? What are its features?
9. Briefly describe each type of Internet tool that aids written communications.
10. What is a Usenet? When would you use a Usenet?
11. What are some ethical dilemmas that Usenet newsgroups can create?
12. Describe the elements in an e-mail address. What does ".com" at the end of an e-mail address stand for? What does ".net" stand for?
13. Describe the World Wide Web. What are some key WWW terms?
14. What is a Web browser and what are some of its features? What is a search engine?
15. Describe a Web site.
16. What is an intranet? What is an extranet? What technologies do they use?
17. What is the difference between an Internet, an intranet, and an extranet?
18. Explain how companies use intranets and extranets to achieve their goals.

KEY TERMS

Archie (p. 193)
browser (p. 197)
chat room (p. 196)
e-mail (p. 193)
extranet (p. 204)
file transfer protocol (FTP) (p. 191)
firewall (p. 202)
Gopher (p. 192)
home page (p. 199)
hyperlink (p. 201)
information superhighway (p. 189)
intranet (p. 202)
mailing list (p. 195)
the Net (p. 187)
scalable (p. 189)
search engine (p. 193)
telnet (p. 195)
Usenet (p. 195)
Veronica (p. 193)
WAIS (p. 193)
Web site (p. 199)
World Wide Web (WWW) (p. 196)

DISCUSSION QUESTIONS AND PROJECTS

1. The advantages of the Web are obvious to many. However, the Web also brings some unique problems into the workforce. For example, the use of the Internet at the workplace for fun and games is an issue that the corporate world is struggling to tackle. Companies are developing policies for appropriate Net use and enforcement methods, including monitoring and filtering employee activities. Other companies fear that the company may face legal battles if an employee finds images from a pornographic or racist World Wide Web site on a colleague's system and complains about a hostile working environment. Companies are adopting different measures to avoid such situations, from monitoring usage to using products that block access to inappropriate sites.[34]
   a. Would you be reluctant to work for a company that monitors your Internet activities? Why or why not?
   b. Find out if your educational institution or workplace has blocking software. If not, examine the Internet policies, if any, of the educational institution or company.
   c. Develop a set of Internet policies for a local company and make a presentation to the Board explaining why such policies are important.

2. Dairy cooperative Land O'Lakes is a $4 billion company in Arden Hills, Minnesota, which supplies dairy products to members and farmers in 15 states. The company relies on databases containing information on trade promotions, internal sales, and other subjects which food brokers and regional sales managers access from their notebook computers through dial-up links. But Land O'Lakes was not able to send some critical information electronically to its retailers because of incompatible technologies.

   "You need access to all that data to make sure your stores have the best products available at the best price in the right markets," says Adam Krauter, manager of information and technology at Land O'Lakes. Instead, the company would print out the data and send it via courier to regional sales managers and food brokers, but that did not go over very well. "You have this 2-inch-thick stack of paper to lug around, and most sales managers don't have time to dig through that stuff," Krauter quips. Also, by the time the sales managers received the printouts, they were 2 weeks old and not current enough to be helpful.

   Krauter decided to build an extranet so the scanner data could be accessed over the Web. Both local and remote users now access data and reports on the server using Windows 95 and Microsoft Internet Explorer. They can drill down to various levels of information and look at products by brand name, size, or whatever other criteria they're allowed to use. "It's easy to drill down to data over the Web, and it eliminates the problem of carrying paper reports with you," Krauter explains. Also, users can access new data as soon as received, rather than having to wait for up to 2 weeks. He says: "It's hard to measure how much we've saved with the new system, but it's a question of, if you don't do it, you get to be toast."

   a. Why is this Land O' Lakes system an ideal extranet application?
   b. Why do you think it might be difficult to measure the effect of extranets? What are some ways to convince management to invest in an extranet even though it may be difficult to place a dollar value on the returns?

3. "But I'm just one person! How could what I'm doing affect the whole Internet?" Dr. Bernardo Huberman, a researcher at the Xerox Palo Alto Research Center and a professor of physics at Stanford University, has heard those words from the lips of too many Internet users. To convince such skeptics that their actions do indeed have a big impact on network traffic, Huberman and graduate student Rajan Lukose came up with a mathematical model to track "storms" of Internet use that lead to bursts of congestion, long waits, and frustrated users. Then they put their findings in a social context, arguing that Internet congestion occurs when users who pay the same amount no matter how much information they need take a greedy, all-you-can-eat approach to the Internet. Their proposed solution: Put a price on the information.[35]

   a. What is your opinion about the proposed solution to put a price tag on information? Discuss.
   b. Putting a price on information defeats the basic premise of an Internet. Discuss.

4. **(Web exercise)** Use any search engine and click on the "Travel" link. Pick a place anywhere in the world. Explore how to book an airline ticket, make hotel reservations, and identify local points of interest. Write a two-page report about your experience.

5. **(Web and software exercise)** Natural language processing is one important area of an artificial intelligence system. Try to use two search engines—such as Yahoo, Excite@Home, Infoseek, and HotBot (www.hotbot.com)—to find three products that can translate English to Chinese. Use appropriate software to create a table to report your result. Include the fields product name, supplying company, hardware platform, and Web link.

Case 1: Changing the World One Camper at a Time

Technology skills can translate into economic power. To avoid social class barriers, then, technology should be accessible to the rich and the poor. Outdoor Online is a program that introduces cutting-edge Internet technology to children ages 10 to 17 of all socioeconomic backgrounds from all parts of the world. Its founders hold positions in government, politics, entertainment, and business. The program, held in the California Sierras (near Lake Tahoe), encourages exercise, teamwork, natural challenge, personal growth, and respect for nature and others.

The Outdoor Online curriculum gives students a technological education using state-of-the-art equipment. Each student contributes to the camp electronic newspaper, builds a personal Web page, explores advances in multimedia, and conducts research using the Internet. In addition, several guest speakers challenge students to consider issues of safety, intolerance, crime, and etiquette in "cyberspace." Students are also challenged in the outdoor arena, both physically and mentally. Along with high-adventure sports, they conduct environmental studies during nature hikes and explore survival skills during several overnight trips.

Students work on a network of personal computers connected to the Internet through a network connection provided by MCI Telecommunications. The operation of this connection is no small feat, given the 8,000-foot elevation of the Sierras and the erratic weather conditions. Other Internet-related tools that students use include Web-development software, various browsers, multimedia tools, digital cameras (used to capture outdoor experiences and apply them to the Web page), video and audio software to convert sound and video to the World Wide Web, scanners, and antivirus software.

The goal of this project is to help children from all walks of life understand and use information technology. However, the program helps students develop more than IT skills. They are challenged to reason, create, interact, play, and work in a diverse environment and ultimately to understand where technology fits in the human experience. Hopefully, they translate these experiences into success after they finish the program and share their knowledge with their teachers, parents, colleagues, and friends.[35]

1. The Internet can be used as a tool to help individuals better themselves. Discuss.
2. Technology is meaningful only if the social context in which it operates is taken into account. Discuss.
3. What recommendations, if any, would you make to the founders of this program to enhance and enrich more lives?

Case 2: The Angry Voice of the Web

Drew Faber was irked. When he signed up at a Bally Total Fitness health club, he had negotiated to upgrade his plan so that he could use other clubs in the Los Angeles–based Bally Total Fitness Holding Corp. chain when he traveled to other cities. But when he cut a check for the upgrade just before a trip to Chicago, the club simply tacked a few extra months on to his membership. Bally told him his plan did not qualify him to use its Chicago club.

Faber, a freelance photographer, already maintained two World Wide Web sites to promote his work. He wasted no time launching a third—one that promoted his complaints about the chain. He called it Bally Total Fitness Sucks (www.compupix.com/ballysucks/). He topped the page with the health club's logo, across which he scrawled the word "sucks." "I thought a Web site would be the easiest way to get a response from Bally's," Faber says. "If I just wrote letters, they would just ignore them, but it wouldn't be easy to ignore the Web site."

In vast numbers, consumers are taking their grievances about companies, products, and services to the Web, and they aren't being coy about it. *GTE Sucks; The I Hate McDonald's Page; Toys R Us Sucks; I Hate Bill Gates!, I Hate Microsoft, I Hate Windows, The Official Packard-Bell Hate Page;*and *Why America Online Sucks* are just a few sites started by unhappy consumers.

Public relations consultants estimate the number of such rogue sites could be close to 1,000. Nike knows the spectrum. The company is targeted by at least eight different sites, which mainly criticize the Beaverton, Oregon, company for alleged labor abuses in Southeast Asia. "Some of them are so completely over the edge, in our opinion, that it seems pointless to even try to counterpoint what they say," Reames says. "Some are actually well thought out and have offered us a different point of view."

"Avoid 'testosterosis,' or the urge to hit someone in the face because they are doing something you don't like," counsels Jim Lukaszewski, president of The Lukaszewski

continued

Case 2: The Angry Voice of the Web, *continued*

Group in White Plains, New York, which advises Fortune 500 companies on how to deal with public relations crises. "It's a free country, and the Web is completely unregulated. Don't get angry and think about doing foolish things." But because consumer hate sites upset corporate employees and boards of directors alike, there is a natural tendency to get lawyers involved. That can be a mistake. Those who operate hate sites adore posting letters from lawyers threatening them with legal action unless they stop their activities. Once made public, such letters can cast another negative spotlight on the company.

Faber heard from scores of other unhappy Bally members within months of launching the Bally Total Fitness Sucks site. He added their complaints and other suggested content to the site. If Bally had contacted him right away, Faber says, he probably would have let the site die a quiet death. But Bally did not respond for months. By then, the site had developed a life of its own. Today, it boasts more than 300 messages from other members.

Faber eventually accepted a settlement offer from Bally and now belongs to another health club. However, Bally then sued him for trademark violations. The case was dismissed.

Experts give the following advice to deal with—or not, as the case may be—rogue Web sites:

- Do not ignore the sites; monitor them. Designate a responsible party in your Web development group, legal department, or public relations organization and establish a line of communication among the three departments.
- If you can verify that complaints at the site are legitimate, address them.
- Resist the impulse to wage a war with the site operator. Instead, focus on substance.
- Create an area on-line that presents your side of the story. If you addressed the concerns voiced at a site, consider linking to it from your own site. That will diminish the effect of the attack.
- Keep in mind that any correspondence you send to the site will end up posted on it.
- Take action against site operators only when the material meets the guidelines for copyright infringement or is absolutely libelous.[37]

1. Do you believe it is appropriate for customers to set up such sites? What ethical or legal issues are involved? Now assume the site attacks a person, not a business. How does your analysis change, if at all?

2. If your company were the target of such a site, what measures would you take to do damage control besides the ones recommended in the case?

3. **(Web exercise)** Use a search engine to locate such a site and comment on the site's merits. If possible, find the site of the business that is being attacked to see whether that business addresses any concerns raised in the rogue site.

You can't just build it, because they will not come.

Cliff Conneighton, CEO of Icoms Inc.

CONTENTS

ELECTRONIC COMMERCE FOR SUCCESS

Shopping will never be the same again, thanks to the Internet. Having to drive to a store, find a parking space, shop during the hours of store operation, fight the crowds, and search for what you want is no longer the only option for consumers. On-line shopping can take place from the comfort of your home or office, day or night, with a few simple keystrokes and a credit card. The computer monitor is now a window to a world of shops and galleries. This shift is due to electronic commerce, also known as e-commerce or simply "EC," where shopping for goods and services occurs over the Internet.

How does EC differ from traditional shopping? Unlike shopping in a retail store, no paper money is involved in an EC transaction. There is no need to wait in long lines or do battle with other customers. Instead you can shop when you want and where you want, and you can comparison shop quickly by visiting competitors' Web sites to make sure you are paying the lowest price.

Individuals with and without technology backgrounds are actively participating in electronic commerce as a way to save time and money and to learn about competitive products. Marketing giants are targeting key consumer decision makers—especially female Web users—and are eager to sell everything from soaps to sauces and perfumes to pasta.

Unilever, whose brands include Lipton tea, Ragu sauce, and Close-Up toothpaste, is planning to spend at least $50 million over 3 years to promote its brands on America Online and other Internet sites. Their targets: the 22 million women who surf the Web from home or from the office.[1] And that number keeps growing. Web traffic by women has more than doubled in the past 2 years, and women now account for about 43 percent of the on-line popula-

Chapter 8

Electronic Commerce

AFTER STUDYING THIS CHAPTER, YOU WILL BE ABLE TO:

- Define electronic commerce and explain how it works
- Distinguish between different types of EC models
- Specify the guidelines for an effective EC site
- Summarize the opportunities and challenges of EC
- Outline global EC issues

tion, according to Forrester Research, an on-line consulting and research firm.[2]

Although the benefits of Internet shopping include convenience and speed, many businesses believe EC offers them a more meaningful way to reach and connect with consumers. "Any new medium that can help us deepen [the company's] bonds with families and offer them new benefits is, by definition, of tremendous interest to us," observes Denise F. Beausejour, Procter & Gamble's vice president for worldwide advertising.[3]

The impact of EC on businesses has been, and will continue to be, profound. Both small and large businesses now view the Internet as essential to their business success because it expands their opportunities. "This Internet is great. I could live on the North Pole and sell bikinis and do a booming business," says Scott Girner, owner of Aloha Pools and Spas in North Little Rock, Arkansas. Aloha's Web site generated $100,000 in business—3 percent of Aloha's usual annual revenue—within the first year, all of it from outside the state. "I've yet to get any orders from the moon or Mars, but I've gotten them from everywhere else," Girner quips.[4]

Many small businesses such as Aloha Pools maximize the ability to reach more customers affordably over the Internet. In fact, many small businesses invite, entertain, educate, please, and retain customers. They use their Web sites to create the same sense of warmth and caring that many mom-and-pop stores do. "Come in and stay a while" is the general theme of some of these sites.

What's more, small companies can teach big business a few lessons about what works in on-line commerce. They usually take a greater interest in checking e-mail received from their Web visitors

TECHNOLOGY PAYOFF

Estée Lauder Sells Beauty

Estée Lauder, a cosmetics company that sells more than $4 billion worth of products each year, is now selling one of its flagship brands directly to consumers over the Internet. Selling goods and services over an electronic medium such as the Internet is called "electronic commerce" or "e-commerce" (EC).

Estée Lauder's Web site (www.clinique.com) lets consumers place orders for Clinique products with the company directly or with one of several hundred national retailers linked to the site. The choice is a boon to customers who avoid buying cosmetics in a store because the experience is too intimidating or time-consuming. The site tries to encourage retail store visits, however, by recommending that customers test products at a store counter before making a purchase. Customer e-mail feedback and orders suggest that the convenience, choices, and simplicity offered through Estée Lauder's Web site create a positive consumer experience.

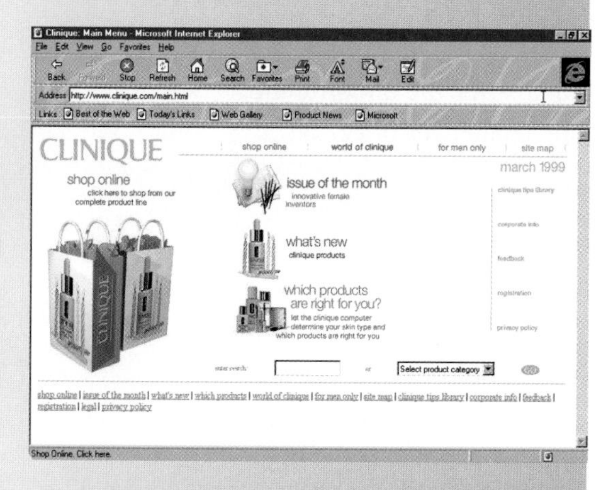

But on-line shopping has its drawbacks. It's tough to re-create the in-store impulse buys that occur when someone visits a Clinique counter to buy one product and ends up buying two or three. Estée Lauder is experimenting with ways to encourage impulse buying over the Web but has not yet found the perfect solution. In addition, many customers shy away from making purchases over the Web because they're concerned about their privacy and the security of the buying process.

On balance, Estée Lauder believes its Web site provides a win-win scenario. Many customers win because of the convenience,

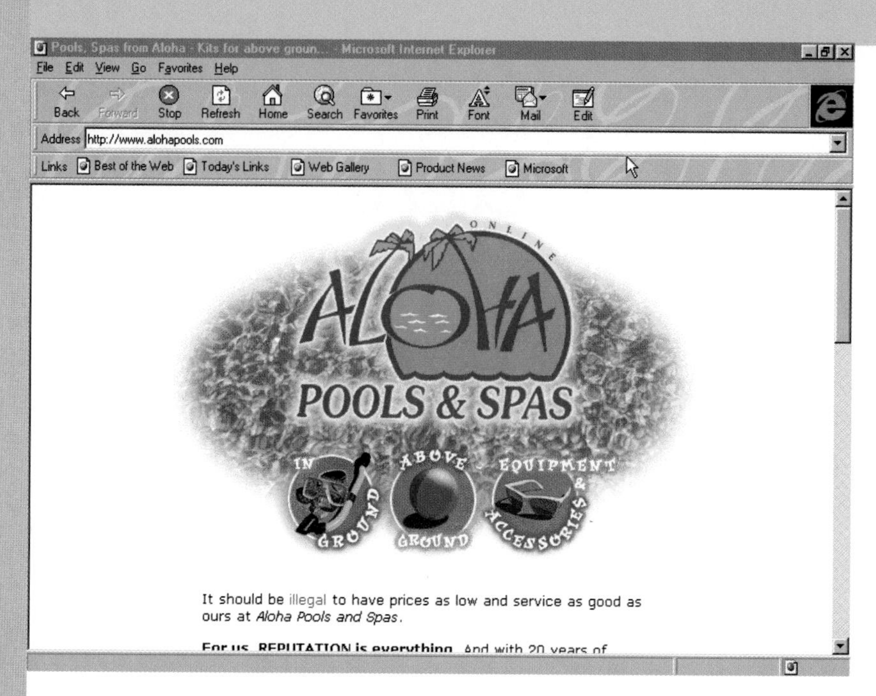

Aloha Pool's Web site has generated out-of-state business that it could otherwise not have obtained from its Arkansas headquarters.

and are frequently more responsive to customer requests than are mega corporations, according to Minda Caesar, marketing manager for IBM's Home Page Creator, a do-it-yourself Web site publishing package aimed at small businesses.[5]

EC also helps companies sell to customers affordably because growing the business with EC requires an investment in technology and a core sales staff rather than an investment in real estate, buildings, and employees at all locations handling similar responsibilities. In 1981 Tech Data Corp., a family business that sells office and computer products, employed about a dozen people in Clearwater, Florida, and operated out of a small warehouse. It was a traditional catalog operation: customers called Tech Data's salespeople and those salespeople placed the orders, tracked shipments, and configured products by price, availability, and compatibility.

Through careful planning and a shift to electronic commerce, Tech Data has grown to a $4.6 billion Fortune 500 company serving 55,000 dealers with more than 45,000 products from 900 manufacturers; they now employ more than 2,700 people. The company does a significant share of its business on the Net. With a few keystrokes, customers can view catalogs, select their purchases, and pay over the Internet. Salespeople are freed from the mundane order-taking tasks and can focus instead on attracting more customers both on and off the Web.[6]

EC sites that meet the communication needs of their patrons can improve business processes. At the supplier's request, a marketing manager could access a company's EC site to determine which products are selling fastest so that the supplier can plan its manufacturing schedule to keep pace with demand. Or, a key client in the fast-paced stock market industry who obtains quick answers on an EC Web site to questions about market fluctuations becomes more loyal to the stock-trading firm. Ultimately, many consumers and business partners may be unwilling to do business with a company that lacks an EC site.

When we think of "commerce" most of us think money. But some people are using EC to help the poor and the underprivileged. For instance, a new Web site lets you buy "goats, geese, or an arkful of animals on-line," at Heifer Project International, a nonprofit group (www.heifer.org). The charity based in Little Rock, Arkansas, sends farm animals to poor families worldwide so that they can sustain themselves. It also teaches them how to raise and care for these animals with the hope that it may lead to their economic betterment.[7]

EC is also providing alternative learning methods. MicroAge, an Arizona-based company that provides computer-consulting services to its global clients, created innovative training programs for its salesforce. Instead of relying on traditional training methods in which individuals are sent to a specific location to receive training on a set topic at a given day and time, the company trained its salesforce over its Web site. One of the main objectives of the new program was to train the salesforce to sell Internet products both on and off the Web. Within the first week of one of its courses, the company saw a 50 percent increase in sales for one of its key products.[8]

Because EC touches so many aspects of business and our lives, we need to understand how EC works, different ways to conduct electronic commerce, guidelines for effective EC sites, and EC's opportunities and challenges. In addition, because EC is by its very nature a global business activity, we explore cultural and technological factors that affect EC.

speed, and hassle-free nature of on-line shopping. Estée Lauder wins because it can reach customers who want to avoid a trip to a retail store. The company can also gather valuable information about its Web customers' preferences so that it can respond to customer demands effectively.

Source: Sharon Machlis, "Estée Lauder Tackles Web, Channel Conflict," *Computerworld,* July 6, 1998, 79.

How Electronic Commerce Works

What is **electronic commerce**? It is the process of exchanging something of value—such as products, services, or information—through electronic means, mostly the Internet. Vladimir Zwass, Professor of Information Systems at Fairleigh Dickinson University, applies this definition broadly, stating that electronic commerce is sharing business information, maintaining business relationships, and conducting business transactions by means of telecommunication networks.

Electronic commerce

The process of two or more entities engaging in commercial transactions through electronic media, usually the Internet. These transactions include the exchange of something of value, such as money, goods and services, or information.

The exchange transaction may occur between individuals, businesses, and organizations. Note, though, that E-commerce does not refer only to transactions and information exchanges between consumers and businesses. It may also refer to transactions and information exchanges between internal business divisions or with external business partners.

When we define EC in such broad terms, both intranets and extranets may become a subset of EC. The question is not, "Are intranets and extranets part of EC?" They may or may not be. What tells us if an extranet or an intranet is an EC application is whether it helps and promotes the company's goals of conducting business over the Internet. If a company has an extranet application that promotes EC, then the extranet is an EC application.

Electronic commerce is not a new idea. In fact, e-commerce was originally (and still is) conducted via electronic data interchange (EDI) over value-added-networks (VANs). However, the idea of engaging in electronic transactions did not gather full steam until hardware and software advances in the 1990s made personal and professional commercial transactions using electronic media more affordable and feasible.

Let's explore in simple terms how EC works. Electronic commerce is based on the idea that all transactions can be done electronically, as Figure 8-1 illustrates. In electronic commerce, entities do not meet in a physical location. Instead, they "meet" in cyberspace. There are few, if any, paper transactions because most transactions are executed electronically.

Here are common steps that an individual or business undertakes to buy or sell goods on the Internet:

Step 1: A customer logs onto the Internet. The customer uses search engines to identify companies that offer products of interest. As you may recall, some popular search engines include InfoSeek, Alta Vista, HotBot, Yahoo!, and Lycos.

Step 2: Next, the customer studies and analyzes different sites that the search engine yields and narrows the choice to a few companies that meet his or her needs. The customer visits the Web sites of selected companies. This process is often called "surfing" because the customer moves from one site to another to locate items of interest.

FIGURE 8-1 **The Steps Involved in an EC Transaction**

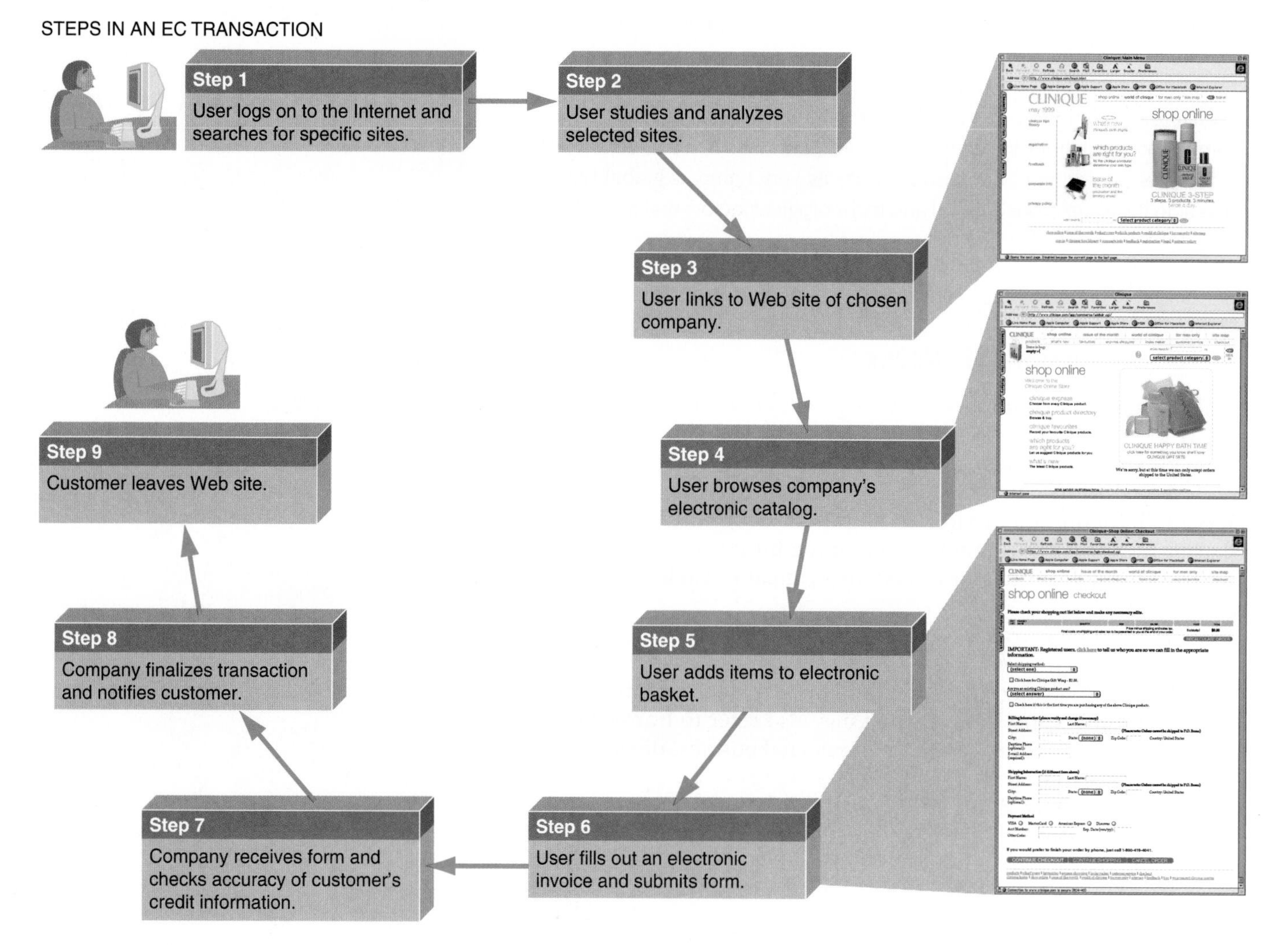

Step 3: The company's Web site has links to the "on-line store," which is basically an electronic catalog of the company's goods and services.

Step 4: The shopping experience begins as the customer "flips" through electronic pages of the catalog to identify relevant goods and services.

Step 5: The customer adds the item he or she is buying to a "shopping basket." The customer continues to accumulate items in the basket, similar to what customers do in a grocery store.

Step 6: Once the shopping is complete, the customer checks out by simply clicking on a button labeled "Done," "Proceed to Checkout," or something of the kind, which takes the customer to the electronic cashier. The electronic cashier requests the customer to verify the items in the basket by showing the customer an "electronic invoice." At this point, the customer has the choice of adding or deleting items from the basket. Once the invoice is finalized, the cashier produces an electronic invoice that summarizes items bought, quantities, state taxes, and shipping and handling charges.

Step 7: The cashier then requests that the customer fill in an electronic invoice form that provides detailed information about the customer and financial details relating to the transaction. The "electronic cashier" requires information such as customer name, shipping address, telephone number, and credit card number to complete the transaction. If customers are reluctant to share credit card information, they can place the order electronically and mail the company a check. The customer then submits the electronic invoice by simply clicking on the button labeled "Submit" or something similar. The cashier verifies the information and records the transaction. Estée Lauder, featured in the Technology Payoff, processes the orders it receives on its Web site in this way.

Step 8: The company receives the invoice, processes the order, receives payment from the customer, and ships the item to the customer. The company may sometimes use middlemen to process the order, although the customer is unaware of this behind-the-scenes transaction.

Step 9: The customer can now leave the Web site, with his or her shopping done.

Although these steps seem uncomplicated, the technology behind electronic commerce is anything but. "A Web site is like an iceberg," observes Delta AirLines CIO Charles Feld, a longtime IT executive with experience at Frito-Lay and Burlington Northern. "What you see looks small and simple, but below it you have infrastructure integration issues with maybe 40 or 50 databases. So building a Web infrastructure can be a pretty serious risk for older companies [that may have outdated technologies]."[9]

The steps just described form the basis of all electronic commerce transactions. However, there are several variations or "models" of the EC process that we examine next.

Models of Electronic Commerce

Several models of the EC process help businesses understand and apply electronic commerce principles effectively. Which model is most effective depends on the situation and the parties involved. For instance, a business transacting with other businesses would rely on a slightly different EC model than an individual selling directly to a consumer.

Here are three EC models that differ based on the parties involved in the transaction:

1. The supplier is a business and the consumer is also a business (business to business)
2. The supplier is a business and the consumer is an individual or a business (business to consumer)
3. The supplier is an individual and the consumer is also an individual

Figure 8-2 shows these different EC models, which we explore in more depth in the following sections.

These models show that not all EC sites are the same. Some sites deal exclusively with other businesses, some deal exclusively with nonbusinesses, and some deal with both. The nature and scope of transactions, the method of payment, and other such related factors may vary depending on the model used.

Business-to-business EC models

A model of commercial electronic transactions between two businesses in which the businesses do not negotiate each transaction.

Business to Business

With a **business-to-business model** EC, sometimes called an interorganizational information system (IOS), two business entities engage in EC transactions. This model is

FIGURE 8-2

The Three Models of EC

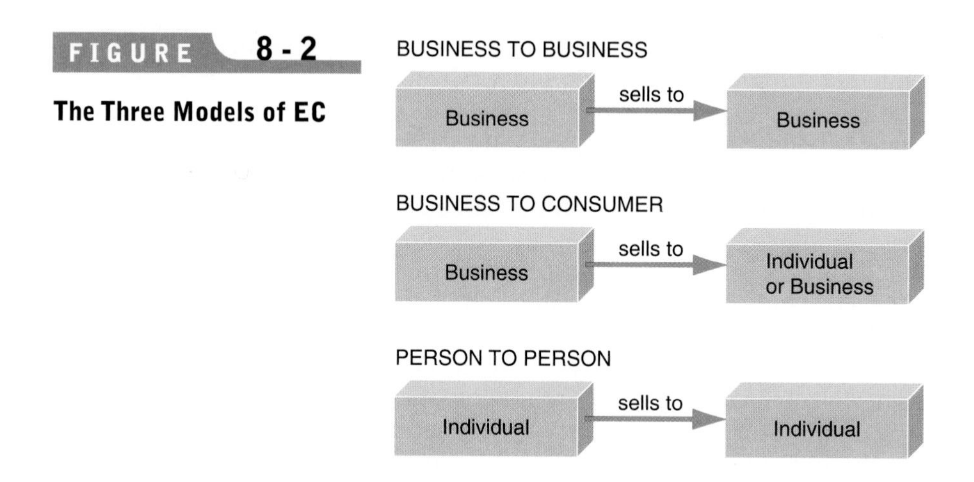

fairly common. In fact, we have already looked at some business-to-business models in earlier chapters. EDI is a business-to-business model in which two businesses exchange documents electronically. However, in the case of EDI, the information travels over VANs (value-added networks), not the Internet. Extranets, covered in Chapter 7, can be either a business-to-business or a business-to-customer model in which one business gives its business partners access to company information over the Internet.

The business-to-business EC model is quite complex, although it may not appear so on the surface, for several reasons. First, usually several business entities are involved in each transaction. For example, a manufacturer may have numerous suppliers that provide parts and multiple distributors that deliver its products. Once the manufacturer receives an electronic order, it may forward that order to a chain of business entities that in turn must do their part to execute the order. Second, in business-to-business EC, the systems linking two or more businesses must be compatible.

Note that under this model the businesses do not negotiate each transaction. Instead the two businesses agree on a set of terms and continue to follow those terms in each transaction.

Business to Business/Individuals

Business-to-business/individual EC models

Models in which commercial electronic transactions occur between a business and another business or individual, and all transactions are open to negotiations.

Another type of EC model is the **business-to-business/individual model,** also referred to as electronic markets, in which a business engages in electronic commerce with another business or individual consumer. That is, the consumer may be either a business or an individual.

The primary difference between the business-to-business model and the business-to-business/individual model is that, unlike the business-to-business model, each transaction may be open to negotiation in the business-to-business/individual model. The negotiation occurs because the consumer solicits bids, processes and negotiates the bid, and agrees on a set of terms for each transaction, which are then executed.

Individual to Individual

In some cases, individuals may engage in electronic commerce transactions with other individuals. In this case, the two individuals determine all terms relating to the transaction.

Building and Maintaining Effective Electronic Commerce Sites

Electronic commerce requires more than launching a Web site that has an on-line store. Businesses that engage in EC must give potential customers a reason to visit their site, feel comfortable with the purchasing process, and become loyal customers. In this section, we examine guidelines for developing effective EC sites.

Keep the Site Interesting

"The Net is like TV with 10 million channels. You can't just hope that someone surfs by,"[10] says Cliff Conneighton, CEO of Icoms, a company that has developed EC sites for Houghton-Mifflin, Hasbro, Fujitsu, and other companies. Even if people visit your site, that doesn't mean they will become customers. Unfortunately for many businesses,

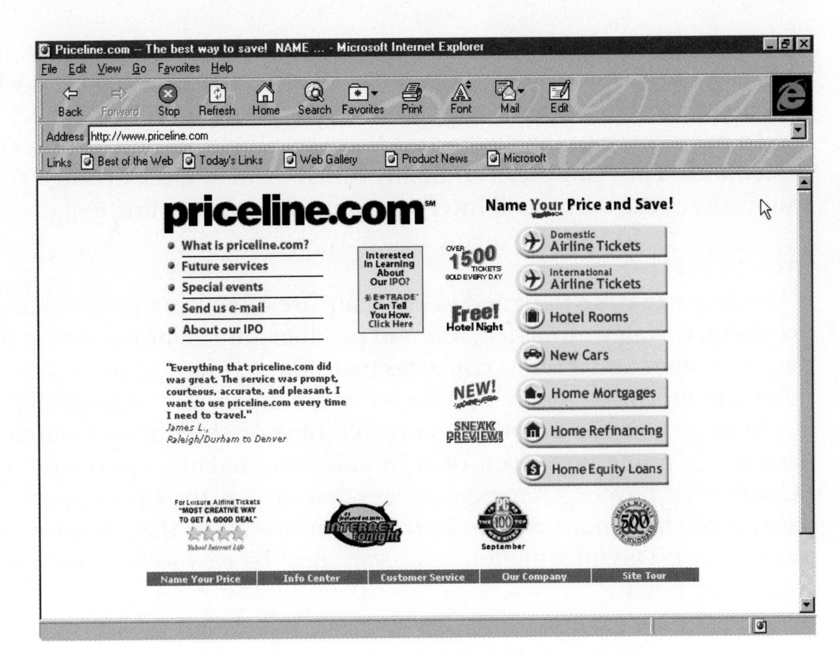

Priceline offers customers a "buyer-driven commerce" service in which buyers offer a price they're willing to pay for items such as a hotel room. Priceline searches for a seller willing to accept that price. The company's contacts with national sellers provide consumers a distinct benefit.

"surfing" still describes the way most people use the Web, where surfers are the equivalent of window-shoppers—those who look but don't buy.

Successful EC sites convert uncommitted surfers into buyers by grabbing their interest; allaying their fears and concerns; providing valuable, hard-to-find information; and delivering high-quality, reliable products and services. "You need to offer a compelling consumer benefit to get people to shop on-line," says Jay Walker, chairman and CEO of priceline.com, a buying service that connects buyers with sellers willing to accept the price the buyer offers.[11]

Walker's company lets customers name their price for an airline ticket and find out within an hour (or 24 hours for an overseas destination) whether 1 of 15 airlines is willing to sell a seat for that price. Priceline sold 10,000 tickets in its first 6 weeks of operation and in July 1998 began inviting New York–area shoppers to name their price for new cars and trucks. "To get consumers to behave in a new way, you have to offer a price benefit, a convenience benefit, or a service benefit," says Walker. "Or, like us, you have to invent something that you fundamentally can't get anywhere else."

In essence, good Web sites grab attention by offering something of value you can't get elsewhere. "We've shifted from a money-based economy to an attention economy, in which the most valued commodity of exchange—and also that which is in shortest supply—is attention," says President and CEO Nat Goldhaber. "If [companies] want your attention, they should compensate you for it."[12]

Ensure Privacy and Security

The most common reasons that potential customers opt out of the Internet shopping experience is concern about loss of privacy and security. Sending personal information or credit card data over the Net is unnerving for many individuals, who want to safeguard such information. Good EC sites address these fears openly and candidly. They often explain in nontechnical terms how the company protects personal and financial data from unwanted eyes, assure customers that their data will be closely guarded, and provide phone numbers to call in case customers have unanswered questions. According to Adam Geiger—a Web developer who created an EC site for the 1998 Tibetan Freedom Concert, selling 4,000 tickets in just under 4 hours—companies should tell customers how it will use the information that Web site visitors offer.[13]

Reputable companies state their privacy and security policies clearly. Typically, these companies will ask permission to share information about you with companies that may sell related products. For instance, if you buy golf balls and clubs from an EC Web site, the company will ask your permission to share your interest in golf with a golf clothing manufacturer. If you decline, the company will not share the data.

Unscrupulous companies may sell the data without asking your permission. There is no easy way to know how a company will use private data. This is why it is important to deal only with reputable companies when engaging in EC.

To protect themselves, consumers are turning to products that keep their identity anonymous. For example, a company called Privada has a product that safeguards the anonymity of the user on all Internet transactions, including e-mail and e-commerce.[14]

Inform First

EC Web sites that are designed to entertain are often less successful than those designed to inform. Giving visitors rich, relevant product information is one of the best ways to attract customers and address concerns that shoppers have about a product or service. EC sites must inform to capture the essence of the experience of shopping at a physical store.

Imagine going to a clothing store. Nothing on the Internet can match the exact experience of trying on a dress or shirt and then making a purchase decision. Effective EC sites offer buyers other experiences that surpass the store experience, such as comparison pricing, more detailed product information than a store would provide, or lower prices. The information, however, must be easy to find and formatted to match customers' needs.

Encourage Price Comparisons

"As a buyer, I need to know that I'm getting a fair price," says Keith Halloran, vice president of marketing at NECX, a reseller of computer hardware and software based in Peabody, Massachusetts.[15] Savvy companies like NECX make comparison pricing a part of their on-line strategy. NECX visitors can click on a "Compare Prices" link on any product page to see how NECX's price stacks up against the competition. The site also provides links to competitors' sites.

Similar to traditional shopping, customers like to price shop on the Internet before buying a product or service. "From our perspective, we didn't want people to have to leave the site to get that information," explains Halloran.[16] Once customers leave the site, they may get distracted and not come back. Halloran admits that users will buy from a competing site when the price is lower, but contends that the feature has increased customer loyalty. His proof? The company's revenues have increased steadily over the past 2 years.

Develop a Great Electronic Sales Team

Think about the personal attention you receive from an upscale store. In a similar fashion, quality Web sites have dynamic virtual salespeople who cater to the whims of visitors. Several Internet technologies help companies provide exceptional customer

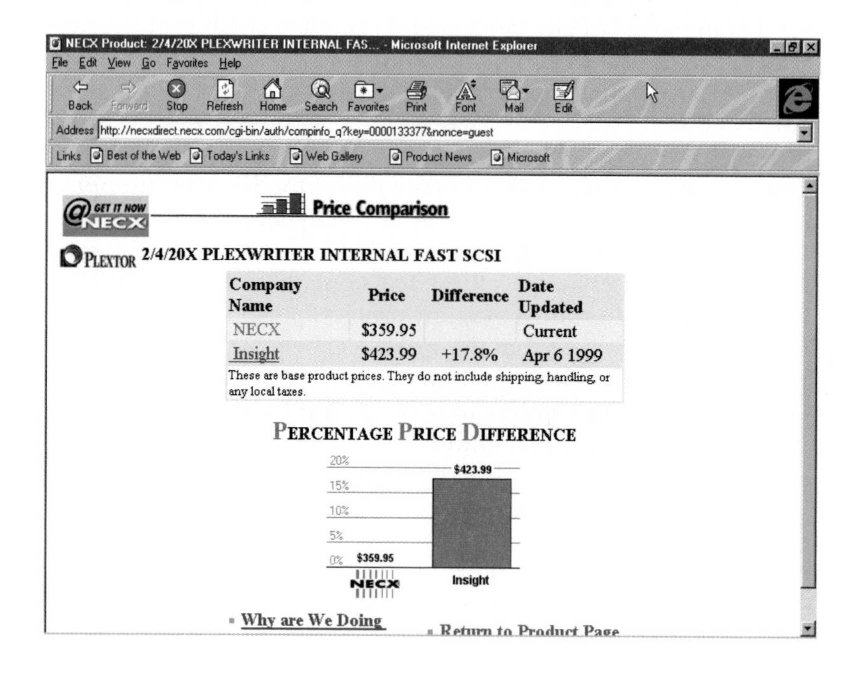

The EC site for NECX links to competitors' sites to make comparison shopping easy.

service. Some technologies help companies provide easy-to-access product and service information, track customers' purchase preferences, remind them when it is time to replace a product or service, refer customers to related products and services, quickly address customer complaints, and act on their feedback to improve their shopping experience. It's everything a great salesperson would do in the real world.

At sneaker.com, an on-line sporting goods store, David Yip is striving to deliver as much service as that real-world salesperson—if not more. Yip is developing software that will estimate "factors such as how long it takes you to wear out a shoe based on how often you run or work out, and will send you an e-mail reminder when it's time to come back to our site."[17] His Massachusetts-based company is seeing many repeat customers who have purchased from the site 9 and 10 times during its 3 years of operation.

Sneaker.com provides customers with clear, step-by-step instructions for ordering shoes. If a customer has a question about a product, he can e-mail a salesperson who will promptly respond. The customer can also hold a telephone conversation with a salesperson. In other words, although this is a virtual experience, the company tries to make the shopping experience as real as possible for the customer.

Other businesses provide superior customer service by developing ways to save customers' time. Several companies offer customers a fast-track service that allows them to skip steps that first-time or undecided buyers must go through. Repeat NECX customers do not need to select each product that they want to buy. Instead NECX offers a service where shoppers can bypass the catalog of products and select from their "frequently purchased" list of products. "That lets people who are in a hurry do an express checkout," says Halloran.[18]

Suppose you are a frequent shopper at NECX or Amazon.com. Once you enter your user identification and password, the system retrieves information about you such as Social Security number, mailing address, details about the last credit card used, and so on. If the customer knows exactly what she wants and is a previous user of the Web site, the entire transaction may take just a few minutes. Similarly, autobytel.com, the on-line network of car dealerships maintained by Auto-By-Tel Corp. in Irvine, California, has a button on its front page—"Ready to Buy"—for people who want a price on their dream vehicle as quickly as possible.[19]

Keep It Simple

One reason for the popularity of electronic commerce is convenience. Companies, then, should keep their sites so simple to use that customers find shopping on the Web site a pleasant, time-saving, hassle-free experience.

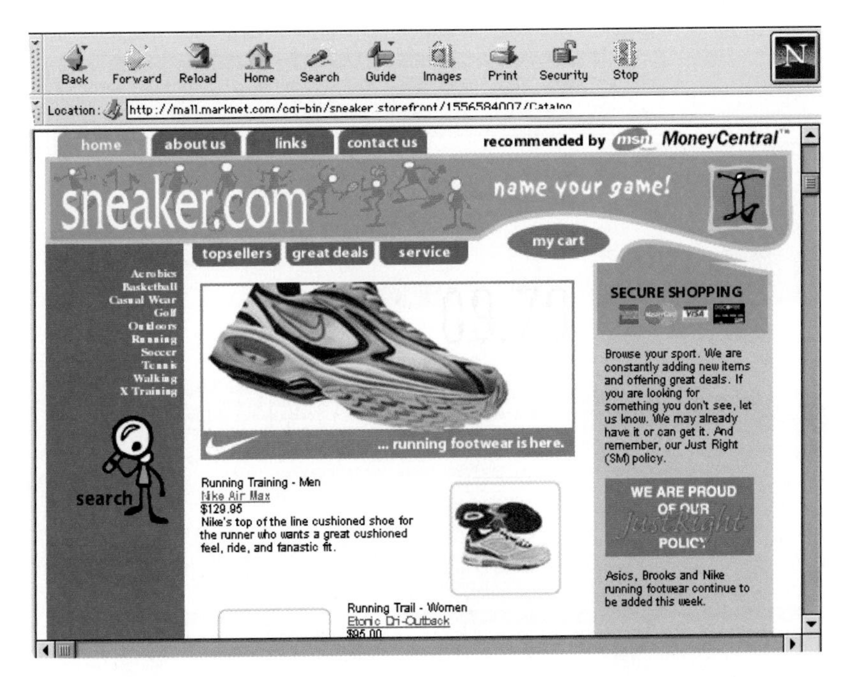

The EC site for sneaker.com offers customers top-notch service through responsiveness and attention to their needs.

Simplicity means that customers can locate company and product information quickly, including a statement about how the business uses customer information, obtain all information necessary for a purchase decision, and learn how to contact a company representative for further information via e-mail or telephone. Customers should also be able to retrace their steps as needed, add and delete things from their electronic basket without a hitch, and change their mind at the last minute.

What happens if a site is too complicated? Visitors leave the site. The Wall Street Journal Interactive Edition realized that its original subscription form was too long and involved; users were dropping out of the process after two or three screens. The form was trimmed. The Journal now has more than 200,000 paying subscribers.

Encourage Customers to Visit the Physical Store

Some EC sites encourage customers to visit the physical store of the company. Sixty-one percent of franchised new car and truck dealers have Web pages, but dealers sell an average of only 5.3 vehicles per month over the Internet, according to a survey conducted by the National Automobile Dealers Association (NADA).[20] This is not unexpected. "The focus of dealers that have [an EC site] is to market their dealerships and get people to come in, not necessarily to complete a transaction [on-line]," explains Tom Webb, chief economist at Washington-based NADA. Dealers are using the Net to build relationships with prospective customers and strengthen bonds with current customers, he adds. This approach is worthwhile: If a customer is hesitant to buy a high-cost item on-line, such as a car, the company still gets the business if the customer visits the physical store.

Site visits could increase if auto industry experts are correct in their prediction that dealerships will gradually decrease spending on mass advertising and instead will advertise on their Web sites.[21] The Web sites, then, should entice customers to visit the physical store. Giving information such as store location, work hours, and a contact person at the physical store is helpful.

Build Cyberspace Loyalty

The number of company EC sites continues to grow. This is good news for customers, but it increases competition for businesses on the Net. Hoping to avoid this profit squeeze, on-line companies are spending heavily to try to create brand loyalty in cyberspace. They are pumping up ad budgets, developing on-line communities of potentially loyal customers, and trying to make it hard for new visitors to go anywhere except their site.

Optimists hope that Internet branding will give companies the clout of a Nike or a Gillette. Cyberspace loyalty, however, requires more than advertising and an attention-grabbing home page. Customers demand a quality product or service, a strong com-

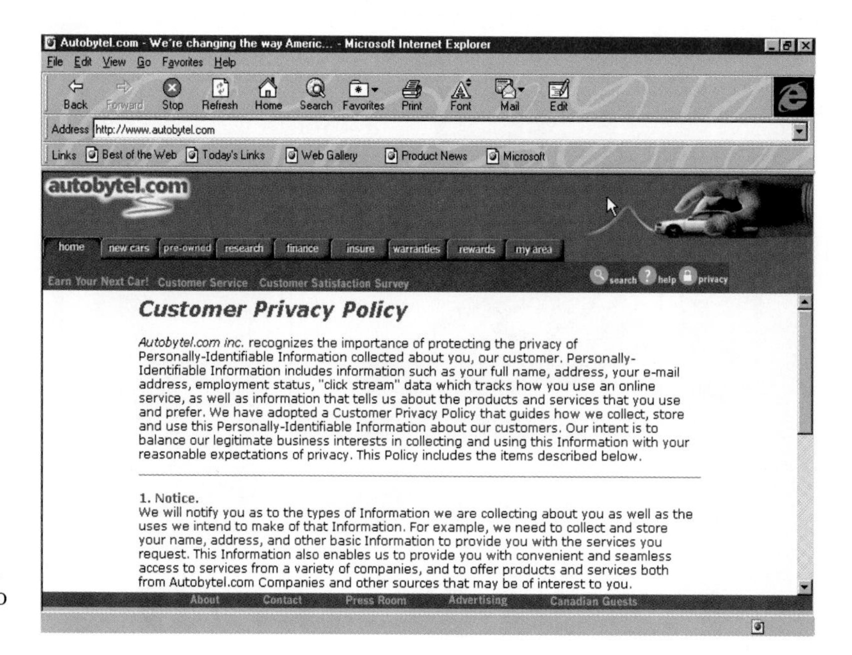

The autobytel.com site allows customers to access information quickly, even information about their privacy policy. Note, too, that the site offers a "contact" button for those who want further information.

pany image that they respect, trustworthy and relevant information, and attention to site simplicity, price benefits, customer service, and security. The complexity and cost of branding a Web site is often too steep for companies to bear—especially as competition on the Internet intensifies.[22]

Building a successful electronic commerce site takes vision, creativity, and a willingness to continue investing in the site for years to come. Yet, companies that take EC seriously can reap many benefits, the focus of the next section.

Promises of Electronic Commerce

Businesses are viewing electronic commerce as a technology idea that can, quite simply, change the face of business. Not only businesses, but individuals and society also stand to gain a great deal from EC advances. It holds greater promise than any other technological innovation in recent history. In this section we explore four benefits of EC: greater consumer power, a worldwide marketplace, improved business efficiency, and stronger loyalty between suppliers and customers.

Creates Customer Power

Information is power, and the Internet provides consumers with much information. Electronic commerce, then, gives individual customers more purchasing power. Customers can shop anywhere in the world for a specific product and in many instances can negotiate price or other terms with a business over the Internet.

Further, customers can join electronic communities and see what other users think of a product, a service, or a company. These communities can spread information about unpleasant business experiences quickly. Think back, for instance, to Chapter 7's case on Bally Fitness in which one unhappy customer developed a site at which hundreds of people posted complaints about Bally.

EC gives consumers more ability to comparison shop and find the best deal for the product or service they seek. Doug Galen, vice president of sales and business development at E-Loan, a Web-based mortgage loan originator in Palo Alto, California, offers customers one place to compare mortgage loan products. E-loan provides customers with a wealth of information so that they feel comfortable applying for a mortgage over the Web.

Information such as comparing loan products of different financial institutions, an assessment of good loan packages, and loan packages customized to individual needs are some of the services the company provides. In the Web business since mid-1997, the company gives customers the choice among 10,000 loan products and claims to save consumers up to 75 percent off loan originating fees (that computes to roughly $1,500, on average, per transaction).[23]

On-line customers can reap the benefits of mass customization. Chipshot.com, a Sunnyvale, California, startup company lets its on-line customers configure the perfect golf club from several million possible combinations of golf club parts. When customers enter their orders on the company's electronic commerce site, the orders are fed directly into Chipshot.com's manufacturing system. The customized golf club is manufactured and shipped to the customer from the plant floor.[24]

The World Is Your Marketplace

Electronic commerce blurs the boundaries of time and space. When General Nutrition, a Pittsburgh maker of nutrition supplements and health products, expanded globally, distance and time-zone differences slowed the order and fulfillment process. In one case the company's 200 overseas franchisees waited several hours just to get questions answered.

CIO Tom Smith decided to use e-commerce technology to let the company's 2,500 franchisees find out whether products were available, reserve them, or look at alternatives, all in real time. He also wanted to let franchisees customize product listings so they wouldn't get lists with products they couldn't sell or in a format different from their own. EC has paid off for General Nutrition: "Real-time response gave us . . . a more satisfied customer base, and slightly larger orders," Smith says. "And franchisees in Asia, where there is a 12-hour time differential, can deal with us according to their working hours."[25]

The ability of an organization to conduct business with any individual or business with Internet access anywhere in the world at any given time is almost equivalent to building stores in every city in the world! EC will continue to expand the reach of businesses as more people gain and use Internet access.

Increases Business Efficiency

Electronic commerce is not only about selling more goods and services or reaching more customers; it is also about increasing the efficiency of a business. Auto maker Daimler-Chrysler has lowered operating costs as a direct result of its investment in electronic commerce. An extranet that aids Daimler-Chrysler's EC, called Supplier Partner Information Network (SPIN), provides suppliers with invaluable data such as design changes, parts shortages, packaging information, and invoice tracking; these improve decision making and response times.

John Kay, manager of Daimler-Chrysler's electronic commerce, says about 3,500 of the company's 12,000 suppliers are connected to SPIN, which has not only helped the company streamline product delivery but also shorten the time it takes to respond to suppliers' questions and communicate process or design changes. Even a $1 per vehicle cost reduction translates into significant savings for the company. With millions of cars and trucks rolling off Chrysler's assembly line, those dollars add up.[26]

Builds a Closer Bond between Suppliers and Customers

When J. Crew, a global retailer and cataloger of clothing fashions, set up shop on the Web in 1997, it realized that it would not succeed with a business-as-usual approach. The company, which has a reputation for quality clothing, was eager to get repeat business from its customers. So J.Crew started at square one: repeat visits are necessary to generate repeat business. To encourage repeat business, the company added interactive games to its Web site that featured new products, catalogs, special promotions, and an archive of past catalogs that allows visitors to walk down memory lane.

The site makes sure that customers are not left guessing. It tells customers whether items are out of stock, when they will be available for back order, and recommends products to users based on past purchasing habits. The result? Customers love the site, visit it often, and remain loyal to the company through repeat purchases.[27]

Although EC offers many benefits, there are also technical and managerial challenges for businesses that implement EC. We take a brief look at these challenges next.

Challenges of Electronic Commerce

Because EC is still relatively new, the path to success is neither sure nor well-paved due to technical, managerial, and social challenges. However, researchers and scientists are working hard to address them so that in a few years some of these issues may no longer pose problems. We analyze seven current EC challenges faced by businesses.

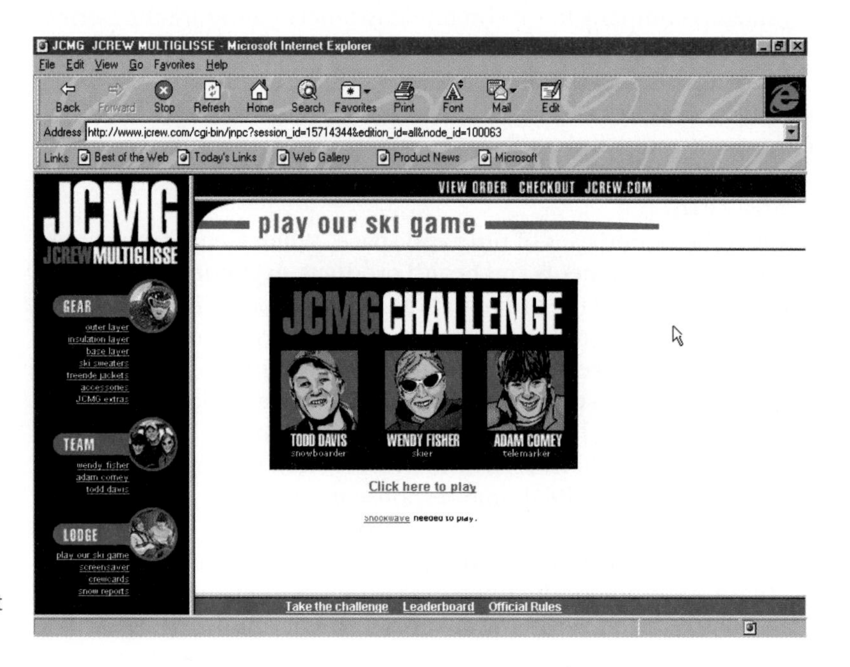

J.Crew's site shows how EC sites can entice repeat business through fun entertainment and quality products.

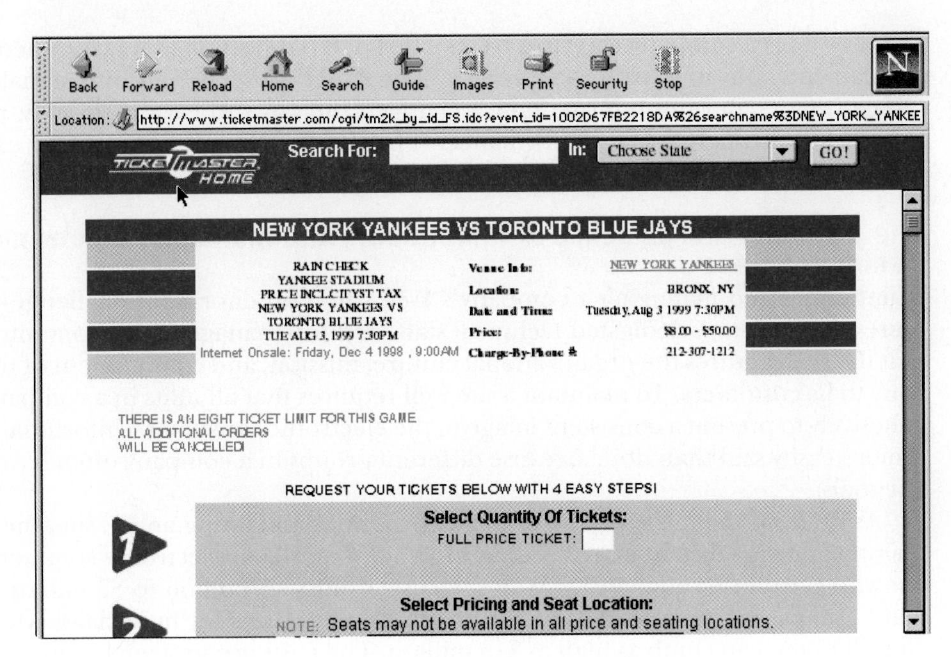

The New York Yankees' Web site links baseball ticket purchasers to Ticketmaster's site—in part to avoid coping with technology issues that can arise during heavy periods of ticket purchasing transactions.

Immature Technology

The technology to support heavy on-line trading is still immature. Companies need mammoth servers that are reliable and up and running 100 percent of the time. Also, the software to aid customer transactions has to be easy, intuitive, and reliable. Such software is expensive, and usually smaller companies simply cannot afford to make such large investments. Finally, reliable telecommunication links are the key to EC. However, running and administering these networks is difficult because networks are highly complex technical entities that require in-depth technical, business, and managerial knowledge.

Ticketmaster Multimedia, which sells tickets on-line to major shows and events, felt the effects of immature systems technology when selling Chicago Bulls tickets in 1997. "The response was so huge, it crashed the system," says Alan Citron, president and chief operating officer at Ticketmaster Multimedia.[28] The New York Yankees' on-line ticketing service also faced severe technical glitches on its EC site and reportedly lost 6 days' worth of ticket orders just before the start of the 1997 baseball season. (The Yankees.com site no longer has an on-line ticket infrastructure and instead links to Ticketmaster's site.)[29]

E*trade, an online securities trading firm, suffered huge revenue losses because its computer systems could not handle the increased number of customer visits as trade volume grew from 43,000 to 70,000 trades per day. Customers sometimes had to wait sometimes 20 minutes or longer to access the Web site and one time for more than an hour. Internet customers, who are renowned for their impatience, often flock to a competitor when delays last more than a few seconds. E*trade is taking an aggressive approach to improve the system supporting its EC site.[30]

The cost of these glitches is sometimes tough to determine because a loss in EC revenues accounts for only part of the damage. Many customers don't return to an EC site after a system goes down, the cost of which is almost impossible to assess. However, for those organizations that don't run into systems trouble, success means revenues. The San Francisco Giants sold $500,000 worth of tickets on the Internet last year—and that revenue should increase this year.[31]

Consumer Distrust

Trust is not easy to engender in the electronic world. As consumers deal with companies around the globe, the fear of being duped is large and real. Ed Chavez, a marketing manager at i-Escrow, an electronic middleman between individuals buying and selling over the Internet, sums up the distrust this way: "[B]etween individuals, electronic commerce is like a standoff; the seller doesn't want to ship first and the buyer doesn't want to pay first."[32]

How does a company earn this trust? The good old-fashioned way. "In theory, anyone can enter any market in e-commerce," says Paul Gaffney, VP of commercial sales at Office Depot. "But the Internet hasn't changed the way you earn credibility, not one iota. That's through actual performance. It has leveled the playing field for exchanging information only."[33]

The Difficulty and Expense of Maintaining and Managing Electronic Commerce Sites

Maintaining and managing a company's Web site is an enormous challenge that requires time, money, dedicated technical staff, and top management's commitment so that the site captures the organizational culture, mission, and commitment of the company to its customers. To maintain a site well requires that all units in a company work cohesively to present a consistent image to the electronic consumer. Unfortunately, this is more easily said than done because different groups in a company often have different goals.

Aside from the difficult task of managing and maintaining an EC site, the cost of maintenance is substantial. According to Bruce Guptill, an electronic commerce analyst with Gartner Group, an EC Web site costs from $1.5 million to $3 million.[34] And many companies spend considerably more than that. Costs for financial-services sites, Guptill notes, can climb as high as $15 million. The costs are so steep because the Web site is supported by a complex, interwoven set of technologies and systems. For example, the company's on-line setup must tie its ordering system to an inventory system and a distribution system.

Security Concerns

Security on the Internet is still a major concern for both consumers and companies. Consumers hesitate to disclose confidential data, such as home address, Social Security number, and credit card number, over the Internet. This concern often translates into lost sales. Intellipost, a Web direct-mail advertising vendor, found that of customers who declare their buying intentions, nearly 75 percent change their minds when they have to provide personal and credit-card information, according to President Steve Markowitz.[35]

Businesses have deep-rooted security concerns. They don't know how to protect themselves against crackers (often erroneously called "hackers") and cyberattacks because information on the latest on-line crime trends is not available, according to security experts at the 1998 World Conference on Computer Security.

John Austin of Computer Crime Consultants in London explains that the culprits in information theft "don't carry guns, and they don't have broken noses." Instead, they may be toting backpacks or briefcases. "Gathering information is the new crime." The lack of information about those crimes is what's making companies more vulnerable to attack.[36]

Eric Ellen, the Interstate Commerce Commission's chief executive of the Commercial Crime Services unit and head of the new Cyber Crime Bureau, is building a global team of crime watchers who will track which companies are getting hit, what problem or weakness was exploited, and how the gaps were plugged. "Governments aren't doing a good job of handling this, and most law enforcement agencies, like Scotland Yard, just don't have the expertise," Ellen notes. "And most companies are not just looking at hacking. There are money laundering, pyramid schemes, fraudulent ventures. It's all on-line."[37]

Societal Challenges

EC poses new societal challenges and exacerbates some old ones. First, several industries are likely to face major downsizing as EC sites partially replace front-line staff, such as travel agents and retail salespeople. Second, more people are likely to face bankruptcy and criminal charges as shopping addicts make major purchases with a few mouse clicks. EC sites that cater to gamblers are already experiencing such problems with gambling addicts. Third, as marketers target children, society faces the challenge of regulating (or not regulating) the free-wheeling Internet medium. Finally, EC poses privacy challenges, as the Ethics feature highlights.

Ethics for success

Is Privacy Sacred on EC Sites?

"Most people would be astounded to know what's out there," says Carole Lane, author of *Naked in Cyberspace: How to Find Personal Information Online*. "In a few hours, sitting at my computer, beginning with no more than your name and address, I can find out what you do for a living, the names and ages of your spouse and children, what kind of car you drive, the value of your house, and how much taxes you pay on it."

On EC sites, "cookies" cause ethical concerns because they track consumers' on-line behavior without regard to privacy issues. "Cookies represent a way of watching consumers without their consent, and that is a fairly frightening phenomenon," comments Nick Grouf, CEO of Firefly, a Boston software company. A "cookie" is a text file that companies use to track visitors on their Web sites. When you visit a site, a cookie is written to your hard drive and allows the site to "recognize" you when you return there. Some people are concerned that cookies might also allow outside access to data on their computers, but such fears appear to be misplaced. However, numerous people object to having any information about them collected automatically.

In place of cookies, some companies use the Open Profiling Standard, which creates an electronic visitor "passport." The user creates the passport, which identifies his or her preferences without disclosing a name and allows the freedom to share as little or as much information as he or she wants to reveal.

This option protects visitors from intrusive marketing techniques. Businesses engaged in EC benefit because they learn about their customers' tastes without intruding on their privacy. "The future is in electronic commerce," says Ira Magaziner, President Clinton's point person on Net and EC issues. All that's holding it up is "this privacy thing."

YOU DECIDE

1. Do you think it's ethical to use cookies without consumer knowledge?
2. Let's say that a business informs EC site visitors that it uses cookies but doesn't explain how the process works or offer another option that protects privacy. Do you think that approach is ethical?
3. Do you think EC sites should be regulated to give visitors the option to do business without disclosing private information? Explain pros and cons of such regulation.

Source: Adapted from Joshua Quittner, "Invasion of Privacy," *Time,* August 25, 1997, Vol. 150, No. 8, http://cgi.pathfinder.com/time/reports/privacy/cover4.html.

Ambiguous Laws Governing Electronic Commerce

Laws governing electronic commerce are nonexistent, ambiguous, or in their infancy. The validity and application of these laws are being tested in courts all over the world. Regulations concerning state and federal taxes, information privacy requirements, transmission of data, and communication protocols, to name a few, are still being tested. Companies find that they have few or no guidelines when it comes to EC legalities.

Staff Shortages

To grab consumers' attention, EC sites are including exciting, fun features such as free e-mail, chat rooms, animation, search engines, games, and giveaways that require talented and dedicated technical staff who are up to date in the latest technologies. Unfortunately, many companies are short-staffed when it comes to qualified technology professionals. "[T]he technology behind [e-commerce] changes so very fast that it's difficult to keep up with," explains David Perl, CEO of Pro-Soft I-Net Solutions Inc., an $8.8 million electronic-commerce training organization in Santa Ana, California.[38]

Further, EC requires professionals with a blend of technical, marketing, and management skills—and such professionals are in short supply. For instance, many marketing professionals are being asked to help with Web site design, which requires some technical knowledge. "Many companies did not realize that a Web site needs a compelling marketing program to go with it," explains Sheldon Laube, chief technology officer of US Web, a Web systems integrator. And equally, if not more, important is the marketing of the Web sites themselves in traditional media. "Let's face it: People still watch TV and read magazines," says Laube. "Building a site is just one piece of the puzzle."[39] The Careers segment features a growth job market for people who blend technical, managerial, and marketing skills.

Global Electronic Commerce

Electronic commerce is revolutionizing business in developed and developing countries. In fact, EC may change the economic status of some nations as they become active in electronic commerce. However, countries and individuals face severe obstacles as they struggle against high technology costs, poverty, lack of education, primitive infrastructure, and restrictive government regulations. Despite these challenges, there will be more "world" in the World Wide Web by 2002, according to U.S.–based consultancy Gartner Group.[40]

EC site developers also face the challenge of customizing a site so that it can meet the local needs, preferences, and value systems of many different cultures. Why customize? Even though anyone anywhere in the world can access an EC site, once a visitor is on the site it becomes a window into the company's offerings and products. The company must communicate with the local customer in a meaningful way. This means that a site based in Canada that wants to target Argentineans must do so in a culturally sensitive manner by changing the language, offering products that its target audience prefers, and giving users viewing options that suit their technological sophistication.

EC developers, then, must analyze the similarities and differences among cultures and adapt the site accordingly. Andersen Consulting, for instance, researched the best way to offer travel services via electronic commerce. It discovered that African and German travelers respond to promises of adventure and danger, whereas U.S. travelers were motivated by an emphasis on nature and family. In response, Andersen changed its site to reflect local preferences and tastes.

In this section, we explore the progress of electronic commerce in five parts of the world. We look at Asia—with a special focus on Japan, Singapore, Malaysia, Thailand, and China—Europe and the United Kingdom, Latin America, Australia, and Africa.

Careers for success

Web Master for EC Sites

A Web master for an EC site is fully responsible for that site's design, development, and maintenance. This position involves technical, managerial, and marketing issues related to the site. "It helps to have a diversified background," advises David Young, electronic-group manager at United Parcel Service of America, based in Atlanta. "We look for people with a lot of experience with Internet projects or with communication systems. And we look for people who have worked with both business systems and IS, so they understand how the IS life cycle works and what the business community wants and why. We absolutely look for breadth."[41]

What does a Web master do? A typical day might entail intense interactions with internal customers (the marketing and sales team, for instance) and visits with external customers such as America Online and the Microsoft Network. Web masters also have to work closely with marketing, sales, legal, and financial professionals, yet still focus on technology opportunities and limitations. "Our marketing people come up with an idea almost every day, and those ideas have to be analyzed very quickly to understand the scope of each," says one Web master for an EC site.[42]

Cecila Pagkalinawan is a former Web master. She came from a communications rather than a technical background. As a media specialist at a public relations firm, she saw the possibilities of the Internet for her clients and shifted gears. She took a job position at K2 Design, where she supervised the creation of sites for such clients as Toys R Us.

Now president of Abilon, a leading Internet company, Pagkalinawan's firm provides integrated creative and technical solutions "everything from strategies to application development."[43] She urges more women to use their brainpower and determination to enter this wide-open field of opportunity. And, once there, she believes women should help other women gain a foothold through encouragement and training.

Sources: Rochelle Garner, "Electronic Frontiers," *Computerworld,* December 15, 1997, www.computerworld.com; Sharon Bermon, "Web Work: A Gal Thing," *Computerworld Online,* November 10, 1997, www.computerworld.com.

Asia

Asia is a land of economic, political, and cultural contrasts—and nowhere is that more apparent than on the Internet. According to Nikkei BP Biztech, a global business and high-tech news provider, Asia's 5 to 10 million Internet users will surge to 100 million in 5 years. Asian factories manufacture everything from sweaters to semiconductors, and their Western business partners want them on the Web to "shrink the time and cost of the supply chain and update requirements," says Russ Craig, a partner at Andersen Consulting.[44]

Supplier communication is only one reason for the growth of Internet use in Asia. General Electric Information Services targeted Asian businesses with its Trading Process Network, a Web-based trading service that links raw material suppliers with manufacturers, the first region outside the United States to become an integral part of the service network. The company targeted Asian businesses "because a lot of manufacturers in Asia want to get materials from a [Web-based] purchasing service," explains John Berry, a spokesperson at General Electric Information Services.[45]

Many nations in Asia are friendly to global electronic commerce, such as Japan and Singapore, says Jeevan Kumaran, marketing manager of Internet Business in Digital Equipment Corp.'s Asia-Pacific region. He believes they are friendly because these countries are prosperous, educated, globally oriented business centers with advanced telecommunications infrastructures and "a rate of Web progress similar to the U.S." In fact, many Asian countries have implemented network infrastructures faster than the United States in an effort to modernize. We look briefly at a range of Asian nations—Japan, Singapore, Malaysia, Thailand, and China—to spotlight the contrasts in Asian EC development.

Japan

Until recently Japan lagged in its EC development, largely because it depended on U.S. information technology products. The product support literature had to be translated into Japanese, which slowed development. But now Japan is growing its on-line consumer shopping market successfully. First, it already has the distribution setup to deliver goods purchased over the Internet because of its strong transportation and financial infrastructure. Second, its culture supports gift giving, but its stores are often crowded. As a result, many consumers welcome the convenience of the medium. Table 8-1 shows projected EC growth in number of users and dollars in Japan.

Japan, like so many other countries, is facing the enormous challenge of integrating the Internet, companies' intranets and extranets, and more specifically, EC sites, with its business systems and culture. This challenge exists whether the company is trying to engage in domestic or international Web business.

Yukihiro Kayama is a general manager of technology for the IS services group of Mitsubishi Corp. in Tokyo and a member of the board of directors of JapanNet, Japan's government-sponsored directive to develop a secure electronic commerce infrastructure for international trading. He believes that the biggest obstacle for Japanese companies that want to conduct electronic commerce is the conversion of mainframe systems so they can connect to the Internet.[46]

A study conducted by the Japan Development Bank, however, suggests another obstacle: Consumer confidence in the Internet is low. The confidence levels occur in part

TABLE 8-1

EC Forecasts for Japan

	1998	2002
Users buying goods and services over the Web (in millions)	1,717.1	7,524.0
Year-end commerce revenue (in U.S. millions)	$1,545.6	$26,031.1

Source: International Data Communications, *The Global Market Forecast for Internet Usage and Commerce,* June 1998, www.headcount.com.

One major EC player in Japan is Kinokuniya Book Web, an on-line Japanese bookseller.

because security is still perceived as unreliable. In addition, shipping costs are steep and data-transmission speeds are slow. The slow transmission can produce images that do not match the actual color or shape of a product, leading to disappointed customers who receive their purchases—after having paid hefty shipping fees.[47]

Singapore

In contrast to Japan, in Singapore, "it is not the culture to purchase via mail order, much less via the Web, unless [the product] is not available in shops," explains Yean Fee Ho, a manager in the IT division at Star+Globe Technologies Pvt. Star+Globe is a vendor of multilingual information authoring and retrieval software products. As a result of the cultural values, Star+Globe's Web site—similar to many other Singaporean sites—is informational only.

Yet Singapore, with 105,000 Internet users, the third-largest number in Asia, has the technological infrastructure to support an EC boom. The government is installing ISDN cables in every home, and most households have a PC. Although Internet access charges are still high, there is a price war going on that may eventually benefit customers.

Malaysia versus Thailand

The Malaysian government supports EC development but lacks sufficient Internet infrastructure. The government recently initiated a major drive to raise PC literacy, liberalize the telecommunications industry, and encourage information technology development. However, the demand far exceeds the supply of Internet connections.

Thailand's government actions sharply contrast with Malaysia's. The Communications Authority of Thailand (CAT), a government agency, levies huge fees on Internet Service Providers (ISPs). These providers pay CAT 60 times more than what they pay in most other countries. In addition, businesses must pay the authority nearly $5,000 a month to maintain a site, which explains why only 200 or so firms own and operate Web sites based in Thailand.[48] These government policies have greatly restrained the development of Thailand's electronic commerce.

China

E-commerce forecasts for China show rapid growth. Even so, a relatively small portion of the country is engaged in EC, as we see in Table 8-2. The Chinese government, however, is strengthening the country's telecommunications infrastructure in an effort to make China the world's largest "cyber nation."[49] Web business proponents and analysts say that governmental influence has been largely positive. "I have talked to progressives [in China] who are trying to pull [foreign] companies in for joint ventures and bring

TABLE 8-2

EC Forecasts for China

	1998	**2001**
Users buying goods and services over the Web	19,969	292,745
Year-end commerce revenue (in U.S. millions)	$11.69	$847.84

Source: International Data Communications, *Market Forecast for Internet Commerce, 1996–2001,* October 1997, www.headcount.com.

in technology, and they are very upbeat," notes Russ Craig, a partner at Andersen Consulting. "They say the market there for PCs is bottomless."[50]

In contrast, some experts say that China is too technologically backward and politically isolated to become a serious player in the EC market. Building a network is still a tedious, bureaucratic, and nightmarish experience for many businesses. Access to the Internet is costly and the process of getting an Internet account itself can be quite intimidating. Users must register with the Chinese government before they are approved for an account.[51]

Europe

The European community remains culturally, linguistically, and monetarily fragmented, as does European Web commerce. However, global industries that are largely undeterred by national boundaries rely on the Web for trade, marketing, and information sharing, observes Chris Champion, an analyst at the European division of The Yankee Group consulting firm. European Web hosts (companies that provide hardware and software to host Web sites)are growing at double-digit annual percentage rates across Europe. Countries such as Portugal, Belgium, Denmark, Spain, and Italy are experiencing growth rates of more than 100 percent.

Companies that want to conduct electronic commerce with Europeans must tailor their Web sites to match the language, culture, and monetary units of each European country or risk losing their audience. Companies must balance the need to target different nationalities against the need to present a strong, unified corporate image, analysts say. Take Kao Infosystems, which makes CD-ROMs and floppy disks for the software industry. The company is putting up a European site to promote communication with its business partners. Jonathan Rawle, an IT manager, says his group is now figuring out how to design a site that "enhances the differences [between different countries], but not in a negative way that makes people scared of a bifurcated company."[52]

The cost of localizing services combined with the low number of European households with Internet access (just 3.5 percent this year, according to The Yankee Group), may preclude significant EC development, especially in the small business sector. "You need a critical mass [of potential customers] to be selling into any market," explains Yankee Group's Rick Champion.

EC development in Europe is also inhibited by customer charges for Internet access. Customers are charged by the minute rather than by the hour, day, or month. As a result, consumers "will only visit a site if they are getting something out of it, instead of surfing," notes John Fox, head of editorial services at ABB Group in Zurich.[53]

Also, government bureaucracy and authority stifle technology innovation in several European countries. Italy has one of Europe's most primitive infrastructures, says Jupiter Communications, a research firm in New York, because government-supported telecommunications monopolies have kept network service prices up and high import tariffs have kept PCs and Web software prices high.

However, research suggests that the political climate and IT infrastructures in many European nations are changing in ways that will foster EC. A recent study by Forrester Research rated Germany, the United Kingdom, the Netherlands, Belgium/Luxemburg, Austria, Switzerland, and Scandinavia a 4 or 5 on a scale of 1 to 5 in terms of technology penetration and political climate.[54]

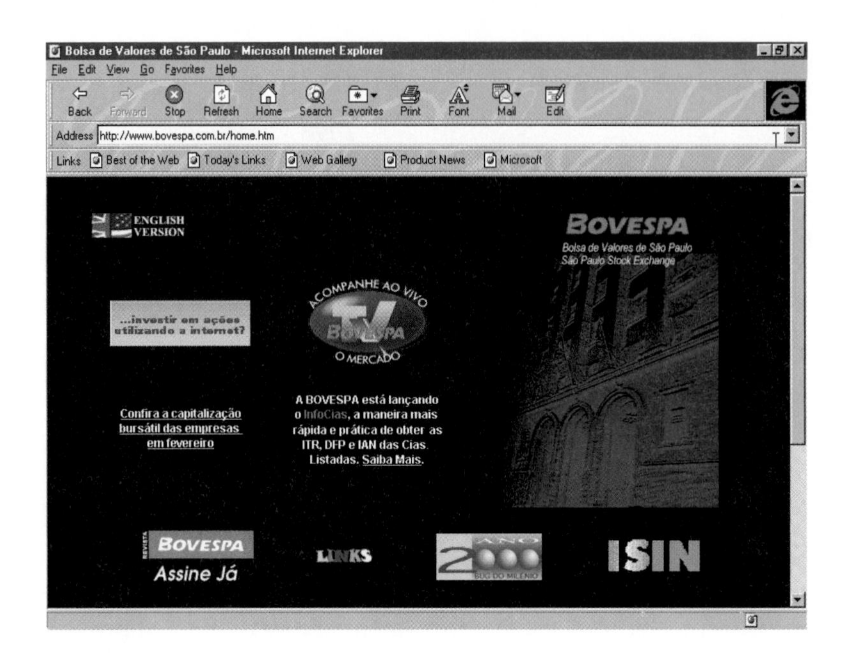

Bovespa, the largest stock exchange in Brazil, is on the Web.

Latin America

The Internet market in Latin America is booming; companies around the world are eager to do business with Latin America and companies in the region are eager to join the world of EC. Growing competition in telecommunications markets, a rising middle class, favorable demographics, and the availability of cheap PCs make it a region to watch.

About 10 million of the region's estimated 500 million inhabitants surf the Internet—up from 1 million 2 years ago, according to international advertising agency Saatchi & Saatchi. By 2000, the region's Internet surfers should swell to 30 million. However, conducting electronic business in Latin America has its pros and cons.

Although IT talent and the awareness of IT's value to the region's economy is growing, Latin America has some problems that inhibit electronic commerce. First, it has an aging telecommunications infrastructure. Rigid government rules and regulations, private monopolies, high phone charges for local and international connections, and corruption in the utilities industry and the government are additional obstacles to EC development.[55]

A word of warning: Because of cultural, political, regulatory, and technological differences, businesses cannot paint the entire region with the same brush. Chile has a digital phone system that makes quality telephone connections easy and inexpensive. Argentina, Uruguay, and Peru are slowly following Chile's lead. Further, the cost of Internet connections in these countries is decreasing significantly.

In contrast, Mexico and Brazil are emerging from years of protectionist policies that guaranteed jobs at good wages. Corruption exists and civil servants are apt to "intervene in productive sectors' daily lives," notes Kenneth Richard, president of Latinrep Associates, a sales and marketing firm based in Oakland, California, that does business with Latin America. Brazil is "by far the most complicated, frustrating and difficult" place to do business, Richard says.[56] However, Internet access is growing at a constant rate in Brazil; it surpassed 1 million users in mid-1997 and grew to more than 1.3 million users by the end of the year.[57]

Jaime Graterol, MIS director of Foote Cone & Belding Advertising in Latin America, offers this advice: "Realize the subtle differences among countries, expect delays in getting permits or hooking up telephone lines in some of the larger markets, and make friends among civil servants." The native Venezuelan continues: "To set up a shop, you need a lot of permits, and it's going to help you if you have contacts. . . . What can I tell you? That's the reality."[58]

Australia

Alan Stockdale bemoans the fact that while "many companies are using electronic marketing techniques, have a home page or are using other network IT applications . . . in

Australia, generally, the current pace of activity in electronic commerce is too slow." The United States and other countries such as "Sweden and Ireland are using electronic commerce more extensively and more creatively then we are," says Stockdale, the city of Victoria's Treasurer and Minister for Multimedia.[59]

This concern may be the result of Australia's high standards for the pace of adopting and using technology, because indicators suggest that Australia has the conditions for explosive EC development. Four million Australians in 2 million homes use computers, according to the Australian Bureau of Statistics. That's at least 20 percent of a total population of between 18 million and 20 million. And 55 percent of all households have PCs with CD-ROMs and modems. It's no surprise, then, that Australia has one of the highest per capita Internet usage rates in the world: 20 percent, up from 12 percent a year ago, says the Centre for Electronic Commerce at Monash University in Victoria.

The high Internet penetration rate helps make up for what Forrester Research in a recent report defined as Australia's major Web commerce weakness: a small regional population that translates into a limited local market pool. Australia's user base makes up in quality what it lacks in quantity: English as a first language, a well-established passion for consumer electronics, and generally high levels of education and disposable income.

Many Australians see the Web as a place to strategically position themselves and sell real products and services—not just market them. And in the retailing sector, a growing number of sites offer users Web-based shopping. At David Jones, one of Australia's oldest clothing and household goods stores, shoppers can browse through different sections of an on-line catalog or search by department—clothing, toys, housewares—or by person, price range, or keyword. The site helps customers who are geographically isolated from the store to shop. Damian Eales, national home-shopping manager at David Jones, says: "[W]e did some advertising of our site in the U.K. and Asia so that relatives and friends of people living in Australia could use this service to purchase Christmas gifts over the Web instead of paying to ship such products overseas."[60]

The main obstacle to EC growth is the lack of readily available, affordable bandwidth. "We can't send [users] the graphics we'd like" because response time would be unacceptable with current modem rates, he explains. The cost of telecommunications is also prohibitive, with some services costing as much as 10 times the same offerings in the United States. But improvements are on the way. The Australian federal government has sponsored several EC awareness-raising initiatives and has announced that it will purchase all government supplies and services electronically. "That's a $30 billion [Australian government] market—quite a carrot. And the stick is, if you don't adopt the required technology, your competitor most likely will and, at worst, lock you out of the market."[61]

Africa

In all reports that analyze worldwide Web use, Africa shows up at the bottom of the list. "The problem throughout Africa is that marketplaces are generally underdeveloped, so they have a limited attraction for major [foreign technology companies] to set up presences there," explains Michael Portlock, an independent telecom consultant who works in Africa. Further, "in many parts of black Africa, telecom systems are so bad that the likelihood of setting up any type of Internet capability is very low."[62]

The big exception is South Africa, which already has about 900,000 Internet users and is expected to reach the 1 million mark soon. This number represents 86 percent of all Internet users in Africa.[63] By the turn of the century, the South African Internet site development and advertising market could be worth $215 million (U.S.), with online transactions exceeding the $425,000 mark, according to IDG South Africa. "South Africa is the wealthiest of African countries, with the white minority possessing the overwhelming majority of capital," Portlock notes. "That English is widely spoken is a factor in on-line usage."[64]

South Africa also has a decent telecommunications infrastructure, at least in its major cities. Also, major computer suppliers that operated through agents in the apartheid era are beginning to have direct involvement in the country. Several major South African banks have recently introduced Internet-based services, including access to account balances and statements, account payments, interaccount transfers and checkbook requests, and secure, on-line banking transactions.

Tanzania is one other exception in Africa, but it lags far behind South Africa. Nevertheless, Internet use is on the rise and the infrastructure is emerging. "There are quite a number of companies/institutions providing Internet services there," says Hassan Ali, a Tanzanian expatriate now living in Canada.[65]

Although electronic commerce is a worldwide phenomenon, businesses must understand and adapt to the business, technical, and cultural landscape before they can target their EC sites to people in other parts of the world. Once that homework is done, the site should be customized to adapt to these environmental factors but still present a strong brand image.[66]

Business Guidelines for Electronic Commerce Success

Similar to other information technologies, electronic commerce requires strategic thinking, planning, and commitment from top management. However, unlike other technologies, EC is so new that planners and managers cannot draw from past experience. We examined several practical tips for effective e-commerce sites in an earlier section of the chapter. Here we consider some big-picture considerations that affect EC success.

Timing Is Everything

What is the right time to launch an EC site? The answer is not simple. "All of electronic commerce right now is so turbulent. It's hard to determine when is the right time," notes Erica Rugullies, an analyst at Giga Information Group in Cambridge, Massachusetts. Timing often depends on "what industry you're in."[67] Businesses should analyze if consumers in their industry have access to and the education to use on-line technology. If so, are they comfortable doing business on-line? They should also consider if their customers are willing to buy without visiting a store.

Another key question is whether industry competitors are on the Web. Borders bookstore's entry into the EC world seemed late compared to Amazon.com and Barnes & Noble. A late entrance is not necessarily bad, but there is a tradeoff. Latecomers have an opportunity to learn from the experience of their predecessors, but typically they have to invest significantly more resources in their site to play catch-up with the market leaders. "Buyers limit their choices," said Ray Satterthwaite, an analyst at Gartner Group, in Stamford, Connecticut. "That's why there's Coke and Pepsi and everybody else."[68] Newcomers should therefore try to find a niche by offering something valuable to their customers that no one else offers.

Borders developed a competitive advantage by being the first bookstore to offer music and videos on their site, explains Scott Wilder, director of on-line services at Borders Online, in Ann Arbor, Michigan. It also developed shipping procedures and facilities that give it another advantage—customers' orders are fulfilled and mailed quickly.[69]

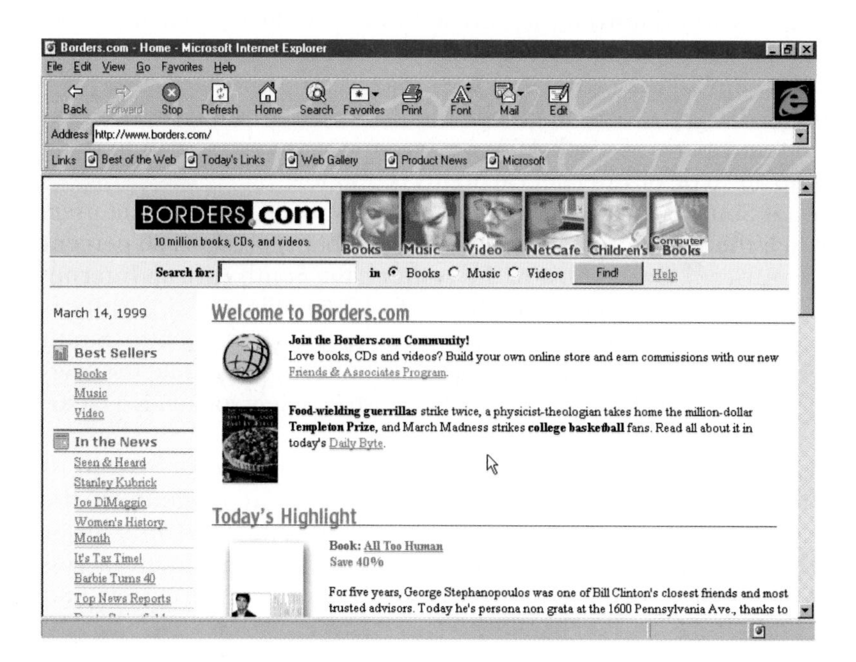

Although Borders' entrance into the EC arena was late compared to its top competitors, it believes it has a competitive advantage because of its speed and additional offerings of music and videos.

Avoid the Bandwagon Mentality

Although there are compelling arguments to engage in electronic commerce, there are equally compelling reasons to be cautious. Businesses should analyze their customer base and weigh cost and customer concerns against the benefits of an EC site. For instance, if customers do not want to shift to an electronic medium to do business, offering an EC site does little good.

In addition, many companies have effective alternatives to reach consumers and business partners, so they lack a compelling reason to shift to EC. Maytag Corp., for example, finds that EDI with its suppliers and distributors works well, so it has put electronic commerce via the Internet on hold. Maytag VP of IT Ed Wojciechowski notes, "We have informational Web sites where we can engage the customer, and we see commerce as an option in the future. But it's not strategic for us yet."[70] Businesses should analyze the "to be or not to be"-an-EC-player decision carefully.

Plan for and Invest in Customer Service

Customer service is essential to electronic commerce success and can also distinguish the business. Before launching an EC site, businesses must assess how much and what type of customer service support the site will provide to users. After the site has been launched, they need to stay flexible to meet the demands of their Internet customers.

Jim Coane, president and chief operating officer of New York–based on-line music retailer N2K, learned this lesson the hard way. Coane discovered that the company had seriously underestimated the level of service its customers would expect. N2K's six service representatives had trouble satisfying people who clamored for everything—from information about the order process to help finding a certain album containing a lyric from a song they'd heard years ago. "We were surprised," Coane admits, "that people on the Internet wanted to talk to a live person." After learning from its mistakes, the company has remedied the situation.[71]

"A lot of companies think they can just throw up [an] e-mail [address] on their Web site, and that is customer service," notes Maria La Tour Kadison, a senior analyst at Forrester Research. "But there needs to be a mechanism in place to handle that e-mail in a prompt, effective fashion. Sometimes that means an immediate response or personal attention. Often it means both."[72]

Think Globally but Act Locally

Although a Web site can attract customers from around the world, building and maintaining an international audience base requires an understanding of and sensitivity to people with different cultural, political, economic, technological, and business backgrounds. Plunging ahead without thinking about these situational factors can hinder business effectiveness.

"Where's the other bottle?" This question from Japanese customers perplexed Virtual Vineyards, which markets wine and specialty foods over the Internet. The company was confused. The customer had ordered only one bottle of wine, so why were they asking for another? Virtual Vineyards, a privately held firm in Palo Alto, California, did some investigation and found out that the problem resulted from shipping single bottles in two-bottle packages. Although this is not unusual in the United States and other Western countries, it confused Japanese customers because in Japan packaging is an intrinsic part of a prestige product. Cultural values affect consumer perceptions—a key factor in marketing and selling products—so it is critical for EC.

SUMMARY

1. **Define electronic commerce and explain how it works.** Electronic commerce is commerce done through electronic means, mostly the Internet. Electronic commerce involves different kinds of transactions between individuals, businesses, and organizations that are of value to both parties involved in the transactions. Due to hardware, software, and telecommunications advances and the declining prices for these components, electronic commerce has begun to surge. There are several steps involved in

EC transactions. They are logging onto the Internet and identifying companies of interest, visiting their Web sites, entering the on-line store and browsing through the catalog, identifying items of interest, adding the item to the shopping basket, filling out an electronic invoice, and having the cashier verify the information. The company then processes the order.

2. **Distinguish between different types of EC models.** There are three types of EC models based on the parties to the transaction. They are (1) the supplier is a business and the consumer may also be a business (business to business); (2) the supplier is a business and the consumer may be an individual or a business (business to business/individual); and (3) the supplier is an individual and the consumer is also an individual.

   The first two models are the most widespread. In business-to-business models, the contract is prenegotiated and the terms are fixed for separate transactions. With the business-to-business/individual model, negotiations may occur for each transaction.

3. **Specify the guidelines for an effective EC site.** Several practical guidelines can increase an EC site's success rate. These guidelines include the following: keep the site interesting, ensure customer privacy, provide useful information, encourage price comparisons, develop a great electronic sales team, make the site simple and easy to use, encourage customers to visit the physical store, and build cyberspace loyalty.

4. **Summarize the promises and challenges of EC.** Like most other technologies, EC offers both promises and challenges. EC benefits include creating customer power, expanding a company's market, increasing business efficiency, and building a closer bond between suppliers and customers. The challenges of EC are immature technology, customer distrust, the difficulty and expense of maintaining and managing a Web site, security, ambiguous laws governing EC issues, staff shortages, and negative societal effects.

5. **Outline global EC issues.** Although EC is by its nature a global activity, conducting business around the world presents cultural, legal, political, business, and technological challenges. EC developers must consider the challenges and opportunities in various countries and regions throughout the world to assess their chances of success in each area. However, one issue is clear: Countries around the world are increasing their use of and belief in the potential of EC.

KEY TERMS

business-to-business EC models (p. 219)
business-to-business/individual EC models (p. 220)
electronic commerce (p. 217)

REVIEW QUESTIONS

1. Define electronic commerce. Identify any two benefits of EC.
2. What are some benefits of EC to individuals, businesses, and society?
3. How is Estée Lauder, featured in the Technology Payoff, using electronic commerce to attract more customers to the stores that sell its products? Why do you think Estée Lauder wants to encourage consumers to visit stores when it has an EC site?
4. How is EC different from traditional shopping? Describe three similarities and three differences.
5. Are small businesses embracing electronic commerce? What are some advantages that EC provides to a small business?
6. Explain how EC works. What are some of the complexities involved in the steps of electronic commerce?
7. Discuss the three models of EC. Under which model would the Estée Lauder site fall?
8. What are some guidelines for an effective EC site? Discuss the opening quote, "You can't just build it, because they will not come!"
9. What are some security concerns related to EC? How would you tackle some of these concerns?
10. What are some characteristics of a great electronic sales team?
11. What are some benefits of EC? How does EC empower customers? How does EC enhance business efficiency?
12. What are some challenges of EC? Why is it so challenging to manage and maintain EC Web sites?
13. Select a country highlighted in this chapter and discuss its EC potential. Consider the technical, political, business, socioeconomic, and cultural factors that affect electronic commerce.

DISCUSSION QUESTIONS AND EXERCISES

1. One challenge in building effective EC sites is integrating a whole host of applications to operate the site. Some of these applications include ordering, inventory, distribution, marketing, legal, and human resource systems. Businesses often take a piecemeal approach to EC, which is one of the reasons why so many companies are achieving only limited success. The piecemeal approach doesn't work, says analyst Ted Schadler, of Forrester Research. "It gets pretty ugly pretty fast." In contrast, companies that integrate their applications into a cohesive system have a lot to gain. If they unify the ordering and customer service systems, for instance, they can learn about customers' ordering and complaint histories and track customer preferences and needs. This, in turn, can give sales and customer service personnel crucial information that allows them to provide better sales and service.[73]
   - **a.** Identify a company in your local area that has an EC site and interview the IT manager to see how they deal with systems integration issues.
2. Recreational Equipment Inc. (REI) launched its on-line store in September 1996. Just 1 year later, on-line store manager Matt Hyde boasted that "our on-line store is beating some of our physical stores in sales." "That's impressive," says Kate Delhagen, senior analyst at Forrester Research. "We believe a good benchmark for on-line retailers is to meet and quickly exceed the revenue of a real-world store." Hyde noted that an on-line store is essentially a startup business, and he allowed that few startups make money in their first few years. In general, businesses spend between $1 million and $3 million to accomplish what REI has done.[74]
   - **a.** What are some lessons that a company can learn from a successful EC site that it can use to improve its stores?
   - **b.** What are some reasons why you, as a customer, may prefer to shop over the Internet rather than visit a physical store?
   - **c.** What are some reasons why you might prefer to shop traditionally?
3. Many people think that an EC site gives small companies instant access to global markets. Access is one thing; leveraging it is quite another. Smaller companies frequently do not have a global brand image, so access doesn't necessarily translate into sales. Large companies with strong existing brands have a hefty on-line advantage in overseas markets because consumers already have brand familiarity, "whether they're Boeing, Eastman Kodak, or Pepsi," says Randy Meyer, VP of financial services and e-commerce at Compaq. Although any company can enter the EC market, few become a cyberspace name brand.[75]
   - **a.** What are some challenges that a small business may face in building a brand in the EC market?
   - **b.** How can the company overcome some of these challenges?
4. Many companies that invest millions of dollars in their Web sites are counting on advertising revenues to keep their electronic ventures healthy. And that is the core of the unusual lawsuit Ticketmaster Corporation filed against Microsoft Corporation in the spring of 1997. Microsoft drew Ticketmaster's ire when it provided links from a Microsoft Web page to a ticket-buying page deep within Ticketmaster's Web site.

   In the physical world, a vendor might be thrilled to have another company driving ready-to-pay customers to its doorstep. But in the digital world, Microsoft's direct link meant customers would not view ads posted along Ticketmaster's path to its purchasing page. Microsoft's links, Ticketmaster charged, threatened as much as $1.3 million of its 1997 Web site advertising revenue.

   The conflict is rooted in the way Web sites generate ad revenue. Advertisers flock to the most frequently visited sites and pay rates based on "impressions" or hits. A hit refers to a count of the number of visitors to a link on a Web site. Netscape Communications Corporation's site was getting 6 million visitors a day in 1998 and as many as 135 million daily hits, recalls Larry Geisel, senior vice president of IS and CIO. Naturally, Netscape's ad space generates a healthy secondary source of revenue. Based in part on such success stories, Forrester Research predicts Web-based ad revenue will reach $4.8 billion by 2000.[76]
   - **a.** Do you read the Web ads on the EC sites that you have visited so far? Why or why not?
   - **b.** A few years from now, traditional advertising may face a serious decline in revenue. Discuss.
5. **(Web exercise)** Visit two Web sites that offer an opportunity to electronically auction goods and services. Evaluate how each company addresses your security concerns. What are the strengths and weaknesses of each site?
6. **(Web exercise)** Visit two major clothing retail EC sites. Discuss the shopping experience on each site. Write a note to the CEO or Web master explaining two improvements that you would make to one of the sites.

Case 1: Michelin Is on a Roll!

Michelin North America realized that a delivery receipt from a dealer might languish for 3 or 4 weeks before being processed. The company turned to Web-based technology to increase its customer responsiveness. To develop the Michelin "Bib Net" Web site—named for the 100-year-old inflated "Bibendum" Michelin man—the company assembled a cross-functional team from its marketing, sales, customer service, and information technology departments.

The team also enlisted Michelin's independent tire dealers, visiting 55 of them and bringing 15 to 20 to South Carolina to brainstorm a technical wish list and help design the user interfaces. "They gave us carte blanche to draw up what we wanted," explains Leo Zannetti, director of purchasing at Belle Tire, a chain headquartered in Allen Park, Michigan. "They did a great job taking in our input. Most companies would say, 'Here's what we have.' I guess corporate America's changing every day."[77]

Dealers now can access Michelin's Bib Net Web site to order products, schedule deliveries, check order status, make real-time inventory inquiries, receive advance shipment notices, create claims, scan pricing, and see a national account directory. Dealers can also check their 2-year history of purchases in dollars and units, make real-time invoice inquiries, do warranty adjustments, and better manage their orders because the system will spot errors in item numbers. A total of 286 dealers—90 percent of the 318 the company initially targeted—are using the system so far, reports Lynn Melvin, manager of electronic-commerce application development at Michelin.

All told, Melvin notes, Michelin has spent more than $5 million on its Bib Net since May 1995, when the project team started planning. Some savings have been realized in printing materials, reduced order errors, and, to a small degree, customer service. "We didn't really go into this to save money. Basically, we wanted to create close partnerships with customers," says Melvin.[78]

Erica Rugullies, an analyst at Giga Information Group, claims the site was a good competitive investment for Michelin, given that probably all tire dealers will have Internet access some day. Further, such sites have helped companies reduce the cost of processing an order from the $8-to-$25-range to the 3-cents-to-$1 range. Finally, tire dealers also benefit. Reduction in order errors alone can translate into significant cost savings.[79]

1. Michelin's goal in building the site was not so much to cut costs as it was to create close partnership with its clients. In your opinion, did Michelin achieve this goal?
2. Assume you are a Michelin dealer. What are some benefits that this site offers you?

Case 2: Deutsche EC Trailblazers

Europe has experimented longer than the United States with electronic commerce. But Europe's business traditions have been limited in the past by regional and linguistic factors, a lack of common currency, and telecommunication monopolies that are only now being deregulated. Nowhere has this been more true than in Germany, which was unified less than 10 years ago after almost half a century of existing as two separate states, each belonging to a different political system. Each of the two German states had large companies, but no company was terribly successful with electronic commerce.

Otto Versand, the world's largest mail-order catalog group, is using the Internet to diversify its products and service offerings and create alternative channels to reach its ever-widening, pan-European customer base. Otto began to do business on-line late in 1996. Today it offers its entire catalog (primarily apparel) on the Internet and reports that 6 percent of its total sales come from some form of electronic commerce. Its on-line catalog consists of more than 26,000 items in still frames or video. Although the company takes orders on-line and offers a wide range of delivery options, all articles are shipped cash on delivery, according to Susan Jeschke, an Otto spokeswoman.

Here's how Otto's site works: Customers create shopping carts and browse its catalog. Orders are processed and deliveries managed on a mainframe. Otto, like all German companies, maintains a very complex firewall system to protect customer data, as German law requires.

In its electronic commerce Otto adheres to an old, trusted system in which a consumer is guaranteed the right to accept or reject an article on physical delivery, just as if they'd placed a phone or mail order from the print catalog. That the article might have been seen and ordered over the Internet changes absolutely nothing from the consumer standpoint. And there is certainly a comfort factor in knowing that one's package will be

continued

Case 2: Deutsche EC Trailblazers, *continued*

delivered by the same service, in the same time, probably by the same delivery person that a consumer has grown to know and trust.

The "Otto Model" may seem very tame, safe, and "inside" the envelope, but it has made the transition to electronic commerce smooth and maintains the company's reliable image. Chris Stevens, an analyst at Aberdeen Group in Boston, agrees that cyber merchants often underestimate the comfort factor. "Companies that go on-line often forget that at the end of the day, what they are providing is a service, and that service has to be comfortable for the consumer to use."[80]

1. **(Web exercise)** What are some things that an EC site should have to make you feel comfortable with shopping on-line? Visit any four EC sites of your choice and identify four comfort factors.
2. By not accepting payment on-line, Otto may actually be encouraging more shoppers to shop on-line. Discuss.

Part 4 Creating and Managing Business Data and Information

Client/servers have little to do with technology, and everything to do with competitive business processes.[1]

Charles Pelton, information systems commentator

CONTENTS

CLIENT/SERVER SYSTEMS FOR SUCCESS

Business managers search for tools that help meet their goals as effectively as possible. One potentially valuable tool, if properly developed and implemented, is the client/server system because it makes it easy to share information and other computer resources with both internal and external parties. Remember, the Internet is one of the best client/server models there is!

To make wise client/server system decisions, users must first understand the controversy that surrounds this technology. Advocates claimed that client/server systems could solve all business IS issues, replace mainframes at a much lower cost, and make information readily and easily available to decision makers. Client/server systems are a powerful business tool, but they have advantages and disadvantages that need to be carefully weighed against the alternatives to make the best possible IS choices for the organization and to avoid costly mistakes.

Many of you have worked with or are likely to work with client/server systems, so an understanding of what these systems are and how they differ from mainframe or other types of systems is helpful. Client/server technologies are widespread. In fact, electronic mail, the Internet, intranets, and extranets are applications of client/server systems. "When you look at the Fortune 500 market, about 40 percent have made client/server software purchases [for internal company systems]," explains Neil J. Herman, an analyst at Salomon Brothers, a New York brokerage firm.[2]

The push for client/server systems is being driven by end-user demand for graphical interfaces and user-friendly systems and by the need to analyze large volumes of data. Client/server systems, if implemented properly, can handle these demands and can improve the speed and quality of business operations. In 1990 AT&T Universal

Chapter 9

Client/Server Computing

AFTER STUDYING THIS CHAPTER, YOU WILL BE ABLE TO:

- Describe client/server computing and the reasons for its growth
- Compare and contrast client/server and LAN environments
- Identify some popular client/server applications
- Summarize key advantages and disadvantages of client/server systems

Card Services Corp. in Jacksonville, Florida, launched the AT&T Universal Card (now owned and operated by Citibank)—a credit, calling, and ATM card all rolled into one. Although the marketplace is filled with rivals, the company feels it has a competitive advantage because of its superior customer service.

To cope with the 250,000 daily calls from Universal Card users, AT&T used a client/server system—cleverly titled UWIN—to support the Universal Card customer service team. UWIN accesses and consolidates information from various AT&T databases and presents the information to sales associates through a standardized, user-friendly, graphical interface. The effect of the system is prompt, exceptional customer service.

Here's how the UWIN system works: Let's say a customer calls to report a lost or stolen card. The associate simply clicks the mouse on a "lost or stolen" icon, and the system automatically retrieves the necessary information. Under the old system a service rep had to search through hundreds of document pages before responding to a customer.

AT&T used a client/server application to give its Universal Card customers superior service.

TECHNOLOGY PAYOFF
Strong Link in the Chain

Joe Wisdo is helping to improve relations between Nabisco and grocers. Wisdo, senior director of sales and logistics information, began his 25-year Nabisco career as an inventory analyst fresh out of Pennsylvania State University. Now he's known as a technology guru at Nabisco's U.S. Foods Group, where he is working on a client/server project that Nabisco and the whole food industry are watching.

A client/server refers to an information system in which two or more networked computers "serve" one another. Usually, one computer is the server (it holds all the information and files) and clients (other computers on the network) obtain the necessary information from the server.

Wisdo represents a rare "combination of technological understanding and business acumen," says Joe Andraski, Nabisco's recently retired vice president of customer development. He relied on that combination of skills to spearhead an avant-garde client/server sales forecasting collaboration with Wegmans Food Markets, a 57-store grocery chain and major Nabisco customer based in Rochester, New York. The system cost Nabisco between $100,000 and $200,000 but the returns are manifold.

Interest in developing such a system actually grew out of a new industry initiative called Collaborative Planning, Forecasting, and Replenishment (CPFR), which was designed to improve supplier/retailer partnerships by helping both parties share meaningful information. The main goal of Wisdo's project was to help Nabisco and Wegmans exchange sales and promotional data so that the two partners could arrive at a joint sales forecast for Nabisco's Planters nut products.

Both parties stood to gain a lot from such a system. Nabisco's payoff was that it could match its inventory of Planters products to Wegmans' needs; Wegmans' payoff was that it no longer panicked and overstocked because of promotion-related spikes in demand. In just 13 short weeks, Wegmans found that its sales of Planters products increased by 36

More than 12 million customers appreciate the high-quality service that UWIN provides.[3]

In addition to AT&T and others in the telecommunications industry, many retailers use client/server systems to analyze voluminous transaction data. Judy Newdom, a principal at Computer Sciences Corp.'s retail practice in Newton, Massachusetts, explains that many retailers learned that client/server systems could help them analyze extensive data strategically, a necessity in a fiercely competitive market. For instance, retailers can see what merchandise is selling quickly or slowly, what items are being returned at a higher-than-average rate, and what products sell best in certain regions or at different times of year. "It's no longer a game of keeping track of transactions," Newdom says. "It's now a game of being able to analyze the data for competitive advantage."[4]

This chapter provides a broad overview of client/server computing and explores the reasons for its growth, its advantages and disadvantages, and client/server security issues. In addition, we identify the technical and managerial issues companies face as they shift from mainframes to client/server environments.

What Is a Client/Server System?

A **client/server system** consists of a client and a server that are linked through a network and special software that helps the client and server communicate. A **client** is a computer that requests a service from another computer, often called the server. The **server** is the computer that provides the requested service to the client under a given set of conditions (see Figure 9-1).

Many systems that you use on an everyday basis are client/server systems. The Internet, intranets, and extranets are systems based on the client/server model. Your machine (for instance, your PC) requests a service and a group of machines (servers) provide the service. The communication between the client and the server takes place over the network. A special kind of software, called middleware, conveys the client requests to the server and vice versa.

Take, for example, a company's intranet that holds phone numbers and addresses of all company employees. Sitting at your PC you

FIGURE 9-1 Client/Server System

The client computer sends a request for service to the server over a network.

If the client's request is appropriate, the server provides the service.

Networks

Client

Server

can request the server (the computer that holds the directory-related files) to "serve" you the phone number of a specific individual. Your request is conveyed over the network to the server, which then responds with the appropriate answer.

Another example of a popular client/server system is financial software that allows a bank's clients to access information about their bank accounts from their home or office PC. The PC is the client and a bank's computer is the server "serving" the information to the individual client.

Client/server systems are highly flexible, responsive systems as compared with mainframe systems (also known as legacy systems). First, extracting highly customized information from client/server systems is relatively easy as compared with legacy systems. Second, because servers are simpler to manage and maintain than mainframes, information on servers is more readily changed to meet decision makers' needs.

Consultant Judith Hurwitz points out that the main difference between client/server systems and other systems technologies is not the technology so much as it is the flexibility and responsiveness that client/server systems provide. "Business technologists want the same flexibility with new hardware and software that other executives have with, for instance, the corporate car-rental company, the stationery supplier, or the janitorial contractor. Client/server is just another way of defining business freedom."[5]

percent. Despite the higher volume, Wegmans says it was able to chop the average time it warehoused Planters products from 14.1 days to 11.6, yet it was able to fill orders more effectively.

In this particular case, the server (a computer onsite at Wegmans) holds information about Wegmans' sales data. Nabisco can access this sales information from its computers (the clients) and make decisions accordingly. This information system has helped forge a stronger, more profitable partnership between these two businesses.

Source: Nancy Dillon, "Strong Link in the Chain," *Computerworld*, January 25, 1999, www.computerworld.com. Copyright © 1999 Computerworld, Inc. Framingham, MA 01701. Rights reserved.

Interactions between Client and Server

A number of rules guide the interactions between a client and a server. First, when a server receives a request from a client, it checks to see if the client is authorized. For example, if a salesperson requests the server to list the salaries of all employees in the company, the server will check to see if the employee has the authority to do so and responds accordingly. If not, the server will turn down the request. If for some reason the server cannot find the information, it sends a message to the client computer for the user to read. Figure 9-2 shows these preliminary steps in client/server interaction.

Second, a server can serve multiple clients at the same time and, conversely, a client may request services from multiple servers. Although there are certain limits on the number of clients that a given server can process (some systems support up to 150,000 concurrent users), the ability to cater to multiple clients is a key benefit of this technology. Figure 9-3 shows the ability of the server and client to serve and request service from multiple computers.

Third, client processes are independent of server processes. This independence means that the client may be processing one application, say desktop publishing, while the server is processing another application, such as payroll. This independence maximizes the computing power of both the client and the server. Thus, the client calls on the server only when it needs a specific service that the server can provide.

Client/server system

A system that links a client and server through networks. The client requests the server for a given service and the server provides the service if a predetermined set of conditions is met.

Client

A computer that asks the server for a specific service (such as data, programs, or applications) that it needs to perform a task.

Server

A computer that stores and serves, on request, frequently used data, programs, and applications to computers requesting the service.

FIGURE 9-2

Preliminary Steps in Client/Server Interaction

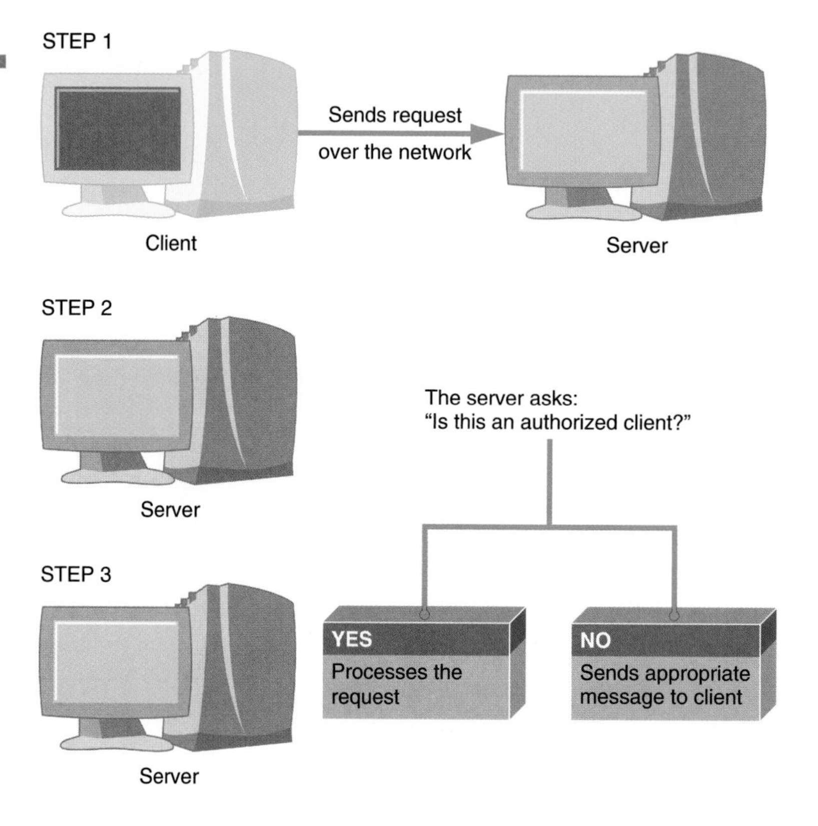

This independence is one of the biggest advantages of client/server technologies. It allows clients to be added to or deleted from the network without affecting either the server or other clients in the network. Moreover, system administrators can make changes to the server without affecting clients on the network.

Dumb terminal/Host processing

A client/server situation in which the server does all the processing work.

A client/server system divides a task between the client and the server so that two or more machines share the work. However, work can be apportioned differently depending on the circumstances. In some applications, the server may do all the processing. In such cases, the client is called a **dumb terminal** or dumb client and the processing is referred to as **host processing.** The client could either be a terminal linked to a mainframe or be a PC that acts as if it were a dumb terminal.

FIGURE 9-3

(a) Servers Can Serve Multiple Clients and (b) Clients Can Request Service from Multiple Servers

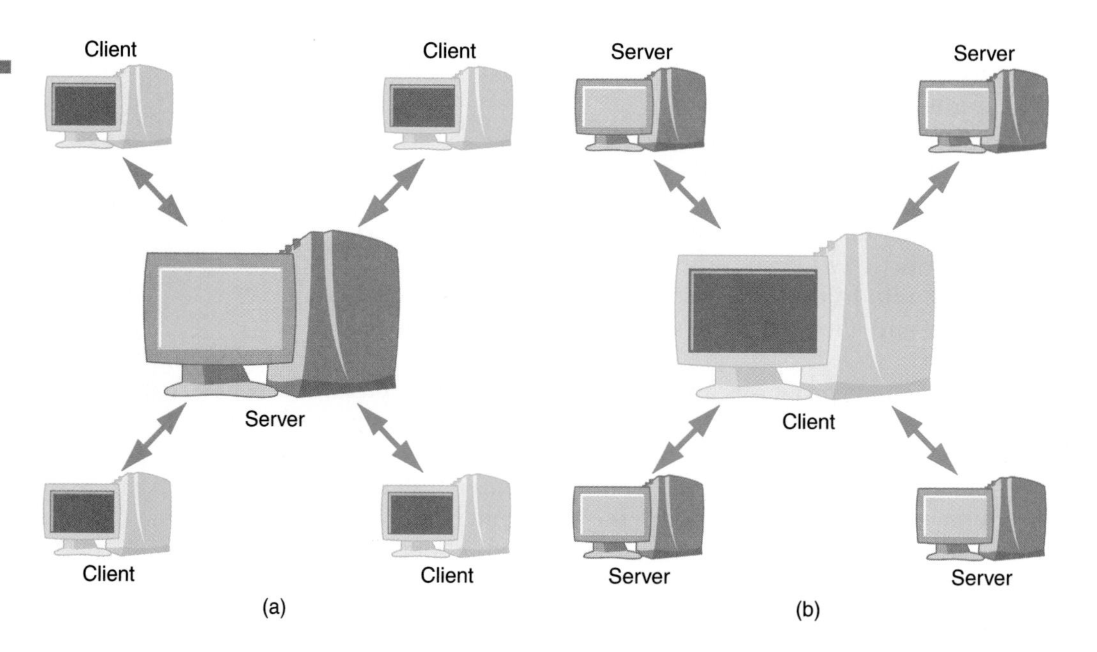

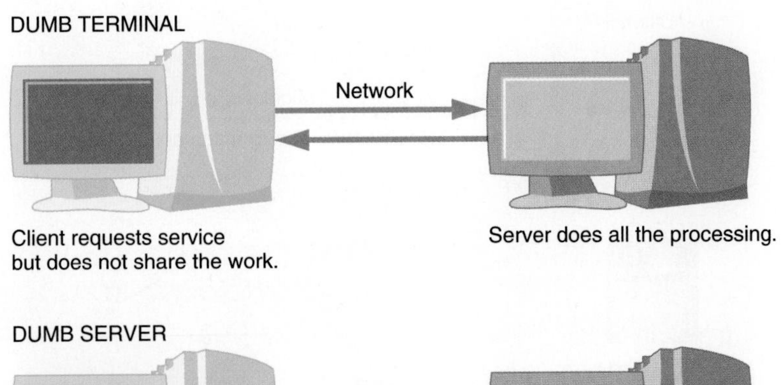

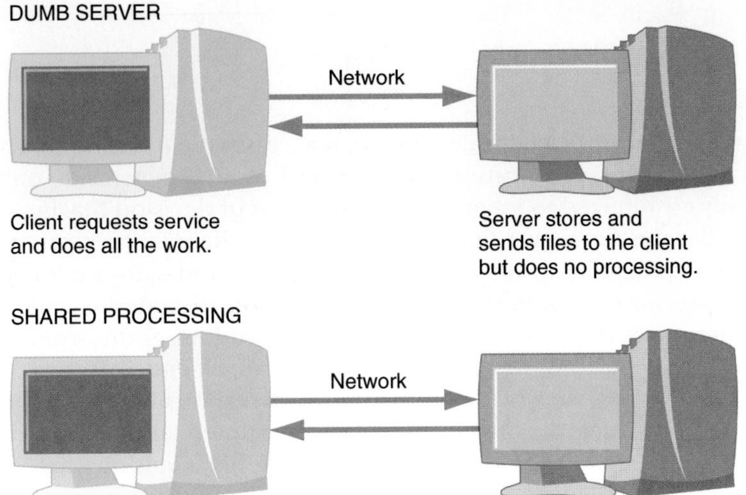

FIGURE 9-4

Dumb Terminal, Dumb Server, and Shared Processing in a Client/Server System

The other extreme in job apportionment is a **dumb server.** In this case, the client does all the processing; the server simply provides the data or the files that the client requests. For example, a file server may simply house and deliver the files when a client needs them but not process the file. So, depending on the application, the client/server system may have a dumb server, a dumb terminal, or an environment in which the processing is shared between the client and the server (Fig. 9-4).

Dumb server

A client/server situation in which the server does not do any processing but delivers the data or files to the requesting client, which does all the processing.

Client/server hardware has changed over time. In the early years of client/server technologies, the client was almost always a smaller machine, such as a PC or workstation, while the server was a larger machine, such as a midrange computer. Today, that is not the case. A client can be as large as or even larger than the server, depending on the application.

Think for a moment about a fax server, a server that stores all the faxes that a company receives and then distributes them electronically to the right recipient. Usually a fax server is a PC. A person who uses a midrange computer or a workstation may access the fax server to see if she has any faxes. In this example, the client is bigger than the server is.

Another hardware change is the use of mainframes in client/server systems. Experts initially predicted that client/server systems would eventually replace mainframes. However, client/server systems have led to a resurgence of mainframes because their reliability and scalability make them ideal servers. Recall that scalability means that system performance will not slow down as the number of users increases.

Note, however, the distinction between a mainframe-based IS application and a client/server system in which the mainframe is the server. In the former case, the entire application is designed, developed, and implemented on the mainframe. Programs are written in a mainframe operating system environment, processing is done on the mainframe, reports are generated by the mainframe, and the application is maintained on the mainframe.

In the case of a client/server system that uses a mainframe as a server, the mainframe stores data and information. The interface to the application may reside on the client

FIGURE 9-5

Client/Server System Software

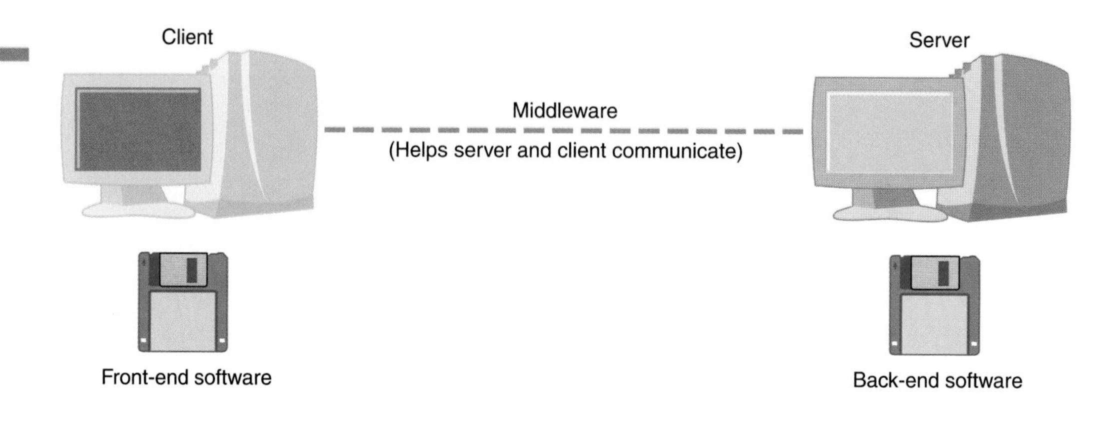

and whenever the client needs data, it accesses the mainframe. Unlike a mainframe environment, the application interface and reports may reside on the client and can be easily customized to meet the unique needs of decision makers.

Besides the server and client hardware, client/server systems require special software for the client, called front-end software, and software for the server, called back-end software (Fig. 9-5). **Front-end software,** designed to make the system easy for end-users, is responsible for accessing data and programs from the server and presenting them in the right format to the user. **Back-end software,** designed to help programmers and network administrators, is responsible for getting and managing the data, preventing the data from getting corrupted, and recovering lost information.

Front-end software

Software that resides on the client and accesses data and programs from the server and then presents it in a user-friendly format for client users.

Back-end software

Software that resides on the server and helps to manage and protect the data and other files on the server.

Middleware

Software that helps the client communicate with the server to ensure the smooth functioning of different components in a client/server system.

Another element in client/server systems is **middleware,** which is software that helps the client and server communicate. This software is considered to be the glue that holds together different client/server elements or components. It is called middleware because it resides somewhere between the client and the server and supports communications, data access, security, and other features. Table 9-1 highlights the key components of front-end, back-end, and middleware software.

Note that the front-end and back-end software and middleware help to manage, maintain, and access databases. The ability to retrieve and manipulate data and provide managers with good information is a critical function of a client/server system.

The Growth in Client/Server Computing

The rapid growth in client/server computing can be traced to three powerful forces: (1) the ubiquity of PCs, (2) the interest in corporate downsizing, and (3) the high cost of running and maintaining mainframes, particularly for smaller organizations.[6] First, PCs have become as common as telephones in the workplace. PCs help with the arduous task of building integrated systems, namely, systems that communicate with each other.

TABLE 9-1 Uses of Front-end, Back-end, and Middleware Software

Type of Software	Who Uses	Responsible for . . .
Front-end	End users	Database management systems Network security Application integrity backups Disaster recovery
Back-end	Programmers, network administrators	User interfaces Application development tools Document management Data access
Middleware	Users, programmers, network administrators	Smooth communication between the client and server

Integrated systems are the key to providing decision makers with consistent, reliable information and networked PCs can help. W. Eric Harris, senior vice president in charge of financial systems and reengineering at First Chicago NBD Corp., recalls business meetings where half a dozen bankers would show up with half a dozen different figures for the same thing. "Someone would say, 'Here's my number for profitability,' and someone else would say, 'This is my number for profitability,' " recalls Harris. Then they would spend half the meeting deciding whose number was best.

This problem, which is not unique to First Chicago, often arises because many organizations have disconnected systems, resulting in inconsistent information. PCs have made it possible for companies to link disparate systems and find the common information thread.

Second, the 1980s and 1990s will be remembered in corporate history as the years of layoffs due to business downsizing or (to put it more nicely) "rightsizing." To cut costs, businesses fired workers and reengineered their business processes to become leaner, meaner, and stronger. Reengineering requires companies to take a close look at what they do and ask the question, "Why do we do what we do?" This process helps companies to eliminate inefficiencies in the way they operate.

Companies can no longer afford to accept the answer "That's how it's always been done." Instead, employees are simply expected to do more with less. Client/server systems are one way to increase employee productivity. They increase productivity by helping companies to deliver customized information as and when needed to decision makers at all levels in the organization.

To illustrate how customized information that client/server systems deliver improves productivity, take a look at CS First Boston Corp. This corporation switched to client/server systems to increase sales and enhance the productivity of its salesforce. CPTrade, a client/server system for short-term securities, helped reduced the time for creating a portfolio of financial products from 30 minutes to less than 3 minutes.

The new system was designed and developed to respond to the information needs of salespeople. Before the new system was installed, salespeople relied on reports from mainframes that were not as responsive as a client/server system. By distributing the information among different servers and customizing the information to meet the needs of salespeople, productivity increased significantly—so much so that a salesperson can now handle seven investors in the time it used to take to handle one.[7]

The third factor accelerating the client/server movement is the rapid pace of technology. New and powerful technologies are hitting the marketplace at lightning speed. Today, less hardware can accomplish more at a lower cost. Computers, networks, and operating systems have all become more powerful and more flexible, thus allowing companies to put more power and more features in the hands of the user. Today's computer has become an "intelligent electronic companion" to employees at all levels and functions in an organization. Client/server systems have contributed to that reality in significant ways.

Before client/server technologies evolved, information was often isolated, compartmentalized, and hidden in huge computerized databases or, even worse, in manual systems. This isolation led to data redundancies and information bottlenecks. Although these problems have not been eliminated, they have been significantly reduced through client/server systems.

Hyatt Hotels' client/server reservation systems allow agents to check room availability at 156 hotels, quote rates to customers, and book any one of 80,000 rooms worldwide, all within a matter of seconds. Before the system was installed, each hotel kept a giant, handwritten diary of all room bookings. Booking a room required phone calls and faxes between hotels located in different parts of the country. If a customer called Hyatt headquarters in Chicago to book a room in San Francisco, employees in Chicago would call the manager in the San Francisco hotel to find an open date. Telephone tag and mail delays took so long that customers had to wait hours, and sometimes even days, to receive a reply or confirmation. Annoyed customers took their business elsewhere.

Today the new client/server system is so successful that it is estimated to generate an additional $20 million per year in revenues and reduce the cost of booking rooms by over $4 million a year. That's an impressive return on a system that cost a little over $500,000 to build.[8]

The Hyatt's investment in client/server systems has paid off in terms of faster, more accurate customer reservation services.

Comparing the Client/Server and Local Area Network Environments

In this section we examine the relationship of the client/server environment to a local area network (LAN) environment. In a LAN environment, just as in a client/server environment, multiple desktop PCs are linked to one or more servers. However, in a LAN environment, each PC views the server as nothing more than a storehouse of data and programs, similar to a dumb server in a client/server environment. That is, the PC treats the server as if it were another disk drive.

When the client requests data, programs, or applications from the server in a LAN environment, the entire file is transmitted across the network to the client, be it a word-processing application, database, or any other program. All the processing is done on the PC. This unprocessed file transfer can cause major bottlenecks on the network, especially during hours when numerous employees use the network.

To illustrate, in a client/server environment (with host processing), the "processing" is shared by both the client and the server. Let's say that a client requests the names of salespeople whose last names begin with the letters M to Z. The server will send a list (M–Z). In a LAN environment, the entire A–Z list will be sent to the client and the client has to process the file to find the M–Z names. In this situation, the LAN files transferred to the user are larger than the processed files of a client/server system would be. This transfer of the entire file (or entire application or program) can clog up the network.

Although the processing workload may differ from one system to another, the potential for sharing the processing work exists in a client/server environment. This logical separation of the processes that the client performs from the processes that the server performs is the key reason why client/server systems can support multiple users without burdening the network.

In summary, in a LAN environment, the central computer is simply a storage mechanism, not a processing mechanism. In a client/server environment, the server is a pro-

Global IS for success

Freighting Instead of Fretting

Andrew Tidd, information technology manager at Panalpina World Transport, the Switzerland-based freight company, has converted 100 users in eight U.K. offices to client/server systems. His enthusiasm for client/server systems has spread to the rest of his organization. Panalpina is implementing client/server technologies in 66 countries to reach two-thirds of Panalpina's 9,500 employees.

Tidd's department is responsible for supporting 200 users at ports and airports around the United Kingdom. Most of the work is simple data entry, such as logging the arrival or departure of freight shipments and inputting data related to each shipment. Just a few years ago, each of those offices used their own PCs to enter the data and then moved the information to a centrally located midrange computer.

This process meant that the central IT department had to travel around the country providing assistance when PCs needed upgrading, when systems broke down, or when someone introduced a virus by loading an infected floppy disk. Tidd and his team had a big management headache trying to service thousands of PC users.

Then Tidd found a client/server system that allows multiple users to run applications on a single server. All the processing happens on the server, eliminating the need for data duplication and disjointed processing. Although the system cannot solve all problems, it has been the right choice for Panalpina. "We have saved three or four staff in the IT department and have just three people to run 450 devices across the U.K. and Ireland." More than that, the problems associated with managing an army of PCs have been eliminated.

QUESTIONS AND PROJECTS

1. What are some problems that Panalpina's client/server system has solved?
2. Why do you think it would be advantageous for multiple users in Tidd's department to be able to access the shipping information system?
3. After reading through the next two text sections, determine whether an alternative to a client/server system could have solved Panalpina's problems effectively.

Source: Adapted from Ron Condon, "Thin Is in for This Freight Forwarding Company," *Computerworld*, March 30, 1998, www.computerworld.com.

cessing mechanism that can process different applications and programs for clients on the network. This is not to say that client/server systems are better than LANs. A number of factors, such as type of application, user requirements, and number of users, influence the choice between LAN and client/server.

Keep in mind that "client/server" is a term that refers to how an organization brings together a set of technologies and applies it to solve a problem. The key point is that in a client/server system the processing is shared by the client and server. In a LAN, it is not. A word of caution: Wide area networks (WANs) and metropolitan area networks (MANs) are terms that refer only to the distance that a network covers. A client/server, then, may use a MAN or a WAN to link clients separated by significant geographical distance.

Client/Server Applications

As a student of IS, you need to understand the difference between client/server models and client/server applications. For example, an extranet or an intranet follows a client/server model of a server and client linked by a network. The same is true for the Internet. In the case of the Internet, there is a whole network of clients and servers. When you search your computer (the client), it requests different servers that are connected to the Internet, for the information that you are requesting.

In contrast, the use of a client/server system to address a specific business problem is a client/server application. The Technology Payoff featuring Nabisco's sales forecasting system is a client/server application. AT&T's customer service information system, UWIN, is also a client/server application.

FIGURE 9-6

Client/Server Database Applications

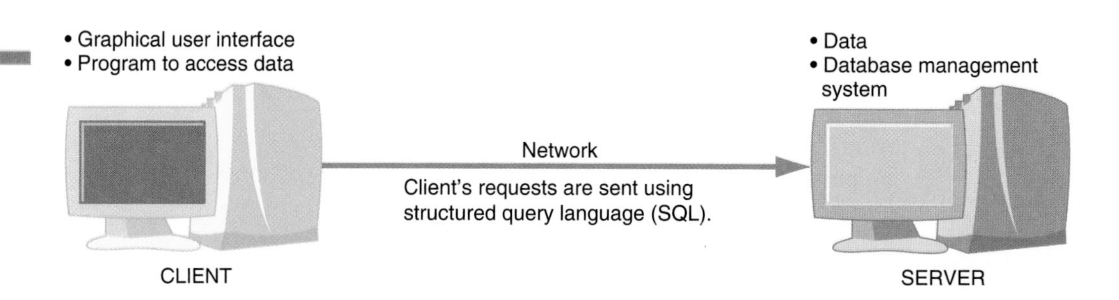

There are a wide variety of client/server applications. The most popular application is a database application. The data and the database software run on the server while the program that can access and manipulate the data is usually stored on the client. The client end usually has a graphical user interface that makes it easy for users to retrieve and manipulate data from the server. The client requests the necessary data using structured query language (SQL). The server processes the queries and presents the results to the client. Figure 9-6 illustrates the client/server database application process.

Another popular client/server application is transaction processing. Although these systems are covered in detail in the next chapter, we take a brief look at them here. A transaction is an exchange between two entities. When you buy a product at a store, a transaction occurs between you and the retailer that must be recorded in the retailer's system, known as a *transaction processing system.*

In the context of a client/server environment, a transaction is an all-or-nothing proposition, which means that all updates associated with a transaction must be completed or the transaction will be voided. If incomplete, the server must "clean the slate" and begin processing the transaction all over again. Although transaction processing was once considered exclusive to mainframes, today powerful client/server systems are slowly becoming ideal for transaction processing.

Electronic mail (e-mail) is another popular client/server application. An e-mail software package stores the e-mail on the server and then sends it to the client on request. When there are a large number of users, a server is dedicated exclusively to sort and deliver mail.

We see how broad the range of customized applications is as we move through the rest of this chapter. In the next section, we assess the advantages and disadvantages of client/server systems.

Advantages and Disadvantages of Client/Server Systems

Businesses that recognize the promises and challenges of client/server systems will be better prepared to implement and use them effectively. In this section, we'll investigate the advantages and disadvantages of client/server systems listed in Table 9-2 and their implications for managers.

TABLE 9-2 **Advantages and Disadvantages of Client/Server Systems**

Advantages	Disadvantages
Data are readily accessible to decision makers	Resistance to change
Reduced operating costs	High training costs
Reduced system development and maintenance time	Extensive planning required
Increased organizational responsiveness	Inadequate standards
	Susceptible to security violations

Advantages of Client/Server Systems

Client/server systems, if implemented effectively, have four key potential advantages. First, they can make data more accessible to decision makers. Second and third, they can reduce operating costs and can save system development and maintenance time. Fourth, they can increase a business's ability to respond to changing customer demands or other changes in the environment, a key factor in maintaining a competitive edge.

Data Are Readily Accessible to Decision Makers

Accessibility to reliable, up-to-date information when needed is one of the hallmarks of responsive organizations. Timely information can often translate into tangible benefits, such as increased profits or reduced operating costs, and intangible benefits, such as greater customer satisfaction.

Consider Lutheran Hospitals in Chicago, an organization with 6,275 employees and $682 million in revenue. The hospital is an integrated health-care firm that believes information technology and good patient care must fit hand in glove. Using client/server systems, the hospital delivers comprehensive, computerized patient information to health-care specialists in the hospital.

The patient information includes medical history, current medications, and other specialists the patient visited, along with diagnoses of existing or past illnesses. Insurance information is also available to the health-care providers to aid administrative decisions. The information access not only has improved the quality of health care but has also won patient approval because patients no longer have to spend time repeating the same information to different health providers.[9]

The system works this way: All data relevant to a patient are stored on a server, which in this case is a mainframe. A doctor treating a patient logs onto his or her PC, which is networked to the server, and pulls up relevant information relating to the patient. Because each and every health-care worker who comes into contact with the patient sees the same information, there is little room for misrepresented data or lack of data about a patient's condition, treatment, or history.

Reduced Operating Costs

In the long run, the cost of information processing may be cheaper for client/server systems than for mainframe systems, thereby lowering overall operating costs. Toyota's Camry division, based in Georgetown, Kentucky, replaced its proprietary mainframe-based manufacturing system mandated by Toyota headquarters in Japan with a graphical, client/server information system.

The client/server system links Camry's manufacturing, finance, and administrative departments with 175 suppliers, both domestic and international, resulting in increased efficiency and reduced operating costs.[10] Today, the company uses client/server technology for car design, communications, and workflow design and analysis.

Reduced System Development and Maintenance Time

Overall, client/server systems tend to be easier to develop than mainframe systems, in which one machine (the mainframe) does all the processing. With proper planning and the necessary expertise, developers can create client/server systems more quickly and efficiently than mainframe applications. In large part, this is because packaged client/server applications are more readily available than mainframe applications.[11] Also, in many cases (but not all) client/server applications are less complex than mainframe applications.

Changes or additions to an existing client/server system can be made without too much disruption because server applications are independent of client applications. For instance, a server application such as payroll can be updated or refined without adversely affecting a client application and vice versa. As result, client/server system maintenance time is reduced as compared with systems that must be shut down to make upgrades or perform maintenance.

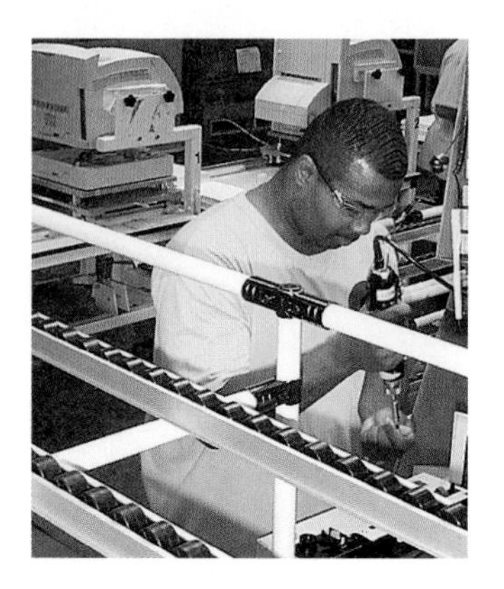

Lexmark uses a client/server system to integrate different business functions.

Increased Organizational Responsiveness

Halfway through developing client/server systems many companies realize that they need to rethink the way they do business. Designing a client/server system often compels managers and employees to search for more efficient, more effective business practices. As we saw in the opening section, a client/server system helped AT&T offer its Universal Card Services to a profitable niche in the competitive credit card industry.

As AT&T developed the system, however, the company realized that it was not enough to simply give the salesforce more data. Its salespeople needed more decision-making authority and access to more complete information. Even though the company was used to delivering piecemeal data to salespeople, the client/server system led managers to consolidate information from different databases and deliver the "big picture" to sales representatives so they could make quick decisions and serve customers better. The result of this new thinking and the support from the client/server system was an increase in market share for AT&T credit card services.[12]

Stanley Works, a manufacturer of home improvement products, demonstrates another way in which a client/server system helped a business respond to customers' demands to improve service. Stanley Works customers were complaining because they often received multiple invoices, from each of the company's six divisions, for a single order. The company decided to build a client/server system to address this problem.

The new system integrates several databases to consolidate the ordering application, which has helped increase efficiency and customer responsiveness. The order processing application now resides on a server and different client computers access necessary information from the server. Employees are able to provide consistent information to customers because of the consolidation of the ordering application on the server.[13]

Lexmark International, a Kentucky-based maker of ink-jet and laser printers, also turned to client/server systems to become more responsive to customers. Lexmark is a make-to-order business—no easy task when assembling $4,000 laser printers. The company uses a highly integrated client/server system that links production, marketing, finance, and human resources. Because of the integration and the ability to provide accurate and consistent information, the system has helped the company reduce manufacturing cycle times from 4 hours to 24 minutes. Inventory is now turned over 59 percent faster. Floor space has gone from 6,000 square feet to 4,500 square feet and volume per shift has increased 33 percent, from 225 units to 300 units.[14]

Disadvantages of Client/Server Systems

Client/server systems, in spite of their significant advantages, have significant risks and cannot solve all problems. Many organizations venturing into client/server environments realize too late the challenges in successfully developing and implementing such systems. Preparation and careful planning are key. We examine five disadvantages: transition difficulty, steep training costs, significant planning time, lack of standards, and susceptibility to security violations.

Resistance to Change

The transition from a mainframe environment to a client/server environment is fraught with obstacles. Says one industry expert, "It is like asking two people who don't speak the same language to describe to one another the inner workings of a lawn sprinkler!"[15] Although this analogy may be somewhat exaggerated, it is clear that the knowledge, experience, and expertise guiding these mainframe and client/server technologies are quite different.

The real challenge lies in encouraging professionals who move from one area of expertise to another to be flexible and open-minded. Although many mainframe proponents resist the move to client/server systems, mainframe programmers should remain open to a shift, both for their own benefit and their company's. "If you are not riding the wave of change, you'll soon be beneath it," claims Bob Rothenberger, assistant director of computer operations at Provident Mutual Life Insurance Co. in Berwyn, Pennsylvania.[16]

Doron Cohen, Chief Information Officer at TransCanada PipeLines, knows all about helping people make the transition from a mainframe environment to a client/server environment. With the help of the right technologies, he transformed the Calgary, Alberta, company from a sleepy, regulated utility to an aggressive, $10.8 billion (Canadian dollars) global competitor. In the process he also changed IS from a much-hated support function to a true business partner with a can-do, aggressive attitude. Such feats are not easy to accomplish and require instilling a strong business sense in people who otherwise may have their technology blinders on.

Rebuilding a corporate information system from a mainframe to a client/server system "does not come just by gazing at navels and feeling nice," Cohen quips. "There is a very, very hard core of no-compromise business sense that can only allow touchy-feely up to a point. Then the steel blade comes in."[17] Growing up in Tel Aviv, Israel, "my childhood inclination was to wire things up," Cohen remembers. He has developed ballistic missile guidance systems and run large mainframe data centers. Today, he focuses on people. He says, "people are what make or break you. How you get people to change over time, and to keep changing, is far more important than either technology or even business issues."

Cohen and a brainstorming team identified four key values that guided the transition from a mainframe to client/server system. They are "partnership, teamwork, the energetic pursuit of results and integrity," he says. Anyone who can't or won't live by them is invited, as Cohen puts it, to "find happiness elsewhere." That's what happened to 34 data center veterans who, in early 1987, threatened to quit unless he reversed plans to unplug the mainframe. He called their bluff, even though he still needed the mainframe for critical business functions.[18]

Resistance to change is a big obstacle to the transition from legacy systems to client/server systems. A company must be prepared to meet the challenge. Its IS team must work with end users, plan carefully, allow sufficient lead time, and communicate the shared business values that drive the shift to client/server systems.

High Training Costs

Users need extensive training to successfully use and manage client/server environments. Because these systems often change the dynamics of the business environment, training must be comprehensive and include both the business and the technology side. People need training in technology but—even more important—they also need training in using the technology to improve the way business operates. Such training is critical, quite expensive, and long term.

Forrester, a consulting group, estimates that it costs a company $25,000 to $40,000 per employee in out-of-pocket expenses and lost productivity for an initial round of training in basic client/server technologies such as relational databases, applications integration, and data access. It costs an additional $5,000 or so every 18 months for refresher courses and to update skills.[19] Companies must be prepared to invest heavily in the training necessary to equip users with adequate client/server skills.

Extensive Planning Required

Client/server systems are like mushrooms. They tend to grow fast and in unexpected places. As a result, a business must plan carefully and develop a strategic plan for a client/server system. Without a plan, the system becomes an ad hoc collection of systems that don't integrate information and streamline business processes. Instead, the ad hoc system causes more problems than it solve.

American Express's experience is illustrative. The company implemented client/server computing several years ago. Suddenly it found that it had more than 70 client/server applications, some of which were obsolete, even before the system was fully implemented.

Now the company has a growth plan that clearly identifies the role of client/server systems in achieving the company's strategic goals. The plan identifies hardware issues, such as the nature and type of networking, operating systems, and hardware platforms; and broader issues, such as data management, development tools, system security, user

Nordstrom implemented a client/server system because the technology matched its management style of giving employees at all levels decision-making authority.

training, and access methods. An unexpected benefit of the plan was that developers at American Express were able to reuse parts of the code because they could see the big-picture view of where the organization was going with its information systems technology.

Another example is Nordstrom, a company reputed for its superior customer service. The company developed a technology plan and switched to client/server systems when it saw a nice fit with its decentralized management style. The plan forced users and developers to answer the fundamental question about the match between technology and the company's business style and needs. In the words of a CIO who emphasizes the importance of planning and having a vision, "It's up to [the CEO] to provide the vision of where you want the business to go, and it's up to me to help you get there [with the right technology]. If you don't know where you're going, I can get you there, too, like the pilot who says 'We're lost, but we're making good time.' "[20]

Inadequate Standards

Like any other new and evolving technology, client/server systems lack standardization in terms of system management, maintenance, and security, resulting in some reinventing of the wheel. Developers become burdened with a host of issues that in other environments would be a standard part of the hardware and software package. Standards and procedures available in a mainframe environment, such as security, are not fully developed in the PC environment in which the client/server system functions. Without standards and a proven record of what works and what doesn't, companies may end up playing a guessing game, resulting in huge losses and sometimes irrecoverable setbacks.

Susceptible to Security Violations

Security of information systems—protecting valuable trade secrets and intellectual property—is vital for the health of the organization. In the case of client/server systems, security concerns are even greater because such systems are prone to security violations. There are several reasons for this, including lack of standardization, a decentralized organizational structure, and the nature of the technology.

Ironically, the same features that make the client/server flexible, modular, open, and responsive also make it risky and vulnerable. "Client/server computing is a double-edged sword. You get great productivity, but all of a sudden everybody is a systems developer and administrator, tinkering with their own applications. Without any point of centralized tracking and control, companies will end up with worse chaos than [that which arose] from the proliferation of minicomputers in the early 1980s."[21]

The first step in building system security is to ensure that only authorized users have system access. "Let's say I have a phone book for sales. I will let just about everyone look at it, but only a couple of people will be allowed to put anything into it. Here integrity is a high-level issue and confidentiality is low. You don't necessarily let one issue drive the other," says security expert Steve Bellovin.[22]

Some organizations rely on customized user interfaces that allow users to access only certain data fields. This restriction prevents users from putting "muddy, curious paws on restricted data."[23] Many companies let employees know that their network activities will be monitored to deter inappropriate activities, such as sharing passwords, copying programs, and releasing proprietary information.

An IS director relates an incident in which a large bank made its retail bankers responsible for maintaining the files for its client/server–based, VISA credit-card system. Retail bankers—who were clearly not well versed in the intricacies of file maintenance—inadvertently set the credit limit to zero on all the cards. "All customers trying to charge items to their VISA accounts that day were turned down, including the CEO's daughter, [who] went out to buy her wedding dress."[24] Not only did the bank incur losses in millions of dollars, but generated ill will and suffered serious damage to its reputation.[25] This understanding includes knowledge of how client/server systems interface with people, existing systems, and the business environment. Let's examine these success factors next.

We see, then, that client/server systems have both advantages and disadvantages. Companies must carefully consider all factors before investing in client/server systems so they can plan for, develop, and implement the systems successfully.

Business Guidelines for Client/Server Success

Similar to other technologies, reaping the benefits of client/server technologies begins with a solid understanding of the factors that lead to system success. This understanding includes knowledge of how client/server systems interface with people, existing systems, and the business environment. Let's examine these success factors next.

Know Thy Business and Its Goals

The key question at the heart of successful client/server systems is "Why do we do what we do?" If a company builds a system before determining how to make its operations as efficient as possible, it cannot reap the full rewards of client/server systems technologies. As the popular saying goes, "If you automate a mess, you get an automated mess!" But evaluating all operations from an efficiency standpoint takes time, personnel, and commitment.

Norfolk Southern Railway Co. asked the key question, "What is our business and how can we improve it?" before investing a penny in the Strategic Intermodal Management System (SIMS), a client/server system that has earned the company high marks in the transportation industry. The system replaced tedious, error-prone paper-shuffling processes for coordinating intermodal traffic (the movement of truck trailers and shipping containers by train). "[Because of the system] we got rid of the angry drivers blocking the gates, the delivery delays and the errors that caused lost containers, and congestion in our yards," explains Lee Durham, manager of information systems development at Norfolk Southern in Norfolk, Virginia.

The challenge was "to drastically boost how we used our assets so we could compete not just with other railroads, but with long-haul truck companies," says Hugh Starling, manager of client/server systems. The company was not interested in blindly investing in a client/server system but instead was looking for ways to improve its business processes and realized that a client/server system was one way to achieve that goal.

Improvements through SIMS helped the intermodal unit become the fastest-growing part of the business and contributed to record revenues, officials claim. Managing intermodal freight has gone from "totally inadequate" to "deadly accurate." Now the intermodal department estimates it could lose $50,000 per hour if access to SIMS were denied.[26]

Plan, Plan, Plan

The success of client/server technology, like other complex technologies, depends on careful planning. A technology roadmap that shows the role of client/server technology in achieving the corporate mission is vital. The plan should identify the areas in the company that will lend themselves well to automation and then specify client/server technologies that will meet those automation needs. Some evaluation procedures to measure the return on investment should also be included in the plan.

Although the plan may not provide exact answers to all questions, often the process itself is therapeutic. It gives employees an opportunity to voice their "technology wishes" and concerns. It also gives people an opportunity to see what they must do to help the company succeed and help them realize the challenges of fulfilling that mission.

Sears has produced over 20 client/server applications that provide leading-edge support for 200,000 associates and 800 stores. Planning was the key to the success of these systems. For each project, a strategic and technical planning group at the corporate level evaluates and recommends hardware and software. Still, officials say it's hard to estimate a payback on client servers. "We don't have a totally concrete foundation to stand on other than our best judgment, tied to a very cautious [plan]," admits Mary Elizabeth Ferraro, a Sears systems manager in the strategic and technical planning group.[27]

Training Is the Key

Even the best client/server system will fall short if employees are not trained to see both the business aspects and the technology aspects of the application. Reengineering almost always precedes the development of client/server systems. As a result, employees are faced not only with a new system but also with a new or a different way of doing business. Proper training becomes a pivotal part of reaping the benefits of client/server systems.

Consider the training at United Airlines' Catering Division. Providing snacks and meals to flight passengers is no small task. United Airlines' Catering Division handles 75 million in-flight meals a year, with 17 kitchens and 250 food contractors worldwide. Until a few years ago, United's food inventory management system relied on standalone PCs. The system was tedious and grossly inefficient. Every time the menu changed, the information had to be manually entered at each site. Service Level guides, which provide specific details on everything from brownie ingredients to the number of servings per plate, ran hundreds of pages long and had to be printed and mailed four or five times a year to each location.

With the help of an integrated client/server system, the airline developed an online tracking and monitoring system. An extensive database on food items and food preparations is stored on a server and remote kitchen sites dial into the database for a variety of information. The system was an instant hit with employees because United Airlines spent significant dollars training individuals not only in how to use the system but also about how good food service translated into higher levels of customer satisfaction.[28]

Make Sure the Data Have Integrity

Data are essential to good decision making. The best of systems is only as good as the data that go into it. As Comedy Central found out, good data lead to market power. Comedy Central's salesforce's customer-tracking system was "nothing to smile about" before it left MTV. "We had access to nothing," observes James Walley, vice president of information technology.

Normally, salespeople requested account information from MTV, which competes with Comedy Central for subscribers. That information was delivered on spreadsheets. In January 1998 the company invested in a client/server system so that salespeople had accurate and current data about their customers. Sarah Louise Hale, who works with building relationships with affiliates, critiques the old system, "The worst thing as far as affiliate relations goes is to send out a pitch letter to someone who left five years ago. That is embarrassing." Poor systems can lead to significant losses for the company. By ensuring data integrity and timeliness of customer information, the company hopes to increase its subscriber base by 5 million homes.[29]

Comedy Central's client/server system enhanced its market power by delivering accurate customer information to salespeople.

Establish Standards

The importance of establishing standards for information systems is especially critical for client/server systems. Managers must address standards relating to both hardware and software. For example, they should ask questions such as:

- What kind of hardware are we going to use for servers?
- What kind of hardware are we going to use for clients?
- What software will the company use to establish communications between clients and servers?
- What kind of applications will run on clients?

If these and other issues are not carefully considered, client/server systems quickly become a hodgepodge of incompatible systems.

Client/server systems are powerful tools that can support company goals and help the business gain a competitive edge in delivering information quickly. The ability to carefully align the technology with business goals is the key to client/server success. Finally, client/server systems are not just about technology. They are about bringing people and technology together in unique and innovative ways.

SUMMARY

1. **Describe client/server computing and the reasons for its growth.** Client/server systems are ones in which the client and the server share the processing work. The client requests the service from the server, which provides the service, if certain conditions are met. In a client/server environment some or all of the processing may be shared between the client and the server. Although once clients were always smaller than servers, today that is not necessarily the case.

   There are three main reasons for the growth in client/server systems. First, due to their widespread use, many employees are comfortable with PCs as productivity tools. Further, PCs have made it easier to integrate and deliver timely information to users. Second, when corporations downsize their workforces, companies are forced to do more with less. This often results in rethinking the business processes and client/server systems can help in this effort. Finally, the rapid pace of technology has made the client/server movement a natural choice for many companies.

2. **Compare and contrast client/server and LAN environments.** In a LAN environment, like a client/server environment, a number of PCs are networked. However, in a LAN environment, the server does not do any processing; it is simply a storehouse of data and programs. When a client requests the service, the server simply passes the data or the program to the server. In a client/server environment the processing work is usually shared between the client and the server. Although the extent of processing may vary from one application to another, the work in a client/server environment is almost always shared.

3. **Identify some popular client/server applications.** Client/server applications include databases, transaction processing, e-mail, and other customized applications.
4. **Summarize key advantages and disadvantages of client/server systems.** A client/server system is a technology that helps organizations to become more agile, responsive, and effective. It has the potential to make information available in a timely and useful manner to decision makers, reduce operating costs, increase the efficiency of different processes, reduce the time it takes to develop systems, and increase organizational responsiveness. The disadvantages are making the transition from a mainframe environment to a client/server environment, extensive employee training, long-range system planning, inadequate standards, and security.

KEY TERMS

back-end software (p. 248)
client (p. 245)
client/server system (p. 245)
dumb terminal (p. 246)
dumb server (p. 247)
front-end software (p. 248)
host processing (p. 246)
middleware (p. 248)
server (p. 245)

REVIEW QUESTIONS

1. What are some reasons for the increase of client/server systems in business?
2. Describe what is meant by client/server technology. What is a server? What is a client?
3. A client is always a larger machine than a server is. Further, a server will provide whatever service the client requests. Comment.
4. What is meant by front-end software and back-end software? Are both essential for a client server to function?
5. What is middleware? Why is middleware needed in a client/server system?
6. What is the key difference between a client/server environment and a local area network environment? Is one better than the other?
7. Why is it important to have a plan before investing in client/server applications?
8. What are some of the advantages of client/server systems?
9. What are some disadvantages of client/server systems? What are some hidden costs associated with this technology?
10. How did TransCanada PipeLines help its employees transition from a mainframe environment to a client/server environment?
11. What are some difficulties that a company may face in transitioning from a mainframe environment to a client/server environment?

DISCUSSION QUESTIONS AND EXERCISES

1. Recall that the Internet is one of the best client/server models. Here is an example of how one insurance company developed a Web-based client/server system. Workers Compensation Fund of Utah (WCFU) allows its policyholders to submit worker injury claims using a standard form on the Web. The benefits of this system include significant reduction in the cost of processing each claim and an increase in customer satisfaction because the claim process is so simple and fast. Before the system was implemented it took the company about four weeks to process a claim. In the meantime, injured clients would visit several doctors and explore different treatments that might not be appropriate. The new system allows claims investigators, sometimes within minutes, to look into a claim and recommend the most appropriate course of action for the client. The Internet-based client/server system is giving the company a significant edge in a tough marketplace.[30]

a. Why is the Internet a good example of a client/server system?

b. What are some benefits that the company derived from this system?

c. What customer and employee concerns might have caused resistance to the shift from the old paper-based system to the new client/server system? After making a list of these potential concerns, develop responses to address the concerns.

2. Identify a local firm that has moved from a mainframe environment to a client/server environment. Interview one of their managers and identify the problems that the company faced, if any, during the transition.

3. PeopleSoft is one of the most popular client/server packages. Research the company's client/server products and identify some product features that the company offers.

4. **(Software exercise)** Find an article on a client/server application. Write a one-page report on the technical issues covered in your article and make a PowerPoint presentation to your class about this application.

Case 1: The Reengineering Blues

In this true story the name of the company has been changed to maintain confidentiality. A multibillion-dollar diversified U.S. company was using mainframe and PC LAN technology to provide on-line services for more than 1,500 users. However, senior management was concerned that the company might be left behind in the massive shift to client/server systems. They had read articles about how other firms had scrapped their mainframes and seen advantages such as big cost savings, improved productivity, faster time to market, empowerment of end users, and more flexible access to information. So they asked their specialists about overhauling their existing information technology infrastructure. The carefully considered reply? "Absolutely not!"

Unconvinced, management immediately hired an independent consultant for an objective, tie-breaking opinion. Not surprisingly, the consultant's advice was, "Reengineer everything, shed the mainframe—keep up with your competitors." Management took the hook. A New Age chief information officer was hired to replace the Iron Age incumbent. The incoming CIO, assuming the obsolescence of the information technology staff, hired outside consultants to work directly with end users. He also put a freeze on any spending for mainframe technology.

After spending $30 million and 2 years on a carefully phased migration, the firm declared the client/server system production-ready. But there was one problem: It did not work. Critical, end-of-year financial reports could not be generated. No contingency or parallel plans had been implemented. Within a week, the New Age CIO resigned.

Senior management then turned to the company's mainframe professionals for help. The mainframe "graybeards" completed the operation in 8 weeks, cut storage requirements by 60 percent, and cut response time in half. And the system could actually do a trial balance. However, now fearful of aftershocks, end users in the business units wanted nothing more to do with the client/server system.[31]

1. What went wrong in this situation? What should management have done to avoid this situation?
2. What role, if any, do you think IS and IT staff should play in reengineering efforts?

Case 2: Art Goes High Tech

The National Gallery of Art (NGA) is second only to the Smithsonian's Air and Space Museum as the most popular tourist attraction in Washington, D.C. It houses and displays a collection of approximately 80,000 objects, and engages in educating and informing the public. It holds local, national, and international exhibitions and runs a National Lending Program to share works of art with major government offices, including the White House, the Supreme Court, and U.S. embassies and consulates around the world.

In 1978 the NGA was one of the first organizations to create a computerized catalog. Since then the NGA has provided technology leadership in the field. The computerized catalog, called the Art Information System, was an efficient way for the NGA to collect and store data about each and every item in its collection. However, by the late 1980s, the world of information technology had changed so much that the catalog became inflexible and tedious. Today, the company has a sophisticated, state-of-the-art client/server system, called the Collection Management System (CMS), that keeps the organization on the leading edge of art and technology.

The CMS supports a wide variety of functions, such as administration, operations, and general information for a wide variety of departments: the curator, the registrar, exhibitions, insurance, education, and general information. Users have access to information that is relevant to all departments and information unique to their department. For example, curators maintain information about each work of art, and sometimes each work of art may require more than 600 distinct pieces of information from different sources.

Two key museum responsibilities became subsystems of the CMS: Movement and Acquisition. The Movement subsystem helps the Museum's registrar to plan, monitor, and coordinate shipments of loaned or borrowed art, both inside and outside the gallery. It helps address the special shipping and handling directions that often accompany art packages.

The Acquisitions subsystem catalogs hundreds of new lots every year, each containing one or more art objects, with basic information such as donor, source, funding acknowledgment, and official date of approval by the museum board. This subsystem is also responsible for

continued

Case 2: Art Goes High Tech, *continued*

managing the art exhibitions. Because art shows are sometimes planned as many as 10 years in advance and involves hundreds or even thousands of art objects, it is a tedious and detail-oriented task. The Acquisitions subsystem tracks the permission necessary to move art objects, insurance or indemnity arrangements, shipping, and other factors. A significant advantage of this system is that it helps administrators manage their fiduciary responsibilities, such as insurance costs for borrowed items.[32]

1. Identify some of the benefits to the NGA from its client/server system. Would a LAN environment be suitable for this problem?
2. What are some security issues that must be addressed in this system?

Building information trust may take us further than building information technology empires.

Kenneth A. Kozar, professor, University of Colorado

CONTENTS

BUILDING INFORMATION SYSTEMS FOR SUCCESS

Information systems and technologies are critical to VW's business success around the world. For many businesses, information systems are valued as much as land, capital, and human resources.[1] In fact, some countries, like India and China, view IT as the road to economic prosperity and world leadership. "There's little doubt that technology is good for the corporate soul. Indeed, most organizations would be consigned to purgatory without it."[2]

Consider the opening example. Volkswagen could not have delivered custom-made Beetles without the support of its information sys-

VW's information systems altered its design and production processes so that it could deliver made-to-order Beetles in an error-free, affordable manner.

Chapter 10

Information Systems for Managerial Decision Making

AFTER STUDYING THIS CHAPTER, YOU WILL BE ABLE TO:

- Explain how different types of information systems aid decision makers
- Outline how transaction processing systems support operational decision making
- Specify how management information systems help managers make tactical decisions
- Discuss how intelligent support systems support mid- and top-level managerial decision making

tems. Those systems, like those of so many businesses, moved well beyond storing records and other company-related data for easy access. Instead, VW's information systems improved design and production processes, customer service, sales information, and distribution.

Systems that once were capable of doing only standard, routine tasks can now perform sophisticated tasks such as playing chess or serving as a manager's "thinking hat" during decision making. Systems can support decisions or offer expertise, giving managers succinct, relevant, timely information that helps personnel at every level make choices that affect business success.

This chapter describes how all employees, regardless of what job they do for the organization, can use information systems to make effective decisions. Different types of systems cater to the different information needs of employees. As we discussed briefly in Chapter 2, different kinds of systems aid different types of decisions.

The three types of information systems (Fig. 10-1) that support management decisions are:

1. Transaction processing systems (TPS)
2. Management information systems (MIS)
3. Intelligent support systems (ISS) (This category includes decision support systems, executive information systems, and artificial intelligence and expert systems.)

Let's briefly look at these three systems. Every business is driven by transactions, which are exchanges between two business parties such as a sale, refund, or request for information. A **transaction processing system (TPS)** captures data about different transactions in a

TECHNOLOGY PAYOFF
Beetle Mania

Fire-engine red. Water-bug black. Every minute, two shiny built-to-order Volkswagen Beetles glide off the all-new computerized factory floor in Mexico. In a single day up to 1,000 cars—some days, no two alike—are manufactured to meet the specifications of adoring customers worldwide. Some are willing to wait months for the metallic-silver one.

Behind the Beetle's rebirth is the largest information systems renovation in Volkswagen AG's history. VW increased the technology budget from $10 million per year 4 years ago to $35 million per year today. "The increase of VW model's production in Mexico couldn't have been done with the old technology," explains Gerhard Rieder, director of finance at Volkswagen Mexico. "It was clear to us that without investing heavily in IT, we would not have been able to fulfill our objectives."

Using an all-new automated factory information system, Volkswagen revamped its entire production process. The company's sophisticated information systems ensure that the production is smooth, error-free, timely, and efficient. To ensure outstanding customer service, a network links Mexico's 170 VW dealers directly to the factory. This Dealer Communication System handles everything from consignment to shipment orders to invoicing to dealer credit information. "I think it will help us sell more cars," says Sam Cortina, operations manager at a dealership. "We can get an order number and status of cars on the waiting list. We can show this information to customers right on the screen. It helps build trust."

What is so notable is that Volkswagen built this sophisticated automated factory without missing a single day of production. To Volkswagen, great cars and great information systems go hand-in-hand.

Source: Julia King, "Beetlemania," *Computerworld,* June 8, 1998, www.computerworld.com.

company. Generally, these systems support routine, operational decisions made by lower-level managers.

Managers use management information systems to view different types of reports about the organization's performance. TPS and MIS are closely linked because the output from a transaction processing system often becomes the input to a management information system.

Both middle and upper management need systems that support semi-structured and unstructured decisions. **Intelligent support systems** refer to a set of systems—decision support systems, executive information systems, and artificial intelligence and expert systems—that help managers integrate data, judgment, and intuition into their decision-making models. These systems also help organizations to capture and preserve the knowledge of its employees.

Is one type of system better than another? The answer is no. The type or types of information systems that an organization uses depend on the organization's information needs. For example, a large hospital may need all three types of systems, whereas a florist shop may need just a simple transaction system. The information needs of a hospital are typically much broader and more complex than those of a florist shop. In a hospital, information from a wide variety of sources must be integrated and the information must be highly accurate. In contrast, the information needs of a florist shop tend to be much less complex and require less accuracy.

For organizations that have complex and exacting information needs, TPS, MIS, and ISS systems contribute to their well-being. To maximize the benefits of all three types of systems, organizations must make sure that the systems communicate with each other to avoid forming "islands of information." When systems in a business cannot communicate with one another, the information in each becomes isolated, so users can't access information from one location but must do so from each island.

The critical factor for organizational IS success is not so much the type or the number of systems, but *how* people use these systems in a way that adds value to their professional or personal life. Integrated TPS, MIS, and ISS systems add value to the decision-making process because they present information not on a piecemeal basis but in a comprehensive and meaningful way so that decision makers can make better decisions.

In this chapter we examine transaction processing, management information, and intelligent support systems in depth. We also explore how managers select systems that meet the organization's needs.

Making Operational Decisions with Transaction Processing Systems

Transaction processing systems capture transaction data that are vital for the survival and growth of a company. Recall from Chapter 2 that managers make operational decisions (decisions about how to operate the business), such as how many products to produce and how many people to hire, based on transaction data.

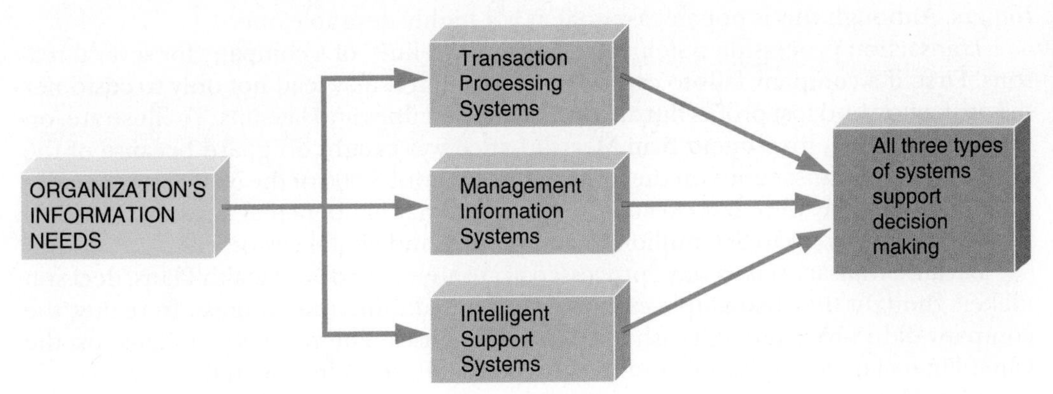

FIGURE 10-1

The Three Types of Systems That Support Employee Decision Making

Transaction processing system (TPS)

A system that records company transactions, in which a transaction is defined as an exchange between two or more business entities.

Intelligent support systems

A set of systems that help managers integrate data, judgment, and intuition with their decision-making models and captures and preserves the knowledge of a company's employees.

For example, Nasdaq, the electronic stock exchange, handles up to 1,000 stock transactions *per second.* Losing or corrupting these data is unthinkable. This transaction data help Nasdaq managers make decisions about the value of a stockholder's portfolio, the amount of taxes owed to the government, the number of a company's stocks sold and at what price, and other financial information that affects its business and individual customers. To ensure its continued success, Nasdaq has one of the most sophisticated transaction processing systems in the world.

Transaction systems were one of the earliest computerized systems that organizations used to capture valuable decision-making data and to conduct everyday business. Almost all organizations, regardless of their size and nature, have a manual or automated transaction processing system. We see examples of transaction processing systems every day at places such as the local coffee shop (the transaction is the sale of coffee), the bank's cash machine (the transaction is the withdrawal of funds from or the deposit to your account), and the doctor's office (the transaction is payment for the doctor's services). The coffee shop, bank, and doctor's office have systems that process the organization's transactions to aid decisions about what coffee beans to buy, which type of account is most profitable, and how many claims to file with insurance companies, respectively.

Transaction processing systems are considered the backbone of many organizations. Without them, managers couldn't make basic decisions about how much inventory to stock, how to staff, how to budget, and how many customers to expect. The volume of company transactions has increased exponentially, thanks to a booming economy, mergers and acquisitions, and the ability to do business on the Internet. Nasdaq's system, for instance, handles 5.5 million trade-related requests and transactions per day. "In an electronic society where cash withdrawals, retail purchases, and airline bookings are now just a few key strokes away from many consumers, IT departments quickly find themselves suffering transaction overload."[3]

Consider the volume that other transaction processing systems must handle. AT&T's transaction processing system handles 240 million voice calls on an average day, and each call requires 10 to 20 transactions to route it to the right destination. Each voice call also triggers a transaction in the billing database![4] Visa International processes more than 30 million credit-card-related transactions per day. The SABRE airline reservation system handles more than 5,000 transactions per second. Bill Gates, CEO of Microsoft, predicts that soon companies will need systems that support a *billion* transactions per day.

Transactions can be *internal* (occurring inside the organization) or *external* (originating outside the organization). When Maria in the accounting department orders office supplies from Kevin in the purchasing department, it is an internal transaction. When a customer places an order from a company catalog, an external transaction has occurred.

Until a few years ago separate transaction systems existed for each department in a company. That is, marketing had its own TPS, finance had its own TPS, and so on. Now many organizations are integrating the TPS systems of each department so that users can see the how their decisions affect other parts of the organization and their customers. Although this is not an easy goal, it is a highly desirable one.

Transaction processing systems are the "data lifeline" of a company for several reasons. First, if a company fails to capture a transaction it may lead not only to customer dissatisfaction and lost profits but also to serious penalties and lawsuits. To illustrate, on October 28, 1997, investment firm Merrill Lynch was caught off guard because of the high volume of transactions on the stock market. About 3,000 of the 50,000 stock trades it handled that day were not executed promptly. What happened as a result? The firm is expected to pay up to $10 million to compensate individual customers.

Because transactions weren't processed accurately at Oxford Health Plans, decision makers thought they had ample cash to spend on running the business. In reality, the company didn't have enough cash to cover its expenses. The systems problems cost the Chief Financial Officer his job and the company suffered a loss of credit.[5]

Second, transaction processing systems become the source of data for other systems in the organization. If analyzed and integrated, the captured information gives businesses key information about how and when customers use its products and services so that it can better plan how to meet customers' needs and preferences.

Third, a TPS is a link between the organization and external entities, such as customers, suppliers, distributors, and regulators. A TPS helps a company to study and analyze how much business it is doing with different clients. Successful companies use information from these transactions to serve their customers better and to identify new market opportunities.

Let's look at a real-world transaction processing system. "Bank on-line. Not in line" is the motto of Dollar Bank, a Federal Savings Bank that was nominated for the prestigious Smithsonian Award for computer innovation. The philosophy at Dollar Bank has always been "We Never Forget Whose Money It Is." True to its philosophy, the company uses information systems to deliver the best bang for the buck. Says one customer, "Now I know why I never wanted to bank anywhere else. This new NetBanking is easy and a lot of fun, plus it is up-to-the-minute. I used my debit card and when I got home ten minutes later and started using my computer, my account was current just that fast."[6]

What does Dollar Bank's NetBanking do for customers? Customers can access information on every aspect of their banking situation, including the status of their consumer loans, credit cards, home mortgages, checking accounts, savings accounts, and so on. Customers can access up-to-the-minute information on checking, statement savings, and money market accounts. They can check their available balance, individual

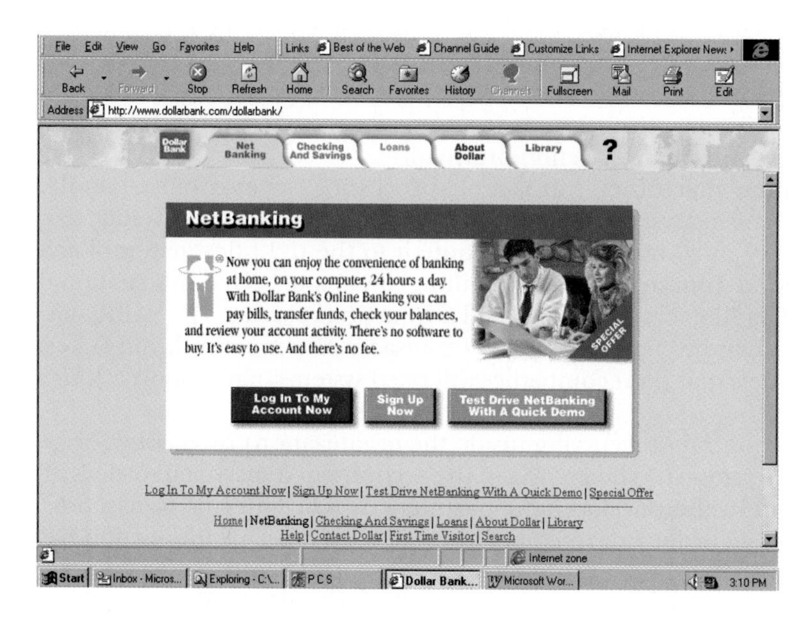

A transaction system allows Dollar Bank to keep accurate account of its customers and their transactions with the bank.

deposits, and withdrawals at any time from their personal computer. Customers can also pay bills and transfer funds between accounts. If they see that they don't have enough money in checking to cover an outstanding check, they can point and click to move an adequate cushion from savings to checking. Funds can be transferred to other insured depositories (banks, for example), insurance companies, mutual funds, and broker/dealers. And loan payments can be made to Dollar Bank or other lenders.

Perhaps the most popular feature of NetBanking, however, is the capability for paying bills with the touch of a computer key—no paper, no envelopes, no stamps, no fuss. Payments can be set up on a future-dated basis, either for a single payment or recurring ones. So, for example, when Dollar Bank's NetBanking customers go on vacation, they can pay their bills automatically, accurately, and on time.

NetBanking from Dollar Bank is available 24 hours a day, 365 days a year, subject to normal maintenance. Customers can use it anywhere there is a personal computer connected to the Internet through a secure browser—at home, in the office, or while traveling overseas. Even U.S. missionaries in Malaysia can use the NetBanking system to make long-distance payments on bills back home without incurring phone charges.

Each time a Dollar Bank customer does business on the NetBanking system a transaction occurs. This transaction must be captured in an accurate, timely manner in the transaction processing system. If Dollar Bank fails to capture each transaction, it could result in missed payments, inaccurate balance statements, and bounced checks for customers. The end result would certainly be the loss of customers and profits, and might possibly trigger lawsuits from customers who suffer damage.

Steps in Transaction Processing

Companies usually move through six steps to capture transaction information: (1) data entry, (2) validation, (3) processing, (4) storage, (5) output generation, and (6) query support. Figure 10-2 outlines these steps, which we explore next.

Data Entry

Transaction data are entered into the system using input devices, such as a keyboard and mouse. The data for entering into the system can come from a variety of sources. For example, an ATM receipt for a bank transaction becomes a data **source document** for balancing a checkbook.

Source documents

Documents generated where and when a transaction occurs; the source of data for the transaction processing system.

Validation

Validation ensures the accuracy and reliability of data. For example, the NetBanking system must validate the user ID to ensure that the user is authorized to make certain transactions, such as moving money from one account to another. However, even the most sophisticated validation techniques cannot detect some human errors. Say that a data entry clerk enters 12 hours instead of 2 work hours for a part-time employee. The system will not be able to detect this error.

Processing

Once the company validates the accuracy and reliability of the data, the system processes and converts the data into information. Processing may include merging files, adding two columns in a file, and other procedures. The two ways to process transactions are on-line transaction processing and batch processing.

In **on-line transaction processing (OLTP),** the data input device is directly linked to the transaction processing system, so the data are processed as soon as they are generated. Note, however, that an input device at a remote location may be linked to the system via

On-line transaction processing (OLTP)

Transaction data that are processed almost instantaneously.

FIGURE 10-2 Steps in Processing a Transaction

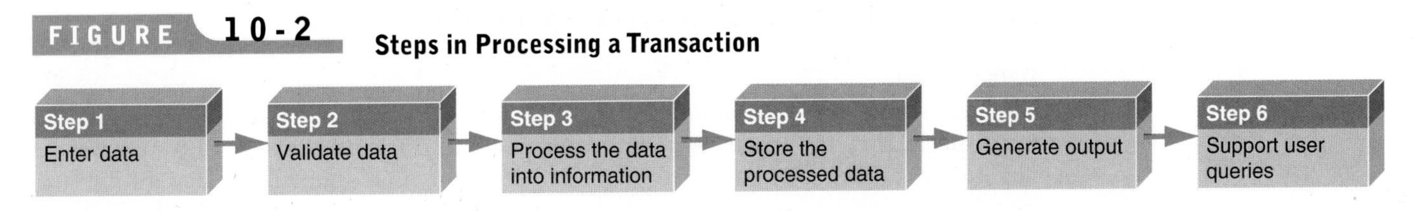

networks or telecommunications. Because the lag time between data creation and data processing in an on-line system is often minimal, the system's information is usually current. NetBanking, an example of an on-line processing system, provides users current information. When customers make transactions (for example, deposits or withdrawals), their accounts are updated immediately.

Some examples of on-line transaction processing include ATM transactions, on-line student registration for classes, and electronic order tracking. Travel agent flight reservation systems are another example of on-line systems that process data as soon as they are input. A travel agent checks for seat availability using the data in a central computer system and immediately notifies the customer about the status of the ticket. Once the reservation is made, the airline system immediately updates the files and sends the travel agent a confirmation. On-line processing is possible because of networks—such as LAN, MAN, and WAN—and different kinds of databases, including distributed databases. Today, many on-line transactions are also taking place over the Internet.

Batch processing

Transactions are accumulated over a certain period of time and processed at periodic intervals.

Batch processing may be done on a daily, weekly, or monthly basis or any other regular time interval that is appropriate for the application. NetBanking may batch process customer bank statements once a month showing all transactions for that month, although each transaction was processed immediately. A computer retailer may process the travel expenses of its employees on a monthly basis and process sales at the end of each day. Once the transactions are processed, the master file, which is a permanent record of all transactions, is updated. A company's master file of travel expenses will show the total travel expenses incurred by the company over the past 12 months or any other period the company chooses.

Until the early 1960s, batch processing was the *only* method available for processing data. It continues to be a popular method because for some applications it is the most sensible, practical approach. Payroll, for instance, lends itself well to batch processing because a paycheck is generated only periodically. Without batch processing, the company would have to pay the employee at the end of every minute the employee works! Clearly, this is impractical. Batch processing results in a more efficient, effective use of computer resources in the payroll system so that payrolls are processed periodically instead of constantly.

Batch processing has some disadvantages. The key disadvantage is the lag between the time the data are created and the time they are processed. As a result, the information in the files may not be up-to-date. Compare the master file of a batch processing system with the master file of an on-line processing system. In batch processing, the master file is updated only periodically. In an on-line system, the master file is updated continually. Another disadvantage of batch processing is that some errors may be detected only after the entire batch is processed; in on-line processing, errors can be detected right away.

Which type of processing is better? The answer depends on the user's decision-making needs. If a user requires only periodic updates, then batch processing is ideal. However, if a user needs up-to-the-minute information to make decisions, then on-line processing is best. Because the batch-versus-on-line-processing choice depends on the user's needs, various organizations may process the same type of transaction differently.

For example, a small computer retailer may batch process its inventory while another company, say CompUSA, may use on-line processing. This is because a small computer retailer may not sell that many computers in a day so its inventory systems may be easily updated at the end of the day. CompUSA, in contrast, has millions of inventory items and must communicate constantly with the suppliers responsible for maintaining its inventory to avoid running out of items. CompUSA's needs require an up-to-the-minute status of the company's inventory.

Table 10-1 describes the differences between on-line and batch processing. Now let's look at the remaining three steps in processing a transaction.

Data Storage

The next step in the transaction process is to store the processed data. If data are stored improperly, they lose their value and usefulness to decision makers, who may not be able to access the information when needed. Further, improper storage can inhibit pro-

TABLE 10-1	On-line versus Batch Transaction Processing
On-line	Data input device is linked to the transaction processing system, so data are processed as soon as they are generated.
Batch	Data are updated at certain intervals, such as daily, weekly, monthly, and so on.

cessing data in the right manner. For example, batch processing versus on-line processing depends heavily on the type of storage medium.

The kind of processing (batch versus on-line) and the type of storage medium are, to some extent, related. To demonstrate, with batch processing, sequential access of data is normal so magnetic tape is often used to store batch-processed data. With on-line processing, data are often accessed in a nonsequential or random manner, so magnetic disks are frequently required.

Output Generation

Once data are converted into information, it should be given to the decision maker in a useful format, which is often a challenge. Different users need input in different formats at different times. Some NetBanking customers, for instance, may want a detailed printout of their transactions whereas others may simply prefer an e-mail. The importance of the output is critical: If the output isn't useful, people will not use the system to make decisions no matter what its level of sophistication.

Query Support

The last step in processing a transaction is to query or ask the system questions. Query facilities allow users to access information that may be unique to their decision or problem. A NetBanking customer may query to see if her loan was approved; another might query to see if his funds transfer went through successfully.

So what is the secret to successful transaction systems? "Be prepared," says Lori Hiricik, senior VP of technology with Chase Manhattan Bank, which processes more than 1 million transactions a day valued at $3 billion.[7] Trouble with transaction processing

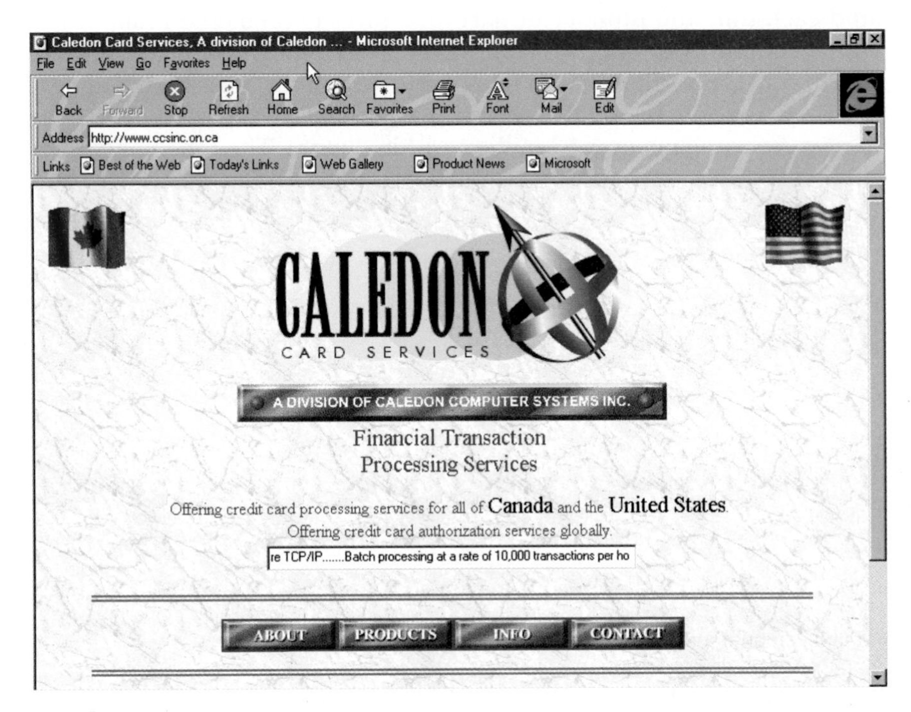

A query allows computer users to obtain specific answers to their questions or queries.

TABLE 10-2

Characteristics of a Transaction Processing System
• Records internal and external transactions that take place in a company
• Is used mostly by lower-level managers to make operational decisions
• Stores data that are frequently accessed by other systems
• Is ideal for routine, repetitive tasks
• Records transactions in batch mode or on-line
• Requires six steps to process a transaction—data entry, validation, data processing, storage, output generation, and query support

systems can spell disaster for decision makers and the entire company, so these systems should be nurtured carefully. Table 10-2 summarizes the characteristics of a transaction processing system.

Management Information Systems for Decision Making

Management information systems (MIS)

A group of general-purpose, well-integrated systems that monitor and control the internal operations of an organization.

Summary report

A report that accumulates data from several transactions and presents the results in a condensed form.

Exception report

A report that outlines any deviations between actual output and expected output.

Management information systems (MIS) provide middle managers with the information necessary to make semistructured decisions. GE Medical Systems, featured in our Global IS for Success segment, shows how an inventory and logistics system can help managers attract new customers and retain existing ones. Usually, the information generated by an MIS helps managers understand the day-to-day operations of the company, such as weekly sales, daily production, and monthly operating expenses. A management information system, then, helps managers implement the tactical goals of the company.

The main input to an MIS is usually the transaction processing system and other internal company sources. **Summary** and **exception reports** are the most common output of a management information system.

For example, a bank manager typically receives a summary report of yesterday's deposits and withdrawals. A sales manager may routinely receive a summary report of products sold last month. A production manager may get a summary report on the total number of products produced last month.

The primary goal of an exception report is to show the difference between actual performance and expected performance. An exception report may list all sales personnel who sold less than $20,000 or more than $80,000 last month. It may be generated each time the number of part-time hires exceeds the number approved by top management. Both summary and exception reports should be succinct, accurate, timely, reliable, verifiable, and in a usable format for decision making.

Kraft Foods has a highly successful MIS that was deployed in 1998 and is expected to save the company over $3 million within 3 years. The food conglomerate, which includes the Kraft, General Foods, and Oscar Mayer brands, handles all information re-

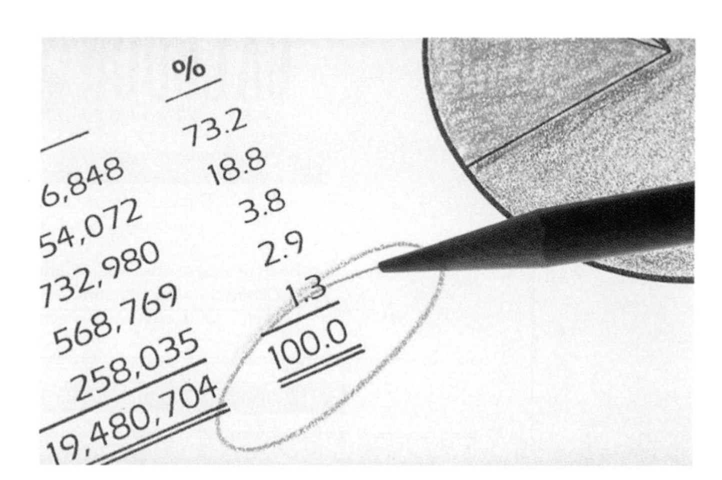

A management report provides managers with timely information to make decisions.

Global IS for success

GE Medical Narrows It Down to Seconds

GE Medical Systems' 5,000 field service representatives phone into its call centers more than 1 million times per year. When ordering new medical equipment parts and checking on the status of orders, they don't want to wait on hold. The company doesn't want them to wait even a few seconds longer than absolutely necessary. "Adding just 30 seconds to 1 million calls translates to an astronomical cost, so response time is critical for our system," explains Ken Accardi, manager of the Global Service Management System division of GE Medical Systems.

GE Medical, a Milwaukee-based division of General Electric Co., makes high-tech diagnostic imaging equipment, including magnetic resonance, digital x-ray, and ultrasound machines for hospitals and clinics around the world.

In 1998 GE Medical invested in an inventory and logistics system to create a global version that keeps precise data about parts close to the parts themselves. The company is replacing its four logistics and inventory systems in North America, Europe, Japan, and Singapore with a new system that will treat its worldwide inventory as a single global asset that can be moved around as needed.

Much of the system uses a client/server module for logistics and inventory control. The system decides which warehouses the parts should come from by linking to three databases in North America, Europe, and Asia. "We didn't feel like a single, distributed database would be robust enough to handle what we want it to do with the speed we need," Accardi says, so each of the three will carry data about all of the parts in that region's physical warehouses.

The system will be able to respond to after-hours emergency calls—routing them to open call centers—but will send the parts orders to the proper region and warehouse. According to Accardi, "The goal of our logistics operation is to deliver any part anywhere in the world within 4 hours, without having lots of parts sitting around on shelves."

Michael Matty, a Wall Street analyst at Capital Reflections in North Granby, Connecticut, believes GE Medical could use the new setup to entice new customers and help retain current ones. Such systems do "tremendous things for users in terms of responsiveness and inventory control" and can help companies differentiate themselves from competition, Matty observes.

QUESTIONS AND PROJECTS

1. What type of a system is an inventory and logistics system? What kind of decisions do you think it supports?
2. How would such a system help to attract new customers and retain existing ones?
3. Identify a local company and study its inventory system. Interview a manager at the company regarding the importance of the system in achieving corporate goals.

Source: Stewart Deck, "GE Part Data Goes Global," *Computerworld*, September 7, 1998, www.computerworld.com.

lated to accounts payable. The new accounts payable system has reduced the cost of paying an invoice from $7 to about $4, productivity has increased by 30 percent, and customer service calls are answered in 3 minutes instead of 15. The system prioritizes invoices and sets rules and decision guidelines for processing the invoices.

"If all the information needed to process an invoice is not there, the system kicks it out as an error, and we are able to reject that invoice back to the requester," says Bernie Kocanda, director of the processing center. The system automatically calculates and adjusts taxes according to a table maintained by the tax department. In the past, tax experts often would be asked to calculate taxes manually.

The system also prints out reports on duplicate invoices, old invoices, and problem invoices. It gives a report on the priority of each invoice and the tax levied. It lets managers know if invoices from certain companies are perpetually on the problem list. It also gives managers a report of invoices that have errors and what errors need to be corrected before the invoice can be paid.[8] These reports give managers pertinent information so they can decide how to correct inaccuracies, plan for taxes, and deal with problem companies.

Kraft relies on timely reports to make good decisions about its products, services, and operations. Its MIS generates the reports.

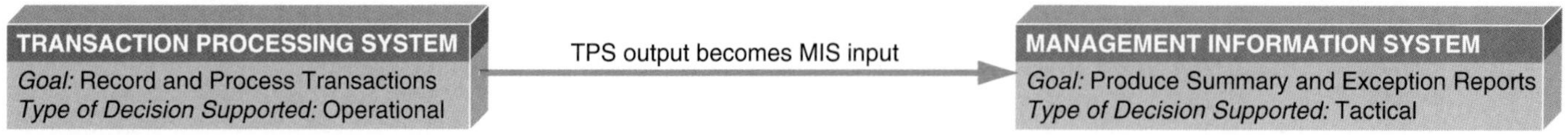

TRANSACTION PROCESSING SYSTEM
Goal: Record and Process Transactions
Type of Decision Supported: Operational

TPS output becomes MIS input

MANAGEMENT INFORMATION SYSTEM
Goal: Produce Summary and Exception Reports
Type of Decision Supported: Tactical

FIGURE 10-3 **Relationship between a TPS and MIS**

TPS and MIS work together to meet the information needs of a business.

Kraft's system generates several types of summary and exception reports. A list of all invoices paid in the past week is an example of a summary report. If the number of rejected invoices far exceeds the average rejection rate, the system will print an exception report to alert managers.

What is the relationship between a transaction processing system and an MIS? Figure 10-3 shows how the two types of systems are intricately linked.

First, the main goal of a transaction processing system is to record and process company transactions, while the main goal of a management information system is to produce summary and exception reports for making tactical decisions. Second, the output of a transaction processing system becomes the input to the MIS, although the transaction processing system is not the only source of data.

Finally, a transaction processing system typically helps managers with operational decisions—decisions made day-to-day to operate the business—while a management information system helps managers make tactical decisions over a longer period of time, such as a year or more. However, both systems must work in harmony to meet the company's information needs.

Intelligent Support Systems

Top managers can make high salaries and earn big rewards if they consistently make sound strategic decisions that strengthen the market position of their companies. To make such decisions, managers must assess a large volume of information and combine it with intuition, judgment, and foresight.

Managers who make complex, long-term decisions need systems that can augment their intelligence and expertise. Such systems are called intelligent support systems (ISS). Here are three types of ISS systems:

- decision support systems (DSS)
- executive information systems (EIS)
- artificial intelligence and expert systems (ES)

Intelligent support systems evolved in the late 1970s and early 1980s for several reasons. First, mid- and top-level managers faced stiff global competition and customer demands for high quality at low cost. Their information needs became more complex as a result, often forcing decision makers to deal with a huge volume of data. The MIS summary and exception reports weren't enough to support highly complicated decisions.

Second, computer costs declined, making it easier for companies to invest in automation. Third, more computer-literate users began to expect more from their information systems departments. These changes led to the development of the three types of intelligent support systems that we investigate next.

Decision Support Systems

Decision support systems (DSS)

A set of interactive software programs that provide managers with data, tools, and models to make semistructured decisions.

Managers who spend time finding answers to "what" rather than "why" questions do not spend their time wisely. Computers are excellent at computations (answers to the "what" question). In contrast, people are excellent at applying intuition and judgment to solve problems (answering the "why" question). A **decision support system (DSS)** uses computer computations and siphons them into models that systematize decision processes. Figure 10-4 depicts a simple version of a decision-making model.

A model is a physical or conceptual representation of reality. Most decision makers use conceptual models to support decision making. Some examples include the for-

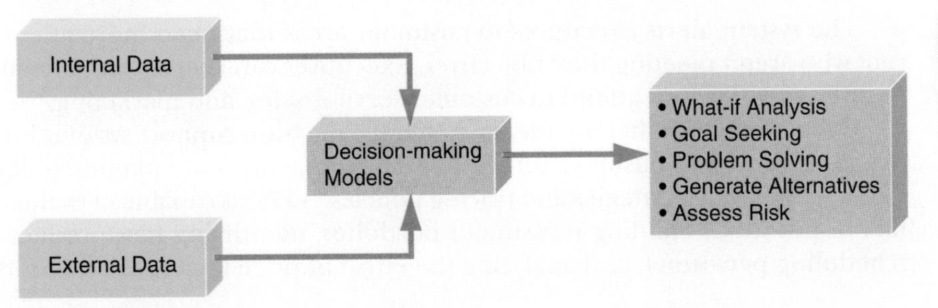

FIGURE 10-4

A Simple Decision-making Model

mula used to calculate interest on a student loan and the method a professor uses to calculate your overall grade in a course. The guidelines that a company uses to decide how many part-time employees to hire during the holiday season are also a model. Some activities that a DSS can perform are selecting the best loan package to meet your needs, identifying an ideal location for a store, and predicting staffing needs.

Preparing a bid is a semistructured task that involves some structured, routine activities (such as assessing the cost of a certain product) and some unstructured activities (such as estimating the competition). The decision maker must consider both internal and external data. Internal data include items such as the cost of raw materials, the number of people required for the job, and the time needed to finish the job. External data may include state and federal taxes, regulatory requirements, and so on. These internal and external data are mostly the "what" part of the problem.

Next, the data are integrated with different decision models, such as financial, accounting, and production models, to arrive at a bid price. This "why" part of the problem may look at issues such as "Why did we lose the last contract?" and "Why would a customer pay a higher cost to do business with our company?" These kinds of questions help managers use their expertise and judgment to solve a problem.

Let's begin by looking at a real-world example of DSS. Dr. Pepper uses a DSS to help sales representatives answer a number of "what if" questions. Dr. Pepper originally hailed itself as "the most misunderstood soft drink," and then in the 1970s became "the most original soft drink ever." Diet Dr. Pepper, reformulated in 1991, is the number-one-selling diet noncola in the United States.

Top management at Dr. Pepper recently issued a directive stating that the salesforce should spend 80 percent of their time with the customer. The company designed a DSS to minimize unproductive paperwork and help the sales representative ("sales rep") provide better customer service.

Here is how the DSS works. Sales reps use their laptop computers to log onto the system to download the customer's sales data, including sales volume over the past 2 to 3 months. The data are color-coded to identify trends and to alert salespeople to potential issues, such as declining sales. The sales rep can also customize the data to answer any specific questions that the customer may have. The system then automatically creates a text and graphical presentation that shows how the customer's company is doing compared to other companies in the region.

This information shows "what" the situation is in the region so that the salesperson can assess "why" the situation occurred. The customer and sales rep can then create a business plan to help the customer be more successful based on this analysis. The DSS has helped sales reps play a key role in their customers' success, which in turn helps to build a large and loyal following of customers.

The DSS has other significant cost and time benefits. For example, before the company installed the system, creating a sales presentation took 3 to 10 days. Today, completing a new presentation takes less than 1 business day. Office support personnel have eliminated many hours of report printing, sorting, envelope stuffing, and mailing. The system also allows sales reps to manage their accounts effectively, track orders, find contact information, assess the number of sales calls made to each contact, and print out a discussion summary. Field personnel no longer need to carry around multiple three-ring binders containing sales information. All material resides in the system.

The system alerts executives to customer areas that need more attention or sales reps who aren't meeting their objectives. Executives can keep a close eye on business to ensure that sales reps attend to customer service, sales, and marketing.[9]

Other problems that are ideally suited for decision support systems include selecting a location for a business, forecasting demand, corporate planning, developing effective advertising strategies and pricing policies. A DSS is capable of evaluating the best mix of products, building investment portfolios, identifying new products to market, scheduling personnel, and analyzing the effect of price increases on profits.

Components of a Decision Support System

How does a DSS work? Three main components in a DSS work together to solve a problem:

1. A **database management system (DBMS)**
2. A **model management system**
3. **Support tools**

Database management system (DBMS)
A piece of software that controls, manages, and maintains internal and external data.

Model management system
A system that stores and processes the models that managers use to make decisions.

Support tools
Tools that help users to interact and interface with a decision support system.

A DSS has five main characteristics. First, this type of system integrates data and models so that it is easier for managers to make good decisions. Second, a DSS helps managers see how decisions interrelate and the effects of one decision on others. Third, it supports a wide variety of decision-making styles. Fourth, it helps managers make decisions under dynamic or changing business conditions. Finally, a DSS allows users to query the system for specific answers.

In the next section we examine the key features of a decision support system.

Features of a Decision Support System

A DSS has three features that are extremely useful to managers: what-if analysis, goal-seeking capabilities, and risk analysis. A manager can do "what-if" analysis to study what effect changes have on a problem. For instance, product pricing is a complex decision. Decision makers must consider many internal items, including material, production, and labor costs, and external items such as competitors' prices and product demand. A DSS can help a manager answer "what-if" questions such as, What if the price of raw materials increases by 3.6 percent in a year? What if demand for the product increases by 10 percent? What if a competitor reduces price for a similar product by 20 percent?

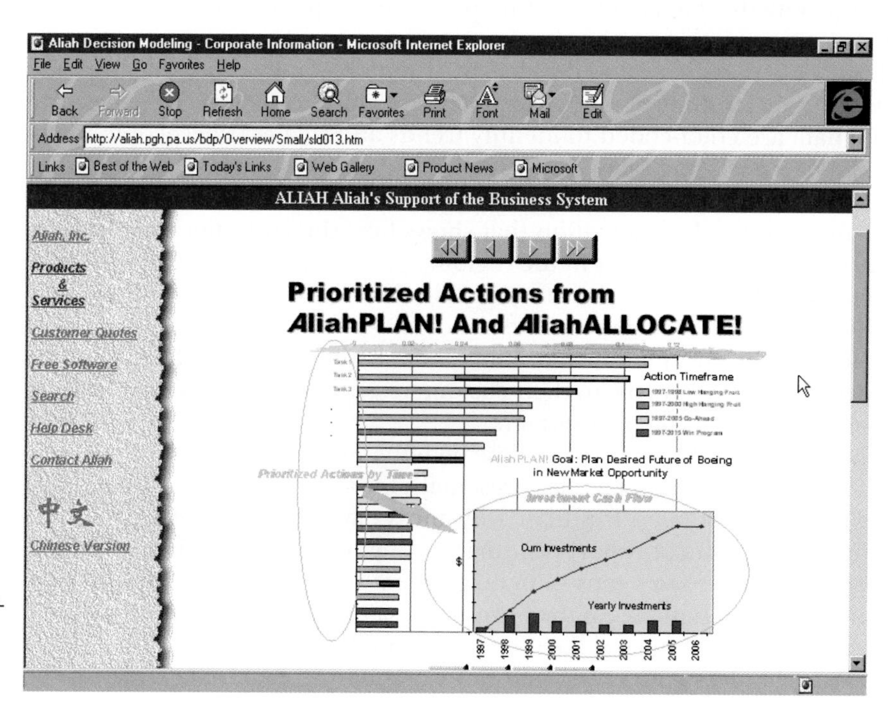

A DSS allows managers to incorporate models, intuition, and judgment into the decision-making process.

The DSS at Dr. Pepper helps sales representatives answer questions such as What happens if Pepsi offers 10 percent more price discount than Dr. Pepper? or What happens if Billy Joel's rock concert is not held in this region?

Goal-seeking capability is another feature that helps managers determine what they should do to achieve a certain goal. Suppose the company's goal is to increase sales of its top-selling product by 10 percent. A DSS can show different ways to achieve that goal. A sales rep at Dr. Pepper can determine how many units to sell at what price in order to achieve a 10 percent profit. A student can use a DSS to determine what grade she must make on the final exam to make an "A" in the course.

A DSS can also help managers calculate the risk associated with different alternatives, a process often referred to as risk analysis. Based on the decision maker's preference for risk (for instance, some decision makers may be willing to take high risks whereas others may be averse to taking risks), a DSS calculates the risk associated with each alternative.

We know that a DSS brings together data and models to make decisions. The database gathers, processes, and manages the data in the DSS while the model management system selects and manages a wide variety of models used to make decisions. Decision makers can use models to design manufacturing facilities, analyze the financial health of an organization, forecast product demand, and so on. Models can be quantitative (financial) or qualitative (self-motivational). A DSS selects the right model and then uses the data in the model to arrive at solutions.

Finally, support tools consist of features, such as pull-down menus, on-line help, graphics, and other features that make the system easy to use. The better the support tool, the greater the chance that users will accept and use the system.

Decision Models

Many different types of decision support models exist. In this section we highlight several common types of models.

Statistical Models

Statistical models are used to perform a wide range of statistical functions, such as average, standard deviation, graphical analysis, regression analysis, analysis of variance, and exploring.

Financial and Accounting Models

Financial models allow decision makers to measure and assess the financial implications of different alternatives. These include, but are not limited to, profit-and-loss analysis, cost-benefit analysis, investment analysis, and capital budgeting models.

Production Models

Production models are mostly used on the shop floor to make manufacturing-related decisions. They aid decisions such as estimating the number of machines to operate, amount of materials required to meet predetermined demands, scheduling, logistics, and evaluating the impact of different inventory policies.

Marketing Models

Marketing models help marketing managers make a wide variety of decisions. Marketing models help managers with decisions concerning product pricing, store location, and advertising strategies, to name a few.

Human Resource Models

Human resource models help managers make decisions that involve company personnel. Some examples of human resource models include personnel planning, benefits analysis, assessing training needs, skills inventory, estimating future personnel needs, labor negotiations, evaluating hiring and firing policies, and assessing the implementation of government rules and regulations.

Group decision support systems (GDSS)

Computer-based systems that enhance group decision making and improve the flow of information among group members.

Group Decision Support Systems

A **group decision support system (GDSS)** is a special type of DSS that is widely used in group decision making. It allows people separated by time and space to interact with each other in an efficient and meaningful way.

Group decision making is quite different from individual decision making. In group settings, it is important for people to feel that their inputs are valued. Further, the inputs from different individuals must be carefully analyzed before a decision is made. Negotiation is also an important part of group decision making. The ability to understand another person's point of view helps teams succeed.

Also, different individuals bring different decision-making styles to the table. For example, some people need all the facts before they can make a decision. Others tend to rely more on their intuition and judgment rather than rely solely on facts. Finally, in group decision making, the team leader weighs different alternative solutions to a given problem and helps the team arrive at a conclusion. Group decision making can quickly become complex, so managers look for system support in these situations.

GDSS is special software that is loaded on a set of computers that are networked together. This network allows all people linked to the GDSS to see and respond to the input of others. A facilitator is someone who helps the group remain focused on the task at hand and work toward achieving the group goal. He may encourage members to listen carefully, summarize key points that members made, and help arrive at compromises where necessary. A facilitator can help enhance communications between groups and among group members. Your instructor plays the role of a facilitator on class group projects.

Here are some key GDSS features:

- Electronic questionnaires—questionnaires that people fill out on their computers rather than on paper
- Electronic brainstorming tools—tools that allow people to express, share, and analyze ideas anonymously using their computers
- Idea organizers—tools that allow groups to coordinate, compile, and prioritize
- Voting tools—tools that allow people to vote for an idea from a set of choices

A group decision support system has several advantages. It fosters an environment conducive to decision making. In one case, an organization had to suddenly initiate Chapter 11 bankruptcy proceedings and was concerned that the proceedings would adversely affect the company's stock price. Managers used groupware (GDSS software) to generate ideas to address this critical situation. "Within 10 minutes, we had 47 excellent ideas. By the end of the hour, we had discussed them, voted on them, ranked them in order of priority, and walked out with printed documentation in hand."[10]

Networked computers loaded with GDSS software allow decision makers to talk and respond to each other on screen.

First, managers were able to address a complex problem quickly because the system encouraged a free flow of ideas in a setting in which the players were anonymous. Second, unlike traditional meetings where talkative or politically powerful people can dominate the shy and the introverted, a GDSS provides equal opportunity for all group members. Third, because users can give feedback anonymously, participants can be open, creative, and innovative without fear of being judged or penalized. This anonymity is particularly critical when addressing problems that are of a sensitive nature, such as sexual discrimination cases.

The Ethics feature discusses a situation that is ideal for a group decision support system. In this particular case, the issue is should single working women be expected to travel more than their married counterparts? This issue is a sensitive one, and individuals may be reluctant to voice their opinion. A GDSS provides opportunities for individuals to voice their opinions (anonymously, if they so desire) and a skilled facilitator can help individuals to arrive at a consensus.

Executive Information Systems

Top managers do not have the time to study and analyze large volumes of data. Instead they need an information system that will analyze the data and present it in an easy and elegant manner so that they can make quick and effective decisions. The system that delivers high-level information in a friendly way is called an **executive information system (EIS).** An EIS consists of a set of tools and techniques, such as color graphics, touch screens, voice-activated commands, and natural language interfaces that help managers to retrieve, analyze, navigate, summarize, and distribute large volumes of data quickly and efficiently.

Executive information system (EIS)
Software that analyzes and presents information to executive decision makers in a useful, friendly, and customized format.

Ethics for success

Would a GDSS Ease This Conflict?

"Why should I get assigned more travel and more special projects simply because I'm single and don't have any kids?" The question startled and stopped the room, touching off a woman-versus-woman debate in an otherwise unabashed female bonding session. The query was met with a sense of astonishment. A second woman said bluntly that it made sense to assign more travel and special projects that required work on nights and weekends to single and childless women and men because kids were much more important than anything else. "What do you have to do that's more important?' she challenged.

"My horse," the first woman responded.

"Oh, yeah, like your horse is really going to miss you if you don't show up one day," the second woman said.

"As a matter of fact, he would. Since I show [him] he will miss our workouts. Otherwise we'd both be out of shape and risk possible injury. I'm single by choice, and why should I be penalized for that?"

Kristin Marks, vice president of Networks Are Our Lives, an information management consulting firm in Sherman, Connecticut, said she got a lot of extra projects shoved at her when she was single and just starting out as an IS manager. "My bosses just naturally assumed I had free time to spare because of my single status—nights, weekends, holidays—and that they could call me to fill in at a moment's notice," Marks recalls. But as she gained more experience, she has protested against such an attitude. "[I]f you're single, you have to state your case up front and push back when necessary. Being single doesn't mean being second class; there are plenty of IS jobs to be had."

YOU DECIDE

1. Outline why and how a GDSS could help improve a group discussion and decision process on this issue.
2. Should single women be given a greater workload than married women?
3. If you were an IS manager, how would you handle the complaint of an employee that she is being burdened with more work because of her marital status?

Source: Laura DiDio, "Singled Out," *Computerworld,* March 23, 1998, 74.

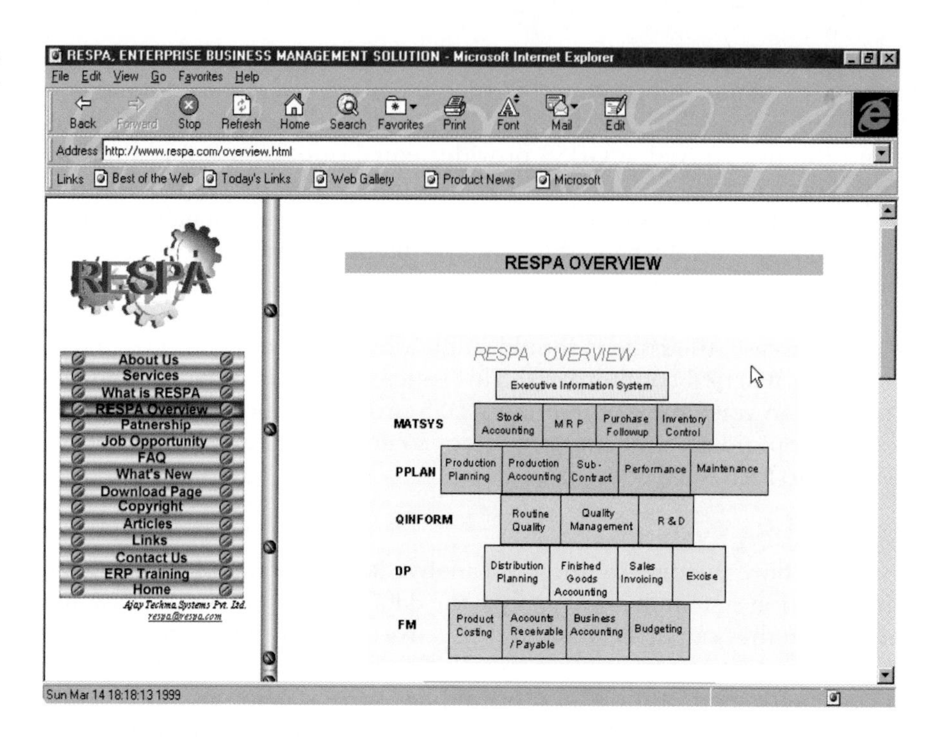

The output of an EIS helps top managers make executive decisions. Information is presented in a concise and comprehensive way.

The primary difference between an EIS and a DSS is that an EIS is used to deliver and display information (information delivery), whereas a DSS is more appropriate for analyzing a problem (problem solving). In fact, today, many systems are a combination of both DSS and EIS; such systems are called executive support systems. The system Dr. Pepper uses is an example of an executive support system.

Drill-down

A system's ability to provide information at the level of detail that the decision maker demands.

An EIS has many of the same features that a DSS has, as well as other special features, such as **drill-down**, which allows employees to obtain summary or detailed data with a few simple keystrokes. The Dr. Pepper system allows sales reps to drill down through the system and get very detailed information about a customer. It also allows a sales manager to view data by region, sales representative, product, and so on, at any level of detail that he or she desires.

EIS business and government applications abound. A few years ago top officials at the U.S. Air Force had to analyze massive amounts of data to decide which air bases to close. The Air Force selected an EIS with excellent graphic and drill-down capabilities, which allowed decision makers to see quickly what needed to be done, saving the Air Force time and money.

Banks and other financial institutions, in particular, are enthusiastic users of EIS. Experts estimate that more than one third of the discretionary technology budgets of banks go toward systems that improve decision making. In fact, EIS is considered such an important technology that some universities in the United States and other countries devote a considerable amount of their research dollars to EIS. The University of Texas at Austin and the Massachusetts Institute of Technology are highly regarded DSS and EIS research centers.[11] Table 10-3 summarizes the characteristics of a DSS and EIS.

Artificial Intelligence and Expert Systems

A company's greatest asset is its people and the knowledge and skills they bring to the workplace. Because knowledge is such a valuable asset, organizations try to capture and preserve that knowledge for the future. This process is referred to as knowledge management, which is covered in detail in Chapter 13. Expert systems—which are a part of the field of artificial intelligence—can help organizations achieve this goal.

Artificial intelligence (AI)

A field of computer science that studies the design and development of computer systems that mimic human intelligence.

The phrase **artificial intelligence (AI)** was first coined by MIT Professor John McCarthy at a 1956 conference that laid the foundation for this field of study. Since those early beginnings, artificial intelligence has grown in scope. Although the word *intelligence* is used frequently in our everyday language, there is no single, universally accepted definition of what it means. Instead, intelligence is best defined as a set of characteristics

TABLE 10-3

DSS and EIS Characteristics

DSS and EIS provide middle and top managers with decision support.

Both DSS and EIS are intuitive, interactive, user-friendly systems.

DSS and EIS are menu-driven and often have excellent color and graphic capabilities.

Both systems use internal and external data to solve problems. Managers at this level tend to rely more on external data than on internal data.

A DSS uses internal and external data and different decision-making models to provide managers with alternatives to a given problem. An EIS provides managers with expert information in the form of analysis and reports.

Both systems are equipped with decision-making tools such as "what-if" analysis and "goal seeking." In addition to these tools, an EIS is equipped with drill-down capabilities.

A DSS can support both individual and group decision making. DSS that support group decision making are known as group decision support systems (GDSS).

or attributes, some of which are outlined in Table 10-4. Artificial intelligence is the study of those attributes.

Artificial intelligence includes several areas of specialization, such as:

- Computer vision—the computer's ability to recognize and identify objects
- Speech recognition—the computer's ability understand a human voice
- Natural language—the ability to communicate with a computer the way humans communicate with each other
- Neural networks—pattern-recognition programs
- Robots—machines capable of human-like movements

One of the most developed fields of artificial intelligence is expert systems, which we examine next. Then we explore one other AI field, neural networks.

Expert Systems

Knowledge appears in different forms in an organization such as an innovative idea for a product, a new way to motivate employees, a new production method, a longer-lasting product, a better way to deliver a service, and so on. The main goal of an **expert system (ES)** is to capture the knowledge of experts in all forms and use that knowledge to solve complex problems for an organization. Expert systems, then, are versatile and can help with many kinds of problems.

Expert systems (ES)

Computer programs that capture the knowledge of a human expert and use it to solve complex problems.

TABLE 10-4

Attributes of Intelligence

Intelligence attributes include the ability to

- think, process, reason, and solve complex problems
- use knowledge, intuition, judgment, and rules of thumb to solve problems
- quickly and efficiently identify all possible solutions to a problem and narrow the array of solutions to a few good alternatives that have a high probability of success
- reason using conflicting, inaccurate, or uncertain information
- learn from experience and modify one's behavior accordingly
- distinguish the trivial from the important when dealing with complex situations

TABLE 10-5

Questions to Answer to Determine Whether Expert Systems Are Appropriate

1. Is expertise in the given area rare and expensive?
2. Is the knowledge that is to be modeled likely to be inconsistent and incomplete?
3. Does the problem-solving process involve intuition, judgment, and trial-and-error methods?
4. Is it possible to state precisely what the system should do?
5. Can the organization benefit significantly if this knowledge is captured and disseminated?
6. Is top management committed to solving this problem?

How does a manager know if a problem can be solved using expert systems? If the answer to most of the questions in Table 10-5 is "yes," then the problem is suitable for expert systems.

Components of an Expert System

How does an expert system capture and apply the knowledge of a human expert? It does so by joining three main components: (1) a **knowledge base,** (2) an **inference engine**, and (3) a user interface. Figure 10-5 shows these components.

Knowledge base

A computer storehouse of knowledge that experts use to solve difficult problems.

A knowledge base consists of facts, theorems, principles, rules, and rules of thumb that experts use to solve a given problem. The information in the knowledge base comes from many sources such as the human experts themselves, books, journals, databases, and electronic media. Managers can also gain knowledge through observation, formal and informal interviews, and questionnaires.

Knowledge acquisition

The process of acquiring knowledge from different sources.

Knowledge acquisition is extremely challenging and time-consuming because experts often have difficulty articulating their knowledge. Explaining *what* knowledge to use and *why* to use that knowledge is not always easy. Because of this difficulty, knowledge acquisition is often viewed as a bottleneck in building expert systems. Figure 10-6 illustrates the different sources of knowledge represented in a knowledge base.

Knowledge representation

The process of representing the knowledge of experts in a language that the computer can understand.

How do we represent the expert's knowledge in a computer system? The process of representing the expert's knowledge in a computer system is called **knowledge representation.** There are different approaches to knowledge representation. One of the most popular ways of representing knowledge is using IF-THEN rules. IF-THEN rules work as follows: IF a certain condition(s) is true, THEN the system will perform a set of actions. Expert systems that use IF-THEN rules are called rule-based systems. Examples of IF-THEN rules follow:

Rule 1

IF	a student's overall grade is greater than 89 percent, AND the student has actively participated in class
THEN	the overall class grade is "A."

Rule 2

IF	car lights were left on, AND car does not start
THEN	the battery is dead (say, 99 percent likelihood).

Inference engine

Software that reasons with the knowledge in an expert system to determine when, how, and what knowledge to apply to solve a given problem.

Once the expert system captures the expert's knowledge in the knowledge base, the second component, a piece of software called the **inference engine,** helps the sys-

FIGURE 10-5

The Three Components of an Expert System

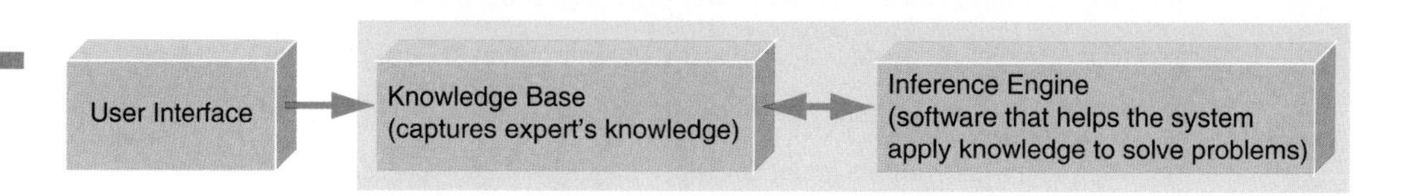

The Different Sources of Knowledge Represented in a Knowledge Base

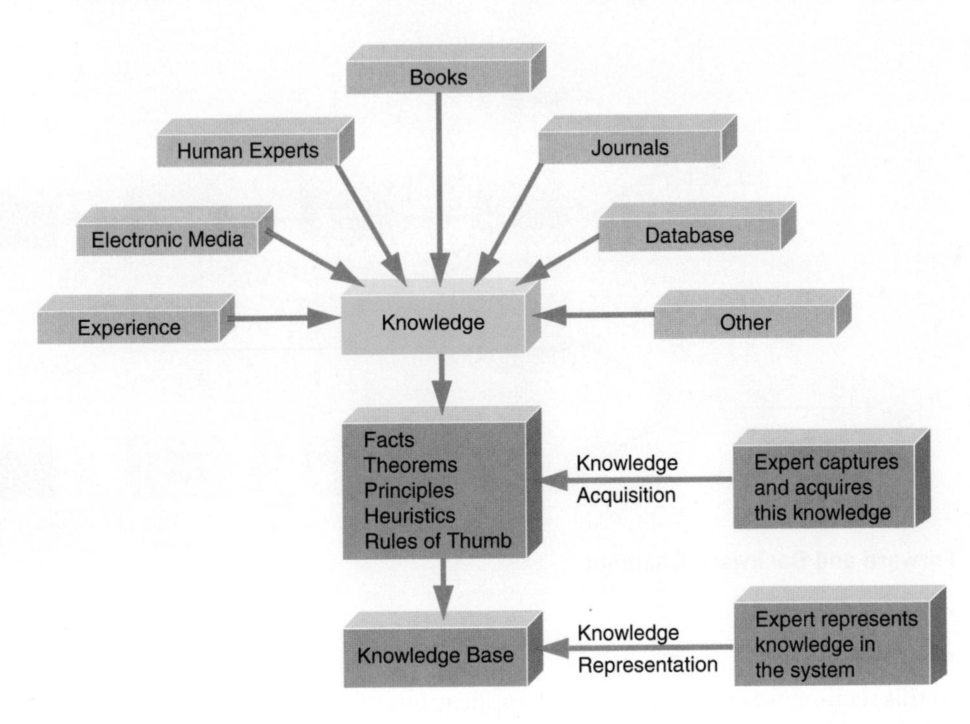

tem apply this knowledge. The inference engine is similar to the reasoning capabilities of the human brain. Two popular reasoning processes that an expert system uses are forward chaining and backward chaining.

In forward chaining, the system begins with a set of known facts (data or initial conditions about a given problem), analyzes the data, and looks for solutions that match the data set. If a match is found, the system executes the actions given in the THEN part of the rule.

Consider the rule

IF number of hours worked by part-time employee is greater than 20 OR
number of hours worked by full-time employee is greater than 40
THEN Overtime Rates = "Yes."

If Tom, a part-time employee, worked 23 hours, the system uses these data to pay Tom overtime.

In backward chaining, the inference engine begins with a goal and searches for data, facts, and other evidence that support this goal. Note that we use the word "goal" loosely in this context. For instance, suppose we begin with the goal that "car does not start." The system then searches for a rule whose THEN part indicates "car will not start," and then looks for evidence that supports this hypothesis such as a bad engine, weak battery, or the like. The rule may state:

IF battery = "dead"
THEN car = "does not start."

Figure 10-7 shows the differences between forward and backward chaining.

Which reasoning method is better than the other depends completely on the nature of the problem to be solved. In fact, most systems use both forward and backward chaining. This combination approach is known as mixed chaining.

Expert systems have a third component that combines the knowledge base and the inference engine in a way that makes it easy for the user to interact with the system. That component is the user interface, a piece of software that includes menus, graphics, touch screens, help functions, and other features that make an expert system easy and friendly to use. An explanation module is another feature in a user interface that helps the system answer questions such as How was the solution reached? Why were certain alternatives rejected? and What pieces of knowledge helped solve the problem?

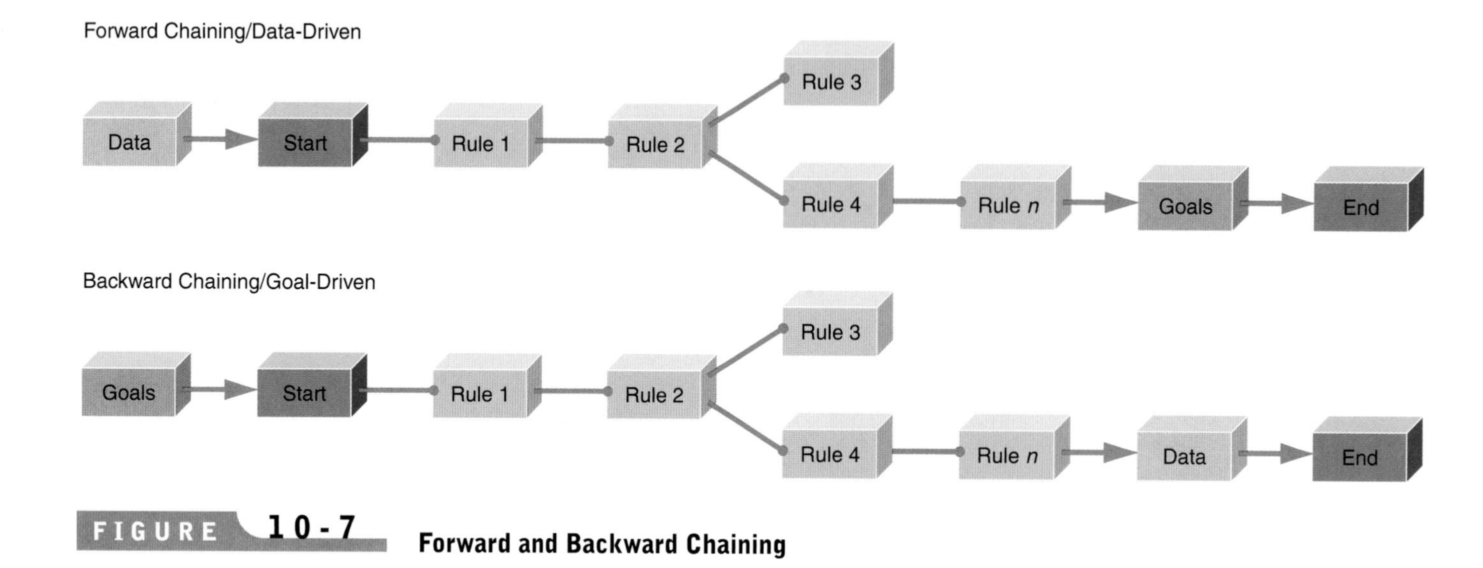

FIGURE 10-7 **Forward and Backward Chaining**

Examples of Expert Systems

In this section, we examine different applications of expert systems: product design, systems configuration, management, and government security. These four examples illustrate the range and versatility of expert systems to aid in strategic business decision making. As indicated earlier, expert systems are ideal for applications in which decision makers need expert knowledge and intuition to solve a problem. In all the examples shown, capturing the expertise helps the organization to increase productivity and serve customers better.

To aid product design decisions, coordinating knowledge from various information sources is challenging. As companies become global, however, this task becomes more difficult, but the payoff can be tremendous. Ford Motor Company in Dearborn, Michigan, coordinates the design knowledge for circuit boards from electrical engineers from seven manufacturing plants around the world. Knowledge coordination—as opposed to keeping design knowledge from one plant separate from another—reduced design revisions from 55 percent to fewer than 5 percent.

An expert system may also configure computers to satisfy users. Configuring implies that a computer is customized to match unique customer needs (memory, RAM, speed, and so on). This complex task requires in-depth knowledge about computers, their design and functioning, configuration mechanisms, and problem-solving techniques. Digital Equipment Corporation captured the knowledge, experience, and intuition of hundreds of Digital computer technicians and engineers in an expert system designed to support systems configuration decisions. The system helped Digital automate the configuration process—which had been highly labor-intensive and error-prone.

Another type of expert system is a business system that manages different business functions, including accounting, quality assurance, and employee scheduling. Mrs. Fields, headquartered in Park City, Utah, uses expert systems to manage its large chain of stores. Its expert systems do everything from running back-office accounting operations and scheduling part-time and full-time employees to ensuring consistency and quality of the cookies. In fact, Mrs. Fields has been so successful with its expert systems that today it consults and sells expert system products to other companies.

The U.S. Customs Service in Washington, D.C., uses an expert system to monitor all imports for illegal cargo. This system helps managers to allocate their time and money wisely and helps customs inspectors prioritize which shipments to inspect. In addition, the system captures the knowledge of experts who know which projects are critical, why they are critical, and the resources required to complete the inspection successfully.

A novice may underestimate the resources required to complete the inspection or may lack the experience to prioritize shipment inspections efficiently. When the system was initially tested at Newark and Los Angeles, the two largest ports in the United States,

TABLE 10-6

Characteristics of an Expert System

An expert system is a software program that captures the knowledge and problem-solving skills of a human expert.

Expert systems are not targeted at any one level of management.

Expert systems are ideally suited for problems that require knowledge, intuition, and judgment.

Expert systems, unlike DSS and EIS, can replace the decision maker.

The three main components in an expert system are the knowledge base, the inference engine, and the user interface.

the number of seizures and the total number of shipments inspected increased. Eventually, customs plans to deploy the system in every U.S. port.[12]

Table 10-6 summarizes the characteristics of an expert system. Next we analyze neural nets, another field of artificial intelligence.

Neural Networks

To make most decisions intelligently requires the ability to see the link or connection between large, diverse data sets. This ability is sometimes referred to as pattern analysis, which is integral to solving problems in all domains from medicine to warfare to business.

A branch of artificial intelligence that helps with pattern recognition is a **neural network.** The word *neural* comes from the word *neuron,* which is a brain cell that processes information. The word *network,* as used in this phrase, conveys the idea of a cluster of neurons joined together to achieve and recognize a pattern. Neural networks mimic the biology of the human brain by manipulating electronic neurons.

Neural networks
Software programs that mimic the pattern recognition capabilities of the human brain.

The power of neural networks lies in their ability to recognize patterns that the human mind cannot detect. Neural networks have the ability to connect, link, and see patterns even if there are hundreds of variables in a problem. Compare this with human beings who (typically) can study and assimilate the relationships between only three to five variables at a time. Although most computer programs process and digest data in small chunks, a neural network digests and processes large chunks of information, making it easier to recognize patterns.

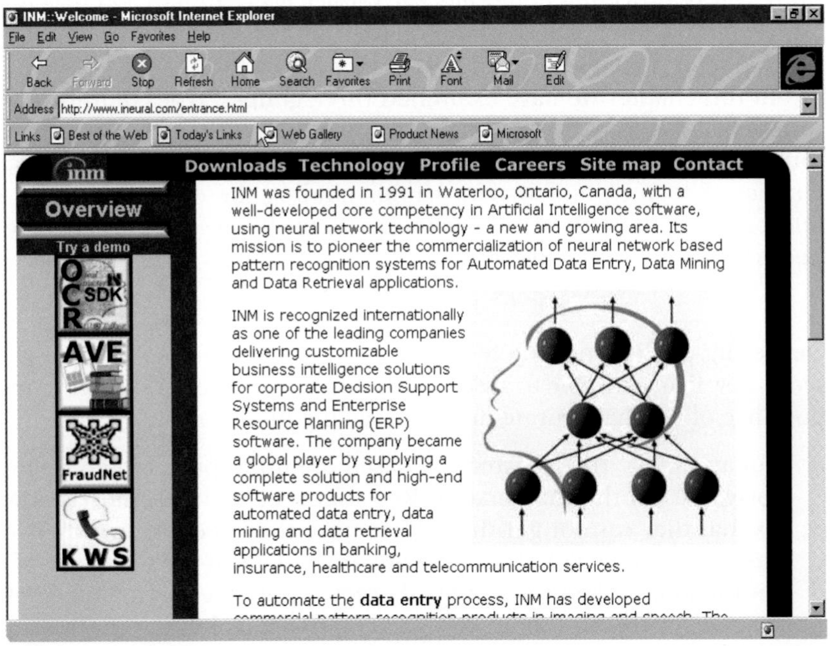

Neural networks such as those used by INM help capture patterns in a sea of data and help decision makers to recognize important issues that may lie hidden in the data.

TABLE 10-7

Characteristics of TPS, MIS, and ISS

System Type	Input	Processing	Output	Users	Examples
TPS	Transaction-related data	Uses procedures and rules Repetitive tasks Control-oriented	Summaries of transactions	Lower-level managers	Sales transactions Credit-card payments Insurance claims
MIS	Output from TPS and other internal data	Measures and monitors operational performance Facilitates tactical decisions	Summary and exception reports	Mid-level managers	Monthly production reports Quarterly travel reports Safety violation reports
ISS (DSS, EIS, ES)	Internal and external data and models Knowledge and experience	Interactive, ad hoc reporting Generates alternatives	Alternative-analysis reports Excellent presentation of information Decision-making information	Top- and mid-level managers ES: Knowledge workers	Investment portfolios Enterprise-wide performance Plant expansion

A good application of neural networks is analyzing customer surveys. Philadelphia-based Pattern Discovery uses neural networks to find what activities affect customers' overall perceptions and preferences in a positive way. As an illustration, Pattern Discovery learned that in a large fast-food company, restroom cleanliness affects diners' perception of overall food quality. When restrooms are clean, people feel better about the restaurant.

At Public Service Gas & Electric Company in Newark, New Jersey, neural networks showed a direct relationship between billing accuracy and how customers rated the reliability of the electric service. "In other words, if you get your billing right, customers think you're providing better electric service even though you haven't spent a cent."[13] Other popular applications of neural networks include fraud detection, financial analysis, character recognition, and text retrieval.

In this chapter we have examined three general types of information systems that support managerial decision making: transaction processing systems, management information systems, and intelligent support systems. Table 10-7 summarizes the characteristics of each type of system. Understanding these characteristics helps managers select and combine these information systems to meet the organization's information needs in the most effective way.

Business Guidelines for TPS, MIS, and ISS Success

Delivering quality and timely information to decision makers is not as easy as it may seem. Few firms are able to accomplish this objective, although they understand the importance of timely, accurate decision-making information.

> Today, in fact, the information-based organization is largely a fantasy. Despite forty years of the Information Revolution in business, most managers still tell us that they cannot get the information they need to run their own units or functions. The CEO of a shoe company put it this way: "On one of my first days on the job, I asked for a copy of every report used in management. The next day, twenty-three of them appeared on my desk. I didn't understand them . . . .

Each area's reports were Greek to the other areas, and all of them were Greek to me. [It was like] each part of the organization had a separate political domain, with its own culture, leaders, and even vocabulary."[14]

Knowledge about different types of systems alone is not enough to build good systems or achieve market success. Information literacy is also essential. If we sift through the best practices of companies that use information systems for decision making, we discover the following guidelines can enhance success.

Get the Commitment of Top Management

One of the most critical factors in the successful adoption of any technology is the commitment of top management. In other words, if the CEO does not understand how systems such as TPS, MIS, and ISS help employees to make better decisions, he or she may not support the technology. Both the chief information officer (CIO) and the chief executive officer (CEO) should understand the core value of information systems and how they help employees to make better decisions. The CIO, once a maintenance manager, is now often a star quarterback who can lead a company in strategic ways. The role of the CIO has changed from an operational one to a strategic one. The CIO, in many companies is in the same league as the CEO and the CFO.

The CIO must convince top management of the link between IS and quality managerial decision making. Once that happens, employees are more likely to understand the power of IS and use information technology to increase their productivity.

The More Integrated the System, the Greater the Benefits

Decisions are not isolated, self-contained entities. Instead, decisions made in one department or by one individual often have a ripple effect throughout the organization. Because companies rely on different information systems to meet different information needs, it is important that systems don't operate as isolated islands. Rather, systems should be well integrated so that different systems can communicate and share information effectively. "You need an application environment that can withstand the velocity of change," says Anne-Lotz Turner, executive director of global technology at the Canadian Imperial Bank of Commerce.[15]

Without integrated systems, decisions will be made in isolation and the net impact will be delayed and often confused decisions. Although most organizations recognize the benefits of integrated systems, this is by no means an easy task.

> Anybody who's ever bought a house knows the frustration of trying to find something that fulfills every domestic requirement. You pay your money, and you compromise. Still, every house hunter dreams of a home with everything—kind of like a CIO with a vision of designing a responsive, innovative IS organization. [And only] the best organizations do it.[16]

Achieving integration may not be easy, but it is certainly one of the most desirable goals for organizations that want their managers to make good decisions consistently.

Benefits Are More than Just Bottom Line

Like any other information system, the cost of any information system depends on factors such as the information needs of managers, the effect of the decision on the organization, the nature and criticality of the application, the number of users, and the hardware and software resources of the organization. The investment in an information system is an ongoing one. "The development of an [information system] can be thought of as an ongoing journey rather than as a destination. The system continues to evolve over time in response to market, industry, and organizational changes that affect executives' information needs."[17]

However, in some cases a simple cost-benefit analysis may not be sufficient to make the investment decision. It is sometimes hard to show the effects of a good decision versus an average decision. Instead, companies may have to ask a two-sided question: Can we afford it, and can we afford not to have it?[18] If some of the great organizations in IS history had focused exclusively on bottom-line results, the world would have missed some great and revolutionary systems. Instead, these organizations recognized the link between these systems and their ability to make better decisions.

This is not to say that investments in IT should not be held accountable to show returns. Paul Strassmann, President of Information Economics Press, emphasizes that IT is not like accounting, which is often not required to justify its budgets or show returns on investments. "Much of IT is an investment with expectations of measurable payoffs and justified accordingly. Accounting is not an investment, but an overhead expense. While information technology is mostly optional, accounting is always mandatory. IT offers economic tradeoffs. Accounting is only an alternative to going to jail."[19]

Business Drives the Choice of Information Systems Technology, Not the Other Way Around

Investing in technology for the sake of technology is a disaster waiting to happen. "Technology is a queer thing. It brings you great gifts with one hand and stabs you in the back with the other," said the late Charles Percy Snow, English writer, physicist, and diplomat. Before a company invests in an information system, it should ask the key question, How is this investment going to help us make better decisions and serve our customers better? IS professionals have the responsibility to maximize the returns from information systems for the overall good of the business.

The sad and startling truth is three out of four IT projects fail to meet the needs of the business. A large reason for this dismal state of affairs is because many IT projects are developed in a vacuum without understanding the real needs of the business stakeholders. "It's surprising how many large companies embark on an IT solution without any concept of its value to the organization," says Patricia Benson, managing director of DCC Technology Management Group, a business unit in Toledo, Ohio.[20]

It is also important to understand the contribution of systems to business goals and objectives. In other words, it is important to answer the question, "What benefits does this system provide to the stakeholder?" Benson tells of a case where she met with top executives from a Fortune 500 company to automate their procurement process. Using a huge wall of Velcro and a handful of placards, she carefully charted out all the steps that had to be implemented to purchase a $50 software upgrade. When she took into account the time and cost for this simple activity, she found that it took 18 days, countless hours of paperwork, and nearly $22,000 in people time to get the product ordered. Automating such a process would have contributed nothing to the business. Quite to the contrary, it would have increased operating expenses.

T Is for Trust

Trust develops when the IS department delivers successful and meaningful IS and IT services that help employees make better decisions and do their jobs better. When there is trust, employees feel that the company is not being judgmental about their decisions, but is instead willing to be a partner and help each employee enhance their decision-making skills. If employees trust, they will risk more to reach the company's goals.

SUMMARY

1. **Explain how different types of information systems help decision makers.** Managers at different levels in an organization make different kinds of decisions, so organizations need different types of systems. The three types of information systems are transaction processing systems, management information systems, and intelligent support systems. The type or types of information systems that an organization uses depend on its information needs. Note, however, that no one system is superior to another, and the different types of systems must be integrated to promote the free flow of information within and outside the organization.

   Transaction processing systems typically support the needs of lower-level managers. Management information systems mainly support the decision-making needs of mid-level managers, whereas intelligent support systems support the decision-making needs of top- and mid-level managers. Operational decisions, typically made by lower-level managers, help to ensure the smooth functioning of a company on an everyday basis. Tactical decisions help companies implement operational decisions to achieve the overall goals of a company.

2. **Outline how transaction processing systems support operational decision making.** Transaction processing systems (TPS) record the transactions that take place in a company. If a company fails to capture information about a transaction it not only may lead to customer dissatisfaction and lost profit but can also lead to serious penalties and lawsuits. Also, the source of most of the information that managers use to make operational decisions originates in the TPS, so we regard these systems as the data lifeline of an organization.
3. **Specify how management information systems help managers make tactical decisions.** Management information systems produce summary and exception reports. Middle managers use these reports to make a wide variety of everyday decisions to monitor and control the internal operations of an organization. The output of a TPS often becomes the input to MIS, so both systems must work together to meet the information needs of lower-level and middle managers.
4. **Discuss how intelligent support systems support mid- and top-level managerial decision making.** Intelligent support systems include decision support systems, executive information systems, and artificial intelligence systems that include expert systems and neural networks. A decision support system integrates internal and external data with decision models to solve semistructured problems. It has several key features such as what-if analysis, goal seeking, and risk analysis. An expert system captures the knowledge and expertise of key individuals in the organization and uses that knowledge to solve complex problems.

    Group decision support systems help the free flow of ideas and information among group members. They also promote an environment conducive to decision making. An executive information system has many of the features of a decision support system and also has a drill-down feature that allows managers to drill down into their systems for specific and detailed information. An expert system is a software program that captures the knowledge of a human expert. The three main components in an expert system are the knowledge base, the inference engine, and the user interface. The knowledge base stores the knowledge, the inference engine processes the knowledge, and the user interface makes it easy to interact with the system. A neural network is a computer program that mimics the neuronal capabilities of the human brain and consists of a network of processors that behave like a neuron. Neural networks are capable of finding patterns that may not be obvious to the human eye.

KEY TERMS

artificial intelligence (p. 280)
batch processing (p. 270)
database management system (DBMS) (p. 276)
decision support systems (DSS) (p. 274)
drill-down (p. 280)
exception report (p. 272)
executive information systems (EIS) (p. 279)
expert systems (ES) (p. 281)
group decision support systems (GDSS) (p. 278)
inference engine (p. 282)
intelligent support systems (p. 267)
knowledge acquisition (p. 282)
knowledge base (p. 282)
knowledge representation (p. 282)
management information system (MIS) (p. 272)
model management system (p. 276)
neural networks (p. 285)
on-line transaction processing (OLTP) (p. 269)
source documents (p. 269)
summary report (p. 272)
support tools (p. 276)
transaction processing systems (TPS) (p. 267)

REVIEW QUESTIONS

1. Identify the system(s) most suitable for structured, semistructured, and unstructured decision making.
2. What are some reasons why companies value their transaction systems?
3. What are the steps in processing a transaction? What is meant by query support?
4. What is the main difference between batch processing and on-line processing? Which method is better?
5. How does a management information system meet the information needs of middle managers?
6. What were some reasons that led to the evolution of intelligent support systems?
7. Describe a decision support system and identify three characteristics.
8. What is a GDSS and how does it aid group decision making?

9. What is an EIS? What are some primary features of EIS?
10. Describe the drill-down function of an EIS, using an example.
11. Review Table 10-7. What are the differences between TPS, MIS, and ISS?
12. What do we mean by intelligence? Describe the field of artificial intelligence.
13. Describe an expert system. Identify some questions to ask to determine whether an expert system will help the business.
14. What are some characteristics of problems that are well suited for expert systems technology? Is tax analysis a good application for expert systems? If so, why?
15. What is the difference between knowledge acquisition and knowledge representation? Why is knowledge acquisition a challenging task?
16. What are the components in a DSS, an EIS, and an expert system? Briefly describe each component.
17. What is a neural network and how does it help in decision making?
18. What are some guidelines for success in using TPS, MIS, and ISS to achieve organizational success?

DISCUSSION QUESTIONS AND EXERCISES

1. Selecting the right software package is a difficult task. Some criteria that can be used to evaluate DSS software include understanding user requirements, evaluating system costs, system friendliness, ease of system maintenance, vendor reputation, and system security from break-ins and theft.[21]

   Based on the information just provided, identify and evaluate any PC-based EIS package. Popular trade journals such as *Computerworld* and *PC World* often do product evaluations on different software. These publications may be a good starting place to find the answer to this question.

2. One of the goals of decision support systems and executive information systems was to reduce, if not eliminate, the use of paper reports. But this is not an easy thing to achieve because people are so used to paper reports and have a burning desire to receive a hard copy of all key information. At PCS Health Systems in Scottsdale, Arizona, David Thompson, vice-president of Internet development, has the tough job of phasing out the printing of four million pages of Cobol-based reports every month. PCS, the largest organization of its kind, manages the prescription drug benefit programs for health insurers and HMOs serving more than 56 million Americans. Thompson is now face with the considerable challenge of what he calls "weaning people off the desire to see paper."[22]

   a. What are some steps that you would take as a CIO to wean people from paper?

   b. How can a DSS and EIS help in this cause? Discuss.

3. Carl DiePietro, a consultant specializing in computer-assisted meetings, indicates that one of the strengths of groupware is its ability to avoid what is called the "Abilene paradox." He explains the paradox as follows:

   A Texas family gathers one Sunday morning to decide what to do for the day. No one has any ideas—or if they do, they are afraid to speak up. Finally, the patriarch of the family suggests going to Abilene, which is 100 miles away, on this hottest day of a Texas summer. Everyone agrees, with relief, and they take a long, hot, joyless trip there and back. At the end of the day it turns out that no one wanted to go to Abilene, not even the person who suggested it. But everyone just fell in line with the suggestion. We make decisions based on other people's behaviors rather than based on our own ideas or beliefs.[23]

   How can a GDSS help organizations avoid the Abilene paradox?

4. As discussed in Chapter 2, Inacom, an Omaha-based technology management services company, snares hot talent by enticing techies to play "Techno Challenge," a high-tech assessment tool disguised as a game, on its Web site (www.inacom.com). The game has three levels of difficulty; players who get to the third level are entered into a quarterly drawing for a $1,500 gift certificate. And their names and contact information are forwarded to recruiting. "We get a list of people who get to the third level—and those are the ones we want to call right away," says Eva Fujan, vice president of technical recruiting.

   More than 3,000 people have played the game since it went on-line. Of those, a couple of hundred have hit the third level, Fujan says. She doesn't know how many have been hired because of the game, but 80 to 90 percent of third-level players have been interviewed.

   The game is also used to prequalify information technology candidates who use traditional channels. "If we're interviewing for 20 systems engineers, we can say, 'Play the game first, and see how you did

[sic],' " Fujan says. The game is part of the company's new approach to recruiting, called Inacom World Tour, designed to appeal to young techies. Inacom sets up the game at recruitment fairs, where potential candidates are urged to test their skills. The company also distributes "game tickets" that look like tickets to a rock concert, urging people to play.

World Tour is the brainchild of Fujan, who took over recruiting for Inacom 2 years ago after 12 years in sales and marketing. "I took a sales and marketing focus," she says. "I watched my son, who is 15, playing CD-ROM games, thinking, 'This is the way you should do these things. Make it fun.' "[24]

a. How would such a system help recruiting managers make better decisions?

b. Would you classify recruitment as an operational, tactical, or strategic decision. Why?

c. What type of a system is this and why? What are some key features of this system?

CRITICAL THINKING • Cases for Success

Case 1: Whirlpool Sets a Swirl on Prices

Imagine having to change the prices on hundreds of items and models each time your competitor made a price change. That was what the world-renowned Whirlpool Corporation, an $8.6 billion manufacturer of stoves, dishwashers, and other appliances, had to do each time its competitors, such as Maytag, changed their prices. The company relied on a flurry of faxes and notes sent by overnight courier to respond quickly to competitors' price changes. Today, Whirlpool can respond to market changes and competitors' moves with a few keystrokes, thanks to a sophisticated product pricing system.

The computerized pricing system cut by more than half the 110 days it took each quarter to reprice its entire product line of 2,000 or more models and be more competitive in the marketplace. "The new system will make it easier to do business with Whirlpool," says Bill Hester, a senior information systems project manager at Whirlpool. Before the system was installed, customers would be quoted one price while their invoices showed a different price. "It creates dissatisfied customers," says Kathleen Descamps, business project manager for the company. Today the same price information is reflected everywhere and sales agents can quickly match a competitor's price. This price matching helps Whirlpool win customers in a rapidly changing market.

Bruce Richardson, an industry analyst, says, "People in manufacturing are starting to realize that pricing is everything. You want to do real-time pricing so you can align the street price of a product with the actual amount it cost you to make a product."

1. What type of a system is the pricing system at Whirlpool? What kind of decisions would this system support?
2. **(Software exercise)** Create a spreadsheet with five appliance models (such as a top-of-the-line dishwasher, mid-to-high-quality dishwasher, a midlevel-quality dishwasher, and so on). Against each model, list the price of the product for Whirlpool, Maytag, Kenmore, and Amana. See the following example chart.

Models	Whirlpool	Maytag	Kenmore	Amana
Model A	$650	$750	$615	$725
Model B	$580	$500	$525	$630
Model C	$890	$800	$925	$875
Model D	$750	$790	$700	$650
Model E	$575	$550	$600	$590

Next quarter, Maytag, Kenmore, and Amana make the following changes to the prices:

Models	Maytag	Kenmore	Amana
Model A	3.5%	-2%	1%
Model B	-2%	3%	-4%
Model C	3%	-4%	1.8%
Model D	2%	2.4%	-2%
Model E	1%	3.2%	2%

Use a spreadsheet to determine how Whirlpool should price its models if it wants to undercut the competition.

3. **(Web exercise)** Check the Web site of any of these companies and see if they advertise sale items on their site. Can you buy any Whirlpool product via their Web sites?

Case 2: UPS Delivers on Its Information Promise

A few years ago, United Parcel Service, the "parcel delivery" company, realized that its employees were spending too much time collecting data. They found engineers were taking information from computer printouts and keying them into spreadsheets and then manipulating the spreadsheets for reporting, auditing, and business analysis. Not only was this tedious and time-consuming, but often yielded nonstandard and inaccurate results.

Now the company has a decision support system, called the Information Library, that helps managers become better decision makers. The system is easy to use, fast, and user-friendly. It provides users with a flexible way to get information, produce reports, and make high-quality business decisions in an increasingly challenging environment. The database in this DSS contains 300 gigabytes of data in 400 tables collected from 13 different

continued

Case 2: UPS Delivers on Its Information Promise, *continued*

UPS functions. Over 1,500 users worldwide access this data on 800 PCs running Windows and Microsoft Office. Microsoft Access (a database) and Excel spreadsheet help users to query, report, analyze, and plan their information needs.

The Information Library has many applications that helps users to generate simple or sophisticated reports. Users can easily make changes to a report and customize it to meet their unique needs.

1. What are some features of the Information Library that make it a decision support system? What are some of its benefits?
2. If a spreadsheet can do the job, why spend money developing a DSS?
3. Suppose you had to make a presentation to top management asking them to invest in this technology. Make a 5-minute presentation that will explain to a nontechnical person the benefits of intelligent support systems.

Part 5 Approaches to Designing, Developing, and Managing IS

The illiterate of the 21st century will not be those who cannot read and write, but those who cannot learn, unlearn, and relearn.

Alvin Toffler, author

CONTENTS

DEVELOPING SYSTEMS FOR SUCCESS

Skills needed for developing information systems are in short supply. In fact, people with good skills in this area can be assured of employment.

Several reasons explain the high demand for systems developers. First, losses from poorly managed information systems (IS) projects can be significant and can quickly become the "bleeding artery" that drains a company's resources. Second, delays or mishaps in IS projects can have a downward spiraling effect in other parts of the organization because information systems serve other functional areas in an organization, as we saw in Chapter 2. Third, most projects in IS require a sharp, trained, and disciplined eye to understand the intricacies of project development.

Fourth, IS system development is still an art, requiring creativity, intuition, and feedback from those who will use the system. Peter Keen, a management expert, summarizes this point well when he says, "Information systems is no longer about 'development,' 'projects' and 'operations.' [Instead] its responsibility is to manage business ventures: commercial activities focused on providing goods and services that satisfy customers. Information systems needs strong brands, marketing, selling, support and, above all, a continued focus on the customer."[1]

Organizations that view IS development as the sole responsibility of the IS department risk failure because they eliminate part of the "art" of systems development—the art of giving users the right tools so they can become more productive. The Technology Payoff demonstrates the importance of this art. Successful IS projects are like good families: everyone in the family does their part so that the family can succeed.

Chapter 11

System Analysis and Design: Methodologies and Tools

AFTER STUDYING THIS CHAPTER, YOU SHOULD BE ABLE TO:

- Describe the systems development life cycle methodology and its limitations
- Discuss the prototyping methodology
- Explain end-user computing and the reasons for its growth
- Outline situations in which companies should use off-the-shelf packages
- Explain why outsourcing is a viable option for building information systems
- Identify and discuss structured tools for system development

As a future professional in business, health care, law enforcement, or another field, you are likely to be influenced by and to influence the design, development, and maintenance of information systems. You may be a member of a cross-functional team charged with developing information systems or an IS project manager accountable for building quality systems. Regardless of your major, it is important to understand the guiding principles and tools of system development.

What can employees do to ensure the development of high-quality systems? First, be knowledgeable about how to use different methods to build information systems. Understand the strengths and weaknesses of these methods so that you can actively and meaningfully participate in system-related decisions.

Second, realize that system development is inherently woven into the fabric of organizational change, and change, by its very nature, is complex.[2] Information systems can change job functions or even the nature of the business, eliminate jobs, demand new skills from employees, and cause fear, resistance, feelings of inadequacy, and morale problems. As a result, developers need to be sensitive to the needs of people.

System development is not limited just to businesses; it also applies to individuals. Many of us develop simple systems at home, such as spreadsheets to keep an account of our income and expenses or word documents to store names and addresses of our friends. If we apply sound design and development principles, the performance of even these systems will improve greatly.

For business, good system development is critical not just for business success, but for basic survival. Take Johns Hopkins Health

System. A few years ago, the 40,000-bed, 270,000-outpatient hospital's information systems department was "juggling priorities without a whole lot of rhyme or reason," notes Stephanie L. Reel, vice president and CIO of John Hopkins Medicine Center for Information Services. Meeting the needs of the Johns Hopkins staff, she says, was the single biggest obstacle to change. "Imagine it is our job to serve 1,000 CEOs, each with his or her own business, each with total autonomy, each empowered to be an entrepreneur who can do whatever it takes to get something done. Each of them can look in the mirror every morning and say, 'I am the best in the world at what I do.' "[3]

Reel knew that the only way to gain acceptance for the changes her department suggested was to empower and involve her users in the implementation process. She formed several technology advisory boards heavily composed of physicians and every change was made slowly and with "a healthy respect for the past," she explains.[4]

One way of leading an IS department is by building effective and successful projects. "Never before has there been a better time to be an industry revolutionary, or a more dangerous time to be an incumbent," comments industry expert Richard Page. "The goal is not to predict the future; the goal is to predict a future that you can make happen."[5] Developing effective systems is an important step in predicting and achieving a future full of promise.

Finally, robust and reliable information systems influence our everyday lives and thus have an impact on society. For example, a poorly designed drivers' licensing system can become an aggravation for citizens; an unreliable airport baggage delivery system can frustrate travelers; a pharmaceutical system for tracking patients' medications that is inaccurate can be life-threatening.

The system development process is so pervasive that the World Bank is stepping in to address some information technology (IT)–related problems that affect society. In recent years, the World Bank in Bangladesh has spent more than $13 million to alert Central Africa states to fight the year 2000 problem, according to a report in the *Cameroon Tribune*. The year 2000 problem, as mentioned in Chapter 4, relates to the inability of some computers to handle dates starting in the year 2000. Most African states weren't fully aware of the issue or had taken few steps to remedy it.

The World Bank encouraged IT specialists from Nigeria, Ghana, Sierra Leone, Congo, Liberia, and the Central Africa Republic to address this problem by offering aid packages of $54,000 for each realistic proposal addressing the problem. It also urged the development of national action plans and the formation of ad hoc committees in each country.[6]

This chapter explores several different approaches and tools for building information systems. Knowledge about different methodologies and their strengths and weaknesses is essential to be a good steward of information systems. Methodologies and system development tools go hand-in-hand.

Similar to an architect who depends on tools to design and develop a home or building, IS developers depend on certain tools and techniques to develop good information systems. Tools play three roles in sys-

TECHNOLOGY PAYOFF

FedEx Pilots Fly off the Handle

Developing information systems requires more than hardware, software, and a team of technical professionals. It also requires a keen understanding of users' needs. If user input is ignored, businesses should beware of the outcome.

A new pilot scheduling information system at FedEx made pilots so mad that they would rather strike than use the system. Surprisingly, the system works well and is widely used in the airline industry by businesses such as Trans World Airlines (TWA), Delta Air Lines, Northwest Airlines, Belgium-based Sabena Airlines, and Air Canada.

So what went wrong at FedEx? System users at FedEx, namely pilots, were not consulted about the system before it was installed. "The system was extremely disruptive, [and] we weren't consulted before it was implemented," recalls Tony Hauserman, communications chairman of the 3,200-member Federal Express Pilots Association union. The FedEx system relies on efficient scheduling to cover all the routes while getting the pilots out of, and then eventually back into, their home bases as quickly as possible.

The pilots were caught off guard because, as Bob Miller, president of the Independent Pilots Association union, explains, past labor contracts weren't written with strict efficiency rules and guidelines about layovers, route preferences, and time away from home. The system, in effect, changed FedEx's labor policies through its emphasis on speed. "Contracts weren't written with this kind of optimization in mind, but they will be in the future. Negotiations between pilots and companies will become more complex as a result of high-tech software capabilities," says Miller.

Sally Davenport, a spokeswoman at FedEx, acknowledges that system implementation was not smooth, but adds that the company has now addressed the pilot's work policy concerns. The moral of this striking tale is to obtain user participation and input before implementing a system to avoid costly problems. Other airlines, like TWA, tested the system for a year before it was installed. This before-the-fact user input is a key factor in system development success.

Source: Adapted from Stewart Deck, "System Implementation May Contribute to Pilots' Strike at FedEx," *Computerworld,* October 26, 1998, 24.

Well-developed information systems ensure that airport baggage delivery and claims are handled efficiently.

tem development. First, they help team members communicate about system issues in a clear and concise manner. Second, they allow developers to experiment with different design and development approaches and learn by trial and error. Third, they help developers understand the impact of new systems on business.

In the following sections, we examine five system development methodologies: system development life cycle, prototyping, end-user computing, off-the-shelf software packages, and outsourcing. Then we explore the appropriate tools for system analysis, design, and implementation.

System Development Life Cycle (SDLC)

Our goal in this chapter is to learn how developers and end users can build effective information systems. Recall from Chapter 1 that the five basic system components are input, processes, output, feedback, and control as shown in Figure 11-1.

FIGURE 11-1 The Five Basic Components of a System

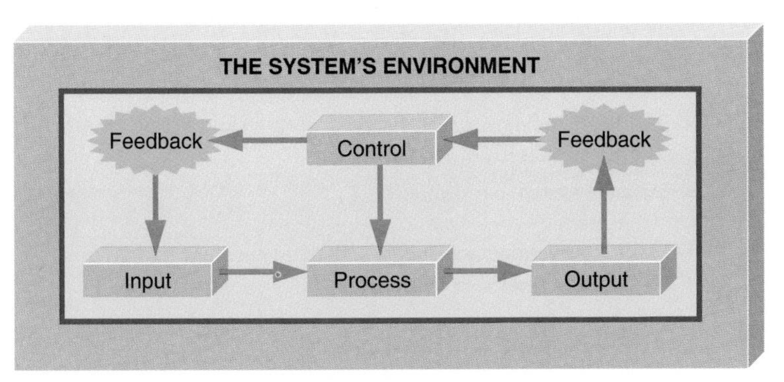

To demonstrate how these components operate, consider a newspaper delivery system. The name, address, and number of newspapers delivered to a customer (subscriber) become system input. Different processes are used to determine total payments. The system output is the customer invoice. Feedback may be in the form of complaints about missing newspapers, vacation notices to stop newspapers, or delinquent accounts. The feedback is fed into the system and the control mechanism ensures that the actual performance of the system meets expected performance levels. Any development methodology should take into account these five components.

System development life cycle (SDLC)

A methodology to develop information systems that consists of these phases: system definition, analysis, design and programming, testing and implementation, and maintenance.

The **system development life cycle (SDLC)** is one of the oldest and most traditional methods for developing information systems. Just as human beings are born, live, and die, systems also follow a life cycle from conception to death—hence the name systems development life cycle (SDLC). The SDLC is divided into five broad phases:

1. System definition
2. System analysis
3. System design and programming
4. System testing and implementation
5. System maintenance

As Table 11-1 illustrates, the five phases are structured and somewhat compartmentalized. However, they are interwoven in the sense that the success of one phase influences the other. The first step, of course, is to define the problem that the system should solve, which is the focus of the next section. In the sections that follow we explore the other phases of the SDLC and the limitations of this system methodology.

TABLE 11-1

The Activities in the Five Phases of the SDLC

Phase	Activities*
System definition	Address the questions: • What problem are we trying to solve by developing a new system? • What are the objectives of the new system?
System analysis	• Gain thorough understanding of the problem • Conduct feasibility study • Determine and establish system requirements
System design and programming	• Explore different designs and select best design • Provide a detailed plan for converting requirements into actual performance • Create logical and physical design specification • Plan, coordinate, control, and manage technical aspects of the system • Convert design specifications into program code
Testing and implementation	• Perform unit, system, and acceptance testing • Decide on implementation strategy: parallel conversion, direct cutover, or phased conversion • Evaluate system performance
Maintenance	• Make modification and enhancements to ensure that system continues to meet user needs

*Sometimes activities in one phase may overlap with activities in others.

System Definition

The **system definition** phase describes what is being built and why it is being built. This phase seeks answers to questions such as "What problem are we trying to solve by developing a new system?" and "What are the system's objectives?" The system definition phase looks into why the company needs a new system and identifies why the existing system, if one exists, can no longer meet the needs of the organization.

The second question identifies the primary goal(s) of the new system, its features and functions, and its limitations or boundaries. Boundaries establish what the system will and will not do. Without boundaries, the project expands without a specific purpose or goal and this often leads to disastrous results. Unfortunately, this critical phase is often overlooked or done shabbily. Once the problem is clearly defined, the next step is to check if the system proposal is feasible and then develop detailed requirements, the focus of the next phase.

System definition

The process of defining the business problem, establishing why a new system is needed, and identifying the objectives of the proposed system.

System Analysis

There are three activities in the **system analysis** phase of the SDLC. Developers must understand the problem thoroughly, examine the feasibility of the project, and establish system requirements. We explore each of these activities in the following sections.

System analysis

A detailed analysis of a new system to be built that helps developers better understand the nature, scope, feasibility, and requirements of a new system.

Understand the Problem

This activity requires that system developers assess and understand the strengths and weaknesses of the existing system, if any. If a system does not exist, developers focus on why the company needs a system. This process helps to identify what information needs are currently not being met and how a new system will help users be more productive. The product of this step is a system proposal that summarizes the strengths and weaknesses of the existing system and outlines the strengths and weaknesses of the new one.

Feasibility Analysis

Next, business managers and system developers determine if the proposed system can be built with the allocated resources. *Technical feasibility* analyzes whether the proposed system is technologically viable given existing technologies. *Economic feasibility* is an analysis of the financial commitment of the project—a difficult assessment because many information systems benefits are intangible, such as greater responsiveness to customer needs.

Operational feasibility analyzes problems that may arise when the system becomes operational. The new system may require extensive training before it becomes fully functional, for instance. *Resource feasibility* is a study of all resources necessary to build the system, such as personnel, time, money, equipment, and so on.

Legal feasibility is an analysis of legal factors such as copyrights, patents, and federal or state regulations that affect the system, if any. In the case of life-threatening systems, legal feasibility can be a deciding factor. Life-threatening systems are those that are potentially harmful to people if they fail, such as those used in military settings, police departments, nuclear power plants, and hospitals.

Finally, *strategic feasibility* is a study of factors such as the ability of the system to increase market share, attain a competitive edge in the marketplace, enhance productivity, create new products, and so on. The outcome of this phase is a project feasibility report that summarizes the technical, economic, operational, resource, legal, and strategic feasibility factors.

Establishing Functional Requirements

The third and final activity in the system analysis phase is establishing **functional requirements** also known as system requirements. Functional requirements answer a set of questions, as outlined in Table 11-2.

Developing functional requirements may appear like a simple task, but it is demanding and time-consuming. For instance, a $7 billion U.S.–based consumer products company decided to build a call center in Europe to handle its customers in Western Europe. One system requirement was the necessity of communicating with customers

Functional requirements

Requirements that identify the who, where, when, and what of the new system. Also known as system requirements.

TABLE 11-2

Functional Requirements Provide Answers to the Following Questions
Who will use the system and for what purpose?
What are the specific information needs and expectations of the user?
Who will provide system input?
Who will receive system output?
Who will monitor system performance?
When should the system be delivered?
When will the system be updated?
What are the maintenance requirements?
What are the training requirements for this system?

in their preferred language to address any product questions or problems they might have. Switzerland seemed a natural choice. Because both French and German dialects are spoken there, company officials reasoned it would be easier to staff the 300-person center with speakers of the major European languages.

"The problem was that the Parisians are very sensitive to accents, and they didn't appreciate some Swiss French speaker giving them service," explains Carter Lusher, research director for customer service and support strategies at Gartner Group in San Jose, California. So the firm had to build a second, smaller call center on the outskirts of Paris.[7] This example illustrates that functional requirements must be based not only on technical system requirements, but also on users' needs and preferences.

Creeping requirements

System requirements that keep changing well past the system analysis phase.

Capers Jones, chairperson of Software Productivity Research in Burlington, Massachusetts, states that **creeping requirements** is a major problem in the development industry. Creeping requirements are functional specifications that change so frequently that it is impossible for developers to build a system that meets users' needs.[8] Creeping requirements lead to employee frustration and animosity and a tremendous waste of corporate resources.

In addition, creeping requirements have an adverse effect on project development costs. The cost problem is a major one because businesses make huge investments in systems development—as Figure 11-2 shows. If the requirements keep changing, then development costs skyrocket beyond the planned investment. Developers, then, should work hard to ensure that users establish all requirements at the outset to avoid inefficient, expensive changes in the middle of a systems project.

Config, an artificial intelligence system designed to configure computer systems, demonstrates one curse of creeping requirements. In Config's case, creeping requirements became an excuse for users to avoid using the system. "Rather than saying they don't want it, they say, 'I think I would use it if it just had this feature or that feature.'

FIGURE 11-2

Systems Development Costs in U.S. Businesses

Source: Computer Sciences Corp., *CIO,* June 1, 1997, 96.

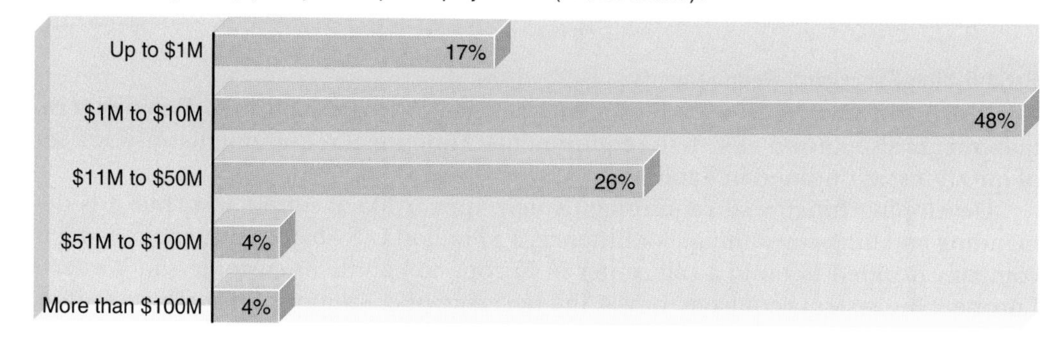

This was evident in a memo written almost 11 years *before* development began. Config's (developers) are concerned that the company's [intended users] are not showing enough interest in the project."[9]

Creeping requirements must be dealt with firmly in the early phases of system development if the project is to succeed. After establishing detailed requirements, the next phase is to actually build the system in the system design and programming phase, described next.

System Design and Programming

In **system design** each requirement that was established in the system analysis phase is converted into a sequence of detailed procedural steps and system specifications. Let's revisit our architect example to illustrate. An architect looks at the blueprint of a house (the building requirements) to identify the amount of concrete, wood, wiring, and so on (the specifications) needed to build the house. Similarly, the system developer looks at each system requirement and determines how to make the system deliver that requirement.

System design

The process of developing a step-by-step map that shows developers how to convert system requirements into a workable operational information system.

For instance, a requirement may state: "Build a user-friendly interface for the payroll system." In system design, this may be converted into "Build a graphical user interface [GUI] with a blue background and drop-down menu. The drop-down menu has the following eight choices (the eight choices are identified). The GUI should also have four buttons at the top: main menu, help, exit, and print."

Recall from Chapter 5 that there are two types of design: *logical* and *physical.* Logical design establishes the relationships among different elements in the system. Imagine for the moment that you are designing a business system for a large retail business. Logical design dictates that the tax department is a part of the accounting department. It also dictates that a copy of every customer invoice should go to the purchasing department. Physical design addresses the physical aspects of the system. This includes input and output devices, memory, storage devices, location, security measures, and so on.

System design involves three major activities:

1. Identify the appropriate technology to implement the system.
2. Involve users in the development process from the beginning.
3. Provide detailed specifications and show how these specification help to meet system goals.

Once this groundwork for building an effective system is complete, developers can begin the development process, which we outline next.

System Development

Although people often associate building information systems with programming, this is only one phase in the system development life cycle. Programming is a highly complex, time-consuming, labor-intensive task that, for some projects, may take years. A team of programmers usually works to develop the programming for large to medium-sized systems. In this phase the functional specifications are written in a programming language, such as C or COBOL. Once the program is written, the next phase is to ensure that it works as planned through testing.

System Testing and Implementation

Testing is one of the most daunting parts of the development process. It requires creativity, persistence, and a thorough understanding of the system to anticipate the many ways in which a program may fail. A difficult question is "How much testing is enough?"

Testing

The identification of system weaknesses and errors by assessing system elements (such as software and hardware) under different situations and environments to see if system performance matches system requirements.

First, developers don't know how many errors are in the system. The number could range from a few to hundreds. Second, no system is perfect. It is perfect only until the next error is found. Third, organizations may be reluctant to commit resources to testing, as they are anxious to get the product out the door as quickly as possible. So allocating resources for testing is always a challenge.

There are three types of testing: unit testing, system testing, and acceptance testing. In **unit testing** each program is individually tested. However, because each program may

Unit testing

The process of testing each program in the system individually.

FIGURE 11-3

The Relative Cost of Mistakes in Each Phase of Systems Development

System testing

The process of testing the performance of the entire system through simultaneous testing of all the system's programs.

Acceptance testing

The process of users testing system performance to ensure that the system meets their requirements and expectations.

Parallel conversion

A system implementation strategy in which the old and new systems run in parallel until the new system is fully tested.

interact with many other programs, testing each program as a separate entity is not enough. So developers do **system testing,** in which the system is tested in its entirety to make sure that the interactions between programs work successfully. Unit and system testing may be done under simulated conditions. In **acceptance testing,** developers and users test the system under actual operating conditions. For example, a user may test to see if the system responds to her query in the desired time. Or a user may test to see if a standard report looks the way he wants it to once all the data have been input.

Many empirical studies show that although it is relatively inexpensive to rectify errors in the early phases of system development, costs for fixing errors escalate by a factor of 10 for each additional phase. In other words, if it cost ten cents to fix a mistake in the analysis phase, it would cost a dollar to fix the same mistake in the design phase, ten dollars to fix it in the programming phase, and one hundred dollars to fix it in the implementation phase! Figure 11-3 shows this cost escalation. If major errors are detected during testing, the cost of the system can quickly escalate.

Once testing is complete, the next step is to implement the system without disrupting the daily operations of the company. When a new system replaces an existing system, there are four types of conversion or implementation strategies:

1. Parallel conversion
2. Direct cutover
3. Pilot study
4. Phased conversion

Table 11-3 summarizes the different implementation strategies.

In **parallel conversion,** the old system and the new system run in parallel until all bugs are identified and eliminated. This approach is ideal for mission critical applications, such as control systems for air traffic control, where failures can have disastrous

TABLE 11-3 Four Implementation Strategies

Strategy	Description
Parallel conversion	• Old and new system run in parallel until new system becomes reliable • Costly but safe approach • Best suited to critical applications
Direct cutover	• Old system is replaced with new system • Less costly but more risky than parallel approach • Best suited to noncritical application
Pilot study	• One department or unit serves as a testing ground • Good for systems that are moderately critical
Phased conversion	• New system is slowly phased into the operational environment • Safe and conservative approach • Well suited to critical systems

results. The disadvantage of this approach, however, is that it is expensive to run two systems in parallel. In the **direct cutover** approach, the old system is removed and the new system is installed. This strategy usually works for small, noncritical systems. Although less costly than the parallel approach, there is no safety net if the new system fails.

The **pilot study** approach uses one department or unit as testing ground before the system is installed throughout the organization. Finally, in **phased conversion,** the new system is slowly introduced into its operational environment by replacing parts of the old system with parts of the new system. This strategy is a safe and conservative approach to introduce a new system and is by far the most popular method of system conversion.

Similar to an automobile that requires regular maintenance, once an information system's installation is complete, it requires maintenance, as we see in the next section.

Direct cutover

A system implementation approach in which the old system is removed and the new system is installed.

Pilot study

A system implementation approach in which the system is piloted in one department or unit first.

Phased conversion

A system implementation approach in which parts of the old system are replaced with parts of the new system.

System Maintenance

System maintenance begins soon after the system is installed and lasts as long as the system is in use. User requests for new features or enhancements of existing features, system errors, changing business needs, and emerging new technologies are factors that affect maintenance. Maintenance costs increase with time and at some point, it is more expensive to maintain the system than to develop a new one.

Maintenance makes up about half of the information systems activity in most companies and is a critical and vital activity. As Peter Salfi, project director for operations and maintenance at SHL Systemhouse, notes, "[Maintenance] is not as sexy as development. Everyone wants to be the artist, but very few want to be curator of the museum. To present the artwork well, however, you have to be a very good curator."[10]

"When the system goes live, the adrenaline rush starts to die down. Hot-shot developers fight this overpowering urge and remain involved, helping shell-shocked users as they begin to use the new system. . . . It's the critical first few weeks after the code is delivered that make or break the project," says Vince Hoenigman, project manager.[11]

We have just examined the system development life cycle, a widely used systems development method that can be adapted to suit a company's needs. In spite of its popularity the SDLC has some limitations that we explore next.

System maintenance

The process of modifying and updating systems currently in existence. Maintenance helps to fix errors, improve performance, and continue to meet the changing needs of users.

Limitations of the SDLC

Although the SDLC is well suited for highly structured systems, such as TPS and MIS, it is in fact, quite rigid and inflexible for certain applications. Information systems expert Joanne Kelleher explains: "Structured methods just don't work. None of that bears any relation to the way things are done today. The way things are done today is fast, cheap and with the maximum amount of reality-checking along the way."[12]

This criticism is really targeted at the step-by-step approach of the SDLC, in which each phase is completed before the next one begins. Further, the SDLC also assumes that system requirements, once developed, can be frozen in time. However, this is rarely the case in a dynamic world where user requirements frequently change. As a result, the SDLC is more ideally suited for stable environments where things are slow, steady, and quite predictable.[13]

One way of overcoming these limitations is to customize the SDLC methodology to meet the unique needs and demands of the organization. Another way is to explore the suitability of other methodologies such as prototyping and end-user computing, which we explore in the sections that follow.

Prototyping

Prototyping (also known as rapid application development or RAD) is a methodology in which the system development phases are executed at the same time, rather than in sequence like the SDLC. There are two types of prototypes: throwaway prototypes and evolutionary prototypes. A throwaway prototype is discarded after several iterations and is mainly used as a learning tool to develop the best possible system. It is ideal for projects involving state-of-the-art technologies.

An evolutionary prototype evolves from a simple prototype into a full-fledged system through expansions and enhancements. Each round of prototype builds on the previous prototype and is ideal for projects in which system requirements are unclear and users' information needs continuously evolve.

Prototyping

A development methodology that relies on prototypes, working or experimental models of a system. Also know as rapid application development.

The first step in prototyping is to develop system requirements, just like the SDLC. However, unlike the SDLC, where we follow system requirements with analysis, design, and development, in prototyping, all these phases are done in parallel. Once the requirements are developed, teams of individuals go to work on the remaining phases to build an initial prototype. Developers then study the prototype and find ways to further improve and enhance it. This leads to the next iteration of analysis, design, and development and is why we call prototyping an iterative method.

As Figure 11-4 depicts, prototyping consists of four steps:

1. Define the problem and identify system requirements
2. Build the initial prototype
3. Use the prototype to refine existing requirements
4. Revise and enhance the prototype

These steps are repeated until the system is completed

Satellite dish provider EchoStar Communications Corp. faced a major crisis when a deal between the company and media mogul Rupert Murdoch went sour. In the months leading up to the collapse of the deal, EchoStar had altered its business plans thinking that the merger would go through. The company now had to regroup quickly. "Just about every analyst on [Wall Street] gave us only a few weeks to live," says Tom Ryan, CIO of EchoStar in Littleton, Colorado.[14] It became clear to corporate executives the company would need to take radical action to stay afloat.

Recognizing that cost was the biggest barrier to getting new satellite dish subscribers, the company cut the consumer's upfront investment from $499 to $199. To make the new deal profitable for both EchoStar and its dealers, EchoStar had to adopt a new commission structure. The whole company mobilized to develop new dealer agreements, marketing materials, point-of-sale materials, and other campaign matter, all targeted to roll out in less than four weeks. Ryan was a central figure in making the new deal work, because his group had to develop a new application for calculating dealers' weekly payments based on satellite receiver activation.

The requirements were steep: The new system had to be able to analyze account information for over 1 million receivers and generate thousands of commission payments each week. "Using a traditional approach of requirements definition, system design, development, testing and deployment would have taken months. We had to have the first components deployed within three weeks," says Brian Carnell, senior NT administrator

FIGURE 11-4

The Prototyping Process

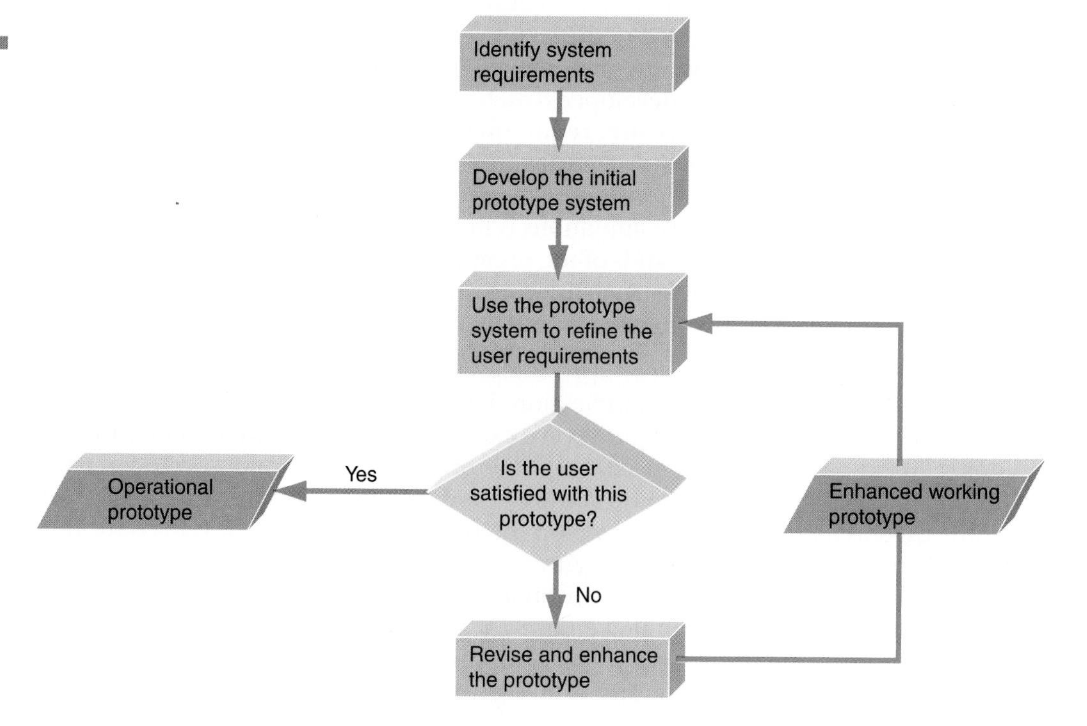

at EchoStar. "Under [Ryan's] direction, we tried something different." The IT team turned to prototyping. Requirements were developed and refined quickly. Prototypes helped to quickly narrow down on a working model. The company was able to meet its tight deadline.[15]

Prototyping has many benefits. This method is useful for building systems with emerging technology or in cases where the requirements aren't clear. It allows users to interact with a preliminary, working model of the system and learn how to improve it. Prototyping relies on four powerful ideas: teamwork, achievable goals, incremental system delivery, and eliminating waste. In prototyping, users, not developers, set system goals. This process makes it easier for users to accept the system.

Developers at the Virginia Department of Taxation, for example, successfully designed and developed a complex tax accounting system that integrated 1,500 programs and 40 databases. Developers attribute the success of the project to "aggressive but achievable goals, set by end users."[16] Prototyping also sensitizes users to the challenges of building information systems, as they are more actively involved in the process. Further, new and better designs often emerge during prototypes, which, in turn, lead to better systems.

The downside is that prototyping is a highly intense development methodology that can lead to employee burnout. IS managers, then, should make specific efforts to reduce stress levels, reward creativity of team members, and require developers to train extensively in prototyping methodologies. Further, prototyping members tend to ignore system documentation, which can lead to serious problems if key developers quit. IS managers must leverage the strengths of prototyping and overcome its weaknesses.

Another development method is end-user development. In this method, end users become both users and developers, as we see next.

End-User Computing

End-user computing (EUC)

Users rather than developers design, develop, and maintain the system.

An end user is someone who uses an information system. There are about seven million U.S. end users, and this number is expected to grow by at least 12 percent each year.[17] **End user computing (EUC)** relates to end users who design, develop, and maintain their systems.

There are several compelling reasons why EUC is becoming popular. Increased demands for timely information, plummeting hardware prices, easy-to-use graphical user interfaces, flexible software tools, overworked IS departments, and computer-literate new graduates all contribute to end users becoming developers. In general, EUC is similar to SDLC, except that the user and the developer are all in one. It is more flexible and less structured than the SDLC.

EUC benefits include shorter lead times, greater control and flexibility, and lower development costs.[18] Further, EUC is a blessing to overworked IS departments as users assume responsibility for their own systems. Finally, because the user knows what he or she wants, defining user requirements is much simpler with this methodology.

On the downside, end users sometimes fail to understand and follow the key principles for building good systems. Further, they often do not spend enough time testing the quality of their systems. When their systems fail, often they expect the IS department to fix the problem. Also, EUC can lead to redundant systems, because two users may build identical systems. Finally, sometimes end users can become secretive or protective of their systems, leading to information hoarding.

The previous sections explored different methodologies for building systems. An alternative to building systems is to buy off-the-shelf packages that minimize development activities. In the next section, we look at the pros and cons of this approach.

Off-the-Shelf Software Packages

Companies that do not have the resources or the inclination to build every part of their systems can buy software packages off the shelf. Note that the software is only part of the information system, but is often a substantial part. Off-the-shelf software packages are well suited for noncritical applications such as word processing, financial analysis, inventory control, scheduling, project management, and employee benefits. They eliminate the need to "reinvent the wheel" and help companies build the software portion of their systems quickly and efficiently. Small businesses, in particular, extensively use off-the-shelf software.

FIGURE 11-5

The Percentage of Businesses that Use Off-the-Shelf versus Custom-Built Software

Source: Computer Sciences Corp. *CIO,* June 1, 1997, p. 88.

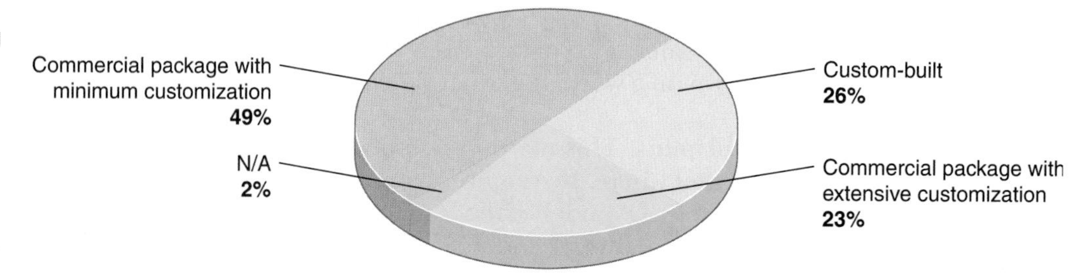

Software packages can be customized to meet the unique information needs of a company. However, permission from the vendor may be required for customizing the software. Figure 11-5 shows the percentage of businesses that use commercial packages with and without customization, as compared to custom-built systems.

In recent years off-the-shelf packages have become highly sophisticated. For example, Kaneb Services, a $200 million pipeline management and repair company located in Texas, does not have an IS department. Instead employees rely on an off-the-shelf database package to perform a variety of sophisticated tasks such as compiling and analyzing financial information from 40 different offices using six national currencies.[19]

The off-the-shelf approach has many benefits too. It reduces the cost and time for developing systems. It helps to overcome some of the problems and limitations associated with other development methodologies. For instance, reputable systems software packages are often free of major errors, reducing the need for extensive testing. Also, reputable software vendors provide training (at a cost) for their software and toll-free technical support. This can be a boon, especially for small companies. Finally, the system maintenance for off-the-shelf packages is usually lower than that of a custom-built software program, an advantage for any company.

The major drawback is that off-the-shelf packages may not meet the unique needs of the organization, although customization can somewhat alleviate this problem. Sometimes companies get desperate and try to fit the problem to the tool, rather than finding a tool to fit the problem. Extensive customization can also increase the cost of the software. In addition, some vendors get the product to the market even if it has errors, and the user company may become the guinea pig for locating the errors and fixing them. Finally, packaged software often has a number of fancy features, many of which users don't use, so companies may spend money for more than they need.

What happens if a company is not inclined to build its own systems and cannot find software that meets its unique needs? One option to consider is outsourcing its information systems, an approach that we turn to next.

Outsourcing

Outsourcing

The process of relying on external experts to meet the in-house information needs of an organization.

When a company uses outside vendors to create, process, manage, and maintain information systems, it is called **outsourcing.** The outside vendor may provide services such as data processing, accessing external databases, systems integration, global networking, and gathering business intelligence. A company can outsource some or all of these tasks.

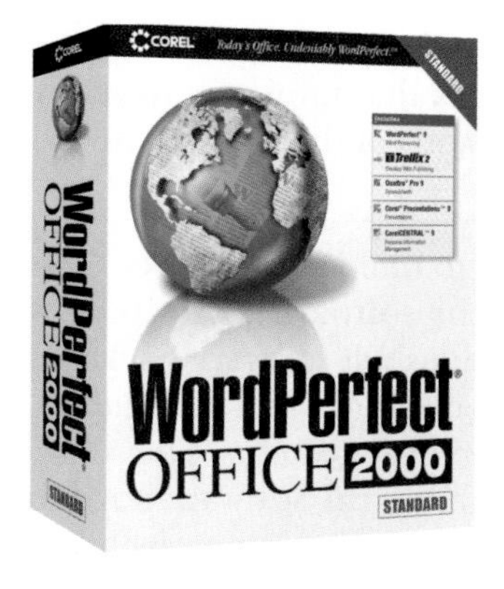

These are three popular off-the-shelf software packages.

TABLE 11-4

How Businesses Outsource IT Functions

Different IT Functions	Outsourcing Percentages
PC desktops and networks	35%
Hardware support	34%
Application development	30%
None	24%
Systems operations	22%
Systems maintenance	19%
Other	19%
Call center management	15%

Source: David Pearson, "Relationships on the Rocks," *CIO,* Section 1, November 1, 1998, p. 28. Reprinted through the courtesy of CIO. © 1998 CIO Communications, Inc.

Sometimes organizations outsource their entire IS department to an outside vendor but mostly they outsource rudimentary data-processing operations (such as data entry, data verification, and the like), general business functions (such as accounting and human resources), and systems that are not in their direct line of business. Rarely do companies outsource critical systems or proprietary systems. Table 11-4 shows the ways in which companies outsource different information technology functions.

Companies can choose the extent to which they outsource the IS function. Here are three popular choices:

1. Outsource system maintenance but use in-house staff to build new systems.
2. Outsource developing new systems but use in-house staff for running and maintaining existing systems.
3. Use outsourcing for building new systems and maintaining existing systems.

Why Do Organizations Outsource?

Organizations outsource for a variety of reasons. These can be classified into four broad categories: strategic focus, economies of scale, market forces, and technical considerations. Organizations may outsource to gain a strategic edge in the marketplace and better focus on its primary line of business. The question "What do we do best and how can we do it better?" may lead to the decision to outsource information systems.

In 1989 Kodak, the photo imaging company, outsourced its data centers, communications systems, and networks to three different vendors. Kodak was looking at ways to better use its limited resources and stay focused on achieving its mission of being the best imaging company in the world.

Companies also outsource for economic reasons. Because outsourcing contracts are usually fixed-price contracts (the fee for service is written into the contract), this eliminates the burden of escalating technology costs. Sometimes market forces may compel organizations to outsource. If the competition outsources its information systems to better leverage its resources and reduce operating costs, other companies may be forced to follow. Mergers, acquisitions, leveraged buyouts, and downsizing are some other market dynamics that lead to IS outsourcing. Finally, technical considerations, such as lack of expertise in certain technical areas, can lead to outsourcing. Greyhound Lines of Canada Ltd. outsourced its information systems when it had difficulty attracting IS talent to its offices in Calgary, Canada.[20]

Like other approaches, outsourcing has advantages and disadvantages. The primary advantage is the burden of developing and delivering quality information systems shifts to the outsourcing vendor. Outsourcing, when carefully implemented, can decrease costs, reduce technologic obsolescence, and provide a competitive edge. The organization can focus on its strategic or primary business and leverage its resources to achieve the maximum benefit. The Ethics for Success feature highlights some steps businesses can take to manage the outsourcing process effectively.

Ethics for success

Some Outsourcing ABCs

A $100 million fraud lawsuit filed against Andersen Consulting offers valuable lessons in how to avoid botched consulting projects. The suit against Andersen stems from work the $3.4 billion consulting giant performed for UOP, an 80-year-old $800 million engineering company that develops technology used to build oil refineries. In the early 1990s UOP hired Andersen to streamline its engineering specifications and cost-estimating processes and develop a series of client/server software applications.

Three years later UOP President and Chief Executive Officer Michael D. Winfield claim that "the difference between what Andersen promised us at the outset and what it actually delivered is staggering." "From the beginning, we were not included in the actual development process," says Eugene Schmeizer, director of support systems centers at UOP. "Andersen insisted on using their own staff for coding and software work. They also kept re-estimating the number of man-hours it would take to complete the project."

Another problem was Andersen's use of inexperienced personnel who ultimately delivered incomplete, defective, and largely unusable systems. Meanwhile, Andersen's periodic progress reports to UOP indicated all was going well. Of the half-dozen former or current Andersen clients contacted, some were not altogether surprised by the charges, especially those about the Andersen consultants' alleged lack of expertise. Other Andersen clients characterized unplanned time extensions as commonplace on their projects and some complained about Andersen's often-undisciplined approach to projects.

First Union Corp., a Charlotte, North Carolina, bank with $77 billion in assets, selected Andersen to head up a call center project. But the bank terminated its $6 million contract with the consulting firm after the first development phase because the work "had become a struggle to complete," recalls Judge Fowler, senior vice president and director of systems development at First Union. The problem was that Andersen did not manage the initiative "with the appropriate project disciplines."

Experts say that there are several important lessons to be learned from this experience.

1. Never leave development contractors to work exclusively on their own. Always insist that some in-house developers be part of the project.
2. Before signing a contract, make sure the outsourcer develops a detailed needs analysis of your organization that includes a list of the exact changes the system requires.
3. Negotiate all costs up front.
4. Have frequent reviews of schedule and performance, especially during the early stages of the process.

YOU DECIDE

1. Revising the cost of a project and the time it would take to complete is not unethical. Andersen Consulting gave the best estimate it could and revised those estimates when necessary. Comment on the ethics of this approach to system development.
2. Based on this case, what do you think are some steps that Andersen Consulting should have taken to avoid the lawsuit? To ensure that its actions were ethical?

Sources: Julia King and Thomas Hoffman, "Lessons From a Lawsuit," *Computerworld,* April 10, 1995, 28; Geoffrey James, "Outsourcing Litigation: Tipping the Scales Your Way," *Datamation,* November 1997, www.datamation.com.

But outsourcing also has some disadvantages, such as layoffs. The remaining staff may find that they are carrying a higher workload and feel demoralized and concerned that they may be next in line, leading to higher turnover. Further, improper outsourcing can lead to lawsuits. For failing to give 580 former employees adequate notice of a computer outsourcing agreement with EDS Corp., Blue Cross, Blue Shield of Massachusetts was ordered to pay more than $7 million in compensation.[21]

Employees may also view outsourcing as a lack of confidence in their technical skills or as a sign of troubled times for the company. Finally, outsourcing to the wrong vendor can result in loss of control over the quality and reliability of the IS function. For example, Texas State Bank in McAllen, Texas, sued Electronic Data Systems (EDS), its outsourcer, for $300 million in exemplary damages and $65.5 million in lost business opportunities. The bank claims that it missed two acquisitions worth $17.5 million and

TABLE 11-5

	Characteristics	Advantages	Disadvantages
SDLC	• Traditional development approach • Sequential step-by-step approach • Five phases	• Suitable for large projects • Provides structure and control	• Expensive • Time-consuming • Inflexible • Limited role of users
Prototyping	• Iterative methodology • Based on building a working model	• High user emphasis • Promotes teamwork • Reduces waste • Flexible	• Sometimes used as an excuse for poor development methods • High stress levels
End-User Computing	• End users assume full responsibility for system development	• Speeds development • Reduces IS backlog • Users become sponsors	• Lack of control results in lax security, uneven quality, and redundant systems
Off-the-Shelf Application Software	• Off-the-shelf packages used for some applications • Can be customized	• Eliminates some development problems • Reduces overhead costs • Speeds up development	• Can be hard fitting the problem to the tool • Allows only limited customization
Outsourcing	• Outside vendors provide full or partial IS-related services	• Business can focus on strategic areas • Cost-effective • Reduces obsolescence	• Eliminates jobs • Potential legal trouble and morale problems • Can lose control over system quality

another $40 million in lost business transactions because of errors in the software, such as calculation errors, formatting errors, and lost or misreported data.

In sum, there are five methodologies for developing information systems: SDLC, prototyping, end-user computing, packaged software, and outsourcing. Table 11-5 highlights the strengths and weaknesses of the five methodologies.

Is any methodology superior to any other? The answer is an emphatic "No." Methodology decisions are guided by a number of factors, including project requirements, technical expertise of in-house personnel, project criticality, resource availability, and corporate culture. Although selecting the right methodology is important for system success, it is not the only factor. If following the methodology becomes an end in itself, it can become unproductive. Says one IS manager, "Methodologies lead you into quicksand. We once spent three years following a methodology and ended up with a diagram that we couldn't code." [22]

There is a strong movement in many organizations to shift the focus from rigid methodologies to focusing on customer needs. Larry Runge conveys this message powerfully:

> Customers . . . are a different breed. All they ask is that we do our job well and efficiently. Then, in return, they pay our mortgages, buy our groceries, help send our kids to college and give us money to buy that boat or stereo we've always wanted. Frankly, if our customers are willing to pay for the good life we enjoy in return for a bit of programming, then they deserve our respect and our best efforts to get them what they want, when they want it. . . . Our measurements and rewards have to be based on meeting the customer's needs. Anything else will be counterproductive to our goal of serving the customer.[23]

So bear in mind that although methodologies are important, they do not operate in isolation. Instead, managers should assess different user needs, training resources, personnel resistance to change, and other factors before making methodology decisions. One way to ensure that methodology decisions are implemented effectively is to dedicate someone to manage an information system, as the Careers feature discusses.

Careers for success

IS Venture Managers

An emerging and evolving career in systems development and management is the venture manager. A venture manager cares for a system, application, or technology area (such as data warehouses or transaction processing systems) in a cross-functional manner. They handle everything that has anything to do with a system, including development, packaging, marketing, support, and enhancement.

Venture managers require an in-depth knowledge of their system, its economics, customers, after-sales/development services, and, above all, the expertise required for running, managing, and maintaining the system. They must be flexible and communicate well. They may or may not have in-depth technical experience but should have a good grasp of technology issues. Otherwise they'll be the "victims of vendors, fad-providers, and 'techies'" who have their own priorities.

IS venture managers not only oversee a system through its life cycle, but also make sure that IS professionals stay customer-focused. IS specialist Peter Keen offers this example: "[A] venture manager would make sure the programming team building a new application thinks of the help desk as an integral component of the venture. After all, the help desk is a top concern for anyone using a system; it should be for the programmers, too."

Similar to brand and project managers in firms such as Procter & Gamble, IS venture managers must coordinate all resources and talents required to build a successful system, whether the sources are outside packaging design firms or the in-house market research team or finance specialists.

The career of a venture manager can be exciting, challenging, and dynamic. The ability to interface and work well with many people, the ability to understand the business well, and the ability to stay focused on all aspects of a product are some key traits of good venture managers.

Source: Adapted from Peter G. W. Keen, "Systems: Not Just a Job—It's a Venture," *Computerworld,* February 9, 1998, www.computerworld.com.

Once a company decides what methodology to use, the next step is to identify a set of tools to develop the system. Note that the tools discussion does not apply to off-the-shelf software packages (unless the company decides to customize them) or to outsourcing decisions.

Decision-Making Framework for Selecting IS Tools

Managers should consider two important factors when selecting IS development tools and techniques.[24] First, developers must envision the future business environment of the company and the role that IS will play in helping the company get there. Second, selecting the right set of tools is a business decision, not just a technical decision, so a wide variety of businesspeople should be involved.

This joint approach is needed because IS tools have the power to create significant organizational change through coordinating information exchange and connecting people to that information. According to researchers John Rockart and J. Debra Hofman, the new system development environment "is not simply one in which bridges are built between previously unconnected systems. Instead, it is now one in which the relations and interconnections between systems are articulated and well understood before they are built so that coordinated systems can be developed, where each system is one component within an integrated framework."[25]

Business and IS professionals must learn to work together if a company is to succeed at building good systems. In the next section, we look at some tools and techniques that support the analysis and design, development, and implementation of information systems.

Top-down approach to system development

The process of taking a conceptual view of a system and breaking it down into subsystems until the system's parts cannot be broken down any further.

Structured Tools

One commonly used approach in system development is the *systems approach,* in which a system is broken down into subsystems. Each subsystem is then further broken down until a subsystem cannot be broken down any further. This view of the system is referred to as the **top-down approach** because users study the system starting from the highest level to the lowest level of detail, from the general to the specific, from the abstract to

Structured Tools Used during Several Phases of Systems Development

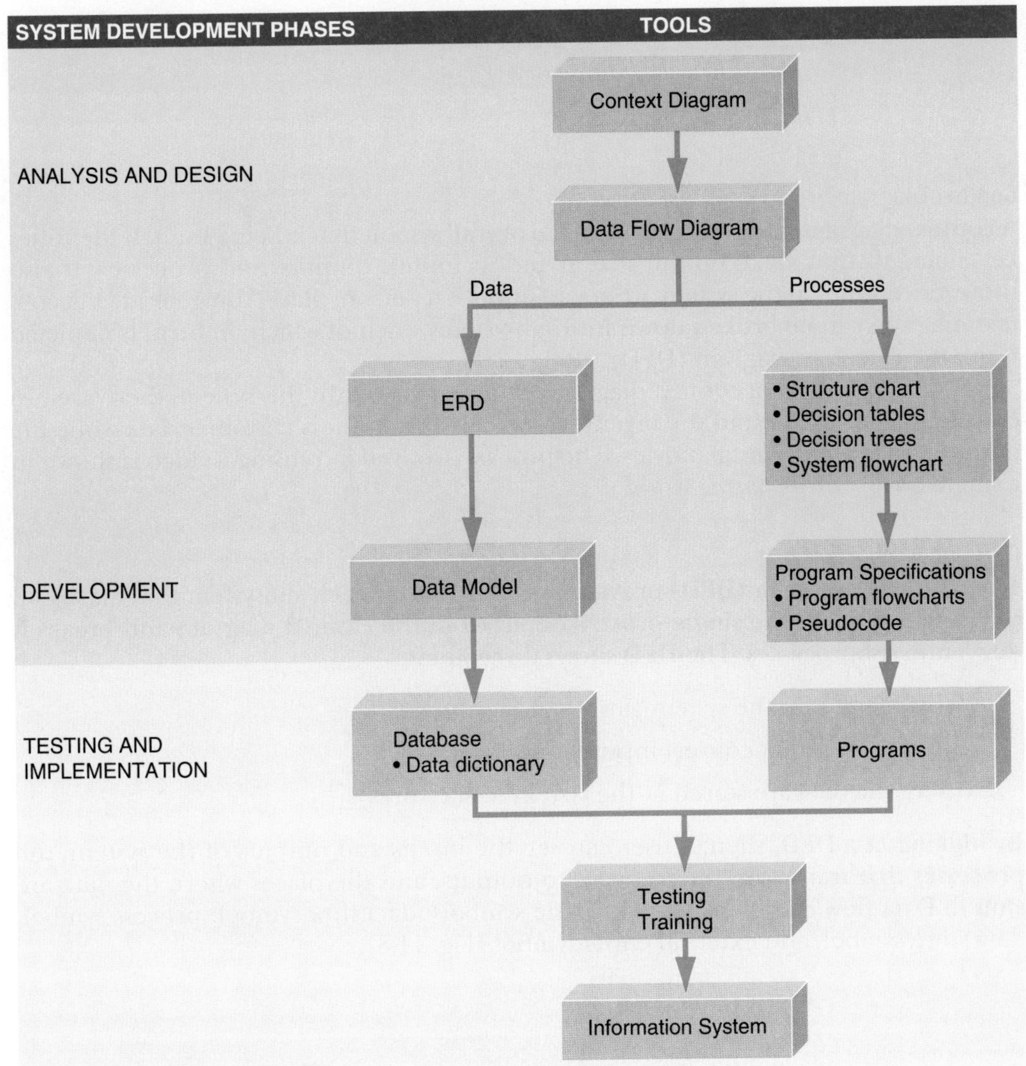

the detailed. This approach helps users to see the "big picture" and breaks down the system into more manageable units.

Structured tools and techniques support SDLC and prototyping. End users developing their own systems can also use these tools. Figure 11-6 highlights different tools used in the system development phases of analysis and design, development, and testing and implementation.

Structured tools
Tools and techniques used to develop a system that supports a top-down approach in which users study the system starting from the highest level of detail and move to the lowest.

The context diagram gives a broad overview of the system, including its major inputs and outputs, to help users see the big picture view of the system. The context diagram, which depicts the overall system, is broken down into smaller and more manageable subsystems. Each of these subsystems, in turn, is described in detail using the data flow diagram (DFD), which captures the flow of inputs and outputs, the processes that transform the data from inputs to outputs, and the data stores—that is, where the data are stored in the subsystem.

The two main elements in the DFD are data and processes. Data are captured using the entity relationship diagram (ERD). Processes are captured using tools such as the structure chart, the system flowchart, decision tables, and decision trees. Each tool is described next in detail.

Tools Used to Analyze and Design Systems

The first phase in designing a system is to gain a broad understanding of the system by addressing questions such as What are the main subsystems? How are these systems related? What are the major inputs, outputs, and processes? The context diagram helps answer these questions.

FIGURE 11-7

A Context Diagram for a Video Store

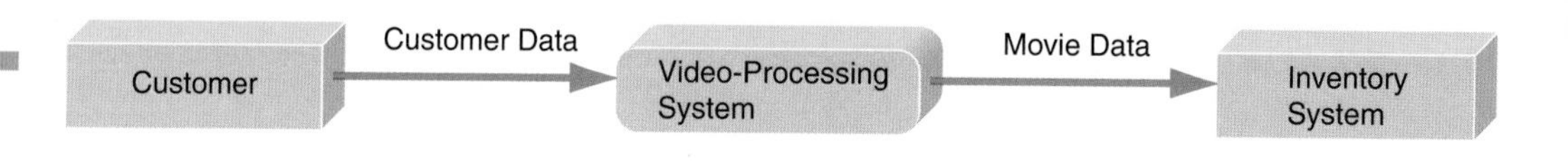

Context diagram

A graphical depiction of the overall system that identifies its major inputs, outputs, processes, and entities.

Context Diagram

A context diagram graphically depicts the overall system that is being built. It identifies key elements that make up the system and its inputs, outputs, and processes. It also shows the entities in the system, where an entity is a person, place, thing, or idea. A context diagram can be broken down into subsystems, each of which, in turn, is depicted using the data flow diagram (DFD).

Figure 11-7 shows a context diagram for a video store. In this system, there are two entities, the customer and the inventory system. The input is customer data while the output is data about rental movies. The process involved in renting a video is shown in a single box, *video-processing system.*

Data flow diagram (DFD)

A graphical tool that describes each of the subsystems in a system.

Data Flow Diagrams

The **data flow diagram (DFD)** provides a closer look at each subsystem that makes up the system. It takes the single process depicted in the context diagram and breaks it down into subprocesses. The DFD shows three items:

1. How data flow in the system (inputs and outputs)
2. The processes that convert input into output
3. Where the data are stored in the system (data stores)

By looking at a DFD, then, a user can see the inputs and outputs of the system, the processes that transform the inputs into outputs, and the places where the data are stored. Data flow diagrams use four basic symbols: data flow symbol, process symbol, data store symbol, and external entity symbol (Fig. 11-8).

FIGURE 11-8

The Different Symbols Used in a DFD

SYMBOL	DESCRIPTION	EXAMPLE
Data flow symbol	Shows the inflow or outflow of data. The name of the data is depicted above or below the arrow. Data can flow between entities, processes, and data stores, or a combination thereof.	Exam grades are input into the calculation of the final course grade. This is an example of inflow.
Process symbol	Describes the process that transforms the data. A numbering system identifies each process. A brief description of the process is indicated inside the rounded box.	The process of calculating the final grade in a course can be described as *Calculate* (verb) *final grade* (noun). Other examples of process descriptions include *Check* (verb) *credit* (noun), *Update* (verb) *system* (noun), *Send* (verb) *notice* (noun).
Data store symbol	Depicts the name of the data and indicates where they are stored, such as in databases, file cabinets, microfiche, and so on. If a data flow (i.e., an arrow) exits from a data store, it means that the process is *using* the data, whereas if it enters a data store, it implies that the process is *updating* or *changing* the data in the data store.	Student grades may be stored in a database (type of storage) called GRADE (name of data).
External entity symbol	An external entity symbol describes the source or the destination of the data.	Examples of entities are employees, products, departments, suppliers, customers, stockholders, the government, and so on.

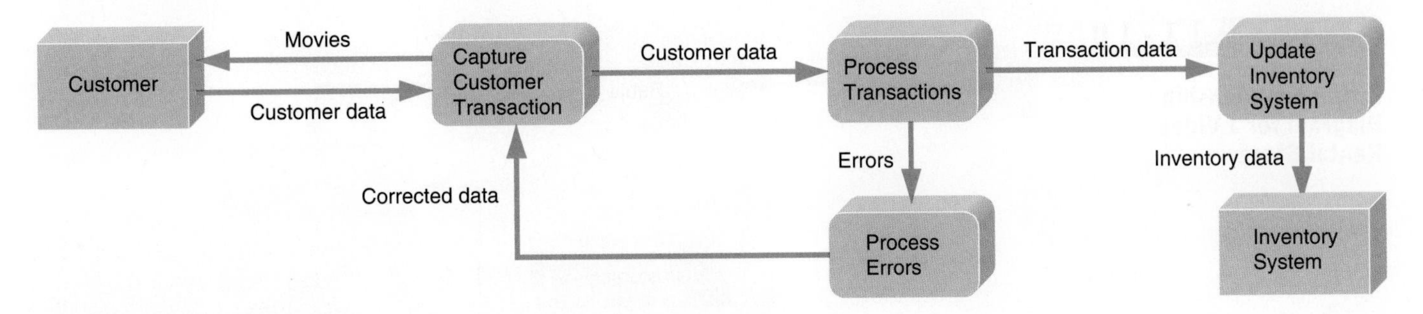

FIGURE 11-9 **The DFD for a Video Rental System**

The DFD for the video-processing system is shown in Figure 11-9. Note that the single process—the *video-processing system*—shown in the context diagram is broken down into four subprocesses:

1. Capture customer transactions
2. Process transactions
3. Correct error
4. Update inventory system

A DFD gives a detailed view of each subsystem that makes up the system. This knowledge about the system is invaluable for everyone who interacts with the system, including developers, users, and managers. It gives a clear idea of the components of each subsystem and this, in turn, helps people to catch errors early on in the development process.

Tools Used to Capture and Represent System Data

Data are an essential and vital component in any information system, and tools that capture and represent data are critical for system development. One such popular tool for capturing data is the **entity relationship diagram (ERD).** Unlike DFDs, which depict both data and processes, ERDs simply capture and depict data without any regard to the processes in the system. ERDs supplement the DFDs and help to provide a graphical overview of a system.

Entity relationship diagram (ERD)

A graphical depiction that identifies the entities of a system and their relationships.

An entity is shown as a rectangle while the relationships between entities are shown as diamonds. Relationships are described using verbs, such as *order, remove, teach, create,* and so on. As you may recall from Chapter 5, there are three types of relationships between entities: one-to-one (1-1), one-to-many (1-M), and many-to-many (M-M). Figure 11-10 shows the entity relationship diagram for the video rental store. The entities, represented by rectangles, are the video store, customer, movies, and inventory system. Diamonds represent the relationships between the entities.

There are five steps in creating an ERD:

- *Step One:* Developers and users work together as a team to identify the different entities in the system. In the video store example, the entities are the video store, customers, movies, and inventory system.
- *Step Two:* Establish the nature and scope of the relationship between the different entities identified in the previous step. Are the relationships one-to-one (1–1), one-to-many (1–M), or many-to-many (M–M)?
- *Step Three:* Describe each entity using a set of data elements. For example, the movie entity can be uniquely defined using the data elements *movie number* and *movie name.*
- *Step Four:* Graphically depict the data associated with each entity and the type of relationship between different entities.
- *Step Five:* Check that no entity is missing and that the relationships between different entities are accurately portrayed. Also, at this point a careful analysis of the data is done to identify and eliminate data redundancies.

FIGURE 11-10

Entity Relationship Diagram for a Video Rental Store

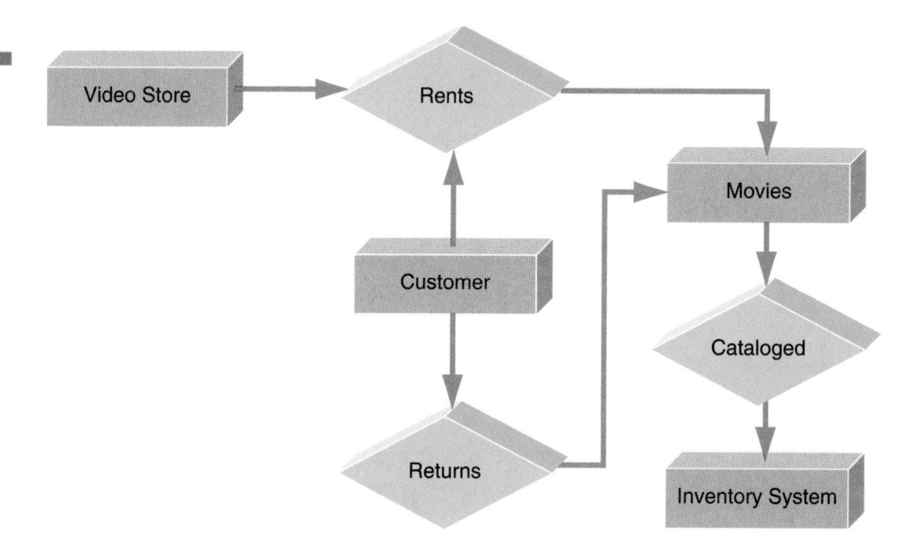

In summary, an ERD supplements the DFD and provides a static view of system data. By graphically depicting the entities and their interrelationships, developers can gain a better understanding of the overall system. In the next section, we describe tools and techniques that help to capture the processes in a system.

Tools Used to Capture and Represent Processes

Structured programming

A tool that shows the processes that convert data into information.

Structured programming is a tool that shows the processes that convert data into useful information. It is based on two key concepts: top-down approach and modularization. Recall that the top-down approach moves from the general to the specific and breaks a system into subsystems. Modularization breaks a software program into smaller and more manageable units called modules. Each subsystem may have a number of modules associated with it. Note that in structured programming, our focus is the software and the software only. In the top-down approach, our focus is on the system, which includes hardware and software.

Structured programming is based on three simple constructs or ideas: (1) sequence, (2) selection, and (3) iteration. A sequence is the set of steps a program goes through to fulfill a given instruction. Here is an example:

```
READ X, Y
ADD X + Y
SET Z = X + Y
PRINT Z
```

This sequence reads the values of X and Y, adds them together, and prints the new value, Z.

Next, the program selects a path, from a variety of possible paths it can take, to implement a given instruction. This is called the selection construct, which helps the program to select the right path. The selection construct is based on the IF-THEN-ELSE clause. For instance, suppose a school gives a scholarship of $500 to a business major whose overall GPA is greater than 3.9. The selection construct would look as follows:

```
IF      Student's GPA is greater than 3.9
THEN      Give award $500.
ELSE     Send thank-you note.
```

In this case, the selection construct helps the program decide whether to award a scholarship or send a thank-you note.

The repetition construct repeats a given operation until it meets a certain condition. The program terminates a specific operation when it meets the condition. Suppose a program calculates the net monthly pay for employees.

FOR EACH Employee
CALCULATE Net Monthly Pay
UPDATE Employee Benefits File
IF Number_of_Employees = 50
PRINT Employee Benefits File

When the program starts, it assigns a value of 1 to Number_of_Employees, calculates the net monthly pay for that employee, and updates the employee benefits file. The program then checks to see if Number_of_Employees is equal to 50. If not, it increases the number of employees to two and repeats the operation. When Number_of_Employees equals 50, the computer terminates the current operation and prints the file.

There are other tools that help us to capture system processes. Let's briefly examine four popular tools: the structure chart, system flowchart, decision tables, and decision trees.

Structure Chart

A **structure chart,** which looks like an organization chart, shows different modules in a program and their relationships. Figure 11-11 shows the structure chart for a program that calculates the overall letter grade for students. This program is divided into four submodules: get record, compute overall course grade, compute average exam and assignment grade, and post grade. By studying the structure chart, a programmer can see that the module called computer average exam and assignment grade has two submodules, weight average exam score by 75 percent and weight average assignment score by 25 percent.

Structure chart

A graphical systems tool that shows the hierarchy of software modules and the relationship among different modules.

System Flowchart

Flowcharts, in general, are widely used in the IS community. **System flowcharts** serve a valuable purpose by graphically depicting the major sources of data and the major processes that make up the system. Further, because processes do not function in a vacuum, but are instead highly interdependent, the flowchart helps developers see the relationships between different processes, a critical part of system development.

Note that the level of detail in a system flowchart can vary. Some users may prefer highly detailed system flowcharts while others may prefer an overview of the processes. Regardless of the level of detail, system flowcharts help users and developers understand the functioning of the system. Figure 11-12 shows the system flowchart for the video rental system. For example, one of the processes in the video rental system is a customer renting a movie.

System flowchart

A chart that shows how data flows in an information system. It also shows the processes, the sequence of the processes, relationships between the processes, and the data required for each process.

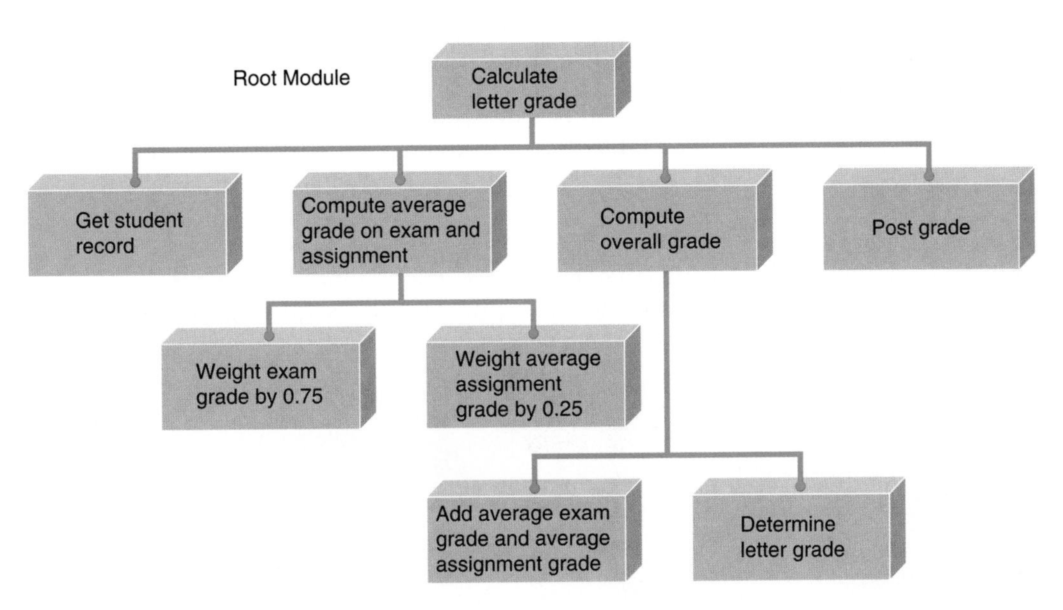

FIGURE 11-11

A Structure Chart for a Student Grade Calculation System

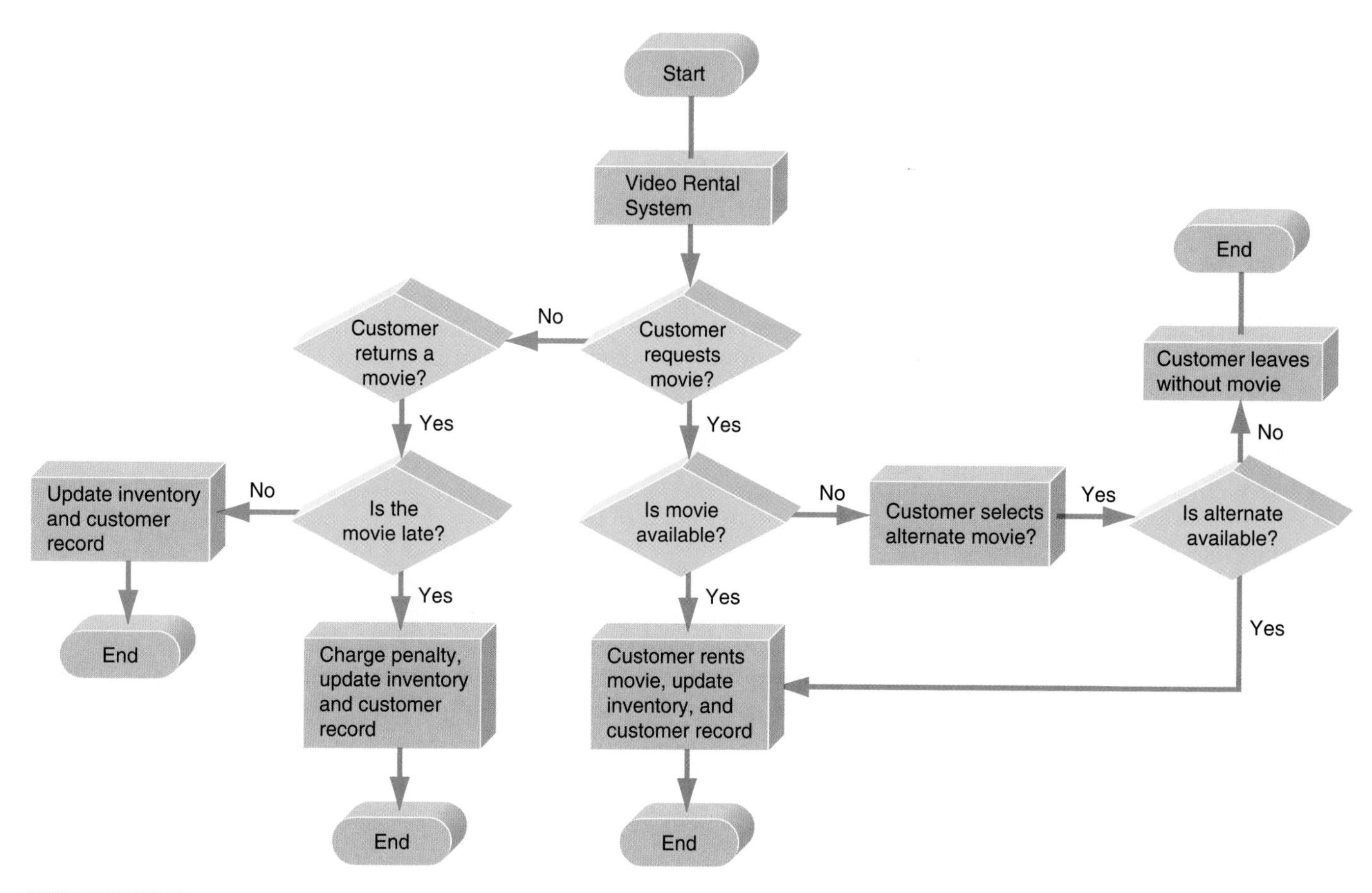

FIGURE 11-12 **System Flowchart for the Video Rental System**

Another flowchart is the program flowchart, which shows the processes within each program in the system. That is, if the system flowchart shows that the system is made up of five key programs, a detailed look at the processes within each program is the program flowchart.

Decision Tables

Decision tables

Rules that capture the logic in system processes using a set of conditions (IF clauses) and actions (THEN clauses) shown in the form of a table.

Another tool that aids structured programming is a **decision table.** A decision table is a set of IF-THEN rules that is shown in the form of a table.

Decision tables are useful if there are clear choices for solving a problem. Figure 11-13 shows a decision table for selecting scholarship recipients. There are three conditions in this table: GPA, income level, and number of years to graduate. Depending on the values of these conditions, two courses of action can be taken: award the scholarship or reject the applicant. The table shows the logic used to make each decision.

Decision Trees

Decision tree

A graphical representation of steps used to solve a problem.

A graphical representation showing different decision points a decision maker will encounter during problem solving is a **decision tree.** Each branch in a tree refers to an alternative. Branches proceed from left to right, and the sequence and number of

FIGURE 11-13

A Decision Table for Selecting a Scholarship Recipient

1. GPA ≥ 3.5	Y	Y	Y	N	Y	N	N	N
2. Income level ≤ 25,000	Y	N	Y	Y	N	N	Y	N
3. Number of years to graduate > 1	Y	Y	N	Y	N	N	N	Y
Approve $500 scholarship	X	X	X	X				
Reject application					X	X	X	X

Decision Tree for Video Rental System

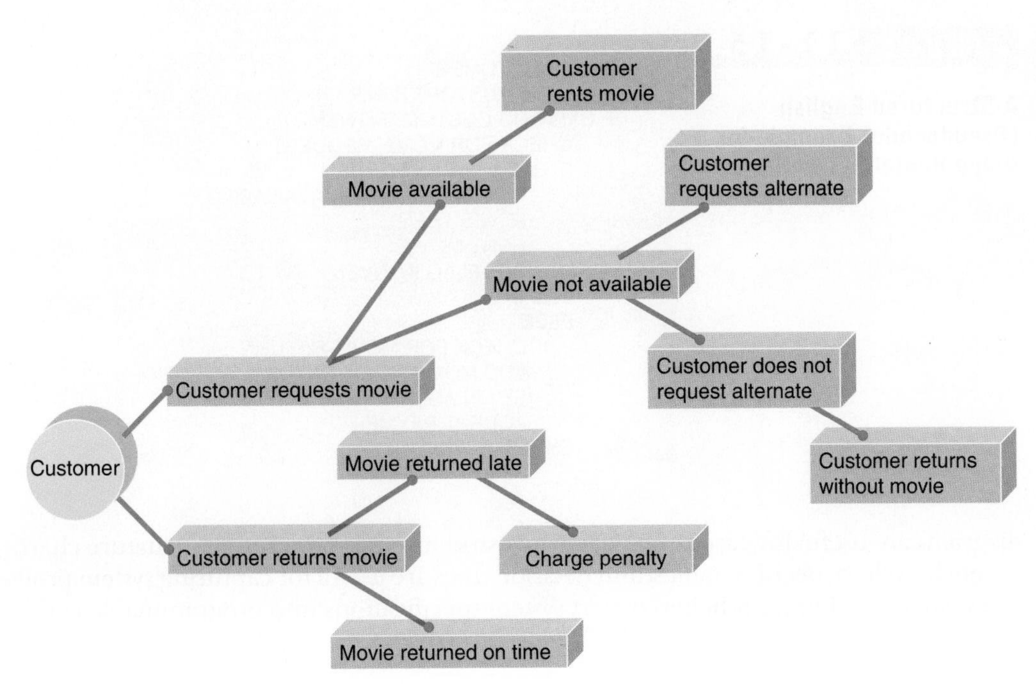

branches depend on the number of steps in the decision-making process. The values associated with each alternative are shown at the end of the branch. The key difference between the decision table and the decision tree is that the decision table shows the alternatives but not the steps behind those alternatives. The decision tree shows the steps to get to a solution.

Figure 11-14 shows a decision tree for the video rental system. The outcome associated with each option (renting a movie and returning a movie) is shown at the end of each branch. Note that the logic flows from left to right and the tree shows the different decision points.

Developers can use one or all of the tools just discussed, depending on their personal preference. The output, however, from these tools are step-by-step instructions (program specifications) that show how to convert the system design into a program. In the next section, we investigate tools that convert program specifications into computer code.

Tools Used to Convert Program Specifications into Code

When program specifications are written in a language that the computer understands and implements correctly, we have a working system. Accurately capturing the requirements of users is only half the battle. We need tools to convert user requirements into computer code. One such simple tool is **structured English,** or pseudocode. Because the computer does not understand English sentences, programmers use pseudocode to convert English sentences into English phrases, which are then used to write programs in a computer language, such as COBOL or C.

Structured English (pseudocode)
A code that converts program specifications written in English sentences into simple, easy-to-understand English phrases.

Structured English is unambiguous and widely used. It is a quick and efficient way to understand the main steps in converting program specifications into computer code. In structured English:

- Statements must be brief and should avoid adjectives, such as *good* or *quick.*
- Statements should begin with a strong action-oriented verb such as *Order, Process,* or *Send.*
- Statements must be formatted using multiple-level indentations.

An example of structured English is shown in Figure 11-15.

To review, a number of tools help developers throughout the development life cycle. The context diagram gives a broad overview of the entire system, while the DFD give a more detailed view of each subsystem within the overall system. Entity relationship

FIGURE 11-15

A Structured English (Pseudocode) Example for Video Rental System

```
VALIDATE_CUSTOMER
    VALIDATE CUSTOMER INFO
    IF EXISTING CUSTOMER THEN
        CHECK FOR MOVIE REQUEST
        IF REQUEST = YES THEN
            CHECK FOR MOVIE AVAILABILITY
            IF YES THEN
            RENT MOVIE
            SET FLAG IN INVENTORY TO OUT
        END IF
        ELSE
            CHECK FOR MOVIE RETURN
            ADD MOVIE TO INVENTORY
            SET FLAG IN INVENTORY TO IN
            ACCEPT PAYMENT
        END IF
```

diagrams are useful for capturing data, while structured programming, structure chart, system flowchart, decision tables, and decision trees are useful for capturing system processes. Structured English helps convert system specifications into programmable code.

Business Guidelines for System Development Success

Systems development is a costly, labor-intensive process that can greatly affect the success or failure of an information system. It is both an art and a science. In this chapter we have examined several methods and tools that build successful systems. However, business managers and developers should adhere to six additional guidelines to ensure that they develop and implement systems strategically.

Every Information System Is a Business System

Many IS projects fail because organizations view them as technology projects, not business projects. "There are no system projects—only business projects enabled by IT," says Karen L. McKemie, executive project director of finance for Tenneco Business Services, headquartered in Houston.[26] When managers understand that the only reason for the existence of information systems is to support and enhance the business, they start to ask the right questions. Tenneco, manufacturer of such diverse products as Hefty trash bags and turkey basters, needed IT to help it come back from a near-death experience in 1991, when the company's stock was at an all-time low and its debt was $9.3 billion.

A benchmark analysis of its competitors revealed that it cost Tenneco twice what it did the competition even to process something as simple as an invoice. The only way for Tenneco to recover was to reduce its manufacturing cost, and that simply could not be done without systems and technologies. The company developed an information system integrating common business functions such as finance, human resources, and marketing to better serve the customer. The new system has resulted in reduced operating costs, organizational flexibility, increased efficiencies, and better customer responsiveness.

The Business of IS Departments Is Change

There is nothing permanent about information systems. As the environment around the system changes, the system must adapt. Otherwise it will die a slow and well-deserved death. Preparing for change is the key to success. Although many companies carefully plan the resources required for developing systems, they are not prepared for the demand on resources placed by change.

Victoria's Secret Stores—a chain of four stores in 1982 compared to the 700-plus stores in 1995—is a business that understands the importance of change. When the company found itself growing faster than it could handle, executives were willing to revamp their information systems. "We're in a fashion business, our culture is all about change," explains Rich Amari, vice president of information systems. The $2 billion division of Limited Inc. altered its information systems completely to help manage change and satisfy customers.[27]

Systems Development Is a Venture, Not an End in Itself

Many organizations view information systems as if they were operating in a vacuum. As a result, many systems exist that do not communicate with other systems, fail to meet user expectations, and cause more problems than they solve.

Management guru Peter Keen laments about the lack of vision in organizations when it comes to system development:

> IS originated as systems development, and its historical organization and career and skill base were built on that. The core of the profession was programming, operations and project management. Development is detached from maintenance; support and education are add-ons. If you think of systems development as a venture, as bringing a product or service to market, you get a very different mind-set and set of priorities than those that mark the mainstream of IS thinking and practice. For example, those shameful toll-free customer disservice lines offered by PC vendors are a heritage of the separation of product development from what's vital to the customer—after sales help.[28]

One Size Doesn't Fit All—Especially in a Global Environment

Running into political, cultural, and technical glitches in global system implementations is very common. The difficulty of achieving a successful global rollout is "infinitely worse" when a corporation's business units are dispersed worldwide, says Chris Jones, vice president and research director of manufacturing applications at consulting firm Gartner Group. In spite of the enormous challenge of building global systems, more and more companies are going global.

"Not only are companies feeling the need to be global, but they are placing much greater strategic value on making sure systems are in place and information available on a global basis," observes Tim Ramos, a senior vice president at Cambridge Technology Partners, a systems integrator based in Cambridge, Massachusetts. And consistency is not always a virtue. More often than not, some practices, including the software for implementing these processes, must be customized to meet the needs of different sites, countries, and product groups.

Perhaps the most important potential payback of a global software rollout is as a vehicle for implementing the best business practices in a consistent manner companywide. Managers at the $3.5 billion Echlin automotive parts manufacturer were building an information system to replace a hodgepodge of manufacturing and distribution systems in 150 business units worldwide. Even though "people are very cognizant of the opportunities and benefits of the project, it's been challenging to get general consensus on the implementation," notes Bill Tilt, director of enterprise systems at the Branford, Connecticut firm. "We have disagreements on what a best practice may be, and people perceive themselves as having a unique set of requirements." In the United States alone, for instance, each site has an individual way of handling inventory receipts.

But Echlin hopes to capture and build on its best practices. In the United States, a 70-person, largely domestic team is spending six or seven months defining best practices. The company will then buy software to model and implement these practices. During the worldwide implementation the company does not expect many challenges. "By going after leading best business practices, we'll make acceptance by other operations much easier." Echlin is actually treating applications at different geographic areas—the United States, the United Kingdom, Mexico, South America, and Europe—as "different projects, different venues." "We call it the localization component, customizing software to adhere to current covenants and government statutes in each country."

Build the Development Team

Developing systems is no cakewalk. To relieve the stress of the job, IS managers must build a culture that fosters creativity, innovation, and teamwork. Brenda Wong of IBIS Consulting explains how a team of developers warded off stress with humor and a sense of community as they completed a $5.5 million IS development project for North America's leading energy company on time.

One team leader's office door had a sign that read "Go home already!" . . . Even the application itself was not spared the team's mischievous humor. The "About" window contains cartoon images of the developers as pigs swimming out of a pipeline, a reference to the mechanical "smart pigs" that scrub the inside of natural gas pipelines.

David Easa, one of [the team's] project developers . . . spent days at the office without going home prior to a critical deadline. When his manager finally ordered him to go home, his teammates left some clothes, a pillow, and food on his desk at work. "Will code for food," says the sign they posted on his door. "It was exhausting, but exhilarating at the same time," Easa says of the experience. "But the sense of accomplishment, of holding things together in perilous times, brought the whole team together."[29]

A culture that encouraged a sense of purpose and fun led to this team's success despite crushing deadlines. How can IS managers help create a culture that promotes creative, effective teamwork?

1. **Select members with care.** Team members should complement one another's business expertise and interpersonal skills. No team will function well if everyone tries to dominate the group or shies away from resolving problems.
2. **Build trust.** Each member should be willing and able to communicate openly, share the workload, and treat people fairly and equitably. After all, a team cannot succeed if its members do not trust each other. To help build trust and improve team performance, managers should consider training employees in teamwork and conflict resolution methods.
3. **Build cohesiveness.** The IS manager should provide ample time for members to interact so that they understand their common purpose, set clear goals, and develop standards for work-related behavior.[30]

It's All about Users

When we think of information systems, most of us tend to think about hardware and software. But what really lies behind a successful system is not just hardware and software but more important, people. This includes professionals who design and develop the system along with system users.

At BMG Entertainment North America, CIO Scott Dinsdale emphasizes that his IS professionals first understand all aspects of the business, including reading profit-and-loss statements and being aware of basic marketing concepts such as branding. Because his company is in the music business, he expects his staff to explain all IT projects not in the context of a "system plan," but in the context of a "music plan." In other words, he expects his staff to explain to users how the system will help them to be a more successful music company.

BMG Entertainment, a company that promotes musicians' recordings and tours, expects its system developers to understand the music business before they build systems.

Dinsdale recently treated his IT directors to a "marketing morning" during which one of BMG's top marketing executives presented an impassioned overview of pop singer Sarah McLachlan's career from her humble Canadian roots to her headlining success on the Lilith Fair tour. The point? To give his IS staff a greater understanding of what people expect from their information systems.

"We have two customers who connect to our processes—the artist and the consumer," Dinsdale explains. "Every process we follow hangs off those two customers. It's easy for our people to think of themselves as music consumers, but what they don't always get is what drives the musicians. If they don't understand what drives the musicians, then they don't understand the company." And if they don't understand the company, they cannot build effective systems. [31]

Designing and developing information systems are complex tasks. Both developers and users must work closely to build truly effective systems. As future employees, you will make a significant contribution if you understand and practice the principles of effective system building

SUMMARY

1. **Describe the system development life cycle methodology and its limitations.** The system development life cycle (SDLC) is a traditional development approach for building information systems. It is made up of five phases: system definition, system analysis, system design and programming, system testing and implementation, and system maintenance. These phases are usually done in sequence. This method relies on a systematic and structured way to develop information systems. The SDLC's limitations include its rigidity and relative inflexibility and the assumptions that the systems development process occurs in orderly, sequential steps and that once system requirements are established they can be frozen in time.
2. **Discuss the prototyping methodology.** In prototyping, different phases of system development are done at the same time rather than in sequence. This methodology is also referred to as rapid application development (RAD) and has four main phases: problem definition and identification of system requirements, building the initial prototype, refining the prototype, and further revising and enhancing the prototype. This method is useful for building systems with new and emerging technologies or in cases where the requirements are not very clear.
3. **Explain end-user computing (EUC) and the reasons for its growth.** In this method, end users design, develop, and maintain information systems to meet their needs. The proliferation of affordable PCs and user-friendly software packages greatly propelled the end-user movement. Often, end users follow the same steps as the SDLC, but the overall approach may be less formal. The benefits of EUC are shorter development times, greater control and flexibility over system development, and lower development costs.
4. **Outline situations in which companies should use off-the-shelf packages.** Off-the-shelf packages are an attractive alternative to building the software portion of an information system. Companies buy ready-made software and sometimes customize it to meet their unique information needs. Companies resort to this alternative if they do not have a large IS department or if there are sophisticated packages in the market that meet company needs.
5. **Explain why outsourcing is a viable option for building information systems.** When a company uses outside vendors to create, process, manage, and maintain information systems, it is called outsourcing. Vendors can provide a wide range of services, from simple to complex. Businesses can choose to outsource some or all of the functions of their IT department. Like other approaches, outsourcing has advantages and disadvantages. The main advantage is that the vendor rather than the company becomes responsible for designing and developing quality information systems. Outsourcing can decrease costs, reduce technologic obsolescence, and provide a competitive edge. The disadvantage is that outsourcing may sometimes result in layoffs, demoralized employees, and cost overruns if the project is poorly supervised.
6. **Identify and describe structured tools for system development.** Structured tools are those that support development methodologies such as SDLC and prototyping. Two tools that support system analysis and design are context diagram and data flow diagram. The context diagram gives a broad overview of the system and identifies the major inputs, processes, and outputs in the system. It allows users and developers to see the "big picture." The data flow diagram (DFD) identifies the inputs, outputs, processes, and data stores of subsystems within the overall system. The DFD uses four symbols to represent data flow, process, data store, and external entities.

   Tools used to capture and represent system data include the entity relationship diagram (ERD), which graphically depicts the data that drives the system. An ERD shows the different entities in the system and the relationship among them, which helps users see how the entities work together to produce an operational system. There are four tools used to capture and represent system processes: structure chart, system flowchart, decision tables, and decision trees. The structure chart depicts the logic that links different modules in a program. The system flowchart shows how data flow in an information system. Decision tables show the condition clauses and their corresponding action clauses, while decision trees depict both the logic and the sequence of steps behind that logic. Finally, structured English, also known as pseudocode, is a tool that translates program specifications into code.

KEY TERMS

acceptance testing (p. 302)
context diagram (p. 312)
creeping requirements (p. 300)
data flow diagram (DFD) (p. 312)

decision tables (p. 316)
decision trees (p. 316)
direct cutover (p. 303)
end-user computing (EUC) (p. 305)
entity relationship diagram (ERD) (p. 313)
functional requirements (p. 299)
outsourcing (p. 306)
parallel conversion (p. 302)
phased conversion (p. 303)
pilot study (p. 303)
prototyping (p. 303)
structure chart (p. 315)
structured English (pseudocode) (p. 317)
structured programming (p. 314)
structured tools (p. 311)
system analysis (p. 299)
system definition (p. 299)
system design (p. 301)
system development life cycle (SDLC) (p. 298)
system flowchart (p. 315)
system maintenance (p. 303)
system testing (p. 302)
testing (p. 301)
top-down approach to system development (p. 310)
unit testing (p. 301)

REVIEW QUESTIONS

1. What are the five components in an information system? Describe each component. Are these components found in other systems also? Explain.
2. What are five different development methodologies for information systems? Why should workers be aware of these methodologies? Briefly describe each methodology.
3. Briefly discuss the five phases in the SDLC. What are the types of systems for which the SDLC is well suited?
4. Identify and briefly describe the three primary activities in the system analysis phase. What are some types of feasibility analysis that are conducted in this phase?
5. Define functional requirements. Explain why it is difficult to develop functional requirements.
6. What are creeping requirements, and why are they such a common problem?
7. Identify and describe three types of system testing. What are the four types of implementation methods that are used to replace existing systems with new systems. Which of the four implementation methods is the safest?
8. Describe prototyping and identify any two strengths and any two weaknesses of this methodology.
9. Define an end user. What are some factors that propelled the end-user movement?
10. What are some advantages and disadvantages of off-the-shelf software packages? When are they recommended?
11. What are some reasons why organizations choose to outsource their information systems? What are some advantages and disadvantages of outsourcing?
12. Why should selecting IS tools be viewed as a business decision and not just a technical decision?
13. Identify any three structured tools and explain how they aid system development.
14. Describe the context diagram and its primary purpose. How is the context diagram related to the data flow diagram?
15. What are the three main tasks of a DFD? What are the four symbols used in a DFD? What do they represent?
16. What is an entity? How are relationships represented in an entity relationship diagram? Does the ERD represent data or processes?
17. An ERD supplements the DFD. Explain.
18. Identify the steps in developing an ERD. Develop an entity relationship diagram using the entities teacher, students, and course grade.
19. Define structured programming and the three constructs on which it is based.
20. Compare the structure chart with the system flowchart. How do these two tools help to capture system logic?
21. What is the difference between decision tables and decision trees? When is the decision tree preferred over the decision table?

DISCUSSION QUESTIONS AND EXERCISES

1. There are two competing viewpoints about the role of litigation in ensuring the quality of software systems.

Viewpoint 1: Competition, not litigation, ensures quality systems. As computers continue to influence all aspects of our personal and professional lives, the implications of faulty systems are serious for both users and developers. Although faulty systems may result in damaging lawsuits, such measures do not necessarily result in better systems. Instead they simply increase the cost of developing information systems, which are then passed on to the consumer. "Competition, not litigation, ensures quality systems."[32]

Viewpoint 2: Responsible lawsuits keep vendors honest. Companies incur devastating financial losses because of faulty computer systems. For example, a company in Massachusetts alleged that it became insolvent because of a faulty computer-based financial system that caused errors in the company's integrated general ledger system, passbooks, and loan statements. The errors were so serious that dissatisfied customers withdrew more than $5 million dollars from the bank and took their business elsewhere. There are other incidents in which faulty systems have created adverse, sometimes even life-threatening, situations. A Boeing 747 had to make an emergency landing because of an error in the plane's autopilot system.

Lawyers and their clients argue that professionals, such as doctors, lawyers, and architects, are held liable and accountable for their actions and so should programmers and system developers, particularly in cases where the software can cause catastrophic losses.[33]

a. Computer programmers, like other professionals, should be held accountable and liable for their actions. Discuss.

b. If a structural engineer uses a software program that miscalculates the stress loads in a building, thereby causing serious injuries to its residents, should the programmer be held liable? Discuss the cost implications if such liabilities are imposed on programmers.

c. Higher liability standards will simply increase the cost of developing information systems with little or no effect on the quality of systems. Discuss.

2. Good project managers are those who can explain to users the cost and scheduling implications of their requests to make changes to the system and if possible, get them to agree to defer them until after the base system is up and running. How would you convince a rather obstinate user to postpone changing requirements until the initial system becomes operational? What policies and procedures should an organization put in place to address users' requests for requirement changes?

3. Many end users and even IS chiefs do not want to be bothered about the details of development methodologies. One IS chief recently commented "I don't care whether we use pencil and paper or crayons and drawing tablets . . . whatever works."[34] Do you agree with this approach? Why or why not?

4. One of the major drawbacks of traditional development methodologies, such as the SDLC, is that the lead-time from product conception to delivery is often too long, somewhere between three and five years. But in today's environment, such development times can put a company at a competitive disadvantage as competitors beat them to the market with new, innovative, and high-quality products. Conversely, high-quality systems take time to develop and cannot be rushed.[35]

Which methodology would you recommend if a system is to be delivered quickly? Why?

5. Review Figure 11-6. Prepare a short memo that explains how each tool supports the systems development phases listed in the figure.

6. Ask the director of information systems at a local company how IS development tools and techniques are selected at his or her firm. Make a short presentation to your class on the strengths and limitations of IS tools.

Cases for Success

Case 1: Building Blocks for a New Age

Many technology managers say that creating a piece of business software is like constructing an office building. In both cases, three elements are essential: construction methods, users' needs, and the overall success of the end product. Unfortunately, existing tools and techniques are often not capable of building applications that support large, complex, mission-critical tasks because the tools were originally designed to work with a limited number of clients accessing just one type of database management system (DBMS).

In today's environment, applications must operate on several hardware platforms and access more than one type of database. Further, many tools lack the group programming features that allow companies to build integrated applications for different business functions, such as programs that link accounting, distribution, and sales systems. However, software vendors are actively addressing this problem. They are building a new generation of development tools that help businesses build more complex, integrated applications that work on multiple platforms.

1. Use your imagination and predict some tools that may be in use in the year 2010.
2. How would you improve on any one of the existing tools covered in this chapter? Discuss.

Case 2: Outsourcing Baggage

According to a survey of IT executives at 85 large companies conducted by Gordon & Glickson P.C., a Chicago-based technology law firm, 80 percent of those surveyed said they are outsourcing their IT functions. Of those who are, 54 percent admitted they are struggling to manage outsourcing relationships that have gone sour. Despite such difficulties as failure to provide desired service, disagreements over the scope of the project, cost overruns, and dissatisfaction with vendor personnel, fewer than 25 percent have renegotiated key points in their contracts, the study found. Only 28 percent reported retaining outside legal counsel to help with crafting an outsourcing contract.

Forty-six IT executives who responded to the survey reported the following problems with their outsourcers:[36]

Customer service adversely affected	40%
Cost to outsource higher than expected	37%
Outsourcer does not understand core business	34%
Outsourcer not responsive	31%
Relationship has not evolved	31%
Lack of management control	28%
Difficult technology changeover	20%
Outsourcer has missed changeover dates	17%
Led to a loss of skilled labor	6%

1. Outsourcing can lead to a decline in customer service. If you were the IS manager for an outsourcing contract, what measures would you take to ensure that this problem does not occur?
2. Hiring a legal consultant to write an outsourcing contract is a wise option, although few companies exercise this option. Make a presentation to your top management explaining why this is important.
3. Do a search in your library for an example of an outsourcing contract that turned sour. Explain how the company could have avoided that situation.

Case 3: Temporary Problem?

IT departments in this country and around the world rely heavily on temporary employees and independent contractors to design, develop, and maintain their information systems. In a case that should hit close to home for many IT departments, the U.S. Department of Labor has accused Time Warner of denying pensions and health benefits to full-time workers by wrongfully classifying them as temporary workers or independent contractors. The case marks the first time the agency has taken on this issue, which could have an impact on all companies that hire contract workers, observers say.

"Employers must deliver promised benefits to all eligible employees, and we believe some misclassified Time Inc. employees did not receive benefits they were entitled to," Labor Secretary Alexis Herman claimed when announcing the suit. Time Warner shot back with a statement that said the Labor Department's claim had no basis in law or in fact.

In the case against New York–based Time Warner, the company is accused of classifying employees as temps even though they worked for Time Warner beyond four to six months, which Time Warner's own guidelines suggest should make them full-time employees. The workers involved include about 1,000 journalists, photographers, and graphic designers who worked between 1990 and the present on the company's publications.[37]

1. Many IS departments hire temporary workers as a way to keep costs down, especially because they do not typically pay for benefits for these employees. Is there anything unethical about this approach?
2. If you were representing Time Warner, how would you convince a jury that you did not do anything wrong or illegal?
3. What are some implications for society if the government wins its suit? If it loses?

There are two kinds of customers: those who have been the victims of computer fraud, and those who will be.[1]

Anonymous

CONTENTS

SECURITY FOR SUCCESS

Computer security affects all of us. Some examples illustrate the negative effects of a security breach. When a bank's computer is broken into, personal information about customers' financial transactions is in jeopardy. If the person who breached the system intercepts personal credit-card information provided to e-commerce sites, individuals can experience huge financial losses.

When unauthorized individuals access medical records of patients via computer, it can lead to loss of privacy and in extreme cases, denial of employment or even medical insurance. In one Florida case, thieves stole computers that housed the medical records of 8,000 carriers of HIV, the virus that causes AIDS. Criminal hackers (crackers) can also harass people by manipulating their phone services. One cracker, for instance, transferred all phone charges from a local hospital to a residential phone line.[2]

Criminal computer security violations are the leading white-collar crime in terms of monetary losses in the United States and around the world, compared to other white-collar crimes such as espionage, pilferage, and illegal trading. The violations are some of the most dangerous, yet most neglected, problems facing organizations around the world. The ramifications of security problems are huge, ranging from financial losses to privacy violations to corporate espionage. Experts estimate that 75 percent of U.S. organizations suffer some kind of security breach. Company employees such as those at King Soopers cause 80 percent of those breaches.[3]

Despite these high crime rates, security experts believe these estimates are probably too low due to underreporting. Many companies do not report security breaches because they are embarrassed, afraid the news might turn away customers, or even worse, they are afraid to admit they were technically too ignorant to recognize when and how the breach occurred.

Chapter 12

Computer Security

AFTER STUDYING THIS CHAPTER, YOU WILL BE ABLE TO:

- Describe computer security and its business importance
- Explain why information systems are vulnerable to security breaches
- Identify different types of security breaches
- Describe measures that organizations take to prevent security breaches
- Discuss the importance and elements of a disaster recovery plan

According to the FBI, fewer than 20 percent of companies report security intrusions to law enforcement. "One of the few constants that we've seen in the last three years is that the percentage of businesses that comes to us to report and investigate hacking incidents has remained steady at 17 percent," explains Special Agent George Grotz in the FBI's San Francisco office. "The overwhelming majority of companies fearing adverse publicity, copycat hacking and loss of customer confidence still prefer to handle their security breaches and problems in-house."[4]

Computer security breaches occur all over the globe. China has detected more than 100 cases of computer crimes in the past two years, the most serious case involving the theft of $1.2 million. In addition, newspaper reports indicate that an inefficient computer police force, outdated computer protection equipment, and the slow development of computer protection products hamper Internet security surveillance in China. This security issue looms large because China has experienced an explosion in Internet use. The country had 620,000 active users at the end of 1997 and projects 5 million active users by 2000.[5]

Security regulations, however, vary from nation to nation, which makes it more difficult to find and penalize those who engage in international security breaches. China did not enact a law criminalizing computer system break-ins until 1997. That law set a maximum five-year prison term for a conviction. Police in the commercial hub of Shanghai arrested China's first suspected computer cracker under the new law in 1998. A 22-year-old had broken into a Shanghai computer network and learned the passwords of more than 500 users.[6]

In contrast, the Norwegian Supreme Court ruled that crackers who try to find ways to access a network or system cannot be punished. In a case involving students who were trying to break into the University of Oslo's network, the Supreme Court ruled that snooping

TECHNOLOGY PAYOFF
Stealing from the King

At first, managers at the King Soopers supermarket chain suspected software bugs were causing the huge number of sales "voids" and other accounting anomalies. The corporate office repeatedly dispatched regional PC manager Jay Beaman, who had virtually unlimited access to computer systems and data, to fix the problems.

But he turned out to be part of the problem. Beaman and two head clerks allegedly stole more than $2 million by manipulating computer records at King Soopers stores in Colorado. This incident is not surprising to industry experts: Employee theft is one of the leading corporate security threats.

In 1998 the Colorado Springs Police Department arrested Beaman, the PC manager, and head clerks David Heinke and David Selaya. Beaman tampered with the bar-code pricing system to overcharge customers and then Heinke and Selaya skimmed the difference out of cash registers after closing. In addition, the group would void entire customer sales and pocket the cash. One week the voids totaled $219,305.11. The trio also rang in thousands of coupons multiple times per day, then took that money out of cash drawers over the course of several months. They were able to skim thousands of dollars from the cash registers with this scheme.

They also set up bogus accounts. For example, a cashier would slide a gallon of milk across a scanner and a price would flash for the customer. It seemed normal. But behind the scenes, the milk purchase was placed in a dummy account. At the end of the day, Heinke or Selaya allegedly would steal the amount of money recorded in the fake account from the registers. Beaman would later erase the category from sales reports. Because of the siphoned cash and fake accounts, the official records made it seem as if no one had purchased any dairy products at Heinke's store for 18 months.

The suspects are charged with conspiracy, computer crime and felony theft. Al-around is okay as long as no information theft occurs. This rule is equivalent "to letting burglars check the doors and windows of a house for locks, but not prosecuting them until they break in."[7]

In spite of the potential for damage, many companies are lax in their computer security, particularly small businesses, treating it as a waste of time and money. Many organizations do not have policies to prevent or remedy security breaches. This strategy usually does not work because security becomes an afterthought rather than a guiding operating principle.

This trend is changing slowly as security breaches skyrocket. A Computer Security Institute study showed that nearly 60 percent of companies surveyed plan to increase their information security budgets in the coming year. The same survey found that security averages just 1 to 3 percent of the overall IS budget.[8]

Protecting information systems is vital to safeguard companies' financial well-being. Computer security breaches can result in colossal financial losses—as demonstrated in the King Soopers Technology Payoff—and may wipe out an entire business. Consider this example: A major bank in New York fixed a computer security breach 26 hours after it occurred. In that time period the bank incurred a loss in excess of $34 *million* and had to borrow several billion dollars to cover financial transactions from the previous day.

To counteract security breaches, several sophisticated security tools are emerging. For example, secure-face recognition technology is being installed in several check-cashing machines throughout the country, making it easier and safer for people to cash their checks. Check-cashing company Atreva is using a face-recognition technology in about 42 check-cashing ATMs in convenience stores and warehouses throughout the southwestern United States. It has almost completely eradicated fraud at those machines and bolstered customer confidence, according to Atreva's top officers.

The face-recognition software works by registering the unique heat signature created by the pattern of blood vessels in a person's face. Scanners at ATMs scan users' faces before they use the machine and compare the images with the file copy stored on a True-Face server. According to Atreva executives, it is more accurate than other techniques such as voice recognition and retinal scans, which can be counterfeited.[9]

In this chapter we explore what computer security is, why information systems are vulnerable to security breaches, and different types of computer security violations. Then we investigate protective measures that companies can take to prevent or remedy breaches, and we close by examining disaster recovery plans for businesses. Everyone who uses information systems in the workplace or at home should understand the risks of security violations and natural disasters and the steps businesses must take to minimize their effects.

What Is Computer Security?

Computers and information systems are so tightly interwoven into our personal and professional lives that if they fail our everyday activities can be seriously disrupted. Imagine what would happen if your bank's computers went down for a week or if doctors were unable to perform surgery because the computers in the operating room were down.

Computer security is important for several reasons. First, the number of computers in use, both at home and at work, has increased dramatically since the early 1980s. Second, with graphical user interfaces and other easy-to-use tools and programs, it is easy for anyone with a little computer background to use a computer. Third, networks are commonplace, and as electrons travel across the globe, protecting them has become a monumental task. Fourth, information is one of the most valuable assets of a business, but it is more difficult to protect than other company assets—such as land, buildings, and equipment—because it can move more freely in many ways.

Computer security is the process of protecting and safeguarding hardware, software, networks, physical facilities, data, and personnel from accidental, intentional, or natural disasters. It includes activities such as accidental input or output errors, theft, break-ins, physical damage, and illegal access and manipulation. It is a seven-day, 24-hour operation. This business function can never afford to go on vacation!

Computer security is a complex, pervasive problem. In large part this is because the range of security violations is so vast and so costly. (Table 12-1 offers a sample range of violations.) Risks from IT malfunctions now rank with earthquakes (a $30 billion to $60 billion exposure) and hurricanes ($5 billion to $15 billion per incident) in potential economic losses. And if one contemplates various failure scenarios, such as a global Internet-borne software plague or deliberate acts of information terrorism, the financial damage estimates are similar to those from a nuclear power plant accident.[10]

Companies often struggle to balance proper security with the cost and convenience of providing it. They need secure environments without stifling or offending their employees. Achieving this

TABLE 12-1 Common Types of Security Violations

- Company data theft by employees
- Gaining access to information stored on computer networks by cracking passwords
- Industrial espionage by criminals eavesdropping on wireless communications or on LANs and Internet connections
- Deliberate, unauthorized modification of software
- Theft of employees' identities to make outrageous or illegal statements on the Internet
- Starting or fueling rumors on the Internet that are designed to harm the company
- Denial of service attacks in which people call a toll-free number or send an e-mail but the number stays perpetually busy or they are denied access

Sources: Adapted from M. E. Kabay, "Prepare Yourself for Information Warfare," *Computerworld,* March 20, 1995, www.computerworld.com.

though this case was difficult to investigate, the police knew something unusual was happening because the suspects traveled, bought numerous cars, and used a lot of cash while the embezzlement was ongoing. The vanity plates on Heinke's red Dodge Viper read, "BYBYCOP"—suspicious activity for employees who earned less than $35,000 per year. "They weren't smart about covering their tracks," notes Anthony Erickson, a nine-year police veteran.

Several years ago King Soopers' switched from a centralized mainframe system to a decentralized system of networked IBM PCs. Few managers were well trained in the new system, so they relied heavily on Beaman's PC expertise. Ron Nissen, Beaman's boss, acknowledged in a police interview that he never checked Beaman's work. Nissen said he would "take at face value" Beaman's claims that he had fixed alleged computer problems at Heinke's and Selaya's stores.

King Soopers' internal security managers tried unsuccessfully to solve the problem themselves before calling police. When security got too close, the trio would switch theft methods and find fellow employees willing to cover for them, police claim. Erickson speculates that if store officials had called police when they first suspected theft, they might have limited losses to under $1 million.

Source: Adapted from Kim S. Nash, "PC Manager at Center of $2M Grocery Scam," *Computerworld,* March 30, 1998, retrieved on-line at http://www.computerworld.com/home/print.nsf/all/9803303D8A.

Computer security

The process of protecting all computer assets through the use of policies, procedures, tools, techniques, and methods.

FIGURE 12-1

Awareness of Security Violations

Has Your Organization Been the Target of Information Espionage?

Base: Survey of 320 Fortune 1,000 companies

Source: Warroom Research, Inc., Annapolis, Md.

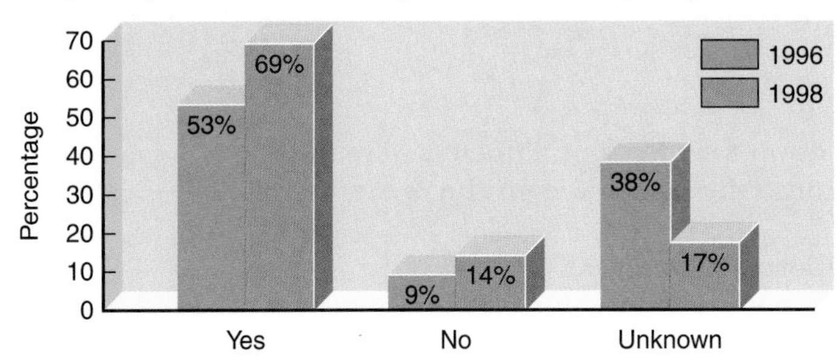

balance requires more than sophisticated equipment, policies, and procedures. It also requires the support of all employees, common sense, good judgment, and shared corporate values of trust and integrity. In particular, it is important to educate employees about the critical nature of security violations and also to sensitize managers to the dangers of computer security violations.

Christine Snyder, a vice president at Price Waterhouse LLP in Baltimore, says that one of the biggest security threats is from company insiders. Educating and training employees in computer security issues tops her list of ways to protect company data. Her staff distributes booklets and updates on company policies and the penalties for users that breach security rules—including dismissal. "As far as I'm concerned, there are no lasting technical solutions to social problems," Snyder comments.[11]

It is equally important to make sure that managers become sensitive to the effects of security violations because such violations are on the rise, as a survey of Fortune 1,000 companies suggests (see Figure 12-1). Almost 70 percent of the companies surveyed reported that their organization had been the target of information espionage. Shockingly, 17 percent of them did not know whether their companies had experienced a security breach.[12]

Investments in security measures may sometimes appear to be a waste because there are no immediate and quantifiable results. How does a business value the cost of a potential break-in? One security manager for a manufacturing company with 30,000 users turned to scare tactics to obtain a larger security budget. He presented an itemized list of all potential network vulnerabilities and the associated cost of repairing damage if a network outage occurred. "I was able to show my CIO that even a simple network outage would require two to three network administrators at least two hours to fix and cost us about $10,000," explains the security manager. "A severe network security breach—one that made us lose data and suffer an outage of one to three days—could run into the millions. That made the extra $75,000 I was asking for look like a pretty good investment. I got the money."[13]

Background checks on IS employees, particularly those who work on sensitive projects, are also essential to minimize security violations. The number of security breaches by IS staff is significant. Twenty-eight percent of the companies reported Internet misuse by IS employees, 18 percent reported internal theft or fraud, and 13 percent reported network security violations.[14]

Security consultant John Case, president of John Case & Associates in Del Mar, California, recalls how a burglar in the IS department of one company had committed a near-identical crime at his previous job, but the new company hadn't checked out his past before hiring him. "Getting a bad apple in IS can be a lot more catastrophic than a bad apple in other areas because of the terrific opportunity they have to accomplish and cover up their activities," notes Case.[15]

Now that we have a general idea of what computer security is and its importance, we investigate why information systems are vulnerable.

Why Are Information Systems Vulnerable?

Information systems are prone to security violations for myriad reasons, ranging from employees who do not understand security policies to hardware and software programs that offer inadequate protection to lax security policies. Further, many users are unable

TABLE 12-2

Five Sources of Security Violations

Source	Examples
Many employees have access to system	Only select employees should have access to payroll systems; if access isn't restricted, a mistake (someone's paycheck gets sent to the wrong bank) or intentional security violation (someone funnels other employees' wages to their account) is more likely to occur.
Increased system complexity	If an information system fails, it could be due to the software, hardware, network, input error, a cracker, or some other problem. The more complex the system, the more difficult it is to locate a violation.
Cyber terrorism on the Internet	Unscrupulous individuals can intercept credit-card numbers and other private information over the Internet.
Network vulnerabilities	Networks rely on many components to function; someone can breach one part—from a cable wire to the software that runs the system—and access the entire information system.
Complacent management	Managers who don't fully understand the importance of computer security or the likelihood that their business is at risk fail to invest in security tools and techniques.

to spot and report security violations because they don't understand the technologic underpinnings of the IS system.

In this section we investigate five key reasons for security breaches: the number of people with access to the information system, system complexity, cyber terrorism on the Internet, the network environment, and complacent management. Table 12-2 summarizes these five threats.

Increased Access to the System

Imagine that you gave hundreds of copies of your house or apartment key to people with whom you work or go to school. Your chances of getting robbed would increase substantially. Similarly, many people have access to information systems in a business. Typically, some of them know enough about IT to pose computer security threats.

Key sources of security breaches are employees, authorized external users such as suppliers, and crackers outside the business who gain illegal access to the information system. Employees who intentionally or accidentally breach computer security are the main source of violations. Employees who have sophisticated technical expertise and the wrong intentions can cause serious damage. Remember the Technology Payoff? King Soopers had no checks and balances to counteract a few unscrupulous, technologically savvy employees. The result was serious financial damage.

Suppliers and other authorized users of intranets and extranets also have access to company systems and pose a threat to company security. Security violations of enterprise systems by outsiders are on the rise. According to the Computer Security Institute (CSI), 57 percent of 521 respondents reported assaults on their systems via the Internet, up from 37 percent in 1998—a 20 percent overall increase. The average cost of each security breach was $1.8 million, according to the 31 percent of survey respondents able—or willing—to quantify financial losses.

The increase is spurred in large part by the growth of Internet and extranet applications "and the disappearance of a clear border between internal and external systems." "The old rule that we would see 80 percent of the penetration coming from the inside, 20 percent from the outside, is outmoded," says Richard Power, editorial director for CSI.[16]

People outside the business without authorized access to company data who pose a threat to computer security are known by many names. Two of the most common terms

Hacker

A person who is knowledgeable enough to break into a computer system or facility but does not cause any harm to the system or organization.

Cracker

A person who breaks into a computer system with the malicious intent of stealing passwords, data, information, mail messages, files, and programs for fun or profit.

are "hackers" and "crackers." Both **hackers** and **crackers** know enough to break into computer systems and commit security breaches. However, hackers do so without the intent to harm or gain profit.

"White hat" hackers, as they are sometimes called, attempt to distinguish themselves from their malicious brethren by claiming that their attempts to find flaws in software are for the intellectual challenge rather than for illegal entry into systems. Sometimes, these people can offer a valuable service. Karan Khanna, a Microsoft product manager who oversees Windows NT security, notes that after her team discovered three security flaws in Internet Explorer within a week, Microsoft contacted a white hat hacker for assistance. "He's extremely helpful; he informs us of any security holes [we might have missed]. That way, we can post a [solution] to customers before a potential hole becomes public knowledge."[17]

In addition, many hackers have Web sites that some vendors and users find helpful. The sites explain how to hack into different systems. "These sites serve a useful purpose," claims Ed Ehrgott, director of IS at Charles Schwab & Co. in San Francisco. "I consider them one more weapon in the fight to keep my networks secure. . . ."[18]

Cracking can cause serious losses for a company or organization. Shakuntla Devi Singla, a former Coast Guard employee, pled guilty to accessing a federal computer without authorization and intentionally causing damage. Her attack on the Coast Guard's personnel database took 115 Coast Guard employees, including network administrators, more than 1,800 hours to restore the lost data, according to the U.S. District Attorney's office. The recovery effort cost $40,000.

Singla gained remote access to the personnel database from her home using another employee's password and identification. She then deleted personnel information, including pay, promotions, awards, and employee transfers from the database. Singla's attorney, Nancy Luque of Washington, D.C., claimed that Singla acted out of frustration that the Coast Guard ignored her attempts to report contractor improprieties.[19]

Increased System Complexity

Security becomes more difficult as system elements become more complex—just as a puzzle becomes more difficult as the number of pieces increases.

Information systems today are much more complex than systems even a few years ago. First, the software has many more functions and features and the hardware has integrated components, all of which must work together to provide overall system security. Just as a puzzle gets more difficult as the number of pieces increases, as the number of elements in a computer system increase, the more difficult it is to guarantee system security.

Second, each operating system has its own security features, so switching to a new operating system can throw previous security measures into disarray. Third, networks are often part of the information system. The highly sophisticated technical environments of networks are prone to security violations. When software, hardware, and networks are brought together in an information system, providing system security becomes more difficult.

Even if information systems managers develop security measures for this complex array of system elements, it is difficult to keep pace with the constant change in technology. When managers eventually identify a good way to secure their systems, they find that hackers have come up with more sophisticated ways to break into a system and the struggle starts all over again. As crackers and hackers try to keep one step ahead of IS managers, developing a system that is totally secure requires constant vigilance.

Cyber Terrorism on the Internet

The Internet is a haven for those engaging in security misdeeds. The Internet connects two million host computers and provides access to a rich and extensive set of data and information to millions of users, with the numbers increasing by 15 percent every month. The Internet transmits more than 100,000 million bytes of data every day. Every country in the world has an Internet connection. The Internet, then, is an ideal target for "cyber terrorists."

Serious security violations occurred on the Internet as early as 1994. Perpetrators had cracked into many company networks and stolen thousands of passwords, allowing illegal access to government, financial, research, and scientific computers around the

United States. "This large scale digital robbery is in a class by itself for scope, audacity, and potential damage."[20] The Federal Bureau of Investigation's Financial Crimes Section Chief testified that in more than 80 percent of the FBI's computer crimes investigations, the Internet was used to gain illegal access to systems.[21]

A new version of international cyberterrorism is called *hacktivism,* in which people violate computers to convey their political or social viewpoints. For example, the Electronic Disturbance Theatre (EDT), a group that is opposed to the independence movement of the Chiapas sector in Mexico, began to protest through "Web site shut-ins." They instructed protesters to open and then keep reloading the Web pages of Mexican financial institutions, leading to denial of service for many customers. Such activities are spreading throughout the world. In 1997 a group called the Hong Kong Blondes in China protested against human rights violations by penetrating Chinese military computers and shutting down China's communications satellites. In India, a group hacked into the country's atomic research center computers to protest against nuclear testing.[22]

Warroom Research Corporation, a security consulting firm based in Annapolis, Maryland, surveyed Fortune 1,000 companies to determine how many companies had been the target of information espionage. The survey found that 70 percent of the surveyed companies had been targeted by people who tried to penetrate their systems either through dial-up connections (telephone connections that allow remote users to dial into their office computers) or the Internet. The survey also found that none of the companies reported the intrusions to police because they didn't trust the ability of law enforcement to investigate the crimes.[23]

Networks Are the Weakest Link in the Chain

Crackers attack each corporate network on average between 12 to 15 times each year, according to a survey by the Computer Security Institute and the FBI. Of the 563 users polled, 73 percent said crackers had broken into their networks. Eighteen percent of those respondents reported that they had no idea if, or how often, their systems had been invaded. The Defense Information Systems Agency (DISA) claims that in some companies nearly 98 percent of attacks on a network go undetected.[24]

There are several ways to establish a network connection in a company. Depending on the type of network, the connection may require modems, cable connections, telephone lines, cellular phones, pagers, and so on. Networks continually become more complex because they rely on numerous integrated technologies. As a result, they become more prone to security violations. "Networks are essentially sieves to anyone with minor technical skills and the desire to retrieve other peoples' information."[25]

First, the various devices on a network, such as cellular phones, radio modems, and sky pagers, create new points of vulnerability in the electronic exchange of information because anyone with a receiver can tune into a company's voice or data transmission. Second, in a distributed environment, hundreds of potential sources for security breaches exist. "In contrast to the fortress-like architecture of the mainframe, security exposures in client/server computing almost defy identifications."[26]

Third, networks transmit large amounts of data and information around the globe. Continuously tracking and monitoring who is doing what, where, when, and how becomes difficult. Fourth, in many organizations network administrators are rewarded for easy access to the network, not for tight security. The twin aims of easy user access and security often do not dovetail.

Finally, many network users are ignorant of network security measures and, intentionally or unintentionally, can cause considerable damage. Users often view security policies and procedures as cumbersome and unproductive, so they try to find shortcuts or ways to bypass security controls. Figure 12-2, shown on the next page, summarizes the reasons for network vulnerability to security breaches.

Complacent Management

In spite of highly publicized cases of security violations, top management teams in some organizations ignore this problem and its potential ability to bring a company to its knees. Top managers are often reluctant to invest in security because it is difficult to see the effect it has on the "bottom line." Unless management takes a vigilant, proactive

FIGURE 12-2

Reasons for Network Security Vulnerability

approach to computer security, experts predict that security breaches will continue to surge, at great cost to business and society.

For example, the U.S. General Accounting Office found security loopholes with the State Department and FAA's flight control centers. "Wide open and vulnerable to attack" is how the report ranked computer security at the FAA. In each case, the GAO cited a lack of risk assessments to identify and check for system vulnerabilities, along with an effective, centralized system for managing security, something that falls within the purview of top management.

In the FAA's case, the GAO said an inspection of a facility that controls aircraft revealed 13 physical security weaknesses and claimed that the FAA hadn't assessed physical security at 187 facilities since 1993. As a result, "the FAA does not know how vulnerable they are." Such vulnerabilities can be catastrophic. Hackers can gain access to secure government data such as defense, top secret data, trade information that could jeopardize America's competitiveness, and so on.[27]

You may wonder why so many examples of security violations relate to the government. This is not to say that these violations and breaches do not happen in corporations. Quite the contrary, most breaches do occur in business, but many companies do not publicize any security breaches they suffer because they question whether law enforcement can be effective with such cases or they fear negative publicity.

In this section we have explored five key reasons for security violations. The next section outlines the different types of security breaches.

Types of Computer Security Breaches

Although hundreds of kinds of computer security breaches occur, they can be broadly classified into three categories: accidental errors, intentional errors, and natural disasters. Table 12-3 describes these categories. Companies should prepare to face breaches in any of these three categories through careful planning and ongoing security enhancements.

TABLE 12-3

The Three Categories of Security Breaches

Types of Security Breaches	Description
Accidental or unintentional errors	Accidents relating to hardware and software. Employees can also cause unintentional security breaches.
Intentional errors	
Cracking passwords	Most common type of security violation, in which individuals intentionally decode passwords.
Breaking into computer hardware	Breaking into computer hardware such as modems, faxes, and cellular phones.
Software virus	Infected software that behaves in unexpected and undesirable ways.
Natural disasters	Tornadoes, earthquakes, and other disasters that cause computer systems to fail.

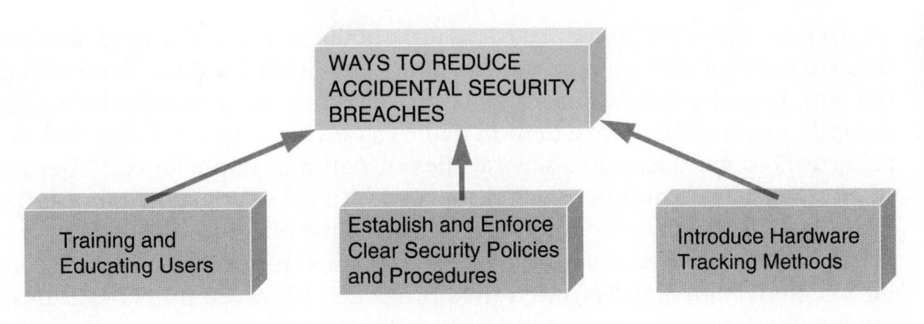

FIGURE 12-3

Techniques for Reducing Accidental Security Breaches

Accidental or Unintentional Errors

The cost of unintentional security damage exceeds the cost of premeditated computer crime. In the case of hardware, components such as memory, network connection cards, network cabling, network servers, and so on, may accidentally fail and cause a security breach.

Cables, modems, faxes, and cellular phones are particularly vulnerable to accidental failures. For instance, cables are installed underground or on rooftops, so they are hidden from the public eye and often forgotten when creating security plans and policies. However, cables can be accidentally cut or destroyed during building repairs and maintenance, resulting in serious security violations, expense, and information loss. Software, another cause of accidental errors, can create security problems through input, processing, output, or storage errors.

Businesses can reduce accidental security violations to hardware or software through education, training, and establishing clear security policies and procedures—such as authorizing only certain individuals to move or change a cable. In addition, a business should introduce methods that help track hardware. Some examples include requiring that a team of individuals be responsible for any movement of hardware inside or outside the company (collective memory is better than individual memory) and requiring frequent inventories of hardware items and their locations. These methods, summarized in Figure 12-3, minimize accidental security breaches.

Intentional Errors

Intentional security violations are common. Many experts believe that IS personnel are the greatest threat to security because they have intricate knowledge about the information system. Examples of intentional violations include illicit entry to a system, accessing valuable and proprietary corporate data, stealing passwords, "listening" to electronic mail, or destroying or appropriating important files. These serious security violations may go undetected for days, weeks, or even months, particularly if the violator is skilled. Let's briefly examine three prevalent types of intentional security breaches: cracking passwords, breaking into computer hardware, and creating or distributing software viruses.

Cracking Passwords

Cracking or decoding passwords, the Achilles heel of computer security, is one of the most common security violations. Crackers can guess passwords or capture them as they travel over the network. Once the password of the *super user* (the user, such as a system administrator, who has access to all other passwords) is cracked, the perpetrator gains full control of the network. She or he can set up pseudo accounts, use the system to uncover more passwords and retrieve confidential and vital information without being detected.

Breaking into Computer Hardware

Modems, faxes, and cellular phones are particularly vulnerable to break-ins. Although modems are central to electronic communications, they are also highly vulnerable to security breaches. To illustrate, a software program known as demon dialers can identify all phone numbers hooked to a modem. It then breaks down the passwords and allows hackers to gain illegal access to the system.

Demon dialers software programs are not illegal because system administrators use them to monitor and manage their systems. The problem, then, is not with the software but with how the software is used. Two crackers in Seattle broke into a federal court computer with the help of a demon dialers software program. Then they decoded user passwords to gain access to several files of national importance.[28] Because crackers often share phone numbers and passwords with other crackers to boost their ego and value in the crackers' community, there is a ripple effect to such crimes.

Faxes are another prime source for break-ins. Information sent over faxes can be intercepted, copied, or rerouted to another fax. However, users never hesitate to give out fax numbers, often because they do not know that they can be a security threat. Nor are they always careful about sending sensitive documents via fax.

A risk management consultant recalls how two U.S. companies' law firms were engaged in merger negotiations. One firm was based in Chicago; the other was based in New York. When clerks in the New York firm faxed sensitive contracts to the Chicago firm, they misdialed the firm's fax number by one digit. The office of the *Wall Street Journal* received the faxed documents instead of the Chicago law offices. The *Journal* made the negotiations public and the merger deal collapsed, resulting in millions of dollars in losses and irreparable damage to its competitive position.[29]

Experts recommend avoiding sending anything confidential or proprietary over the fax. "Assume that everything that you fax could go to the local newspaper," cautions one security expert. Also, documents received over the fax should not be treated as original documents. Using a pair of scissors, a little bit of Scotch tape, and a falsified signature, a cracker convinced a London bank to transfer $600 million into his account! Banks learned an important lesson in the process. Today the U.S. Uniform Commercial Code requires phone call verification for any fax-based fund transfers.[30]

Cellular phones are weak links in communication networks because they are essentially FM radios that crackers can easily scan using a $100 piece of equipment. Experts recommend that users should avoid discussing proprietary information over cellular phones and strongly urge the use of code words to discuss confidential information.

Software Viruses

Software virus

A software program that causes a computer system to behave in undesirable and unexpected ways.

Software viruses are the most common, most threatening intentional security violation. According to a study by research firm International Computer Security Association (ICSA), even though more companies use antivirus software, they're also suffering more computer viruses on their corporate networks.[31] The ICSA surveyed IT professionals from 300 large U.S. corporations and government institutions that represent close to 750,000 PCs and servers. The study found that the rate of infection in 1998 was 48 percent higher than reported in 1997, averaging 86.5 virus incidents per 1,000 machines. "A lot has to do with the fact that more viruses are being created," reports ICSA's Larry Bidwell.[32]

Experts estimate that every day the computer world is infected with 10 to 15 viruses, which makes regular updates of antivirus software critical. According to Alex Haddox, product manager at Symantec Antivirus Research Center, viruses are being generated three times faster than four years ago. In fact, many virus writers are so proud of their work that they sign their name to it. Although the United States is plagued by viruses, other parts of the world suffer, too. For example, in the early 1990s, the Eastern Bloc was a prime source of viruses. [33]

Table 12-4 summarizes key signs of a virus. They include an inexplicable loss of free memory, unusually long times for program loading or execution, changes in file or program size, malfunctioning print routines, computer "freezing," strange beeps or messages, computer reboots in the middle of a process, and corrupt files. When a virus is executed, it makes copies of itself and spreads from one system or application to another through networks and floppy disks. These symptoms explain why many faculty members are reluctant to insert a student's floppy disk in their computers!

Many viruses are also being transmitted through e-mail attachments of word-processing documents or spreadsheets. The growing popularity of e-mail is producing a related surge in the number and type of e-mail–borne viruses.

TABLE 12-4

Eight Symptoms of a Software Virus
Inexplicable loss of free memory
Unusually long program loading or execution times
Changes in program or file size
Malfunctioning print routines
Computer freezing
Unusual messages or beeps
Computer rebooting in the midst of a process
Corrupt files

In late March 1999, the Melissa virus attacked and disrupted businesses around the world. The virus attacks users of Microsoft 97 and 2000 and works in the following way: Users receive an e-mail from a known e-mail address with the subject "Important Message From" and an attachment. When the user opens the attachment, some features of Word are dismantled and the virus proceeds to send e-mail to the first 50 addresses in the user's electronic address book, thus further perpetuating itself. The fastest spreading virus in corporate history caused significant damage and brought work to a standstill in many companies.

Unfortunately, viruses are not easy to isolate or fix. Dan Schrader, director of product marketing at Trend Micro, a California firm, noted that people simply had to shut down their mail servers to avoid spreading the Melissa virus, which affected thousands of computers worldwide.[34]

Software viruses can cause serious and untold damage to companies. When Omega Engineering Corp., a technology defense company, fired one of its programmers, Timothy A. Lloyd, the company did not realize how costly this move would become. Upset at being fired after 11 years on the job, Lloyd, a network engineer in charge of Omega's computer system, decided to retaliate. He quietly planted a virus or a "logic bomb" in the company's computer system. But this was no small virus. Like a bomb it detonated three weeks after he left the company and destroyed valuable and almost irreplaceable data. The virus also damaged the company's network and customized software, among other things. Lloyd's virus is estimated to have caused the company losses exceeding $10 million, and that is just the initial estimate.[35]

Differences in software availability can make it difficult to implement worldwide virus protection strategies. U.S.–based Otis Elevator Company installed the same type of antivirus programs on the computers in its European subsidiaries and U.S. headquarters. Later, after several virus attacks, corporate security officials realized that the same product provided less protection for subsidiaries than it did for personnel at corporate headquarters, according to Alfredo DeFilippo, corporate director for information management. This problem occurred because vendors include different features in the same product in different countries.[36]

Educating users is the most powerful way to prevent the infection and spread of viruses.[37] A simple yet highly effective technique is to teach users not to move disks from one system to another. Restricting disk movement greatly reduces the chance of infecting other machines.

In addition, e-mail users should be taught about potential virus issues and trained to secure e-mail messages that contain confidential information. Another virus called "Papa," a copycat version of "Melissa," had the potential to bring down entire networks. Delivered via Microsoft Excel documents, the virus automatically mails itself to the first 60 people in different electronic address books. Further, by automatically sending queries to external sites, the virus can completely devour all the bandwidth available on a network, causing the network to crash. Because of viruses like Papa and Melissa, experts recommend that users should not open any attachments to e-mail unless they are

Otis Elevator discovered that some employees were more vulnerable to viruses than others because of differences in their antivirus software programs.

confident of the source.[38] Security controls for e-mail include such methods as encryption or the use of software programs that search e-mail messages for suspicious file attachments. As Ken Hetzer, president of Virginia-based TenFour, an e-mail security company, asks: "Would you send a letter and not put it in an envelope—open for everyone to read before it gets to its destination?"[39]

How prevalent are e-mail viruses in the workplace? Such infections rose 48 percent in 1998 relative to 1997 because of the increased spread of "macro" viruses—viruses usually found in Microsoft Word document files attached to e-mail—according to the ISCA. The number of infections per 1,000 PCs is approximately 31.85.[40]

Unbelievable as it may seem, it is still legal in the United States to create and distribute a virus. The lawfulness of these programs occurs because a virus is a software program and writing software is protected by the First Amendment, although federal regulatory agencies are working to change this loophole. Other reasons make it difficult to ban software viruses. For instance, researchers often use viruses for scholarly study, such as testing system security.

Also, the laws prohibiting virus development and distribution are difficult to write because they tend to be overly broad. Say that a law makes it illegal to delete information. This restriction could prohibit the use of the delete function (*DEL *.**) in other software programs—not a desirable result. Further, there is no uniformly accepted definition of a "malicious virus" from state to state, so prosecuting those who create viruses is difficult if the virus crosses state lines—and most do.[41]

For example, how should a court handle a virus hoax distributed through e-mail and the Internet that caused severe damage? Virus hoaxes are often e-mail messages that falsely tell readers that their system is infected with a virus. These hoaxes can be a huge nuisance for IS departments or others who are responsible for computer security. "A user sees a virus hoax and tells four friends about it. And they tell four friends, and they tell four friends, and before long—to paraphrase a line from a Bee Gees song—someone's started a joke that's started the whole world crying."[42]

Consider the Bill Gates virus hoax, which spread so far that finally Gates had to step in and inform people of the hoax. In November 1997 a bogus e-mail chain letter started

Global IS for success

Australia's Telstra

Building secure IS environments is a tremendous challenge for global companies. One way of handling global security issues is to have a broad vision of corporate security that is customized to meet local needs. Telstra Corp., Australia's largest telecommunications company, provides an example of a company with a global security policy that can be adapted to meet specific local issues.

"We try to work to a collective security model which is adapted to prevailing local conditions and circumstances," explains David Harris, general manager for corporate security at Telstra, which conducts business in Asia, Europe, and North America. The company relies on people with skill sets in specialized areas like security, and these individuals become a knowledge resource for others in the company.

The global security approach requires communication between policymakers and policy implementers, notes John Clark, director of Andersen Consulting's information security practice. "I've seen cases firsthand where companies have a central security group in one country, and they distribute [security] policies to other countries [that] have not necessarily bought off on those policies," he says. A business will lose its security battle if branch offices and business partners aren't committed to corporate headquarter's security policies.

Telstra's Harris, for instance, offers this cautionary tip: Avoid relying on business partners when identifying security issues in their region. They often do not want to create a poor impression of their country. Instead, businesses should do their own homework and understand the region's cultural issues.

QUESTIONS AND PROJECTS

1. How can companies achieve stronger commitment to security policies from other divisions located around the globe?
2. Why is it important to localize security policies instead of having a blanket corporate security policy?

Source: Adapted from Tom Duffy, [untitled article], *Computerworld,* March 10, 1997, www.computerworld.com.

circulating. The letter offered recipients $1,000 and a free copy of Windows 98 for forwarding the message—"if it reache[d] 1,000 people." The e-mail claimed to have an "e-mail tracing program" that tracked everyone to whom the message was forwarded. A few weeks later the chain letter spawned a virus hoax when someone sent a follow-up message requesting users' credit-card numbers to compensate for pain and suffering they may have suffered because the original message contained an embedded virus program.[43]

Natural Disasters

The third type of security breach is caused by natural disasters such as lightning, floods, hurricanes, earthquakes, and tornadoes. Sometimes referred to as "corporate heart attacks," natural disasters can wipe out a company's entire information system. Natural disasters can affect power supplies, cooling systems, communication networks, alarm systems, building structures, and other facilities that support computer systems.

How much money should a company invest to protect itself from natural disasters? Although cost-benefit analysis is an important consideration, the question is not "What is the probability of a disaster striking?" Instead the right question is "What is at risk if a disaster strikes?" To assess this risk, companies should answer the following key questions:

- What is the loss in revenue if disaster strikes?
- Will disaster adversely affect the competitive position of the firm?
- How will suppliers, creditors, and stockholders be affected?
- Will customers take their business elsewhere?
- How will the disaster affect the financial health of the organization?

Something as simple as lightning can cause problems when a company is unprepared. For instance, Florida firm Kevin L. Erwin Consulting Ecologists lost about $40,000 worth

Natural disasters such as lightning-triggered power outages can cause serious computer security violations and destroy computer files and data.

of personal computer and network equipment when the company's installed lightning surge protectors failed. The loss, however, was more than monetary. It took the business more than six months to recover from corrupted data problems caused by the lightning.[44]

Power and telephone outages are another common cause of computer downtime and lost productivity. A power failure for just 50 *milliseconds* can result in at least 10 minutes of computer downtime, which in turn can trigger millions in losses for large financial institutions.[45] In fact, almost 50 percent of companies that suffer a prolonged power outage are likely to go out of business within five years.[46] When Cumberland County Teachers Federal Credit Union with 6,800 members in Falmouth, Maine, lost electricity for 6 days in early January 1998, the credit union had to run its computer system on a small portable generator that was refueled every 5 hours. Eventually, it had to borrow a generator from another credit union before it could open its main office. The business disruption caused rampant customer dissatisfaction.[47]

In this section we examined the three types of IS security violations: accidental errors, intentional errors, and natural disasters. In the next section we explore measures that companies can take to build a more secure IS environment.

Computer security controls

Policies, procedures, tools, techniques, and methods designed to reduce security breaches, system destruction, and system errors from accidental, intentional, and natural disasters.

Security Controls

Companies reduce security breaches through **computer security controls.** Note that the key word is *reduce,* not *eliminate,* because it is impossible to eliminate all security violations. Controls can be broadly divided into the following categories, as we see in Figure 12-4:

1. Application controls
2. Development controls
3. Physical facility controls

Let us look briefly at each type of control.

Application controls

Controls designed to provide security to the input, processes, output, and storage phases of any system.

Application Controls

All security policies and procedures that cover the four main phases or stages in any information system—inputs, outputs, processing, and storage—are **application controls.**

FIGURE 12-4

Classifications of Security Controls

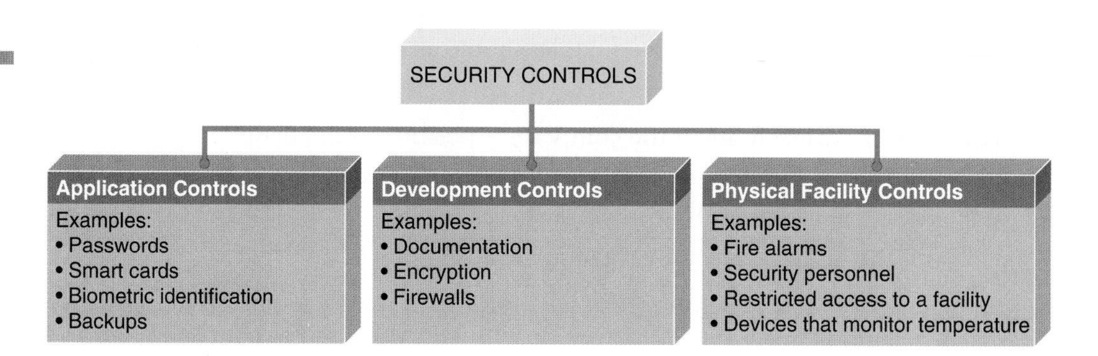

Components of a Smart Card

FIGURE 12-5 Smart Card

For example, one way to ensure that only authorized individuals enter data in a system is through passwords.

Passwords, the most common type of input controls, are controls that prevent users from entering incomplete, erroneous, unauthorized, or inappropriate data. This type of control gives access only to authorized system users through unique user IDs, and also by simply monitoring users logged on to the system. Many companies require employees to change their passwords frequently. Employees should use hard-to-guess or randomly generated passwords.

Passwords

A type of input control designed to ensure that only authorized users access a system and its different features.

To achieve better application security control, some companies such as MasterCard are switching to smart cards. A **smart card,** as shown in Figure 12-5, is a card with a chip embedded in it that provides users with dynamic passwords—passwords that change each time you log in. The card has a tiny digital display with six digits that change every two minutes. When users log on to the information system, they use the password code that appears on the card. Smart cards add "a layer of protection" to existing security features.

Smart card

A plastic card with an embedded chip and a tiny display that provides users with a new password each time they log into a system.

In addition to passwords and smart cards, many companies are switching to biometric identification techniques, which rely on body parts to validate that the user can access the system. Athletes underwent retinal scans (scans of the irises of their eyes) during the 1998 Winter Olympics in Japan. Members of the Purdue Employees Federal Credit Union place their fingers on a plate at one of several automated branches to gain account access. Disney World identifies season-pass holders by the geometry of their hands and travelers entering the United States in some places can opt for computer identification of their facial features or voice to enter the country more quickly.

Despite the promise of biometrics, these techniques have some disadvantages. First, they are still being developed.[48] Jim Wayman, head of the National Biometric Test Center at San Jose State University, notes that two to three percent of the population can't use biometric security devices. "Either they don't have the (body) part or the part doesn't look and work like everyone else's, or something is just off."[49] In addition, people fear the specter of privacy violations as their exact movements in the workplace are monitored with such startling accuracy. Because the technology offers security and convenience, many organizations plan to eventually replace passwords with identities tied to one's body parts. Experts caution, however, that relying on just one security technique often gives a false sense of security and recommend using a combination of identification verification techniques, such as passwords, smart cards, and biometrics.[50]

Process security controls help to make sure that a specific process, such as paying an invoice or recording the vital signs of a patient, are done in a proper manner. Output controls help to make sure that system output reaches the right individual at the right time in the right format while storage controls ensure that data are stored on the right storage mechanism (example: disks versus tapes versus CD-ROM) and that they are accessible as and when needed.

Backups

Creating duplicate copies of a file and storing it on a separate disk or medium or in a separate location.

One storage security control is the practice of creating backups, which are vital for both individuals and organizations. A **backup** is a duplicate copy of a file or a program that resides in a different location (folder or storage device) from the original file. It is of utmost importance to create backups of all important data and files.

Many of us have experienced that scary moment when we think we have lost an important file or term paper. Backups help to protect data and files against accidental deletion, misplacement, and natural or man-made disasters.

Nonprofit agency Wellness Community suffered a scare when its server went down in the midst of an annual fundraising program. The agency could not access its databases and financial application and discovered that no recent system backups had been done. "We were in a real crisis," recalls Sharon Martin, office manager for the organization. Fortunately, a security expert was able to retrieve the data after several hours of hard work. Today, backup is mandatory at this organization.[51]

Many organizations have written policies on the number and frequency of backups and even explicitly state the penalty for failing to create backups. In fact, companies hire individuals whose sole job is to create backups. Patricia Carey of *Small Business Computing & Communications* offers the following tips and examples regarding backups:

- **Treat information like gold.** Information has tremendous value, so a company must have a backup plan to prevent an inconvenience from turning into a disaster that "puts your company on life-support," notes Ms. Carey.[52] Technology director James Luther of the Alpine Clinic, a 30-person medical practice in Lafayette, Indiana, observes that if the clinic's data were ever destroyed "it would take months to replicate on paper what we have stored electronically," which would severely tighten cash flow "in a matter of weeks."[53]

- **Establish a backup routine.** By establishing and following a regular backup schedule, users are less likely to delay or forget backups that are critical. The network at Khera Communications, a Web site developer and publisher, is backed up automatically nightly and weekly. President and CEO Raj Khera believes backups are essential to his business operations and to serve his clients. "Since we host some of our clients' Web sites, if they accidentally delete a file, they can call us and we'll restore it from our tapes."[54]

- **Keep your backups in a safe place.** No one likes to think of worst-case scenarios, but security directors should. Placing backups in the safest possible place is one way to fend off a scenario that negates the usefulness of backups. Alpine Clinic's Luther learned this lesson the hard way. He backed up the company's network daily and then stored the tapes in a fireproof safe on company premises. When robbers broke into the safe and stole the backups, he changed policies. Now only the three most recent tapes are stored on-site. The rest are stored off-site.[55]

Development Controls

Development controls

Security measures that are part of each phase of the development life cycle of an information system.

The second broad classification of security controls is **development controls.** These refer to controls that are built into each phase of the system development cycle, which was covered in the last chapter. System development controls should never be ad hoc and arbitrary; instead they should be deliberate and carefully implemented. Development controls ensure that systems are developed in the most desirable way possible. There are many ways of doing this, including proper *documentation,* securing and protecting system data through *encryption,* allowing only authorized users to access the system through the use of firewalls (discussed on page 202), and preventing any possible conflict of interest among different team members working on the same system.

Documentation

Written manuals, memos, and other documents that describe the features of a system and its processes.

Documentation is a written set of documents (usually a manual) that explains in detail the reasoning behind processes, procedures, and other details related to software and hardware. The more detailed the documentation, the better off the company will be in the future.

The purpose of documentation is to help people monitor and understand system features and operations. Keeping detailed documentation about a system, its functions, features, interfaces, and other elements makes good business sense because it can save companies substantial money in times of disaster as experts try to piece the system back together.

Encryption is another common type of development control. It is a software program that makes e-mail messages, data files, and electronic-commerce transactions secure. The program takes blocks of data (usually 156 bits), called keys, and secures them so that only an authorized party can view the data. Encryption converts data into a secret code before they are transmitted over the network. When the message or file reaches the recipient, the recipient uses a special digital key (such as a code or a password) to unlock (or "decrypt") the message and read the data. "Internet communications and connectivity, especially between companies and their business partners and employees, is driving the need for encryption," says Ed Shapland, senior manager at Ernst & Young LLP's Consulting Group in Washington.[56]

Encryption

A form of security control to ensure that only authorized parties can view confidential electronic documents.

The politics of encryption technology can be a headache for companies with traveling employees. For executives at Australia's Telstra Corp., discussed in the global IS feature, encryption has created a predicament. Telstra's executives carry custom-built e-mail encryption software on their laptops. If their international travel includes a U.S. stopover, they must delete the encryption software from their laptops at U.S. airports or risk a breach of customs regulations. Why? U.S. laws ban the export of encryption technology. Bringing the software to the United States from Australia on the laptop violates this regulation.[57]

Physical Facility Controls

Physical facility controls—the third type of security control classification—refers to policies and procedures that control the physical environment in which systems reside. **Physical facility controls** safeguard the environment of a computer and its related assets. These controls are important because the best of systems can fail miserably if the environment is unsuitable. Controlling the physical environment includes a whole range of factors from room temperature to power supply, from protecting systems from natural disasters, like flood and hurricane, to preventing theft and vandalism.

Physical facility controls

Security measures that protect the environment in which the computer and related assets reside.

Physical controls include posting security personnel, installing fire alarms, security alarms, and hidden cameras, and requiring users to wear badges or use smart cards to gain access to a building. Most facilities also include environmental control devices that monitor and control the air and temperature in a building in which a computer resides.

The physical environment has caused numerous information system failures and some far-reaching effects. When an electrical fire broke out in the Securities Industry Automation Corp.'s (SIAC) Manhattan data center several years ago, the New York and the American stock exchanges (NYSE and AMEX) ground to a halt for hours and delayed transactions worth billions of dollars. Eventually, SIAC discovered that the problem was a faulty alarm that closed down the system.[58]

Similarly, an unexpected environmental problem affected the computer system at Newark International Airport. Power cables that supported the airport's three main terminals were severed when a construction crew driving steel beams into the ground for a new parking facility accidentally cut the cables. The airport had no plan in place to restore power in the event of a blackout. The airport had to close until the next morning when power was restored. In the interim, airlines had to divert passengers to other East Coast airports, which cost Newark and the airlines millions of dollars in lost sales.[59]

The extent of physical controls necessary to protect an environment differs from country to country. For example, physical computer security is stringent in Europe because computer theft is highest there. "It's a very lucrative field at the moment," explains Jackie Hyde, an information security analyst at Datapro in the United Kingdom. "Criminals are targeting large organizations, knowing they're deserted in the evenings. People are gaining access just by walking into the building."[60]

In contrast, computer theft is less prevalent in Turkey. According to Ergun Solemez, an information systems consultant to Turkey's largest advertising agency, Cenajans/Grey, computer theft is rare. In part, this is because criminals cannot sell the machines. "People are only going to buy a computer here from someone they know personally or from a known company," Solemez comments. Thus, physical controls are minimal in Turkey.[61]

Because employees are the main source of security violations, controls should focus first on employee security issues. No matter what type of control—application, development, or facility—the focus should start with regulating, training, and setting clear policies and guidelines for employees. "There's a bigger security problem with insiders than with terrorists or industrial espionage. You can't worry about protecting against external forces if you have not protected yourself from within," says a security expert at Coopers & Lybrand.[62]

In this section we explored several classifications of security controls. Next, we turn to disaster recovery plans, detailed action plans that companies develop to deal with information system disasters.

Disaster Recovery Plan

When the main server in the São Paulo, Brazil, office of Young & Rubicam Advertising crashed late one December morning, it could have been catastrophic. Instead, the company followed its well-detailed disaster recovery plan and business proceeded after a short delay. The company first downloaded its Lotus Notes software application from its New York office via the network. The agency uses Lotus Notes for its creative work, media plans, and strategy. By the end of business that day, the São Paulo system was operational.

David Gutierrez, Young & Rubicam's vice president/regional technology officer for the Southern Hemisphere, is responsible for protecting client data in Latin America. He protected the São Paulo agency's data with four levels of duplicate backups. Due to Gutierrez's disaster recovery plan the agency didn't lose any data when the system crashed.[63]

Given that there are many reasons for and types of security breaches, what are some things that a company can do to protect and secure its computer assets? The company should have a security plan and clear policies in place to prevent security breaches. The next step is to develop a comprehensive **disaster recovery plan (DRP)** to prepare for natural disasters. As we will see, such plans can help a company to restart operations within hours of a disaster.

Disaster recovery plan (DRP)

A plan that details how a company will sustain and maintain its information systems and services in the case of a disaster.

There are seven steps in developing a DRP:

1. Identify specific situations that are classified as a disaster.
2. Name the individuals who have the right and the responsibility to declare a disaster.
3. Identify specific steps for declaring a disaster.
4. Inventory all crucial corporate assets, functions, and resources that are essential to operate the business. Prioritize those assets.
5. Specify the general course of action the business will take when disaster strikes.
6. Develop a specific course of action that each employee must take to make the company operational when disaster strikes.
7. Identify resources required to recover from the disaster, including money, time, personnel, and facilities.

Figure 12-6 summarizes these steps.

A security expert says that DRP is driven by the key question and its answer: "What would we do if that key piece of technology were not there? The wrong answer is: 'We pack up and take the day off.' The right answer is: 'What did we do before we got (that technology)?' [Asking these questions] creates the sense that 'we're unstoppable.' "[64]

An IT manager explains how the DRP worked when his company headquarters was damaged by fire one night. Because the building's stability was in question, his IT team could not set foot in the data center and technical support area for three days. However, the DRP was so well planned that by 8:00 A.M. the morning after the fire, the company shifted from sophisticated networked systems to a fully functional, manual process. Had it not been for the local media, customers would have not have known a fire occurred.[65]

For global companies, developing a DRP offers additional challenges. Attitudes toward security vary from one country to the next. Planners must stay sensitive to cultural values and attitudes to ensure the success of a DRP.

The cultural issues become important for multinational businesses that must adopt disaster recovery plans due to industry regulations. International financial institutions insist on high DRP standards no matter where the bank is located. The plan, then, may be easier to implement in the United States where government banking regulations are strict, compared to Europe and Asia. "In the U.S., the major [international] banks have been doing disaster recovery for 15 years," notes John Jackson, vice president and general manager of Comdisco Professional Services, a leading disaster recovery firm. "Now they're doing it in Europe and Asia even when the local institutions might not be stepping up to it because they don't have the same regulatory requirements."[66]

But developing a plan is not enough. A DRP is effective only if it is well tested, well rehearsed, and up-to-date. Companies should evaluate their disaster recovery plans through testing. Each and every step in the plan should be practiced and tested regularly so employees know what to do in the aftermath of a disaster. The plan should be kept current to specify new IT assets and risks that increase the firm's vulnerability.

To illustrate the value of rehearsing a DRP, consider a disaster that struck London's downtown financial district. An Irish Republican Army car bomb exploded in the district, damaging the buildings and assets of several financial institutions. The headquarters of Commercial Union (CU), an insurance and financial services group, was severely damaged. Its headquarters facilities were destroyed completely, including the main telephone switchboard—which handles 3,600 extensions, 500 terminals, and 100 word processors. However, CU's data center near Croydon, south of London, was about ten miles away.

On Saturday, a day after the bombing, CU executed its emergency plan to sustain critical operations. On Sunday, replacement terminals, fax machines, telephones, and other office equipment were ordered and delivered to various alternative sites around the city. Telephone services were rerouted from the company's central London telephone switchboard to the Croydon site. CU also set up 10 switchboards and a message backup system to handle calls. Four days after the bombing, 631 of the 650 staffers were working at other offices.[67] The company was able to implement the plan so efficiently because all employees knew what they had to do in case of an emergency.

FIGURE 12-6

The Seven Steps in Developing a Disaster Recovery Plan

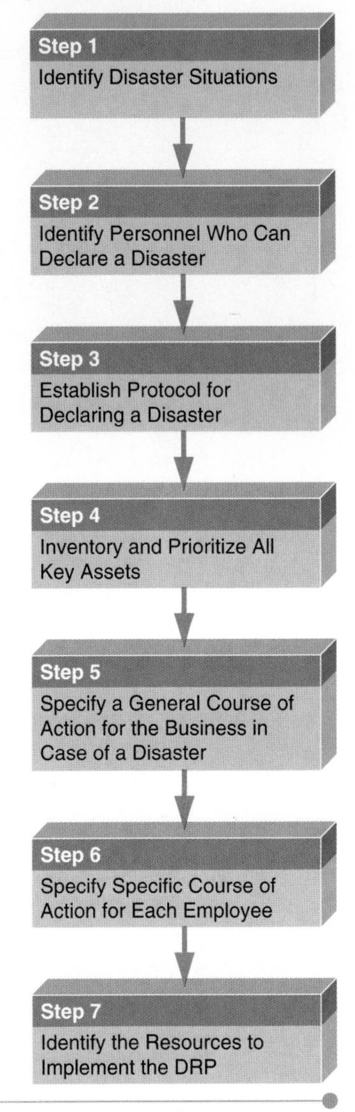

Business Guidelines for Security Success

Businesses that are successful in protecting their data and information systems from unwanted eyes and hands treat security as an integral part of their corporate culture. In such companies, security is not an afterthought, nor is it the sole responsibility of a few individuals. Instead, employees understand how effective security protects the financial stability of the company and behave accordingly. This section identifies some key guidelines for computer security.

Recognize the Symptoms of Security Breaches

Like doctors who cannot treat an illness if they do not recognize the symptoms, IS managers cannot sustain a secure environment if they don't recognize the signs of security breaches. For example, a security director at a major Midwestern consulting firm recently spent a month assessing security risks at two Fortune 100 accounts. "They had no clue when the networks were hacked," he comments. "Both firms averaged one serious hack a week for every 5,000 users. And the losses totaled $5,000 and up. Unfortunately, this is all too typical."[68]

Gary Loveland, a partner at Price Waterhouse LLP's Information Security Risk Management Group in Los Angeles, notes that employees can look for obvious signs to see if the network has been cracked. According to Price Waterhouse Coopers' Operational Systems Risk Management Solutions, some signs include the following:

- unknown accounts added to the system and file server
- an unusual number of log-on failures and dial-in attempts
- unexpected system or network crashes
- unauthorized changes to system software and system files
- high system activity when no users are logged on, especially during off-peak hours[69]

Once crackers have broken into a system, they often create accounts so they can get back in. Many will also try "to give themselves administrator-level backdoor access into the network," Loveland explains. Companies should perform audit and inventory checks, intrusion detection, behavioral anomaly detection, and other checks and balances to search for security breaches.[70]

Be Watchful of Disgruntled Employees

Disgruntled employees or employees who have been fired are often likely to cause security breaches. The first step toward protecting company data and files is to establish clear policies and legal agreements with fired employees. In the case of disgruntled employees, system administrators should keep a close watch on their computer-related activities without breaking any privacy laws. Some simple steps such as immediately removing access privileges to data and files and preventing the employee from entering company premises can also help.

Involve Law Enforcement When You Suspect a Security Breach

If a company is suspicious of internal sabotage, often they tend not to contact the police, fearing unwanted publicity. However, the earlier law enforcement is brought into the picture, the better off the company will be.

If an employee is suspected of computer crime, experts recommend companies take some initial steps to help with a potential criminal investigation:

- Call police immediately. Every day that internal security tries to solve or stop the crime means more evidence gets tainted or destroyed.
- Train employees not to erase, overwrite, or destroy electronic or paper files that the employee used or created.
- Cooperate. Remember that a police investigation requires the time, energy, and cooperation of company staff at all levels, perhaps for many months.
- Quantify damages. Prosecutors don't like cases without a clear idea of the victim's suffering. And some computer crime laws require a certain level of financial damages to warrant prosecution as a felony. Colorado law, for instance, requires a loss of at least $15,000 to bring a felony charge. Anything less is a misdemeanor, which carries far less severe penalties.[72]

Build Security Partnerships

Security protection isn't a one-person job. It depends on partnerships with suppliers and customers, and sometimes the government. Although it's up to the business to create a secure environment, systems vendors can help. Many are starting to embed antivirus software and firewall capabilities directly into their hardware. When making hardware or software decisions, companies should look closely at what the vendor has to offer in terms of security. Careful long-range security planning that includes vendor partnerships helps protect the business.[73]

Convince Top Management That Security Is Not an Option, It's a Requirement

The Ernst & Young/*Computerworld* 1998 Global Information Security Survey of 4,255 IT and information security managers found that of those surveyed, 84 percent responded that their senior management think information security is "important" or "extremely important." But the following results indicate that top managers aren't translating that concern into action:

- Forty-one percent of the survey participants reported that their company doesn't have formal security policies.
- More than half said they lack disaster recovery plans.
- More than a third said they don't monitor their networks for suspicious activity.
- Fewer than one in five use encryption technology to safeguard sensitive information.

The survey also showed that managers still lack a good understanding of security issues. Asked to identify threats, respondents were almost twice as likely to cite crackers over employees as the number one concern, but studies have shown that the overwhelming majority of security breaches come from inside the company.[74]

IS managers that ask top management to invest in security tools and techniques have a tough job because the relationship between security investments and bottom-line profits is neither tangible nor obvious. Many security professionals struggle every day to convince top management of the importance of investing in security. "We've got antivirus software and firewalls in place, but beyond that, it's tough to convince my CEO that security should be built in to the network. They [sic] just don't get it, so I don't get the necessary money and manpower," explains a security manager at an upstate New York Fortune 500 company, who requested anonymity.[75]

Average security spending is approximately 5 percent of IT budgets. The number of companies with published security policies is dropping. In 1992, 82 percent of companies had published policies, compared with 54 percent in 1996. What is troubling is that a number of companies don't have a policy because they think they don't need one. This belief is sometimes attributed to a phenomenon called "information fatigue syndrome."[76] This syndrome occurs when employees and managers are so overwhelmed with information and the challenges that accompany managing information that sometimes they are too worn out to protect that information effectively.

Gus Rogers, director of corporate computer security at Merck & Company in New Jersey, believes that businesses should alter their thinking about security. "Security is not a technical issue; it's about business integrity. Purchasing [security] is a real problem because many organizations don't see beyond the up-front costs."[77] Consequently, many IS managers find themselves unable to deal effectively with serious security violations. Rogers believes that the question to ask management is "Will you be able to run your business tomorrow if all your data were wiped out or if your company's proprietary data is made available to the competition?" If the answer is no, then investing in security is imperative.

SUMMARY

1. **Describe computer security and its business importance.** Computer security is the process of protecting a computer-based information system, often by establishing a set of policies and procedures and implementing security tools and techniques. It protects all elements of a system such as hardware, software, networks, physical facilities, data, and personnel from accidental, intentional, or natural disasters.

   The increase in networks, the growth in PCs and information-related products, competitive pressures from around the globe, and technology advances have all made information one of the most sought-after assets in today's competitive business environment. As our reliance on computers and information systems increases, the importance of securing these systems also increases.

   A computer security breach can cause serious damage to an organization. Security is a complex issue because of its potential cost and vast range of sources, including company insiders. All employees should be trained about security and the effects of a breach.

2. **Explain why information systems are vulnerable to security breaches.** There are several reasons why computer systems are vulnerable to security breaches. The number of insiders and outsiders with access to the systems; the increased complexity of information

systems, including the number of hardware, software, and network choices; distributed or network computing; Internet cyber terrorism; and complacent top management are some key reasons. Networks are highly vulnerable to security breaches. Particular weak links on the network include computers on the network, improper access privileges, network cables and wires, lack of user training, and lack of well-though-out security policies and procedures.

3. **Identify different types of security breaches.** Security breaches can be broadly divided into three categories: accidental errors, intentional errors, and natural disasters. Hardware breaches can be intentional or accidental. In particular, faxes, modems, and cellular phones are vulnerable to security breaches. Computer viruses are a primary threat to software. Finally, disasters can cause security violations. Natural disasters can affect power supplies, cooling systems, communication networks, alarm systems, building structures, and other facilities that support computer systems.
4. **Discuss the importance and elements of a disaster recovery plan.** One way that a company can prepare itself to face security disasters is to develop a comprehensive disaster recovery plan (DRP). A DRP specifies how a company will sustain and maintain the information systems and services necessary for the smooth operations of a business after a disaster strikes. The plan should clearly list and specify the specific situations that warrant the declaration of a disaster and identify the actions that must be taken by each employee when a disaster occurs.

KEY TERMS

application controls (p. 340)
backups (p. 342)
computer security (p. 329)
computer security controls (p. 340)
cracker (p. 332)
development controls (p. 342)
disaster recovery plan (DRP) (p. 344)
documentation (p. 342)
encryption (p. 343)
hacker (p. 332)
password (p. 341)
physical facility controls (p. 343)
smart card (p. 341)
software virus (p. 336)

REVIEW QUESTIONS

1. Define computer security. Explain why employees are an integral part of achieving a secured environment
2. Identify and describe any three reasons for computer security breaches.
3. What is a cracker?
4. What do we mean by security controls? Briefly describe some security control examples.
5. What are some measures that companies can take to ensure that passwords provide the necessary security?
6. What are the three types of security breaches? Give an example of each.
7. What is a computer virus? What are some ways to prevent transmission of viruses?
8. What is a backup? Why are backups an integral part of computer system security?
9. What is a disaster recovery plan? Why should every company, regardless of its business, have a disaster recovery plan?
10. What are some steps involved in developing the disaster recovery plan?

DISCUSSION QUESTIONS AND EXERCISES

1. IT alone cannot ensure secure systems. Computer security relies on common sense, good judgment, and shared corporate values. Discuss.
2. Winning the commitment of top management to allocate resources for security measures is one of the biggest challenges confronting IS managers. Develop a short presentation to convince the board of directors why investing in security measures is like preventing a "corporate heart attack."

3. Identify any small business in your area and interview the CEO about the company's disaster recovery plan. If the company does not have one, identify some reasons why they do not have a plan.

4. **(Software exercise)** There are a number of encryption tools on the market. Search and identify any five such tools. Create a spreadsheet that compares the prices of these different products (make up your own prices, if necessary). Also, develop a security budget for these five tools. Your budget should include the salary for two security experts (salaries $45,000 and $52,000), training for 45 company employees at $450 per employee, and security manuals for the company's 125 employees at a cost of $8 per manual. Finally, add 15% of the price of each product toward product maintenance.

5. **(Software exercise)** Suppose you have to convince top management that a virus attack can be very costly to the company. Develop a PowerPoint presentation to convince management to invest in virus protection software. Your presentation could include the many costs associated with a virus attack, some of which include lost data and files, employee downtime, the cost of hiring a security consultant, customer dissatisfaction, and any other factors you wish to consider.

Case 1: Monitoring Employees

One downside to IS security is privacy violations concerns. For example, security tools monitor user activities to catch crackers and others who may be violating the company's security policies. However, the monitoring also opens doors for abuse of the collected information. This approach to security has raised a host of legal and social issues that have not yet been resolved.

Although communication over public phone lines is considered private and can be tapped only by law-enforcement officials with a court order, communication over telephone lines at the workplace lacks this legal protection. In fact, many managers believe that because their company owns the technology, they have every right to monitor the communication that takes place over those lines, and federal law supports their views. The 1986 Electronic Communications Privacy Act prohibits phone and data line taps with two exceptions: law-enforcement agencies and employers.

Reading e-mail and monitoring keystrokes, unlike telephone communications, has no legal precedent, causing a great deal of confusion and frustration for employers and employees. To rectify the situation, the Computer Systems Laboratory of the National Institute of Standards and Technology formulated guidelines about the legality of keystroke monitoring at the request of the Justice Department. The "Guidance on the Legality of Keystroke Monitoring" bulletin states: "The Justice Department advises that if system administrators are conducting keystroke monitoring or anticipate the need for such monitoring, even for the purpose of detecting intruders, they should ensure that all system users, authorized and unauthorized, be notified that monitoring may be undertaken."

However, written notice alone is insufficient. The Justice Department also recommends that system administrators add to every user's log-in a banner that gives "clear and unequivocal notice that by signing on and using the system, they are expressly consenting to have their keystrokes monitored or recorded. "

"Informed consent" of users is vital to protect them from undue harassment. The Massachusetts CNOT (Coalition on New Office Technologies), a civil rights group, is formulating the CNOT Act. The Act requires businesses to tell employees about the kinds of data that will be collected, frequency of monitoring, how employees can access the data, and if the data will be used toward employee evaluations.

In a study of 686 workers, overwhelming evidence suggests that monitoring lowers employee productivity, increases turnaround, and decreases employee morale. Two-thirds of the workers surveyed indicated that they felt monitoring made it difficult to take a break, even to go to the bathroom. Monitoring may deter workers from taking risks, making mistakes, doing unorthodox things, and using their creative energies.

According to Alan Westin, professor of public law at Columbia University in New York, the issue is beyond that of worker privacy; it is one of human dignity.

1. Many managers believe that because their company owns the technology they have every right to monitor any communication that takes place on that technology. Do you agree with this viewpoint? Discuss.
2. Assume your company provides written notice of monitoring and a log-on banner appears when you start up your computer reminding you of the monitoring process. What, if any, objections would you have to the monitoring?
3. Keystrokes are monitored in an effort to increase productivity. Why do you think there is overwhelming evidence that keystroke monitoring has a negative effect on worker productivity?
4. Monitoring workers is not an issue of worker privacy but an issue of human dignity. Discuss.

Case 2: Disaster Strikes Only the Unprepared

Jeffrey G. Williams conducts seminars on the topic of disaster recovery planning and crisis management. Williams says being prepared for computer-related disasters is no different from training a volunteer firefighter, another activity he's been doing for years. "We used to put the fireman in full gear with a bag around his head and a tape playing with the sound of the fire and a child saying, 'Daddy, save me.' The firemen who were young parents couldn't stand it. You have to find out who can do it and who can't," says Williams, president of Binomial International Inc. of New York. He believes that companies should use similar tactics to train certain employees in computer-related disaster management.

Michael Magee learned about the need for computer crisis planning first-hand. A fire destroyed the manufacturing plant he worked at and the FBI and the Bureau of Alcohol, Tobacco and Firearms would not let anyone in the building for three days. Although the company was able to resume its business operations, it lost valuable time. A disaster recovery plan would have helped the company get back to business more rapidly.

The challenge for disaster specialists is to find all necessary information quickly. Different employees should understand their duties to help the company manage its information system needs quickly. Training is essential to build such understanding. "This was an awakening for me. I've become an evangelist for these plans," says Magee who moved to a new company. When he moved to his current job, he asked about the company's crisis preparation. In response to his question, the CIO assigned him the task of crafting the plan.[78]

1. What is a disaster recovery plan and why is it necessary to train employees in how to enact the plan?
2. Check to see if your school or company has a disaster recovery plan. Identify and describe the key elements of that plan. Identify a local company that does not have a plan and prepare a presentation that you could make to top management about the importance of such a plan.

If we only knew what we knew, we'd be a stronger company.

A common saying[1]

CONTENTS

INFORMATION SYSTEMS AND SUCCESS

Information systems have become indispensable to individuals and businesses around the world.[2] From e-mail to Internet shopping and research to computer games, information systems have become integral in our home, school, and work. In fact, they may become part of us. Professor Kevin Warwick, director of cybernetics at the University of Reading in the United Kingdom, was the first human to host a microchip in his body. During the 20-minute medical procedure, doctors inserted a glass capsule about the size of a pearl into Warwick's arm. The capsule housed several microprocessors. The device (approximately 23 mm by 3 mm) stayed in Warwick's arm a little more than a week to avoid medical complications and because it had limited power.

The professor wanted to see how successfully the embedded chip would communicate with the University of Reading's intelligent building. An intelligent building is one in which microprocessors are embedded throughout the building in doors, windows, computers, and other facilities. Doors that would normally require smart cards to operate swung open for the professor. A system of electronic nodes tracked his movements throughout the building. Lights turned on when he entered a room. His PC greeted him when he walked into his office.

If this idea sounds like an episode from *Star Trek,* consider that many experts predict that chips embedded in our bodies, clothes, and wallets will become commonplace. Chips embedded in human beings could automatically release medicine to heal the body and memory alarms could alert people to events.[3]

Chapter 13

Managing Knowledge, Change, and IS Personnel: The Next Challenges

AFTER STUDYING THIS CHAPTER, YOU SHOULD BE ABLE TO:

- Describe knowledge management and explain its relevance to IS
- Define and discuss the importance of change management in IS
- Explain ways to organize IS personnel to help achieve business goals
- Outline career opportunities and concerns in the field of information systems
- Identify some indications that a good fit exists between a person's talents and values and an IS job

Why have computers and information systems assumed such a prominent role in our lives—and why does that role continue to grow? The reason is simple. They are evolving into tools for managing knowledge and implementing change. For instance, having information is necessary but not sufficient to lead a company to greatness. Instead, the ability to integrate information in a timely manner with the experience, skill, intuition, and knowledge of key personnel gives companies the edge necessary to succeed.

Computers and information systems can also help businesses initiate, manage, promote, and understand change. However, the ability to use computers to create long-term change in an organization requires a shift from the traditional mindset of the computer as an information storehouse or number-cruncher to a new mindset that views computers as relationship-building, boundary-breaking, speed-enhancing, global communication tools. Nicholas Negroponte, director of MIT's Media Lab, says that today's digital world does a lot more than move bits—"it creates new competition, opportunities and [relationships with] people."[4]

Two key themes in this chapter are the use of information systems and IS personnel to manage knowledge and change effectively. Think for a moment of the Harvard Business School example. The school curriculum stresses change and knowledge management. Harvard's IS technology, however, lagged behind its curriculum and changes in the business environment. The school sought to improve students' ability to manage knowledge—that is, it aimed to help students integrate information from different sources so they could apply it effectively.

TECHNOLOGY PAYOFF

Harvard Leads the Way

Dean Kim B. Clark of Harvard Business School can detail why Harvard's previous information technology infrastructure didn't work well. "We had every network protocol known to mankind," Clark critiques. "It got to the point where our networks and systems were a major barrier to using technology in a powerful way."

Harvard's hodgepodge of business systems and networks made information exchange among users difficult. Students working on one system could not integrate data from another system easily. Further, many systems did not support Web-based applications, which meant that students could not rely on the Web for case studies or other class projects.

Harvard Business School knew its system was a problem, so it invested $10 million to develop a new network that could run Web-based applications. The replacement system builds the student community and improves the educational environment in several ways. First, students use a campus-wide intranet to communicate with professors and fellow students, research, complete assignments, and work in teams. Clark believes that Harvard "can bring the world into the classroom (with intranets)."

Before classes start, Harvard offers new students a short course on how the system operates. During that session, students can access a Web site that contains information on the school's background, courses that are offered, activities, and the local community. In addition, students can send and receive e-mail on the site to exchange information. Once school starts, almost half of the school's 66,000 alumni volunteer their time by responding to student e-mail relating to job searches.

Professors use Harvard Business School's information system to offer course material, assignments, and related materials on-line and to exchange e-mail messages with students.

Students seem to enjoy the system's benefits. MBA student Andrea Chen explains: "By using technology every day, we gain an understanding of how it affects managerial think-

Harvard also wanted to be more responsive to changes in the business world and academia, including the use of the Web as a learning and business tool. It relied on its information systems to meet these goals.

Other changes, propelled by computers and information systems, are also affecting the way we live and work. As we saw in Chapter 8, electronic commerce is revolutionizing the way we shop and do business. The Internet is changing the way we invest in the stock market, continuously learn, and access relevant information. The portability of small computers has made these machines an integral part of our lifestyle.

In this chapter we explore the use of information systems to manage knowledge and change. We also examine ways to organize the information systems team to meet business goals and close with a look at IS career issues.

Knowledge Management and Information Systems

As business and society become more digitized, it is vitally important to learn how to use information to empower our personal and professional lives. To use knowledge effectively, we must manage it. In this section, we explore knowledge management and its relationship to information systems.

What Is Knowledge Management?

The most valuable asset for any company, regardless of the nature of its business, is people. Though this may sound like a cliché, more companies than ever are realizing the importance of investing in people and their intellectual capital. **Intellectual capital** is the knowledge that people apply to solve problems and make decisions in their personal and professional lives. This capital is built on textbook knowledge, real world experiences, intuition, judgment, and perception.

Intellectual capital is both extrinsic and intrinsic. We find extrinsic intellectual capital in written or oral reports, databases, patents, organizational charts, manuals, books, and business rules and regulations. Intrinsic intellectual capital refers to knowledge about business that people have gleaned based on their personal experiences, intuition, perception, and judgment.

Intellectual capital must be identified, captured, stored, retrieved, disseminated, and applied if individuals and organizations are to succeed. As John Gantz of *Computerworld* says: "We are awash in data. If we're lucky and can imbue it with some relevance, that data becomes information. And there's still too much of it. Not until we can imbue information with context can we turn it into knowledge."[5] One way of turning intellectual capital into a valuable asset is through knowledge management.

Knowledge management refers to the ability to capture both intrinsic and extrinsic intellectual capital. Knowledge management creates a body of knowledge that can be successfully shared with others and applied within the organization. The process also helps people to understand, interpret, and apply this knowledge for the betterment of the workplace or society.

ing." Dean Clark believes that "[t]echnology is crucial to the future of education," and thinks the school's systems experiences are comparable to those of the Wright brothers. "We're at the Kitty Hawk stage of the revolution."

Source: Megan Santosus, "Wire Education," *CIO Web Business,* Section 2, October 1, 1998, 29–34.

So what does knowledge management have to do with information systems? A great deal, it turns out. According to a report from the Delphi Group, a research firm in Boston, about half the companies in the United States have some kind of knowledge management effort under way.[6] This growth is occurring for four key reasons:

- **Information must be managed so employees can apply it as knowledge.** Many organizations recognize that collecting information does little good unless that information is managed and applied well.
- **Much information is lost because it isn't captured.** The knowledge of an expert frequently isn't written down, so when that expert leaves the business, the information becomes unavailable. Knowledge management prevents this loss from happening.
- **Sharing knowledge creates a more powerful company.** By creating a pool of knowledge and sharing it with others in the organization, employees can develop knowledge faster and more effectively. As a company shares knowledge more, its ability to adapt to change improves.
- **Valuing intellectual capital signals that the company values its people.** By placing a premium on knowledge, the organization sends employees a message that it values their brainpower, wants them to grow, and creates a **learning organization.** A learning organization is one in which learning from past experiences and new opportunities are an inherent part of the corporate culture. This type of organization values knowledge and encourages employees to learn everyday.

Intellectual capital

Knowledge that resides in a person; it is both intrinsic and extrinsic and derived from a wide variety of sources.

Knowledge management

The process of identifying, capturing, storing, retrieving, disseminating, and applying intrinsic and extrinsic intellectual capital for the betterment of the individual, the workplace, and society.

Learning organization

An organization in which learning is an integral part of the corporate culture.

Converting Information to Knowledge

In Chapter 5, we analyzed how data is converted into information. Here we explore how information is converted into knowledge. Unlike converting data into information, converting information to knowledge does not follow a set of structured, predictable steps. The conversion process is similar to what occurs as a person develops wisdom through continuous learning as he or she experiences different situations.

Organizations that convert information into knowledge effectively must meet several prerequisites. First, they must create a learning environment that encourages risk taking and accepts the chance of failure. In such an environment, employees feel comfortable to generate and explore new ideas and confront new situations.

Second, the organization must identify information that is crucial to its long-term success. Because some information that a business generates is not relevant for future decisions, distilling significant information improves employees' ability to solve problems. For example, a transportation company, such as Amtrak, would consider information about train safety essential to its operations.

Third, the business should create a team of cross-functional experts who have the ability to look at core information and translate it into guiding operational, tactical, and strategic principles for all employees. In the case of Amtrak, the ability to show employees how to incorporate safety considerations in all their decisions is one way to convert information into knowledge.

Fourth, the organization should develop ways for all employees to access knowledge and then communicate how and where employees can do so. Many organizations create a repository or "well of knowledge" so that employees can draw whatever they need whenever they need it. At Amtrak everyone from the secretary to the engine driver should have a clear understanding of how his or her decisions influence the company's safety record.

Fifth, the company should develop knowledge management systems that adapt to changes. Companies must have processes in place to modify, correct, update, and add to existing knowledge on an ongoing basis. Converting information to knowledge is a continuous process that requires long-term commitment. For example, safety principles and regulations change frequently. Amtrak, then, should collect, store, and update safety information so that it can share knowledge about the best safety techniques and procedures with its employees and managers.

Figure 13-1 summarizes the five prerequisites that businesses must meet to convert information into knowledge successfully. Now we examine how to use information systems to manage knowledge.

Using IS to Manage Knowledge

IS managers have a dual role to play in the knowledge management process. First, they should ensure that existing information is disseminated and used effectively. Second, they should learn to use IT tools in ways that achieve business goals.

Information technology tools used to manage knowledge include intranets, extranets, the World Wide Web, e-mail, and other communication systems and software. No new information technologies are required to implement knowledge management. All that is needed is the ability to use existing technologies in innovative ways to promote interactive learning.

Intra-organizational systems

Systems that are shared by two or more departments or divisions within the company.

To that end, many knowledge management systems are **intra-organizational systems** that help foster cooperation and collaboration. Because intra-organizational systems often bring together a diverse group of assets and talents, such ventures often result in powerful systems that enhance productivity, reduce operating costs, increase market share, and create new partnerships, especially for companies that conduct business transactions in global markets.

Today intra-organizational systems are used more frequently for several reasons. First, as globalization continues at an accelerated pace, managers are under pressure to quickly access, digest, and disseminate large volumes of information across national and international boundaries. This often requires the cooperation of diverse business units. Second, intra-organizational systems act as a river of free-flowing information between disparate business units and head offices and back out to all the units. Third, as the cost of hardware declines and technology advances, the cost of building intra-organizational systems continues to decrease.

FIGURE 13-1

The Prerequisites to Converting Information into Knowledge

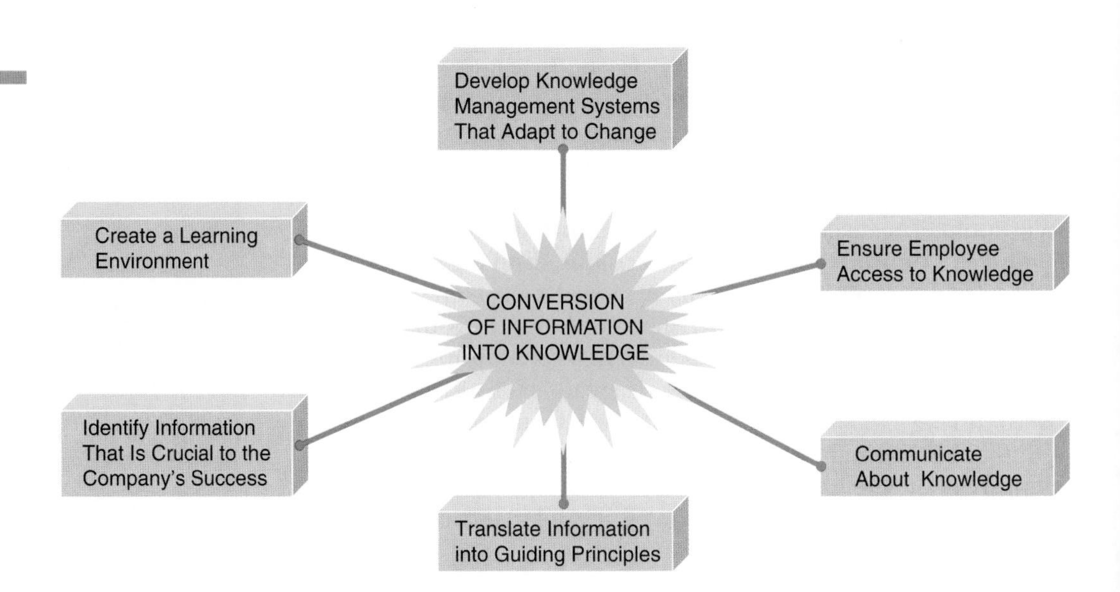

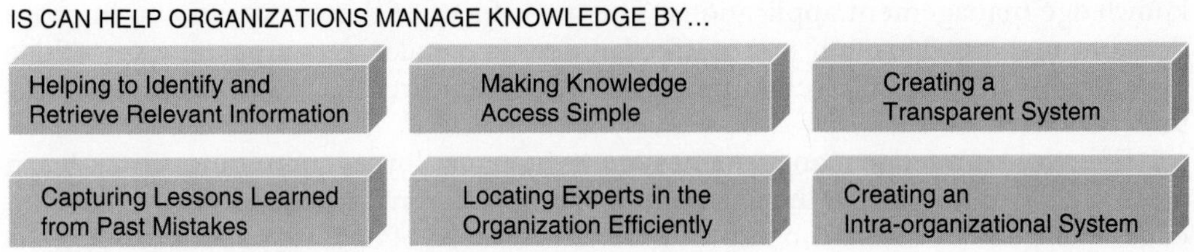

IS CAN HELP ORGANIZATIONS MANAGE KNOWLEDGE BY...

Helping to Identify and Retrieve Relevant Information	Making Knowledge Access Simple	Creating a Transparent System
Capturing Lessons Learned from Past Mistakes	Locating Experts in the Organization Efficiently	Creating an Intra-organizational System

FIGURE 13-2

Methods for Using IS to Manage Knowledge

In most organizations, information systems are central to knowledge management. There are several ways in which information systems can help companies achieve their knowledge management goals, as we see in Figure 13-2.

First, information systems aid knowledge management if they help employees identify and retrieve useful information in a timely, accurate manner. Providing this type of system is challenging. As companies grow, they inevitably end up with a set of mismatched systems. Many managers complain that, although their organizations invest a great deal in IS, often they cannot find the information for which they are looking. The first step toward knowledge management, then, is to plan for and build systems that contain useful information that can grow with the organization.

Second, businesses should build systems that are easy to use. People tend to shy away from systems that are tedious, complex, or burdensome. Third, the systems should be transparent. Transparency in this context means that everyone in the organization understands what others are doing. To promote transparency, employees should be able to exchange information freely.

In addition, the organization should establish procedures to ensure that employees learn of other employees' activities if relevant. For instance, if one team is working on a project, managers or team leaders could inform team members what other employees in the organization are doing that affects the project.

Fourth, the business should develop intra-organizational systems to manage knowledge. Recall that intra-organizational systems are systems that are not divided along functional or divisional lines, but instead view the organization as a whole entity. With this type of system, finance can learn what marketing does and vice versa so that employees can work more effectively toward the overall goals of the organization. Note, also, that an IOS promotes transparency and enhances communications because it encourages electronic discussions in which people engage in "electronic" listening and reflecting on others' ideas.

Fifth, information systems that help employees locate experts in the organization offer value and time-savings. In many companies, employees don't know where to go when they have a problem and often reinvent the wheel (or worse yet, spin their wheels unnecessarily). Visualize a scenario where you as a new employee need information about a specific product that the company makes. How would you find out who the product expert is in the company? The larger the company, the more difficult it becomes to locate the expert.

Sixth, one of the most important tenets of knowledge management is the ability to learn from past mistakes. Effective knowledge management systems help to create a learning organization by capturing and sharing the lessons learned from past experiences. By documenting successes and sharing failures, employees can expand their knowledge.

In addition to the six ways in which IS can help an organization manage knowledge, businesses must learn how to place a subjective value on knowledge management. This task is so difficult that many projects fail because companies cannot show the benefits of this approach.[7] IS managers need to understand what knowledge management is, how knowledge is managed, and perhaps most important, what value knowledge has to the business. To ensure the long-term success and commitment to a knowledge management system, then, they should develop ways to measure the effects of that system.

Strategic Implications of Knowledge Management

Many companies that are adept at managing corporate knowledge achieve a competitive advantage in the marketplace. This section examines the strategic implications of knowledge management applications. The main focus of these systems is to improve decision making. Through more effective decision making, companies can reduce costs, improve product development speed, heighten productivity, and enhance customer service.

Effective knowledge management systems help employees communicate and learn more readily. In companies that have employees in different locations, access to a knowledge management system can improve the effectiveness of decisions about product design and manufacturing. Eli Lilly & Company has measured the effects of knowledge management on its drug manufacturing process and learned that the company has improved speed and lowered costs due to its efforts.[8] The Indianapolis-based corporation has created several knowledge-based applications to help worldwide drug development teams exchange information with business and information technology staffs.

In one application the company uses Lotus Notes, an electronic communication and database tool, to provide researchers, chemists, marketers, and business managers updated access to product information, best practices, cost information, and project time lines. Lotus Notes, a groupware software tool, also allows all employees to create and update information in real time in a database. That way, team members from different parts of the world can tap into the database and view the changes made by other team members. The ability to transfer knowledge easily has significantly lowered manufacturing costs and improved the pace of product development.

IS that is used to manage knowledge can improve the quality of employee decisions and their productivity, often by encouraging collaboration. The productivity, in turn, can improve the quality of product and services. Thailand's National Science and Technology Development Agency (NSTDA) uses an intranet knowledge management system that has improved productivity and group decision making. The NSTDA is a funding and research organization that is the main driving force for rapid science and technology development in Thailand. It supports and implements technology for a range of Thai interests, including those of citizens, the government, and numerous industries.

The NSTDA has hundreds of employees located in offices throughout Thailand. The agency wanted to boost employee productivity by improving communication and collaboration among its staff. Until recently, obstacles hindering the organization's operations included the high costs associated with publishing and distributing documents internally, few opportunities for employees to collaborate easily, and generally poor internal communications.

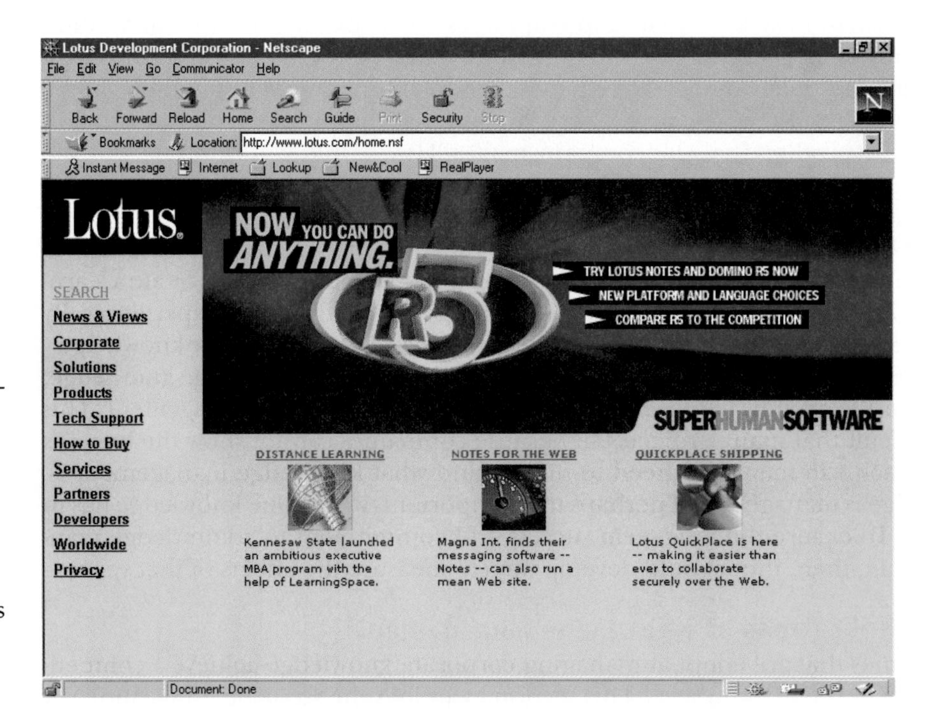

Lotus Notes is a groupware program that enhances organizational communication and fosters knowledge creation and delivery.

Source: © 1999 Lotus Development Corporation. Used with permission of Lotus Development Corporation. Lotus Notes is a registered trademark of Lotus Development Corporation.

Before the intranet was developed, the NSTDA lacked an easy-to-use system for sharing knowledge throughout the organization and working together. Today, the intranet enables the agency to share its ideas and knowledge with employees in different parts of the world and provide solutions more quickly and collaborate efficiently on projects of national importance. By making knowledge available with a few simple keystrokes, the intranet fosters group scheduling, on-line conferencing, an active virtual community, and improved individual and group decision making.[9]

Many businesses use knowledge management to learn more about customers and provide better service, as the Global IS for Success case shows. In some cases, companies can offer better service by sharing its knowledge. Ernst & Young learned that its small business clients wanted access to its financial expertise and developed a customer-oriented knowledge management system called Ernie.

Ernie is an Internet-based on-line business service that offers emerging growth companies a direct, electronic link to Ernst & Young accounting and business consultants. Ernst & Young, specialists in tax, accounting, and management consulting, field questions from subscribers such as "How can I make my accounts payable processes faster and more accurate?" "Can you recommend ways to save costs if electricity deregulates?" and "What is the proper method for valuing our stocks?" Ernie "knowledge providers" (the system that does this work) sort the questions by subject and then route them through Ernst & Young's internal knowledge Web, or "intranet," to the professional who is most knowledgeable about the specific industry, topic, or issue.

Ernie is one of the first on-line consulting resources for entrepreneurial companies. Because many small businesses do not have the resources to pay for expensive consultants, Ernie has been a smash hit. Within four months of its launch, Ernie had successfully answered 1,000 questions and earned $1 million in revenue. The quality of this knowledge management system has given the business a competitive advantage in a niche market. "The site has helped position Ernst & Young as the leading source of innovative consulting service [for entrepreneurs], and a pioneer in redefining the way professional services are delivered," says one management journal.[10]

Remember that knowledge management systems should—first and foremost—improve decision making so employees can solve business problems more effectively. By gathering essential expert information in a system that makes it available exactly when it is needed, organizations can avoid making decisions based on outdated, inaccurate, or incomplete information and can solve problems more rapidly.

An example contrasts the decision-making experiences of personnel who have access to a knowledge management system and those that don't. After a Navy instructor flying a T-45 Goshawk training jet experienced a throttle that jammed and snapped a cable, the training jet fleet was grounded on a Texas airfield until Navy engineers in Jacksonville and Boeing engineers in St. Louis could find the problem. An examination of the engineering drawings didn't help them find and fix what was wrong, though, because the drawings were outdated. Numerous experts pored over the documents to find the problem, to no avail.

Luckily, the story ends well. Engineers eventually discovered the problem by disassembling the throttle, explains Lisa Crawford, technical team leader, extranet administrator, and Webmaster for the T-45 support team at the Naval Aviation Depot in Jacksonville.

Now—instead of relying on Navy drawings that may or may not be out-of-date—an extranet connects several hundred Navy employees and their subcontractors to share engineering and other data as they make repair and design decisions. Using the extranet, a Jacksonville-based engineer can post his repair documents and diagrams online, and a mechanic in Kingsville can start reviewing them days before official repair paperwork makes its way through the system. The constant interaction and updating of information enables engineers and Navy personnel to make more effective, timely decisions that can affect the safety of many lives.

How can you help your company capitalize on its knowledge to achieve success in the marketplace? Knowledge managers rely heavily on three skills: decision making, business savvy, and technical skill. As you learn new technologies, ask yourself the questions "How will this technology help my company better compete in the workplace? What knowledge

Global IS for success

Chocolate, Diapers, and Soaps

Reaching customers used to be easy for U.K. consumer goods manufacturers. Britain had five TV channels, so manufacturers that advertised on a popular prime-time show knew their message would reach a large part of their target audience of British homemakers. Now the United Kingdom's TV viewers have 200 channels to choose from as well as other entertainment media such as PCs and the Internet.

In fact, consumer goods manufacturers have difficulty zeroing in on the average consumer because men and women share household duties, including grocery shopping responsibilities. "The average consumer doesn't exist," explains Phil Barden, relationship marketing director for Unilever UK. Without an average target consumer and more fragmentation of advertising media, mass marketing is a less effective marketing tool.

Unilever, which has headquarters in London and Rotterdam, has an annual marketing budget of £3.6 billion (roughly U.S. $6 billion). It's moving away from "one-size-fits-all" consumer messages. To make this shift, Unilever collaborated with noncompeting companies to research and pool customer data about consumer preferences, motivations, and behavior. The company believed that developing a broad perspective of its customers' buying patterns could enhance its marketing.

"If we learned about people's habits, attitudes and behaviors in completely different [product] categories, we felt that, in theory, we could start to predict how people would behave in our own categories. If I know what videos you rent, where you take your holidays, what books you read and what music you listen to, I can make a reasonable prediction of what fragrance you wear," explains one senior marketing manager at Unilever.

Unilever broached the idea of sharing customer data with three U.K. consumer goods companies that do not compete with it: Cadbury-Schweppes, Bass Brewers, and Kimberly-Clark. The companies quickly learned that they shared common consumers. If the companies could group noncompeting brands in well-planned and carefully executed promotions (such as consumer ads or coupons), they could create a win-win situation for the businesses and their customers. They forged ahead and built a shared consumer database.

To illustrate how knowledge of consumer preferences helped the company, let's take a look at Bass, which makes Carling, the U.K.'s best-selling brand of lager beer. Bass sponsors the F. A. Carling Premiership, a premier English football division. The company partnered with Cadbury and Elida-Fabergé on its Carlingnet Web site (www.fa-premier.com) to offer visitors the chance to send electronic postcards from the site, courtesy of Elida-Fabergé's male fragrance, Lynx, or to participate in a virtual World Cup contest sponsored by Fuse, a Cadbury chocolate bar.

Bass periodically gathers customer data from Carling Club members and shares the information with Elida-Fabergé and Cadbury. These three brands target 18- to-24-year-old men through the Web, a medium that reaches many males this age with appealing content (football). Many consumers willingly gave data.

will we need to make better decisions? And how can I help my company capture and share this knowledge?" This mindset will make you a valuable member of your organization.

Knowledge is not static; it is dynamic and always changing. Individuals and organizations involved in knowledge management must be prepared to change. In the next section we look at change and its relationship to IT.

Change Management and IS

Change is sweeping over our personal and professional levels. But adapting to change is not easy. People are creatures of habit, and the comfort that comes with familiarity is often hard to give up.

Resistance to change is one of the major obstacles in implementing new programs and initiatives, according to a study of more than 100 companies from 20 different countries by ProSci, a business research and publishing firm based in Loveland, Colorado.[11] As researchers and management experts recognized the two inevitable truths, namely, that change is inevitable and change is hard, a new field of study called **change management** evolved. Change management addresses all aspects of initiating, implementing, managing, and rewarding change.

Change management

Management theories, philosophies, and principles that help individuals and companies to deal with all aspects of change.

Before the partnership developed, the companies collected data from surveys, promotions, and customer service center reports. Unilever had a database of close to 1.5 million U.K. households, Kimberly-Clark had a database of information on new mothers, Bass was in the process of building a regional database of beer drinkers, and Cadbury did not have a database. The collaborative efforts have provided a pool of knowledge that has vastly improved the marketing of all involved companies.

QUESTIONS AND PROJECTS

1. By collaborating with different companies, Unilever gained a better understanding of its customers than it would have on its own. Discuss.
2. Why is this an example of knowledge management?
3. Identify any three companies in three different industries and show how collaboration among these three companies could lead to greater market success.

Source: Alice Dragoon, "Looking for Mr. Candybar," *CIO Enterprise,* Section 2, January 15, 1999, 12.

Cadbury-Schweppes, maker of Cadbury chocolate bars, joined with three other U.K. consumer goods companies to develop a shared database of consumer information.

A key aspect of change management is hiring and training employees to make change happen. Employees at all levels should learn to focus on what needs to be done to give the business an edge.[12] One way to help employees anticipate and embrace change is to provide appropriate information technologies.

Technology and Change

"Technology is the biggest driver of change in this country at the moment," says Kevin McCaffrey from PricewaterhouseCoopers. He argues that today what is driving the majority of change in the business environment is the pace and impact of technology. In fact, information systems and technologies are both an external and internal force for change:

1. **Organizations use technology to initiate change inside the organization.** Information systems and IS personnel act as agents of internal change to help the business create a competitive advantage and improve business processes.
2. **Technological changes in the environment are one of several forces that prompts organizations to change to stay competitive.** Technology becomes an external pressure driving an organization to change.

FIGURE 13-3

The Relationship between Change and Technology

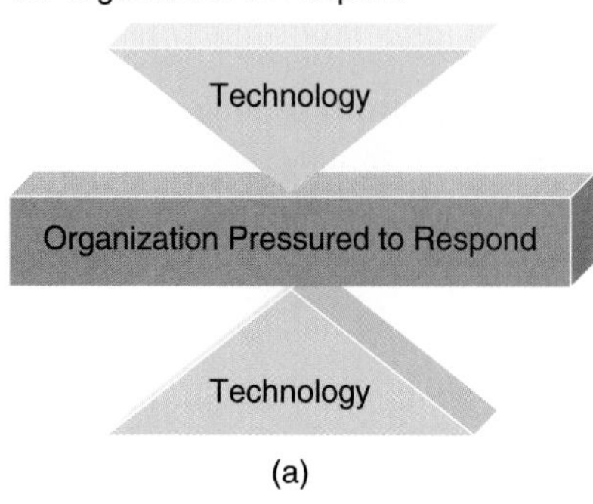

(a)

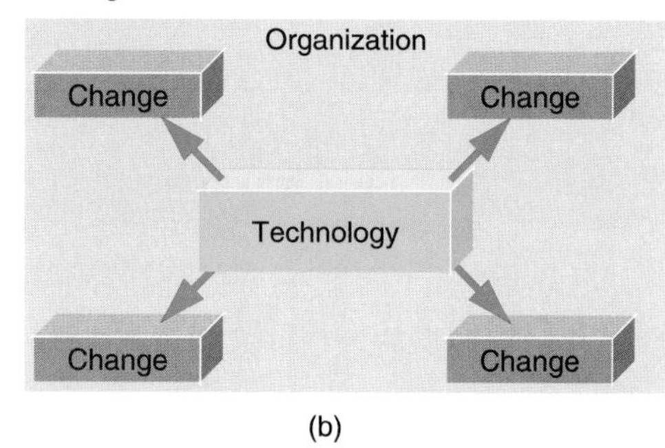

(b)

Figure 13-3 summarizes these two aspects of technology and change. Many organizations experience both aspects—as external advances in information technology occur, they use them internally to create a competitive advantage. Change management strategies can help IS personnel manage changes occurring inside and outside the organization. We examine the strategic implications of change next.

Strategic Implications of Change Management

Societies and organizations that manage change effectively can capitalize on opportunities. Computers and information systems strongly influence the change management process, as we see next.

Think back to Chapter 1's discussion of competitive advantage. Recall that external forces pressure businesses to differentiate themselves from the competition. In response, businesses use various strategies to gain a competitive advantage, such as offering the lowest cost or unique products and services, forging strong customer or supplier relations, or establishing a niche market. With the explosion of new competitors, products, services, and technology, businesses have to manage change on a continual basis to respond to and anticipate changes in the external environment.

Change management strategies differ, depending on the organization, its goals, and the forces in its environment. Although the exact strategies may differ, the overall purpose of change management is to help the organization reach its goals. There are myriad reasons why organizations embrace change, such as global forces, changing the corporate culture, and enhancing employee morale. In this section, we investigate five reasons to use change management, summarized in Table 13-1, including strengthening bonds with customers, keeping pace with scientific and technological advances, lowering cost, handling diversity, and offering more customized products and services.

Managing Change to Strengthen Consumer Relations

Organizations that can forge strong connections with those they try to sell to or serve will gain a competitive edge. Many businesses are using IS and IT to strengthen relations with their customers and with their business partners. Web sites, improved customer service systems, and more accurate customer data management are only a few ways businesses are strengthening their relations with various stakeholders.

TABLE 13-1

Five Reasons to Manage Change
1. Strengthen consumer relations
2. Keep pace with scientific and technological advances
3. Lower costs
4. Manage diversity
5. Provide more customization

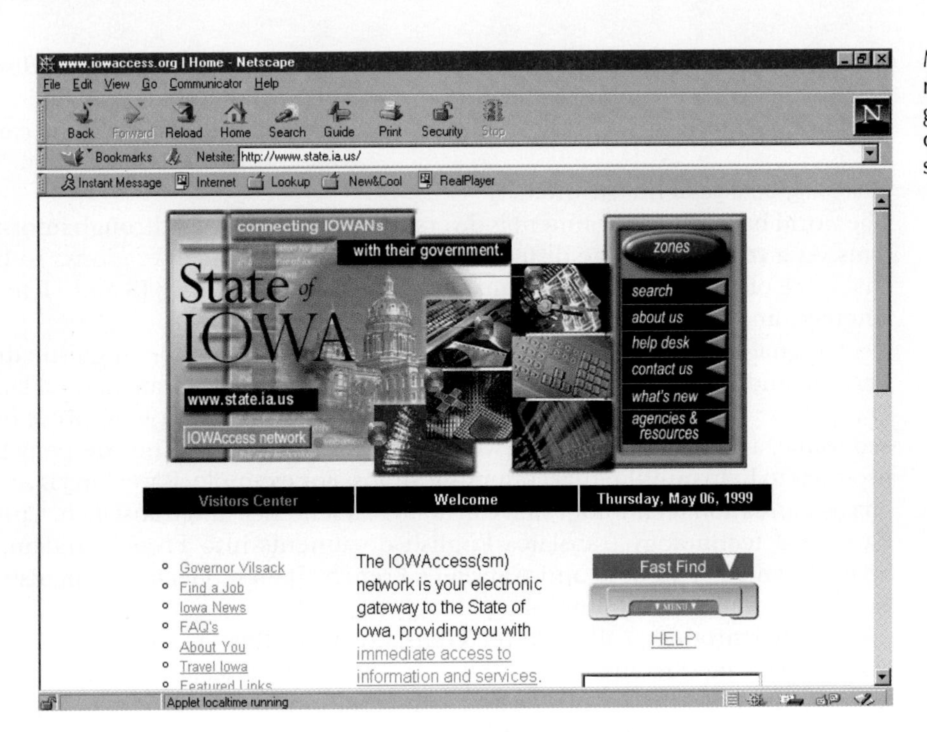

Many state and local governments, such as Iowa's state government, are embracing change management to better serve citizens.

In addition, government entities are using information systems to meet the demands of a populace that is highly diverse, stretched for time, and disenchanted with the government. According to voters, reaching public officials for information or services is difficult, if not impossible. Many agencies are responding with the use of information technology to improve citizen access. The response has been more voter involvement with government.

Voters can now e-mail the President or their congressional representatives with concerns. Youngsters can take a tour of the White House over the Web. Top office holders are developing information systems that help businesses and individuals cut through bureaucratic red tape. Iowa Governor Terry Branstad, for instance, is spearheading an IS project called IowAccess. The project's goal is clear: "Anybody should be able to access services at any time for anywhere. . . . People sometimes think government is too big, too far away and uncaring. We can change that perception by making services more easily available to people on their terms," the governor says.[13]

As part of the project, Iowa officials are working with the Internal Revenue Service and Social Security Administration to develop the State Tax and Wage Reporting System (STAWRS), which will give employers one Web site to report all state and federal employee tax and wage information. The state can then distribute a consolidated report to the appropriate agency.[14] Using information technology to forge stronger bonds with citizens is helping governmental entities at all levels manage changes in their environment.

Managing Change to Keep Pace with Scientific and Technologic Advances

Changes in science and technology have altered the landscape of many industries. Organizations that can stay ahead of the competition in adapting to the changes have the opportunity to gain an advantage. The medical field is undergoing substantial change due to scientific and technologic advances, as well as the onset of managed care and the health care needs of our aging population. Health care professionals, then, experience the pressure to keep costs down yet improve the level of service commensurate with advances in health care and technology. Information systems are helping medical professionals manage these changes, as the next example demonstrates.

Duke University relies on a computerized ultrasound diagnostic imaging system to treat patients with heart problems. The computerized system provides information on pathologies of the heart such as valvular function and congenital defects. The advanced graphic workstations give the physician views and functions of the heart that will have a major impact on the diagnosis and treatment of patients with cardiac diseases. The new system, which combines visualization, two-dimensional image analysis, and three-dimensional imaging, is expected to fundamentally change the practice of cardiology.[15]

Managing Change to Handle Diversity

The world business environment is diverse yet interconnected through information systems. As a result, language differences can stymie business operations. To handle the challenge of increased diversity, many organizations are using IS and IT to overcome language and cultural barriers.

Language translation software can help companies handle linguistic differences. Lernout and Hauspie, a company that builds software to facilitate natural language, allows people and communities to communicate with each other to improve their social, economic, and educational level without language barriers. The company has several products to help multilingual communications. For example, Barcelona is a natural language translation technology that can analyze a sentence and translate it. Currently, the Barcelona technology translates English documents into French, Italian, German, Spanish, and Portuguese and translates French, Italian, German, Spanish, and Portuguese documents into English.

Another product, called Power Translator Pro, allows interactive translations in a word-processing document. In Europe and South America, where there is high Internet use, this tool is invaluable for translating English Web sites into the appropriate language. One company has embedded the Power Translator Pro engine in its Internet chat site, so that people can chat across languages. Another company uses the product to translate e-mail. These information technology products help lower communication barriers and increase tolerance among different cultures.[16]

To cope with increased diversity in the population, Florida and other state and local governments are using information systems to ensure that non-English-speaking communities have equal access to government services. The Florida Department of Labor and Employment Security wants its unemployment claims IVR system—which serves over 80 percent of its customers—to serve everyone, including non-English-speaking users. That information system now generates all critical reports and documents in both English and Spanish. Citizens who use the system can also input data in English or Spanish.

In a state with a large Hispanic population, creating Spanish language scripts was essential, and scripts for Haitian-speaking customers may follow. The department is even considering tailoring the system for the hearing impaired.[17]

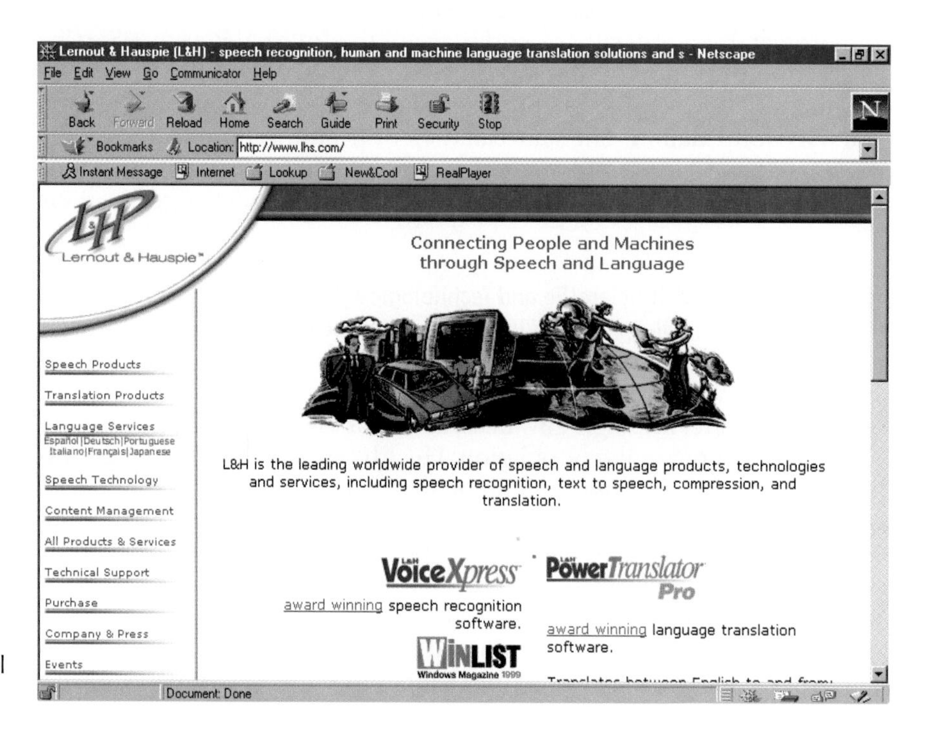

Recognizing the need for global organizations to cope with linguistic issues, Lernout and Hauspie developed natural language translation products.

Managing Change to Lower Costs

Speed and efficiency of service have become critical factors in attracting and retaining customers who want the highest possible value for the lowest possible cost. This change in consumer expectations is forcing businesses to change and streamline their operating procedures. In many circumstances, information systems can help companies lower costs and simultaneously provide high-quality service if planned for carefully and managed effectively.

Disease Manager Plus, a comprehensive medical information system, uses sophisticated database tools to transform medical records into analytical tools that help doctors continuously monitor and analyze the condition of each patient. Disease Manager Plus fully integrates clinical, administrative, and financial data management, which is especially useful in managing complex chronic illnesses. The system has contributed to significant reductions in mortality and morbidity among chronically ill patients and lowered their treatment costs substantially.[18]

Information systems can also lower costs because the person and the information do not have to be in the same location, so the business can eliminate duplicate resources. Take, for example, attorneys looking for case-related information. For years, Allied Signal maintained 23 law libraries in several countries around the world filled with many identical, often expensive, hardbound legal texts. Library maintenance cost several hundred thousand dollars a year. Now more than 95 percent of the company's hard-copy law collection is on-line, according to Joe Vidal, Allied Signal's manager for the Law Information Center.

The company's legal intranet stores legal information, eliminating the need to purchase duplicate books on an annual basis, some of which cost $1,500 per book. The online library's searching capabilities cut research time by more than 85 percent with savings in excess of $500,000 a year. "And you don't have to worry about books walking off the shelves." Vidal observes: "That's a common practice with attorneys."[19] In this instance, the cost-cutting change management strategies worked.

Managing Change to Improve Customization

Technologic changes and increased competition can force a business to change by offering customers tailor-made products. In the media industry, cable company CNN faced the effects of new government regulations, the splintering of the television news audience due to competition from new channels and the Web, and customers who suffered from information overload. Managing these industry changes with the innovative

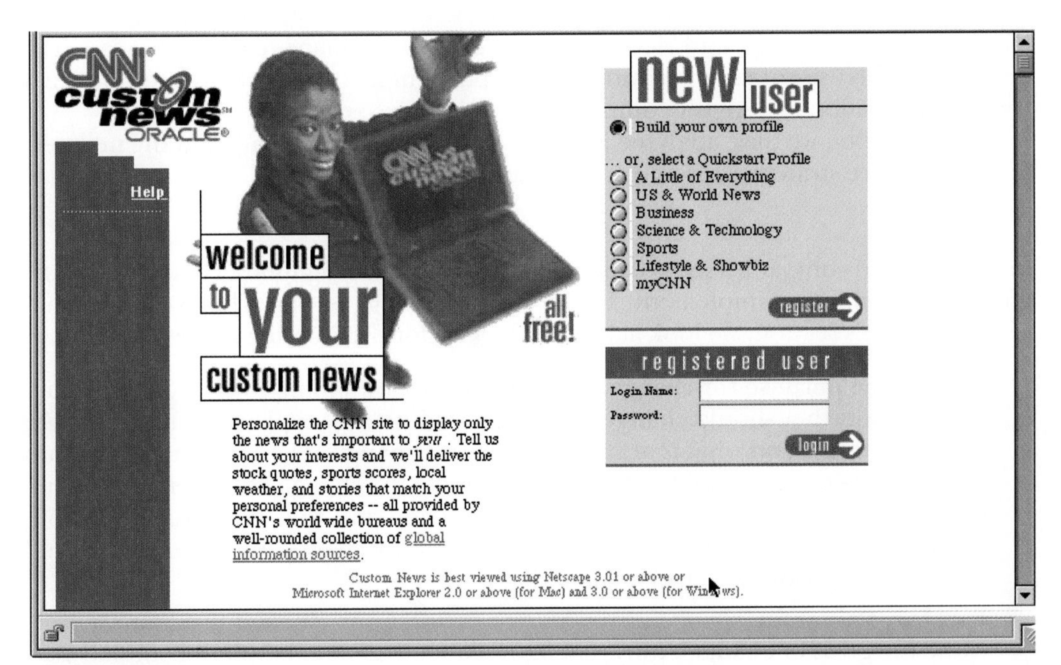

One-news-fits-all no longer works amid the competition in the news media. Now news can be customized to meet an individual's needs and tastes, as this CNN Web site shows.

By being prepared and willing to change, Capital One became a market leader in the banking industry.

use of information technology means that CNN can offer viewers a more customized news service that meets their needs better than competitors do.

CNN now offers the CNN Custom News, a Web site that meets the personal information needs of an individual anywhere in the world. To achieve this, CNN Custom News filters more than 100 news sources and stores them in a searchable database organized by categories that CNN's editorial experts define. The database content can then be used to build a customized news site for each individual user so that viewers only see and read the news that interests them. The issue is choice: The person, rather than the news media, controls what she or he views instead of being bombarded with irrelevant or uninteresting news.[20]

In the financial industry, managing the change of demanding customers who want superior service has forced many businesses to shift from storing volumes of customer data to analyzing and mining it to meet the needs of various customer segments better than competitors. Organizations that can learn what the needs of customers are and meet those needs can beat the competition.

A decade ago the future CEO of Capital One Financial Corp. started approaching banks with an idea to analyze customer data to develop credit cards with features that targeted the needs of various market segments. Nobody was interested in changing its one-size-fits-all approach to credit cards except a small regional bank in Virginia.

Now, billions of dollars later, that bank's credit-card division has spun off into Capital One, one of the largest credit-card issuers in America. Capital One analyzes terabytes of consumer data to pinpoint just the right credit card for the right individual. "At Capital One . . . it's almost impossible to talk about a new business strategy without talking about IT strategy, and vice versa," says one senior manager.[21] In this case, the bank's ability to use database technology to implement a business change resulted in a leadership position in a highly competitive marketplace.

In this section we have analyzed five reasons for managing change. In the next section, we explore strategies for managing change.

Strategies for Managing Change

Individuals and companies strive to keep up with the changing times. However, change is not easy to initiate or implement. Table 13-2 lists the biggest obstacles to change management. In this section, we look at some strategies for overcoming those obstacles.

- **Identify the purpose for change.** Most employees are willing to change if they understand why they should change. The organization must explain what the purpose of the change is and what is at stake if it doesn't change. Then it should follow up with employees to see whether they can commit to the change. When employees understand the reason why change is being initiated and they buy into the reason, change becomes much easier. If employees resist the change, management should uncover the reasons and tackle them directly.
- **Stay focused on the change goals.** Many organizations' change programs fail because the goals of change efforts change frequently. For example, a company may

TABLE 13-2

Change Management Obstacles

Obstacle	%
Employee resistance to change	39%
Management behaviors not supportive of change	33%
Inadequate resources or budget	14%
All other obstacles	14%

Source: Management Review, December 1998, 1–2.

start a change program with the intention of improving communication patterns in the company. If the company has a closed-door communications policy that requires change, it is important to stay focused on this effort unless and until it is successfully completed. Shifting priorities midstream often sends the message that the company lacks a commitment to or doesn't fully understand the goals of its change management project.

- **Top management should lead the charge.** As Table 13-2 suggests, one reason why many change efforts fail is because top management fails to support it. Top managers can derail and hamper efforts to initiate change if they do not actively practice change themselves. Successful change management efforts, however, almost always begin with top management. Employees who see top managers who are willing to embrace change are more likely to adapt to changes effectively. Top management, then, should "walk the walk and talk the talk."
- **Communicate clearly and consistently.** Clear, consistent, truthful communication is essential to companies trying to initiate and implement change. A U.S. research company investigated 531 organizations undergoing major change and asked the CEOs, "If you could go back and change one thing what would it be?" The most frequent answer was "The way I communicated with my employees."[22] Experts recommend that management communicate openly with all employees and tell them the truth about the reason and possible effects of the changes. For example, in some cases change may lead to turnover. It is important to discuss this effect with employees so good employees don't leave the company in a panic.
- **Acknowledge that change is continuous.** Change is not a one-time effort. It is a constant. To maintain a competitive advantage, a company must continuously devise new and better ways to operate. As Randall Mott, senior vice president and CIO for Wal-Mart Stores, says, "differentiation in your business is something you have to work on every day to keep."[23] When a company reaches one goal, management should anticipate, plan, and initiate the next change management program to ensure market leadership.

Figure 13-4 summarizes change management strategies. We turn next to ways that businesses organize the IS team and follow with a section on managing an IS career.

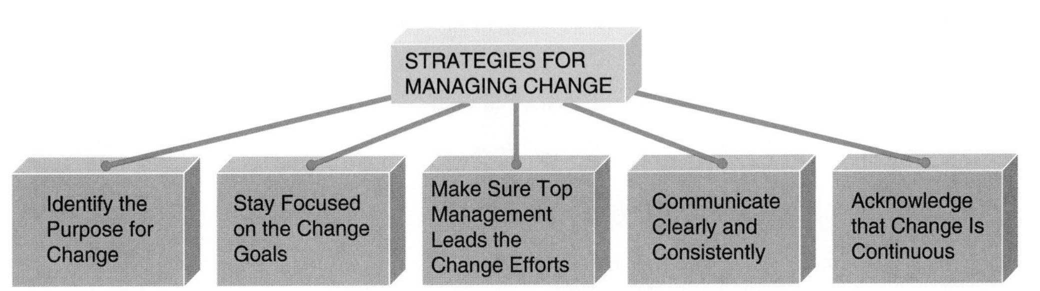

FIGURE 13-4

Change Management Strategies

Organizing the IS Department

Businesses have many options for organizing IS personnel. No one option is better than another. Instead, the key to organizing the IS team is to assess the business goals, how IS relates to those goals, and the best way to organize the IS staff to meet those goals. As simple as this sounds, the organizing task is a difficult one, especially because business goals and how IS relates to those goals can change frequently.

In a small business with only a few IS employees, one person is likely to be responsible for multiple functions. Most businesses of all sizes have a chief information officer, an individual who holds overall responsibility for the smooth functioning of the IS staff. This person is in charge of all aspects of information systems and technologies, some of which are listed here:

1. Make versus buy decisions regarding systems and technologies
2. Managing IS personnel and managers
3. Training IS staff and employees
4. Evaluating emerging technologies
5. Ensuring that information technology is aligned with business goals and needs
6. Making outsourcing decisions
7. Budgeting
8. Maintenance of existing systems
9. Ensuring that all governmental and legal regulations are met
10. Security of systems and facilities

The chief information officer, whose title may sometimes be vice president of information systems, may report to the chief operating officer, to the chief financial officer, or in some cases directly to the chief executive officer. The reporting structure varies from one organization to the next, depending on a number of factors, including company size, industry, and criticality of IS.

The organization of the IS function also varies greatly from one company to the next. For example, in one company, the IS department may be organized simply by IS function, including managing current applications, developing new applications, and maintenance. This simple organizational structure is shown in Figure 13-5(a). As depicted in Figure 13-5(b), larger organizations that depend strongly on IS may have separate departments to manage different technologies such as database, telecommunications, emerging technologies, client/server, and global applications departments.

FIGURE 13-5

Two Ways to Organize the IS Department

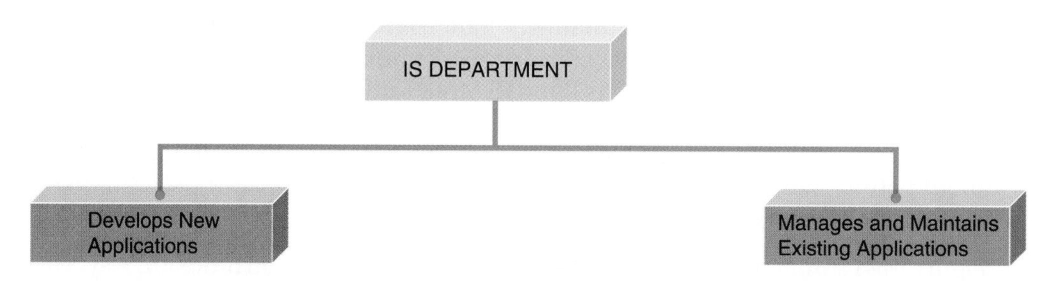

(a) In some companies, the IS department may be organized based on new or existing applications

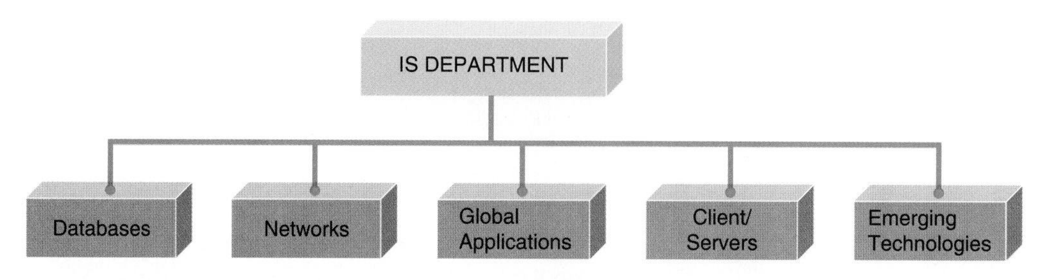

(b) This setup is usually found in large companies with many different, and often large-scale, systems

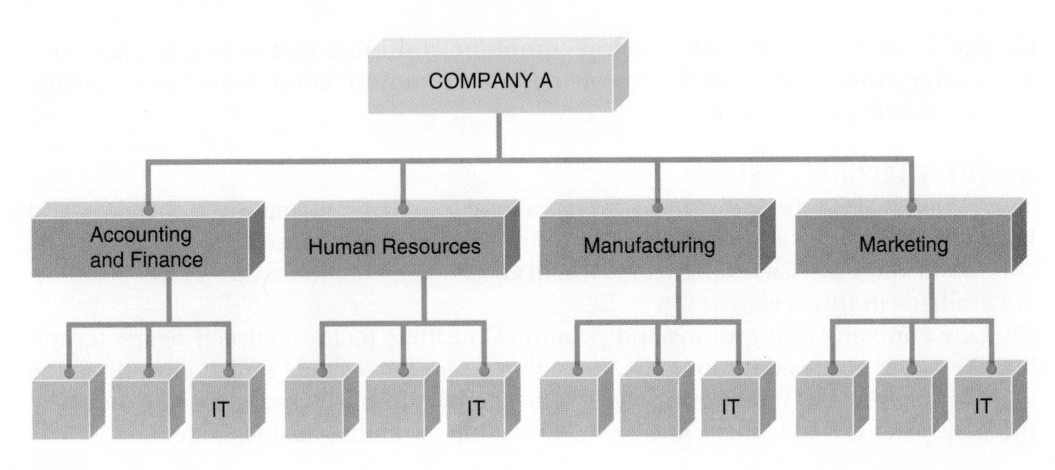

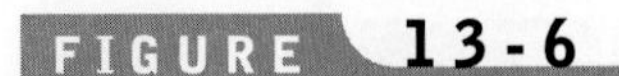
FIGURE 13-6

IS Personnel Organized by Business Function

In other cases companies may have a more complex structure to suit their needs. For example, an international company may have a structure based on regions. It would have several IS directors reporting to the CIO, one for each country.

Another way to organize IS personnel is to integrate them into each business functional area, such as finance, accounting, marketing, production, and human resources, as shown in Figure 13-6. Each area, then, has one or more IS specialists dedicated to support it. This structure allows IS employees to gain a thorough understanding of their assigned functional area and support it exclusively. In such an organization, the IS employee may report to the director of the functional area, to the CIO, or to both.

As the needs of the company change, the structure of the IS team may also change. The ability to keep the IS department organization flexible so that it can adapt to meet company needs is a hallmark of organizations that change effectively. Remember, information systems exist to help companies achieve their goals and objectives. As the company evolves, then, IS departments must change if they are to serve the organization well. However, such flexibility can offer both challenges and opportunities to those in the field of information systems. We close by examining IS careers.

Careers in IS: Achieving Success

The world of information systems and technology is experiencing such radical changes that it affects how people manage their careers in IS. Old titles are out and new ones are in. The IS department is constantly being reorganized as businesses reinvent themselves.

The industrial organization with clearly defined job responsibilities and several levels of hierarchy is being replaced by organizations of **knowledge workers** in which each person needs to think like a business owner to find solutions to problems or spot business opportunities. A knowledge worker is one whose primary contribution to the company is his or her knowledge, talent, and judgment, such as an advertising executive or editor. Compare this with a blue-collar worker whose contribution may be a set of products at the end of the day.

Knowledge workers
Employees whose main contribution to an organization is their knowledge, talent, and judgment.

IS personnel are integral to a knowledge workforce. First, they are knowledge workers. Second, they also support the work efforts of other knowledge workers, as our discussion of knowledge management showed. Many organizations with a knowledge-based workforce have a flat structure (very little hierarchy) and fluid job descriptions that change as the situation demands.

The fluidity of job titles and descriptions in the IS field is rampant. In fact, old job titles such as programmer, systems analyst, database administrator, and so on are beginning to fade. "Job titles are not very important at all," says Professor Emeritus Robert A. Zawacki, president of Zawacki and Associates. "They are stifling—a carryover from the old, bureaucratic organizations."[24] From code juggler to manager of demand creation, from senior completion analyst to director of content analysis, titles reflect a new mindset that IS is here to help businesses and their employees succeed.

This section gives a broad overview of some emerging IS careers and the skills required for managing those careers. What careers will the future in IS hold? The prediction is tough to make because of the rapid pace of business and technological

Business technologists must combine knowledge of technology with problem-solving skills and business acumen.

change. However, those who develop computer and information literacy, business knowledge, and creative problem-solving and communication skills have a strong chance of being in demand.

Business Technologist

This job is ideal for the individual who has a solid grasp of information technology and knows how to apply technology to solve business problems. It requires teamwork and communication skills, a willingness to learn, and business acumen. Entry level positions are available in this area.

One company that grooms and promotes business technologists is Sears. Joseph Smialowski, vice president and CIO, says that when he recruits senior executives, he looks for people with both business and IT backgrounds. Business and IT, he notes, "are the skills you need to foster a business partnership and meet business needs."[25]

Programmer and Systems Analyst

Most people think of these two jobs when they think of IT careers. These are mostly entry level positions that require a good amount of programming knowledge and organizational skills. The ability to listen carefully and interpret the needs of users is vital for systems analysts, who often serve as the liaison between programmers and users.

Although programmers may not have many interactions with others, systems analyst jobs demand close interaction with many user groups. Collaboration skills are vital in this job. "I think of a systems analyst as someone who just does pure analysis—but we don't have much call for that. Most of our positions require people to be capable on both ends. You need to be as solid and up to date in structured programming skills as you do in looking at the overall picture and designing systems from user requirements," notes Marie Clark, a recruiting director at MIS International, an information technology consulting group in Bloomfield Hills, Michigan.[26]

Database Expert

There are many careers in databases including database designers, programmers, and administrators. Today, many other jobs are emerging in this area, including the jobs of data warehouse specialist, Web database expert (one who integrates databases with the Web), and database security specialist.

Regardless of the specific type of database job, all require in-depth knowledge about databases. Database jobs also require knowledge about user interfaces, security issues, an eye for data quality, the ability to integrate multiple systems, a good understanding of the business, and the ability to give users the data they need to do their job successfully.

Networking Specialist

This job is highly technical and requires in-depth knowledge of all aspects of a network, including network management, maintenance, and performance. From installing networks to ensuring that they don't fail, network managers are highly sought after and engage in a wide variety of tasks and activities. They need to have a good understanding of networking hardware, software, and operating systems and should have a keen eye for diagnosing problems. Many client/server systems and projects require highly experienced networking professionals. These jobs usually require some hands-on experience with networks.

Web and E-Commerce Specialist

The Internet and e-commerce has opened the doors to a wide variety of challenging and exciting careers that did not even exist a few years ago. This career specialty includes designing, developing, and maintaining Web pages; integrating Web pages with other applications in the organization; developing and maintaining intranets and extranets; developing e-commerce sites; ensuring the security of Web sites; and processing transactions that the Web generates. Most of these jobs require not just technical skills related to the Web, Internet, networking, and databases, but also a healthy dose of creativity and artistic talent.

Project Manager

Project managers handle all the activities and resources that affect a project, including the schedule, the budget, and the personnel.

Project managers are the "glue" that keep a project together and are in short supply around the world. When a company is developing an IT project, it requires an individual to manage all aspects of the project. This not only includes managing all the activities that were described under the system life cycle model in Chapter 11, but also managing the resources of the project, including budget, time, and people. Given the large number of projects that fail, IS project managers are highly sought after in the IT industry and command high salaries. However, candidates typically must have a minimum of three to five years of experience in the industry.

What are some skills that good project managers should have? Besides technical knowledge, project management requires a set of core competencies, some of which are:

- Interpersonal, teamwork, and leadership skills
- Motivation skills
- Communication skills
- Ability to understand the financial implications of all decisions
- Ability to understand the relationships between different tasks in a project
- Risk assessment aptitude

Knowledge Managers or "Knowledge Czars"

Given the importance of knowledge management, several companies are creating new positions to manage the knowledge cycle in their organizations. This position usually requires several years of experience in the industry in which they will be working, a keen sense of the business, analytic skills, a good understanding of how to deploy technology, and an ability to work with people.

A knowledge czar ensures that learning tools, techniques, and systems are in place for all employees in an organization. New employees must be able to quickly and effectively identify and learn important business practices and core knowledge so that they can contribute quickly to the success of the organization. A knowledge czar is also responsible for informing employees of and creating easy access to experts and specialists. For example, in a pharmaceutical company, employees should know who the experts are in chemical analysis, genetics, sterile manufacturing, physician management, and so on and how to contact them. Finally, knowledge czars are responsible for making sure that organizations learn from past experiences.

Chief Information Officer

A CIO is responsible for the entire IT division or department and ensuring that there is a strong alliance between technology and the business needs of the company. He or she is also responsible for the success of IT projects and their contributions to the overall goal of the business.

Freshly armed with a computer science degree, Mark Brown began his IT career coding COBOL for an auto parts supply company in Chicago. He did well at his first IT job, gaining both new technology and business skills that soon led to a job heading the data processing department at a $50 million paper company. For 12 years he did all the company's systems designs and programming. Brown then tried his hand at consulting, taking an assignment at $50 million Viking Office Products. Brown was soon recruited to run the IT group.

In just three years, Viking's revenue grew from $50 million to $150 million. It had operations in the United States and Europe. The IT responsibilities skyrocketed. Today, as CIO, Brown's responsibilities are providing for the company's IT needs worldwide. That includes managing the IT budget and leading efforts to make sure the infrastructure is in place to support the organization.[27]

These are just a few of the jobs in the information technology field. Many other new careers that we discussed throughout the book are still evolving. Remember that IS careers require technical, business, and social skills. So if you are a "people-person" with some interest in technology, the IS field may have the perfect job for you.

Careers for success

Crafting the Technical Resume

Writing a technical resume differs from writing a business resume. Here are some key guidelines offered by an expert in the field. First, don't oversell your experience. The chances that you have worked with and have in-depth knowledge of more than a handful of technologies is slim. Hiring professionals understand this. Identify the ones that you are prepared and ready to use the first day on the job. It is fair for the interviewer to ask you in-depth questions or give a brief test on those technologies.

Second, relate your experience to technology. Don't divert attention by going into detail about your previous job experience if it is not technology-related. Instead, highlight the technology aspects of your job. For example, if you were a bank teller, emphasize the bank's information systems or programs that you are familiar with. If you are short on technical experience, highlight any class project that involved sufficient use of a given technology. If you had an internship, highlight it and elaborate your experiences in the internship.

Third, distinguish yourself. Once your resume is fully developed, ask this question, "Would I want to pick up the phone and call this individual for an interview?" What is it about your resume that makes it attractive for the employer to invest his or her time in you? You should answer this question as objectively as you can.

Aside from your name, address, and telephone numbers, a properly constructed technical resume has five distinct sections: Objective, Education, Training and Certifications, Technical Proficiencies, and Experience.

Objective: Your objective cannot be too broad ("I want a challenging job") or too high-level ("I want to be a senior manager"). It should be concise yet ambitious and well-thought-out.

Education: After the objective, list your education. It is the first thing many recruiters and hiring authorities look for on a resume. Give the degree title, institution, location, and month and year the degree was conferred, or your expected graduation date. If you have completed multiple degrees, list the highest-level degree first. If you did not complete a degree, list any formal education you have. If you have taken any training classes, list them here.

Technical proficiencies: Identify only the specific products and technologies you work with on a regular basis and are proficient in using. List similar technologies together, with your primary areas of specialty listed first. Remember not to exaggerate.

Experience: This section, the most important part of your resume, should be written in a reverse chronological order with a separate subsection for each employer. Include the months and years you have held each position and your specific title for each. Under each position, include a description of your main responsibilities. Be sure to include pertinent technical details so the reader will be able to understand where and how you used specific technologies. Don't be afraid to include any special recognition you received for doing a great job. Remember to blow your own horn when you can.

Writing a resume is difficult and time-consuming. You must work and rework it until it completely reflects your skills and talents; seek feedback on it from your friends, instructors, and people in the industry. Remember, you worked hard to earn your degree. You must work equally hard to market yourself.

Source: Steve Paris, "Building a Successful Technical Resume," *Computerworld,* May 26, 1997, www.computerworld.com.

The Person/Career Fit

You've landed several great job offers, but how do you know which one is right one for you? Here are some suggestions to follow to ensure that the career fit is a positive one[28]:

- **Enjoy at least 80 percent of the tasks in the new position.** There is hardly a job where someone likes every task they are responsible for. So understand exactly what the job entails and how your time will be divided among the different tasks that make up the job.
- **Become functional in the new position in a reasonable amount of time.** It can become quickly frustrating for both you and your boss if you don't become productive in a reasonable period of time. Understand what is expected of you the first day on the job and what kind of training the company will provide so that you can acquire new skills.

- **Make sure your goals mesh with the company's goals.** Understand and investigate the reputation of the company and see if it fits with your personal goals. This requires some investigation on your part. For example, if you don't like travel, ensure that travel is not an important part of your job.
- **Maintain appropriate chemistry with your coworkers.** This is one of the most important criteria for being successful. During your interview, pay close attention to your coworkers. From their dress style to their attitude toward work, your coworkers can give pointers as to whether you fit with the corporate culture and workplace.
- **Measure your growth opportunity with your personal goals.** If your goal is to reach top management within the next ten years and you find out that the company rarely promotes from within, conflicts can arise. If working on the latest technology is important to you and the company has not embraced new technologies, it sends a message. So ensure that your personal goals align with corporate goals and attitudes. These are just a few factors to consider before you accept your next job.

SUMMARY

1. **Describe knowledge management and its relevance to IS.** Knowledge management is the process of transforming useful information into knowledge by integrating it with experience, intuition, and creativity. It is a process by which intellectual capital, both intrinsic and extrinsic, is identified, stored, disseminated, and nurtured over the long term. To manage knowledge, organizations must create a learning environment, identify and capture information that is crucial to their success, translate that information into guiding business principles, ensure easy access to the knowledge base, and develop knowledge management systems that can change as needed. To implement knowledge management systems, managers rely on IT tools such as intranets, extranets, the World Wide Web, and other communication systems and software. The main focus of such systems is to improve decision making.
2. **Define and discuss the importance of change management in IS.** Information systems and technologies are linked with organizational change in two ways: (1) External technologic changes in the business environment, especially in the IT industry, pressure the organization to respond, and (2) organizations initiate change internally by using IT and IS personnel. Because resistance to change is both natural and common, organizations should find new ways to introduce change in an organization. This is done through change management, which refers to management theories, philosophies, and principles that help individuals and companies to deal with all aspects of change. Businesses have to manage change continually to respond to and anticipate changes in the external environment. Change management strategies depend on the needs of the organization, its goals, and the forces in its environment. Although strategies may differ, the overall purpose of change management is to help the organization reach its goals.
3. **Explain ways to organize IS personnel that help achieve business goals.** IS employees must be organized in the most conducive way to meet the information needs of the organization. Although several organizational structures for managing IS employees exist, no one structure is better than another. It simply depends on the size, information needs, and market characteristics in which the company operates. Some common structures include treating IS as a separate department organized into IS areas such as database and telecommunications, organizing IS personnel by region, or integrating information systems personnel in each functional area of an organization.
4. **Outline career opportunities and concerns in the field of information systems.** IS offers a number of vibrant careers that require considerable interaction with users and impressive rewards. IS personnel are integral to a knowledge workforce because they are knowledge workers and they support the work efforts of other knowledge workers. The jobs and job titles in IS are fluid so those in this field must be able to adapt to change and learn continuously. Most IS careers—from programming and database careers to business technologists and knowledge or project managers—require technical, business, and social skills.
5. **Identify some indications that a good fit exists between a person's talents and values and an IS job.** Some indications that the person/career fit is a positive one is the percentage of job tasks the individual enjoys, the amount of time it takes to become productive in the position, whether the company's goals match the person's goals, the chemistry with coworkers, and the opportunity for personal growth.

KEY TERMS

change management (p. 360)
intellectual capital (p. 354)
intra-organizational systems (p. 356)
knowledge management (p. 354)
knowledge workers (p. 369)
learning organization (p. 355)

REVIEW QUESTIONS

1. Why have computers assumed such a prominent role in our lives? Give any two reasons.
2. What is intellectual capital? What are the two forms of intellectual capital?
3. Why are companies' knowledge management efforts increasing?
4. What is knowledge management? Why is it important to any organization?
5. What are some IT tools used to manage knowledge?
6. Give an example of how knowledge management in a university setting can enhance your educational experience.
7. What are the prerequisites for converting information into knowledge?
8. What is an intraorganizational system? Why do businesses use them?
9. Suppose you are a small business owner. Explain how Ernie could be useful in your business. What are some pros and cons of Ernie?
10. What is change management and why is it important?
11. Give two examples of great change caused by computers in your personal life.
12. What are some changes that companies are going through and how can information technology help them to benefit from this change?
13. What are some societal changes caused by computers? Give any two examples.
14. Can you think of any negative effect that changes due to technology are causing in our lives?
15. What are some skills that managers look for in new IT hires? How can you equip yourself with this skill set?

DISCUSSION QUESTIONS AND EXERCISES

1. Computers influence our behavior in some ways. For example, in 1998 Nielsen Media Research reported that households with Internet access watch television 15 percent less than households without Internet access.[29] For parents with children, this sends an important message: that educational tools can be more enjoyable than entertainment tools.
   a. What are some arguments that you would use to convince a parent that an investment in a home computer is a good idea?
   b. How would you incorporate the theme of change management into your discussion?
2. Executives favor human interaction as an information exchange method. Don Middleberg, the head of a 50-person New York public relations firm, gathers his information face-to-face—and he expects his employees to do likewise. "I keep saying to our people here at the office, if I see you having lunch here [in the company cafeteria] too often, something is wrong," he says. Middleberg practices what he preaches. "Despite all the high tech available, I most value personal relationships. There's no substitute for friends and contacts in the business industry [to find out who] has what account, who is coming and going." Meetings outside his company absorb about half his time.[30]
   a. Face-to-face interactions are considered a great source of knowledge. Identify any one area of study where this is true.
   b. What are some reasons that textbooks and memos cannot replace the value of face-to-face meetings?
3. Executives' strategies for information gathering will be influenced by their industry and will reflect the style of each executive and his or her company's culture. But the one important mission all companies should share is to encourage corporate leaders who develop strategies for bringing knowledge inside the organization. And most of all, we need to talk to a wide range of rigorous sources to find the "better questions."

a. The ability to "think outside the box" is critical if knowledge management is to succeed. This requires looking at the business, not as an isolated entity, but as an integral part of a fast-changing world. Can you think outside the box with reference to your school?

b. What are some changes that are taking place in society that may have a profound influence on your school?

4. **(Software exercise)** Research IT careers and salaries in five or more areas. Make a PowerPoint presentation to your class about IT job salaries.

5. **(Web exercise)** Do a search on the Web and identify a computer job that you did not know about. Write a brief description of this job.

Case 1: Ford Races Ahead in Knowledge Management

"They sped across Florida's Alligator Alley in the middle of the night, headed from the Fort Lauderdale airport to an Internet business conference across the state in Naples. They took notes on a laptop computer and talked nonstop about their mission as they'd been doing for weeks back in Detroit. Later, between conference sessions, they huddled in a hotel room crafting their concise digital document. When they flew home a few days later, they brought with them the rough draft of a manifesto for revolutionizing the way their company—the world's second-largest automobile and truck manufacturer and fourth-largest industrial corporation—conducted its daily business. They were a team of true believers from Ford Motor Co.'s fledgling Department of Enterprise Information Management," writes Ann Stuart, freelance writer of *CIO Web Master Magazine*.

Today, Ford has earned a reputation for being a leader in knowledge management, thanks to an intranet that links 80,000 employees worldwide. Ford has become an agile organization where people quickly disseminate information, share best practices, conduct research, learn from each others' experiences, and collaborate with experts from around the world.

Why is knowledge management important to a company like Ford? The simple reason is that employees cannot make decisions about things that they don't know. Enterprise Information Management Supervisor Jeff Balagna remembers sitting in a conference listening intently as an executive from another company faltered through a case history of his own organization's Web efforts. "He said, 'We have 200 servers—I think. We have 100 home pages—I think. There's business value to it—I think,' [but] he didn't know." It was time to "move to the Ford Intranet as our way of doing business."

"Competitive advantage is what we're after: better quality, better speed, better cost," explains Bob Matulka, director of Ford's Product Development Leadership group. This advantage can be achieved only by creating a knowledge pool, not just reams of reports, that is readily accessible to any employee at Ford. The knowledge pool should help employees engage in continuous learning and enhance the quality of their decision-making on an everyday basis.

Ford previously drowned employees in documents, reports, memos, and manuals, especially in the area of product development and engineering. In fact, there were so many documents that Ford maintains a document-storage facility at a former factory. It could take up to six months for a person to find the right document among the cardboard boxes stacked 15 feet high. And once found, chances are that the document was outdated. Further, different individuals were using different versions of the same document, leading to a further deterioration in the quality of decisions.

Ford decided to embark on an intranet-based knowledge management initiative. Intranets were not a revolutionary idea or a revolutionary technology. Ford had already invested extensively in several Web applications. However, using an existing technology to become a leader in knowledge management was a major achievement. Ford was successful because it understood the importance of involving employees at all levels in its knowledge management efforts. Team members of the knowledge management project estimate that they met with about 20,000 employees at 75 locations around the world in less than a year to determine what knowledge was important to the company and how best to capture it.

The intranet has a directory of categories including News, People, Processes, Products, and Competition. For example, the category on "competition" has valuable documents relating to quality management, auto shows, global market information, competitor news, product-cycle plans, and patent information. Readers can pose questions to experts about each document.

Team members can view a competitor's vehicle components from different angles and at different sizes, and even copy them, mark them up and e-mail them to others. "The Web is the master copy," explains Brad Nalon, a Taurus/Sable program manager. "There's nothing being hidden. . . . Everybody's on the same page."

The company's intranet users bloomed from 2,000 users in early 1996 to 80,000, the digital equivalent of going from 0 to 60 in two seconds. It even allows employees to buy vehicles at discounts. Employees can use the site to check their eligibility, click through option packages, compute monthly payments, place orders, and check order status. An online paint program that is also available on Ford's external site even lets users see how that Mustang convertible would look in Rio Red or Aztec Gold.

A large, company-wide repository of knowledge allows employees to gain a big picture view of the company and its talent. In effect, it is as if each Ford employee, no matter at what level, has all the experts in the company working for the employee. Knowledge management has transformed Ford. What is most powerful about this transformation is that it is ongoing.[31]

QUESTIONS:

1. Why is the intranet an ideal tool for knowledge management? How did Ford use intranets to capture knowledge?

continued

Case 1: Ford Races Ahead in Knowledge Management, *continued*

2. Why is it important for all decision makers to be "on the same page" when making decisions? How does this approach enhance decision-making quality?
3. Why is this a good example of knowledge management?

Case 2: Biting Off as Much as They Could Chew at Dow Chemical

U.S.–based Dow Chemical Company knows all about change and change management. In the past three years, the company has changed its organizational structure, job responsibilities, technologies, processes, and people. With formidable global competition, Dow knew that it had to become more agile in a hurry.

Dow began to change in the early 1990s, when the company's leaders realized that Dow had to centralize its management to become a successful global operation and oversee half of its 43,000 employees, which are located outside the United States. Now almost every product is supplied and priced globally and every business unit operates under global sales targets.

An obstacle to effective centralized management was dispersed information. Many parts of Dow's information systems could not share information because the mainframe systems weren't designed to do so. The first task, then, was to redesign its information systems to centralize the information.

David Kepler, Dow's first CIO, initiated change throughout the company with three main initiatives:

1. Standardization of the desktop on a global basis
2. Consolidation of roughly 70 IS application-development sites into four and 35 mainframe centers into three
3. Outsourcing of systems and operations to achieve greater consolidation

"We bit off about as much as we could chew," says Kepler in retrospect.

Dow's other challenge was to implement IT projects that met company-wide information needs successfully. The company's historical IT project completion rate was poor. To rectify the situation, Dow started to monitor its application development processes, drafted performance goals that included improving productivity and the speed with which employees brought a product to market. In addition, Dow outsourced many projects to Arthur Andersen, in part to learn how to implement IT projects effectively.

But change, no matter how well planned, is never easy. Bob Kasprzyk, Dow's director of executive development in human resources, recalls how President and CEO William Stavropoulos responded to someone complaining of the changes: "He really explained it perfectly, [saying] that we were investing in our future." "People become worried about the future until they sit in it," Kepler adds.

Outsourcing, for instance, led to fears of layoffs. Dow tried to allay this fear by communicating openly and often with its IS employees, including "communicating the why." "You constantly have to reinforce with people why they're changing and what's in it for them," affirms Stavropoulos.

What are some lessons learned? "It was difficult to maintain a positive attitude," Lehrmann recalls. Kepler adds: "Some say the ability for people to absorb change is like a sponge. Once a sponge is full, you can't add more water. You need to make sure that you focus on helping people get through the major changes and don't add activity that is not absolutely necessary." To ensure that change is continuous, the company advocates five principles: assessing employees' change readiness, building a transition team, developing a communications strategy, working with stakeholders, and identifying change leaders.

The effects of the change are widespread. PC costs are down by 30 percent, applications are being developed 20 percent faster, and an IS employee opinion survey found that 75 percent of employees reported that they felt good about the value of their work and were happy in their jobs overall.[32]

QUESTIONS:

1. What are some strategies that Dow used to initiate and manage change?
2. What were some reasons that convinced Dow to change? If you were the CEO, what policies would you enact to help Dow anticipate change?
3. Why is communication important when a company embarks on change? What are some things that you would do as the CEO of Dow to foster open communications in the company?

Glindex

A Combined Glossary/Subject Index

A

B

C

D

F

I

J

K

L

M

N

O

Q

R

S

T

U

V

W

X

Y

Z

Company Index

D

E

F

G

H

I

J

K

L

M

N

O

P

R

S

T

U

V

W

X

Y

Z

Endnotes

Chapter 1

1. John Levey, Editorial Comments, *CIO,* January 15, 1998, 12.
2. "It Soars," *CIO,* Section 1, January 15, 1998, 18.
3. Malcolm Wheatley, "A Global Humanitarian," *CIO,* May 1, 1998, 20.
4. Debby Young, "Pinnacle Brands Sales-Force Automation Systems," *CIO,* January 15, 1998, 72.
5. C. Hilderbrand, "Tricks of the Trade," *CIO,* January 15, 1998, 43.
6. "It Soars," 20.
7. Hilderbrand, "Tricks of the Trade," p. 43.
8. Ibid.
9. Ibid.
10. Paul Strassmann, "Women Take Over," *Computerworld,* February 1, 1999, 54.
11. Barb Cole-Gomolski, "Sky-High Pay for IT Grads Blows Ceiling," *Computerworld,* June 22, 1998, www.computerworld.com
12. Matt Hamblen, "Listen Harder to Customers," *Computerworld,* July 6, 1998, 35–36.
13. Alan Deutchman, "High Tech Superstars," *Fortune,* October 17, 1994, 197–206.
14. Carol Hilderbrand, "What Is Infrastructure?" *CIO Enterprise,* February 15, 1998, 66.
15. Alan Deutchman, "High Tech Superstars."
16. Ibid.
17. "Computerworld Smithsonian Awards: 1997 Innovation Collection," *Innovation Network, 1997,* http://198.49.220.47/texis/si/sc/innovate/+aoeV+Iq+wB-mearvyXeCxwww/full.html
18. John Zachrisson, "The Swedish Method," *Computerworld,* August 24, 1998, www.computerworld.com
19. Michael Porter, *Competitive Strategy* (New York: Free Press, 1980).
20. Michael Porter, *Competitive Strategy. See also,* Michael Porter, *Competitive Advantage* (New York: Free Press, 1980).
21. Jennifer Bresnahan, "What Good Is Technology," *CIO Enterprise,* Section 2, July 15, 1998, 25.
22. Kathleen Melymuka, "Old Bank, New Ideas," *Computerworld,* February 15, 1999.
23. Laura DiDio, "Do You Know If You've Been Hacked?" *Computerworld,* July 6, 1998, 39, 40.
24. Paul A. Strassmann, "For IT Assurance, Get Some Insurance," *Computerworld,* November 2, 1998, 76.
25. Tim Ouellette, "Technology Keeps Tab on Stress," *Computerworld,* April 20, 1998, 43.
26. Laura DiDio, "Computer Crime Costs on the Rise," *Computerworld,* April 20, 1998, 55.
27. "F.Y.I.: A $42 Million Question," *Computerworld,* April 20, 1998, www.computerworld.com
28. Frank Hayes, "It's All Negotiable," *Computerworld,* June 1, 1998, 12.

Chapter 2

1. Christopher Koch, "Value Judgments," *CIO,* February 1, 1998, 31.
2. Todd Datz, editor, "Industry Fat Cat," *CIO,* February 15, 1998, 14.
3. Sharon Machlis, "IT Lends Skills to Nicaragua Crisis," *Computerworld,* November 16, 1998, 6.
4. Rick Saia and Allan E. Alter, "Good Advice Cheap," *Computerworld,* April 20, 1998, 68.
5. Julia King, "Are You Being Served?" *Computerworld,* October 18, 1993, 107–108, 124.
7. Tom Duffy, "The Support Burden Anytime, Anywhere—No Way, No How," *Computerworld,* June 9, 1997, 26.
8. Jennifer Bresnahan, "Improving the Odds," *CIO Enterprise Magazine,* November 15, 1998, www.cio.com
9. Ibid.
10. Robert Simson, "GM Turns to Computers to Cut Development Costs," *The Wall Street Journal,* October 12, 1998, B4.
11. Malcolm Wheatley, "How Can We Help You?" *CIO,* August 15, 1998, 80–81.
12. Ibid.
13. Eric Torbenson, "As You Like It," *CIO,* February 15, 1998, 61–64.
14. Art Jahnke, "A Doctor in Every House," *CIO Web Business,* February 1, 1999, www.cio.com
15. Torbenson, "As You Like It" 61–64.
16. Ibid.
17. Jennifer Bresnahan, "The Incredible Journey," *CIO Enterprise Magazine,* August 15, 1998, www.cio.com.

18. Craig Stedman, "ERP User Interfaces Drive Workers Nuts," *Computerworld,* November 2, 1998, 1, 24.

19. Tom Field, "Vested Interest," *CIO,* October 15, 1997, 14–18.

20. Ibid.

21. Carol Hildebrand, "This Bill's for You," *CIO Enterprise,* Section 2, May 15, 1998, 49–52.

22. Ibid.

23. Ibid.

24. Kathleen Melymuka, "Playing the Recruiting Game," *Computerworld,* November 2, 1998, 76.

25. Stewart Deck, "TWA Scheduling System Pays Off on Bottom Line," *Computerworld,* October 12, 1998, www.computerworld.com

26. Ibid.

27. "It Takes a Village," *CIO Enterprise,* Section 2, May 15, 1998, 26.

28. Matt Villano, "A Lead-Pipe Cinch," *CIO Magazine,* March 25, 1999, www.cio.com

29. Ibid.

30. Nancy Weil, "Global IT Economy Nears $2 Trillion," *Computerworld,* October 9, 1998, www.computerworld.com

31. Lawrence Aragon, "Crisis In Asia," *Computerworld,* September 14, 1998, www.computerworld.com

32. Ibid.

33. Lenny Liebmann, "Going Global," *Internet Week,* Issue 721, June 29, 1998, special insert, 1–14.

34. Ibid.

35. Ibid.

36. Jennifer Bresnahan, "The Elusive Muse," *CIO,* October 15, 1997, 50–54.

37. Carol Hildebrand, "Techcrastination," *CIO,* February 15, 1998, 22.

38. Ibid.

39. David M. Rappaport, "The Press for More Options," *CIO,* June 1, 1997, 30–34.

40. Cheryl Dable, "Solution in Store," *CIO,* October 15, 1997, 12–18.

41. Rappaport, "The Press for More Options," 30–34.

42. Lauren Gibbons Paul, "High-Wire Acts," *CIO,* June 15, 1998, 50–58.

43. Kim Girard, "Stats Not Good For Sales Technology," *Computerworld,* April 6, 1998, www.computerworld.com

44. Tom Davenport, "Serving Up ERP Value," *CIO,* February 1, 1998, 26.

45. Carol Hildebrand, "A Task-Oriented Approach," *CIO,* October 15, 1997, 18–20.

46. Wayne Arnold, "Japan's Daiwa, Trailing in Technology, Turns to IBM," *Wall Street Journal,* October 19, 1998, A23.

47. Carol Hildebrand, "Financial Affairs," *CIO,* March 15, 1994, 62–68.

48. Carol Hildebrand, "IT and the Bottom Line," *CIO,* June 15, 1998, 70–76.

Chapter 3

1. Raju Narisetti, "Now You Can Cook Your Books and Dinner at the Same Time," *The Asian Wall Street Journal,* September 11–12, 1998, B3.

2. Ibid.

3. Meg Mitchell, "Cruise Control," Trendlines, *CIO,* July 1, 1998, 14–16.

4. John P. McPartlin (Editor), "PCs Are A Student's Best Friend," *InformationWeek,* April 5, 1993, 44.

5. Steve Rosenbush, "Tech Leaders Warn of 'Great Divide,' " *USA Today,* June 17, 1998, B6.

6. Randall E. Stross, "Gates Builds His Brain Trust," *Fortune,* December 8, 1997, 84.

7. Logan Harbaugh, "RAID Becomes a Mainstay," *InformationWeek,* December 8, 1997, 116–117.

8. www.techweb.com

9. Kim Girard, "Storage Snafu Grounds Sabre for Three Hours," *Computerworld,* June 29, 1998, 16.

10. Harbaugh, "RAID Becomes a Mainstay," 116–117.

11. Ibid.

12. Brian McWilliams, "Breakthrough in Modernizing CD-ROM Drives," *PC World News Radio,* April 8, 1998.

13. Ibid.

14. Ibid.

15. "Street Talk: Innovation Collection," *Computerworld and Smithsonian Institute Technology Awards, Innovation Network,* 1996, http://innovate.si.edu/1996/96short/96ca24s.htm; *see also* http://home.dti.net/jh47m/StreetsSigns. html

16. www.d-Rom.com

17. http://www.richmedia.com/harry.htm

18. McWilliams, "Breakthrough in Modernizing CD-ROM Drives."

19. Ibid.

20. Polly Schneider, "Father of the Mouse Speaks," *CIO Magazine,* December 17, 1998, www.cio.com

21. Howard Baldwin, "Tech Talk," *CIO,* July 1, 1998, 52.
22. J. Edward, "Speak Easy," *CIO,* June 1, 1997, 102.
23. http://home.dti.net/jh47m/StreetSigns.html
24. Mitch Betts, "Voice Strain Plagues Some PC Users," *Computerworld,* April 24, 1995, 1, 12.
25. James A. Senn, *Information Systems in Management* (Belmont, CA: Wadsworth, 1990), 173–174.
26. Gary Anthes, "Nuclear Again," *Computerworld,* March 23, 1998, 83–84.
27. Ibid.
28. Gary J. Beach, "Publisher's Note," *CIO,* May 15, 1998, 16.
29. Randy Weston and April Jacobs, "Network Computers Can Save Money," *Computerworld,* February 10, 1997, www.computerworld.com.
30. Ibid.
31. Tom Diederich, "CVS on the Road to Wireless," *Computerworld,* June 5, 1998, www.computerworld.com
32. "Time Marches On," *CIO,* June 15, 1998, 20.
33. Kim S. Nash, "Behind the Merced Mystique," *Computerworld,* July 6, 1998, 55–56.
34. Robert Furger, "Look Before You Leap," *PCWorld,* March 1998, www.pcworld.com
35. Richard M. Contino, *Negotiating Business Equipment Leases* (New York, NY: AMACOM Books, 1998).
36. Stephen Simurda, "Deciding on the Dotted Line," *Small Business Computing & Communications,* November 1998, 41–43.
37. Christopher Koch, "A Tough Sell," *CIO,* May 1, 1997, 74–76.
38. Ibid.
39. Jennifer Bresnahan, "Emerging Technology," *CIO,* January 15, 1997, 76.

Chapter 4

1. http://innovate.si.edu
2. Ibid.
3. Lee Gomes, "Microsoft Acknowledges Growing Threat of Free Software for Popular Functions," *USA Today,* November 3, 1998, B6.
4. Harvey M. Deitel, *An Introduction to Operating Systems,* 1st ed. rev. (Reading, MA: Addison-Wesley), 11.
5. April Jacobs, "Windows 98 Hits the Streets," *Computerworld,* June 29, 1998, www.computerworld.com
6. Patrick Dryden, "Brewer Simplifies NT Management," *Computerworld,* June 8, 1998, 53–54.
7. Ibid.
8. Ibid.
9. David Brantingham, Director of Computer Operations and Technical Service, Western Publishing, Racine, Wisconsin.
10. Adapted with permission from David Brantingham, "No Single Solution," *CIO,* May 15, 1994, www.cio.com
11. Jaikumar Vijayan and Laura DiDio, "Getting the Best of NT, Unix Worlds," *Computerworld,* April 20, 1998, 32.
12. Ed Scannell, "OS/2 Pays Dividends to Faithful Bank User," *Computerworld,* September 26, 1994, 39.
13. Ibid.
14. Nancy Weil, "Focus on Substance, Not Hype, Linux Creator Urges," *Computerworld,* April 19, 1999, www.computerworld.com
15. Chuck Appleby, "Norfolk Southern Speeds Up Service," *InformationWeek,* September 26, 1994, 54.
16. William Harder, "The Operational System That Conquered the World," *Unisys Solutions, Special issue,* 1992, 31–34.
17. Sharon Gaudin, "Tales from the Field," *Computerworld,* April 6, 1998, www.computerworld.com
18. Jeff Sweat, "The Front Line," *InformationWeek,* February 22, 1999, 17–19.
19. Mitch Betts, "Postal Software Helps Firms Beat High Rates," *Computerworld,* March 6, 1995, 61.
20. Cynthia Bournellis, "Self-Healing Systems May Cut Help Desk Calls," *Computerworld,* November 2, 1998, 4.
21. David Orenstein, "Java, Visual Basic Seen as Languages of Future," *Computerworld,* March 29, 1999, www.computerworld.com
22. Gordon Ma Ung, "Nabisco, MediSolv Cook Up Application," *Computerworld,* December 29, 1997, www.computerworld.com
23. Rich Levin, "Java for the Enterprise," *InformationWeek,* December 8, 1997, 19.
24. Ibid.
25. Peter Fabris, "Code Word: Project Quality," *CIO,* August 1997, 34.
26. "Sell IT to the Marines and the Navy," *InformationWeek,* March 22, 1999, 14.

27. Lauren Gibbons Paul, "One World, One System," *CIO,* March 15, 1998, 48.
28. Kathleen Gow, "The Support Burden: Software Support: Who Carries Whom?" *Computerworld,* June 9, 1997, www.computerworld.com
29. "Quick Response I.S.," *CIO,* Section 1, September 1, 1998, 34, 36–37, 40–41.
30. Maryfran Johnson, "Beauty and the Software Beast," *Computerworld,* March 20, 1998, www.computerworld.com
31. Ibid.
32. Ibid.
33. Julia King, "Ignoring Development Guidelines Raises Costs," *Computerworld,* May 18, 1998, 37–38.
34. Ibid.
35. Margaret Johnston, "Software Piracy Stunts Job Growth," *Computerworld,* October 28, 1998, www.computerworld.com
36. Ibid.
37. Thomas Hoffman, "Are U.S. Programmers Slackers?" *Computerworld,* April 12, 1999, www.computerworld.com
38. Alice Dragoon, ed., "Trendlines—News, Insight, Humor," *CIO,* May 1, 1997, 24.
39. Craig Stedman, "Gerber Tightens Inventory Control," *Computerworld,* June 8, 1998, www.computerworld.com
40. Lori Valigra, "U.N. Shackled by 30-Year-Old Mainframe System," *InfoWorld,* February 21, 1994, 61.

Chapter 5

1. Ken Sloan, "All Your Assets on Line," *Computerworld,* July 11, 1988, 55–54.
2. Peter Fabris, "A Civilian Action," *CIO,* February 1, 1998, 52–54.
3. Beth Davis and Jennifer Mateyaschuk, "Rapid Response," *InformationWeek,* January 11, 1999, www.informationweek.com
4. Alice Laplante, "The Eternal Project," *Computerworld,* July 13, 1998, www.computerworld.com
5. Craig Stedman, "Handheld Databases Hard to Grasp," *Computerworld,* March 23, 1998, 67–69.
6. Bill Roberts, "English Queries Only," *CIO,* May 15, 1998, 68–74.
7. Ibid.
8. Bruce Caldwell, "In Search of the New Dictionary," *InformationWeek,* April 25, 1994, 51–56.
9. "Years Later, Detectives Hot on the Trail of Old Cases," *AP News Service,* April 3, 1999, www.abcnews.go.com
10. Thomas Hoffman, "Drilling for Financials," *Computerworld,* October 19, 1998, 65, 66.
11. Barb Gomolski, "Health Industry Warehouses Data to Cure Disease, Costs," *Computerworld,* October 19, 1998, 43, 47.
12. David Pearson, "MasterCard: Data Warehouse," *CIO,* May 15, 1998, 62–64.
13. Linda Wilson, "Metadata Standards to Aid Warehousing," *Computerworld,* June 29, 1998, 71–72.
14. Peter Fabris, "Advanced Navigation," *CIO,* May 15, 1998, 51–53.
15. Stewart Deck, "Quick Study: Data Mining," *Computerworld,* March 29, 1999, www.computerworld.com
16. Stewart Deck, "Travel Info Data Warehouse Raises Privacy Concerns," *Online News,* July 10, 1998. (Online site does not provide this information beyond a certain date. However, info is available in the public literature.)
17. Ibid.
18. Ibid.
19. Ron Condon, "Innovation in Action. Tupperware Brings Accurate Forecasts to the Party," *Computerworld,* March 30, 1998, www.computerworld.com
20. Ibid.
21. James I. Cash, "British Air Gets on Course," *InformationWeek,* May 1, 1995, 140.
22. Ibid.
23. Gary H. Anthes, "Competitive Intelligence," *Computerworld,* July 6, 1998, 62–63.
24. Ibid.
25. Gary Anthes, "Learning How to Share," *Computerworld,* February 23, 1998, retrieved online at www.computerworld.com
26. Christopher Koch, "Value Judgments," *CIO,* February 1, 1998, 36–38.
27. Gary H. Anthes, "Competitive Intelligence," 62–63.
28. Patrick Thibodeau, "Bill Offers Legal Protection to Information Databases," *Computerworld,* March 22, 1999, www.computerworld.com

29. Patrick Thibodeau, "Need Info? Help Yourself," *Computerworld,* April 21, 1998, www.computerworld.com
30. David Pearson, "Empire Strikes Back," *CIO,* July 1, 1998, 26–35.
31. Randy Weston, "Data Mart Improves GTE Airfone's Marketing," *Computerworld,* June 1, 1998, 53–54. Copyright © 1998 COMPUTERWORLD, Inc., Framingham, MA. All rights reserved.
32. Ruth Greenberg, "Collecting Its Due," *CIO,* February 1, 1998, 60–62.

Chapter 6

1. Perry Glasser, "Armed with Intelligence," *CIO,* August 1997, 105.
2. Lynda Radosevich, "PDAs to Assist Doctors, Pharmacies," *Computerworld,* March 21, 1994, 77.
3. Neil Weinberg, "Satellite Links Let Cash Flow Out to Sea," *Computerworld,* May 8, 1995, 56.
4. Mariyam Williamson, "Global Snapshot," *Computerworld,* June 1, 1998, www.computerworld.com
5. Stephanie Stahl, "Home Remedy for CDC Networks," *InformationWeek,* May 17, 1993, 22.
6. Herman Manson, "Where Politics, Economics, and the Internet Meet," *Computerworld,* May 18, 1998, 64.
7. Gregory Dalton, "Global Gravity," *InformationWeek,* January 18, 1999, www.informationweek.com
8. Stephanie Stahl, "Home Remedy for CDC Networks."
9. Ibid.
10. M. Fitzgerald, "High Tech Tools Help Report on Low-Tech War." *Computerworld,* October 4, 1993, 38.
11. Stewart Deck, "Global Networking Market at Nearly $15B for '96; To Double by 2001," *Computerworld,* June 30, 1997, www.computerworld.com
12. Ibid.
13. Addie Lundberg, "InBox," *CIO,* September 1, 1998, 10.
14. Stephanie Stahl, "Home Remedy for CDC Networks."
15. Stewart Deck, "DHL Teams with AT&T for On-line Tracking Service," *Computerworld,* September 29, 1997, www.computerworld.com
16. Gary Abramson, "Emerging Challenges," *CIO,* June 15, 1998, 34–47.
17. Ibid.
18. Ibid.
19. Ibid.
20. Ibid.
21. Ibid.
22. Ibid.
23. Gretchen Kres, "High-demand Positions for IT Professionals," *Computerworld,* March 3, 1998, 57.
24. "Airline Grounds Web site . . . ," *Computerworld,* June 29, 1998, 12.
25. Jeanette Borzo, "African-European Network Means Peach Prospects for Capespan," *Computerworld,* March 10, 1997, www.computerworld.com
26. "The Business Re-engineering Journey," Computerworld Smithsonian 1997 Innovation Collection Awards," *Innovation Network,* 1998, www.thunderstone.com

Chapter 7

1. "Plugged In, In Their Own Words," *CIO,* February 15, 1998, 22.
2. "Internet Statistics," *Head Count,* March 1999, www.headcount.com
3. "Clear Days on the Web," *CIO Web Business,* Section 2, July 1, 1998, 40.
4. Joann S. Lublin, "Web Transforms Art of Negotiating Raises," *The Wall Street Journal,* September 22, 1998, B1.
5. Ibid.
6. Bob Wallace, "Car Dealers Adapt to the Web," *Computerworld,* July 20, 1998, 22.
7. Meg Mitchell, "Gender Bender," *CIO Enterprise,* Section 2, May 15, 1998, 18–19.
8. Art Jahnke, "Shame Pays," *CIO,* Section 2, September 1, 1998, 12.
9. "National Wildlife Federation 1998 Innovation Collection Winner, Computerworld Smithsonian Awards," *Innovation Network,* 1999, www.thunderstone.com
10. Preston Gralla, *How the Internet Works* (San Francisco, CA: Ziff-Davis Press, 1997), 6.
11. Ibid.
12. Ibid.
13. Gary Abramson, "Emerging Challenges," *CIO,* June 15, 1998, 34–47.
14. "The Diane Rheam Show," National Public Radio, October 21, 1998.
15. Jeremy Hylton, "David LaMacchia Cleared; Case

Raises Civil Liberty Issues," *The Tech,* February 7, 1995, http://the-tech.mit.edu

16. Sharon Machlis, "Might Makes Right in Name Fight," *Computerworld,* April 20, 1998, 51–52.
17. Publisher's Note, *CIO,* September 1, 1998, 14.
18. Dave Johnson, "Put Your Site on Diet," *Small Business Computing and Communications,* November 1998, 56.
19. Patrick Thibodeau, "Thatcher Urges Governments to Control the 'Net,'" *Computerworld,* June 23, 1998, 46.
20. Ibid.
21. Ibid.
22. Gary Abramson, "Emerging Challenges."
23. Stefanie McCann, "An Effective Barrier to Intruders, But You'll Be Burned without Upkeep," *Computerworld,* October 19, 1998, 54.
24. Joseph L. Levy, "Publisher's Note," *CIO,* January 15, 1997, 16.
25. Steve Alexander, "Project: Rich Products Corp, NT Not Too Rich for Frozen Food Maker," *Computerworld,* June 22, 1998, www.computerworld.com
26. Sharon Watson, "Getting to Aha!" *Computerworld,* January 26, 1998, www.computerworld.com
27. Linda Wilson, "Virtual Training Saves $800K in First Year," *Computerworld,* March 23, 1998, www.computerworld.com
28. Gregory Dalton, "Ford Turns to Extranet," *InformationWeek,* August 10, 1998, 36.
29. John Evan Frook, "Monitoring Purchases via Web," *InformationWeek,* November 23, 1998, www.techweb.com
30. Ibid.
31. Ibid.
33. Mary J. Cronin, *Doing Business on the Internet* (New York: John Wiley & Sons, 1995).
34. Sharon Machlis, "Web Surfing under Scrutiny," *Computerworld,* July 20, 1998, 20.
35. "Trendlines, Decongesting the Net," *CIO,* January 15, 1998, 28.
36. "Outdoor Online, 1997 Innovation Collection, Computerworld Smithsonian Awards," *Innovation Network,* 1997, www.thunderstone.com
37. Leslie Goff, "<YourCompanyNameHere>sucks.com," *Computerworld,* July 20, 1998, 57–58.
38. "3Com Park, 1998 Innovation Collection, Computerworld Smithsonian Awards," *Innovation Network,* 1998, www.thunderstone.com

Chapter 8

1. Tom Field, "New World Orders," *CIO,* Section 1, February 1, 1998, 1.
2. Ibid.
3. Ibid.
4. Leslie Goff, "Put Down the Dust Mop, and Let's Sell Cee-ment Cyberspace," *Computerworld,* August 24, 1998, 58–59.
5. Ibid.
6. Tom Field, "New World Orders."
7. Sair Kalin, "Click, Click, Goose," *CIO Web Business,* August 1, 1998, 16.
8. Louise Fickel, "MicroAge's Internet-Based Training Program," *CIO Magazine,* July 15, 1998, 28.
9. Clinton Wilder, "E-Commerce: Myths and Realities," *InformationWeek Online,* December 7, 1998, www.informationweek.com
10. Ibid.
11. Jennifer Bresnahan, "Plugged In," *CIO Enterprise,* Section 2, May 15, 1998, 24.
12. Ibid.
13. Ibid.
14. Bill Freza, "Privacy Protection Needs to Be Personal Responsibility," *InformationWeek,* March 29, 1999, 34.
15. Ibid.
16. Ibid.
17. Ibid.
18. Ibid.
19. Scott Kirsner, "Recipes for Alchemy," *CIO Web Business,* Section 2, September 1, 1998, 26, 28.
20. Bob Wallace, "Auto Dealers Find Sales Slow on Web," *Computerworld,* October 19, 1998, 51, 54.
21. Ibid.
22. George Anders, "As Many Firms Expand Sales On the Web, They Suffer Weak Pricing and Losses," *The Wall Street Journal,* July 23, 1998, A1.
23. Alan Alper, "Where There Is a Web, There Is a Way," *Computerworld,* July 13, 1998, www.computerworld.com

24. Chipshot.com Web site, retrieved on-line at www.chipshot.com
25. Brian Walsh, "The Nuts and Bolts of Business-to-Business E-Commerce," *Network Computing,* March 1, 1998, www.nwc.com.
26. Jeanette Borzo, "Businesses Discuss Web Payoffs," *Computerworld,* June 1, 1998, 35–39.
27. Alan Alper, "Where There Is a Web, There Is a Way."
28. Clinton Wilder, "E-Commerce: Myths and Realities."
29. Ibid.
30. Saroja Girishankar, "Once Profitable E*trade Sees Red," *InformationWeek,* April 22, 1999, www.techweb.com.
31. Sharon Machlis, "Users: Online Investments Are Poised to Impact Bottom Line, Online Ticket Sales Jump, Outlook Good," *Computerworld,* June 8, 1998, 42, 90.
32. "Overcoming Fear of Buying," *CIO Web Business,* Section 2, July 1, 1998, 28.
33. Mark Halper, "Making Money on the Web," *CIO Enterprise,* Section 2, January 15, 1998, 56–58, 60–62.
34. Mark Halper, "Making Money on the Web."
35. "It's About Time," *Computerworld,* June 8, 1998, 3.
36. Sharon Gaudin, "New Global Team Aims to Thwart Cybercrime Wave," *Computerworld,* November 16, 1998, 6.
37. Ibid.
38. Deborah Radcliff, "The Price of Web Pizzazz," *Computerworld,* November 23, 1998, 62.
39. Clinton Wilder, "E-commerce: Myths and Realities."
40. Rochelle Garner, "Electronic Frontiers," *Computerworld,* December 15, 1997, www.computerworld.com.
41. Ibid.
42. Sharon Berman, "Web Work: A Gal Thing," *Computerworld Online,* November 10, 1997, www.computerworld.com.
43. "Wired World: Notes from Around the Globe," *Computerworld,* December 7, 1998, www.computerworld.com.
44. Elisabeth Horwitt, "Beyond Business Enclaves, Web Use Is Quick to Take Off—and Has Far to Go," *Computerworld,* September 29, 1997, www.computerworld.com.
45. Elisabeth Horwitt, "Asia," *Computerworld,* September 29, 1997, 20–21.
46. Alice LaPlante, "Global Boundaries.com," *Computerworld,* October 6, 1997, www.computerworld.com.
47. Rolf Boone, "Japan's E-Commerce Market Holding Firm (for Now)," *Internetnews.com,* December 11, 1998, www.internetnews.com.
48. Elisabeth Horwitt, "Asia."
49. "China Will Be the World's Largest Cyber Nation," *Nikkei BP AsiaBizTech,* October 6, 1998, www.nikkeibp.asiabiztech.com.
50. Elisabeth Horwitt, "Beyond Business Enclaves, Web Use Is Quick to Take Off—and Has Far to Go."
51. Elisabeth Horwitt, "Asia."
52. Alice LaPlante, "Global Boundaries.com."
53. Elisabeth Horwitt, "Europe," *Computerworld,* September 29, 1997, 21–23.
54. Ibid.
55. Jeffery Zbar, "Oh What a Tangled Web," *Computerworld,* December 7, 1998, www.computerworld.com.
56. Ibid.
57. "Internet Growth in Brazil (1995/1997)," *Internet World Review* 28 (December 1997): 49; "Internet Growth in Brazil (1995/1997)," *Internet World Review* 29 (January 1, 1998): 64.
58. Jeffery Zbar, "Oh What a Tangled Web."
59. Elisabeth Horwitt, "Australia," *Computerworld,* September 29, 1997, 23–24.
60. Ibid.
61. Ibid.
62. Elisabeth Horwitt, "Southern Africa," *Computerworld,* September 29, 1997, 24.
63. "Internet Usage Around the World," International Communications' Headcount.com (December 1998): http:/38.249.210.27/count/datafind.htm?choice=country&choicev[]=South+Africa.
64. Elisabeth Horwitt, "Southern Africa."
65. Ibid.
66. Bob Wallace, "A Twisted Pair," *Computerworld,* September 29, 1997, 33–35.
67. Sharon Machlis, "E-Commerce: Late Is Relative," *Computerworld,* May 18, 1998, 1, 16.
68. Ibid.
69. Sharon Machlis, "E-Commerce: Late Is Relative."

70. Clinton Wilder, "E-Commerce: Myths and Realities."
71. Ibid.
72. Ibid.
73. Sharon Machlis, "For E-Commerce, Integration Is Key," *Computerworld,* November 16, 1998, 43, 46.
74. Ibid.
75. Clinton Wilder, "E-Commerce: Myths and Realities."
76. Mark Halper, "Making Money on the Web."
77. Carol Sliwa, "Michelin Links Dealers, Difficult to Do Business With?" *Computerworld,* November 30, 1998, www.computerworld.com.
78. Ibid.
79. Ibid.
80. Richard Greenfield, "A Tale of Two Deutsche EC Trail Blazers," *Computerworld,* March 9, 1998, www.computerworld.com.

Chapter 9

1. Charles Pelton, "Let's Not Get Caught Up in Semantics," *InformationWeek* (January 31, 1994): 50.
2. Randy Weston, "Client/Server Sales Shoot Up, "*Computerworld,* February 17, 1997, www.computerworld.com.
3. Deidre Sullivan, "Supporting a House of Cards," *Chief Information Officer* (January 15, 1994): 58–62.
4. Randy Weston, "Retailers Dump Big Iron for Client/Server," *Computerworld* (June 30, 1997): retrieved on-line at http://www.computerworld.com/home/print9497.nsf/all/SL26retail.
5. Edward A. Lile, "Client/Server Architecture: A Brief Overview," *Journal of Systems Management* (December 1993): 26–29.
6. Charles Pelton, "Let's Not Get Caught up in Semantics."
7. Mike Ricciuti, "CS First Boston Corp.," *Datamation* (March 1, 1994): 28–29.
8. Mike Ricciuti, "Hyatt Hotels Corporation," *Datamation* (March 1, 1994): 29–33.
9. Chuck Appleyby, "Rx for HealthCare," *InformationWeek* (June 6, 1994): 64–72.
10. Kim Nash, "Car Maker Takes Client/Server Road," *Computerworld* (February 28, 1994): 81–82.
11. Randy Weston, "Client/Server Sales Shoot Up."
12. Deidre Sullivan, "Supporting a House of Cards."
13. Randy Weston, "The Rush Is on to Client/Server," *Computerworld,* March 3, 1997, www.computerworld.com.
14. Randy Weston, "The Rush Is on to Client/Server."
15. Johanna Ambrosio, "Walk, Don't Run With It," *Computerworld* (March 15, 1993): 65.
16. Tim Ouellette, "Mainframe Skills Drive Client/Server," *Computerworld* (September 26, 1997): retrieved on-line at http://www.computerworld.com/home/online9697.nsf/all/970926mainframe1866E.
17. Robert L. Scheier, "Cooking up More Change," *Computerworld* (June 23, 1997): retrieved on-line at http://www.computerworld.com/home/online9697.nsf/all/970623cohen.
18. Robert L. Scheier, "Cooking up More Change."
19. Stephanie Stahl, "Higher-Tech Education," *InformationWeek* (March 21, 1994): 56–57.
20. D. DiPentima, Speech at the Lattane Center's CEO/CIO Roundtable in Towson, Maryland, *Computerworld* (June 28, 1993).
21. David H. Freedman, "To Our Clients, with Best Wishes, From the Servers," *Chief Information Officer* (February 15, 1994): 56–64.
22. Peter Cassidy, "Lines of Defense," *Chief Information Officer* (February 15, 1994): 46–54.
23. Ibid.
24. Daniel E. White, National Director of Information Security Services, in a speech given at Ernst and Young in Chicago, Illinois.
25. Peter Cassidy, "Lines of Defense," p. 51.
26. Patrick Dryden, "Norfolk Southern Readies Freight System for Conrail Branch," *Computerworld* (July 13, 1998): retrieved on-line at http://www.computerworld.com/home/print.nsf/all/9807135a66.
27. Rosemary Cafasso, "Sears, Roebuck and Co.," *Computerworld* (August 1, 1996): retrieved on-line at http://www.computerworld.com/home/online9697.nsf/all/960801SPCSSL9608spcs3.
28. Ellis Booker, "United Airlines Adds Client/Server to Menu," *Computerworld* (January 17, 1994): 51.

29. Kim Girard, "Cable Channel Gets Info Edge," *Computerworld* (June 29, 1998): 1, 100.
30. Barb Cole-Gomolski, "Insurer Saves as Clients File Claims Via Web," *Computerworld*, April 12, 1999, 44.
31. Bill Carico, "The CEO's Role in IT Decisions," *Computerworld* (April 17, 1995): retrieved on-line at http://www.computerworld.com/home/online9697.nsf/all/950417LEADSL9504lead. Copyright © 1995 COMPUTERWORLD, Inc. Framingham, MA 01701. Rights reserved.
32. Rob Gerristen and Estlle G. Brand, "State of the Art Client/Server," *DBMS* (February 1993): 4–60.

Chapter 10

1. Carol Hilderbrand, "The Nature of Excellence," *CIO* (August 1997): 47.
2. Miryam Williamson, "Global Snapshot," *Computerworld:* June 1, 1998, 32.
3. John Foley, "Transaction Time," *InformationWeek* (November 10, 1997): 18.
4. Ibid.
5. Ibid.
6. "Dollar Bank's Interactive Internet Banking, Computerworld/Smithsonian Innovation Award," *Innovation Network,* 1998, *www.thunderstone.com/texis/si/sc/innovate/+HmeQVYz+wB-meKVoOXwww/brief.html.*
7. John Foley, "Transaction Time."
8. Barb Cole-Gomolski, "Oh, I Wish I Had a Better Invoice System," *Computerworld* (May 18, 1998): 54–55.
9. "Dr. Pepper/SevenUp Inc. Decision Support System, Computerworld/Smithsonian Innovation Award," *Innovation Network,* 1997, www.thunderstone.com/texis/si/sc/innovate/+7mel8Yz+wB-meXrvyXJwww/brief.html.
10. Alice LaPlante, "Brainstorming," *Forbes ASP* (September 1993): 46.
11. Thomas Hoffman, "Security Demands Fuel Growing Industry," *Computerworld* (April 24, 1995): 82.
12. Sara Hedberg, "Artificial Ingredients," *CIO* (June 1, 1994): 72–79.
13. Gene Bylinsky, "Computers That Learn," *Fortune* (September 6, 1993): 96–102.
14. T. H. Davenport, R. G. Eccles, and L. Prusak, "Information Politics," *Sloan Management Review* (Fall 1992): 53–65.
15. Jeff Sweat, "The Integrated Enterprise," *InformationWeek,* April 26, 1999, 32.
16. Carol Hilderbrand, "The Nature of Excellence," *CIO* (August 1997): 47.
17. Hugh J. Watson and M. M. Frolick, "Determining Information Requirements for an EIS," *MIS Quarterly* (September 1993): 255–269.
18. Paul Barber and Katherine Gay, "EIS: A Strategic Resource That Can Help Organizations Gain a Clear Competitive Advantage," *CMA Magazine* (March 1993): 23–28.
19. "In Box Feature," *CIO, Section 1,* February 1, 1998, 12.
20. Debby Young, "For Good Measure," *CIO Enterprise,* April 1, 1999, 29.
21. Peter Rubin, "Self-Service Information Retrieval," *CIO Enterprise,* March 15, 1999, 41.
22. Alice LaPlante, "Brainstorming," *Forbes ASP* (September 13, 1993): 45–61.
23. Kathleen Melymuka, "Playing the Recruiting Game," *Computerworld* (November 2, 1998): 76.

Chapter 11

1. Peter G. W. Keen, "Systems. Not Just a Job—It's a Venture," *Computerworld* (February 9, 1998): retrieved on-line at http://www.computerworld.com/home/print.nsf/all/98020952F2.
2. Albert L. Lederer and Raghu Nath, "Making Strategic Information Systems Happen," *Academy of Management Executive,* vol. 4, no. 3 (1990): 76–82.
3. Jennifer Bresnahan, "Makeover Medicine," *CIO* (January 15, 1997): 62–63.
4. Ibid.
5. Ibid.
6. Gideon F. For-Mukwai, "Africa Meets on Y2K," *Computerworld* (November 16, 1998): 40.
7. Tom Duffy, "Anytime, Anywhere—No Way, No How," *Computerworld,* (June 9, 1997), www.computerworld.com.
8. Gary H. Anthes, "Function Points to the Rescue,"

Computerworld (May 2, 1994): 110.

9. Gary H. Anthes, "No More Creeps," *Computerworld* (May 2, 1994): 107–108.
10. Leslie Goff, "A Vanishing Breed," *Computerworld* (April 11, 1994): 119.
11. Ibid.
12. Joanne Kelleher, "Quick Isn't Dirty," *Computerworld* (July 19, 1993): 32.
13. Jerrold M. Grochow, "Tidal Wave Approaching," *Computerworld* (September 20, 1993): 41.
14. "Quick Response I. S." *CIO,* section 1 (September 1, 1998): 34, 36, 37, 40, 41.
15. Ibid.
16. W. Burry Foss, "Fast, Faster, Fastest Development," *Computerworld* (May 31, 1993): 81, 83.
17. Bruce Caldwell, "Who Needs Programmers?" *InformationWeek* (April 25, 1994): 23.
18. Robert L. Leltheiser and James C. Wetherbe "Service Support Levels: An Organized Approach to End-User Computing," *MIS Quarterly* (December 1986): 337–348.
19. Bruce Caldwell, "Who Needs Programmers?" 30.
20. Michael Fitzgerald, "Greyhound Outsources IS to Get the Best Staffing Talent," *Computerworld* (February 28, 1994): 74.
21. John P. McPartlin, "Crossed Up," *InformationWeek* (January 31, 1994): 12.
22. Alan Radding, "To Methodology or Not to Methodology," *Computerworld* (June 14, 1993): 114.
23. Larry Runge, "What's Wrong with Us," *Computerworld* (September 20, 1993): 139–140.
24. John F. Rockart and J. Debra Hofman, "Systems Delivery: Evolving New Strategies," *Sloan Management Review* (Summer 1992): 21–31.
25. Ibid.
26. Jennifer Bresnahan, "Makeover Medicine."
27. Ibid.
28. Peter G. W. Keen, "Systems. Not Just a Job—It's a Venture."
29. Brenda Wong, "What's Fun Got to Do with It?" *Computerworld* (June 15, 1998): retrieved online at http://www.computerworld.com/home/features.nsf/all/980615car2.
30. Afsaneh Nahavandi and Ali Malekzadeh, *Organizational Behavior* (Upper Saddle River, NJ, Prentice Hall, 1999): 280–283.
31. Tom Field, "A New Tune," *CIO,* section 1 (November 1, 1998): 52, 54–55.
32. Ronald J. Palenski, "Competition, Not Litigation, Ensures Quality Systems," *Computerworld* (March 28, 1994): 86.
33. Bruce A. Bierhans, "Responsible Lawsuits Keep Vendors Honest," *Computerworld* (March 28,1994): 86–88.
34. Jean S. Bozman, "Denver Airport Hits Systems Layover," *Computerworld* (May 16, 1994): 30.
35. Lori Dix, "Cool Under Fire," *Computerworld* (April 11, 1994): 111–113.
36. David Pearson, "Relationships on the Rocks," *CIO,* Section 1 (November 1, 1998): 28.
37. Barb Cole-Gomolski, "U.S. Challenges Temp Status," *Computerworld* (November 2, 1998): 1, 104.

Chapter 12

1. Adapted quote from "Toll Fraud and Telabuse: a Multi-billion Dollar Problem," *InformationWeek* (May 16, 1994): 48.
2. M. E. Kabay, "Prepare Yourself for Information Warfare," *Computerworld* (March 2, 1995): retrieved at http://www.computerworld.com/home/online9697.nsf/all/950301SL9503lead.
3. Bob Violino, "Are Your Networks Secure?" *InformationWeek* (April 22, 1993): 30–35.
4. Laura DiDio, " . . . and Face Rising Hacks, Inside and Out," *Computerworld* (April 27, 1998), www.computerworld.com.
5. "China Slams Net Criminals," *Reuters, CNET News.com* (October 12, 1998): http://www.news.com/News/Item/0,4,27437,00.html?st.cn.nws.rl.ne.
6. Ibid.
7. Andrew Dornan, "Look, But Don't Touch," Data Communications, February 2, 1999, www.data.com/story/DCM19990219S0001.
8. Laura DiDio, "Computer Crime Costs on the Rise."
9. Laura DiDio, "These ATMs Never Forget a Face," April 25, 1998, http://www.computerworld.

com/home/print.nsf/all/9805254F92.

10. Paul A. Strassmann, "For IT Assurance, Get Some Insurance," *Computerworld* (November 2, 1998): 76.
11. Laura DiDio, "Computer Crime Costs on the Rise."
12. Laura DiDio, "Do You Know If You've Been Hacked?" *Computerworld* (July 6, 1998): 39.
13. Laura DiDio, "Computer Crime Costs on the Rise."
14. Kim Nash and Julia King, "IS Employers Skip Background Checks," *Computerworld* (October 27, 1997): retrieved online at http://www.computerworld.com/home/online9697.nsf/all/971030back.
15. Ibid.
16. Amy K. Larsen, "Outside Break-ins Increase," *InformationWeek* (March 8, 1999,): retrieved online at http://www.techweb.com/se/directlink.cgi?IWK19990308S0072.
17. Laura DiDio, "Want to Prevent Break-ins? Just Ask a Hacker," *Computerworld* (March 2, 1998): retrieved on-line at www.computerworld.com.
18. Ibid.
19. Laura DiDio, "In U.S. First, Court Convicts Female Hacker," *Computerworld* (July 6, 1998): 10.
20. Winn Schwartau, "Hackers, Sniffers, Worms, and Demons," *InformationWeek* (May 16, 1994): 39.
21. Gary H. Anthes, "Internet Panel Finds Reusable Passwords a Threat," *Computerworld* (March 28, 1994): 50.
22. Down with Hacktivism, *Computer Security Magazine* (February 1999): retrieved online at http://www.infosecuritymag.com/.
23. Laura DiDio, "Do You Know If You've Been Hacked?"
24. Ibid.
25. Winn Schwartau, "Hackers, Sniffers, Worms, and Demons."
26. "Users Still Struggle to Manage LANarchy," *InformationWeek* (March 7, 1994): 37.
27. Patrick Thibodeau, "GAO Slams State Department's Computer Security," *Computerworld* (May 21, 1998): retrieved online at http://www.computerworld.com/home/online9697.nsf/all/980521gao1F972.
28. Winn Schwartau, "Hackers, Sniffers, Worms, and Demons."
29. Mary Thyfault and Stephaine Stahl, "Weak Links," *InformationWeek* (August 10, 1992): 27.
30. Ibid.
31. Tim Clark, "Boom in Computer Viruses," *CNET News.com* (September 14, 1998): retrieved online at http://www.news.com/News/Item/0,4,26312,00.html?st.cn.nws.rl.ne.
32. Patrick Thibodeau, "Workplace Computer Virus Infections on the Rise," *Computerworld* (September 14, 1998): retrieved online at http://www.computerworld.com/home/news.nsf/all/9809141icsa.
33. Lee Bruno, "Sick Jokes," Data Communications, September 7, 1998, www.data.com/issue/980907/jokes.html
34. Kathleen Ohlson and Ann Harrison, "Melissa Mutates," *Computerworld,* March 29, 1999, www.computerworld.com.
35. McDonnel Lausch, "Hold Your Fire," *Information Security Magazine* (July 12, 1998): 12.
36. Tom Duffy, [untitled article], *Computerworld* (March 10, 1997): retrieved on-line at http://www.computerworld.com/home/print9497.nsf/all/SL97glob9.
37. Gary Anthes, "Viruses Continue to Wreak Havoc at Many U.S. Companies, " *Computerworld* (June 28, 1993): 52.
38. Ann Harrison, "Deadly 'Melissa' Copycat Virus Can Bring Down Networks," *Computerworld,* March 29, 1999, 24.
39. Ibid.
40. Patrick Thibodeau, "Workplace Computer Virus Infections on the Rise."
41. James Daly, "Virus Vagaries Foil Feds," *Computerworld* (July 12, 1993): 15.
42. Leslie Goff, "Hoax on You," *Computerworld* (May 25, 1998): retrieved online at http://www.computerworld.com/home/features.nsf/all/980525idx.
43. Ibid.
44. Elisabeth Horwitt, "The $40,000 Bolt from out of the Blue," *Computerworld* (May 25, 1993): cover page and 14.
45. Elliot M. Kass, "Playing with Fire, " *InformationWeek* (April 2, 1990): 48–54.
46. Ibid.
47. Eileen Courter, "Lights Out!" *Credit Union Management,* May 1998, Volume 21, Issue 5, 14–16.

48. Joan H. Murphy, "Taking the Disaster out of Recovery," *Security Management* (August 1991): 61–66.

49. Elizabeth Weise, "Body May Be Key to Foolproof ID," *USA Today* (April 6, 1998): B6.

50. Ibid.

51. Loretta W. Prencipe, "A Graceful Recovery," *Network World,* February 15, 1999, Volume 16, Issue 7, 26.

52. Patricia Carey, "Five Signs You Need Better Backup," *Small Business Computing & Communications.* (November 1998): 39.

53. Ibid.

54. Ibid.

55. Ibid.

56. Tim Oulette, "Quick Study: Encryption," *Computerworld* (January 25, 1999): retrieved online at http://www.computerworld.com/home/features.nsf/all/990125qs.

57. Peter Young, "Outlaw Executives," *Computerworld* (March 10, 1997): retrieved online at www.computerworld.com.

58. Elliot M. Kass, "Playing with Fire."

59. Thomas Hoffman, "Newark Airport Blackout Exposes Systems Flaws," *Computerworld* (January 16, 1995): 6

60. Tom Duffy, [untitled article].

61. Ibid.

62. "Are Your Networks Secure?" *InformationWeek* (April 12, 1993): 32.

63. Tom Duffy, [untitled article].

64. "Technology Does Not Save the Day," *Datamation* (January 21, 1994): 12.

65. "Technology Does Not Save the Day."

66. Tom Duffy, [untitled article].

67. Philip Hunter, "London on Its Knees," *InformationWeek* (May 4, 1992): 17.

68. Patrick Thibodeau, "Corporate Strategies News: FBI Sees Growing Criminal Threat to IS," *Computerworld,* March 26, 1998, 46.

69. Paul Strassmann and John Klossner, "Feeling Vulnerable?" *CIO* (August 15, 1998): 26.

70. Patrick Thibodeau, "FBI Sees Growing Criminal Threat to IS."

71. Patrick Thibodeau, "Computer Security Woes Come From Outside as Well as Within," *Computerworld* (February 19, 1998): retrieved online at http://www.computerworld.com/home/online9697.nsf/all/980218computer1CEBA; *See also,* Peter Fabis, "Safe Exits," *CIO,* Section 1, (June 15, 1998): 32.

72. Patrick Thibodeau, "Computer Security Woes Come From Outside as Well as Within."

73. Laura DiDio, "Security Onus Put on Vendors," *Computerworld* (April 13, 1998): retrieved online at http://www.computerworld.com/home/print.nsf/all/980413424E.

74. Gary Anthes, "Lotsa Talk, Little Walk," *Computerworld* (September 21, 1998): retrieved online at www.computerworld.com/home/features.nsf/all/980921mgt.

75. Tom Duffy, [Untitled article].

76. Ibid.

77. Ibid.

78. "Quick Response I.S.," *CIO,* Section 1 (September 1, 1998): 34, 36–37, 40–41.

Chapter 13

1. Mary Brandel, "Global Innovators," *Computerworld* (December 8, 1997): 4.

2. Nancy Kendall, "Technology Inches Toward the Boardroom," *CIO Enterprise* (August 15,1998): 18.

3. Sam Witt, "Professor Warwick Chips In," *Computerworld* (January 11,1999): 49–52.

4. Tom Field, "IT Triage," *CIO* (January 1999): special insert.

5. John Gantz, "Knowledge Management: Some 'There' There," *Computerworld* (October 12, 1998): http://www.computerworld.com/home/print.nsf/all/9810126E2.

6. Barb Cole-Gomolski, "Knowledge 'Czars' Fall From Grace," *Computerworld* (January 4, 1999): http://www.computerworld.com/home/print.nsf/all/990104czars.

7. Roberta Fusaro, "Rating Intangibles No Easy Task," *Computerworld* (November 30, 1998): retrieved online at www.computerworld.com/home/print.nsf/all/9811307F22.

8. Roberta Fusaro, "Rating Intangibles No Easy Task," *Computerworld* (November 30, 1998): retrieved online at http://www.

computerworld.com/home/print.nsf/all/9811307F22.

9. "NSTDA Intranet, 1998 Innovation Collection of the Computerworld Smithsonian Awards," *Innovation Network,* http://innovate.si.edu
10. "The Evolution of Ernie, 1998 Innovation Collection of the Computerworld Smithsonian Awards," *Innovation Network,* http://innovate.si.edu
11. Michael Hickings, "Running the Change Gauntlet," *Management Review* (December 1998): 7–11.
12. Sherrill Tapsell and Gillian Law, "The Challenge of Change and Fear of the Unknown," *Management,* August 1998, Vol. 54 Issue 7, 60.
13. "Three Dimensional Visualization of the Heart, 1998 Innovation Collection of the Computerworld Smithsonian Awards," *Innovation Network,* 1998 http://198.49.220.47/texis/si/sc/innovate/+kokdejEmwBmMehfLDwwww/full.html.
14. Peter Fabris, " . . . and Just Is for All," *CIO Magazine,* section 1 (April 1, 1998): 53–56.
15. "Three Dimensional Visualization of the Heart, 1998 Innovation Collection of the Computerworld Smithsonian Awards," *Innovation Network,* 1998 http://198.49.220.47/texis/si/sc/innovate/+kokdejEmwBmMehfLDwwww/full.html.
16. "Automated Language Translation Technology, 1998 Innovation Collection of the Computerworld Smithsonian Awards," *Innovation Network,* http://198.49.220.47/texis/si/sc/innovate/+foer0lIWwBmevLo0Xowww/full.html.
17. Peter Fabris, " . . . and Just Is for All."
18. "Disease Manager Plus, 1998 Innovation Collection of the Computerworld Smithsonian Awards," *Innovation Network,* http://198.49.220.47/texis/si/sc/innovate/+OoelCHIWwBmeRBo0Xwwww/full.html.
19. Art Jahnke, "Steal This Book," *CIO Web Business,* section 2 (October 1, 1998): 22–25.
20. "CNN Custom News, 1998 Innovation Collection of the Computerworld Smithsonian Awards," *Innovation Network,* http://198.49.220.47/texis/si/sc/innovate/+XoeoxlIWwBmerSo0Xwwww/full.html.
21. Jennifer Bresnahan, "A Ten-Year Tradition of Excellence: The CIO-100," *CIO Magazine* (July 1998): 32–35.
22. Sherrill Tapsell and Gillian Law, "The Challenge of Change and Fear of the Unknown."
23. Jennifer Bresnahan, "A Ten-Year Tradition of Excellence: The CIO-100."
24. Gary Anthes, "Moniker Mania," *Computerworld,* May 18, 1998, http://www.computerworld.com/home/features.nsf/all/980518mgt.
25. Natalie Engler, "The New Business Technologists," *Computerworld* (November 16, 1998): 43.
26. Emily Leinfuss, "Systems Analysts: Everyone Wants Them Whatever They Are," *Computerworld* (March 20, 1998): 54.
27. Lina Fifard, "So You Wanna Be a CIO," *Computerworld* (December 7, 1998): 49.
28. Jim Seeton, "What You Should Know Before You Take Your Next Offer," *Computerworld,* July 20, 1998, http://www.computerworld.com/home/features.nsf/all/980720car.
29. Ibid.
30. Gary Abramson, "The Thrill of the Hunt: An Executive's Search for Strategic Information Requires an Arsenal of Tactics," *CIO Enterprise,* Section 2 (January 15, 1999): 29.
31. Anne Stuart, "Under the Hood at Ford," *WebMaster Magazine* (June 1997) retrieved online at http://www.cio.com/archive/webbusiness/060197_ford.html.
32. Polly Schneider, "Finding the Right Chemistry," *CIO* (November 1, 1998), retrieved online at http://www.cio.com/archive/110198_change.html.

Photo Credits

Chapter 1

4 Kim Furnald/Tim Gray Photography;

3 Courtesy Michael Loots;

6 Food For Survival, Inc.;

16 Andy Snow/Andy Snow Photographics;

19 TSM/Peter Beck, 1997;

24 Cindy Charles/Liaison Agency, Inc.

Chapter 2

32 (bottom) Miro Vintoniv/Stock Boston; (top) Gregory Bull/AP/Wide World Photos;

42 Mark Segal/Tony Stone Images;

43 (top) John Maier, Jr./The Image Works; (bottom) Nati Harnik/AP/Wide World Photos;

45 BARBIE is a trademark owned by Mattel, Inc. © 1996 Mattel, Inc. All Rights Reserved. Used with permission. College names and logos owned by their respective universities and used under license from the Collegiate Licensing Company or Collegiate Licensed Products;

49 Working Assets Funding Service, Inc.;

52 Mary Butkus/AP/Wide World Photos;

55 Walter Hodges/Tony Stone Images.

Chapter 3

64 (bottom) AP/Wide World Photos; (top) Ed Bock/The Stock Market;

67 Shuttle Computer Group, Inc.;

69 (top) Courtesy of International Business Machines Corporation. Unauthorized use not permitted; (bottom) Courtesy Western Digital Corporation;

71 (top) 3M Corporation; (bottom) Courtesy of International Business Machines Corporation. Unauthorized use not permitted;

73 MicroTouch Systems, Inc.;

74 Dragon Systems, Inc.;

77 CRAY SV1 image courtesy of Silicon Graphics, Inc. Silicon Graphics is a registered trademark of Silicon Graphics, Inc. CRAY SV1 are trademarks of Cray Research, Inc., a wholly-owned subsidiary of Silicon Graphics, Inc. Used by permission;

78 (top) Courtesy of International Business Machines Corporation. Unauthorized use not permitted; (bottom) Sun Microsystems, Inc.;

81 Zigy Kaluzny/Tony Stone Images;

82 Koji Sasahara/AP/Wide World Photos.

Chapter 4

94 David Young-Wolff/ PhotoEdit;

97 Alan Levenson/Tony Stone Images;

105 James Leynse/SABA Press Photos, Inc.;

106 Mark Richards/PhotoEdit;

112 NASA/Lyndon B. Johnson Space Center;

117 Bob Daemmrich/The Image Works.

Chapter 5

130 (bottom) Richard Mackson/FPG International LLC; (top) Jose Pelaez/The Stock Market;

134 Najla Feanny/SABA Press Photos, Inc.;

145 Courtesy Black & Veatch;

148 J.L. Bulcao/Liaison Agency, Inc.;

150 John Dunn/AP/Wide World Photos.

Chapter 6

159 Mark Peterson/SABA Press Photos, Inc.;

160 Gino Domenico/AP Wide World Photos;

168 Richard Sheinwald/AP Wide World Photos;

173 Dan Bosler/Tony Stone Images;

176 Reuters/Corbis.

Chapter 9

243 Cydney Conger/Corbis;

244 © Teri Stratford. All rights reserved;

250 Myrleen Cate/PhotoEdit;

254 Lexmark International, Inc.;

256 Amy C. Etri/PhotoEdit;

259 Steven Borns.

Chapter 10

264 Courtesy of Volkswagen of America Inc.;

266 Ed Bailey/AP/Wide World Photos;

272 F. Pedrick/The Image Works;

273 Michael L. Abramson Photography;

278 Courtesy Ventana Corporation.

Chapter 11

296 George Hall/Corbis;

297 Martin Rogers/Stock Boston;

306 (bottom left) Corel Corporation; (bottom center) © 2000 Lotus Development Corporation. Used with permission of Lotus Development Corporation. Lotus and 1-2-3 are registered trademarks of Lotus Development Corporation; (bottom right) Microsoft Corporation;

320 John Bellissimo/Corbis.

Chapter 12

328 David Zalubowski/AP/Wide World Photos;

332 David Young-Wolff/PhotoEdit;

338 Chris Corsmeier Photography;

340 Rohan Sullivan/AP/Wide World Photos.

Chapter 13

354 Brooks Kraft;

361 © Teri Stratford. All rights reserved;

366 Mary Steinbacher/PhotoEdit;

370 Jeff Zaruba/The Stock Market;

371 Charles Thatcher/Tony Stone Images.